Human Biology and Behavio

Human Biology and Behavior

AN ANTHROPOLOGICAL PERSPECTIVE

Fourth Edition

Mark L. Weiss
Wayne State University

Alan E. Mann
University of Pennsylvania

LITTLE, BROWN AND COMPANY
Boston Toronto

Library of Congress Cataloging in Publication Data

Weiss, Mark L.
  Human biology and behavior.

  Includes bibliographical references and index.
  1. Physical anthropology. 2. Human evolution.
I. Mann, Alan E. II. Title.
GN60.W44 1985   573   85-158
ISBN 0-316-92894-1

Library of Congress Catalog Card No. 85–158

ISBN 0-316-92894-1

9 8 7 6 5 4

MV
Published simultaneously in Canada
by Little, Brown & Company (Canada) Limited

Printed in the United States of America

Cover: Electron micrograph of normal human skin epidermis (magnification ×4600) by
Dr. George Szabo and Evelyn A. Flynn, Harvard School of Dental Medicine.

Acknowledgments

The authors and publisher gratefully acknowledge the following sources for permission to
reprint their material:

Figures: **Chapter 2:** 2.1 From Francisco J. Ayala and John A. Kiger, Jr., *Modern Genetics*
(Menlo Park, CA: Benjamin Cummings, 1980), p. 339. 2.14 Redrawn from Irwin H. Her-
skowitz, *Genetics*, Second Edition (Boston: Little, Brown and Company, 1965), p. 339, by
permission of the author. **Chapter 3:** 3.4 Adapted from P. L. Workman, B. S. Blumburg,
A. J. Cooper, "Selection, Gene Migration, and Polymorphic Stability in a U.S. White and
Negro Population," in *American Journal of Human Genetics*, Vol. 15, Issue 4, pp. 429–
437, by permission of the University of Chicago Press. Original © 1963 by Grune and
Stratton, Inc. 3.5 From P. E. Volpe, *Understanding Evolution*, Fourth Edition (Dubuque:

(continued on page 594)

To Our Parents,
with Love

Preface to the Fourth Edition

Human Biology and Behavior is intended to introduce students to physical anthropology. The book begins with a brief history of anthropology and its integration within the social and political history of the last two hundred years, followed by a discussion of general evolutionary thought. With evolution as a framework, we then deal with long-term biological and behavioral trends in primate and human evolution, ending with the hows and whys of modern human variation.

We believe that an introductory text should emphasize two major themes, adaptation and evolution, and their interrelationships with successful behavior. We have tried to present the basic data of modern physical anthropology within a framework of these themes, concentrating on being intelligible and on using a minimum of jargon, but not oversimplifying. We have not given neat conclusions to problems to make it easy for the reader. If a question, such as the origin of anatomically modern humans, is currently unresolved, we list the alternative hypotheses, summarize the data, and then allow the readers to draw their own conclusions. We have also made every effort to integrate material from branches of anthropology, such as archaeology and ethnology.

Since many introductory students may not encounter another anthropology course beyond this one, we have tried to convey how anthropological thinking can be applied to help answer significant questions: Not just how but why do people differ at every level, from molecules to behaviors? How much of our behavior, if any, is built into us? What is a proper diet? Why do some people have certain diseases? What does playing accomplish? The uniqueness of anthropology lies not so much in its data — which often come from other disciplines — as in its way of analyzing and interrelating the data. We hope that the comparative, evolutionary view of human existence comes through in the book and that readers will use the perspective in analyzing current and future issues.

The fourth edition is marked by significant updating as well as attempts at increased clarity where necessary. The discussion of genetics (Chapter 2) has been expanded to lay the groundwork for the application of biotechnology to the study of primate evolution (Chapter 5). The genetics chapter now preceeds any significant discussion of evolutionary mechanisms (Chapter 3). The introduction to evolution has expanded coverage of classic Neo-Darwinian thought and of recent challenges to traditional ideas about the rates and modes of evolution. The vertebrate evolution section (Chapter 4) provides a discussion of the suggested events that marked the Mesozoic/Cenozoic boundary, as well as additional comparative illustrations. The coverage of the primates is now organized into three chapters (5, 6, and 7), with an introductory overview of taxonomy and distribution followed by chapters on evolution and behavior. The primate evolution chapter (6), like those devoted to hominid evolution (Chapters 8, 9, and 10), reflects the reevaluation of primate and human evolution necessitated by recent fossil discoveries, with the fall from grace of "Ramapithecus" perhaps being the most noteworthy. The section on modern human variation has been updated to include information derived from molecular biology, as for sickle-cell hemoglobin and restriction enzyme polymorphisms, and expanded for greater coverage of growth and development. Throughout this edition we have tried to improve clarity of passages deemed difficult by students. The glossary too has been significantly modified, and the first text mention of a listed word is presented in italics. A complimentary Instructor's Manual is available to instructors requesting it from the publisher on school letterhead.

Students are often justifiably awed by the appearance physical anthropology gives of covering virtually everything about people and evolution. As might be imagined, no one person can cover all the relevant areas with a high degree of expertise; hence our coauthorship. Although each of us concentrated on his own area of specialization, we cooperated throughout the book's development. Being trained at the same institution helped provide the necessary commonality of background.

In addition to the students and colleagues who provided much sound advice during the preparation of all four editions, we (MLW) would particularly like to thank Alain Blanchetot, Paul Barrie, Stephen Harris and Alec Jeffreys for their aid in pursuing the applications of molecular biology to physical anthropology. We extend our gratitude to the reviewers of the fourth edition: Claud A. Bramblett, University of Texas at Austin; Marcia Carman, San Diego City College; Marc R. Feldesman, Portland State University; Roger M. LaJeunesse, California State University, Fresno; Joseph A. Mannino, University of Wisconsin-Green Bay; Louanna Pettay, California State University, Sacramento; David Glenn Smith, University of California, Davis; Robert W. Sussman, Washington University. One of us (AEM) would especially like to thank Janet Monge for her help in all the phases of preparation of this edition. In guiding this edition to final published form, Lauren Green was a thoroughly professional editor, for which we express our genuine thanks. Thanks also to Brad Gray, Anthropology Editor, his assistant Anne Bingham, and Kim Rieck Fisher and Janice Friedman, all of Little, Brown College Division. We also express our appreciation to Linda Darga and Karen Davis for preparing the Instructor's Manual. We especially thank Professor S. L. Washburn for his encouragement and help during our apprenticeship at Berkeley and for his contributions to anthropology.

Finally, thanks to Emily, David, Evan, and Laura, and to our wives Sandy and Michelle.

Contents

Human Biology and Behavior

Chapter 1

The Perspective of Physical Anthropology

The world is not as simple a place as people used to think it was. Five hundred years ago, a European could look around his world and believe he truly understood much of what he saw; what he could not see was not meant to be understood. Animals and plants, it was supposed, looked as they always had and always would. The rivers and oceans, mountains and deserts were just where they always had been. European man was the highest creature, created to rule the planet; woman was made to be his helpmate in the background, raising his children and always there to provide solace and a hot meal. It was a comfortable world to believe in, but it could not last. In the seventeenth century, people started asking why things were as they were, and how they got to be that way.

It took more than a century for natural historians and scientists to break through the established ideas of European thought. In the early nineteenth century, Charles Lyell, a British geologist, showed that even the earth's appearance is not fixed for all time; its topography is slowly but constantly changing. Charles Darwin and Alfred Russel Wallace proposed a theory of organic evolution that not only accounted for the diversity of life, but also suggested that life changes over time in response to the demands of the environment. Nowhere was the change more drastic than in the way humans viewed themselves. An important consequence of the Age of Discovery in the sixteenth century was that returning explorers brought reports about the great variety of other human societies and races. Europeans, however, believed that their way of life was the ideal way; their ideological and social systems were the best; and they alone had been created in God's image. It was understandably unsettling to hear that human existence was as diverse as wildflowers in the fields. The idea that humans, like other animals, had descended from more primitive forms was anathema to many nineteenth-century minds.

People in Europe were fascinated by the tales the travelers brought back of peoples living in strange lands with even stranger ways of life. Many individuals from Africa and the Americas were exhibited to incredulous Europeans (Figure 1.1). The strangers were regarded as imperfect copies of their European counterparts in social organization, religious thought, and physical appearance. The French natural historian, Georges de Buffon (1707–1788), described the Native American: "Although the

Figure 1.1. *Columbus at the court of Barcelona. His reception took place in February 1493; in addition to six Indians, he brought back many items, including their mineral products, food, and clothing.*

savage of the New World is about the same height as man in our world, this does not suffice for him to constitute an exception to the general fact that all living nature has become smaller on that continent. The savage is feeble, he has neither hair nor beard, and no ardor whatever for his female; although swifter than the European because he is better accustomed to running, he is, on the other hand, less strong in body; he is also less sensitive. . . ."[1]*

Buffon's inaccurate knowledge of Native American populations did not discourage him from describing them in derogatory terms. Fortunately, other European and American writers were not so biased, and they compiled accurate data on the living patterns of non-Europeans. Information, both biased and unbiased, on the variation among human populations around the world was gathered throughout the eighteenth and nineteenth centuries. The modern science of anthropology began with the attempts to understand and relate these accumulated data.

*See page 561 for notes to Chapter 1.

The word anthropology is a fairly modern compound of two ancient Greek words (anthropos = man; logia = study of) that was first used in the sixteenth century, although humans were studied long before the subject had a name (Figure 1.2). Travelers could not help noticing differences in behavior, physical appearance, and technologies. The ancient Greeks and later the Romans wrote vast studies about the habits and manners of their neighbors. Like the later Europeans, their comparisons of culture and appearance were usually flattering to themselves. The Roman historian Tacitus (55–120 A.D.), one of the earliest to compose a study that might be called anthropological, described the Germans of his time in terms very similar to those Buffon applied to Native Americans seventeen centuries later. Of one tribe he said that "all are dirty and lethargic: the faces of the chiefs, too, . . . wear to some extent the degraded aspects" of other German tribes.[2]

Early writers compared all other people and their cultures to their own; they considered any differences to be signs of imperfection in the other group. It has taken anthropologists a long time to alter the ethnocentrism, or cultural self-centeredness, expressed in these early studies.

Today we understand that human groups, living in their very different environments, must use many means to survive. Anthropologists study the dynamic interaction among human cultures, biologies, and environments. For them to speak of "inferior" or "superior" societies or races is pointless. Success is wholly relative; anthropologists measure it by the human group's ability to adapt, biologically and culturally, to the demands its environment makes. As a scientific discipline, anthropology covers a very broad range of investigation; it is divided into four subfields, each examining humans from a slightly different angle, yet working with similar assumptions. The subfields are called cultural, linguistic, archaeological, and physical anthropology. Each documents the dynamic process of adaptation in an effort to explain why some attributes are found in some environments but not in others. Humans are in some ways the most complex organisms on the planet; if we wish truly to understand ourselves, why we look and behave as we do, we need the resources that all four anthropological specialities can contribute.

Figure 1.2. *The famous drawing of man, by Leonardo Da Vinci (1452–1519), illustrates European concerns in the fifteenth and sixteenth centuries. His work provided an important source for later biological and physical scientists.*

Cultural Anthropology

Most early cultural anthropologists spent their working lives recording the ways of life of "primitive peoples." By the late nineteenth century, however, some observers realized that many non-western human cultures in the Pacific, the Americas, Australia, Africa, and many parts of Asia were disintegrating under the impact of European colonialism and technology. Anthropologists undertook "salvage" work to rescue all that remained of the traditional crafts, languages, and social relationships. Since that time, many of the cultures have in fact ceased to exist; they survive only in the records of field anthropologists. In some cases, disease, genocide, and the helplessness created by cultural collapse have resulted in the elimination of not only the culture, but also the people themselves.

Recently, cultural anthropologists have also begun to investigate modern technological societies, adapting the field techniques developed in studying primitive groups. The most important is participant observation: an anthropologist studies a society by living among the people, using the language, and attempting to understand what it means to be a member of that group.

Among the things a cultural anthropologist wants to discover is which kinds of behavior people in the society believe is appropriate. The anthropologist asks: What is normal, accepted behavior? Children learn these normative behaviors during the process of socialization. By the time they reach adulthood they know, but usually not consciously, what they must do to meet the expectations of others in their culture. The individual follows the traditions of the group, worships the correct gods in the proper way, marries the right person, farms the right crops in the acceptable fashion, and hunts the right animals during the correct season. Employing these learned standards of acceptable behavior, individuals behave in ways that have worked well in the past in that environment; they also carry the culture on to following generations.

Human culture, then, is based on learned behavior, which can be modified in response to changes in the environment. Such innovations in behavior are important to the cultural anthropologist, for they ultimately alter the culture.

Cultural change can profoundly alter a population's biology. In a society based on agriculture that, for economic reasons, suddenly shifts from growing food crops the people can eat to a cash crop they can sell, such as cotton, diet and health may suffer. New patterns of migration can expose the migrants to new diseases, diets, and choices of possible mates.

The group's biology can also affect the culture. People who are starving do not behave like those who are well fed. Biological and cultural changes are interdependent. By analyzing how human cultures try to cope with the environment while keeping social groups stable, cultural anthropologists help us immensely in understanding humans.

Linguistic Anthropology

Linguistic anthropologists also study human behavior. The development of their field, like that of cultural anthropologists, accelerated when they found they had to transcribe many non-western spoken languages before those languages disappeared. Anthropological linguists helped preserve many of these languages. Analyzing them for their common elements can help reveal, among other things, biological relationships among the speakers.

All human beings are capable of learning to use language, that is, a spoken, open-ended communication system. At about eighteen to twenty-eight months, a child usually will begin spontaneously — without parental guidance or help — to learn to speak the language it hears being used around it. By open-ended we mean that language can communicate any concrete or abstract thought the speaker wants to get across, even if the thought has never been said before. All human languages are capable of communicating any thought or feeling within the culture; "primitive" groups do not have "simple" languages.

Starting in the 1950s, Noam Chomsky and his associates expanded the study of language with a far-reaching theory. According to this theory, a speaker who knows the structure of language and has a vocabulary can generate an infinite number of grammatically correct and understandable sentences. This ability is founded in structures in the human brain and vocal cord system — there is a biological basis for language capability — and its development was crucial for our evolution, for only with an open communication system could human cultures evolve.

Linguists are also interested in the naturally occurring communication systems evidenced by our close animal relatives, and in addition they have recently attempted to teach true languages to apes. We will return to this subject in Chapter 7.

Archaeological Anthropology

Prehistoric archaeology, another part of anthropology, extends the study of cultural anthropology back through time. The remains of past human cultural activity are a message the archaeologist tries to decipher; they can tell us how extinct societies interacted with their environment, the dynamic interaction between a human society and its environment which results in the long-term successful adaptation of that culture in that place. Unfortunately, what is normally left of past cultures are the remnants of technology, such as stone and bone tools, pottery, broken animal bones, and fire-blackened rock. Given this very incomplete record to work with, archaeologists increasingly have turned to sophisticated methods of analysis to discover every bit of evidence they can about an ancient culture. Even with this help they can do little to reconstruct social systems, religious beliefs, and marriage practices from the few scraps left in the ground after a culture disappears. Sometimes the archaeologist must draw conclusions from what is not present, gaining insight, for example, into the nature of our very earliest direct ancestors from the absence of burials, fire, and other signs of complex behavior.

In reconstructing extinct cultures, archaeologists can use the data amassed by cultural and physical anthropologists. Some groups living today do not get their food by farming but by gathering vegetables, fruits, insects, and birds' eggs, and by hunting animals. Until agriculture was invented about 10,000 years ago, all human cultures were based on this economic level; thus many sites an archaeologist investigates contain the remains of gatherers and hunters. By understanding how modern gatherers and hunters handle the problems in their way of life, researchers can reconstruct and help us understand prehistoric cultures. Conversely, besides documenting the material remains of extinct groups, such behavioral reconstructions help us to better understand modern peoples. Insights into cultural development help us explain why people today show particular biological and cultural attributes. The archaeological data can help us to understand the role of such factors as migration patterns, population density, diseases, and subsistence patterns in the molding of modern human society.

Physical Anthropology

Paleoanthropology, the branch of physical anthropology that documents the biological history of humans, can also help the archaeologist to reconstruct past human behavior. Examining the fossil evidence for human evolution, paleoanthropologists have begun to understand how intimate the relationship between biology and behavior really is. They have found a biological basis for culture in the size and complexity of the brain, in upright posture, and in other anatomical evidence. When these facts are described and documented by the paleoanthropologist, they help archaeologists with their reconstructions.

Other subjects that physical anthropologists study are the evolution and behavior of the nonhuman primates (our closest animal relatives), human variability today, and the ways in which humans adapt biologically to their environment.

Physical anthropology gained much from the mass of information about non-Europeans gathered in earlier centuries, especially in the seventeenth century when skilled anatomists like Edward Tyson (1650–1708) dissected the bodies of human beings and apes and described the similarities between them. Modern physical anthropology derives directly from Charles Darwin's *The Origin of Species,* published in 1859.

Darwin's work on evolution changed the discipline's emphasis and point of view markedly, though not as rapidly as one might like. Before, and even for a long time after Darwin, physical anthropologists studied people by classifying them according to racial stereotypes, invariant pictures of human populations, with everyone assigned to one of the categories. Physical anthropologists measured living people to find how tall a typical European was, how big a typical Asiatic's brain was, what color a typical sub-Saharan African's skin was. The fossil evidence was categorized in the same way: if a fossil excavated in China did not look exactly like one found in Java from the same period, the two fossils were assigned to different species. Behavior patterns, too, were handled inflexibly: sub-Saharan Africans were lazy, Jews greedy, Asiatics inscrutable, but contemporary northern Europeans beyond reproach. Variability within a group was disregarded; differences between groups were all-important and considered ancient. Thus were a series of stereotypes, or typologies, established.

Colonialism fed this typological view of humans and spread it abroad. Europeans eased their consciences when they exploited others by proving "scientifically" that the subjugated people were, and always had been, less human than they. It was easier to think of people as unchanging.

Our understanding of past and present human variability has changed radically in the last few decades, partly because of advances in genetics, paleontology, and ethology (the study of animal behavior), and partly because of changes in social values. We now appreciate human variability, and we no longer search for stereotypes because we recognize that they do not allow for that variability. Physical anthropologists today study real populations, not imagined ideals. In both living and extinct populations, variation within a group interests us as much as variation between groups. Looking at both kinds of variation seems the best way to reconstruct the path along which we evolved and to recognize how we are changing today. The direction of evolution is to produce adaptation to an environment, to make the hunt for food easier, and to give protection against climate, predators, diseases, or anything else in the environment that affects our ability to survive and reproduce. From an evolutionary point of view, it is a good thing that all people are different, for variability ensures the ability of our species to survive in a constantly changing environment. Some people have bigger teeth, some resist diseases better, and some are taller. If people did not vary, groups could not adapt to changes in their environment.

We adapt to changing conditions in ways similar to those of other animals. We can adapt biologically via biological evolution and we can adapt culturally by changing our behavior. The two means are not unrelated, for our biological makeup greatly affects our cultural abilities. Our ancestors 3 million years ago may have been biologically incapable of controlling fire, burying their dead, or communicating as we do today. Alternatively, the highly technological, urban environment most of us live in may be placing demands on us that we are biologically ill-equipped to handle. Thus we see that the interaction between our biology and our culture is complicated and that physical anthropology has relevance to some of our present problems.

Until recently, western humans treated nature as something that could and should be dominated. We were just one step below the gods, and the world and all things in it were there to be exploited. We now see the truth many non-western peoples knew long ago: humans are part of nature, not apart from it; to survive we must learn to live within the restrictions imposed by the environment. The fact that our culturally determined uses of the environment must mesh with our biology is at last gaining acceptance in our society. The world is not infinitely plentiful and the human body is not infinitely adaptable. If we are to endure, our biology and our behavior must complement each other. Some have suggested that our biological legacy adapts us best to live in small groups, that we are overstepping our adaptability when we squeeze hundreds of thousands of people into a few square miles, and that the frustration, unrest, and violence in our urban areas are the price we pay for living in conditions for which we are not biologically suited.

Another question anthropologists pursue about the roles of biology and behavior concerns our propensity for warfare. Is it purely learned behavior dictated by our culture, or did we evolve as predators? Are our awesome weapons merely cultural substitutes for large teeth and long claws? To prevent future holocausts we must know more about the causes of human aggression, a subject much studied by physical anthropologists. Has evolution built aggression into our brain structure as some have suggested? Or, as is more likely, is a behavior such as aggression learned during socialization? Our brain allows for a tremendous amount of variation; physical anthropologists must seek the limits of this variability.

What are our cultural and biological limits? To find an answer we must look at what we are today and how we came to be that way. The physical anthropologist's three major specialties — the fossil evidence for human evolution, primate biology and behavior, and modern human variability — all contribute toward providing an answer to this question, and we can add information from the other divisions of anthropology and from the life sciences and the social sciences.

By looking at *hominid* (our "human" ancestors) fossils we can try to reconstruct our ancestors' appearance. Were they large-brained? Could they walk on two legs? Equipped with the answers to these basic questions, physical anthropologists can attempt to answer more intriguing questions: How was our ancestors' anatomy related to their behavior? If they were bipedal (walking upright on two feet), what does this reveal about how they lived? Does it imply that they needed to use their hands for things other than getting around? Did they use their hands for carrying food and tools? What does the ability to make tools tell us about their social organization? How might using tools have affected our ancestors' biological evolution? Why are all humans able to make tools and speak languages?

We can find some answers to these questions by looking at the biology and behavior of our close relatives, the monkeys and apes, particularly our closest relatives, the chimpanzees. What does their behavior reveal to us about human evolution? Do chimps ever walk upright? If so, why and when are they bipedal?

We know that people are variable today, but how do they differ, and why? How have the evolutionary processes molded the genetic differences between groups? To what extent have people adapted to environmental problems by nongenetic means?

These questions can be of pragmatic as well as academic interest. Not all people can digest the sugar in milk; drinking it makes them ill. In fact, this is true of most of the world's adolescents and adults. What sense does it make, politically or biologically, to send milk to people suffering from malnutrition? Knowledge of normal human variation can aid in the diagnosis and treatment of disease, assessments of a child's growth and development, investigations of nutritional adequacy, and help to determine public policy.

The Emergence of Evolutionary Theory

Clearly, few ideas have changed our thinking about ourselves and the world around us more than the idea of evolution. It is the foundation on which physical anthropology, and indeed, all the life sciences are built; the framework within which information about any living entity can be organized and made understandable. We find it hard to imagine how scientists studied humans and other forms of life without knowing anything about evolution. Although some still claim that evolution remains only a theory, we have more than enough evidence to demonstrate that evolution is a fact, and that it has affected, and continues to affect, every living thing. All animals and plants, including the living, dead, and extinct, are ultimately related, by being descended from the first life forms on the planet. Evolution is a fact, but the mechanisms that underlie its operation continue to be investigated and debated. The study of evolution, like evolution itself, is a dynamic process, with new patterns of understanding emerging all the time. Chapter 3 will examine many of these debates, and the new ways of looking at the process of evolution.

It has only been a little more than a century since Charles Darwin and Alfred Russel Wallace provided the world with the first workable explanation of evolution. Until then, many natural historians and philosophers assumed that animal and plant species modify their physical appearance over the generations, but they did not understand the forces that cause these changes. Like many great ideas that revolutionize our understanding, evolution by natural selection is quite simple. In the past several decades, molecular geneticists have refined our knowledge of evolution from the level of the species and the individual, at which Darwin and Wallace worked, to the level of the individual cells and further still to the chemicals within those cells that specify how hereditary material is transmitted from one generation to the next.

Before we go from full-sized people down to molecular structure, which will be the subjects of Chapters 2 and 3, it will help to see how a viable theory of evolution was developed. Only with such an understanding will we be prepared to look at the molecular, cellular, individual, and populational basis for evolutionary change.

Pre-Darwinian Theorists

Theories of evolution preceded Darwin and Wallace by about a hundred years. Until the mid-eighteenth century, natural history was a gentleman's pastime. Studying all the things around us, the plants, animals, soil, and water, was fascinating as a hobby, but these studies only raised new questions. Europeans who had set out in the Age of Discovery to almost every part of the earth returned with precious metals, gems, spices, and silks. They also brought back samples of the flora and fauna (plants and animals), and, sometimes, "strange-looking" human beings as well.

By the year 1700, natural historians knew about staggering numbers of plants and animals from Africa, the Americas, and Asia; it was becoming almost impossible to keep track of them. Some new items that became known to people in general kept their native names: potato, yam, tobacco, orangutan, and gorilla were adopted in European languages. But most native names, if known at all, were unpronounceable for European tongues. One solution was to give animals and plants names that could be understood by all educated Europeans. Those would have to come from the "universal" languages, Greek and Latin.

Figure 1.3. *Carolus Linnaeus in 1775 (engraving after the portrait by Alexander Roslin).*

Linnaeus One eighteenth-century naturalist assumed the enormous task of classifying and naming all living things (Figure 1.3). Carolus Linnaeus (1707–1778), a Swedish botanist, noticed similarities in the structures of many kinds of animals. He believed these might reflect "ideal ground plans" that were followed when the animals were created. Finding only a few kinds of structural organization in many kinds of animals, Linnaeus attempted to group all living things by placing them in categories based on their common ground plans. He thought of these categories of animals with similar physical features as fixed, permanent groupings. As he set up his taxonomy (system of classification), Linnaeus did not think of animals with similar structures as being closely related by descent; all they shared was the same general plan.

Linnaeus published his taxonomy in 1758 as the *Systema Naturae* ("System of Nature"), a hierarchic arrangement of all known animals and plants, in descending categories assigned by common physical features (see Table 4.1 for an example of the Linnaean taxonomy). Linnaeus felt his classification reflected the Creator's use of numerous ground plans, but others saw in the groupings some sort of evolutionary association. They thought these physical resemblances might indicate actual biological relationships. Later natural historians incorporated his taxonomy into a viable theory of evolution.

Cuvier A few decades later, another scientist was spending his years carefully comparing the structures of one animal with those of another. Baron Georges Cuvier (1769–1832) contributed much to our growing understanding of the living world. Under his direction one of the major biological sciences, comparative anatomy, came into being. While he worked in his laboratory, the limestone quarries of the Paris Basin were being worked for the "plaster of Paris" that fed a great building boom in France's capital. Mineralized animal bones and teeth found in the limestone quarries were given to Cuvier to identify. He demonstrated that the bones did not belong to any known living animal. Bones of extinct animals had been turning up for centuries, and people had debated whether or not animals could become extinct, a reasonable question given the traditional belief that all the animals ever created were still alive.

Cuvier was convinced by the bones that some animals had become extinct. But how? Religious faith worsened his dilemma. To resolve this problem he proposed an intriguing theory, *catastrophism*. According to this theory, in the past the planet had gone through a series of worldwide catastrophes, in which all living things were destroyed. A new creation followed each catastrophe, and the newly created animals and plants survived, fixed and unchanging, until the next catastrophe wiped them out. This ingenious idea protected Cuvier's religious faith yet made certain that the evidence of extinct life would no longer be denied. Recently, the idea of worldwide animal catastrophes has been revived as a way to explain the sudden disappearance of the dinosaurs about 65 million years ago (see Chapter 4).

Lamarck Cuvier was not the only Frenchman interested in the relationships between living and extinct animals. Baron Jean Baptiste de Lamarck (1744–1829) saw that animals were not fixed in appearance, but changed in response to the needs of life in that environment. He asked himself what caused these changes and how they were continued. His answer was that acquired characteristics are inherited. If an animal changes its appearance in response to the demands of its environment, the change will be passed on to the offspring, which will be better suited to life in this environment. The most famous example, though one that Lamarck himself did not use, is the giraffe's long neck. At one time, according to this theory, giraffes had necks like other animals. When the leaves on which they fed became harder and harder to reach, the giraffes stretched their necks, making them longer, to reach the food. This length of neck was passed on to the next generation, and bit by bit the elongated neck of today's giraffe was attained. With slight modifications, this theory was accepted in the Soviet Union until very recently. Modern geneticists have found, however, that acquired characteristics cannot be inherited.

Lamarck was only one of the thinkers of his time who saw how important the environment's influence on animals and plants could be, and that living things can survive in their habitat because they possess biological features that permit them to exploit a particular set of resources in that environment — in a word, they are adapted to that way of life. Others, including Charles Darwin's grandfather, Erasmus Darwin (1731–1802), also wrote about these subjects. What they did not understand was the mechanism by which the environment influences animals and plants. It was to this question that Lamarck's suggestion of the inheritance of acquired characteristics was directed. Although his ideas gained some support, most scientists of the day remained unconvinced.

Lyell While Lamarck was presenting his theories, a Scotsman whose main interest was the planet itself was developing different lines of evidence. Charles Lyell (1797–1875) traveled all through Europe, and parts of the newly independent United States, tracing the stratigraphic (rock strata) history of nations. He amplified the ideas of another British scientist, James Hutton (1726–1797), who had studied many of the geological formations in England and concluded that the earth's physical features were the result of natural forces operating in a uniform manner. Lyell also observed the effects of nature on the earth's surface, noting the weathering action of wind, rain, and temperature, and the meanderings of rivers slowly wearing away their beds, forming terraces as they gouged deeper and deeper. Lyell believed these natural forces had made the planet look the way it does, slowly but constantly altering the world's topography.

Lyell called his theory *uniformitarianism*, suggesting that most environments are exposed to slow change. If these forces of change made the plains and valleys, the hills and mountains, working at their incredibly slow pace, then a very long time must have passed while they were at work. Lyell's hypothesis broke away from the ideas of early nine-teenth-century Europe, which accepted the world, like the animals and plants, as forever fixed and unchanging. Europeans were shaken by the idea of the earth being extremely old. Many continued to hold with Archbishop James Ussher, a seventeenth-century prelate, who counted back through the genealogies in Genesis and determined that the world had been created in 4004 B.C.; another churchman later added the de-tail that it had happened on October 23 at 9 A.M. Lyell did not specify how long it had taken to carve the earth into its present appearance, but if natural forces were responsible, many millions of years would have been required. In 1830, Lyell published all his evidence in his *Principles of Geology*. A copy of this book found its way in 1831 into the cabin of a young naturalist, Charles Darwin (1809–1882), as he was about to sail from England on a five-year, round-the-world scientific voyage on H.M.S. *Beagle* (Figure 1.4).

Charles Darwin

Figure 1.4. *Charles Darwin in 1840, at the age of 31, four years after returning from his voyage aboard the* Beagle.

The Voyage of the Beagle That Darwin was even on the *Beagle* when it sailed for South America and the Pacific Ocean was due to a series of coincidences and good fortune. Darwin had just finished his studies at Cambridge University, and, like many other sons of well-to-do families in early nineteenth-century England, he planned to enter the ministry. Although he exhibited no strong conviction for the ministry, young Dar-win did have a passion in life: from the time he was a child he had been a highly enthusiastic naturalist, collecting rocks, butterflies, plants, and animals of all kinds. At Cambridge he had developed friendships with several outstanding scientists of the day, including John Henslow, a noted botanist, and Adam Sedgwick, a professor of geology. It was Henslow who recommended Darwin for the post of unpaid naturalist on the *Bea-gle* voyage. On 27 December 1831, after several earlier attempts to sail out of Plymouth harbor had been thwarted by bad weather, the *Beagle* finally stood out from the land and headed southwest, toward the Atlan-tic coast of South America. The *Beagle* would not return to England until 2 October 1836, nearly five years later (Figure 1.5).

As an amateur naturalist, Darwin had read some of the important books on zoology. Although he probably knew about Lamarck's views, he did not doubt the prevailing view of the fixity of animal species. His observations on this voyage were what led Darwin to develop a work-able theory of evolution. Tracing those observations and the specula-tions they inspired will give us greater insight into the genius of Darwin and help us understand how the idea of natural selection grew and took shape in his mind.

On the voyage across the Atlantic, Darwin, dreadfully seasick then and throughout the five-year trip, managed to read Lyell's book. Unifor-mitarianism and the view of a constantly changing, ancient earth im-pressed him. The observations he made during the voyage increasingly modified his ideas about the traditional interpretations of life.

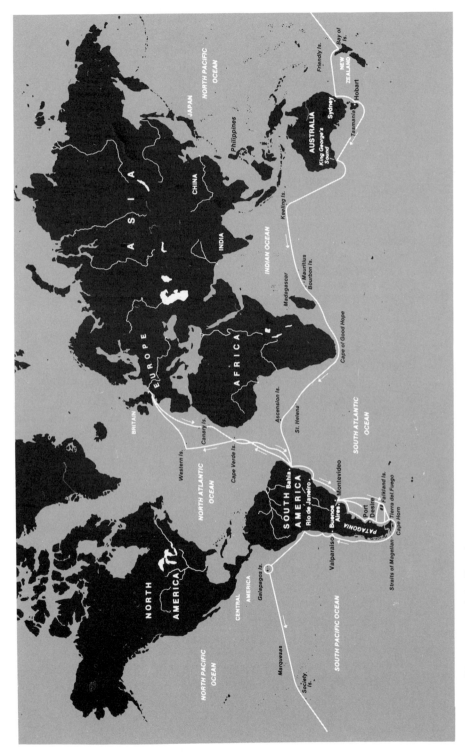

Figure 1.5. The voyage of the Beagle.

SOUTH AMERICA The *Beagle* was to chart the lands and sea along the coast of South America. Much of the time, the ship and its crew beat back and forth taking soundings and making maps, giving Darwin a chance to visit much of southern South America. In 1832, he discovered bones of extinct fossil animals in a cliff on the ocean coast of Punta Alta, south of Buenos Aires, in Argentina. Although the animals no longer lived in any part of the world, Darwin was sure that the fossil bones of the giant ground sloth he had found belonged to a creature much like the living, though smaller, tree sloths in South America. He wrote in his journal: "This wonderful relationship in the same continent between the dead and the living will, I do not doubt, hereafter throw some light on the appearance of organic beings on earth and their disappearance from it."[3] Both at Punta Alta and on the Argentine pampas, Darwin found extinct forms of animals that were like living animals in many ways. These discoveries raised doubts that species are fixed and that all animals ever created were still alive. Darwin found horse bones in geological contexts that left no doubt about their great age. Although the horse was not known to have existed in the New World until the Spanish introduced it early in the sixteenth century, it obviously had been in South America earlier but had become extinct. (We now know that the horse actually evolved in North America, eventually spread to Asia, and became part of the animal life of Eurasia and Europe, but became extinct in the New World about 10,000 years ago, only to be reintroduced by Spanish explorers seeking the "City of Gold.") Darwin wondered why the horse and the other animals were no longer to be found in these areas.

Problems like these occupied Darwin as the *Beagle* sailed up and down the Atlantic coast of South America. After visiting the very tip of the continent, Tierra del Fuego, the *Beagle* rounded Cape Horn and sailed up the Pacific coast, making more surveys, while Darwin examined the geology of the Andes. Darwin's exploration of the mountains coincided with a tremendous earthquake which caused great damage and loss of life. The modifications to the land produced by the earthquake reinforced in Darwin's mind the notion of change brought about by natural forces. Darwin was extremely eager to return home, doubly so because an insect bite had given him a rare disease that was to afflict him for the rest of his life. The *Beagle* prepared to sail home via the Pacific, stopping at several places along the way.

THE GALAPAGOS The ship's first landfall after leaving South America was the Galapagos Islands, fourteen volcanic islands 600 miles west of Ecuador. The life forms here gave Darwin one of the indispensable keys for his theory. He had already gathered huge quantities of field notes and preserved animal specimens that had raised significant questions about how animal and plant forms relate to their environment. The Galapagos animals pointed him toward an explanation of these questions.

The Galapagos Islands contained one of the earth's most exotic animal populations. Reptiles abounded, including iguanas (dragonlike lizards), some of them living on the land, and others adapted to life in the shallow waters just offshore (though they came ashore when danger threatened). Huge tortoises rambled everywhere on the islands. American whalers sailing from New England had made good use of these creatures, capturing and securing them on deck, where they could survive without food for many weeks until seamen ate them. (This practice, unfortunately, was one of the major factors in the near extinction of these giant reptiles.) Birds, too, were everywhere, among them many finches. Darwin spent as much time as possible collecting specimens and making observations.

Just before the *Beagle* set sail, Darwin had dinner with the governor of one of the islands, a Mr. Lawson, who said he could identify which island a tortoise came from simply by looking at the color and design on the shell. On the long voyage across the Pacific to Tahiti, Darwin thought about this remark, and began examining more closely the animal specimens he had taken from the different islands. He had been cataloging these specimens without regard to which island they were from. Now he realized that tortoises and especially finches from the different islands looked different.[4]

David Lack, an English ornithologist, studied the finches of the Galapagos, now called Darwin's finches, more than a hundred years after Darwin had visited the islands. He confirmed much of what Darwin had seen, and added interesting new information. The Galapagos have fourteen species of Darwin's finches. Although they are different species, they do not have markedly distinct physical features. Their plumage is rather dull, varying from gray to black to green. The only definite differences among the species are the size and development of their beaks; some are short and stoutly built, others are long and slender. In a series of experiments, Lack demonstrated that the finches identify members of their own species for breeding and territorial purposes by differences in beak shape and size. Their plumage and all other features are so similar that, unlike other birds, they might have trouble finding mates (the selection process is called mating preference). Thus, differentiation in the beak has sustained reproductive isolation among species.

Darwin had seen that diversity in beak shape permitted the different species of finches to adapt to different environmental niches. It seemed reasonable to think also that the finches had such diversity because the islands did not have a normal complement of other kinds of birds with which they would have had to compete. If the islands had woodpeckers, for example, the woodpecker finch probably would not have appeared (Figure 1.6). Because this finch does not have the woodpecker's strong, hard beak, it uses a twig, held in its beak, to pry up bits of tree bark and reach the insects underneath. The finches (including a ground-feeding, seed-eating finch) seemed to have developed adaptations to ways of life led by other kinds of birds on the South American mainland, but which were not present on the islands. These finches appeared only on the Galapagos, and they differed in slight but meaningful ways from the mainland finches. Darwin was convinced that the environment shaped

Figure 1.6. The woodpecker finch of the Galapagos, using a cactus spine to extract an insect from a tree branch.

the physical features of animal species. The finches also showed that species can modify their appearance over time, because all must have been descended from a common ancestor.[5]

After visits to Tahiti, Australia, and South Africa, the *Beagle* finally sailed into Falmouth harbor on 2 October 1836, where Darwin left the ship, never to leave England again.

Evolution by Natural Selection Although Darwin had learned on the voyage that animal species apparently adapt to their environment, he still could not say how the environment can influence the development of physical features in a species. He began to study domesticated animals, and soon confirmed his earlier observations that individuals in virtually all animal populations are not identical. The differences in appearance may be very slight, but they do exist. Could this variability be connected to the ways by which animals adapt to their environment? The answer to this crucial question came to him from reading Thomas Malthus's essay on population.

Malthus (1766–1834), an economist, writing about how population sizes are kept stable in animal groups, observed that many more individuals are born into an animal species than ever reach maturity: the number of adult animals remains more or less constant. High infant mortality must prevent most of the young individuals from reaching adulthood. This was the key Darwin had been seeking. Could the choice of which young individuals reached adulthood depend on their ability to survive? Could their ability to survive be related to their physical features? If all animals in a species varied in physical features, perhaps some variations permitted a better adaptation to the environment. The environment, then, would select the individuals whose variations made them better able to survive. These animals would stand a better chance of surviving to maturity, and thus of reproducing. The variations that permitted these animals to survive would be passed on to the next generation. In contrast, variations that were not as adaptive would be weeded out by the environment. Darwin's name for this weeding out process was *natural selection*, but he also thought of it as survival and reproduction of the fittest, a process which could account for the changes in appearance of animal species.

Darwin and Alfred Russel Wallace Darwin had the outlines of natural selection in mind by the late 1830s, and he began accumulating data to support his hypothesis. He was aware of the controversy such a theory would engender in scientific and theological circles, and he was not eager to be in the center of the battle. Working quietly, he corresponded with sympathetic scientists, describing his discoveries. They urged him to publish his findings, but he probably would have held his work to be presented after his death, if it had not been for an ironic circumstance.

During the 1850s, while Darwin considered the wisdom of publishing his theory, along with the formidable array of data he had accumulated for twenty years, another Englishman was about to force his hand. Alfred Russel Wallace (1823–1913), like Darwin, was a natural historian. He had traveled widely to study animal and plant life and to collect specimens for European zoos and museums. According to his autobiography, while on such a trip to the Malay archipelago in southeast Asia, Wallace contracted malaria, and during a fever delirium, a theory of evolution almost exactly like Darwin's had come to him. Wallace, too, communicated his ideas on evolution to scientists in England.

Darwin's friends, aware that he was working in much the same direction, at last persuaded him to announce his theory publicly, and in 1858, Darwin and Wallace jointly announced their findings in a paper presented to the Linnaean Society. A year later, Darwin published his book, *The Origin of Species*. He avoided referring to human evolution in this work, except for a cryptic sentence at the end: "Much light will be thrown on the origin of man and his history."

The storm Darwin had expected soon broke. Refusing to be drawn into the controversy, he retired to his home and left the fighting to such men as Thomas Henry Huxley, an anatomist superbly qualified to carry on the battle (Figure 1.7). Huxley himself published *On Man's Place in Nature* in 1863, carefully analyzing the anatomical similarities between man and the apes, and describing the remains of a primitive, extinct human found at Neandertal in Germany, as evidence for human evolution. In 1871 Darwin's *Descent of Man* confirmed Huxley's views and presented a strong case for considering humans and all other life as subject to evolutionary change (see Figures 1.8 and 1.9).

Examination and explanation of evolutionary theory and its application to humans in particular will form the heart of this book. Before looking at modern ideas about evolution we'll first set the stage by looking at some of the information Darwin did not have, specifically that of the science of heredity, or genetics.

Figure 1.7. *Thomas Henry Huxley.*

Figure 1.8. Carica-
tures of Charles
Darwin (left) and
Thomas Huxley
which appeared
during the contro-
versy over evolution.

Figure 1.9. Another caricature of Darwin, by W. H. Beard. Titled "The
Young Darwin," it suggests a scene in which the details concerning modern humans' relationship to the apes are told to Darwin by two very
intelligent and human-looking apes.

Summary

Specialists in the three major branches of physical anthropology — fossil studies, studies of modern human variation, and studies of our closest living relatives — try to answer questions about human evolution by interpreting information gathered from different vantage points on the ancient and modern worlds. This book will tell the story of human evolution, past and present. Humans are animals whose biology is like that of other animals, but we alone have immeasurable potential for learned modification of behavior. This ability to learn and the specific things we learn depend on, and can affect, our biology.

In all cases physical anthropology is an evolutionary science focusing on the process of adaptation. In order to appreciate the processes that effect human populations, and have influenced their development over time, an understanding of evolution is essential.

Although there were earlier evolutionists, the climate of the mid-1800s and the genius of Darwin and Wallace resulted in the flowering of an evolutionary view of life. Darwin and Wallace proposed a theory of evolution based on differential reproduction, or natural selection. According to this theory all populations in nature show variability in physical features, which in turn determine who survives and reproduces and who does not. The individuals whose variations let them adapt more fully to the environment have a better chance to survive, mature, and reproduce. The hereditary material they carry may in time characterize the entire population.

Although this concept has formed the foundation for our understanding of evolution, discoveries in the twentieth century — especially the mechanisms that underline the transmission of the hereditary materials from one generation to the next — have provided a much more detailed picture of the way evolution operates. These mechanisms and how they affect the process of evolution will be described in the next two chapters.

Chapter 2

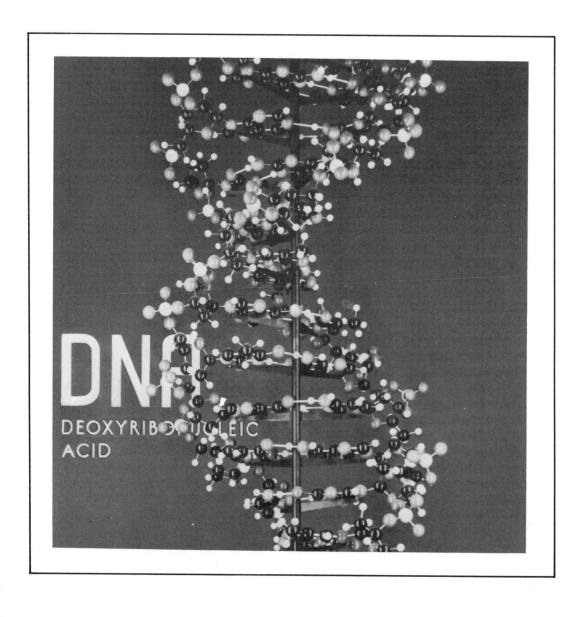

DNA
DEOXYRIBONUCLEIC
ACID

Genetics: The Study of Heredity

The microscopic events that intrigue geneticists seem far removed from the impressive alterations that we often think of when evolution is mentioned. Most associate evolution with large-scale changes: from water to land animals, from reptiles to mammals, from apelike to human organisms. Yet these massive reorganizations in body form (morphology) are the visible evidence of small alterations accumulated over millions of years.

At the base of all evolution is genetic or hereditary change. In fact evolution means change: more specifically, change in the genetic makeup of a group. George Gaylord Simpson, an eminent evolutionary theorist, has referred to the process of evolution as "the stream of heredity,"[1]* a stream flowing through time from generation to generation and constantly changed by the forces of evolution.

A clear appreciation of the flow of our evolution and all it implies about us comes only with an understanding of the behavior and functioning of the hereditary material, genes, and the processes of evolution. This is the case whether we are interested primarily in explaining the variation within and among modern human populations, or in attempting to understand the evolution of pan-human traits such as tool use and language skills.

Genetics has three ways of analyzing the material that gives living things the power to reproduce themselves: biochemical, chromosomal, and populational. At each level of analysis we are looking at the behavior of genes, the hereditary units, but at a different stage of magnification. Biochemistry tells us what the genes are, what they do, and how they change, or mutate. The chromosomes are aggregates of genes that pass from one generation to the next. Chromosomal genetics helps explain why we all resemble our relatives in one or another way, yet why nobody looks exactly like someone else. This area focuses on the mechanisms that allow the stream of heredity to flow across the generations. Population genetics shows us how evolutionary forces can change a gene's frequency. Physical anthropology is an evolutionary science and it is the population that evolves. We take to the grave the same genes we were

*See page 561 for notes to Chapter 2.

born with — an individual does not evolve. The makeup of the group, however, can change over time; population genetics helps demonstrate the hows and whys of this alteration.

Genetics: The Transmission of Information

Before progressing into a discussion of biochemical genetics let's consider what exactly is transmitted from generation to generation in Simpson's stream of heredity.

During the eighteenth and into the nineteenth century, the theory of preformation held wide acceptance. This theory stated that either the sperm or the egg held within it a preformed "homunculus," a microscopic version of the person yet to be (Figure 2.1). Upon fertilization, this homunculus was somehow stimulated to start growing, ultimately to become an adult. Preformation owed much of its favor to vivid imaginations and to optically poor microscopes.

The knowledge that has since been uncovered through the work of many scientists has, of course, discredited the preformation theory. We now know that the material passed via sperm and egg is a coded set of instructions, much like a written language. Chemical counterparts of letters are put together to make words, words are cast into sentences and sentences into paragraphs. If paragraphs of words constitute a set of directions, they can be followed to produce an end product. Likewise, as we shall see, the chemicals of the hereditary material can be strung together in almost infinite arrangements to form directions as well. The sperm and egg, when united, form a book of directions for the development and functioning of an organism. The blueprints are read and interpreted by biological machinery, thus assembling chemical building blocks into new individuals. A book with one general pattern of direc-

Figure 2.1. Three "homunculi." In earlier centuries it was thought that sex cells carried a minute, preformed person within.

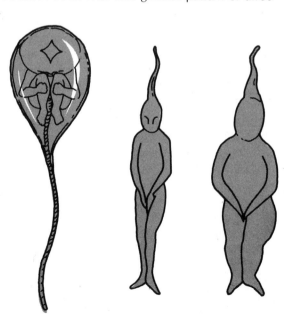

tions may make a person, with another pattern, a butterfly. Variation among people in part depends on relatively small differences in the chemical words. Additionally, while these genetic instructions are quite specific and usually followed faithfully, environmental forces can enhance or interfere with the assembly scheme, thus making the final organism the outcome of both hereditary and environmental factors.

Biochemical Genetics: The Genetic Material, DNA

The average animal cell is composed of a variety of microscopic structures that perform different roles (Figure 2.2). Among these are the cell membrane, which controls the passage of materials into and out of the cell; the mitochondria, where biochemical reactions generate energy for the cell; and the nucleus, which houses the genes. Other cellular structures carry out still other roles. For the moment it is the nucleus that interests us for, with the exception of mature red blood cells and reproductive cells, each of the trillions of cells in the human body has exactly the same amount of genetic material: deoxyribonucleic acid, or DNA. This material has three irreplaceable roles. As the *genetic* (originating) material, it transmits information. This transfer occurs on two levels, both from parents to offspring and from the single original cell, the fertilized egg, to each of the billions of descendant cells. These two functions, passing information from generation to generation of individuals, and from generation to generation of cells within the individual, are very similar. Its third function lies in the content of the information it transmits, for DNA instructs the cells about which proteins to make, and how and when to make them. Proteins are molecules with special chemical properties that are involved in the body's construction, development, and functioning. Because the genes direct production of proteins, all the anatomical changes throughout human evolution ultimately result from changes in our ancestors' proteins.

The Structure of DNA

In structure, DNA is a double helix; it looks like a ladder twisted into a spiral. Like a ladder, DNA has two important elements: the supports (or backbone) and the rungs. The DNA supports are made of sugar and phosphate molecules while the rungs are made of four chemicals called *bases:* adenine (A), thymine (T), guanine (G) and cytosine (C).

The sugars of the backbone are linked via phosphate bonds in a highly regular fashion. Without going into details of organic chemistry, we can simply say that the sugars are joined so that the backbone has a direction to it, as shown in Figure 2.3. At the left of the backbone is the flat side of a schematic sugar; at the other side is a pointed end. In the language of genetics what is shown as the flat end is called the 5' (read as "five prime") end. The pointed end is called the 3' end. Since DNA is a *double* helix, it has two strands of sugars, or two backbone molecules. While one strand has its 5' end on the left, the other strand will have 5' to the right (Figure 2.4). The two strands are linked together by the rungs, called bases.

Figure 2.2. *A schematic view of a cell and a transmission electron micrograph showing some of these structures in a bat pancreatic glandular cell. The plasma membrane is the boundary of the cell and selectively allows substances to enter and leave. The mitochondria are involved in producing energy for the cell, while proteins are actually constructed at the ribosomes. The nucleus contains the chromosomes, which are made of DNA—the genetic material. Symbols in micrograph: N = nucleus; M = mitochondria; G = Golgi complex; ER = rough endoplasmic reticulum.*

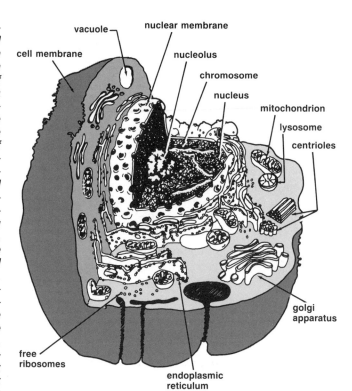

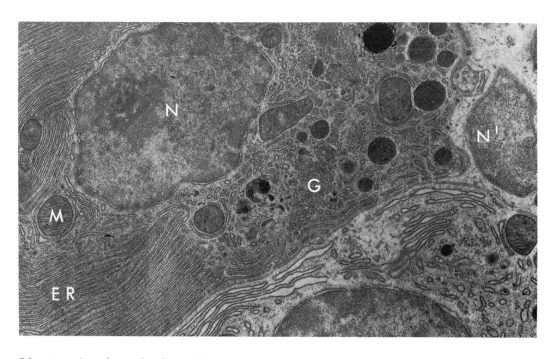

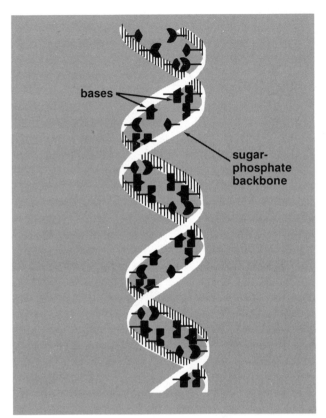

Figure 2.3. *The double helix of DNA. The backbone is composed of sugar and phosphate. The cross links are chemicals called bases.*

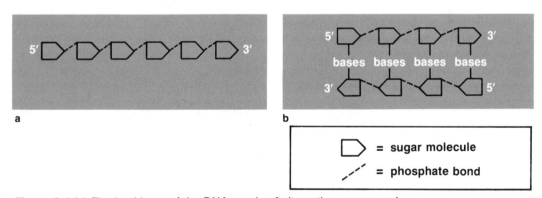

Figure 2.4 *(a) The backbone of the DNA, made of alternating sugars and phosphate bonds, has a directionality. (b) The double helix has two backbones running in opposite directions and linked via bases.*

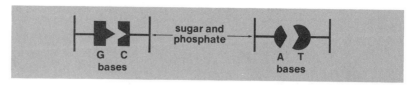

G   C
bases

sugar and
phosphate

A   T
bases

Figure 2.5. *The DNA bases pair in a very specific fashion: A with T and G with C.*

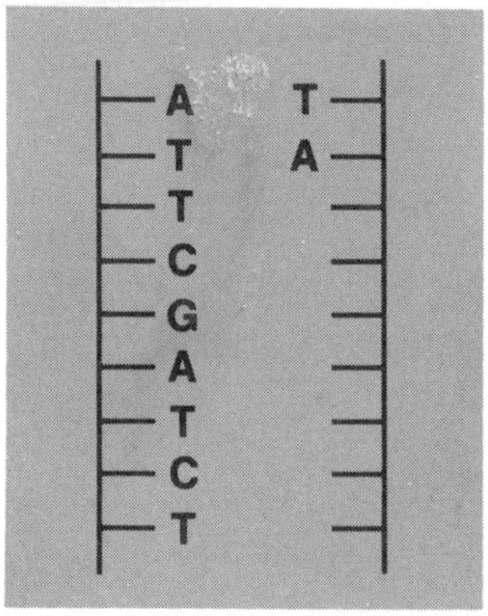

```
A    T
T    A
T
C
G
A
T
C
T
```

Figure 2.6. *With the sequence of one strand of the DNA known, the sequence of its complement can easily be determined. As an exercise, fill in the letters for the empty rungs on the right.*

While the backbone fulfills a structural role, all of DNA's informational activities rest on the rungs or bases. Because of specific physical-chemical factors, A normally pairs or bonds with T and G with C to form a rung (Figure 2.5). Once the sequence of bases making up one side of the helix is known, it is easy to figure out the base sequence in the complementary strand (Figure 2.6).

New Copies of Genes

Whenever the body produces new cells, including the sex cells, one segment of the DNA helix is "unzipped" (Figure 2.7). Bases on each of the resulting DNA strands attract matching, complementary bases (for example, A attracts T) along with their sugar and phosphate supports, forming new halves of the helix. The new DNA bases that are chemically attracted to their complements during DNA replication come from a constantly replenished pool within the cell. Thus, one helix, through DNA replication, can form two helices: each strand directs the production of a new copy of its complementary strand. Now having doubled the gene copies, the cell can divide in two, apportioning to each new cell an identical copy of the genetic material via a process called *mitosis*. Mitosis thus produces two cells from one.

A somewhat different chain of events follows DNA replication in the formation of sex cells. This process, *meiosis*, yields cells which are involved in the passage of instructions to offspring.

Almost always the replication of DNA proceeds smoothly; on rare occasions, however, something goes wrong so that the sequence of bases in the new DNA is altered. This altered sequence is a *mutation*.

DNA Function: Making Protein

Functionally defined in general terms, the gene is the unit of DNA that produces a functional chain of chemicals; the chain is either a functioning protein or a subunit that combines with other such chains to form a functioning protein. Proteins are a large group of complex molecules that regulate and promote the body's development and functioning. Among other roles they work as enzymes, accelerating biochemical reactions; as transporting agents, carrying iron, oxygen, and hormones to the tissues; as structural supports, for example in bones; as antibodies, fighting off disease organisms; and as regulators of gene action, turning genes on and off during development.

Almost every cell in the human body carries a full complement of genes, with more than a yard of DNA squeezed into the nucleus. Depending on where the cell is in the body, however, some of its genes are "turned on" and others are "turned off": only some of the genes direct the production of proteins; the rest are inactive. This is why the

Figure 2.7. *When new cells are formed by cell division, new copies of the DNA are produced as a result of the base complementarity. The original helix opens up and the bases of each strand attract new complementary bases: A attracts T, T attracts A, C attracts G, and G attracts C. Thus, from one double helix of DNA, two double helices are produced.*

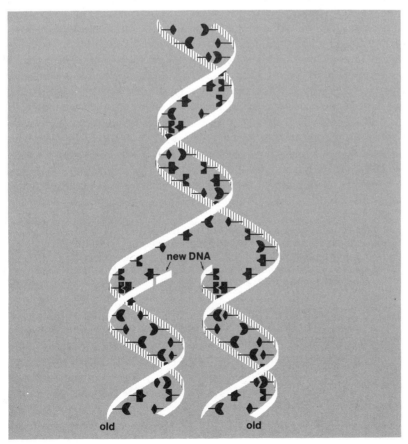

Table 2.1. Amino acids and their abbreviations.
*Proteins are constructed out of building blocks called amino acids. All
amino acids share some common properties, which allow them to bond to
form long chains. A chain that is capable of performing some function is
called a protein. The essential amino acids (boxed) are those which must
be present in the diet; we cannot manufacture them from other substances.*

Amino acid	Abbreviation	Amino acid	Abbreviation
Alanine	Ala	Leucine	Leu
Arginine	Arg	Lysine	Lys
Asparagine	Asn	Methionine	Met
Aspartic acid	Asp	Phenylalanine	Phe
Cysteine	Cys	Proline	Pro
Glutamic acid	Glu	Serine	Ser
Glutamine	Gln	Threonine	Thr
Glycine	Gly	Tryptophan	Trp
Histidine [a]	His	Tyrosine	Tyr
Isoleucine	Ile	Valine	Val

[a] Histidine is essential for children.

red blood cells contain hemoglobin (the oxygen carrying protein), the
stomach cells produce digestive proteins, and the gonadal cells do all
sorts of strange and wonderful things. The processes controlling and regulating this functional differentiation are still very much open to debate.

All proteins are molecules constructed out of twenty smaller building blocks called *amino acids* (Table 2.1 and Figure 2.8). A gene provides for building a protein by specifying the order, number, and kinds
of amino acids that are to be hooked together. In rough outline, the production of proteins is relatively simple, although one has to pay attention to the terminology. The sequence of bases in the DNA guides the
construction of a related molecule called messenger RNA, which carries
the DNA's coded instructions to the region in the cell where the protein
is actually constructed. At the production site the protein is fabricated
out of the amino acids.

Figure 2.8. *Diagrams of two amino acids. Notice that, while all amino acids
share a common part, the distinctive nature of each amino acid is determined by the part of the molecule called the variable sidechain.* C = carbon,
O = oxygen, H = hydrogen, N = nitrogen.

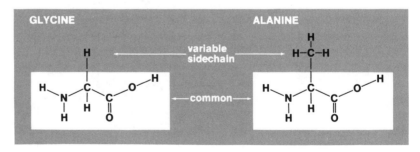

The processes which are collectively referred to here as *protein synthesis* are constantly going on inside you. However, the determination of which protein is being made at what moment and in which cell is the outcome of many complex regulatory mechanisms. Though beyond the scope of this book, these mechanisms are intensely studied by molecular biologists who have demonstrated that many enzymes are involved in the processes summarized below (Figure 2.9). It is also clear that not only is the form of the protein product of importance in normal development and functioning, but the regulation of amounts of protein made and their timing can be of great evolutionary significance.

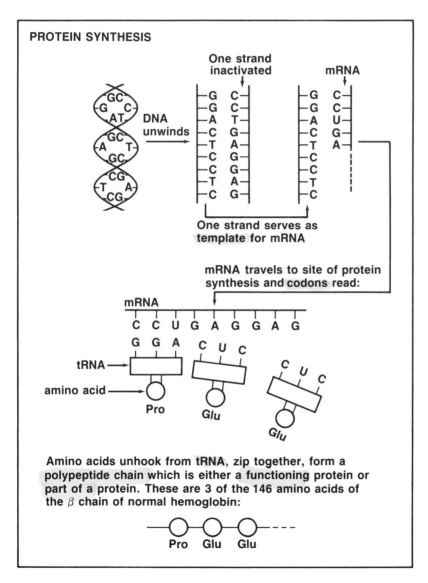

PROTEIN SYNTHESIS

Figure 2.9. A diagrammatic representation of the construction of a protein.

During protein synthesis a portion of the DNA helix opens up to expose the bases in each strand of the DNA. One of the strands (it is always the same strand) attracts free-floating bases to it, just as in DNA replication. But there are two major differences between protein production and DNA replication. For one, now DNA base A does not attract T but pairs with the base *uracil* (U) instead. Also, the sugar molecule in RNA is slightly different from that in DNA, so that the substance produced is ribonucleic acid (RNA). (The prefixes "ribo" and "deoxyribo" refer to the kind of sugar in the backbone.) Because this RNA carries the genetic message, it is called specifically *messenger* RNA or mRNA. mRNA is a complement of its DNA. Wherever the DNA strand has A, the mRNA has U; where DNA has T, the mRNA has A; and so on.

When the mRNA strand is completed, it detaches from the DNA. The two DNA strands reunite to re-form the double helix, and the single strand of mRNA moves to the site where protein is manufactured (the ribosomes in Figure 2.2). Upon its arrival, the information contained in the sequence of mRNA bases directs the gathering and joining of amino acids to form the protein. The process is accomplished by "reading" the bases of the mRNA in "words" of three "letters" (bases). The word UUU, for example, specifies the amino acid phenylalanine; CAA, the amino acid glutamine (see Table 2.2). These three letter words of the mRNA are often called *codons*. They are always three letters long and are read without overlapping: the cell reads bases 1, 2, and 3 as one word, and 4, 5, and 6 as another; the second word is never composed of bases 2, 3, and 4.

The message in the RNA is translated into a protein by the pairing of mRNA bases and those of a molecule called transfer RNA (tRNA). The tRNA can be viewed as a short molecule with three bases jutting off one side and with an amino acid on the opposite side. If the mRNA contains the word UUU it will attract the tRNA with the bases AAA, which always carries the amino acid phenylalanine. After the tRNA pairs with the mRNA, the amino acid is bonded to its neighboring amino acid, and the process continues until a whole string of amino acids is formed. At this point the amino acid chain, either a functioning protein or a subunit of a protein, separates from the mRNA. We can now formulate a more specific functional definition: A gene is the series of codons that constitutes a sentence of directions for the production of a protein.

We have discussed two aspects of protein synthesis: what happens and how it happens. The "what" involves the transfer of information from DNA to mRNA, the subsequent pairing of mRNA with specific tRNA's carrying specific amino acids, and the final coupling of amino acids to form the protein. "How" revolves around the ability of G's to bond only with C's, A's with T's or U's. The genetic code, as we see in Table 2.2, is redundant: more than one word can specify the same amino acid. This results from the need to code for twenty amino acids. If the words were only one base long, the language would only have four words (A, U, C, G) and could code for only four amino acids. If the words were two

Table 2.2. The genetic code.
Each three-letter word in the mRNA either specifies a particular amino acid, or tells the cell's machinery to end the chain of amino acids (here called punctuation words, or pun). To convert this table of mRNA words into its complementary DNA sequence, substitute an A for U, G for C, T for A, and C for G. However, the normal convention is simply to convert to the DNA sequence of the inactive strand by substituting T for U. Thus, the mRNA word UUC, coding for phenylalanine, is said to correspond to a DNA sequence of TTC.

First position	Second position				Third position
	U	C	A	G	
U	Phe	Ser	Tyr	Cys	U
	Phe	Ser	Tyr	Cys	C
	Leu	Ser	Pun	Pun	A
	Leu	Ser	Pun	Trp	G
C	Leu	Pro	His	Arg	U
	Leu	Pro	His	Arg	C
	Leu	Pro	Gln	Arg	A
	Leu	Pro	Gln	Arg	G
A	Ile	Thr	Asn	Ser	U
	Ile	Thr	Asn	Ser	C
	Ile	Thr	Lys	Arg	A
	Met	Thr	Lys	Arg	G
G	Val	Ala	Asp	Gly	U
	Val	Ala	Asp	Gly	C
	Val	Ala	Glu	Gly	A
	Val	Ala	Glu	Gly	G

bases long (AA, AU, AG, AC, etc.), there would be words for only sixteen. Three-letter words provide sixty-four possibilities, with the result that many triplet words may specify the same amino acid: UCU, UCC, UCA, UCG, AGU, and AGC all code for serine, for instance.

The code also has multiple "punctuation" words, codons that do not specify any amino acid; they provide the period at the end of the sentence. When one of these codons is reached, an amino acid is not plugged into the chain, and the sequence is terminated. Likewise, there is an *initiation codon* (AUG) that starts the formation of all mRNAs, though the amino acid methionine may be cut from the final protein.

In sum, the DNA directs the assembly of mRNA, which in turn attracts its complementary tRNA. Each tRNA carries a specific amino acid, and the amino acids, ultimately under the direction of the DNA, are bonded together to make a protein.

Gene Structure

With the advent of more sophisticated techniques for studying and manipulating genes, it has become apparent that in many forms of life the structure of genes is more complex than what we have described here. It was discovered in the late 1970s that genes in eukaryotes (organisms

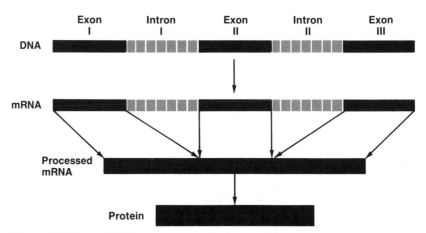

Figure 2.10. *The DNA for some proteins is split into segments that are transcribed into mRNA (exon) and segments that are not (intron). When first made the mRNA has parts corresponding to the introns. These are then cut out to produce the processed mRNA.*

with nucleated cells) normally are subdivided alternating into sequences that code for protein and sequences that do not (see Figure 2.10). Since this structure was first discovered, it has become apparent that most, though not all, eukaryotic genes are "split" into alternating stretches of coding and non-coding DNA. The sections of a gene which code for protein are called *exons* (for expressed), while the non-coding portions are referred to as *introns*, intervening sequences, or IVS for short.

In brief, the whole gene is transcribed into mRNA; however, again, with the aid of enzymes, the mRNA corresponding to the introns is spliced out. Prior to being read, the mRNA counterparts of the exons are bonded together and then the amino acid chain is constructed as described.

One implication of this discovery is that there is much DNA which does not direct the structure of protein. A typical hemoglobin gene is interrupted by 2 introns, the first being roughly 125 bases long while the second is 800 to 900 bases long. Some genes have dozens of introns.

Surrounding the genes, too, there are known to be immense stretches of DNA with no known function. These intergenic sequences (between the genes) might be of significance in relation to the regulation of gene action. Regardless, to the degree that we can judge from well-studied areas of the DNA, it appears that only about 10 percent of the DNA actually codes for protein, about another 10 percent is found in introns, and the remaining 80 percent is intergenic.

This knowledge of the DNA has many implications for understanding the hows and whys of evolution, for as we mentioned earlier, evolution is the accumulation of changes in the DNA through time.

DNA and Mutation   The evolutionary process which can generate new genes is called mutation. Mutations are alterations in the sequence of bases in a gene. Such alterations can come about in a number of ways including the insertion of new bases into the sequence, or the deletion of bases. Bases can also be interchanged between the two DNA strands.

One well-documented example drawn from humans has to do with the base sequence of a small part of the DNA coding for part of the hemoglobin protein, the molecule that carries oxygen through the blood. The contrast between the normal form and the altered version which produces sickle-cell hemoglobin illustrates not only mutational events, but also the ramifications of mutations for individual development and functioning. As we will later see, there are also major effects on the person's population.

The only difference between the normal and sickle-cell versions of the gene is that the codon for the sixth amino acid in the normal gene specifies glutamic acid but in the sickle-cell gene it specifies valine. (Figure 2.11) The difference is created by a 180° rotation of the indicated base pair, mutating the genetic word CTC (in the normal form) to CAC. The altered base sequence in the mRNA (GAG→GUG) attracts a different tRNA, one that carries valine rather than glutamic acid. An apparently minor change in the initial sequence, affecting a base less than a hundred millionth of an inch long, causes many secondary effects in the people who have sickle-cell disease. Because this form of hemoglobin does not carry oxygen well, the heart has to work harder than normal to get enough oxygen to the tissues. The heart becomes enlarged. Red blood cells with sickle-cell hemoglobin are shaped like sickles instead of the usual circular forms and they clog up the small blood vessels (Figure 2.12). The clogging in turn causes bleeding into some joints; abdominal pain; underdevelopment and deformation of the bones; damage to the brain, liver,

Figure 2.11. *DNA sections for normal human hemoglobin and sickle-cell hemoglobin compared. These sequences show the only difference between the genes for these two hemoglobins. This base pair difference results in a difference in the amino acid sequence, which in turn causes functional differences. The lefthand strand of the DNA in each diagram is the strand that directs the production of the protein. To use the genetic code table, it is necessary to convert the DNA triplets into mRNA words.*

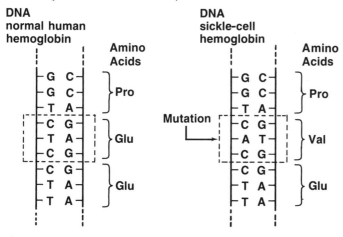

Figure 2.12. Micrographs of normal (left) and sickled red blood cells. It is apparent how the sickle-cell disease got its name. (Normal cells magnified × 5,100; sickled cells × 4,800).

and kidneys; and ultimately death. These secondary effects result from the close relationships of all the body's parts; if one structure, such as hemoglobin, is changed, development or functioning in other parts can also be altered.

Proteins may also be mutated by deletion or insertion of genetic material. These processes, depicted in Figure 2.13, may drastically alter the structure and functioning of an amino acid chain.

Mutations are caused by a *mutagen,* any agent that can break the DNA and allow pieces to drop out, change position, or be inserted. The best-known mutagen is high-energy radiation, such as X rays and ultraviolet light; but almost any source of energy, even high temperature and visible light, can break the genetic material. (It has even been suggested that wearing briefs instead of boxer shorts increases testicular temperature and therefore mutations.) Many chemicals and some foods can also produce mutations. Mustard gas, a nerve gas used during World War I, is a powerful mutagen. Even caffeine can cause mutations under some conditions.

Mutations are evolutionarily important only if they can be passed from one generation to the next; they must be present in the sex cells. A mutation in any cell other than a sperm or an egg cannot affect one's children. Shielding of the gonads (the sexual organs, testis and ovary) from X rays does matter; children are derived from these cells.

Spontaneous mutations, which probably are produced by some unidentified mutagen, occur at a rate of about 1 in 100,000 to 1 in a million; a specific new mutation appears in approximately 1 out of every 100,000 to one million sex cells.

Because of the vast number of genes (estimated to be several tens of thousands per cell) with which we are endowed, roughly one out of every twenty sex cells carries a newly mutated gene; a sizable proportion of the world's people have a mutant gene. Taking a broad view of mutation as any change in the DNA, intronic and intergenic as well as ex-

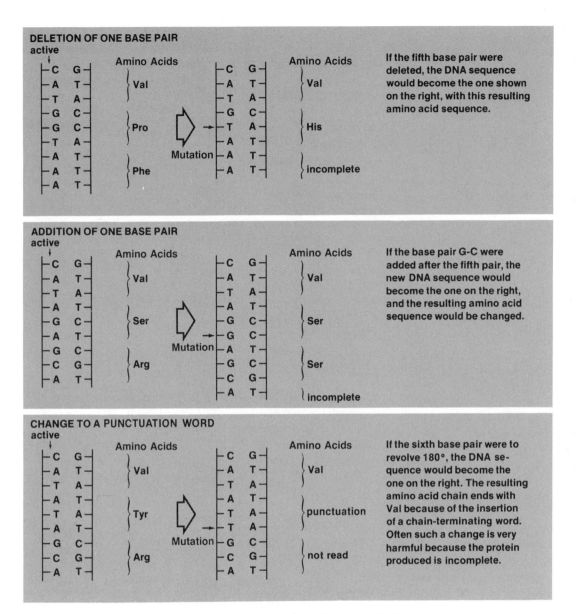

Figure 2.13. Three possible types of mutations. On the left are hypothetical pieces of DNA and the amino acid chains that the left strand would produce; on the right are mutated forms of these strands and the amino acid sequences that the mutant forms would produce. In using the genetic code table, it is necessary to convert the DNA triplets into mRNA words. These diagrams do not illustrate all possible mutations; for instance, more than one base pair could be lost or gained at one time.

onic, an even greater number of mutations could be said to exist. *Back mutations,* or reversions from a mutant back to the original type, do occur, though rarely. As mutations occur more or less at random, and there are millions of bases, it is easy to see that the likelihood of exactly reversing a previous mutation, and thereby reverting to the original form, is quite low.

A rudimentary knowledge of biochemical genetics helps dispel misconceptions about mutants. Most noticeable mutations are simply a change in one amino acid in a protein. Such a change can result in deformities, but rarely would a person carrying a mutant gene show the abnormalities dreamed up for late-night horror movies, and even more rarely would one so malformed survive for any length of time. When we also realize that several of the people we encounter during a day have a new mutation, it becomes clear that mutations do not generally cause horrifying physical deformities. More often they make very minor changes in the visible anatomy, and these come from developmental disruptions caused by altered formation and function of a protein. The resultant disorder may vary all the way from unnoticeable to lethal. An extreme example of a "silent," or harmless, mutation in an exon is the case in which a base change does not result in an amino acid substitution. For example, mutation of the codon UUU to UUC still results in the incorporation of phenylalanine into the protein.

Cloning and Recombinant DNA

In the last ten years we have witnessed a revolution in molecular biology with the advent of recombinant DNA technology. Though a full understanding of the techniques and theories of this burgeoning field is far beyond the scope of this text, it is worth sketching some of the major points of the process, for molecular biology has much to contribute to an understanding of human evolution. In the last chapter, we will also consider some of the ethical ramifications and the medical potential of this field.

A clone is a population of cells derived from a single ancestral cell. Biologists have studied and worked with clones for many years, but molecular cloning techniques in conjunction with recombinant DNA have greatly expanded the capabilities of researchers. Consider the potential of techniques that could allow people to grow and harvest millions of copies of a particular piece of DNA. On the medical front, these copies could be used to produce proteins that are lacking in people with various diseases, such as diabetes. DNA copies might be inserted into important plants to provide them with disease-resistance genes or genes which increase their yield. The benefits, humanitarian and economic, are tremendous. On the research front, too, the availability of millions of copies of a specific piece of DNA would be of great value for molecular studies.

How then to accomplish the goal of millions of copies of a specific, desired piece of DNA? Geneticists considering this question made use of viruses and several techniques developed since the late 1960s. Vi-

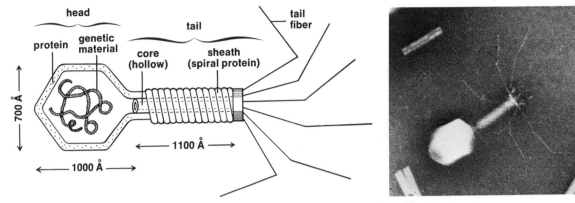

Figure 2.14. *A virus can be viewed as a protein casing enclosing a piece of genetic material — either DNA or RNA. About 250 million angstroms (Å) equal an inch. On the right is an electron micrograph of a virus that infects bacteria (×110,000).*

ruses are little more than small pieces of nucleic acid inside a protein coat (Figure 2.14). Some types of virus contain DNA, while others contain RNA. In either case, a virus infection involves the injection into a host of the viral nucleic acid. Once inside, the nucleic acid replicates itself many times over and directs the production of new virus shells. Each new shell takes in one copy of the viral nucleic acid, and, when many new viruses have been produced, the host cell bursts, spewing forth the new, genetically identical viruses. Here then was a possible factory system. If one could attach DNA of a species of interest to the viral nucleic acid, a molecular factory could be developed. When the virus reproduced, the attached DNA of interest would be produced too.

How then to manufacture DNA which is a hybrid of virus DNA and that of a species of interest? This was accomplished by using a class of enzymes called restriction endonucleases or restriction enzymes, for short. These enzymes recognize specific sequences of bases in DNA and break or cut the DNA wherever that sequence appears. Dozens of such enzymes are now known. The enzyme called Eco RI cuts DNA wherever it sees the sequence: 5'GAATTC3'; and it cuts between the G and A. Now picture the complementary strand to this. Remembering that the 5' end of the complement will be to the right, it reads 3'CTTAAG5' — the exact same sequence! It too will be cut between the G and A. Thus, the double helix is broken by Eco RI as shown in Figure 2.15. This leaves what are called sticky ends — short strechts of bases able to attract their complements.

The DNA of a virus is rather short and in many sorts of viruses there may be only one enzyme recognition site. The DNA of a human, being much longer, may be broken into thousands and thousands of pieces of different lengths. All of the pieces, though, will have these sticky ends. If the viral and human DNAs are mixed, some of the viruses will attach to a piece of human DNA to form recombinant DNA.

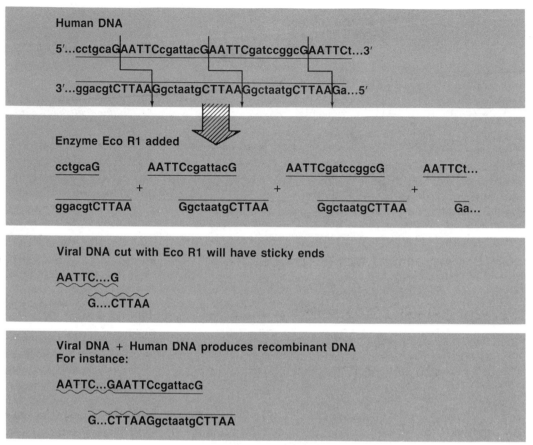

Figure 2.15. Restriction enzymes cut DNA wherever they see a specific sequence of bases. Eco RI cuts the sequence GAATTC at the spot indicated by the arrow. Upper case letters are used to show sites where Eco RI will cut this sequence. Any sequence of DNA is indicated by: . . . . After being cut, the unpaired bases can attract and stick to a complementary "sticky end."

By appropriately adjusting reaction conditions not only can these hybrid molecules be formed, they can be packaged into virus protein coats. These new, recombinant viruses are functional and able to infect and grow in bacterial hosts. The growing virus not only makes copies of itself, but it also makes myriad copies of the attached piece of human DNA. By relatively simple techniques, it is possible to identify which virus has been attached to a particular gene of the species of interest, and thereby to study the gene and its protein product in great detail.

Looking back, biochemical genetics shows us how information is transmitted in an orderly, highly reliable way from one generation to the next, how this information can be altered, and how it serves to direct protein synthesis. If we keep in mind the manner in which DNA is replicated, we will see in the next level of analysis how genes pass from parent to offspring and how the one-cell egg results in the adult with trillions of cells.

In 1856 a Moravian priest, Gregor Mendel, failed his examinations at the University of Vienna for the second time. Although he suffered severe depression because of his failure, science benefited from it. Giving up all hope of receiving a diploma, Mendel decided to indulge his interest in natural history by conducting plant breeding experiments in his monastery garden. It was Mendel who initially described how biological information is transmitted from one generation to the next (Figure 2.16).

Until Mendel's work was published, and for some time afterward, it was generally thought that we inherit a blend of traits from both parents. Darwin believed that each part of the body produced a germ that passed through the bloodstream to be concentrated into one unit in the sex cells; when the sperm and egg united, the parental hereditary units blended like different colors of paint in a bucket, producing a new individual. Even today this is a widely held but incorrect assumption; we all know of cases in which a child seems to be an intermediate between the parents. Skin color in particular would seem to follow this blending pattern. But although outward appearances may seem to hint at blending, the genes are chemical molecules that retain their individuality.

From his experiments with pea plants, Mendel learned that blending does not occur, that the sex cells carry a combination of genes, which are inherited as discrete units and keep their individuality. Mendel noticed that mating a line of peas that always had yellow seeds with a line that always had green seeds invariably produced second-generation offspring with yellow seeds: the yellow character dominated over the green (Figure 2.17). Mating plants from a line that had only smooth seeds with plants that came from a wrinkled seed line produced only smooth-seeded offspring. In all, Mendel made observations for seven traits; luckily, these were traits that are inherited in a simple way. Many other traits, such as height in humans, are affected by more than one gene and also by the environment.

After he made these initial crosses (cross-matings), Mendel, a very patient observer, crossed the offspring with themselves. As other naturalists had noticed, this crossing produced plants with both seed colors and forms. Whatever was producing green seed color or wrinkled seed shape in the initial parental plants had not been lost or blended out of existence in their offspring; it had simply been hidden. Besides noticing that the parental traits did not blend together in the offspring, Mendel also saw the arithmetical ratios in the third-generation plants, and from these ratios deduced what was actually happening genetically. In the experiment involving seed color, a cross of second-generation, yellow-seeded plants produced 6,022 yellow-seeded and 2,011 green-seeded offspring. Mendel realized that this was a close approximation to a 3:1 ratio, the small departure being due only to chance. In fact, for all seven traits that he studied, crossings of members of the second generation produced a third generation in the 3:1 ratio; three members showed one form of the trait for every one showing the alternative form. So close

Mendelian, or Chromosomal, Genetics

Mendel's Unit of Inheritance

Figure 2.16. *Gregor Mendel, the father of modern genetics.*

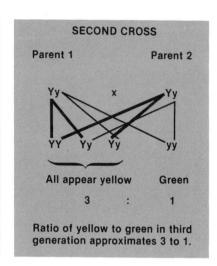

Y = yellow

y = green

FIRST CROSS

Parent 1
Yellow

Parent 2
Green

YY   x   yy

Only passes
on Y

Only passes
on y

Yy

All offspring appear yellow
but have green gene.

SECOND CROSS

Parent 1   Parent 2

Yy   x   Yy

YY   Yy   Yy   yy

All appear yellow   Green

3   :   1

Ratio of yellow to green in third
generation approximates 3 to 1.

Figure 2.17. The inheritance of seed color in peas, one of Mendel's classic experiments.

was the approximation to the 3:1 ratio that some have suspected that Mendel or one of his aides fudged the results to fit the observed to the expected outcomes more convincingly, to help prove his case to an unbelieving scientific community. Several investigators prior to Mendel had conducted similar experiments, but finding that the results were not always exactly the same, and lacking Mendel's insight, decided that inheritance had no general explanation.

How can one explain this approximation to a 3:1 ratio in the third generation? Certainly not by blending. Mendel hypothesized that each plant must contain two units (now called genes) for each of the seven traits, with one gene inherited from each parent.

Suppose two Yy pea plants are mated (Figure 2.17) where Y signifies the gene for yellow seed coat and y that for green. What, Mendel asked, might be expected in the offspring? If, as he thought, each parent contributes only one gene, there is a 50 percent chance that parent 1 will pass on Y and a 50 percent chance that parent 2 will contribute Y to the offspring. This results in a 25 percent chance (50 percent × 50 percent) of producing a YY. The likelihood of a yy offspring is also 50 percent × 50 percent or 25 percent. Yy offspring can come about in two ways: Y can come either from parent 1 or from parent 2; thus, the total chance that these two parents will yield a Yy offspring is 50 percent. The YY and Yy offspring look the same (they both have yellow seed coats), and there are three plants with yellow seed coats for every plant with a green seed coat. The postulated mechanism agrees with the observed results; the old idea of blending is not, for there are no yellowish-green seed coats.

Good examples of the absence of blending can also be found in our own species, for as Mendel hypothesized, each of us has two genes for each simple trait (see exception, page 56), having inherited one copy from each parent. The gene that determines the shape of the earlobe, for instance, has two alternative forms (Figure 2.18): one produces a protein that ultimately results in attached earlobes and the other causes unat-

Figure 2.18. *The boy on the left has two genes for attached earlobes. The boy on the right has unattached earlobes; he has at least one gene for this form of the trait.*

tached earlobes. Each of us has either two attached-earlobe genes, two unattached-earlobe genes, or one of each. If you inherit the attached earlobe gene from one parent and the unattached gene from the other, you will not have half-attached lobes, or one attached and the other unattached; nor will you pass on an intermediate, blended, "half-attached" gene. You will have both earlobes unattached (because of dominance; see page 52), and you will pass on either the attached-earlobe gene or the unattached-earlobe gene; chance determines which one it will be.

As the biochemical geneticist defines a gene in terms of its DNA, the cellular geneticist defines it in terms of its inheritance as a discrete unit. In Mendel's first law, the *law of segregation,* he stated that genes keep their individuality and pass on to the next generation unaltered. The effects of some genes may be undetectable in some individuals because their presence is masked, but they are there nevertheless.

Chromosomes

The DNA sequences, or genes, are not structurally separate, completely independent units. They are strung together to form chromosomes (*chroma* = color; *soma* = body). We pictured a gene as a string of bases, and we can think of a chromosome as a string of genes contained within the cell's nucleus. Figure 2.19 sets out the physical hierarchy that has been discussed in reference to genes. Each of the trillions of cells in the body, except the sex cells, has a full complement of these chromosomes. In humans, the full complement is 46 (Figure 2.20); chimps and gorillas have 48, while another ape, the gibbon, has 44. The numbers do not necessarily mean chimps are more advanced than we are or gibbons less advanced. Chromosome number alone is a very poor indicator of structural or genetic complexity; some plants have well over a thousand chromosomes. The full complement of chromosomes is very important because it guarantees that development will be properly regulated. The loss or addition of a chromosome usually results in gross malformation, if not death.

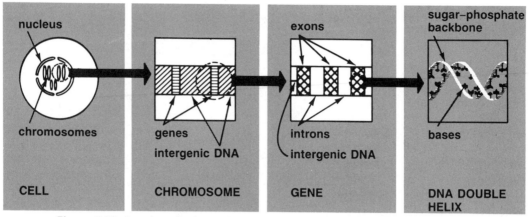

Figure 2.19. *A series of schematic, exploded views of genetic material physical structure.*

Earlier we discussed at the molecular level the ability of DNA to transfer information from one generation to the next. We saw how the DNA can be replicated so that parent and offspring can each have a copy. Here at the chromosome level, we see the process by which the copies of DNA are parcelled out to the next generation of individuals in a sexually reproducing organism. As noted earlier too, once formed, a fertilized egg must be able to duplicate its DNA and pass copies on to each new generation of cells, a second process to be discussed.

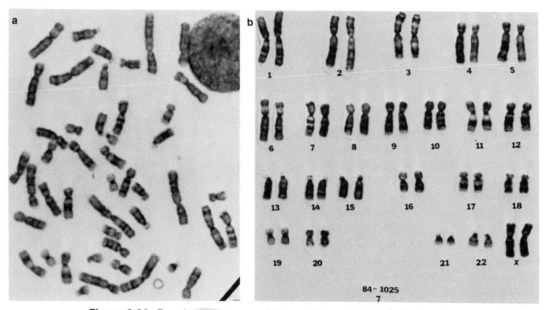

Figure 2.20. *Four karyotypes, or pictures of chromosomes: A photo is taken through a microscope of a person's chromosomes (a). The photo is cut up and the chromosomes lined up in pairs (b) to make a karyotype, here of a normal female. Note the 2 X chromosomes (see next pages). (c) The 46 chromosomes in a normal human, here*
(caption continues on p. 46)

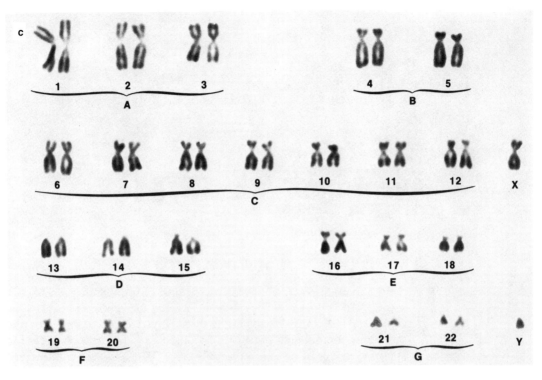

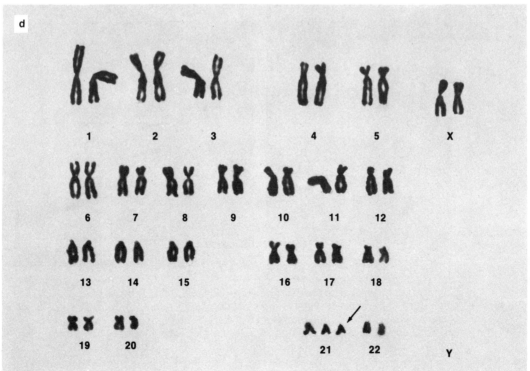

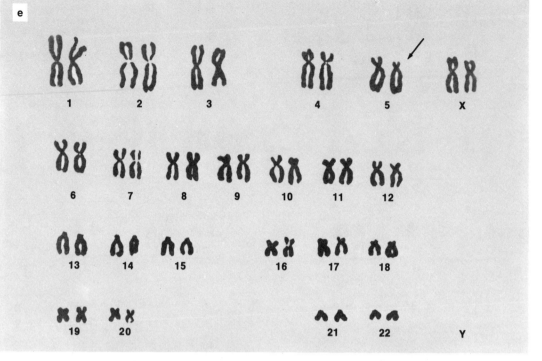

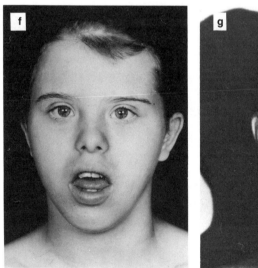

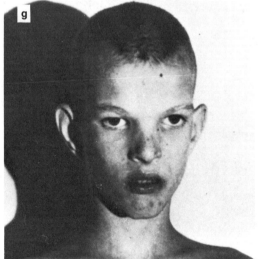

(caption continued from p. 44)
a male. (d) The chromosomes of a person suffering from Down's syndrome. Notice the extra copy of the twenty-first chromosome. (e) The chromosomes of a child with cri du chat *syndrome. Notice that part of the fifth chromosome is lacking. (f) The abnormal appearance of a person with Down's syndrome results from the extra chromosome. (g) The abnormal appearance of the child with* cri du chat *syndrome, characterized by low-set ears, a saddle nose, and epicanthic folds (page 467), results from the lacking chromosome part.*

The fact that sexually reproducing organisms such as humans have two copies of every gene presents a problem. If each parent contributed a full set of genes to the offspring, the child would have twice as many genes as either parent — an impossibility simply because the nucleus doesn't have room. Most higher animals have solved this problem by forming sex cells with half the normal chromosomal complement. When a fertilized egg is formed by the union of egg and sperm, the full number is restored.

But not just any twenty-three chromosomes enter a human sperm or egg. The chromosomes in all but our sex cells occur in pairs, each member of the pair carrying genes that control the same traits. As the two chromosomes of a pair have the same linear arrangement of genes, they are said to be homologous chromosomes or homologs (*homo* = same; *logos* = proportion) for they are similar in structure and function. One member is paternally derived, the other maternally. Mendel's peas each had two genes controlling seed color, with one gene located on each of a pair of chromosomes; two other genes controlled seed form, and so on. Each sex cell must have one and only one member of each chromosome pair so that when two sex cells unite, the fertilized egg will contain the chromosomes in pairs. The sex cells are formed by *meiosis*. A consequence of this process is stated in Mendel's second law, *independent assortment*. The member of one pair of chromosomes that enters a sex cell is unrelated to which member of any other pair of chromosomes enters that cell. For instance, you have one member of chromosome pair 1 derived from your mother and one paternally derived. Likewise, one member of pair 2 is maternal and one is paternal in origin, and so on for the other pairs. When you form sex cells, the law of independent assortment states that your chromosome pairs sort into gametes (the sex cells) without regard to their origin. Members of chromosome pairs you received from your mother need not stay associated when you make sex cells. Thus, considering only two chromosome pairs, some sex cells will have chromosomes 1 and 2 of maternal origin, some will have both of paternal origin, and some will have one from the father and one from the mother (see Figure 2.21).

Though we each have 23 pairs of chromosomes, for simplicity, Figure 2.22 follows two sets of chromosomes (four chromosomes) through meiosis, ending with four sperm, each with two chromosomes. Before meiosis begins, the chromosomes are not visible as distinct units. After they appear, the chromosome pairs line up along the middle of the nucleus; then the members of each pair separate, or segregate, moving to opposite poles of the nucleus. The cell then divides, producing two daughter cells, each with half the original genetic complement. The chromosomes have meanwhile duplicated themselves, and the cells split again, yielding four sperm, each with one member of every pair of chromosomes. In the female the procedure is the same, except that of the four sex cells produced, only one forms a functioning egg. When the sperm and egg unite, the full chromosomal complement is restored.

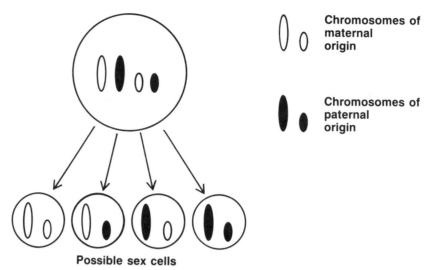

Chromosomes of maternal origin

Chromosomes of paternal origin

Possible sex cells

Figure 2.21. Mendel's law of independent assortment. The maternally and paternally derived members of different chromosome pairs sort independently when entering sex cells during meiosis. With two pairs of chromosomes four different combinations are equally possible.

On occasion, sex cells are formed with either too many or too few chromosomes. Down's syndrome is caused by an extra copy of the twenty-first chromosome and results in mental retardation and other defects. Down's syndrome can occur if during meiosis the members of the twenty-first pair of chromosomes do not enter separate cells but end up in the same sex cell in one of the parents. If the sex cell with two copies of the twenty-first chromosome fertilizes a normal sex cell, the resultant fertilized egg has three copies (one and one-half pairs) of this chromosome and develops into a person with the disorder.

Cri du chat (cat's cry) syndrome, named for the catlike sound an afflicted infant makes, results from the lack of part of the fifth chromosome. This too can result from a mistake during meiosis. Parts (e) and (g) of Figure 2.20 illustrate the morphological or visible changes that these anomalies produce, along with a picture of the chromosomal makeup (karyotype).

The larger chromosomes carry so much genetic information that too many or too few of them is incompatible with life. Abnormal numbers of chromosomes are not unusual in fertilized eggs, but most of these fertilized eggs are spontaneously aborted.

Mitosis: Duplicating Cells

After the normal fertilized egg is formed, another process must allow this one cell to divide and thereby produce the trillions of cells in the adult; this is accomplished by *mitosis,* or cell duplication. During mitosis all the chromosomes line up along the equatorial plane of the nucleus, duplicate themselves (by DNA replication), and the cell splits into two cells, each with the full number of chromosomes (Figure 2.23). As a result, the preponderance of cells in an adult have the identical, complete comple-

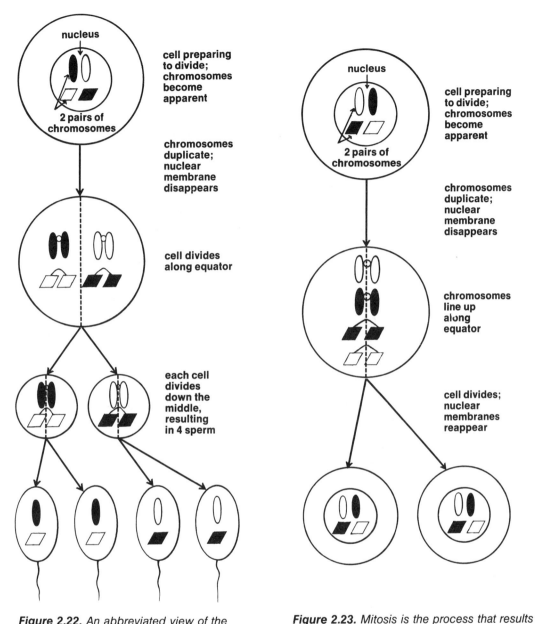

Figure 2.22. *An abbreviated view of the process of meiosis. This process results ιn the formation of sex cells that contain one member of each pair of chromosomes. Meiosis in a sperm cell line is shown. Eggs are produced in a similar fashion except that only one of the four final cells is a functional egg.*

Each pair of ovals and parallelograms stands for a pair of chromosomes. A dark oval or parallelogram represents the member of the pair inherited from the father.

Figure 2.23. *Mitosis is the process that results in the complete duplication of a cell. In humans, mitosis of a cell with 46 chromosomes (23 pairs) produces two cells, each with 46 chromosomes. This process is constantly occurring in all human body cells (except the sex cells). Thus, mitosis does not pass genetic information from parent to child, but from one generation of cells to the next within one person.*

ment of chromosomes. As with meiosis, mistakes do occasionally happen. Sometimes, for instance, the mechanism that controls mitosis goes awry, with one group of cells dividing much too often. This is a cancerous, uncontrolled growth. At other times, a cell does not divide properly, producing one daughter cell with an extra chromosome and the other with one too few, as a pair of chromosomes "sticks" together (Figure 2.24). Because of this mistake, called nondisjunction, some of the cells will not contain the proper 46 chromosomes. If this happens very early in the development of an embryo, ultimately a large percentage of the cells will be abnormal. If the cell shown in Figure 2.24 represents the fertilized egg, it is apparent that all the subsequent cells will be aberrant and the embryo will probably not survive.

Mitosis, then, is cell duplication; it does not normally change the number of chromosomes. It ensures that each cell will have all the genetic material present in every other cell except the sex cells. Sex cells undergo meiosis and incorporate only one member of each pair of chromosomes into each sperm or egg.

Alleles: Variant Genes   We have been discussing members of pairs of chromosomes as if they were identical. In a way they are, because both carry genes affecting the same traits. As Mendel noticed, however, the form of these genes can

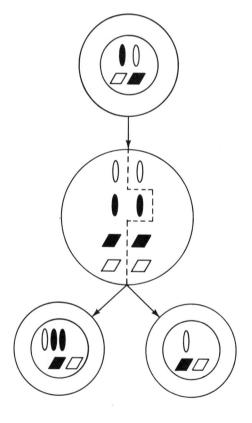

Figure 2.24. *One example of a malfunction during mitosis. This results in some of a person's cells having too many chromosomes and some too few. Cells undergoing normal mitosis continue to yield normal cells.*

vary. Mendel studied the inheritance of alternative forms of the genes affecting seed form, seed color, and other traits. We noted alternative forms of a gene affecting human hemoglobin, the normal and the sickle-cell forms. The variant, or alternative, forms of a gene are called *alleles*. Alleles for a genetic trait are related in that they affect the same characteristic (such as seed color), but they have different effects on that trait (yellow or green seed color). Because each individual has two genes for every genetic trait, one inherited from each parent, the individual can have two identical alleles (two yellow or two green) or it can have two different alleles (one yellow and one green). Individuals with identical alleles are called *homozygotes* (either homozygous yellow or homozygous green; *homo* = same, *zygote* = fertilized egg); those with both kinds of alleles are called *heterozygotes* (*hetero* = different). All allelic variation can be traced ultimately, at least in theory, to mutation. Alleles are important in evolution because they provide the genetic alternatives that natural selection can "choose" between. One of the central questions of physical anthropology is why some alleles are very common in certain populations; African populations, for example, have substantial frequencies of the sickle-cell hemoglobin allele, which is virtually absent in many other populations of the world. The answer lies in the evolutionary history of human populations. Before considering such examples of human differentiation, however, we must discuss several other genetic factors and terms.

We are now in a position to predict the proportions of various types of offspring resulting from matings that involve simply inherited traits. Meiosis (Figure 2.22) ensures that the sex cells will carry one gene for each trait. If a person is a heterozygote for hemoglobin, carrying one normal and one sickle-cell allele, half the sex cells will contain the member of the chromosome pair carrying the normal allele, and half will have the sickle-cell allele. Homozygotes for a trait can produce only one type of sex cell for that trait.

Predicting Genetic Results

    If two homozygotes for normal hemoglobin mate (abbreviated AA × AA), both parents can contribute only a normal hemoglobin allele; therefore, assuming no mutation, 100 percent of the offspring will be AA. If the mating is between an AA parent and a heterozygous AS (S = sickle-cell allele) parent, the AA parent again produces A-carrying sex cells, while 50 percent of the time the other's sex cells will contain A and 50 percent of the time, S. The offspring can then be either AA or AS, and they will occur in a 1 : 1 ratio. The mating of two heterozygotes will yield 25 percent AA; 50 percent AS; 25 percent SS. The most helpful way of showing these matings is in the matrices, as in Table 2.3. It is important to remember that these ratios refer to genetic constitution. Mendel's 3 : 1 ratio (75 : 25 percent) referred to appearance; as we'll see in the next section, because of dominance, appearance does not always reflect genetic makeup.

Table 2.3. Computing distribution of genotypes.

The table below at left shows the distribution of offspring of two heterozygous parents. In the table at right, compute the distribution of the mating AA (father) × AS (mother).[a]

	Alleles in egg	
	A	**S**
A	AA	AS
S	AS	SS

Alleles in sperm

Percentage equals
25% AA; 50% AS; 25% SS

	Alleles in egg	

Alleles in sperm

[a] 50% AA, 50% AS

Dominance: Masking Alleles

That genetic makeup is not always discernible from outward appearance was realized by Mendel. Often two individuals may seem to have the same form of a trait but are genetically different; the visible or detectable appearances of the two individuals are the same but the underlying genes are different (Figure 2.25). This happens most often when one allele is dominant over the other. *Dominance* is the ability of one allele to mask the presence of the other when both are present in the heterozygote. Mendel could not actually see the difference between a pea plant that had two alleles for yellow seed color (the homozygote) and a plant that had one yellow and one green seed allele (the heterozygote). The action of the yellow allele in the heterozygote covered up the presence of the green allele; he had no way of telling the difference between the heterozygote and the homozygote for the dominant yellow allele. Homozygosity for the recessive (nondominant) green allele, however, is easily spotted: the seeds are green.

For the sickle-cell and normal hemoglobin alleles, our techniques are refined enough to distinguish the heterozygote for sickle-cell hemoglobin from both homozygotes. These two alleles are said to be codominant: neither masks the presence of the other. Dominance, then, affects our ability to detect the differences in the structure and function of proteins produced by alleles. At the molecular level, a dominant allele produces a protein we can detect directly or indirectly; recessive alleles do not.

Organisms with different genetic makeups may look the same because of dominance. The visible, measurable, or otherwise detectable appearance, known as the *phenotype,* is the same in the heterozygote and in the homozygote for the dominant allele. The dominant allele is by definition expressed and the recessive is not. Hence, when faced with an organism displaying the dominant form of a trait, we cannot specify its genetic constitution, or *genotype.* The only way to distinguish heterozygotes and homozygotes for the dominant allele is to look at close

Figure 2.25. *An albino from Melanesia. The lack of skin pigmentation is caused by homozygosity for a recessive allele. The relatives of this person who carry one dominant and one recessive allele are normally pigmented as are those who carry two dominant alleles; that is, these two groups look the same but are genotypically different.*

relatives to try to infer the genotype. Because the homozygous recessive has a distinctive phenotype, we immediately know its genotype. The genotype is also directly perceptible for traits that do not display dominance, such as the hemoglobin variation in humans.

Deduction of a person's genotype from information about relatives can be particularly important in medical counseling. Geneticists often must compile genetic genealogies in attempting to inform clients of their risks of bearing a child with a particular disorder. Cystic fibrosis is a hereditary disorder that interferes with proper digestion and respiration and leads to an early death. It is caused by homozygosity for a recessive allele (ff), while nonsufferers are either homozygous dominant (FF) or heterozygous (Ff). The genotype of normal individuals is impossible to decide in the absence of further information. However, if two apparently normal individuals give birth to an affected child, then each parent must be heterozygous: each passed an f allele to the offspring and, since the parents are not diseased, each must also have an F allele.

Many human characteristics nicely illustrate the consequences of dominance and recessiveness on the phenotype. Some of these result in phenotypes often described as inherited disorders like cystic fibrosis, while other dominant-recessive situations have no known benefit or detriment attached to the phenotypes. One such is produced by a dominant allele (abbreviated W) that results in a white forelock: the hair just above the center of the forehead is white, while the rest of the hair is normally pigmented. The alternative recessive allele (w) does not produce this pattern. Here, then, there are three genotypes: WW (homozygous dominant), Ww (heterozygous), and ww (homozygous recessive). Because of the presence of the dominant W allele in the first two genotypes, the appearance, or phenotype, of these people is the same: both have a white forelock. Because of the similar appearance of these two people, it is impossible to identify their genotype simply by looking at them.

Most of us fall into the third genotypic class: lacking the allele W, we do not have a white forelock and yield a second phenotype, normal hair pigmentation. People with the recessive genotype reveal it in their phenotype.

Dominance and recessiveness have to do with the expression of the alleles. Dominance does not mean that the dominant allele is the most common; the w allele for hair pigmentation is the most common even though its effect is recessive. In other cases, the dominant allele is most common. To reiterate, genotypes with one or two dominant alleles will express the dominant trait and thus be indistinguishable. Those lacking a dominant allele, the homozygous recessives, exhibit a second phenotype.

That environment can complicate the expression of genotype is illustrated by people who use hair bleach, cosmetic surgery, or a toupee. Their phenotypes have been drastically altered, but their genotypes are unchanged. This example illustrates that for many traits, hair color being one, the phenotype is the end product of the genes and environment. The hair color specified by a set of genes can be greatly modified by dyes, sun exposure, and other environmental factors. We shall see that many traits are quite complex in their determination; often several sets of alleles and environmental features interact to produce the phenotype.

Linkage: Connected Inheritance

Mendel was lucky to study traits controlled by only one set of alleles. He was also fortunate in choosing traits controlled by genes on different pairs of chromosomes, traits that are inherited independently of each other. The sex cells of a heterozygote for both seed color and form could therefore be of four types: a yellow and a round allele, a yellow and a wrinkled, a green and a round, or a green and a wrinkled allele. In other words, the alleles that the sex cell contained for one trait had nothing to do with the alleles it contained for the other trait.

If, on the other hand, the genes for seed color and form were linked, that is, if the alleles for both traits were on the same pair of chromosomes, the traits would not be inherited independently. If the green and round alleles were on the same chromosome and the yellow and wrinkled were on the other member of the chromosome pair, the plant could not produce a sex cell with yellow and round or green and wrinkled alleles (Figure 2.26).

At times the sequential relationship between linked genes may be altered by crossing-over and recombination. During meiosis, when the

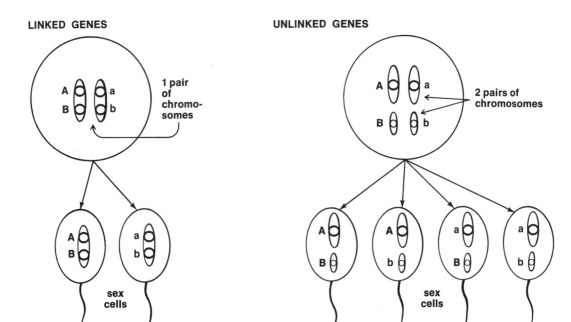

Figure 2.26. Linked and unlinked genes. If genes controlling two traits appear on the same chromosome the genes are said to be "linked." A and a and B and b are two sets of genes controlling two genetic traits. Because both sets are on the same chromosome pair, there are only two probable sex cells produced during meiosis.

Genes controlling two traits appearing on separate chromosomes are inherited independently and are "unlinked." Again, A and a are alleles controlling one genetic trait, while B and b control a second. When a cell like this divides during meiosis, four different sex cells can be produced.

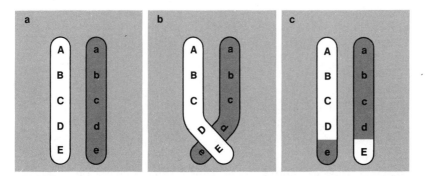

Figure 2.27. Crossing over (b) and recombination (c) between members of a pair of homologous chromosomes (a). (a) Members of a pair of chromosomes line up in a cell dividing by meiosis; the letters A and a, B and b, C and c, and so on signify a pair of alleles. (b) A crossover occurs with both members of the pair breaking and cross-reuniting. (c) The sex cell will contain one of these chromosomes, either of which has a new combination of alleles.

Mendelian, or Chromosomal, Genetics 55

members of a pair of chromosomes, or *homologs*, come together, they often break and cross exchange genetic material (Figure 2.27). This results in new combinations of the genes on a chromosome, but the genes themselves have not been altered.

Sex Determination and Sex Linkage

Another important service that the chromosomes perform is determining an individual's sex. In fact, one pair of chromosomes, the X and Y or sex chromosomes, regulate sexual development. Figure 2.20 shows the chromosomes in a normal male, one X and one Y. The normal female also shown has two X chromosomes. Because females have only X chromosomes, the eggs they produce must contain an X. Of the millions of sperm in the normal ejaculation, half carry an X and half carry a Y. If an egg is fertilized by an X-carrying sperm the child will be a girl (XX); a Y-bearing sperm will produce a boy (XY).

As Figure 2.20 shows, the sex chromosomes are unlike members of other pairs of chromosomes, for they are not of equal size, and most genetic traits represented on the X chromosome are absent from the much smaller Y. This has major implications for the association of certain genetic disorders with an individual's sex. Hemophilia, the inability to form blood clots properly, results from a rare recessive allele found on the X chromosome. Because this allele is quite rare, a female is very unlikely to inherit two copies, one on each of her X chromosomes, so that female hemophiliacs are very uncommon. The Y chromosome is blank for this trait; it cannot have either the dominant, normal allele or the recessive, hemophilia allele. Males are much more likely to be bleeders than females, for the male has to receive only one hemophilia allele (on the X from his mother) to display the disorder.

Geneticists have traced the passage of an allele for hemophilia from Queen Victoria through subsequent generations of European monarchs (Figure 2.28). Three of her six daughters were carriers of the trait; they were phenotypically normal and did not have trouble with clotting, but genotypically one of their X chromosomes carried the recessive allele. They could give birth to hemophiliac sons. One of Victoria's three sons, Leopold, inherited the harmful allele and therefore exhibited the disease. One daughter of Victoria, by marrying into the Hessian nobility, spread the allele to the German royal line and from there on to Russia. Another daughter married into another noble German line; from her offspring the gene eventually entered the Spanish royalty.

In addition to the few people who have too many or too few copies of a nonsex chromosome, there are some who do not have a normal complement of sex chromosomes. Some females have only one sex chromosome. These XO (read it X, Oh, but it means X, Zero) individuals with Turner's sydrome have small breasts, no pubic hair, partial development of the external genitalia, do not ovulate, and are sterile. Anatomically they are obviously female, however. Superfemales, XXX, are also known to occur. Generally, they too have small breasts and infantile external genitalia, and reach menopause very early in life.

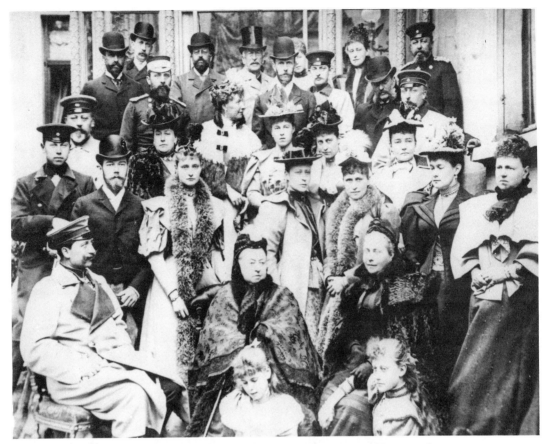

Figure 2.28. *Queen Victoria pictured with some of her descendants. The genealogy (page 58) traces the passage of the sex-linked gene for hemophilia, a disease that slows blood-clotting. Women are carriers but seldom suffer from the effects of the disease.*

Genetically defective males also occur, usually either XXY (Klinefelter's syndrome, Figure 2.29) or XYY. Klinefelter males usually have subnormal intelligence and a dysfunctional genital system. Much research has also been done recently on the XYY males. The results are not at all conclusive, but these individuals may be much more likely to be incarcerated for antisocial acts than normal males. We do know that the presence of one or more Y chromosomes dictates "male," and it is said that males are generally more aggressive than females, although this is a vast oversimplification. Scientists have reported that one out of eighty tall males in the general population is XYY, compared to one out of eleven tall men in institutions for the criminally insane. Results such as these may support a theory of partial genetic control of aggression, but more research is needed. It is still unknown whether XYY men are in institutions because they are genetically antisocial or because their general

Figure 2.28. continued.

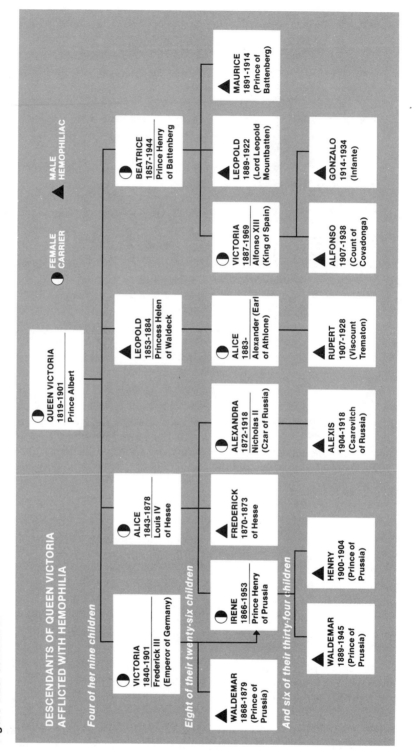

DESCENDANTS OF QUEEN VICTORIA
AFFLICTED WITH HEMOPHILIA

Four of her nine children

Eight of their twenty-six children

And six of their thirty-four children

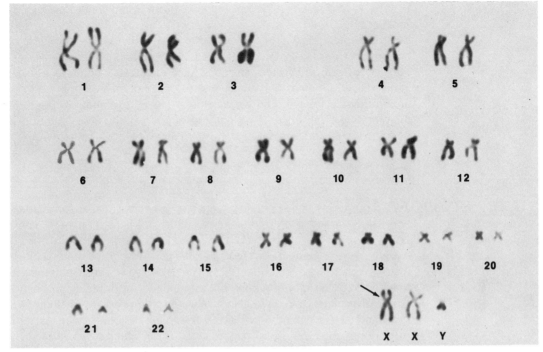

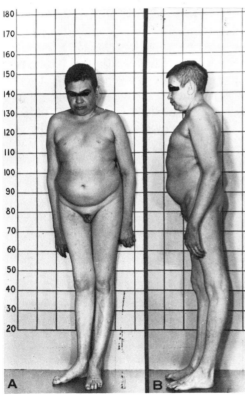

Figure 2.29. A typical karyotype of Klinefelter's syndrome. Men with this chromosomal abnormality have long limbs and broad pelves; they are XXY. They also show some feminization; they have sparse body hair and femalelike breast development.

features — severe acne, often below-average intelligence, awkward-looking body build — make them social outcasts.

In Chapter 15 we will look more thoroughly at the question of aggression and sex. It may be that we have been asking the wrong questions. Just because Western societies have idealized women as passive and sweet and men as bravely aggressive does not mean that these roles are worldwide. Nor should we assume a genetic explanation based on the presence or absence of a Y chromosome. In all the cases mentioned here, however, the sex chromosomes are in a delicate balance: an extra nonsex chromosome produces gross aberrations, and deviation from the normal complement of sex chromosomes is highly deleterious.

Polygenic and Pleiotropic Traits

Two more terms that relate to Mendelian genetics warrant some attention. These are *polygenic* and *pleiotropic* traits. Polygenesis (*poly* = many; *genic* = origin), which is very common, is the control over a trait by more than one gene. Skin color, height, and weight are among these plurally determined characteristics. The genetics of these traits is extremely complex, and environmental influences also affect the phenotype. Polygenic traits require elaborate statistical procedures to study their inheritance. The second term, pleiotropy (*pleio* = more; *tropic* = turn, in response to stimulus) is the extension of an allele's one immediate effect on the structure of a protein to effects on the structure and function of many other features. The sickle-cell allele, for example, affects not only the hemoglobin molecule but also indirectly the shape of red blood cells, heart size, and survival; this allele has pleiotropic effects.

When we look for the causes of pleiotropic and polygenic traits at the molecular level, we find that probably every gene is at least somewhat pleiotropic, and that few, if any, major anatomical traits are simply inherited. Many of the proteins that genes produce are enzymes that speed up the biochemical reactions constantly going on in our cells. The simplified diagram in Figure 2.30 depicts the human biochemical pathway necessary to form melanin, the primary pigment in our skin. In people

Figure 2.30. A simplified biochemical pathway for the synthesis of melanin (skin pigment).

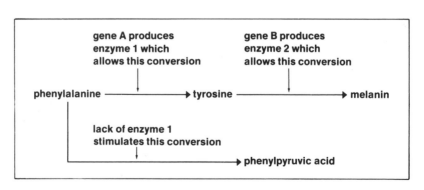

who do not have a functioning enzyme 1, the path is blocked and melanin production drops. Also phenylalanine builds up in the bloodstream, and the accumulating amino acid is shunted to produce more phenylpyruvic acid; which causes mental retardation (pleiotropic effects of lack of enzyme 1); a disorder called PKU. The lack of enzyme 2, by a somewhat different means, also causes reduced melanin formation, and thus variation in skin color. Thus, skin color can be considered a polygenic trait, for both genes A and B must be present for normal pigment production, as well as genes affecting other steps in the formation and deposition of pigment.

As we have seen, the genetic functions make possible the passage of information on how to build a new body from simpler molecules. Basically, the division and reunion of the pairs of chromosomes in sexual reproduction provides for carrying on the species and also constantly reshuffles the genes. When we consider also the modifying factors such as dominance, linkage, and pleiotropy, we see that *ontogeny*, the development of the individual, is an intricate and delicately balanced process.

Genetics and Individual Development

Allelic variation provides alternatives upon which selection can operate. Additionally, because the individual's overall phenotype is made by all his or her genes acting in consort and interacting with the environment, meiosis, by forming new genotypes in each generation, provides for many gene combinations that selection will either favor or weed out.

Population Genetics

The last subfield we must consider before applying genetics to evolutionary theory is population genetics. We need Mendelian and biochemical genetics to understand how genes work and how they are transmitted from one generation to the next. But it is very important also to know about how genes behave within the population, because populations of human beings, not the individuals, do the evolving. In fact, evolution is best studied as changes in allele frequencies. Is the allele becoming more or less common and why? If its frequency is not changing, we are also interested in finding out why and how it is kept from changing.

The basic construct of population genetics is the *population*. This group has been classically defined as "the community of potentially interbreeding individuals at a given locality."[2] In nonhuman animals this group is relatively easy to delimit. Humans, however, because of their great mobility and cultural biases, confound attempts to outline their populations.

The boundaries dividing our species into populations are of two sorts, geographic or social. In Franklin County, Pennsylvania, a small religious isolate of 350 people known as Dunkers, an old German Baptist Brethren community, has kept itself in rather strict isolation from the surrounding peoples since the early 1700s. Since 1850, most of their marriages have been with other members of this group, for this is the socially preferred pattern. Thus, the maintenance of a cultural practice qualifies the Dunkers as an *isolate,* or a population.

Other boundary lines are not quite so clear, however. American Jews, for example, are not a breeding population to the extent that the Dunkers are, because interreligious marriages involving Jews are not rare. In fact, part of the problem in trying to outline breeding populations and determine the boundaries between them is that people do not necessarily mate in a specific group, at least in Western societies. Any American Jew has a reasonably high probability of mating with a non-Jew, and vice versa.

Along with cultural factors, geography often determines the likelihood of matings: people living in Africa, at least before the Age of Exploration, were not likely to encounter an Asiatic. However, geographic and social barriers are not really so cleanly divided from each other. In the United States, social values have produced a definite geographic division in many metropolitan areas, between predominantly white suburbs and minority populated inner cities. The distance separating the two may be small, but the barrier to interbreeding is great. On the other hand, some earlier geographic barriers may now be eliminated by technological advances.

We are interested in the *breeding population,* sometimes called the Mendelian population: the group within which most matings will take place for geographic or social reasons.

We know the theoretical unit we want to study. Yet for the reasons referred to above it is often difficult to outline the boundaries of this group. In fact there may be various levels of "potentially interbreeding individuals." Are sub-Saharan Africans a population? They are when contrasted with Europeans or Asiatics. On the other hand, no one denies that a San Bushman in South Africa is much more likely to mate with another San Bushman than with an Ibo, who lives in West Africa. Generally the solution to such complexities will simply depend on the research project at hand and such practical matters as the availability of subjects, money, and time, as well as biological considerations. This question will be reconsidered in Chapter 14.

Gene Pools, and
Gene and
Genotype
Frequencies

For now, let us consider the idea that usually defines a population, the *gene pool,* or all the genes present in a population, and the relative frequency of each type of gene. Strictly speaking, we are talking in circles: the population is defined as the members of a gene pool and the gene pool is the sum of a population's genes. Another complication is the fact that one person can belong, at least potentially, to several pools. For simplicity, let us assume that we can define our population; that usually makes it very easy to describe at least part of the group's gene pool. The simplest case is a two-allele codominant trait. All we have to do is test a big enough sample of the people and express each allele as a proportion of the whole. The MN blood group system is a good example of such a trait. The MN alleles result in the attachment of molecules to the surface of red blood cells.

The two alleles for MN are M and N. The three genotypes MM, MN, and NN are distinguishable; there is no dominance and there are three phenotypes. Because there is no dominance, the number of phenotypes is equal to the number of genotypes. A person with two M alleles makes only the M type molecules, which can be detected in a laboratory. The NN homozygote has detectable N type molecules on the red blood cells, while both the M and N molecules can be detected on the red blood cells of the heterozygote. To describe the population's gene pool, all we need do is count the number of M alleles in the sample and divide by the sample's total copies of the alleles in the system (Table 2.4). We can find the frequency of N in a similar manner. Using an alternative method, we know that the frequency of M plus the frequency of N must equal one; therefore N equals one minus the frequency of M. Allele frequencies are the way a population's gene pool is described. When dominance is present or if there are more than two alleles, computing allele frequencies is slightly more complex, but these problems can be handled, as will be seen below; given the time, desire, patience, and money, one can describe the gene pool for many genetic characteristics. Related, but distinct, parameters of a population's genetic makeup are genotype frequencies. These are simply statements of the frequency of occurrence of each genotype; how common is each homozygote and the heterozygote? Two populations could have identical allele frequencies, but the alleles could be put together to form different frequencies of the genotypes.

The Hardy-Weinberg Equilibrium

We have said evolution can be looked at as changes in gene frequency. Without evolution, the allele frequencies do not change. This idea was formalized by two early researchers in the mathematics of genetics, G. H. Hardy, an English mathematician, and W. Weinberg, a German physician; it is called the Hardy-Weinberg equilibrium. It says that allele and genotype frequencies will remain constant in an infinitely large, randomly mating population in which selection, mutation, and mixture with other groups are not occurring; an infinite population means that chance fluctuations in allele frequencies (genetic drift — see Chapter 3) are so rare that they can be disregarded. In this ideal nonevolving population, how often members of two particular genotypes will mate is a function of probability.

In turn, the genotypes of offspring produced conform to the rules of probability and Mendelian genetics. Thus, Hardy-Weinberg is a probability statement; given allele frequencies and assuming that the group is not subject to any evolutionary forces, it predicts the genotype frequencies in a population. The prediction is that if in a randomly mating population selection, mutation, migration, and genetic drift are not occur-

Table 2.4. Computing allele frequencies.
When dealing with a simple two-allele, codominant trait, such as MN blood types, computing allele frequencies is simple arithmetic, as this example shows.

Number = 200				Suppose 200 people in a population were tested for their MN blood type.
Phenotypes and genotypes	MM	MN	NN	As there is no dominance, the genotypes are the same as a person's phenotype.
Number in each category	98 ↓	84 ↓	18 ↓	Suppose that in this particular case the people fell into the phenotypes as listed.
	Each person has 2 M alleles	Each person has 1 M allele and 1 N allele	Each person has 2 N alleles	To get the number of M alleles, count the number of M alleles in MM and MN people. Count the N alleles in NN and MN people.
		M = 98 people × 2 M alleles per person = 196 + 84 people × 1 M allele per person = 84 280 N = 18 people × 2 N alleles per person = 36 + 84 people × 1 N allele per person = 84 120		
Total number of alleles			280 M +120 N 400	As each person has two genes for this trait, 200 people have a total of 400 alleles.
Frequency of M	280/400 = .70			The frequency of M alleles is the number of M alleles divided by the total number of alleles. As the frequency of M + the frequency of N must total 1.0, N equals 1.0 minus the frequency of M. The frequency of N can be computed in the same way as for M.
Frequency of N	1 − .70 = .30 or 120/400 = .30			

ring, the genotype distribution in the next generation will be unchanged. As the genotype distribution is unchanged, the allele frequencies will also be unaltered.

To understand these ideas better requires a look at probability. A probability statement involving tossing two coins 100 times is this: if two unweighted (honest) coins are flipped 100 times, the single most likely outcome is that 25 times both would land heads up, 50 times one would land head up and one would land tail up, and 25 times both would land tails up. The probability of getting two heads is the chance of the first one coming up heads (.5) times the probability that the second also lands heads up (also .5); .5 times .5 is .25, or 25 percent. The probability of two tails is likewise 25 percent. The probability of having the first coin land on heads and the second on tails is .5 times .5. However, one can have a head and a tail combination by having the first land on tails and the second on heads. Therefore, the total probability of a head and a tail is two times .5 times .5, or 50 percent. Extending these percentages to 100 repetitions, we arrive at the 25 : 50 : 25 distribution mentioned above.

Although this distribution is the most likely outcome with unweighted coins, if one allows for chance, it would not be particularly surprising to have results such as 24 head-head combinations, 52 head-tail combinations, and 24 tail-tail combinations. This small deviation from expectation is not significant and should not make one suspect the reliability of the results. If the results were significantly different from expectation, say 90 : 10 : 0, the honesty of the coins would be very doubtful.

Thus, we can state a hypothesis about the coins (they are honest), predict a distribution of head-tail combinations (25 : 50 : 25), carry out an experiment (flip them), and compare the actual with the expected results to see how well they agree. Last, we can state how well the initial hypothesis predicts the actual outcome and, based on this comparison, accept or reject the hypothesis. Hardy-Weinberg does the same thing but in respect to the ways alleles come together to form offspring. It yields expected genotype distributions of the offspring in a given population assuming no evolution, which can then be compared to the real, observed distribution (Chapter 3).

Hardy-Weinberg states that given the allele frequencies of a population, the genotype frequencies in the next generation will conform to the rules of probability. These expectations are the probability of having two identical alleles coming together to form one type of homozygote, the probability of two different alleles uniting to form a heterozygote, and so on. The actual probabilities will depend on the actual frequency of the alleles. If the M allele of the MN blood type is very common, then MM people will be formed quite often; if M is rare, it will be very unlikely to form homozygotes.

We have used a matrix to predict the offspring of a mating. By modifying it slightly, we can use the same technique to predict the genotype

Table 2.5. Predicting genotype distribution.

Assuming that the conditions of the Hardy-Weinberg equilibrium are met, we see that allele frequency and genotype distribution do not change from the parental generation to the offspring.

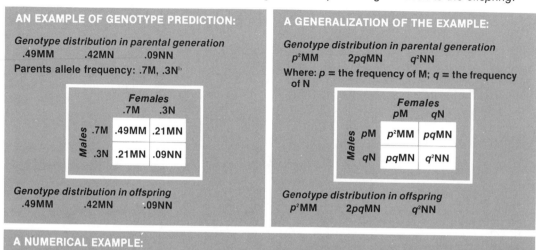

AN EXAMPLE OF GENOTYPE PREDICTION:

Genotype distribution in parental generation
.49MM .42MN .09NN
Parents allele frequency: .7M, .3N[b]

		Females	
		.7M	.3N
Males	.7M	.49MM	.21MN
	.3N	.21MN	.09NN

Genotype distribution in offspring
.49MM .42MN .09NN

A GENERALIZATION OF THE EXAMPLE:

Genotype distribution in parental generation
p^2MM   2pqMN q^2NN
Where: p = the frequency of M; q = the frequency of N

		Females	
		pM	qN
Males	pM	p^2MM	pqMN
	qN	pqMN	q^2NN

Genotype distribution in offspring
p^2MM   2pqMN q^2NN

A NUMERICAL EXAMPLE:

Population size: 100[a]

Observed genotypes: 49MM 42MN 9NN

Genotype frequencies: .49MM .42MN .09NN

Total number of M alleles:
49 people × 2 M alleles per person = 98
+ 42 people × 1 M allele per person = 42
 140 M alleles

Total number of genes:
100 people × 2 alleles per person = 200

Frequency of M allele (allele frequency of M):[b]
140/200 = .70 = p

Frequency of N allele (allele frequency of N):[b]
1 – .70 = .30 = q

Predicted frequency of MM offspring:[b]
.70 M × .70 M = .49 MM = p^2

Predicted frequency of MN offspring:[b]
2 × .70 M × .30 N = .42 MN = 2pq

Predicted frequency of NN offspring:[b]
.30 N × .30 N = .09 NN = q^2

[a]Although this population is not infinite in size, to simplify, we will assume that genetic drift is not occurring.
[b]Because the predicted frequencies are the same as the observed distribution, we would conclude that there is no evidence for the operation of evolutionary forces.

distribution for a population of offspring, if we know the allele frequencies in their parents. If an infinite population has an M allele frequency of 70 percent and an N frequency of 30 percent, and if it fits the other Hardy-Weinberg stipulations, the frequencies of the three MN genotypes in the children can be computed as in Table 2.5. In this hypothetical population all matings are occurring at random; thus, the frequency with which children obtain an M allele from the father is equal to the frequency of M alleles in males (.7). The chance of receiving an M from the mother is here also .7; the probability of a particular child being MM is .49. Put another way, 49 percent of all the children in this group are expected to be MM. Similar reasoning shows that 9 percent should be

NN. The frequency of heterozygous children should be the frequency of the M allele multiplied by that of the N, *times two,* because the heterozygote can be formed in two ways. The M could come from the mother, N from the father, or vice versa. These genotype frequencies in the children can be shown (as on p. 66) to correspond to allele frequencies of $M = .7$, $N = .3$ just as in the parents. If evolution is ignored, we see that the allele and genotype frequencies do not change from one generation to the next. This is true by definition, as evolution means change: no evolution, no change.

Usually the Hardy-Weinberg rule is stated more generally. If the frequency of one allele, let us say M, is p and that of the other allele (N) is q, under Hardy-Weinberg conditions the genotypes occur in the proportion:

$$p^2MM : 2pqMN : q^2NN$$

This ratio is the expected distribution of genotypes given allele frequencies of p and q, if evolution is not operating.

Using Hardy-Weinberg to Estimate Allele Frequencies The Hardy-Weinberg law can be used to estimate allele frequencies when dominance is present. Counting alleles (Table 2.4) is not possible because there is no way to distinguish the homozygotes for the dominant allele from the heterozygotes. Using the earlobe example (U = unattached; u = attached), while we do not know the genotypes of those with the dominant unattached phenotype, we do know that all of those with attached earlobes are genotypically uu. Assuming that the population is in Hardy-Weinberg equilibrium, we can reason that the frequency of u equals the square root of uu. That is, for a population in equilibrium, if the frequency of the homozygous recessive genotype is the gene frequency squared, the reverse holds true too. Thus we obtain the recessive allele's frequency by taking the square root of the frequency of the homozygous recessive. Because the frequencies of the two alleles must add up to 1.0, the dominant allelele's frequency is obtained by subtracting the recessive's frequency from 1.0 (Table 2.6).

A key concept linking genetics and evolution is *genetic fitness,* or the *Genetic Fitness* average reproductive success of each genotype. Fitness in the genetic sense does not correspond to "healthy"; a sterile person in the pink of health is nevertheless an evolutionary failure. Fitness is a measure of the average worth of each genotype in reproductive terms, caused either by differences among people in ability to survive or by differences in fertility. As such, fitness is a function of both the environment and the genes, for a combination of alleles might be very helpful at one time or place, but harmful at another. There are no alleles that are "good" under all circumstances.

The basis of fitness, or reproductive success, can be judged in two ways. Taking a simple two-allele codominant situation with its three

Table 2.6. A numerical example for computing allele frequencies when dominance is present.

Number = 200			Suppose 200 people in a population were observed for earlobe type.
Phenotypes: Genotypes:	Unattached UU; Uu	Attached uu	Because there is dominance, there are two phenotypes corresponding to the three genotypes.
Number in each category	150	50	Suppose the observed numbers were as noted.
Percentages	.75	.25	Then these are the percentages.
Frequency of recessive allele	uu = .25 u = √.25 u = .5		To obtain the frequency of the recessive allele, take the square root of the frequency of homozygous recessives.
Frequency of dominant allele	U = 1.0 − frequency of u = 1.0 − .5 = .5		Because the allele frequencies must add up to one, the frequency of the dominant allele is obtained by subtraction.

genotypes, one can compute the average absolute reproductive success of each alternative. If AA individuals average 1.1 offspring, AA' 1.2, and A'A' .9, these absolute figures can be taken as measures of fitness.

We can also set the most prolific genotype equal to 1; it is the optimal in these conditions. We can then compute relative fitnesses. If 1.2 offspring is equivalent to 100 percent success, the relative fitness of AA (1.1 offspring) is .92 and that of A'A' is .75. Although absolute fitnesses are more accurate reflections of reality, the relative fitness values are much easier to deal with mathematically, and therefore are more commonly used. The average fitness of a population is, simply, equal to the fitness of each genotype weighted according to how often it occurs within the population. A population with equal numbers of AA, AA' and A'A' people would have an average relative fitness of $\frac{1.0 + .92 + .75}{3}$ or .89.

Summary An understanding of evolution, the change in the frequency of genes in a population, demands a knowledge of genetics. Although we cannot reduce anatomical and behavioral factors to the level of genetic analysis except by inference, we can study the current evolution of modern human populations by their alterations in gene frequency.

We can analyze the behavior of genes at three levels: biochemical, chromosomal, and populational. From biochemical genetics we learn that DNA, the genetic material, directs the production of proteins. The proteins are the basis of many functional requirements of life. The synthesis of proteins occurs through a series of biochemical steps: the inherited blueprint, the DNA, is "read" and its directions translated into a string of amino acids, a protein.

The evolutionary phenomenon known as mutation is the change in the structure of a piece of DNA, which can in turn alter the structure and function of a protein. Most mutations involve only a small rearrangement of the DNA, but because of the interconnectedness of the systems of the body, a small chemical change can have large effects on survival and reproduction. The constantly and randomly occurring changes in the genetic material provide for genetic alternatives from which natural selection can choose the better adapted and discard the poorly adapted forms. The gene's degree of adaptation depends on the environment in which it is present.

Chromosomal or Mendelian genetics involves several indispensable terms: alleles, genotype, phenotype, dominance, linkage, pleiotropy, polygenesis, and meiosis. All have to do with the way in which the DNA is passed from parent to offspring or with how the genes function. We find that for many traits the genotype and environment interact to produce the individual's phenotype. Genes set certain limits on the degree of skin pigmentation, but the phenotype is affected also by environmental factors, such as exposure to sunlight, diet, and state of health.

In sexually reproducing organisms, such as humans, we see that meiosis allows for the maintenance of the correct number of genes in every generation by producing sex cells with one gene for every trait. The union of sperm and egg creates a normal individual with two genes for each trait. Proper development depends on having neither too many nor too few copies of the genes. Because sexual reproduction has major effects on evolution (see Chapter 3), a knowledge of Mendelian genetics is important.

Population geneticists analyze the changes in gene frequencies that result from evolutionary processes. The basic concept of population genetics, the gene pool, describes the population's genetic makeup by means of allele frequencies and genotype frequencies.

The Hardy-Weinberg equilibrium makes use of information about the gene pool to predict how the genotypes would be distributed in a population that is not undergoing evolution. We see that the distribution is based on probabilities and that in this ideal population, allele and genotype frequencies do not change. The Hardy-Weinberg equilibrium can also be used to compute allele frequencies for traits showing dominance.

In the next chapter we will consider genetics, especially population genetics, and the evolutionary processes in some detail.

Chapter 3

Evolution in Action

An analysis of human history in an evolutionary framework assumes that we accept evolution as an appropriate model for interpreting the data. Certainly, not everyone accepts this view, and several times in this century, the United States has been the home of anti-evolution movements. Though the reasons why this country should foster such movements are intriguing, the question of import is whether there is any truth to the claim that evolutionary biology is not scientific. In order to respond, first we will review what makes a methodology a science, and then see whether evolution fits.

How Science Works

As a first approximation, we can say that the scientific method is a structured way of solving problems. The structuring involves the formulation of a hypothesis—a statement of the problem—which is subject to testing and is potentially falsifiable. Data are generated by one or another forms of experiment and the hypothesis is examined in light of the data. At this point, the hypothesis is viewed as either: (1) supported by the data, (2) disproven, or (3) requiring modification.

Mendel's work with inheritance in pea plants is a good example of this process. Mendel formulated rules about the integrity of genes and their ability to segregate (see page 41). He performed experiments by breeding thousands of plants, then looking at the results and concluding that his initial hypothesis was supported. Unfortunately for Mendel, no one else paid any attention to his work at the time, but that's another story. Later, others did rediscover his publication, checked his results, and started to ask questions that extended and modified his conclusions. Some of the phenomena they discovered, such as linked genes, didn't accord with Mendel's initial statements. In a treelike fashion, one question led to others, and the answers and more questions formed the field of modern genetics.

This rather sketchy and simplistic view of one scientist's work does illustrate a few key features of science in general.

1. Scientific hypotheses are fertile. They generate many new questions and areas to be investigated.
2. It must be possible for a hypothesis to fail tests to be considered

scientific. If a statement can't be tested and potentially disproven, it's not scientific.

3. The validity of a hypothesis is judged by its predictive success. How well does it predict solutions to new questions?

4. Thus, scientific hypotheses, even when supported by testing, are tentative. They are not immutable, but subject to refinement. We must always be open to modifying the hypothesis to fit future information.

Granted, this is a brief and admittedly "Alice in Wonderland" view of the way science and scientists operate. Scientists are real people too, with egos and ambitions as well as ethics. The methodology sometimes goes awry in real life, but another feature is that it is self-correcting. Scientists are always checking each other's work, and inaccuracies are sooner or later corrected.

How well does evolution fit these criteria? How well have its conclusions been supported? It has been argued that evolutionary hypotheses cannot be tested, for they deal with past events and therefore can't be predictive. This is inaccurate for several reasons. For one, evolution is constantly going on and, in fact, experiments can be designed to test the predictive success of evolutionary hypotheses. When dealing with an organism with a short generation, we can actually see evolutionary changes and check how well predictions fit observations.

Secondly, when dealing with past happenings, evolutionary studies can be retrodictive; that is, hypotheses can be generated about past events and tested against new data as they are uncovered. For a long time, physical anthropologists felt that human evolution was characterized by the early appearance of a large brain, followed by the later development of the ability to walk on two legs. Fossils unearthed over the span of several decades have clearly shown this to be false, in fact, 180 degrees off. The big brain developed late in our evolution. This revelation has in turn led to many other questions which form large segments of this book. Evolution is a very fertile discipline. As new hypotheses are generated, they are also subject to testing by the criterion of predictive (or retrodictive) success and are eminently scientific.

A criticism often made of evolution is that, "After all, it's only a theory." Such comments indicate a prominent misunderstanding of the qualities of a scientific theory. In science, a theory is not simply someone's off-the-top-of-the-head thoughts. It is a set of general principles which have developed out of massive amounts of hypothesis testing and, as such, has the great weight of supporting evidence. We all have "theories" about why our favorite baseball team lost the pennant last year or why the government is pursuing a particular course of action. Such usage of the word "theory" should not be equated with the much more rigorous usage in the phrase "theory of evolution." The latter is not just educated guesswork, but has been developed, tested, and refined through millions of hours of human intellectual endeavor.

In Darwin's original formulations, primacy was given to natural selection as the driving force of evolution, and he was largely correct. Natural selection is not synonymous with evolution. It is but one of the processes that can cause changes in the gene pool of a population, and can subsequently cause evolution. The term natural selection implies a choice or variation. The variation that Darwin observed in natural populations had to have an origin and, of course, that second evolutionary process is mutation.

As was seen in Chapter 2, mutations can lead to alterations in the structure and functioning of the individual. Variation, once having arisen by the process of mutation, can then be worked on by natural selection. Some mutations are adaptive; they help the individual survive and reproduce in a particular environment. Natural selection results in an increase in the frequency of this new, beneficial mutant gene. As we noted previously, this is simply a consequence of the fact that those individuals with genes well suited for survival and reproduction in a particular environment will, on the average, out-reproduce those with less well-suited genes. The better adapted genes become more frequent as time goes by. The flip side of this process is that selection can work to rid a gene pool of harmful genes. This differential reproduction of genotypes is natural selection. This is quite different from Darwin's view of selection as "survival of the fittest," for it is not whether you survive that is important, but rather the number of offspring you produce relative to the number produced by other members of your population. Living to be one hundred years old without ever mating and reproducing not only would be less fun but also would be an evolutionary failure compared to having five or six offspring during a life span of fifty years.

Viewed in modern terms, we see that much, though not all, of evolution is the result of the interactions of these two forces of evolution, selection and mutation. Several important implications follow from knowledge of these two forces.

To reiterate, evolution's direction is the production of organisms that possess genes that are well-suited to survive in a particular environment. The force pushing in this direction is selection. It is the only evolutionary process to be said to have a direction. At the beginning of this century, some geneticists felt that large, single mutations could result in the appearance of whole, new species, a theory called *mutationism*. We now know this to be false, that the appearance of new sorts of organisms requires many genetic events and that these events are ordered to increase adaptation by selection.

From this, it follows that humans are not the goal of evolution. We are not the endpoint of evolution, nor are other animals working their way up a ladder of life to become like us. Chimpanzees are not going to become people someday. Each organism is evolving to survive in its own niche, in its own life-style, whether it is in the trees or underground, eating this food or that, active at night or during the day. Life forms are dispersing into different environments and ways of living and the only goal is for each to be able to deal with its own problems. People are evolving to survive and reproduce in a very broad range of environments, but all require the ability to use a language, live in a cultural setting, make tools and so forth. Apes and monkeys have quite different requirements and are evolving constantly to live in their niches.

As adaptation to an environment is the goal, and as environments are always changing, evolution has no end. What is beneficial at one time and place will become obsolete as the environment changes. As we cannot predict how environments will change, we cannot predict what course evolution will take. Will future humans be bald-headed and large-brained as some science fiction stories picture them? Only if those with less hair and bigger brains are better adapted for survival and reproduction in future human environments. Even if we could state with certainty that these two human traits would be highly advantageous in the future, there is still no guarantee we would evolve along this route. Mutations occur at random, not because they are needed. The organism cannot sense a need and order up the requisite mutation. Should an appropriate mutation simply not happen, natural selection would not have the raw material with which to work: no variation, no selection.

Mutations, as we saw in Chapter 2, do not yield the bizarre creations so popular in fiction. Grossly abnormal individuals who have multiple mutations or chromosomal defects usually do not survive. In fact, as pointed out earlier, it appears that there are many neutral mutations. These neither harm nor benefit the individual; thus they do not affect the chances of surviving and reproducing (Figure 3.1). The neutral mutation classification can also be pictured as including those mutations which only affect fitness to a very limited degree. The fate of these genes is determined not by selection, but by a third process called genetic drift.

Genetic drift, the third process, refers to random fluctuations in the frequency of a gene from generation to generation. Initially a new mutation exists only within one individual. The odds that this mutant gene will get passed on to the next generation, the following one, and so on, are vanishingly small. Nevertheless, the possibility exists and, given the appearance of a large number of neutral or nearly neutral mutations, one can mathematically predict that a percentage of these mutations will, just by chance, achieve 100 percent frequency in a population.

As you might expect, the smaller the population, the more likely it is that genetic drift will be effective. Taking a different case of drift, the loss of a fairly common allele via chance, imagine a small population, say fifty people, in which 10 percent have one form of a genetic trait (blue eyes) and the other 90 percent have the alternative (brown eyes). If one day an earthquake swallows up 10 of the members, including all those with blue eyes, the frequency of the trait will have been markedly altered: the population has evolved, or changed genetically. If the population is larger, say one million people, and 10 percent (100,000) are blue-eyed, the death by accident of 5 of these blue-eyed people will not produce a significant alteration in the genetic composition of the group;

Figure 3.1. *Many mutations have invisible effects and do not significantly affect a person's ability to survive and reproduce. Some have visible effects and still do not noticeably affect normal functioning. This child has a rare dominant gene that causes polydactyly, more than five digits per hand and foot.*

its evolution will not be affected. These are not examples of natural selection, for the eye color of the individuals has nothing to do with their chance of surviving the accident. Thus drift, too, can change the genetic composition of a group; its general tendency is to reduce the variation within the group.

A fourth cause of evolutionary change is *gene flow*, or admixture, achieved through migration and interbreeding, when individuals from one breeding population leave and join another. The movement and mating of people are often related to social values, to conflicts within or outside groups that result in fragmentation, to mating patterns, and to other aspects of social organization as well as to geography.

The effect of immigration on the genetic makeup of a population is directly related to the size of that population. In a small population, the frequency of many genes may be significantly altered, whereas a large population can absorb a sizeable number of immigrants before showing a noticeable change. Emigration (outward migration) may also change the frequency in the original population; in small populations, emigration may ultimately cause total loss of certain genes.

Gene flow not only can alter the frequency of genes previously present in the receiving population, but also can, like mutation, introduce totally new genes into the group.

Evidence for Evolution

What then is the evidence that has been generated in support of the contention that these processes cause evolution? This is a very broad question which could take several lifetimes to answer. Fortunately the evidence falls into several categories which we can briefly review at this stage.

Comparative Sciences

The popularity of a zoo's ape house indicates that we all recognize marked similarities between the inhabitants and ourselves; the behavior of chimps often reflects our own, and they certainly bear anatomical resemblances to us. We also recognize that other mammals share fewer similarities, while the reptiles are quite unlike us in anatomy and behavior. These observations are essentially evolutionary ones. Why are chimps so much like us? Because until very recently we and they were the same animal. We and chimps diverged from each other relatively recently (5 to 15 million years ago; the exact number is debated in Chapter 6); as a result the two of us share many traits. Because chimps and humans on the one hand and, say, tigers, have not shared a common ancestor for upwards of 75 million years, we and tigers have diverged more. Reptiles and mammals last had a common ancestor over 150 million years ago and so are even less alike in anatomy and behavior. By and large, the more similar organisms are, the more recently they shared a common ancestor.

Comparative sciences can thus provide evidence of evolution. Comparative anatomy was one of the earliest to do so: Darwin and his contemporaries drew heavily on it. Comparative embryology, the study of embryos and their development, was also used quite early. Recently, comparative biochemistry and immunology have provided information on evolutionary relationships; we now know that humans and chimps are very similar in molecular makeup. Behavioral comparisons are also very informative.

Fossil Evidence

A direct line of evidence for major evolutionary changes is the fossil record. Fossils are mineralized remains that show us what past life forms looked like. Most fossils are parts of the skeletal anatomy or teeth, but lately even fossilized footprints of our ancestors have been uncovered. Fossils record the changes in the anatomy of our ancestors. By understanding our anatomical evolution we can try to deduce the alterations in behavior. Evolution is adaptive; anatomy changes so that the organism may better perform certain behaviors. Our thumb lengthened because of selection pressures for finer manipulative skills; selection altered our pelvis and legs to accommodate better upright walking.

We also have firsthand evidence of evolution: we have seen it happen. Many observational accounts deal with insects or microorganisms that have short generations and can change rapidly.

Over the last fifty years we have seen the development of many antibiotics, chemicals like penicillin and streptomycin that can kill or retard the growth of certain microbes. Though miraculous, these drugs are self-defeating to a degree, for the widespread use of an antibiotic leads to the evolution of a strain resistant to that drug. Ingenious experimental designs have demonstrated that the initial microbial resistance to a drug is not induced by exposure to the antibiotic; rather, the antibiotic results in the increased frequency of this resistance by operating as a selective force.

Bacteria, like all living things, are biochemically variable. Some bacteria contain mutant genes which, among other effects, allow them to survive in an environment containing a particular antibiotic. When this antibiotic is invented and distributed, the mutant becomes highly beneficial to the survival of the microbe. Those containing the mutation can infect a person, survive the antibiotic treatment, reproduce, and spread to other people. This form of the organism becomes very common; the bacteria without this mutation are killed and do not spread. With the evolution of microbial strains resistant to penicillin, streptomycin, and other antibiotics, it becomes necessary to discover new antibiotics capable of checking the evolved bacteria. The fact that physicians are reluctant to prescribe an antibiotic every time we have an infection is based on knowledge of this evolutionary process; if they blunt the usefulness of an antibiotic by using it to treat minor infections, they are only leading to the appearance of a microbe for which they may have no treatment.

A similar process has resulted in the appearance of insects resistant to the effects of DDT and other insecticides. DDT has been used to control populations of many insects, including houseflies, lice, and malaria-carrying mosquitoes. Each of these applications has led to the evolution of strains capable of surviving in environments with the insecticide.

An even more intriguing example, with a moral for our present ecological problems, comes from the attempt by Australian farmers to rid that continent of rabbits (Figure 3.2). Before European contact, Australia had no rabbits; very few placental mammals were found there. In the 1800s a variety of rabbits was accidentally introduced and, having rabbits' habits, rapidly spread through much of Australia, eating crops as they went. By 1928 there were 500 million rabbits on the continent. Farmers and shepherds, much perturbed by their economic losses, asked the government how they could reduce the rabbit population. Scientists came up with the apparently brilliant idea of introducing a disease, myxomatosis, which was lethal to almost 100 percent of these rabbits. The release of rabbit-biting mosquitoes carrying the myxomatosis virus almost eliminated the natural population. However, a few Australian rabbits had a mutation that made them resistant to the disease, and from

Figure 3.2. *A view of the destructive capabilities of rabbits in Australia. Running down the center of the photograph is a rabbit-proof fence. On the left, rabbits have eaten all the plants they could reach. In the process they destroyed land otherwise suitable for cattle and sheep grazing.*

these few survivors the population started to rebuild. The virus, too, was evolving. The disease organism's evolutionary strategy is not to kill off its host, but to coexist with it. The viruses that could infect a rabbit without killing it were also selected for. In a fairly short time, the rabbits' gene pool was modified for increased resistance, and the virus's genetic structure was selected for decreased virulence. Very soon after the epidemic, the rabbit population recovered (Figure 3.3).[1]*

These small-scale, visible cases of evolution have been said to be quite different from those alterations seen in the fossil record. Actually the difference is usually said to be only one of degree, a quantitative difference. Most feel that the large changes seen when examining the fossil record reflect the accumulation of many, many small changes over immense periods of time. However, while it is relatively straightforward to tie DDT or myxomatosis resistance to the genes, it is not so easy to decipher the complex interrelationship of genes and the sorts of *morphology* (and behavior) we see in the fossil record. While the major shifts in life forms seen in the fossils are undoubtedly the result of the evolutionary forces, there have been and still are debates as to the relative importance of the different forces and the rates at which they cause change to come about. We will return to this debate later.

Although they are brought about by the same processes, the large changes seen in the fossil record, or *macroevolution* (*macro* = large),

*See page 562 for notes to Chapter 3.

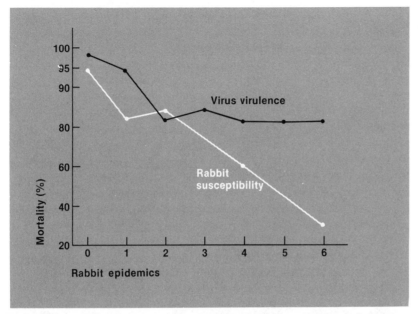

Figure 3.3. The decreasing susceptibility of Australian rabbits is illustrated by the rapid decrease in the percentage of rabbits that died upon exposure to a standard, highly virulent (disease-causing) myxoma virus. As the Australian strain of the virus underwent natural selection, it declined noticeably in its ability to kill laboratory rabbits. The time scale refers to the number of epidemics to which the population was exposed.

are generally studied by one group of people, with the small alterations in the frequency of alleles in a population, or *microevolution* (*micro* = small), studied by another. Macroevolutionists tend to be specialists in areas such as paleontology, geology, and comparative anatomy, while microevolutionists usually concentrate more on genetics and physiology. This is, however, something of an artificial distinction and one of convenience. The standard interpretation of evolutionary mechanisms today, the Neo-Darwinian (*neo* = new) or synthetic approach, relies on the integration of knowledge of genetics, paleontology, and evolutionary principles.

Macroevolution

Two Definitions of Species

Although the details of classifying animals will be dealt with later (Chapter 4), in order to understand the evolution of species we must first know what a species (plural: species) is. The definition of a *biological species* appears to be straightforward: animals are members of the same species if normal males and females are actively or potentially capable of mating and producing fertile offspring.[2] All humans are members of one species, for fertile offspring result from matings between members of any populations. The horse and donkey are not classified as members of one species, for although they can produce offspring, these offspring (mules) are sterile; they are evolutionary dead ends. It is not possible for the genes of a horse to flow into the donkey's pool of genes, or vice versa. It is at least potentially possible for Eskimo genes to enter the pool of any other human population.

In theory it is easy to decide whether two living animals are members of the same species (though even this involves some difficulties). But this definition of a biological species cannot be applied when at least one of the animals is represented only by fossilized remains. We cannot know if the people living 2 million years ago could have interbred with us. We do know that they looked quite different from us, particularly from the neck up, and had a different technology and different diet. Because of these differences we somewhat arbitrarily agree to call them a different species.

It appears that 2 million years ago there was more than one kind of human (Chapter 9). Again from anatomy, tools, and inferences about diet and behavior (but not breeding patterns, for these do not fossilize), we must decide how many species of humans coexisted. A definition of species based primarily on anatomy is called an *evolutionary, paleo* (old) or *chrono* (time), species concept. One expert defines an evolutionary species as a group of ancestor-descendant populations with its own evolutionary trends and tendencies.[3]

Origins of Species

There are two routes by which new life forms appear; both are forms of the process called speciation (Figure 3.4). One, straight-line evolution, or *anagenesis* (ana = upward; genesis = origination), is the gradual change of one form of animal into another form: one species replaces another. In anagenesis the number of species is not altered; one simply

Figure 3.4. A chronospecies can through anagenesis evolve into another species: I→II→III. Through cladogenesis, a chronospecies can evolve into several more chronospecies and/or biological species:
$$A \begin{smallmatrix} \to B \to D \\ \to C \to E \end{smallmatrix}$$

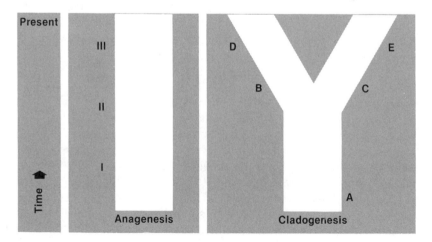

changes into the other through time due to the gradual accumulation of genetic change.

When we look at the history of our species, we will see that the fossil record supports the contention that at least for some time our evolution proceeded by anagenesis. One-half million years ago our ancestors were different enough from us to be called a different *(chrono)* species. Over time this species evolved enough — mainly in respect to cranial features — to warrant being called by a different species name. The changes came about largely as a result of selection favoring mutations which increased brain size, ability to use a language, and so forth. One species evolved into one, new species; this is anagenesis.

The second pathway is called *cladogenesis* (*clado* = sprouting), or branching evolution; one life form yields two or more new ones. One species is subdivided into two or more genetically isolated populations by the appearance of some geographic barrier. Depending on the kind of animal under consideration, isolation might follow a change in the course of a river, the appearance of a mountain or desert, the building of a city, or simply distance — anything that will effectively prevent mating between members of the populations. Because no two places on the earth are exactly the same, the inhabitants of the two (or more) areas will be subject to more or less different selection forces: they may have different food sources, be affected by different diseases, exposed to different amounts of rainfall, preyed upon by predators with different habits. We can expect members of the groups to become more and more different as time passes. It is also unlikely that the mutations that occur in one area will be duplicated exactly in the other; hence more difference. Either at the time of or subsequent to isolation, drift also may cause the groups to differ genetically. Because interbreeding is not occurring, there is nothing to counteract these dispersive forces. The groups will ultimately become so different that even if the geographic barrier was removed the animals could no longer produce fertile offspring. When this condition is achieved, speciation is said to have occurred.

Geographic isolation is a prerequisite for branching evolution; nothing else that we know of can begin cladogenesis. Once geographic isolation and the ensuing divergent evolutionary changes have established two distinct species, other isolating mechanisms maintain the reproductive isolation even if the initial geographic barrier has been removed. Isolating mechanisms operate in two main ways to separate species. In the first, interbreeding never occurs. Such premating barriers include different courtship procedures or habitat differences that preclude the two from meeting. Second, if interbreeding does occur, post-mating barriers come into play: the sperm of one does not fertilize the other's egg; the egg does not develop; or hybrid animals (offspring that come from interbreeding) are not able to compete with individuals of the parental groups or are biologically weak or even infertile, like the mule.

Thus, over time, a variety of mechanisms develop to maintain the separation of two distinct species. In this way evolution, once having produced an array of genes that adapts an animal to its way of life, prevents disruption of the adaptive combination, which could follow breeding with other forms.

Very early in the evolution of our species, cladogenesis occurred. Several millions of years ago a group of human-like animals became subdivided into geographically isolated populations. Each pursued separate evolutionary paths, adapting to somewhat different ways of life and, as will be seen, evolving into separate, contemporaneous species. Only one of these has continued through time, ultimately to become us.

Semispecies Just as there are difficulties in applying our apparently straightforward definition of a biological species to long-dead animals, there are difficulties in defining species that are in the process of becoming reproductively isolated, for although members of the diverging groups may not be very successful at interbreeding, fertile offspring are occasionally produced.

There are many known examples of the inability of classification to reflect totally the complexities of speciation. Among our close relatives, the monkeys of Southeast Asia, are the rhesus monkey and the crab-eating monkey. The rhesus is found primarily in the Indian subcontinent, but outlying populations are found in Thailand. Crab-eating monkeys are common through the Malay Archipelago and Malaysia but also have outlyers in Thailand. In this small area of overlap, human disturbance of the environment results in occasional contact between the species, and interbreeding and fertile young are known. With how many species, then, are we dealing? Although the uncritical application of the biological species concept would define these animals as one species, most researchers regard them as two very closely related species, or *semispecies*. They reason that the interbreeding is so rare as to have virtually no effect on the vast majority of the animals in the central areas of the species' range. The interbreeding does not result in significant gene flow between the groups.

Rates and Patterns of Evolutionary Divergence The aftermath of speciation is divergence. Once two animals have split and evolved isolating mechanisms, there is no way for them to evolve back into the same species, for the differences which have come into being are so complex that it is impossible to relive all the changes in reverse sequence. Greater and greater differences build up with the passage of time. This is known as *divergent evolution;* all cladogenesis is divergent.

Adaptive Radiation Evolution does not happen at a constant rate (but see page 208); sometimes the rate of divergence can be quite rapid and the number of new species formed quite large. When an animal enters an environment which offers a number of unused new ways of life, or unoccupied *niches,* it may diverge quickly into many newly formed, geographically isolated populations, and evolve biological features that adapt it for each of these ways of life, resulting in a lot of cladogenesis. This evolutionary pattern is called an *adaptive radiation*.

The finches Darwin observed in the Galapagos Islands gave him one of his clearest leads for formulating a theory of evolution. Today about fourteen species seem to have evolved from one ancestral species, which was derived from a mainland South America species. The first finches probably began their life on the Galapagos when a few mainland birds reached the islands by chance. They then spread to all the islands, and because finches do not normally fly great distances, each island's populations remained isolated from the others. The Galapagos have few other species of land birds and thus provided the finches with many vacant adaptive niches. In time, the finches underwent an adaptive radiation, a lot of cladogenesis, evolving to lead many new ways of life. The ground finches of the *Geospiza* group evolved heavy beaks suited for cracking seeds. Generally speaking, the larger beaked birds are those that chose larger seeds for the preponderance of their diet. The tree finches are vegetarians with shorter, thick beaks, while the warbler-like finch *(Certhida)* is insectivorous with a slender beak. The woodpecker-like finch (Figure 1.6) evolved a behavioral adaptation for feeding. In each case, the finches specialized through the interplay of mutations and selection so as to use the available foods. For instance, when a mutation that slightly increased the robustness of the beak appeared in a bird that had to crack large seeds for its supper, it was increased in frequency through selection. Thus evolved the rather specialized beaks seen in Figure 3.5, as well as other features. Once the birds are no longer capable of interbreeding, even when living in the same area, we say they have speciated. This large amount of rapid speciation to take advantage of new ways of life is an adaptive radiation.

Convergent and Parallel Evolution Although all cladogenesis is divergent when investigated carefully, occasionally two animals superficially come to resemble each other more and more. The porpoise is a mammal whose ancestors lived on land. Over millions of years, after going back into the seas, the porpoise has come to resemble the shark in several ways: it has *converged* on the evolution of the shark. The porpoise has evolved streamlining for speed, strong tail fins for locomotion, and large teeth for predation. Yet internally the porpoise is nothing like a shark: it gets its oxygen from the air, not water; it has internal fertilization and a uterus for incubating the embryo; its fins contain modified forms of the same bones present in our limbs; and the cellular structure of its skeleton is quite different from that of the shark. The porpoise's superficial similarities to a shark reflect only the fact that, as marine predators, both animals face some similar requirements and natural selection has produced some common answers in both groups. Similar effects are seen in an aquatic reptile too. *Convergent evolution* refers to the appearance of superficial similarities in unrelated species as both adapt to deal with similar environments (Figure 3.6).

Figure 3.5. *After inhabiting the Galapagos Islands, the finches underwent an adaptive radiation — a lot of divergent evolution. Among other features, the modern finches have come to differ in beak shape as the species specialized to eat different foods. To-day there are four main groups (genera — see chapter 4) and fourteen species.*

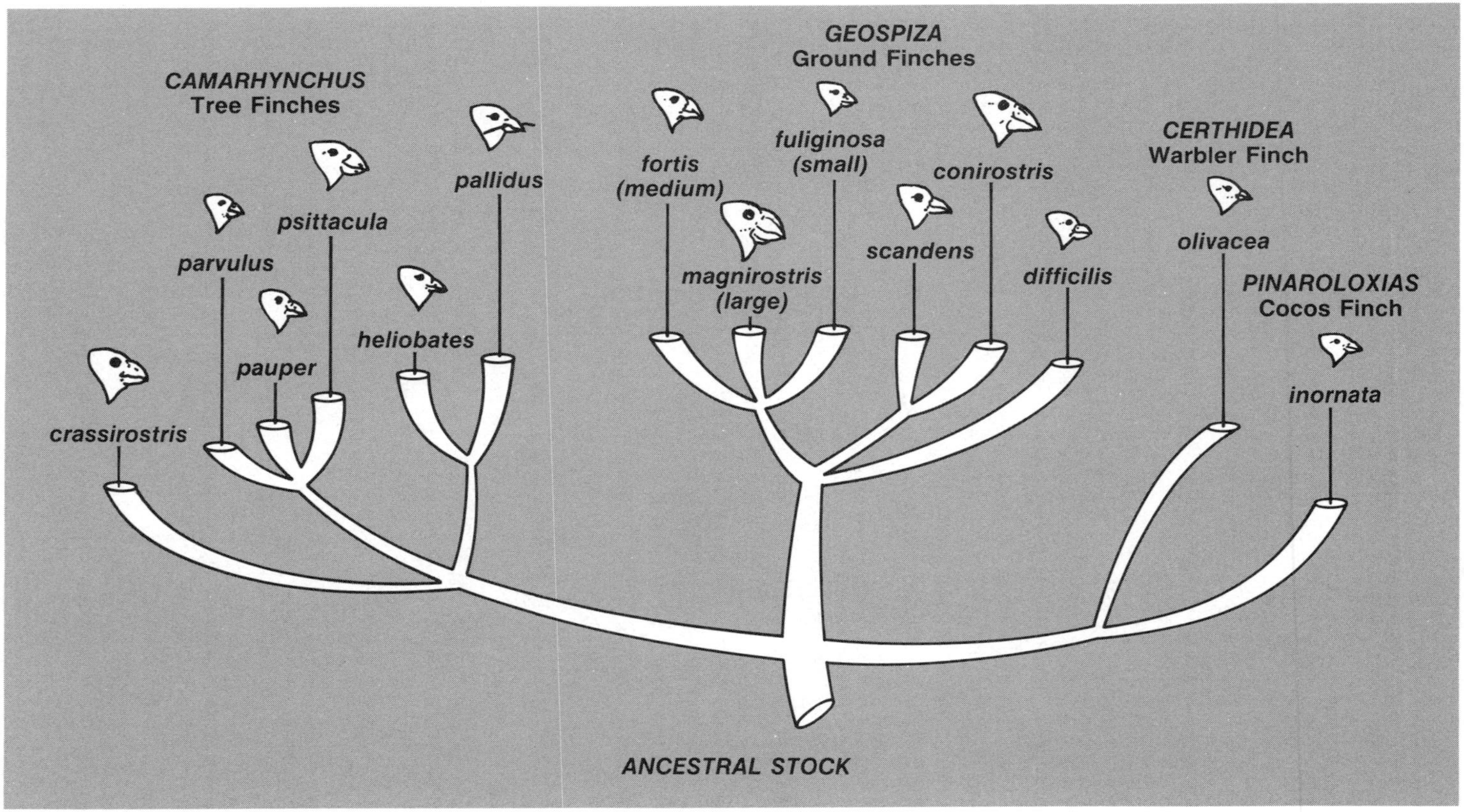

Figure 3.6. *Convergent evolution can be seen by comparing three animals which, though only very distantly related, look very similar. All three evolved superficial features as a common adaptation to life as fast swimming predators. From top to bottom, a fish (shark), a reptile* (Ichthyosaurus), *and a mammal (porpoise).*

An analogous situation involves two closely related animal species that are already similar due to recent common ancestry. Their evolution of further similarities as they adapt to comparable environmental conditions is known as *parallel evolution*. Again, the animals are not becoming genetically more alike, but they are evolving similar ways of coping with similar stresses. The monkeys of the Old and New Worlds are a good example. Though genetically quite distinct (Chapter 6), they have evolved some similar locomotor and behavioral adaptations as both attempt to survive in tropical forests. Different human populations, when faced with similar problems, likewise evolve similar solutions. Yet when we investigate these populations in detail, we find that the specific mutations involved are usually different in the different groups; they have evolved in parallel, achieving the same net goal by different routes.

Variation among species is a result of the process of speciation, as different mutations, coupled with different selection pressures, accumulate genetic differences in geographically isolated groups. Within a species variation is of prime interest and the ways in which the evolutionary forces

Microevolution

Maintaining Variation

increase or decrease the level of genetic variation is an important concern of the synthetic theory.

A species with little variation is in a very precarious evolutionary position. Should the environment of such a group alter rapidly, it is likely that extinction will occur. The presence of variants, even those with no obvious value, provides a valuable defence against future disaster.

Theodosius Dobzhansky, among others, has shown that much variability is hidden in the gene pool.[4] He demonstrated this using fruit flies (Drosophilia) in selective breeding experiments designed to bring out hidden variation. The genetic trait Dobzhansky decided to study was the flies' preference for light or dark passageways. He started with flies from one population which he randomly divided in half. Initially, the two subgroups showed similar numbers of flies prefering light or dark passages. Then, in one strain, Dobzhansky selected only flies that preferred the light routes as parents for the next generation. In the other strain, only those preferring the dark were allowed to reproduce. As this pattern was kept up for several generations, there appeared a very marked difference in the preferences of the two strains. One chose the light the vast majority of the time, and the other principally chose the dark. This indicates that the original population had a large amount of hidden variation present which could provide the basis for, and be made apparent by, selection. Such large amounts of concealed variability can provide the necessary paths to new adaptations. In part, this hidden variability was the result of recessive genes being brought to light. Recombination, by physically associating the genes in new arrangement, can also produce new variants.

Because of the significance of variation, it is important to understand the evolutionary processes that increase or decrease variation in populations. The examples we will use are on a small scale, involving slight shifts in the frequency of an allele controlling one or another blood protein. This is not to say that there were no variants for brain organization, pelvis structure, hand dexterity; it is just that knowledge of genetic variations in complex anatomical and behavioral features is very rudimentary. The much simpler protein variants are better, though by no means perfectly, understood. It should be possible to imagine that the forces to be described were important in the evolution of a large brain size, upright posture, and other major trends discussed in the next several chapters.

Polymorphisms Traits that show genetic variability are described as *polymorphic* (*poly* = many; *morph* = shape). For a trait to be called a genetic polymorphism it should meet two criteria. First, each form of the trait must be more common in a population (greater than 1 percent) than would be likely just from recurrent mutations. If one expression of the trait occurs in 99.99 percent of the people and the other is found in one out of every 10,000 people, the trait is not considered a genetic polymorphism. Second, the two (or more) forms of the trait must be *discontinuous;* that is, the expressions of the alleles must fall into discrete categories. There can be type M, N, or MN blood, but nothing else. Hence, the MN system is a genetic polymorphism when both alleles are found in a gene pool. Stature is a polymorphism, but it is not a genetic polymorphism because the differences in height among people in a population do not fall into discrete classes: there is a range between 5'1" and 5'1.1". In addition, a person's height is determined by very complex interactions among many sets of alleles (stature is polygenic) and many environmental factors. The discrete, discontinuously distributed genetic polymorphisms are not subject to much environmental modification. However, the genes involved in producing both continuous and discontinuous variation are probably maintained in a population by the same sorts of evolutionary processes.

Polymorphisms can be preserved in several ways. The first and least realistic way of preserving variability is to have no evolution. Allelic frequencies will not change from one generation to the next in a randomly mating group in which natural selection, mutation, drift, and migration are not active, that is, when the population is meeting the rules of the Hardy-Weinberg equilibrium. But we know that the Hardy-Weinberg law's criteria make it an idealization. There is no infinitely large population that practices random breeding, lacks migration, and is not subject to selection and mutation. The rule is useful, though, because it allows us to compare observed data with an expectation (page 63).

In the real world, if we do find a deviation from expectation based on the Hardy-Weinberg model, we can go on to try to identify the factor(s) causing the departure. These factors may be of two sorts. Either the deviation is caused by chance due to errors in sampling or it may be caused by one or more of the four evolutionary factors (Table 3.1). The chance referred to is not the same as those chance forces underlying genetic drift; here the chance is that the sample we draw does not accurately reflect the gene frequencies in the whole population. In drift, chance factors at the time of fertilization are changing the population's genetic makeup all the time.

Small departures of observed genotype frequencies from what we expect are more likely to come from errors in sampling, but large deviations lead us to think some evolutionary force is operating. To be more objective, we use statistical tests to help decide whether any deviation is likely to be due to chance or not. A statistical test cannot tell us that the difference definitely comes from one or the other alternative; it does tell us the odds that a departure from the expected result is caused by chance. The deviations have to be rather large before the statistics "tell" us that evolutionary forces are the most likely explanation; it is hard to detect evolutionary effects (Table 3.2).

Given that variation will not be maintained in the real world because of the absence of evolution, how can evolutionary processes ac-

Table 3.1. A numerical example for predicting genotype frequency.

Suppose that you tested a population sample of 100 people for MN and found the phenotype and genotype distribution to be:

MM = 14   MN = 52   NN = 34

a   What are the allele frequencies (M = .4, N = .6)?

b   What is the expected genotype distribution according to Hardy-Weinberg?
    (MM = .16,   MN = .48,   NN = .36)

c   How might you explain the difference between observed and expected genotype frequencies? (Most likely: chance. Other possibilities include selection for the heterozygote or nonrandom mating.)

Answer a, b, and c, given this observed genotype distribution:

MM = 50   MN = 0   NN = 50

Answers
    a   M = .5, N = .5
    b   MM = .25, MN = .50, NN = .25
    c   Likely answer: selection against the heterozygote. Less likely: nonrandom mating or chance.

count for variability in real, natural populations? One situation is referred to as a *balanced polymorphism*. There appear to be many traits for which the heterozygote is the best adapted, at least under certain environmental conditions, and of course, to have heterozygotes, you must have variation. The situation in which each homozygote is less genetically fit than the heterozygote is known as a *balanced polymorphism*. Here selection is performing a balancing act by favoring the alleles when they are contained in the heterozygote state and working against them in the homozygotes. In this situation, a point of balance, or equilibrium, is reached just as one can be attained for water level when a partially filled bathtub has the water turned on and the drain opened so as to balance water input and outflow. (Do not try this at home, as Murphy's Law states that you will flood your bathroom.)

As you might imagine, this aspect of population genetics can be dealt with mathematically, and Table 3.3 steps through an example related to

Dr. D. F. Roberts and colleagues gathered data on the MN blood group system for several groups in northwest India. The sample of Brahmins from Rajasthan state comprise 94 people distributed so:

M = 38 MN = 42 N = 14

The gene frequencies are thus:

$$M = \frac{2(38) + 42}{2(94)} = .627$$

$$N = 1.0 - .627 = .373$$

The expected genotype frequencies, assuming Hardy-Weinberg is met:

$$MM = (.627)^2 = .393 \qquad MN = 2(.63)(.37) = .468$$

$$NN = (.373)^2 = .139$$

As there are 94 people, these percentages translate into *expected genotype numbers* of:

Expected: MN = (.393)(94) = 36.9
Observed: 38
Expected: MN = (.468)(94) = 44.0
Observed: 42
Expected: NN = (.139)(94) = 13.1
Observed: 14

We can conclude that the agreement of observed and expected is so close that there is no evidence of evolution.

Data from: S.S. Papiha et al. (1982). *Annals of Human Biology*, 9(3), 235 – 251.

Table 3.2. An actual example of the application of the Hardy-Weinberg equilibrium.

sickle-cell hemoglobin. The pleiotropic effects of the sickle-cell hemoglobin allele and the reasons why sickle-cell disease kills have already been mentioned (page 35). For some time it was not clear why the frequency of this allele was rather high, up to 20 percent, in certain African populations. If the allele is deadly, why hadn't selection reduced its frequency? The rate is high because those with normal hemoglobin are subject to severe cases of malaria; those who are heterozygotes are largely resistant to severe malaria infection and they do not die of sickle-cell

Table 3.3. Allele frequencies and selection in a balanced polymorphism: the sickle-cell case.

BEFORE SELECTION

Fitnesses: It is noted by observation that in malarial areas AA people have about 90 percent as many children as AS individuals. SS individuals rarely survive and reproduce. If the fitness of AS, the optimum, is set at 1.0, then the fitness of AA = 0.9 and SS = 0.0.

Let us *assume*:
Population size: 121

Gene frequency: $A = \dfrac{10}{11}$ $\qquad\qquad\qquad\qquad S = \dfrac{1}{11}$

Then genotype frequency according to Hardy-Weinberg:

$AA = \left(\dfrac{10}{11}\right)^2 = \dfrac{100}{121}$ $\quad AS = 2\left(\dfrac{10}{11}\right)\left(\dfrac{1}{11}\right) = \dfrac{20}{121}$ $\quad SS = \left(\dfrac{1}{11}\right)^2 = \dfrac{1}{121}$

These conditions comprise an equilibrium point. Below we show that when selection operates, it will do so in such a way that the allele frequencies are not changed.

SELECTION

	AA = 100	AS = 20	SS = 1
Number of people before selection (assuming N = 121):	AA = 100	AS = 20	SS = 1
Selection:	0.1	0	1.0
People lost due to selection:	10 (malaria)	0	1 (sickle cell)
Number of alleles lost:	20 A	0 A or S	2 S
Survivors after selection:	90 AA	20 AS	0 SS

AFTER SELECTION

New gene frequency:

$A = \dfrac{\text{number of A alleles}}{\text{total number of alleles}}$

$= \dfrac{2 \text{ A alleles} \times 90 \text{ people} + 1 \text{ A allele} \times 20 \text{ people}}{2 \text{ alleles} \times 90 \text{ people} + 2 \text{ alleles} \times 20 \text{ people}}$

$= \dfrac{2 \times 90 + 1 \times 20}{2 \times 90 + 2 \times 20} = \dfrac{200}{220} = \boxed{\dfrac{10}{11}}$

$S = \dfrac{\text{number of S alleles}}{\text{total number of alleles}}$

$= \dfrac{1 \text{ S allele} \times 20 \text{ people}}{2 \text{ alleles} \times 90 \text{ people} + 2 \text{ alleles} \times 20 \text{ people}}$

$= \dfrac{1 \times 20}{2 \times 90 + 2 \times 20} = \dfrac{20}{220} = \boxed{\dfrac{1}{11}}$

anemia as do the SS homozygotes. The point of balance that is obtained is determined by the relative disadvantage of each homozygote. If one homozygote is ten times better off than the other, its allele will be maintained at a ten times higher frequency. This is not a magic trick; it simply follows from the fact that the homozygote with the higher fitness will be better able to reproduce, and as a result, that allele will have a higher frequency. Certainly the balance is not ideal: people still die from malaria and an unfortunate few succumb to sickle-cell anemia. But, all in all, the populations of malarial areas are better off with, than without, the polymorphism.

As might be predicted, when the environment changes, either by eradication of malaria or by migration into nonmalarial areas, the frequency of S drops. The black population in the United States was originally drawn from African populations in which the S frequency was between 8 and 15 percent. Today the frequency of S in the American black population has declined to between 2 and 6 percent. Part of this decline was due to the infusion of A alleles from whites, particularly in northern areas, but some of the change comes from changing selective pressures.

Much to the chagrin of physical anthropologists, sickle cell is the only balanced polymorphism they can talk about with great assurance. Scientists have hints and hunches about the causes of variation in some of the blood groups, blood proteins, and gross morphological traits, but they are not entirely convinced that those explanations are correct (Chapter 11).

Several other polymorphisms are thought to be maintained in equilibrium by malaria: hemoglobin variants like Hb^c and thalassemia (a complex anemia), and a red cell enzyme variant known as G-6-PD deficiency. If this is indeed the case, it indicates that there is often more than one evolutionary answer to a problem. Malaria's role as a selective agent is more impressive when we realize that even today more than a million people die each year from this disease. Before something was done to control it, the mortality rate was much higher.

Mutation All these polymorphic conditions, whether they come from balancing selection pressures or not, can be traced to mutation, the ultimate source of all new alleles. Even in traits generally not considered polymorphic, there is some variation caused by mutation. Many of the genetically caused disorders, such as phenylketonuria (PKU), alkaptonuria, and hemophilia, are as frequent as rates of mutation would lead us to expect them to be. Many of these deleterious mutations are recessive, which increases their variability by shielding the mutants from natural selection.

While mutation is responsible for the appearance of new genes, we have seen (page 47) that meiosis can also account for much variability in phenotypes. Combining already existing alleles in new arrangements provides a large store of variation.

Admixture The last mechanism preserving variation in a population that we will consider is admixture, or mixing genes from two or more gene pools. A flow of genes from one pool into another may not only change the frequencies of alleles in the recipient population but also introduce into it previously absent alleles. Mutation ultimately accounts for the appearance of new alleles, but migration and subsequent interbreeding can spread a new allele from one population to another.

The fate of a newly introduced allele generally is determined by selection. It seems fair to assume that an allele that reaches a noticeable frequency in a population has done so because it was selectively advantageous in the environmental conditions. Transplanting that same allele into a new population with a different genetic environment and possibly a different external environment may or may not be selectively beneficial.

Mixing genes derived from two or more parental populations may also form a new population, as it has with the American blacks. If we look at the frequencies of several genetic traits in American whites, blacks, and in West Africans, it is clear that the allele frequencies in the American blacks fall between those of the ancestral populations (Table 3.4). Because American blacks are somewhat isolated from West Africans and American whites, for geographic or social reasons, their gene pool, formed by admixture, reflects the formation of a new population, different from both ancestral populations.

Reducing Variation To complete our theoretical picture of variation, we must consider the several ways in which it can be reduced. Natural selection, a primary force in evolution, is the most obvious.

Selection Complete selection against a dominant allele will completely obliterate that allele in one generation. All who have the allele are prevented from reproducing. If selection is not this severe, elimination will

Table 3.4. Approximate frequencies of a few alleles in West Africans, American blacks, and American whites.

Allele	West African blacks	American blacks	American whites
A	.15	.17	.26
B	.15	.12	.07
O	.70	.71	.67
G-6-PD deficiency	.19	.11	.00
HB^s	.11	.04	.00
cDe	.59	.44	.03
CDe	.07	.16	.41
cde	.21	.26	.39
Hp^1	.69	.53	.43
S	.13	.17	.35

Adapted from P. L. Workman, B. S. Blumberg, and A. J. Cooper, "Selection, Gene Migration, and Polymorphic Stability in a U.S. White and Negro Population," *American Journal of Human Genetics* 15: 430.

take longer. Much more common is selection against a recessive allele, which reduces variability in a population. The rate at which selection can decrease the frequency of a recessive allele is much slower than it can work against a dominant. Suppose a population has two alleles controlling a trait. G is the dominant allele and its frequency at some time in the past was .8; the frequency of the recessive allele (g) was .2. Then some shift in the environment made the homozygous recessive (gg) a lethal genotype; selection did not operate against GG or Gg. Under the new conditions we can obtain the proportional contribution of each genotype to the next generation by multiplying the frequency of each genotype by its fitness (Table 3.5).

The new g frequency (after selection) is equal to the contribution of the g alleles from the heterozygotes because the gg people do not reproduce. As the frequency of the g allele drops, the probability of forming a gg homozygote decreases in accordance with the Hardy-Weinberg rule, reducing the rate at which selection can rid the population of the allele. As the frequency of the g allele drops, most of the g alleles will be found in heterozygotes where they cannot be selected out. At a g frequency of .01, only one in 10,000 people would die and all other copies of the gene would be in genetically fit heterozygotes. If, however, g were more common, say .1, one in every 100 people would be open to selection.

Mathematical analysis shows that the initial drop in the frequency of g is quite rapid and then starts to tail off. After one generation of selection against only the gg homozygotes, the gene frequency drops from .2 to .16; in the second it drops to .1344; from the twentieth to the fiftieth generation it drops only from .04 to .018. In humans the intervening thirty generations would take several hundred years to realize only a 2.2 percent drop in gene frequency.

After long selection, the frequency will eventually reach an equilibrium at which the rate of loss of the g allele is balanced by the production of new g alleles by mutation. Then every g allele lost because of natural selection against the homozygous gg will be replaced by the creation of new g alleles by random mutations. Such an equilibrium seems

Table 3.5. Selection against a recessive allele.

Gene frequency	$G = p$		$g = q$
Genotype frequency before selection	$GG = p^2$	$Gg = 2pq$	$gg = q^2$
Fitness	1	1	$1 - x$ (x = deaths due to homozygosity)
Genotype frequencies after selection. (That is, genotype distribution of those who will produce the next generation.)	p^2	$2pq$	$q^2(1 - x)$

to have been reached for genes causing metabolic disorders such as PKU. Eugenicists (those who want to improve our species genetically) have never been able to solve this problem satisfactorily when they try to explain how they propose to accomplish their goals.

When selection or drift causes a relatively common gene to become scarce, the variation does not disappear immediately. While diminishing, it illustrates a *transient* polymorphism. The variation is still there, but it is approaching the 1 percent level at which it ceases to be a polymorphism. Transient polymorphisms, such as the sickle-cell allele in American blacks, tell us a population is in the midst of significant evolutionary change.

In the example we have considered, selection operates directly by biological means: a person with sickle-cell anemia (SS) rarely lives long enough to reproduce. Society, too, applies selective pressures against traits it cannot or will not tolerate. Many non-Western groups practice infanticide, often on those born with obvious congenital defects; a group leading a marginal existence cannot tolerate the economic drain of nonproductive members. It is difficult to judge how such practices affect evolution, but they certainly would reduce the frequency of genetically caused disorders.

Genetic Drift Genetic drift, or random fluctuation in gene frequencies in a small population caused by chance phenomena, also causes loss of variation. Drift will decrease variability in any population, but it will increase the variability *among* populations. Because drift is effective in small populations (page 74), it probably was of greater significance in our hunter/gatherer past.

While drift eventually fixes alleles at either 0 or 100 percent in a population, it maintains variability among populations. Consider 100 small populations, each with two alleles, A and A', at frequencies of .8 and .2. After a long period of drift, the most likely outcome would be 80 populations with A at 100 percent and 20 populations fixed at 100 percent A'. After drift has rid all the populations of internal variability, drift is no longer possible. Variation among groups, however, would still exist. Although it is hard to prove that drift has occurred, it is difficult to imagine that it has not. Illustrating drift with data on humans essentially involves proving the negative, showing that differences among populations are not caused by selection. Evidence that closely related populations have little variation within groups, but marked variation among groups, certainly does imply drift. It is impossible, however, to demonstrate conclusively that the variation is not caused instead by undetected selection pressures.

A subtype of drift known to have affected human beings is the Founder's effect, or the Sewall Wright effect. Here, variability is reduced in newly founded, isolated populations by sampling error; that is, the founding population, which could be as small as one pregnant woman,

Figure 3.7. A family of Pitcairn islanders.

does not carry all the alleles at exactly their frequency in the original large population.

Several island populations today have limited variability because they are the descendants of a few stranded sailors. The nine mutinous crew members of H.M.S. *Bounty,* six Tahitian men, and eight or nine Tahitian women founded a population on Pitcairn Island in 1790 (Figure 3.7). After a falling-out between the Tahitian men and the English, the population was reduced to Alexander Smith, the women, and some children. With such a small founding group, the genetic variability today is quite limited. It would be impossible for nine English men to carry all the alleles present in England or for fourteen or fifteen Tahitians to represent truly the Tahitian population. Even if the population had rapidly expanded, the genetic bottleneck that it passed through greatly limits variability in later generations. Harry L. Shapiro vividly describes the history and biology of this new human population in *The Pitcairn Islanders.*

Inbreeding and Homozygosity Another phenomenon that may diminish variability in populations is inbreeding, or mating between ancestrally related individuals. If we go back far enough genealogically, any pair of individuals shares at least one ancestor; to measure inbreeding, then, we have to specify a base population, such as the original inhabitants of Pitcairn Island, as a starting point.

All homozygotes for a trait have two functionally identical alleles, that is, two pieces of DNA which synthesize a protein with the same amino acid sequence. The likelihood of being homozygous for any particular allele is related to the frequency of that allele. A person whose parents are genetic relatives represents a special case wherein the chance of homozygosity is somewhat greater; the amount by which it is greater is related to the closeness of the parents' genetic ties. Here the alleles can be identical because they are descended from one allele in the parents' recent common ancestor. This is homozygosity by descent. The smaller the group from which mates can be drawn, the greater the amount of inbreeding.

Figure 3.7 diagrams a case of inbreeding between first cousins. Child A may be homozygous because a gene in one of the great-grandparents was passed to both grandparents and both parents, as the hypothetical example illustrates for the X' allele; the child could be homozygous X'X' by descent. Thus, a child born to genetic relatives has a greater probability of homozygosity than does a child born to two unrelated individuals. Inbreeding therefore reduces genotypic variability and increases the chance of homozygosity.

In a population comprised of inbred lines, the genetic variation in the population as a whole may be maintained, but the variability within family lines is decreased. If one inbreeding lineage within a population contains only the X allele and one only X', variation is still present in the population's gene frequencies, but there is none within lines. Also there are no heterozygotes. Socially preferred mating patterns may subdivide a population into many inbred lines, further reducing genotypic variability.

Sharing ancestors, as do the parents in Figure 3.8, can be important socially as well as biologically. Almost all human societies have incest taboos that limit choice of mates, though the matings considered incestuous often vary. On the other hand, common ancestry can confer social importance, as it does for those who trace their heritage back to the Pilgrims. Socially, ancestors can be recognized for hundreds of years into the past and may even involve descent from an imaginary common ancestor, as in Australian Aborigine clans. But a common ancestor more than four or five generations back has little genetic effect; a mating between individuals who share a great-great-great-great-great-grandparent probably will not cause homozygosity by descent.

The layman may think that inbreeding always results in retarded or otherwise defective children. Inbreeding can indeed bring about mental retardation and other disorders by bringing together in one individual

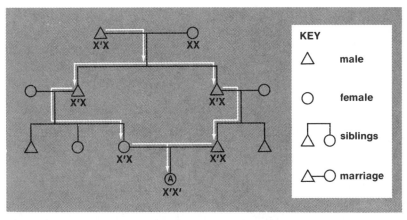

Figure 3.8. *A geneaology showing how homozygosity for the allele X' in person A results from inbreeding. A's parents are first cousins.*

two copies of a harmful gene. But if such a gene either is not present in the lineage, or has not been passed on in it, inbreeding does no harm. If homozygosity for a gene is advantageous, inbreeding will be beneficial.

As far as we know, inbreeding does not seem to have had any great effects on human populations. Some of the most extensive inbreeding is recorded in rural Japanese villages. Consanguineous ("blood"-related) marriages are encouraged, perhaps partly because in the small villages the choice of a mate may be limited to a relative. In some villages more than 25 percent of the marriages involved related individuals, and often more than half of these involved first cousins. Even so, the overall risk of deleterious disorders in the children of first-cousin marriages is not tremendously greater than in the children of unrelated parents. Obvious congenital defects appear in about 1.02 percent of the children of unrelated mates; they appear in 1.69 percent of the offspring of first cousins. The latter group shows about a 60 percent greater risk of congenital defects, but the traits still are not very common. The mortality rate for the children of first cousins increases about 3 percent over that for children of unrelated parents. Also in Japan, inbred individuals are slightly lower in birth weight, shorter as adults, and lower in IQ. William Schull, one of the preeminent researchers in this subject says, "The picture [of the effects of first-cousin marriage] is one of small but pervasive effects." Schull also says that the number of live births for the consanguineous marriages is greater than that for the unrelated marriage group. The number of children who eventually reach the age of twenty-one, though, is about the same for both groups, meaning that the related individuals produce "extra" children to compensate for those who will die because of inbreeding.

The Japanese are one of the most extreme cases of inbreeding, yet on the average the amount of inbreeding is roughly comparable to what one would expect if everyone were marrying his or her third or fourth cousins. Very high levels of inbreeding occur in several small isolates. Among the Juruna Indians of Brazil about 73 percent of the marriages have both partners coming from within the group. Because the group now has only fifty-eight Jurunas, many of them are, to no one's surprise, related by descent. Mathematical computations show that their inbreeding is roughly equivalent to everyone marrying a second cousin. In fact, half of the twenty-two marriages studied involved people who are related through more than one line of descent and one couple is related through eight lines.

Another group is the people of Tristan da Cunha, a small island in the middle of the South Atlantic Ocean. It was first settled in the early nineteenth century by several English seamen. The population was increased both by importing wives and by saving several shipwrecked sailors. The population was about 300 prior to its evacuation in the 1960s. Luckily one of the founders liked and encouraged accurate record keeping, so that today it is possible to trace, via birth and marriage records, almost everyone's ancestry. With the records in hand, Derek Roberts of England was able to compute not only the amount of inbreeding but what brought it about. Figure 3.9 shows that for the first three decades after its founding no inbreeding occurred. By then, however, inbreeding was almost inevitable. One man, age twenty-two, had to pick a wife, and of the eight eligible women, only three weren't related to him. Choosing one of his first cousins, he started inbreeding on Tristan. Often in later years one had no alternative but marrying a relative. Although Tristanians preferred to marry nonrelatives, the closed population and its small size voided this alternative. In fact, the only cases of outbreeding since 1930 have been illegitimate births after a male came visiting. Again, as in Japan, full medical surveys indicate that congenital abnormalities are

Figure 3.9. *The degree of inbreeding in the Tristan population, by the decade of birth. The gradual increase in inbreeding reflects the gradual decrease in unrelated possible mates in this small population. F is a measure of the amount of inbreeding.*

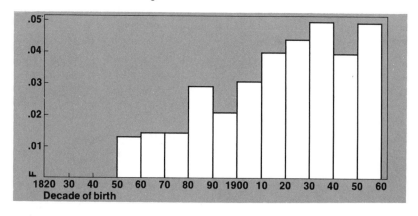

somewhat more common than in outbreeding communities. Inbreeding does not, however, guarantee that a medical problem will arise.

Like drift, inbreeding probably was more significant in the population structure of our ancestors. Given that the size of a population was very small for much of our history, probably ranging between twenty-five and one hundred persons, the number of nonrelated potential mates would have been very small, making inbreeding very likely. The practice of village exogamy, marrying a person from outside one's own village, is quite common among modern hunter/gatherer peoples, possibly as a mechanism to retard the effect of inbreeding.

Admixture: Reducing Differences We have seen that admixture can increase variation within a population; it can also decrease the differences among populations. Native Americans today have much higher frequencies of some blood types than they are thought to have had in pre-Columbian times, mostly because of interbreeding with whites. The Native American gene pool now is more similar to that of American whites. Gene flow among populations can be an extremely important evolutionary phenomenon, for it can spread new genes from population to population, thus reducing the differences between the populations.

Evolution in the Real World

We have seen how some evolutionary movements affect the genetic structure of populations. We have considered most of them as separate, each having specific effects on a population's evolution. In the real world, all the factors are more or less busily working. The most obvious interaction is that between selection and mutation. Mutation creates new alleles, which are then selected for or against in a specific environment.

Through drift, a newly arisen, beneficial mutation may disappear simply by chance; a newly hatched, extremely fit, mutant bug, for example, may be unintentionally stepped on. By this chance occurrence, the rare but highly advantageous allele has ceased to exist and so cannot be selected for. Alternatively, drift can override selection against a harmful allele and cause its frequency to rise to high levels in a small population.

Selection and admixture also are intertwined. The forced migration and subsequent admixture of Africans in the New World and the altered selective pressures have resulted in a greater decrease in the frequency of S than selection or admixture alone would have accomplished.

Mutation, selection, and gene flow can also operate to produce *clinal* variation. A cline is regular variation in a trait over space, shown by the alteration in the frequency of one or more traits from population to neighboring population. A new, beneficial mutation (Q) may arise in one population. Because Q is advantageous, it is increased in frequency by selection. Meanwhile, gene flow carries Q to neighboring groups, and eventually to more distant populations where it also gradually increases in frequency. As a result, Q is highest in frequency in its group of origin and lower and lower in frequency in further and further removed groups. Selection pressures that change over space may also cause clines.

Sewall Wright and the Evolution of Populations

Evolution is not the result of selection, migration, mutation, or drift, but of all of these interacting. Nor do these forces produce their effects on isolated genes; genes can be selectively advantageous at extremely subtle levels. Genes for seemingly different traits may be interacting to influence the total fitness of the individual. Part of a gene's environment is the constellation of other genes present in the person.

Since the 1930s, Sewall Wright, dean of American population geneticists and evolutionary theorists, has been refining a framework by which to view the effects of evolution on the genetic structure of populations. Wright came up with a topographic, or surface, view of adaptation. Populations of organisms with well adapted gene pools, genes that work well with one another in an environment, are thought of as occupying adaptive peaks on a surface; the complexes that are maladaptive are thought of as selective valleys.

In Wright's view, to consider the fitness of a genotype is an oversimplification to the point of inaccuracy. It is a whole person, not a genotype, who either does or does not reproduce. The benefits or disadvantages of a particular genotype are not determined only by the physical environment; often the value of a set of alleles is affected by the person's alleles for many other traits. We have considered the worth of the sickle-cell allele (page 89) by itself. This allele is even more adaptive in groups where an allele for reduced amounts of an enzyme (G-6-PD) is also present; it is less beneficial where certain other hemoglobin alleles are found (page 91). The sickle-cell allele and the enzyme-deficiency allele are *coadapted:* they mix well with each other in a population's gene pool.

The overall fitness of various combinations of two genes can be plotted on a three-dimensional graph. Two of the axes show the gene frequencies while the third shows fitness, producing a surface of peaks and valleys. In a malarial area, the combination of 15 percent sickle-cell and 30 to 60 percent enzyme-deficiency allele produces a very high peak; this combination is very adaptive. Other combinations would be of varying heights. A high frequency of the enzyme deficiency coupled with zero percent sickle cell is not as adaptive; it is a lower peak. One hundred percent sickle cell is a deep valley, for everyone dies, at least given today's medical environment (Figure 3.10). In an area without malaria the surface would be very different.

Because of the tremendous number of genetic traits, there are actually many peaks and valleys of varying altitudes. How do the evolutionary processes determine the placement of a population on this surface? Will all groups eventually possess the best adapted gene pool and inhabit the highest peak? What is the best position for the species as a whole? According to Wright's reasoning, selection will keep a population on a peak, but not necessarily on the highest one. Selection, not

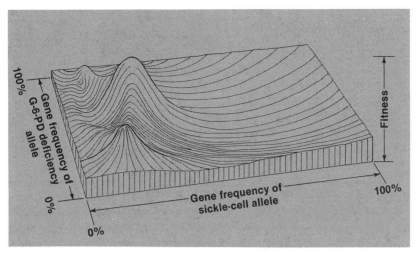

Figure 3.10. A topographic view of adaptation, based on the example described in the text. Each point on the surface corresponds to a combination of the genes for sickle-cell hemoglobin and G–6–PD deficiency. The degree of adaptation of genes is reflected by the height of that point. The heights are only approximations. Should the environment change, a peak could become a valley, and vice versa.

having foresight, cannot anticipate that by becoming less adapted for a short time — moving into valley B (Figure 3.11) — the population can eventually move from low peak A to the higher summit C. If drift, mutation, or admixture changed the structure of the gene complex from A to point A', selection would bring the population back to A. How then can a group at A get to C? According to Wright, this is one situation in which drift can make a big difference. If the population at A is small, it is likely that drift will sooner or later displace the group to a point (C') on the upslope to C. Selection will then bring the population's genetic structure back into equilibrium and from C' the only peak that selection can attain is C. Selection acts as a stabilizer — constantly trying to keep the group on a peak — retaining the adaptive status quo. Drift, mutation, and migration are not directed toward producing adaptation — they often, though not always, result in movement into the valley.

What is the best evolutionary situation for the continued success of a species? In the short run, a species inhabiting one very high peak, one with no interpopulational variability, is best off because all the populations are highly fit. Their continued isolation ensures that a maximum number of species members will contain a well-adapted genotype. The species that continues on this evolutionary course, however, is routed onto a dead end; we know that inevitably environments do change and an invariant species, no matter how high the peak it now inhabits, may find itself unable to reach a new peak when an environmental shift occurs. On the other hand, a species divided into many smaller groups among which there is a little interbreeding is in a much better position

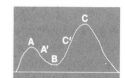

Figure 3.11. A topographic surface exhibiting two peaks. Movement of a population on this surface, caused by the evolutionary processes, is discussed in the text.

for long-term survival. Even if none of the peaks this species occupies is exceptionally well adapted, it occupies so many peaks and the range of variability between populations is so great that one or another of the well-adapted gene complexes can tolerate almost any environmental change. If the survival of one group is threatened by environmental change, another group (or at least its genes, via interbreeding) can surmount the altered conditions.

We have greatly oversimplified the situation by thinking of the surface as having only three dimensions and considering only two variable traits. With three interacting variables the surface is four-dimensional; with four variables, five dimensions are needed.

Questioning the Theory

Dogma, it was pointed out, is a word that does not apply to science. Though the previous sections present a rather standard and traditional view of genetic and evolutionary processes (the Neo-Darwinian view), this does not mean that all such phenomena are fully understood and agreed upon. Now we will touch on a few of the current areas of debate surrounding topics of evolutionary significance. We will start out with a question initially raised decades ago, but recently revived: Is macroevolution really as gradual as traditional treatments would have it? If not, there are many interrelated implications as to:

1. The role of adaptation in macroevolutionary trends;
2. The ways in which new species appear; and,
3. The relationship of microevolutionary forces to those of macroevolution.

The ways in which these modern questions are resolved will then affect how one views other aspects of evolution; for instance, "How and why did sex evolve?" or "To what degree is macroevolution a result of structural changes in proteins as opposed to changes in the timing of gene action?"

Punctuated Equilibrium

Charles Darwin based his ideas of evolution on the mechanism of natural selection. He visualized this process as operating on each generation, slowly and gradually perfecting the adaptation of the population by selecting the most fit individuals, and weeding out those that were not as well adapted. In the Darwinian view of evolution, a population gradually changed over time, constantly accumulating modifications that altered its biology; eventually enough changes occurred so that a new species could be said to have appeared.

Although this view has come to represent the dominant theme in evolutionary thought, it has not been accepted without serious criticism. In the years prior to the publication of *The Origin of Species* in 1859, Darwin spent considerable time amassing evidence in support of evolution and discussing the basic concepts with scientific friends. One of these was the geologist, Charles Lyell, who was introduced in Chapter 1 in the context of uniformitarianism. Lyell's contributions to the study of geology also included the construction of a relative chronology of earth history (Figure 3.12, showing the subdivisions of the geologic record). Lyell wished to identify rock strata from various parts of the world and place them in a time-ordered sequence, from the earliest to the latest. It was already an established observation that if a geologist wished to distinguish one rock formation from another, the identity of the rock itself — limestone, standstone, or whatever — was of limited value, since the same kind of rocks have been laid down at very different times. The most effective way for Lyell to accomplish his goal was to use the fossilized remains of extinct animals that were found embedded in the rocks. So although the earth was formed about 4.5 billion years ago, the chronology of the earth shown in Figure 3.12 only presents subdivisions of earth history covering the last 600 million years. Prior to this time, fossilized remains become rarer, and finally disappear altogether, so that they cannot be used to distinguish one rock strata from another.

Lyell's examination of many rock strata had convinced him that the fossil species found in one rock deposit could be easily distinguished from those in deposits above and below it. He also found that there was virtually no change in the biology of the fossil animals from their first to their final appearance. Animals seemed to appear abruptly, remain unchanged throughout their presence in the record, and then disappear just as suddenly, to be replaced by a new series of animals in the next higher strata.

Lyell pointed out to Darwin that these observations did not support his proposed notion of gradual change, but rather showed sudden appearance, relatively no change, and then sudden disappearance. Darwin remained unconvinced, arguing that the fossil record was incomplete, that strata which showed the transitions between different animal species had been destroyed, and that eventually the transitional animal forms linking animals from one rock strata to those above and below it would be found.

Over 100 years after the exchange between Lyell and Darwin, biologists, including Nils Eldredge, Steven Gould, and others, have suggested that perhaps Lyell was right after all. These writers have emphasized the fact that a considerable amount of investigation has failed to bring to light the transitional forms Darwin was sure would be found, and that even now the fossil record continues to show animal species which abruptly appear, remain relatively unchanged, and then disappear. Fossil evidence of gradual change of one fossil species into another is exceedingly rare, leading Eldredge and Gould to propose that the Darwinian model of gradualism over time should be modified. In its place, they suggest a different pattern, one they have termed *punctuated equilibrium*.

In contrast to Darwinian notions of the gradual change of one species into another, Eldredge and Gould argue that most species evolve very quickly, changing dramatically in a very short period often via nonselective mechanisms, so swiftly that it is unlikely that fossil evidence

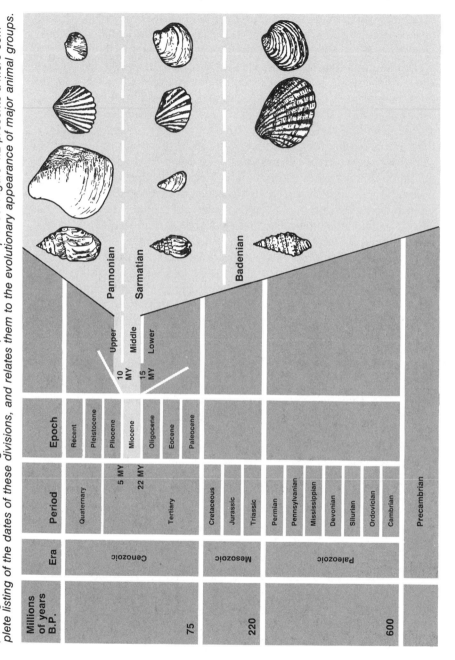

Figure 3.12. *Example of the development of a relative time scale of earth history. Pictured are three distinct time-ordered groupings of fossil mollusc species found in geological deposits representing an extension of the Mediterranean Sea which covered parts of Central Europe between 5–15 million years ago. Identification of the species of shellfish present also identifies the deposit and places it in the overall sequence of earth history. Here, the three groupings are called Badenian, Sarmatian, and Pannonian. Based on their relative position to other fossil-bearing rock strata that are found above and below them, these three are placed in the Middle to Upper Miocene, which in turn is placed in the Cenozoic. The major divisions of earth history noted on the left of the figure are thus the result of placing hundreds of rock strata together in their correct, time-ordered sequence. Figure 4.2 presents a more complete listing of the dates of these divisions, and relates them to the evolutionary appearance of major animal groups.*

will be found in the record. They further propose that once a species has evolved, and has reached a state of equilibrium with its environment, selection will then operate to maintain the species in that form, and thus will work to prevent the accumulation of the gradual changes that in the Darwinian model lead to the appearance of a new species. The punctuated equilibrium model visualizes a species appearing with a burst of change, moving into a time of little or no change, a period of "stasis," and then abruptly being replaced by a new species (Figure 3.13). Thus the original species disappears from the fossil record.

An important aspect of this idea, and one that further differentiates punctuation from gradualism, is the emphasis on nonselective agencies as being responsible for the origin of new species. Eldredge and Gould suggest that other mechanisms may be more important than natural selection in the rapid evolution of a new species. A variety of models have been constructed, and several have been tested in the laboratory, which show that over a small number of generations significant differences can develop between two previously interbreeding populations, and that these differences can appear without the action of natural selection. Punctuated equilibrium therefore views natural selection as operating mainly to maintain stasis or lack of change in a population, while the rapid development of new species is accomplished with little or no influence of selection.

The notion of punctuated change is a reflection of the difficulties that are encountered when we study the evidence for the evolution of life. There is an abundant record of fossil remains of extinct life, but these fossils are often times extremely difficult to arrange into a reasonable sequence of evolutionary change. In the study of human evolution, for example, there are sites where several rock strata contain the fossil bones of our ancestors. The bones from one rock strata differ in a number of details from the bones deposited above and below them. Just how much change is sufficient to demonstrate the action of gradualism? How little change permits us to conclude that stasis is the pattern? How much time is required to document a gradual or a punctuated change from one species to another? These are questions that are most difficult to answer

Figure 3.13. The classic idea of evolution by gradual change (left) is now being rechallenged by a view involving abrupt changes.

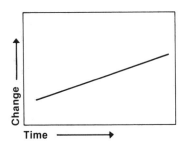
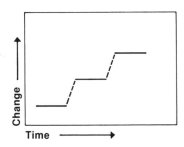

looking at the question of punctuation from the perspective of the fossil record, but even more difficult questions arise when we attempt to utilize this concept in the study of living populations. A geneticist studying a living population would consider 50,000 years to be an exceedingly long time, but a paleontologist studying the evolution of the mammals would consider 50,000 years merely an instant. How micro- and macroevolutionary phenomena can be reconciled is therefore a serious modern concern. Likewise, if you adhere to the gradualist school, your view of a lot of other debates will be quite different from the view of those supporting the punctuated equilibrium model.

The Evolution of Sexual Reproduction

Having looked at the generalities of the punctuated-gradualist debate, let's look at a particular example dealing with a subject near to the hearts of most: sex, and why it ever evolved.

At face value, an observer might predict that sex should never have evolved. We've seen that from an evolutionary standpoint, the winner in the evolutionary race is the individual who passes on more genes to the next generation than other individuals. For a species such as our own, which reproduces sexually each time an offspring is conceived, this is a particularly "expensive" proposition, especially for the female. Female mammals (and especially primates) invest a tremendous amount of time and energy to ensure the survival of their offspring, yet half the genes they are protecting aren't even theirs! Even in a species whose maternal investment isn't so great, the parents still have to devote some limited resources toward the production of sex cells which are only of value after union with those of the other sex. Wouldn't it be a tremendous evolutionary advantage if an individual could simply reproduce asexually: every offspring would be a 100 percent return on the parent's "investment," not 50 percent? It certainly seems that the answer to this question is "yes." Thus, since sexual reproduction does exist, we must try to understand its function.

Asexual reproduction is a common reproductive mechanism in many microorganisms. Essentially, it is reproduction by mitosis: the individual replicates its genes and then divides. One individual spawns two genetically identical offspring — or clones — and each cell line is separate and unique. Again, why did our ancestors abandon this seemingly efficient method of reproduction more than a half billion years ago?

To date, there have been a variety of answers to this question, but none has received unanimous acceptance and each would appear to have potential pitfalls.

An early explanation for the evolution of sexual reproduction was proposed in the 1930s by Sir R. A. Fisher, a famed evolutionary theorist, and H. J. Muller, a Nobel Prize winning geneticist. Basically, Fisher and Muller felt that sexual reproduction allowed for quicker and more adaptive evolutionary change. Imagine, for instance, a situation where mutations A, B, and C would benefit survival in a particular environment.

An asexual organism would have to have these mutations appear in succession in one cell line. As asexuality does not allow for mixing of genes between individuals or lines, all three would have to appear as a unit, in one line, a very unlikely event.

One result of sexual reproduction is the constant shuffling of genes every generation. Thus, even if mutation A happened in one individual, B in a second, and C in a third, the recombination of genes can relatively rapidly bring all three together in one individual. Put in other terms, this view holds that each new mutation is tested out for its worth in many different combinations, while asexuality tests it in only one array of genes.

This view has not gone without criticism, though there are certainly those who still stand by it. Some say that this advantage of sexuality only holds true under very limited conditions. For instance, computer simulations seem to show that sex would work this way only in very small populations. A theoretical criticism is that the Fisher-Muller view is based on group selection; that is, its benefit is not to the individual, but to the group. The Neo-Darwinian theory holds that selection will not favor traits which are beneficial to the group but harmful to the individual. Fisher himself had great difficulty on this point and ultimately concluded that sexual reproduction was the only legitimate example of group selection; sex conferred no advantage for the individual, just the group.

One alternative relates to the flip-side of the Fisher-Muller hypothesis. Not only does sexual reproduction put new gene combinations together, it is also constantly breaking them up via meiosis. This too can be viewed as beneficial when the environment is undergoing change, as indeed it always is. If an asexual organism hit upon a very beneficial array of genes and its descendants became very common by outcompeting other cell lines, a change in environment could quickly result in extinction if this one genotype ceased to be adaptive. Determining whether sex is really beneficial here, in part, depends on how radically environments are likely to change and how rapidly the organism can reproduce in the new situation.

These explanations of sexual reproduction are generally gradualistic in nature. Taking a punctuated view of macroevolution suggests other possibilities. Steven Stanley has proposed that the advantage of sexual reproduction is not to the individual or species, but to whole groups of species. How would this work?

We know that environments constantly change and that groups poorly adapted to the new conditions become extinct. How can sufficient diversity be generated to ensure that one or another group will survive in one or another changed condition? For asexual organisms, variation must result from different mutations in different cell lines. This process is not likely to yield tremendous diversity between related "species" (as the species definition relates to interbreeding, which is, of course, impossible in asexual organisms, the word is in quotes; the determination of species in bacteria is based on other criteria). Remember that in the punctuated view most diversification and evolution comes about at the

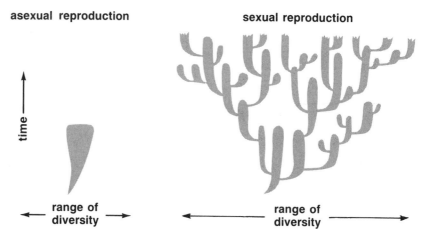

asexual reproduction

sexual reproduction

time →

← range of diversity →

← range of diversity →

Figure 3.14. Sexual reproduction leads to much speciation and thus much interspecies diversity, according to Steven Stanley.

"instant" of speciation. As only sexual organisms can speciate and thereby generate a lot of diversity within the group of related species, it is the sexual organism that is likely to have sufficient variability (not internal to a species but between related species) to survive through time (see Figure 3.14).

So today, we are still in the position of reiterating the question "Is sex necessary?" And if so, "Why?" We do see that the different models of evolution yield differing views.

Macro- and Microevolution   Generally, the modern debate on evolution is put in terms of gradual versus punctuated change. Yet these sides are not necessarily contradictory. It is certainly possible to have rapid change and then stasis brought about by the same forces as have been found to cause slow change within a population. There is nothing in classic Neo-Darwinian theory that states a steady, slow rate of change is the only pattern possible. In fact, the traditionalist would maintain that the rate at which species change would be affected by the particulars of each case: Is the climate changing rapidly? Is the vegetation changing rapidly? Is the geography changing rapidly? and so on.

The key issue, we feel, is not then the rate or pattern of change but the forces that are bringing about the changes.

Gradualists say that new species appear as selection, mutation, and drift cause the gene pools of isolated populations to diverge, with selection being particularly important. E. Mayr, a major name in evolutionary studies, states that: "The proponents of the [Neo-Darwinian] theory maintain that all evolution is due to the accumulation of small, genetic changes, guided by natural selection. . . ."[5]

Eventually, the gene complexes of different populations become so different as to prevent interbreeding. Speciation here is the result of a lot of microevolution accumulated over long periods.

According to the punctuated view many new species rapidly appear and then compete for survival. The large, rapid shifts in morphology and functioning are proposed to come about as the result of a few mutations with large effects (see below) and/or the random fixation of variants due to genetic drift. Significantly altered constellations of genes appear rapidly in small, marginal populations which quickly become incapable of breeding with other such groups — a lot of speciation occurs. These species then compete with each other and the parental group. The survivor, which is morphologically quite different then spreads out geographically, comes to be the norm and remains essentially unchanged for long periods of time. The small microevolutionary changes, brought about by selection causing one allele to be substituted for another, have little or nothing to do with the major trends seen in the fossil record. In this view, the trends of macroevolution arise largely as a result of species selection, a situation wherein selection favors one species over another in contrast with the traditional view that selection favors one individual over another.

Given their viewpoint, it is not surprising that gradualists look to explain morphological and behavioral trends in terms of adaptation. Thus, in future chapters, you will see comments to the effect that primates evolved stereoscopic vision as an adaptation to life in the trees or that bipedalism evolved in our ancestors as an adaptation to life on open grasslands. Yet many punctuationists view these sorts of statements as "just so stories." They say that the gradualists see a trait in a living species and then put together a tale to explain how it came to be. Certainly, there are times when these stories are accurate reflections of past events, but punctuationists assert that many times they are at best unproven and often wrong. The mere existence of a feature is not sufficient reason to state that the feature therefore *must* somehow be adaptive. The ability to put together a plausible story which can account for the evolution of a trait doesn't prove that the scenario is a true reflection of history.

Adaptation

Sometimes, the punctuationists say, features come into existence as a byproduct of development or past evolutionary directions. Stephen Gould and Richard Lewontin of Harvard University use an architectural analogy.[6] Spandrels are triangular spaces formed by the right angle intersection of two rounded arches (Figure 3.15). In Venice's St. Mark's Cathedral, there are four such spandrels, each elaborately decorated with religious art. These areas were not purposefully designed into the cathedral so as to accommodate the artwork. The basic architecture called for intersecting arches and the spandrels were an unavoidable byproduct which was then a likely spot for decoration. Likewise, if you square a circle four distinctive triangular shapes are produced; there is no way to avoid it.

Some see evolution in similar terms of cause and effect. Is everything, punctuationists ask, an adaptation or might some biological traits simply be byproducts of other phenomena? Given that the punctuated

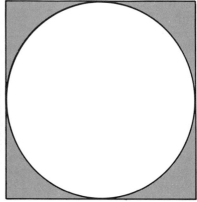

Figure 3.15. *Not everything in the world is adaptive. Spandrels (left) are a necessary byproduct of putting a dome on top of rounded arches. Likewise, when a circle is squared, the gray triangular shapes (right) are produced.*

view does not see microevolution and adaptation as the primary mover in the appearance of new species, it is not surprising that its proponents do not see adaptation as the cause of all traits. The nonadaptationist would argue that many (though certainly not all) changes which occur in the evolution of an organism come about for one or another of several nonadaptive reasons. In direct analogy to the spandrels, architectural changes in one part of the body may create structural changes elsewhere. In human evolution, as the brain enlarged and the head became rounder, the forehead appeared as a byproduct.

This sort of effect might also pertain to behavioral shifts. Ralph Holloway considered the reasons why the human canine tooth has diminished in size relative to that of most other primates. It has been experimentally shown that the levels of male hormones in a developing primate affect the growth of its canine tooth; the more male hormone, the bigger the canine. We also know that one important aspect of human evolution was the increasing ability to live peacefully within a social group. Holloway put these two pieces together with a rather speculative bridging assumption: that the amount of male hormone in a primate affects that individual's aggressiveness. Assuming for present purposes that this point is reasonable, Holloway said that natural selection would favor the survival and reproduction of those males with lower levels of aggression and lower levels of male hormones. A side effect would then occur, for as the average male hormone level dropped from generation to generation, the canines would get smaller. Thus, selection would not be responsible directly for decreasing canine size. There was no advantage to small canines; they just came about as a byproduct of other changes.

The nondirective evolutionary forces of drift and mutation can also cause nonadaptive changes to become common — even the norm — in groups. When a neutral or nearly neutral mutation occurs in a small population, there is a low probability that by accident it will become more common over time. It is, in other words, subject to genetic drift (page 94). The chances that such a mutation will come to be present at 100 percent frequency (fixed) in any individual population is quite low. However, if mutations with small selective effects occur often, there is a high probability that some mutations will be fixed. Such a mutation is a prime example of genetic change that is not adaptive.

Gradualists do not say that such events never happen. They do maintain that adaptation is a key feature of large-scale changes and, again, that large changes (from an ape to a human, for instance) are largely due to the accumulation of many smaller changes over long periods of time.

How much change is involved in going from an apelike animal to a human? This is another sort of question bearing on this debate which presently has no definitive answer. Yet it is possible to make some educated guesses along these lines. In Chapters 6 and 7, we will describe some of the anatomical and behavioral differences between apes and humans. As will be seen, these are numerous and literally range from the top of the head to the bottom of the feet. A list of traits pages long could be compiled which would document all the fine details by which humans differ from an ape, such as the chimp. Yet contrasting these dissimilarities are molecular studies comparing human and chimp proteins which conclude that the two are more than 99 percent identical (the methods for determining this are dealt with in Chapter 6). M. C. King and A. Wilson proposed an intriguing solution to this apparent paradox.

Proteins are the products of genes that control the structure of a molecule. There also appears to be a class of regulatory genes which act as on and off switches and control the timing of structural gene activity. The tremendous degree of similarity between gorilla or chimp and human proteins reflects high levels of structural gene similarity but does not necessarily imply anything about the timing of gene function. Experimental evidence indicates that a small alteration in the timing of gene function can produce significant alterations in morphology, even when structural genes might not be mutated.

It has long been recognized that the development of a modern human exhibits *pedomorphism*. This rather impressive word refers to the retention of juvenile features *(pedo = child; morph = shape)* into adulthood. In many primates, during early life the head is quite large relative to body size (see Figure 3.16). As nonhuman primates grow and develop, their body proportions change quite noticeably as the growth of the head tapers off while other body parts grow at a great rate. The end result is a relatively small head on top of a large body. In modern humans the newborn's head is also large, but it continues to grow and to maintain a relatively large size into adulthood. Thus, the human adult maintains something of the body proportions seen only in juveniles of other primate species.

Other examples of pedomorphism abound. As adults our heads are not only large, but also quite round compared to that of a gorilla (Figure

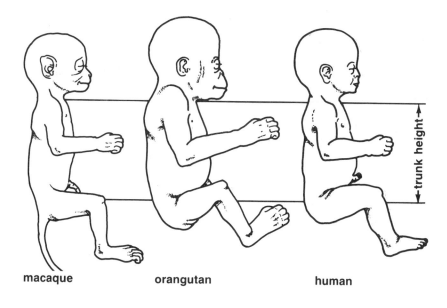

macaque   orangutan   human

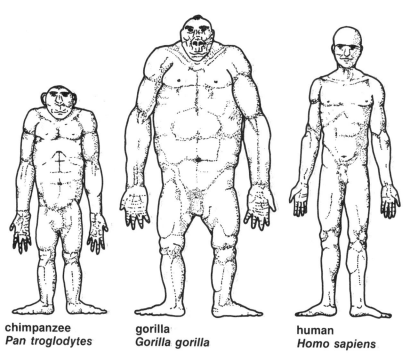

chimpanzee   gorilla   human
Pan troglodytes   *Gorilla gorilla*   *Homo sapiens*

Figure 3.16. *Compared to other primates, the relative size of the head is not particularly great in newborn humans. The size of the head relative to body size is maintained to a greater extent in developing humans than in non-human primates however. Here the three newborn primates are drawn such that their trunk lengths are equal, while the adults are drawn to scale.*

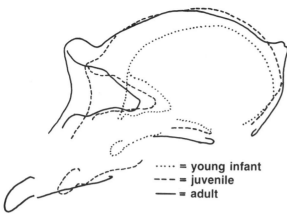

····· = **young infant**
- - - = **juvenile**
——— = **adult**

Figure 3.17. *Superimposed sketches of the outline of the skull of an infant and adult female gorilla. As the gorilla grows, much of the skull's roundness disappears.*

3.17). Yet, if you look at a juvenile gorilla you find that its head is also quite round. We maintain into adulthood the juvenile form found in the gorilla. It is certainly reasonable to consider that the pedomorphism results from alterations in the timing of gene operations rather than from changes in the products of the gene. Some genes which come into play at the time of sexual maturity in the gorilla may never be turned on in us, thus affecting the rates at which different body parts grow, and hence, their final shape.

King and Wilson suggest that the seemingly contradictory situation they describe can be solved by maintaining that much of the difference between us and chimps comes about due to changes in regulatory genes.

Regarding the punctuated-gradual debate, one could maintain that a relatively small number of alterations in regulatory DNA could rapidly come to characterize a population. These alterations, which could greatly effect morphology, could contribute to the rapid appearance of a new species in accord with Gould's model. Nevertheless, one could also argue that such a process does not contradict more traditional views of evolution: it simply constitutes a case of rapid evolution brought about by the processes (selection, etc.) that Neo-Darwinians have generally called upon as explanatory. Again, the so-called gradualists never said that all changes are equally slow or that all evolutionary change chugs along at some constant, slow rate.

Summary

We started this chapter with a consideration of the scientific method for solving problems. Several features characterize a scientific statement.

1. It generates new questions.
2. It can be tested.
3. It is predictive.
4. It is subject to change.

In all features, evolutionary statements are scientific. The original statements of Darwin and other early evolutionists have generated many new questions; some have since been firmly answered (and the answers produced new questions), others are still open to debate. In any case, there is much evidence from the fossil record, comparative sciences, and observed cases, that evolution actually does happen.

The forces of evolution (natural selection, mutation, genetic drift, and gene flow) are discussed, both in terms of what they are and what they are not. Selection is a directed force, producing adaptation, but it is not technically "survival of the fittest." Mutations are random in occurrence and they do not appear as they are needed. Mutation is particularly important as it creates much of the variability upon which selection can act. Drift is also random: it is the fluctuation in allele frequency brought about by chance. Gene flow is the result of interbreeding between groups.

Macroevolution refers to large evolutionary changes, such as the appearance of new species. The definition of a biological species applies to animals actively or potentially interbreeding and producing fertile offspring. Extinct animals, on the other hand, must be defined by a concept of evolutionary species, based largely on anatomical similarities. New species appear by straight-line evolution, or anagenesis; and by branching evolution, or cladogenesis. It is cladogenesis that has resulted in the diversity of life forms. For branching evolution to occur, a species must be subdivided by a geographic barrier into two or more isolated populations. Each evolves along its own lines until they become so different as to preclude interbreeding even if the geographic barrier should be removed. The inability to mate successfully may be due to one or more isolating mechanisms, which may be behavioral as well as anatomical or physiological. When a lot of speciation occurs quickly, it is referred to as an adaptive radiation. Although virtually all evolution is divergent, causing greater differences to accumulate between species, it sometimes appears that two are becoming more alike (convergent) or are maintaining a high degree of similarity (parallel). These similarities, which come about as species try to adapt to similar environmental problems, are only superficial.

The unending process of evolution has only one directional force, natural selection, which produces adaptation. Because alternatives are basic to the operation of selection, the analysis of the effects of evolution on genetic variation deserves much attention. Selection can maintain variation in a population by favoring the heterozygote; this mechanism is known as balanced polymorphism. While the lack of evolution would also preserve variation, all groups are evolving. Notwithstanding the fact that evolution is always occurring, by knowing what the genotype frequencies should be in the absence of evolution (Hardy-Weinberg expectations), we can identify those traits that are obviously undergoing change. Mutation, admixture, and the shuffling of genes by recombination also serve to increase a population's variability. Selection, when it favors one homozygote, works to reduce a population's store of variation, as does drift. Within family lines, inbreeding also reduces genotypic variability. In the real world these forces are all interacting constantly and in very complex ways. As human population size and structure have changed, so has the impact of the forces.

To see these interactions better, Sewall Wright devised a topographic view of evolution; the degree of fitness of a combination of genes can be pictured as a peak or valley on a complex surface; the movement of a population up and down this surface results from the operation of evolutionary forces. As the environment changes, the surface also is altered. The analysis of evolution at this rather fine-tuned level is called microevolution.

Though many decades of investigation have gone into the attempt to understand evolutionary mechanisms and patterns, the answers are not engraved in stone. As with science in general, we must constantly reanalyze our present knowledge as new insights and information become available. Such is the case with regard to the punctuated equilibrium model. This view holds that macroevolutionary changes occur in jumps, interspersed with long periods of quiesence. There are many ramifications of the punctuated or gradualist views which affect how one then looks at particular questions such as the evolution of sexual reproduction or the role of adaptation in evolution.

Chapter 4

The Evolution of the Vertebrates

In earlier chapters we introduced the mechanisms of evolution, the ways in which animal species modify their physical features over time in response to the demands of the environment. Numerous examples illustrate how these mechanisms have operated to lead to the diversity of living forms that we see today. One group of animals, the vertebrates, offers especially good evidence of evolution; because all vertebrates possess an internal skeleton and most have hard, distinctively shaped teeth, structures that fossilize well, we have a very good fossil record of their biological history. Humans, along with many other animals, are classified as vertebrates. Many of our biological systems were elaborated during vertebrate evolution: the general proportions of the limbs, the number of digits on the hands and feet, the internal bony skeleton, eyes, skin, teeth, brain, and most of the internal organs, as well as the basic plan of body organization. For example, it is difficult to understand the evolution of the uniquely human mode of movement, bipedalism, without an appreciation of the development of the vertebrate bony skeleton and its adaptation to the requirements of life on land.

Evolution works on what is present, and rarely in the history of life do we find the evolutionary introduction of radically new features. Rather, evolution modifies the physical structures that are already a part of an animal's system. The skeletal elements and muscles that controlled movement in the early vertebrate ancestors of modern humans permitted them to be successfully adapted to their environment. These elements were there because the animal needed them to interact successfully with its environment, not because they were going to evolve into human bipedalism. All its organs and systems had specific functions as parts of an interrelated complex that helped the living organism adapt to its environment. In the context of this book, an understanding of vertebrate evolution patterns provides an essential background for examining human biological and behavioral systems, like bipedalism.

Vertebrate Taxonomy

A *taxonomy* (from the Greek *taxis* = arrangement; *nomia* = distribution), or classification, is a hierarchic arrangement of animals and plants into various groups to show how all of them are related (a taxon — plu-

Table 4.1. A taxonomy of modern humans.

Taxonomic category	Category to which humans belong	Main biological features used to categorize humans
Kingdom	Animalia	Humans are animals (as distinguished from plants).
Phylum	Chordata	Humans are chordates; that is, they have concentrated nerve fibers running along the midline of the back.
Subphylum	Vertebrata	Humans are vertebrates, with internal, segmented spinal columns, and bilateral symmetry.
Class	Mammalia	Humans are mammals, with hair and mammary glands; they are warm-blooded and nurture their young after birth.
Order	Primates	Humans are primates, sharing with other primates specialized structures in the ear region and enhanced blood supply to the brain.
Suborder	Anthropoidea	Humans are anthropoids, along with the monkeys and the apes. They are social-living, daylight-active primates.
Superfamily	Hominoidea	Humans are hominoids, sharing characteristics of the other living hominoids (the apes), with similar back teeth, shoulder muscles, and bones; they lack tails.
Family	Hominidae	Humans are hominids, with the anatomical equipment permitting habitual bipedalism.
Genus Species	*Homo sapiens* }	Placement in this genus and species is based on details of brain and tooth size.

ral, taxa — is a taxonomic category). The Swedish natural historian, Carolus Linnaeus, made the first systematic attempt to classify all living things (see page 12). He anticipated no changes in his classification because he thought that all animal and plant species were immutable; once formed, they would not change. The organization of the taxonomic system in Table 4.1 is generally the same as the one Linnaeus devised 200 years ago.

Linnaeus grouped the animals according to a number of shared biological characteristics. Working our way down the hierarchic categories, we see that the common biological characteristics become more and more specific, from the most general category (kingdom), where humans are classified with all other animals, down to the genus level *Homo*, which humans share with only one or two extinct ancestors.

The subphylum Vertebrata includes all animals that possess these features, among others: *bilateral symmetry* (the right half of the animal is, more or less, a mirror image of the left half); an internal, segmented vertebral column, with nerve tissue shielded inside the column; and an enlargement of this nerve tissue (a brain) at the anterior (front) end.

The class is the next grouping in the taxonomic hierarchy. The vertebrates are divided into eight classes (Figure 4.1): four adapted to the water and four adapted mostly to life on land. The four water-adapted vertebrate classes are the Agnatha, the jawless fishes, of which the lamprey eel is one of the few living examples; the Placodermi, or armored fishes, all of which became extinct several hundred million years ago; the Chondrichthyes, cartilaginous fishes with skeletons that lack rigid bony tissue, whose main living representatives are the sharks and rays; and the Osteichthyes, or bony fishes, an extremely successful group made up of most of the living ocean and freshwater fishes. The four land or partly land-adapted vertebrate classes are Amphibia (frogs, toads, salamanders); Reptilia; Aves (birds); and Mammalia. Animals in each of these classes are distinguished by biological features that are common to virtually all animals in their group.

Most mammals have constant internal body temperature, a four-chambered heart, and fur. All mammals have mammary glands to nurture the dependent young after birth; the young also undergo a postnatal

Figure 4.1. *Representatives of the major vertebrate classes. The names of the classes appear in parentheses.*

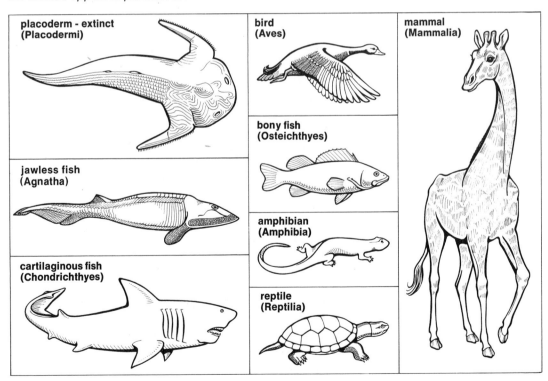

placoderm - extinct (Placodermi)

jawless fish (Agnatha)

cartilaginous fish (Chondrichthyes)

bird (Aves)

bony fish (Osteichthyes)

amphibian (Amphibia)

reptile (Reptilia)

mammal (Mammalia)

period during which they depend on adults for food. Some mammals, grouped together as the placental mammals, have a placenta, which attaches the developing young to the mother's uterus, providing a system for nourshing the young and disposing of the fetus's metabolic wastes. Other mammals, the *marsupials,* such as the kangaroo, have no placenta but instead nurse their young in a pouch from a very early stage in their development. Finally, some mammals, the *monotremes,* have continued the earlier vertebrate pattern of egg laying.

The taxon below class is order. The class Mammalia contains over twenty orders, some of them extinct. Rodentia, the rodents, including squirrels, rats, mice, and beavers, is one order. Carnivora, the carnivores, including dogs, cats, weasels, badgers, foxes, bears, seals, and wolves, is another. Each order of mammals is distinguished by shared biological characteristics. Another of the mammalian orders is the Primates, in which humans are placed. The biological features that primates have evolved to suit them to their adaptive niche have made them very difficult to define. We will examine their biology and behavior in the next chapter before trying to define primates. The human suborder Anthropoidea and superfamily Hominoidea will also be discussed and defined in later chapters.

The human taxonomic family is the Hominidae; members of the family, which normally includes humans and their immediate ancestors, are called hominids. The main distinguishing biological feature of hominids is our specialized mode of locomotion: *bipedalism,* or walking on two feet.

Below the family level are the most specific categories, the genus and species. Every living and extinct animal and plant is given a binomial, or two-part name, which exactly identifies that particular life form. The binomial of modern humans is the genus name *Homo* (Latin for man) and the species name *sapiens* (Latin for wise), together: *Homo sapiens.* All taxonomic binomials are written in italics to indicate that they refer to specific animals.

The species is the smallest working unit generally recognized in the taxonomy of animals and plants. A smaller category, the subspecies, or variety, is sometimes employed in detailed analyses of particular animals; it is roughly equivalent to the breeding population, and it is written as a trinomial. For example, modern humans are often classified as *Homo sapiens sapiens,* to distinguish them from close extinct hominid ancestors who are also classified as *Homo sapiens,* as in *Homo sapiens neanderthalensis.*

Taxonomy and
Evolution

A number of major changes have occurred since Linnaeus proposed his taxonomic system. Many living animals have been discovered, identified, and incorporated into the system; extinct animals, too, have been added. Linnaeus considered the animal world as fixed and unchanging: all animals that had been created were still alive. Although Linnaeus did not recognize evolutionary relationships, we recognize today that animals' features are the result of the operation of evolutionary mechanisms, and that similarity in biological characteristics often indicates a close relationship in the past. Animal species placed in the same genus have a closer evolutionary relationship than animals outside that genus; animals in the same family are closer in descent than those not classified in that family; and so on through the hierarchy.

Scientists have yet to identify the ancestors of the vertebrates. They certainly came from the large group of animals in the phylum Chordata. We believe the earliest true vertebrates evolved in the early part of the Paleozoic era, for there is fossil evidence of them by the Ordovician period.

The Water
Vertebrates

In the Paleozoic era, as now, the planet was composed of seas and land, but their arrangement was very different. During the past twenty-five years a great deal of evidence has been amassed by geologists and other scientists to show that the continents and·other major land masses are subject to movement, termed plate tectonics, or more commonly *continental drift*.[1]* Apparently the earth's land masses have always drifted very slowly in relation to one another, so the distances between continents today are merely their positions at this time. We know, for example, that the North American plate, the mass on which much of the North American continent sits, is slowly drifting westward toward Asia and away from Europe, thereby increasing the size of the North Atlantic Ocean, and reducing the size of the Pacific. At one time North America and Europe were joined in one large continental land mass that broke apart finally some 50 million years ago.

Knowledge of continental drift has helped us understand some of the geologic forces that have shaped and continue to shape the surfaces of the continents. The earthquake zone along the California coast results from the pressures that build up where the westward-moving North American plate is in contact with another, smaller plate, that is moving northward. The geologic origin of many mountain chains can be attributed to the forces unleashed when two continental plates collide. Geologic studies tell us that during the latter part of the Paleozoic era, at the end of the Pennsylvanian and the beginning of the Permian periods, all the continents were gathered into two "supercontinents" (Figure 4.2). The southern land mass was *Gondwanaland* and the continent more to the north was *Laurasia*. These broke apart later, during the Mesozoic era; the pieces moved to the north, separated, and gradually formed the configuration we know today.

Geologists believe that during the Ordovician period, when vertebrates first appear in the fossil record, the planet's land masses were in a still different arrangement, though the exact configuration has yet to be worked out. The topographic features of the continents were very dif-

*See page 562 for notes to Chapter 4.

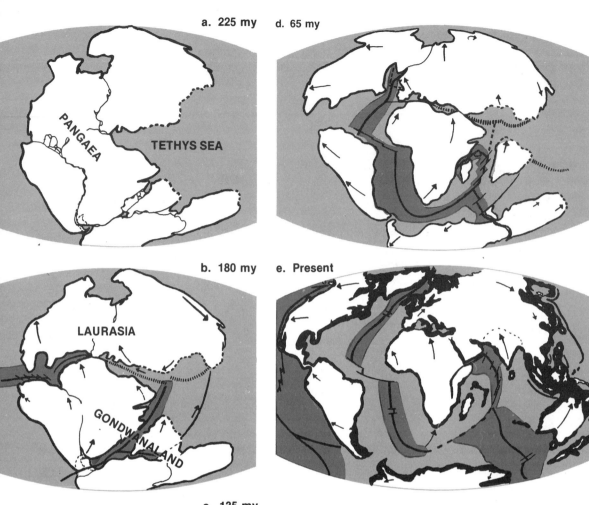

a. 225 my

PANGAEA

TETHYS SEA

b. 180 my

LAURASIA

GONDWANALAND

c. 135 my

d. 65 my

e. Present

Figure 4.2. Diagrams showing a series of changes in the positions of the earth's land masses, oceans, and seas brought about by continental drift. (a) Reconstruction of continents at end of the Paleozoic, some 230 million years ago, grouped together into a large, supercontinental land mass called Pangaea; (b) the continents at the end of the early part of the Mesozoic, the Triassic, some 180 million years ago, when the formation of Laurasia and Gondwanaland seems to have begun (darker gray regions are opening ocean basins; arrows show drift directions); (c) position of continents at the end of the Jurassic, some 130 million years ago; (d) position of continents at the end of the Mesozoic and the beginning of the age of mammals, the Cenozoic, some 65 million years ago; (e) position of the continents today.

ferent from those we see today, which were formed much later. At that time, over 400 million years ago, no plant or animal life had yet developed on the land, but there was life to be found in the waters. Plants had evolved, along with some nonvertebrate animals.

The first vertebrate we know to have joined this assemblage was fish-like, probably fairly slow at swimming, and perhaps lived in the shallows along the shore. These early vertebrates have been placed in a class called Agnatha (meaning jawless). Most of these animals are extinct; the best known of the few living agnathans are the lamprey eel and the hagfish. These animals may seem completely unrelated to humans, but they possess some features, though now highly modified, that are a part of our biology. Generally in the evolution of the vertebrates, including humans, we will see few radically new characteristics being introduced. Evolution operates by modifying structures that are already present. The gills of these early fish are controlled by muscles that, in the evolutionary continuum leading to humans, have moved up the neck, along the face, and now control facial expression. The nerves that supply these areas in humans are like those found in the early vertebrates; the structures remain, but they serve different functions.

In most features the Agnatha are very different from us (Figure 4.3). They have neither jaws nor teeth. Like all vertebrates, however, they possess an internal segmented vertebral column and are differentiated from their prevertebrate ancestors by an enlarged area of the nerve cord at the front of the animal. The brain in the lamprey eel's larva shows three enlarged areas on the nerve cord, specialized to deal with different sensory data. These are divided into a forebrain (or forelobe), a midbrain, and a hindbrain, which control smell, sight, and coordination and hearing, respectively. Later in the evolution of the vertebrates, this basic plan was modified and enlarged. When vertebrates evolved for life on land, one of the most important areas that changed was the front of the forebrain, which controls the sense of smell. Eventually, in the mam-

The Jawless Fishes

Figure 4.3. *Lamprey. Notice the lack of jaws. Members of the Agnatha, the lampreys are specialized descendants of the early jawless fishes. Living animals are about 28 cm (11½ in) long.*

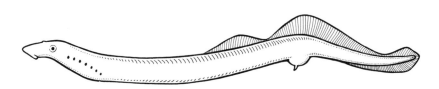

mals, it became the grossly enlarged cerebral cortex and completely covered the rest of the brain.

There is a break in the fossil evidence between the agnathans from the Ordovician period and the middle and latter parts of the next period, the Silurian. Fishlike members of the Agnatha became much more numerous and varied in the Silurian, suggesting that they underwent an adaptive radiation.

Fishes with Jaws The fishes continued their expansion in the Devonian period, but we know little about the evolutionary relationships between the newly evolved forms and the continuing agnathans. Four classes of vertebrates existed then, all adapted to the water but with some different biological traits. The Placodermi, or armored fish, had a bony shield covering the head region like that found in the agnathans (Figure 4.4). The placoderms differed from the jawless fish in having movable jaws, formed from the first gill arch bones, that lay flat instead of in the normal vertical position. The dermal (skin) armor, hard plates covering the placoderm (and agnathan) head, was made of a substance called *dentin,* which forms the major part of vertebrate teeth. In many vertebrates, such as the mammals, the dentin in the teeth is covered with a thin layer of a harder, denser material, enamel. Vertebrate teeth appear to have had their origin in an inward folding of the dermal armor in the mouths of these early vertebrates. The first teeth were nothing more than small spikes sticking up from the inner surface of the mouth. Later in the evolution of the vertebrates, the teeth were restricted to the sides of the mouth and became firmly anchored in the jawbones.

The placoderms became extinct just after the Devonian period closed. The other two vertebrate classes that evolved in the Devonian had better fortune. By the early part of this period, the class Osteichthyes, the bony fishes that came to dominate the lakes and seas of the planet, had appeared. Toward the middle of the Devonian, members of the class Chondrichthyes turn up in the fossil record. These two classes differ, among other things, in the materials composing their internal skeleton.

The bony fishes have skeletal elements made of hard, rigid bone; the Chondrichthyes, of which the sharks and rays have survived to our time, have a skeleton of more flexible cartilage. Because cartilage is laid down first in the embryonic development of many vertebrates, later being replaced by bone, scientists used to think that the bony fishes evolved from the cartilaginous fishes. Many now reject this idea, arguing that the bony fishes may be more representative of the ancestral condition and that the cartilaginous fishes keep the infantile condition into adulthood.

These two vertebrate classes are very successful animals. They underwent a series of adaptive radiations early in their evolutionary development, filling many marine and freshwater niches. The first land vertebrate seems to have evolved from the bony fishes. By the end of the Devonian, there is fossil evidence of a vertebrate at least partially adapted to life on land.

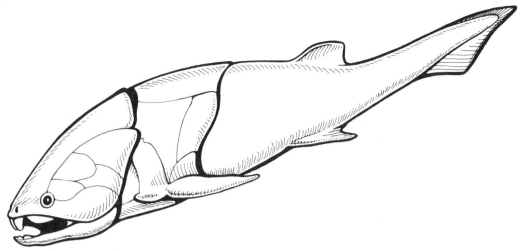

Figure 4.4. *Reconstruction of a placoderm from the Devonian period (actual size about 45 cm, or 1.5 ft). Notice the armor plating and the lower jaws of this member of the only known vertebrate class that is extinct.*

The vertebrates' evolutionary transition from existence in the water to existence in the air was an incomparably important event in the history of life. It set in motion the evolution of the reptiles, birds, and mammals. But a number of vital changes had to occur for animals adapted to water to evolve into land dwellers.

Transition from Water to Land

Air Breathing First, the vertebrates had to evolve a structure that could take oxygen directly out of the air. It would replace the gills, which work like filters, absorbing oxygen from the water. As it happened, some primitive fish had lunglike structures, and thus a complex had already evolved that could give land vertebrates one of the basic necessities of life.

Evolution of Terrestrial Physical Features

Body Fluids Another important condition had to be met. Body cells must have a watery environment or they will die. For a vertebrate living in the water this is not a problem, but a vertebrate that lives on land, surrounded by air, must keep its body moisture from escaping through the skin. Terrestrial adaptation, then, demanded waterproof skin to retain body liquids and an efficient system to recirculate and purify the fluids. Most water vertebrates had such a kidney system, but it is more highly developed in the land forms. The kidney continually filters metabolic waste out of the blood, converts it into uric acid or urea, and stores it in the bladder for later excretion.

Reproduction Life on land also had to evolve a new system for reproduction. The water-dwelling vertebrates, with several specialized exceptions, reproduce outside the body, using the water as an integral part of the process. A female fish deposits her eggs on the sea floor, or in the water, and the male passes over them, releasing sperm and fertilizing the eggs. The soft and gelatinous eggs develop into miniature versions of the adult. The eggs and young fish far outnumber the adult fish, but because the adults do not take care of their young, the mortality rate is extremely high, and only a very few of the young reach sexual maturity. (This point was recognized by Malthus, as we noted on page 18, and Darwin later used it in formulating natural selection.) Fertilization must be performed in water, which transports the sperm to the eggs. The eggs also need water all around them to dispose of metabolic wastes. They are not sealed capsules, but are open to the environment.

Locomotion Water-dwelling vertebrates move in a highly specialized way. Fishes have body fins on their top, bottom, and sides, and strong tail fins. The body fins are used for stability and turning, but not for locomotion. The body itself, undulating from side to side, snaps the tail fins back and forth and propels the fish through the water. Some of the ear-

Figure 4.5. *Skeletons of an early amphibian and a lobe-fin showing the similarities in structure, particularly between the amphibian's front limb and the lateral fin of the lobe-fin.*

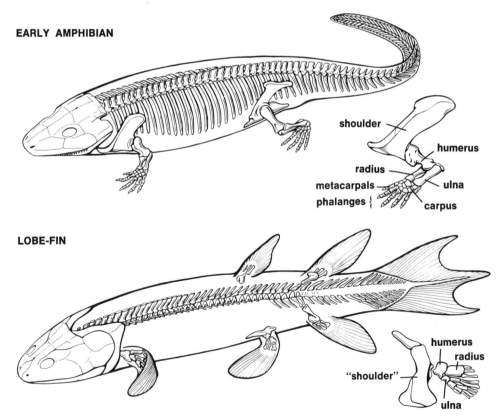

EARLY AMPHIBIAN

shoulder
humerus
radius
metacarpals
phalanges {
ulna
carpus

LOBE-FIN

humerus
radius
"shoulder"
ulna

liest land vertebrates may have moved over the land by swishing the tail back and forth and using the side appendages to keep the body stable, but not to move or to lift the body off the ground; these vertebrates moved with their bellies resting directly on the ground. A more efficient method of locomotion on land called for keeping the body off the ground and developing the fins into limbs strong enough to support and move the body's weight. The body fins of most fish are too weak to support that weight; normally the skeletal elements inside the lateral (side) fins are made of cartilage, too flexible to carry weight. One order of bony fish, the lobe-fins (order Crossopterygii), had lateral fins of a different sort. Because they are bottom-feeders, their lateral fins contain bony elements developed to hold the animal stable while it rests on the bottom. The lobe-fins first appear in fresh water deposits of Devonian age, and were thought to have become extinct by the end of the Mesozoic. Thirty years ago, however, a living lobe-fin was caught in waters off the coast of South Africa.

The first land vertebrates may have evolved from the lobe-fins. The bony elements of the lateral fins have the outlines of the terrestrial vertebrate limb system (Figure 4.5). The pattern, much modified, is still found in many modern mammals, including humans (Figure 4.6). A large supporting bone at the upper end of the fin became associated later in ver-

Figure 4.6. *Whales are mammals that have adapted to a life in the sea. As a result, the terrestrial vertebrate skeletal system has modified to permit these creatures to move effectively in the water. Note the presence of the land vertebrate front limb bones (like all whales, this sperm whale has lost its rear limbs) with the typical number of bony elements.*

Like the fishes, whales move in the water by powerful strokes of their tail fins, but while fish undulate their vertically oriented tail fins from side to side, whales, descendent from land vertebrates, possess muscles and bones which move their horizontally oriented tail fins up and down. Not to scale.

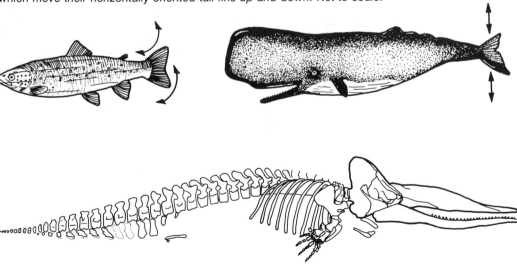

tebrate evolution with the vertebral column and evolved into the shoulder blade *(scapula)* of the front limb system and the pelvic bone *(innominate)* of the rear limbs. The limb system itself consists of one upper-limb bone *(humerus* in the front limb, *femur* in the rear limb); two lower-limb bones *(radius* and *ulna* in the front limb, *fibula* and *tibia* in the rear limb); a wrist and ankle complex; and a hand and foot of five digits each. The major elements of this design, common to all terrestrial vertebrates, can be seen in the ancient lobe-fins of the Devonian seas.

Early Land Vertebrates The first terrestrial vertebrates appeared in the latter part of the Devonian period. They were primitive members of the class Amphibia, the amphibians. Their familiar and very specialized descendants are the frogs, newts, and salamanders, but the earliest of their kind were far more primitive. Like their relatives living today, these primitive amphibians had not completely evolved the necessary equipment that would fully adapt them to life on the land. Their skins were not watertight, their reproduction was still external, and their eggs had not developed a tough shell. Virtually all amphibians, both then and now, reproduce in the water, where their eggs develop.

Thus, in many ways, the amphibians are a transitional form, different from the wholly water-adapted vertebrate classes that preceded them and from the later, completely terrestrial, reptiles, birds, and mammals. However, the amphibians should not be viewed as unsuccessful animals, dozing in late Paleozoic ponds waiting to evolve into a fully terrestrial vertebrate. The amphibians are well adapted to the environmental niches they exploit. Seen in the overall context of vertebrate evolution, these animals represent the continuum between the water and land forms.

The Reptiles The reptiles evolved in the Pennsylvania period, probably from one of the early groups of amphibians. They were the first well-adapted class of land vertebrates, with waterproof skins, four limbs sturdily supporting the body, and profound changes in their reproductive system. Their fertilization was internal, the male placing the sperm in contact with the eggs inside the female. When the female laid fertilized eggs, they were encased in a tough shell, which protected the developing embryo. Inside, along with the yolk for nourishment, was an extremely important membrane, the *allantois,* which served as a collector of metabolic wastes. The growing reptile's tough-shelled egg sealed it off from the outside world, unlike earlier vertebrate eggs, which needed the water outside to flush away wastes. This self-contained incubator could be laid on land; this change, with the other reptilian evolutionary developments, provided the biological basis for a land vertebrate.

With a whole planet of empty terrestrial adaptive niches, the early reptiles quickly evolved a wide array of forms to exploit the diverse terrestrial adaptations open to them. Through the next 150 million years, they were the dominant terrestrial animal life, numbering among them the incredible and highly diverse group of reptiles we lump together as the dinosaurs, but which actually represented many different kinds of plant and flesh-eating forms. The living reptiles — snakes, lizards, turtles, crocodiles, and alligators — are only a pale reminder of the large numbers of their ancestors that once roamed the planet.

One of the earliest reptile groups to evolve was the order Therapsida, who are termed the mammal-like reptiles because of their biological features. The therapsids were primitive, lacking the specializations found in living reptiles; yet many of their traits are so clearly mammalian that we may conclude they were the ancestors of the mammals. By the latter stages of the Triassic period, there is evidence suggesting that true mammals had evolved from the therapsids. The first mammals did not have a full complement of mammalian biological features; those took time to evolve, and even members of this class that are still alive, such as the monotremes and marsupials, do not have biological complexes common in most other mammals. That is why we have great difficulty in determining exactly when the earliest mammals appeared.

The Mammals

Some 65 million years ago, at the end of the Cretaceous period, the last period of the Mesozoic, the dinosaurs, including such successful Cretaceous forms as the horned dinosaurs and the truly terrifying meat-eater *Tyrannosaurus rex,* suddenly disappeared, and not one trace of any of these creatures has ever been found in succeeding Cenozoic geologic deposits. Recent discoveries have suggested a possible explanation for this apparently instantaneous mass extinction.[2] Geologic deposits in various parts of the world that represent the very end of the Cretaceous period have been found to contain a very high percentage of the rare element Iridium. Meteors and other rocks of extraterrestrial origin also possess relatively large amounts of this mineral. It has been suggested that a large (4 to 10 km in diameter) object struck the earth and, along with hundreds of millions of tons of earth rocks, was vaporized at the point of impact. This resulted in the formation of a temporary worldwide dust cloud, reducing the amount of solar radiation reaching the earth, and significantly lowering atmospheric temperatures. The cold-blooded reptiles would have had great difficulty surviving even a short period of lowered temperatures, while the warm-blooded mammals could live through it more successfully. Although this seems to be a reasonable theory, problems remain. Analysis of some dinosaur bones indicates that some of these reptiles were, like mammals, warm blooded; why did they too become extinct? Perhaps lower temperatures and less solar radiation resulted in plant extinctions as well.

The Cenozoic: Age of the Mammals

Mammals had been an inconspicuous part of the Mesozoic animal world, many most probably adapted to a *nocturnal* (active at night), *arboreal* (living in trees), and *insectivorous* (a diet of insects) niche. At the beginning of the Cenozoic, the mammals begin a series of adaptive radiations, expanding into the now-vacant niches left by the dinosaurs. Early in the Cenozoic, the bones of large terrestrially adapted mammals begin appearing in the fossil record, and the stage is set for the evolutionary developments that will create the familiar modern mammal world. Among the most primitive mammalian orders still living are the insectivores, such as the shrew; at some time in the Cretaceous period the primates may have branched off from this group. Unlike most other mammal groups, however, the primates apparently maintained the primitive tree-dwelling insectivore adaptation, and as a result maintained the general vertebrate biological features that were lost or modified in other, more specialized mammal groups.

Mammalian Biological Patterns In discussing the biology of the mammals we will concentrate on the attributes that are most important in understanding the biology and evolution of humans. Like all living organisms, a mammal is a complex of interrelated anatomical systems, each having an influence on the others. We will discuss individual systems, such as reproduction or locomotion, because it is more effective to look at one system at a time, but no system works independently of the others.

The hard palate, the bony roof of the human mouth, is a good example. It separates the breathing opening of the nasal cavity from the mouth. Many reptiles have no hard palate and cannot breathe effectively when they eat and swallow; their intake of oxygen is interrupted by a mouthful of food. Mammals, though, are more active, maintain a constant body temperature and a high metabolic rate, and also have a larger, more complex brain. The constant supply of oxygen that these systems need has led to the hard palate and to other anatomical structures that permit continuous breathing even while the animal is eating. By itself the hard palate may not seem significant, but as part of a complex, interrelated system it is indispensable. It is also representative of an animal, the mammal, whose biology is significantly different from that of most reptiles. That difference is fundamental to the mammalian pattern and essential to the subsequent evolution of humans. Distinctive mammalian characteristics involve many other areas, such as growth and development, locomotion, reproduction, activity, behavior, and dentition.

Dentition From its origin as a folding in of the placoderm's armor, vertebrate dentition evolved to the condition that we see in living reptiles, amphibians, and fish: a long row of pointed or sharp-sided, undifferentiated teeth *(homodont)* that are completely replaceable. Most reptiles have this kind of teeth (Figure 4.7). The mammalian pattern, which evolved in the therapsids, shows significant differences. One of the most important is the close relationship of the teeth in the upper and lower jaws. Mammal teeth in the opposing jaws have evolved to fit and operate together as a unit: they *occlude,* that is, the chewing surfaces of the teeth are so constructed that the upper and lower teeth are able to

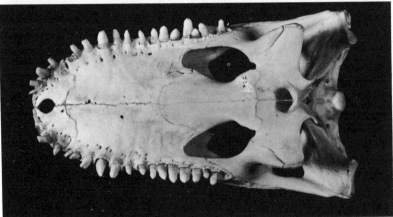

Figure 4.7. Reptile teeth (alligator) shown in two views. Notice in the top photo that with the upper and lower jaws together, the teeth do not occlude.

fit precisely together, cutting, crushing, grinding, or shearing the food caught between. The reptile's homodont teeth in the upper and lower jaws usually operate independently, preventing most reptiles from chewing their food; they have to swallow it whole.

In nonmammal vertebrates, if one tooth falls out, another will take its place. In some reptiles the teeth are replaced periodically throughout the animal's life, with new teeth replacing the old in a wavelike progression starting in the front and working backward. Mammalian teeth are replaced only once; as a young mammal develops, the milk, or *deciduous* (falling off) teeth erupt from the jaw bones. Later the milk teeth are replaced by the permanent dentition. If a permanent tooth is lost or broken, no new one will take its place.

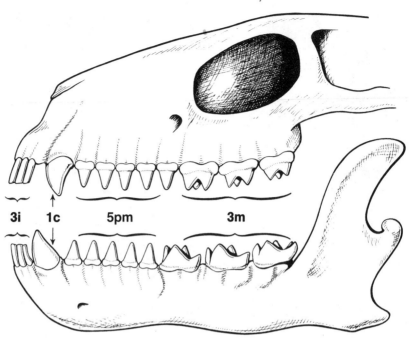

Figure 4.8. Dentition of a hypothetical early placental mammal, showing the kinds of mammalian teeth, their number, and their position.

The mammals also evolved differentiated teeth *(heterodont)*. The therapsids, like the mammals, had four kinds of teeth — incisors, canines, premolars, and molars — with distinctive shapes and different functions in chewing (Figure 4.8). The incisors occupy the front of the tooth row in the upper and lower jaws. They are normally flat, chisel-shaped teeth that meet in an edge-to-edge bite; their function is cutting, slicing, or gnawing food peices into manageable bits to fit into the mouth for further chewing. Directly behind the incisors are the canines. In many mammals the canines are pointed, tusk-shaped teeth, projecting beyond the level of the other teeth. In the carnivores they are primarily an offensive weapon for bringing down prey. In other mammals, such as some of the monkeys and apes, they are used to split open bamboo shoots or other hard-surfaced food.

At the back of the tooth row are the premolars and molars. Depending on the particular mammal and its diet, these two kinds of teeth prepare pieces of food to be swallowed by grinding, shearing, or crushing. In herbivorous mammals (Figure 4.9), whose diet is coarse, fibrous foods like grass, fruit, and leaves, the premolars and molars have ridged, corrugated surfaces which grind foods much as a millstone would. Carnivores, whose diet is primarily meat, have pointed-cusped premolars and molars, with sharp sides (Figure 4.9). When the upper and lower premolars and molars are brought together as the jaws close, the sides of the upper and lower teeth slide past each other, and meat that is caught

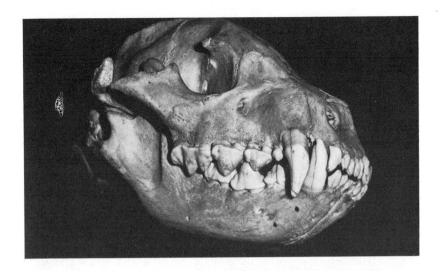

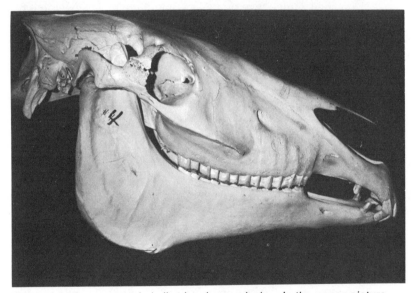

Figure 4.9. *Two mammal skulls showing occlusion. In the upper picture, that of a carnivore, a hyena, the back teeth, the sharp-edged premolars and molars, occlude by sliding past each other, slicing or shearing meat between them much as scissor blades cut. The large, pointed canines also slide past each other, permitting the jaws to close. The lower picture, that of a herbivorous mammal, a horse, shows occlusion in mammals who use their back teeth to grind food between the flattened, millstonelike chewing surfaces. The canines in the horse are much smaller than those in the carnivore, reflecting their relative lack of importance in herbivore dentitions. Many herbivore species no longer possess canines. The incisors in the two mammals are also different, reflecting the different uses these teeth have in the adaptation of these animals.*

between them is cut or sheared as though by scissors. Primates, along with a number of other mammals, have bulbous projections, called cusps, on the chewing surfaces of their teeth. These cusps, which were part of the dentitions of the earliest placental mammals, orginated as part of an insect crushing complex, and have evolved in the primates to permit a wide variety of dietary adaptations (Figure 4.10).

These specialized teeth are found in the same order in every mammal. Furthermore, every mammalian species has a specific number of each kind of tooth, whereas in most reptiles the number can vary among individuals of the same species. Recent discoveries indicate that the earliest placental mammals may have had a total of forty-eight teeth; no living placental mammal has this many. To identify the number and kind of teeth in species of mammals, we use a simple formula: separate the upper and lower jaws and divide each jaw down the middle; count the number and kind of teeth from the incisors in the front to the molars in the back. The ancestral mammals' dentition (total forty-eight) is stated as three incisors, one canine, five premolars, and three molars (Figure 4.8), representing one quadrant of the total of upper and lower jaws. The dental formula is often abbreviated as 3i, 1c, 5pm, 3m, or an even shorter way: 3.1.5.3. This is the greatest number of teeth found in any known placental mammal. All living mammalian groups have lost one or more teeth from this maximum. The human dental formula is 2.1.2.3, meaning that in the evolution of our ancestors, one incisor has been lost from each quadrant, for a total of four; and three premolars have been lost from each quadrant, for a total of twelve. The human total of permanent teeth is thirty-two.

Because mammalian teeth are specialized for different functions, many mammal groups have lost types of teeth not needed in their adaptation. The form of the teeth, too, has undergone evolutionary modification in response to the needs of specialized feeding or other adaptations. Over time, different mammal groups have evolved distinctive dental features, both in the number and type of teeth, and in the shape and size of the chewing surface.

The evolution of a differentiated occluding dentition has enabled the mammals to adapt to a wide variety of niches, and to efficiently process the large amounts of food necessary to fuel the high activity levels, constant internal body temperature, and large brain that are the essential basis for mammalian adaptive success. The mammal's dental complex is also related to the other unique traits, and one reason for the mammal's limited number of teeth, fixed for each species, is the mammal pattern of growth and development.

Growth and Development Mammals and reptiles differ fundamentally in their growth patterns. Reptiles are born as miniature adults and continue growing until their death. This is one explanation for the continuous eruption of new teeth in reptiles; as they get larger, the animals' jaws have room for additional teeth. The mammals' growth period, on the

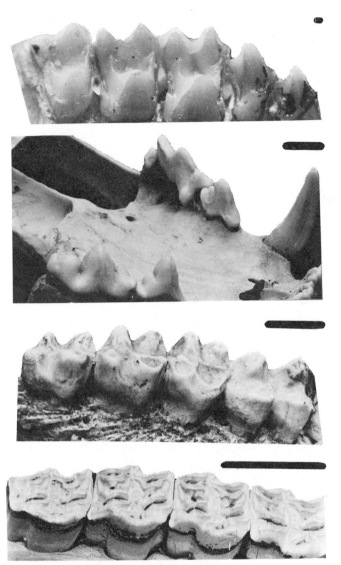

Figure 4.10. *From bottom to top, the upper molars of a horse, a gorilla (a primate), a lynx, and a tarsier (a primitive primate), illustrating the variation on the cusps of mammalian molars.*

Horse molars have a flat corregated surface that is effective in grinding coarse vegetable foods. Like many primates, gorillas, apes closely related to modern humans, have molars with large, rounded, relatively pointed cusps capable of chewing a wide variety of foods. Note the "hollows" where cusps should be; these are pits worn in the enamel from hard usage, exposing the underlying dentin. The lynx, a carnivore, has sharp edges on the sides of the molar teeth which are efficient in cutting meat. The tarsier, although a generalized feeder, possesses molar teeth much like the earliest insectivorous mammals, with high pointed cusps accompanied by sharp edges along the sides and deep "basins" in the middle of the tooth. Pointed cusps from the lower teeth fit into the basins, crushing, and with the sharp edges, cutting food caught between.

Photos not to scale; the black lines indicate the true size of one molar.

other hand, has definite stages: in infancy the young mammal depends on adults for care and nourishment; in childhood it begins to develop independence; in adolescence strong growth occurs; and in adulthood all growth stops. This distinctive system applies to many other biological complexes in mammals.

Bone growth, for example, is very different in reptiles and mammals (Figure 4.11). As a reptile grows, the bones of its skeleton get longer as new bone tissue is laid down at the ends of each bone; this method hinders the development of an efficient *articulation*, or joint, with the adjacent bone, because growth takes place at the joint. Mammal bones develop the articular ends early in life, and the ends grow little after that; growth occurs in an area just behind the articulation, where it connects

Figure 4.11. *Bone growth in a reptile and a mammal compared. Long bone growth in a reptile: (a) bone in an early embryo, composed entirely of carti- lage; (b–e) stages of growth, with cartilage being replaced by bone. Bone growth occurs at the ends of the bone and can continue throughout the animal's lifetime. Long bone growth in a mammal: (a) bone in an embryo, composed entirely of cartilage; (b–c) stages of growth, with cartilage being replaced by bone; (d) condition when most longitudinal growth occurs, with new bone being laid down between the ends and the shaft of the bone; (e) adult stage when ends and shaft have fused and little further longitudinal growth is possible.*

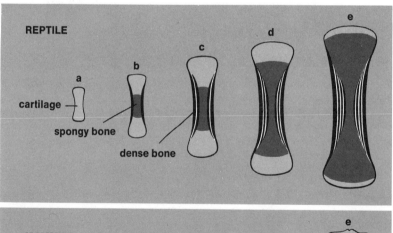

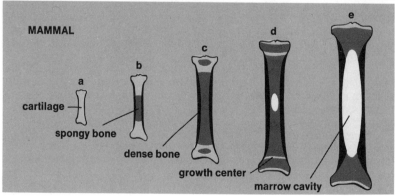

with the shaft of the bone. As a mammal develops, the skeletal bone lengthens by the addition of bone tissue in these areas, not at the ends. As adulthood nears, the growth centers get smaller and smaller, disappearing altogether when the articular end of the bone fuses to the shaft. At this adult stage, the bone can lengthen no further.

Locomotion Growth and development of the long bones have much effect on locomotion (Figure 4.12). Reptilian locomotion, except in specialized snakes and the bipedal dinosaurs, depends on support and propulsion by the four limbs. In most reptiles these limbs are not directly beneath the animal but extend straight out from the shoulder and hip joints, the elbow joint and knee joint making a 90° angle to put the front and rear limbs in a supporting position. Most mammals, too, rely on four limbs, but their limbs are underneath the trunk, and the elbow and knee joints are tucked in under the body rather than out to the side. One of the anatomical changes that made this possible was the angulation of the ball of the upper bone of the front (humerus) and rear (femur) limbs, making a bend that permits the limbs to be placed in an efficient position to support and move body weight.

Reproduction and Childhood Development Profound evolutionary changes have affected mammalian reproduction. As in the reptiles, fertilization takes place inside the female. The developing embryo remains inside the mother's womb, attached by the placenta, which gives nourishment and takes care of the embryo's wastes. Almost all mammals have this system, except the marsupials, whose young are transferred to a pouch at a very early stage of development, and the duck-billed platypus (a monotreme), which still lays eggs. The monotreme's ancestors indirectly illustrate the transition from the egg-laying reptiles to the placental

Figure 4.12. *Reptilian and mammalian stances compared. The transition from a reptilian stance to a mammalian one meant that the limb bones were repositioned in order to elevate the body, which changed the limbs' function from merely propelling the body to supporting it as well. The bones were remodeled and their articulation was changed; their coordinated movement was gained by changes in musculature. See Figure 5.2 for the primate limb pattern.*

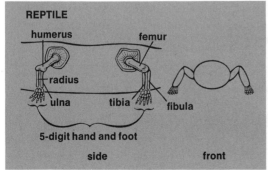
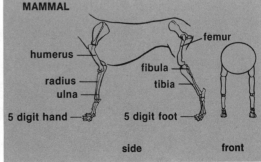

mammals. Like other mammals, the platypus cares for its young after they are born.

Placental mammals give birth to live young that are relatively help-less at birth. Every mammal goes through a dependent stage, requiring food and care from adult animals. Female mammals possess mammary glands, which begin producing milk after their offspring are born. The dependency period gives the young mammal time to learn many of the behaviors it will need for survival. Reptilian females generally lay their eggs and then leave them, never to return. A young reptile must be equipped to deal with its environment from the moment it leaves the comparative safety of the shell. It must know what to eat and what to avoid: everything it needs in order to survive in a hostile world. This necessity limits its possible actions, leaving little room for developing learned behavior. Having a reproductive biology conducive to learned behavior is one triumph in the mammals' evolution, for they can modify learned behavior rather quickly to respond to the environment's de-mands. Reptiles, relying more on biologically programmed or instinctive behaviors, must do without this flexibility. The mammals' reproductive biology and the dependency of their offspring were basic to the subse-quent appearance of humans, to whom a complex of learned behaviors is essential for survival.

Brain and Behavior Crucial to the ability of a young mammal to learn adaptive behaviors during its dependency period was the evolution of the mammalian brain. One of the greatest differences between the rep-tiles and the mammals is the size and complexity of their brains. All ver-tebrate brains perform a number of functions, including the regulation of the animal's internal systems, such as respiration, digestion, and heart rate. In addition, the vertebrate brain is the centralized location where information from all the animal's sensory systems — the eyes, ears, nose, and touch receptors — is received, sorted, and analyzed, and where sig-nals to the muscles originate in response (Figure 4.13). The brain acts as a link between sensory input and the motor output to the muscles, the result of which is behavior. As the brain became more complex in ver-tebrate evolution, its ability to initiate more flexible responses to sensory data increased. What this amounts to is the evolution of intelligence, in contrast to instinctive or biologically programmed behavior. H. J. Jeri-son, a biologist who has studied the evolution of the vertebrate brain, defines intelligence as *the ability of an animal to construct a perceptual model of reality.*[3]

To understand the significance of this definition, let us briefly review the findings of the noted animal behaviorist, Niko Tinbergen, who in his 1951 book, *The Study of Instinct,* reported his observations of the mat-ing behavior of a small European fish, the stickleback (Figure 4.14). Tin-bergen discovered that during the spring mating period, the female stickleback's belly became swollen with eggs, creating a distinctive bulging appearance. The sight of this swollen appearance prompted a male to

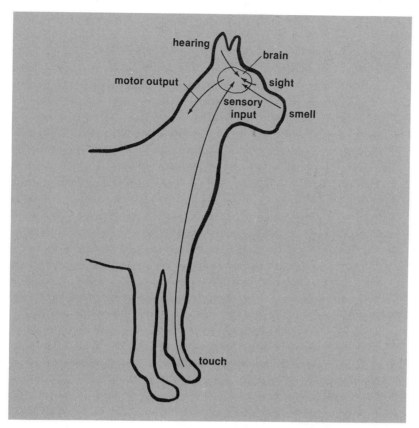

Figure 4.13. *A generalized mammal illustrating the relationships between sensory input and motor responses, and the mediating function of the brain.*

perform a specific behavior, a zig-zag "dance." The response of the female to this dance in turn triggered an appropriate response on the part of the male, all culminating in the female's depositing of her eggs in a nest the male had prepared, which in turn resulted in the male's passing over the eggs, to fertilize them. Tinbergen suggested that this series of behaviors was a fixed pattern, with each action directly triggering the next. He described the sequence thus: each behavior acts as a *sign stimulus* that serves as an *innate releasing mechanism* in the brain of the other animal and produces the next behavior in the series, a *fixed action pattern*. This fixed action pattern in turn acts as a sign stimulus to the other animal, which as a result produces that next fixed action pattern in the series, and so on. All of this suggests that these behaviors are biologically programmed in the brain, so that the receipt of sensory information (in this case by the eyes) of a particular behavior leads directly to a specific motor response or behavior. These are not learned behaviors; Tinbergen found that even sticklebacks raised in an aquarium away from other fish were capable of performing these actions successfully and in proper sequence. Thus, there seems to be a direct link in the brain

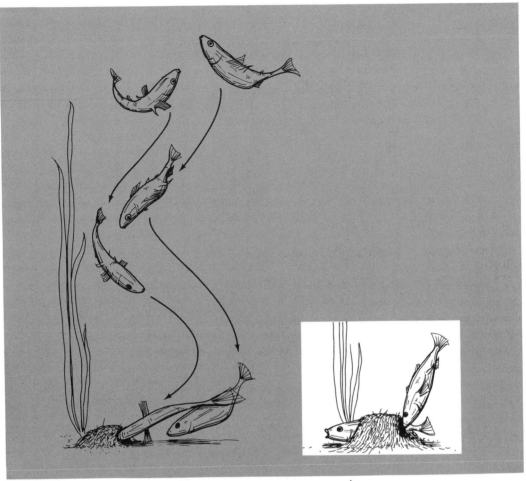

Figure 4.14. Stickleback mating behavior.

between specific stimuli and particular responses. Since Tinbergen made his observations, we have found that the relationship between what an animal senses and what it does are sometimes more complex than those in this example. It seems clear, however, that this sort of biologically programmed behavior is characteristic of many nonmammal vertebrates.

In mammals there appear to be far fewer direct links between sensory input and behavioral response. During the childhood dependency period, a young mammal, not having to survive on its own, can learn how to react appropriately to stimuli in the environment. As Jerison noted, the young mammal develops a concept of its environment and learns to deal with it successfully by observing the actions of its mother and other adult members of its species. Thus, the mammalian brain has taken on an increasingly important role in mediating between sensory perceptions and behavior. Instead of responding in accordance with genetically fixed patterns, the mammalian brain receives the sensory input, compares it to the model of reality constructed on the basis of previous experiences, and then initiates patterns of behavior it has learned will be appropriate in that particular context.

The biological basis for flexible patterns of behavior is the evolutionary development of the mammalian brain, especially the *cerebrum* (Figure 4.15). In the early vertebrates, three specialized areas developed to

Figure 4.15. *Evolution of the human brain. The complex and highly refined sensory apparatus that is the human brain has been built on the structure shown in the fish: a relatively large forebrain concerned with the sense of smell so important to fish; a midbrain with vision; and a hindbrain with balance and hearing.*

The reptile's brain is more complex; because hearing and vision have become more important, the midbrain and hindbrain have enlarged, with the midbrain coordinating the reptile's greater sensory activities.

The mammal's brain is of still greater complexity. Sense coordination has shifted to the forebrain, which has developed a folded cerebrum on top that deals with memory and learning. The hindbrain has developed a marked cerebellum to coordinate the mammal's more varied actions.

The human midbrain and hindbrain have not increased in size in proportion to the forebrain. The large cerebrum dominates the brain and handles the functions that are unique to humans, including abstract thought.

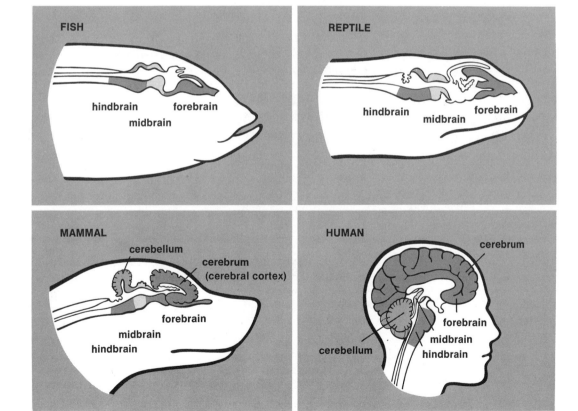

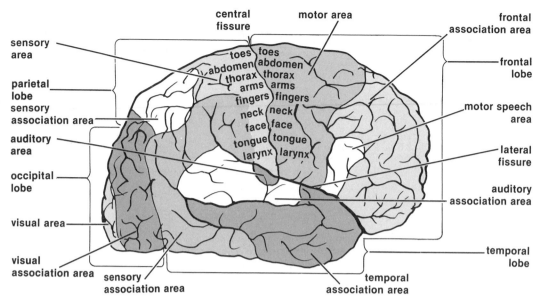

Figure 4.16. *Human cerebral cortex (cerebrum) illustrating specialized areas.*

deal with varied sensory information: a forebrain for smell, a midbrain for vision, and a hindbrain for hearing and balance. In most early vertebrates, this sensory information was passed to the midbrain, where motor responses were initiated; in these animals, the midbrain was in control. In the mammalian brain a number of major changes have occurred; the most important is the elaboration and expansion of the forebrain into the cerebrum, or cerebral cortex. In the mammals all sensory information now terminates in the cerebrum, bypassing the hindbrain and midbrain, and it is there also that behavioral responses are initiated. Figure 4.16 is an illustration of the human brain, the most complex mammalian brain yet to evolve. The large cerebrum is convoluted to permit a greater number of nerve cells to be packed into a given volume; the other parts of the brain, especially the midbrain, have decreased in size, although the *cerebellum* continues to be an enlarged area because of its role in the coordination of muscular activities. The human cerebral cortex, like that of other mammals, possesses specialized areas that are responsible for the receipt of specific sensory information, the storage of memory data, the association of sensory data, the analysis of sensory information, and the issuing of motor commands to the muscles.

In the evolution of the human brain, certain areas of the cerebrum have become elaborated as part of the human emphasis on complex learned behavior and tool making. The frontal lobes, where deliberate, rational thought is controlled, and "choice" decisions are made; the lower parietal lobe, where complex associations of sensory and other data occur; the temporal lobe, where memory is stored; and the lower frontal

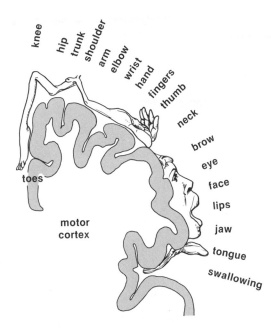

knee
hip
trunk
shoulder
arm
elbow
wrist
hand
fingers
thumb
neck
brow
eye
face
lips
jaw
tongue
swallowing

toes

motor
cortex

Figure 4.17. *Human motor cortex, illustrating the areas devoted to various parts of the body.*

lobe, where the motor speech area is located, have become especially developed. The motor control area in the back of the frontal lobe has undergone differential enlargement, and of an interesting sort. The nerve tissue controlling the muscles in various parts of the body is arranged in what would seem to be reverse order: the nerves controlling muscles of the toes and feet are located on top of the cortex, and those controlling head and facial muscles are at the bottom (Figure 4.17). In most cases, the areas of the human motor cortex that control muscles in various parts of the body are comparable in size to those of our nearest primate relatives, the great apes. The two areas of the motor cortex where there has been elaboration control hand and finger movements and the tongue and lips. The reason for these particular expansions are clear: an important part of human adaptation is based on our ability to make and use tools, which requires fine muscular dexterity of the hands. Another of the unique attributes of modern humans, as we saw in the first chapter, is articulate language, which necessitates highly developed control of tongue and lip movements. An enlarged cerebellum is also a part of this complex. Apparently the motor cortex of the cerebrum issues raw command signals which are then translated by the cerebellum into a definite sequence of orders for the activity of specific muscles at specific times. The cerebellum is thus responsible for habitual motor movement patterns (behaviors), such as brushing teeth, eating with utensils, driving a car, and a thousand other everyday behaviors. When we realize how many muscles are working, and in what extremely complicated sequences, for even the simplest routine behaviors, it is clear why the human cerebellum is a large, complex organ.

The Mammalian Biological Complex   Mammalian growth and development, high levels of activity, high metabolic rates, and a constant internal body temperature are intimately related to the reproductive system and the enlarged brain. So, too, are the teeth that enable the animal to chew its food, and the hard palate. Because its complex brain requires a constant supply of oxygen and nutrients, a mammal must be able to breathe continuously and to obtain nourishment on a regular basis; thus the high activity levels of most mammals. Conversely, the complex mammalian brain provides the basis for a flexible, responsive adaptation, permitting mammals to exploit a wider variety of environmental niches. It is clear that without the evolution of the mammalian pattern of reproduction, with a period of childhood dependency, the development of the complex brain and intelligence would not be possible. These traits, however, are biologically expensive, for they require an additional investment of parental time and energy. Because of this, mammals have also evolved a distinctive reproductive strategy. In most earlier vertebrates, adult population size is maintained by the production of large numbers of sex cells and immature individuals, the vast majority of which never reach adulthood because of the very high mortality rates (see Malthus's observations in Chapter 1). The mammals' strategy is to produce far fewer offspring, whose better chance of reaching reproductive maturity in turn ensures maintenance of the adult population.

These new, interrelated traits evolved on the foundation of previous vertebrate biology, but not at the same time or at the same rate. The therapsids, mammal-like reptiles, had some mammalian traits, and other traits and animals developed eventually; we cannot isolate one characteristic, instant, or individual as the origin of the mammals. The evolutionary transition from the therapsids to the mammals took millions of years, and even when mammals had evolved, they remained less important than the reptiles for many millions more. All these mammalian biological features were crucial to the subsequent evolution and successful adaptation of the primates and humans.

Summary   We have reviewed briefly the biological history of vertebrates. The vertebrates give us an excellent perspective on humans because many modern human biological features were first elaborated in earlier vertebrates.

The first fossil evidence of vertebrates is found in rocks of Ordovician age; by the Devonian period, all the known water-dwelling vertebrate classes had appeared. Primitive land vertebrates are known from the upper Devonian, but well-adapted terrestrial forms did not evolve until the Pennsylvanian period.

The vertebrate class to which humans belong, the mammals, developed from primitive, mammal-like reptiles, and are known from geologic deposits of the upper Triassic Age. At first they were subordinate to the reptiles, but by the beginning of the Cenozoic era they had become the dominant terrestrial vertebrate group.

The mammals differ from the reptiles in dental, skeletal, reproductive, neurological, and other traits. This biological complex forms the foundation for the evolution of mammalian intelligence, which has permitted mammals to learn appropriate ways of dealing with the environment, in contrast to the more fixed behavioral pattern of other vertebrates.

Chapter 5

An Introduction to the Primates

Fossil evidence and a comparison of biological traits make it clear that the primates evolved before most of the other mammals alive today. Our place within the order Primates has been recognized for a long time; when Linnaeus published the tenth edition of his *Systema Naturae* in 1758, he classified humans in the order Primates, with the monkeys and the few apes known at that time. The chimpanzee was not named until 1816 (the genus *Pan*), and not until 1847 did the gorilla get its scientific name (genus *Gorilla*). It is intriguing to think about the fact that this largest of the living primates had escaped the notice of scholars, and was not officially recognized by science, until almost the middle of the nineteenth century. However, by the time Thomas Huxley wrote his 1863 book, *On Man's Place in Nature,* enough was known about this animal for Huxley to write in some detail about the strong anatomical similarities between humans and the African apes, concluding that these creatures were our closest living relatives; Darwin agreed with that notion. A hundred years of biological research, including comparative biochemical and genetic studies, have reinforced Huxley's ideas about our close relationship with the other primates.

This chapter will introduce the members of the mammalian order Primates, and will briefly describe the biological, including molecular, features which are used to include a mammal within this order. Subsequent chapters will deal with the fossil evidence for primate evolution, and with their naturalistic behavior.

Defining the Order Primates

As was noted in the general discussion of taxonomy in the last chapter, except at the species level the separation of animal groups into categories does not represent a reality of nature, but rather an attempt on our part to reflect broad evolutionary relationships. The order Primates furnishes an example of the difficulties involved in attempting to define a large grouping of animals on the basis of specific morphological traits. Despite the difficulties in establishing precise criteria, however, there is a good deal of agreement on which living animals can be considered primates (Table 5.1). An exception is the tree shrews of Asia, whose primate status was long uncertain; on the basis of recent analyses, they have been placed in the insectivore order.

Table 5.1. Classification of living order Primates.

Suborder	Infraorder	Family	Genus	Common name	Location
PROSIMII (lower primates)		Tarsiidae	*Tarsius*	tarsier	Asia
		Lemuridae	*Lemur*	lemur	Malagasy Republic
			Lepilemur	sportive lemur	
			Hapalemur	gentle lemur	
			Microcebus	mouse lemur	
			Cheirogaleus	dwarf lemur	
			Phaner	fork-marked dwarf lemur	
		Indriidae	*Indri*	indri	Malagasy Republic
			Propithecus	sifaka	
			Avahi	avahi	
		Daubentoniidae	*Daubentonia*	aye-aye	Malagasy Republic
		Lorisidae	*Galago*	galago, bush baby	Africa
			Loris	loris	Asia
			Nycticebus	slow loris	Asia
			Perodicticus	potto	Africa
			Arctocebus	golden potto, angwantibo	Africa
ANTHROPOIDEA (higher primates)	PLATYRRHINI	SUPERFAMILY CEBOIDEA (New World monkeys)			
		Cebidae	*Cebus*	capuchin	tropical New World
			Saimiri	squirrel monkey	
			Ateles	spider monkey	
			Brachyteles	woolly spider monkey	
			Lagothrix	woolly monkey	
			Alouatta	howler monkey	
			Callicebus	titi	
			Aotus	night monkey, douroucouli	
			Pithecia	saki	
			Chiropotes	bearded saki	
			Cacajao	uakari	
			Callimico	Goeldi's monkey, callimico	
		Callithricidae	*Callithrix*	marmoset	tropical New World
			Cebuella	pygmy marmoset	
			Saguinus	tamarin	
			Leontideus	golden lion tamarin	
	CATARRHINI	SUPERFAMILY CERCOPITHECOIDEA (Old World monkeys)			
		Cercopithecidae Cercopithecinae (subfamily)	*Cercopithecus*	vervet, guenon	Africa
			Erythrocebus	patas	

Table 5.1. Classification of living order Primates (continued).

Suborder	Infraorder	Family	Genus	Common name	Location
ANTHROPOIDEA (continued)	CATARRHINI (continued)	Cercopithecinae (continued)	Cercocebus	mangabey	
			Papio	baboon, hama-dryas baboon (into Asia)	
			Mandrillus	drill, mandrill	
			Theropithecus	gelada	
			Macaca	macaques	Asia, Africa
			Cynopithecus	black ape	Asia
		Colobinae (subfamily)	Colobus	guereza, colobus	Africa
			Presbytis	langurs, leaf monkey	Asia
			Pygathrix	douc langur	
			Rhinopithecus	golden snub-nosed langur	
			Simias	Pagi Island langur	
			Nasalis	proboscis monkey	
		SUPERFAMILY HOMINOIDEA (apes and humans)			
		Pongidae	Pongo	orangutan	Asia
			Pan	chimpanzee	Africa
			Gorilla	gorilla	Africa
		Hylobatidae	Hylobates	gibbon	Asia
			Symphalangus	siamang	
		Hominidae	Homo	humans	worldwide

Adapted from W. G. Osman Hill, *Evolutionary Biology of the Primates* (1974). Copyright by Academic Press Inc. (London) Ltd. Used by permission of the publisher and The Royal College of Surgeons of England.

Although there is general agreement on the position of living animals within the primate order, this agreement does not extend to fossil animals, for no one characteristic seems to separate all primates from all other mammals. This is especially true of the animals considered to be the earliest primates. Placed in a separate category, the Plesiadapiformes, these very primitive mammals show few characteristic primate traits.

One rather general definition applies after a fashion: primates are mammals that climb by grasping. One of the most important characteristics of the primates is the manipulative hand and foot. Also, most primates have the ability to oppose the thumb with the other fingers in a grasp; this facility is enhanced in many primates by the possession of nails instead of the claws found in many other mammalian orders. These features enable primates to climb and move in trees by grasping tree limbs. This ability is based on the retention in the primates of many of the elements of the primitive vertebrate limb bone system. Most other mam-

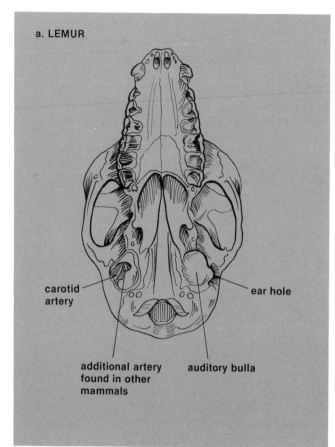

a. LEMUR

carotid
artery

ear hole

additional artery
found in other
mammals

auditory bulla

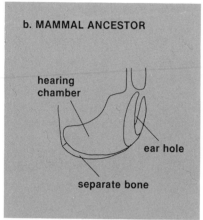

b. MAMMAL ANCESTOR

hearing
chamber

ear hole

separate bone

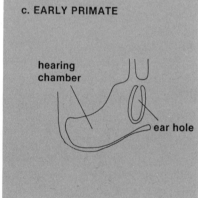

c. EARLY PRIMATE

hearing
chamber

ear hole

Figure 5.1. *(a) The base of the skull of a prosimian primate, a lemur, illustrating two major features often used in defining the Order Primates. On the
right, the bulbous hearing chamber, the* auditory bulla, *where sounds are
received and passed on to the brain, can be seen. On the left, this bony
bulla has been cut away, showing some detail on the inside of the chamber. The auditory bulla in all primates is made up of the same bone that
forms the roof of the hearing chamber. (b) A cross-section view of the hearing chamber, illustrates the structure most probably found in the early mammal ancestor of the primates. Note that the auditory bulla is a separate
bone. (c) illustrates the condition seen in early primates. The significance of
this change is not clear.*

*On the left side of (a), the arrow points to the internal carotid artery,
which is an important blood supplier to the brain. In other mammals, there
is another branch of this artery (see dotted lines) which also passes through
the auditory bulla on its way to the brain. Primates have lost this artery. The
reasons for this difference are debatable, but it seems likely that a single
large artery can supply more blood to the brain than two smaller ones, and
this difference may reflect the evolutionary development of larger brains in
the primate line.*

mals have developed specialized limb systems based on the elaboration of only some of the limb bones, with the rest being lost or reduced in size. It has been suggested that climbing by grasping was important to the primates because very early in their evolutionary history they apparently evolved as *arboreal* (tree-dwelling) animals.

Recent attempts at using morphological traits to define the primate order have focused on the base of the skull in the region of the ear; here, primates appear to possess several distinctive features, including a bulbous, inflated, bony chamber of the middle ear that is composed of bone derived from one part of the skull (Figure 5.1). In addition, several of the arteries in this region have become enlarged, and one has been lost. These changes appear to reflect distinctive adaptive requirements of the primates in hearing, vision, and increasing brain size as they began to exploit new niches.[1]*

Although these shared traits of the skull base would appear to provide objective criteria for defining animals who are primates, some continue to believe that primates cannot be defined on the basis of descriptive lists; that, because they are generalized mammals and thus retain some general vertebrate characteristics, no descriptive lists are specific enough. These primatologists prefer a definition based on trends in primate evolution.

In the evolution of primates, certain biological features have been crucial in their adaptation and have become more pronounced through natural selection. According to this viewpoint, a definition should be based on a listing of these changes in primate biology.

The late Sir W. E. Le Gros Clark, a leading comparative primate anatomist, suggested that the primates could not be defined on the basis of any specializations that they possessed as a group, but rather by a lack of specialization. Clark's opinion was that a number of evolutionary trends, many of which he believed were related to the primates' primary adaptation to life in the trees, distinguished these animals from other orders of mammals:[2]

1. A generalized limb structure (Figure 5.2)
2. Mobile digits, especially the thumb and big toe (Figure 5.3)
3. Flattened nails and sensitive pads on the fingertips, instead of claws
4. Sharper vision, color vision, and depth perception (Figure 5.4)
5. A foreshortened snout (Figure 5.4)
6. Less dependence on the sense of smell
7. Fewer teeth than ancestral mammals
8. An expanded and elaborated brain, particularly the cerebral cortex

These trends are progressive in that they have continued to develop in the primate order, all living primates do not have every one of them, and the farther back we look through the primates' biological history, the fewer of these features we see shared by the early primates.

*See page 563 for notes to Chapter 5.

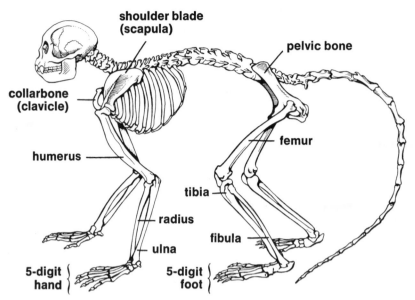

Figure 5.2. *Skeleton of Old World monkey (genus* Cercopithecus*), showing limb segments and proportions (one-seventh actual size). Compare this with Figures 4.5, 4.12, 6.5, and 6.10. Note that primates have retained all of the limb bones of primitive vertebrates.*

Living Primates: Taxonomy and Distribution

The order Primates can be divided taxonomically in a number of ways, depending on how different primatologists view the evolutionary history of the order. The traditional division is into two suborders, the Prosimii and the Anthropoidea, also called the lower and higher primates (presented for living primates in Table 5.1). This approach, however, has a number of limitations. It places the tarsiers with the lorises, galagos, and Madagascar lemurs into the prosimian category, and, as we will see, some scientists believe the tarsiers should be considered evolutionarily intermediate between the other prosimians and the anthropoids, or even more closely aligned with the higher primates.[3] The prosimian/anthropoid division of the primates also does not take into account the extinct, very primitive, earliest members of the order, who share few biological features with later-in-time primates. In a recent encyclopedic survey of primate evolution, E. Delson and F. Szalay argued for a third suborder, the Plesiadapiformes, to accommodate these early primates and indicate the major difference between these early forms and later primates.[4]

The problems associated with this traditional primate taxonomy have led many primatologists to abandon it in favor of a division into the suborders Plesiadapiformes, Strepsirhini (prosimians without the tarsiers) and Haplorhini (tarsiers and higher primates; see Table 5.2). This difference of approach once again draws attention to the difficulties involved in cutting across natural, continuous phenomena in an effort to establish neat categories. Although most working primatologists today prefer the

marmoset

macaque

chimpanzee

Figure 5.3. The hands of three different primates, showing the importance of nails to manipulative ability. The marmoset, a New World monkey, is one of the few higher primates having claws, which limit fingertip to fingertip touching, an ability both macaque and chimpanzee possess.

Strepsirhini/Haplorhini taxonomy listed in Table 5.2, use of the terms "prosimian" and "anthropoid" or "higher primate" in discussions of evolution and behavior make it more convenient and understandable in this text for us to use the traditional classification presented in Table 5.1.

Prosimian Primates

The name prosimian (*pro* = before; *simian* = ape) suggests how the lower primates were viewed when they were first examined; the German word for them is Halbaffe (half-ape). They have a number of living representatives and a great deal of fossil material representing extinct members of the suborder. Living prosimians are limited to parts of Af-

Figure 5.4. Primate skulls. The skulls of Aotus, *left;* Loris, *lower right;* and Tarsius, *small center skull, are those of nocturnal animals. This trait is reflected in their large orbits.*

Table 5.2. Strepsirhine/Haplorhine classification of living order Primates.

Suborder	Infraorder	Superfamily	Family	Subfamily
Plesiadapiformes*				
Strepsirhini	Lemuriformes	Lemuroidea (lemurs) Indrioidea (indriids) Lorisoidea (loris)		
Haplorhini	Tarsiiformes (tarsiers) Platyrrhini (New World monkeys)		Callithricidae (marmosets) Cebidae (spider, howlers, etc.)	
	Catarrhini	Cercopithecoidea (Old World monkeys)	Cercopithecidae	Cercopithecinae (baboons, macaques, etc.) Colobinae (langurs, colobus)
		Hominoidea	Hylobatidae (gibbon, sia-mang) Pongidae (chimp, go-rilla, orang) Hominidae (humans)	

*Included here for comparison is the suborder Plesiadapiformes, an entirely extinct group of primates.

rica, Asia, and the Malagasy Republic on the island of Madagascar, although fossil finds in North America and Europe show that they were once much more widely distributed (Figure 5.5).

Living prosimians are all fairly small, ranging from no bigger than a mouse to a little larger than a house cat. Generally, they are *nocturnal* (active at night, see Figure 5.6), completely arboreal, normally solitary, and have specialized diets. Biologically, most prosimian primates possess rather sharply pointed, three cusped molar teeth similar to the insectivorous teeth of early ancestral mammals. Many prosimians have developed a "tooth comb"; the lower front teeth have become horizontal and are used by the animal to comb through its fur (Figure 5.7). They possess large eyes in orbits that tend to be very large for the size of the animal (Figure 5.4), and lining the back of the orbit is the tapetum, a reflective surface found in many noctural mammals that maximizes the low light intensity common at night. These animals rely on the sense of smell to a much greater extent than the higher primates, and they possess larger snouts. All prosimians possess nails on their hands and feet, but some have a claw, on the index toe, which is used in combing through the fur, and is therefore termed a "grooming claw."

These traits apply to all the prosimians of mainland Africa and Asia: the lorisiformes, including the lorises of Asia and Africa and the galagos

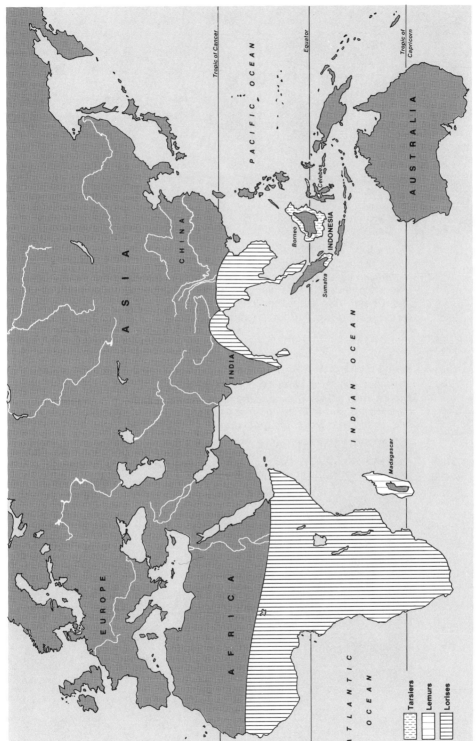

Figure 5.5. Distribution of living prosimians.

Figure 5.6. Two living prosimians. The galago (left), limited to sub-Saharan Africa, is nocturnal, arboreal, and mainly insectivorous. The ring-tailed lemur (right), like all lemurs, is limited to the island of the Malagasy Republic. The diversity of prosimian life may reflect its relative isolation in the southern Indian Ocean. This lemur lives in social groups and spends considerable time on the ground foraging for the vegetable material that is its basic dietary food.

Figure 5.7. The skull of an indriid, one of the lemurlike prosimians from the Malagasy Republic. Note the horizontal placement of the lower front teeth into a dental comb. The inset shows the comb when the jaw is closed. In most lemurs and indriids, there is a large gap between the two middle upper incisors into which the tooth comb fits; this allows the jaw to close fully.

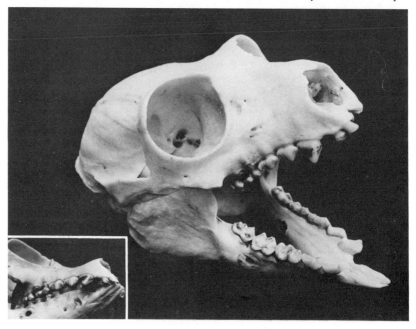

Table 5.3. *Ecological chart of prosimians in the Malagasy Republic (formerly Madagascar), with the range of adaptive niches they occupy.*

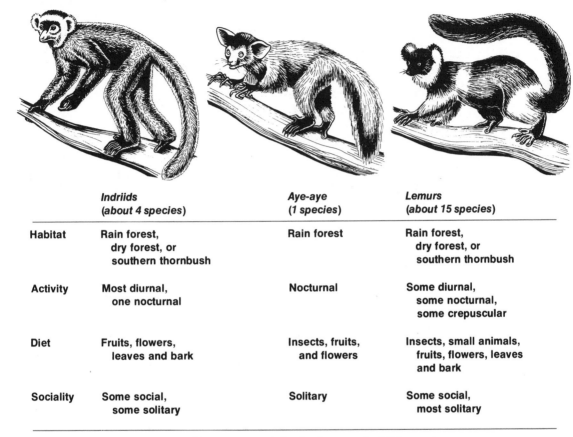

	Indriids (about 4 species)	Aye-aye (1 species)	Lemurs (about 15 species)
Habitat	Rain forest, dry forest, or southern thornbush	Rain forest	Rain forest, dry forest, or southern thornbush
Activity	Most diurnal, one nocturnal	Nocturnal	Some diurnal, some nocturnal, some crepuscular
Diet	Fruits, flowers, leaves and bark	Insects, fruits, and flowers	Insects, small animals, fruits, flowers, leaves and bark
Sociality	Some social, some solitary	Solitary	Some social, most solitary

of Africa; and the tarsiers of East Asia. While the lemurs, indriids, and aye-aye of the Malagasy Republic possess many of these biological features, they are much more varied in their adaptations. Living isolated on the large island of Madagascar in the Indian Ocean off the coast of southern Africa with no other mammals to compete with, the lemurs underwent an evolutionary radiation and filled varied niches. Of about fifteen species of lemurs, indriids, and aye-aye (Table 5.3), some are nocturnal like the mainland prosimians, but others are *diurnal* (daylight active), and still others are *crepuscular* (twilight active). Most lemurs, indriids, and aye-aye are solitary, again like the mainland prosimians, but several lemurs and indriids live in social groups, like the higher primates. Most lemurs, indriids, and aye-aye are arboreal, but several lemurs and indriids spend time foraging on the ground. Some lemurs are arboreal and some terrestrial. Although most lemurs and indriids are insectivorous, like mainland prosimians, several have a significant amount of vegetable material in their diets. Matt Cartmill has even suggested that the nocturnal aye-aye, the only living representative of the family Dau-

Living Primates: Taxonomy and Distribution   157

bentoniidae (see Table 5.1), may occupy the adaptive niche exploited by the woodpecker in other parts of the world.[5] The aye-aye, perhaps the most specialized of the living primates, possesses long, curved, rodentlike incisor teeth, with which it gnaws away the bark on branches to reveal insect holes; and it has a very elongated thin middle finger on the hand, which it uses to insert into the insect holes to capture insects.

While the tarsiers possess many of the features commonly found in the other prosimians, like high cusped pointed molar teeth, they lack the dental comb, and in some features of the dentition, face, and skull, they are more like the anthropoid higher primates.

Anthropoid Primates   The suborder *Anthropoidea* (*anthropos* = man; *oidea* = like: manlike) can be grossly divided into two major categories which correspond to the worldwide higher primate distribution: the Platyrrhini, higher primates of the New World, and the Catarrhini, or Old World higher primates. Platyrrhine monkeys are placed in the superfamily Ceboidea, while the catarrhine primates are divided into the superfamily Cercopithecoidea, the Old World monkeys; and Hominoidea, the apes and humans (Figure 5.8 and Table 5.1). The living members of Anthropoidea are the higher primates; they are social, diurnal animals. Many of them are arboreal, but others have evolved to fill terrestrial niches.

Biologically, living higher primates can be distinguished from the prosimians in a variety of ways. These differences range from the dentition (higher primates normally have much lower, more rounded molar cusps, no dental comb, and spatulate, chisel-shaped incisors rather than the more rounded prosimian incisors), brain, skull, locomotion, even to such features as differences in the placenta, to name the most notable.

The New World Monkeys   The New World monkeys, or Ceboidea, are widely distributed from southern Mexico through Central and South America to northern Argentina. The New World monkeys are separated into two families: the Callithricidae, the marmosets and tamarins, which possess some rather primitive features such as claws, and only two molars in each quadrant; and the Cebidae, which include all other New World monkeys, among them the spider (Figure 5.9). All New World monkeys are arboreal. Those that have been studied live in social groups, some as small as a single family unit. All are active during the day except the night monkey (genus *Aotus*), the only nocturnal higher primate (Figures 5.4 and 5.10). Some New World monkeys have prehensile tails (adapted for wrapping around branches).

The New World monkeys seem to vary more than those of the Old World in many behavioral and anatomical characteristics; this may mean that they evolved earlier. Although we have evidence suggesting that the Old and New World monkeys had a common prosimian ancestor, some recent evaluations, based on continental drift and mammal fossils found in both South America and Africa, suggest that the Old and New World monkeys may have had a common higher primate ancestor.[6]

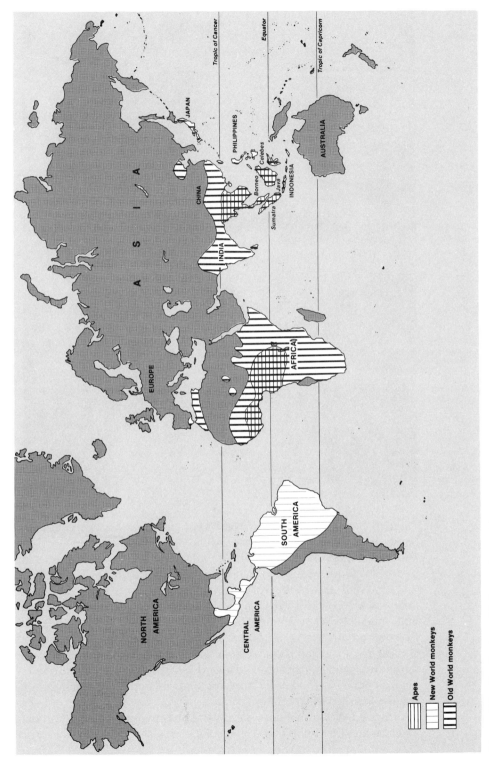

Figure 5.8. Distribution of living anthropoids.

Figure 5.9. A New World monkey, the spider monkey.

The Old World Monkeys The Old World has two groups of higher primates: the Old World monkeys, and the apes and humans. They differ from the New World higher primates in a number of ways, in particular the dental formula; all Old World higher primates have a formula of 2.1.2.3, while the New World variety have either 2.1.3.3 or 2.1.3.2 (marmosets). The Old World monkeys are exceedingly successful, and unlike the completely arboreal New World monkeys, they have adapted to both arboreal and terrestrial niches. They are widely scattered throughout Africa (and on Gibraltar at the southern tip of Europe), through the Indian subcontinent, and eastward into Southern Asia and the islands of Southeast Asia. All Old World monkeys are quadrupedal walkers and lack prehensile tails.

The Old World monkeys are divided into two groups, the Cercopithecinae and the Colobinae. The colobine monkeys, the langurs of India

Figure 5.10. The night monkey (Aotus). *Notice the large size of the orbits for vision at night.*

and Ceylon and the colobus monkeys of Africa (Figure 5.11), have been called the leaf-eating monkeys, for they possess specialized adaptations of the stomach and teeth permitting them to chew, digest, and derive moisture from large quantities of leaves. These traits permit them to live in areas that lack standing water, places closed to exploitation by the cercopithecine monkeys.

Cercopithecine monkeys are found in both Africa and Asia (Figure 5.12). Africa is the home of the baboons, terrestrial monkeys who are adapted to the savanna and forest and depend on strong social organization and large, aggressive males for protection from predators. The terrestrial patas monkeys, savanna dwellers whose protection is speed,

Figure 5.11. *A group of Old World monkeys, langurs (genus* Presbytis). *These Asian members of the leaf-eating Old World monkey subfamily, the colobines, are widely distributed through parts of South Asia. Like many other Old World monkeys, langurs are adapted to an arboreal existence but spend considerable time on the ground.*

and a number of more arboreally adapted monkeys, the *Cercopithecus* monkeys, are also found in Africa. The macaques, the terrestrial monkeys of Asia and North Africa, resemble the baboons in many ways, living in large social groups and depending on a rigorous social order.

Old World monkeys can be distinguished from apes and humans on the basis of a number of features. Virtually all Old World monkeys possess a tail, and all are equipped with very distinctive molar teeth. Apes and humans possess in common numerous specialized anatomical traits of the shoulder joint related to an ancestral adaptation of hanging in the trees suspended by the arms.

The Apes and Humans The living apes and humans are placed in the superfamily Hominoidea. Although it is clear from an examination of their anatomical features that all the hominoids evolved from an arboreal ancestor that used its arms to hang underneath branches, most, but not all hominoids today spend the daylight hours on the ground. The superfamily Hominoidea consists of three families: Hylobatidae, Pongidae, and Hominidae. The hominids include modern humans *(Homo sapiens)* and

Figure 5.12. *An Old World monkey, the pigtail macaque* (Macaca nemestrina). *Macaques are widely distributed through Asia, North Africa, and the tip of southern Europe (Gibraltar). Like many other Old World monkeys, but unlike New World forms, macaques spend much of their active period on the ground.*

our immediate ancestors. The Pongidae include the great apes of both Asia and Africa. The African varieties are the chimpanzee (genus *Pan*) and the gorilla (genus *Gorilla*). The Asian pongid is the orangutan (genus *Pongo;* see Figure 5.13). The pongids are usually distinguished from the family Hylobatidae, the smaller or lesser apes, by a number of morphological and other features. The hylobatids, found in the forests of Southern Asia, are the most arboreal of the apes; they consist of the gibbon (genus *Hylobates*) and the siamang (genus *Symphalangus*).

Most of the taxonomic relationships we have just discussed are based on anatomical comparisons between living animals. Clearly, the as-

Figure 5.13. *An orangutan. This primate, the only great ape in Asia, is limited to the islands of Sumatra and Borneo. Like the African apes, the chimpanzee, and the gorilla, the orangutan spends considerable time on the ground. Orangs apparently do not socialize to the extent observed in other pongids.*

sumption in all such taxonomic statements is that the closer two animals are in the classification, the closer their evolutionary history has been. But just how close is close? And are there any techniques that can establish quantifiable levels of comparison? The recent developments in molecular biology offer the possibility of estimating living primate relationships more directly, and providing additional insight into the patterns of primate evolution.

Using the techniques of molecular biology, we cannot only establish the relationships between living species more firmly, we can also analyze better the organization of the genes in these species and the processes which result in genetic alterations. With recombinant DNA methods, we can now directly determine the base sequence of specific genes in different species for comparison. Many anthropologists feel that this closer scrutiny enables them to understand living primate relationships more fully, to reconstruct our order's evolutionary history more accurately, and to comprehend better the operation of some genetic and evolutionary forces.

Molecular Anthropology

An underlying assumption of evolution is that as genetic differences between living species increase, so does the time since the species last had a common ancestor. Thus, if we can estimate the genetic "distance" between species, we could estimate the time of divergence. Even if the divergence time cannot be expressed in terms of numbers of years before the present, it can be put in relative terms: x and y had a more recent common ancestor than x and z. Here is one area where molecular studies offer a significant advantage over more traditional studies. Though the anatomist can document the ways in which the dental systems of several species differ, and though the anatomist might be able to explain the functional or dietary significance of the differences, they cannot at this time estimate the amount of underlying genetic difference. Yet to reconstruct the path of evolution, it is necessary to be able to measure the amount of genetic divergence. This is perfectly feasible at a molecular level.

Molecules performing similar functions in different species may be given the same name, yet can differ in composition. A variety of techniques are available to measure amounts of similarity among analogous molecules in different species. Some of these, including the first attempts, involve the use of immunology to estimate crudely the level of similarity between comparable molecules in different species. These techniques are not terribly accurate but they can quickly estimate the amount of physical similarity between related proteins. For instance, G. H. F. Nuttall, in the early 1900s, was the first to see that it might be possible to measure molecular differences. His techniques were crude by today's standards, but his insight was highly sophisticated. When foreign molecules are introduced into an animal, the animal's defense system may react by producing a set of proteins, called antibodies, in an attempt to neutralize these invading substances. Nuttall noticed that antibodies produced against the proteins found in the fluid portion of the blood (the serum of the blood) of fowls also reacted, though less strongly, with the serum of pigeons. The reaction made a precipitate, or a solid substance that comes out of a solution. Measuring the amount of precipitate gave Nuttall an estimate of how strong the reaction was. He concluded, correctly, that a strong reaction between an antibody directed against a protein in one species and the comparable protein in a second species indicated a similarity between molecules in the blood of both animals, the strength of the reaction reflecting the degree of molecular similarity. Extending this research to many vertebrates, he was able to establish degrees of relationship between species by their molecular and (because genes produce the molecules) genetic similarity. Immunologists today have many more elaborate techniques, but Nuttall's data and modern data are strikingly similar.

Most of the techniques used today can be separated in two types: those that use immunological methods such as Nuttall's which measure the strength of the reaction between an antibody and the substance against which the antibody is directed (the *antigen*) and those that measure gene differences more directly. All the procedures come to the same conclusion: humans, chimpanzees, and gorillas are very close relatives (which agrees with anatomical evidence) and last had a common ancestor no more than 20 million years ago. Several molecular anthropologists believe that humans and apes separated 5 to 8 million years ago; other anthropologists, who put more faith in fossils, date the split to 15 to 20 million years ago. These differences of opinion will be more fully explored in the next chapter.

Immunological approaches to the study of primate evolution are rapid and generally reliable, but they have one big drawback: antigenic similarity cannot always be equated with genetic similarity. The same protein in two species may look identical immunologically even though its actual amino acid sequence is different in each species. If the amino acid difference is in a part of the molecule that does not function as an antigen, that is, if it is hidden inside a three-dimensional molecule, immunological approaches will underestimate genetic differences.

Biochemical Techniques

Comparing the amino acid sequence of the same proteins in different species is more precise than immunological approaches because the amino acid sequence is directly controlled by the genetic material. Although getting the sequence data is a long and tedious job, several groups of researchers have gathered such information, and we can now compare some sequences directly. Table 5.4 lists the sequences of one of the hemoglobin chains from several species.

Minimum Mutation Distance With a copy of the genetic code (Table 2.2) we can compute the smallest number of mutations needed to change the chain of one species into that of another. One of the human hemoglobin chains differs from the comparable gorilla hemoglobin chain only at position 104 where the gorilla has the amino acid lysine and humans arginine. The genetic codon for lysine may be either AAA or AAG

Table 5.4. Amino acid sequences for part of one of the hemoglobin chains in several primate species.
Only the variable positions are shown.

Species	Position													
	5	6	9	13	21	22	33	50	56	76	80	87	104	125
Human-Chimpanzee	Pro	Glu	Ser	Ala	Asp	Glu	Val	Thr	Gly	Ala	Asn[b]	Thr	Arg	Pro
Gorilla	Pro	Glu	Ser	Ala	Asp	Glu	Val	Thr	Gly	Ala	Asn	Thr	Lys	Pro
Gibbon	Pro	Glu	Ser	Ala	Asp	Glu	Val	Thr	Gly	Ala	Asp	Lys	Arg	Gln[b]
Rhesus monkey	Pro	Glu	Asn	Thr	Asp	Glu	Leu	Ser	Gly	Asn	Asn	Gln	Lys	Gln
Squirrel monkey	Gly	Asp	Ala	Ala	Glu	Asp	Val	Thr	Asn	Thr	Asn	Gln	Arg	Gln

[a]Careful examination of this table in conjunction with a copy of the genetic code (Table 2.2) will indicate that the human-chimpanzee sequence is most similar to that of the gorilla, next most similar to the gibbon, then to the rhesus monkey, and least like that of the squirrel monkey of the New World. [b]Asn and Gln are alternate abbreviations of AspN and GluN.

(shorthand: AAa/g), and arginine may be either AGA or AGG. A change at least in the second letter (base) of the DNA word could account for the difference between human and gorilla. Only one mutation is necessary to change one into the other.

Humans and the rhesus monkey differ at position 87 on one hemoglobin chain, among others, humans having threonine and rhesus having glutamine. At this position, at least two mutations are necessary to convert one into the other: both the first and second bases would have to be changed (Figure 5.14). Adding all the minimum mutations for each position gives a minimum mutation distance (MMD) of 10 between the human and rhesus hemoglobin chains. Like immunological data, MMDs measure species differences. The MMD-derived measure of relationships has the advantage of greater accuracy.

Using this line of reasoning and data on several proteins, especially hemoglobins, M. Goodman and colleagues at Wayne State University have generated trees such as that in Figure 5.15. The "best trees" are those that require the fewest number of mutations to unite all of the protein sequences. We see that humans, chimps, and gorillas form a very tight-knit cluster, while the orang is more distant and the gibbon more distant still. Based on this result, Goodman has suggested a taxonomic revision that would class the humans, chimps, and gorillas together and separate the orang and gibbon groups. The Old World monkeys form a cluster next closest to us, while the New World monkeys are significantly more distant. As we saw, the tarsier has been at times classified in the prosimian category, while the Strepsirhine/Haplorhine classification places it close to the higher primates. Amino acid comparisons class tarsiers with the anthropoids (higher primates); they do not appear to be prosimian. Within the primates, the lemurs and lorises are our most dis-

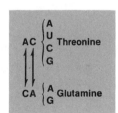

Figure 5.14. Diagram of threonine and glutamine codes. Glutamine is encoded by CAA or CAG; threonine is encoded by ACA, ACU, ACC, or ACG.

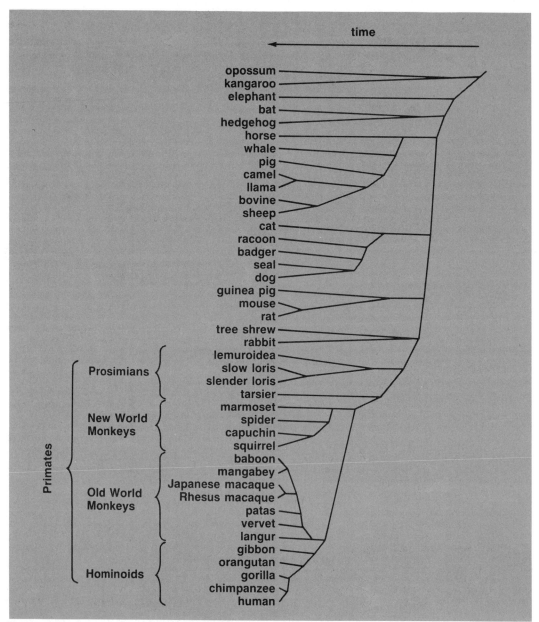

Figure 5.15. *A computer-generated evolutionary tree of some mammals with special emphasis on the primates. The tree is based on sequences of several proteins, including hemoglobins. Note that the primates group along taxonomic lines.*

tant relatives. The tree shrew, which in the past was considered a primate, is outside the primates by amino acid sequence criteria; however, the tree shrew and rabbit do look to be the closest mammalian relatives of the primates.

DNA Hybridization The next molecular technique we will consider, developed in the 1960s by a group at the Carnegie Institute, is known as DNA hybridization (Figure 5.16). After the two strands of helical DNA have been separated by heating, the single strands are embedded in agar. Radioactively tagged single-strand DNA from the same species is added to the agar and allowed to incubate. Because the two sets of separated strands are complementary, much of the radioactively tagged DNA will combine with the embedded DNA during incubation. Washing the agar will remove all radioactive fragments that have not recombined. Because we know how much radioactive DNA was added and how much was washed we can compute the amount that recombined to form double helices (Figure 5.16). This amount is used as a standard for all comparisons between species. When human DNA was used as the standard, chimp DNA hybridized with embedded human DNA as much as the human radioactive fragments did. Gorilla DNA was just marginally less like the human and orang a bit further removed. Gibbon showed 94 percent as much correspondence, rhesus 88 percent, capuchin monkey (genus *Cebus:* a New World monkey) 83 percent, tarsier 65 percent, tree shrew 28 percent, mouse 19 percent, and chicken 10 percent. In other words, the branching order within the primates has chimp and human most closely related, with the gorilla a very close relation (Figure 5.17). These data agree quite well with results derived from protein studies.

Figure 5.16. *DNA hybridization, another method for estimating the relationships between species. Repeat the procedure shown below, using human DNA in the agar, but incubate with radioactive chimp DNA. Compare the recombination of chimp and human DNA with human and human DNA.*

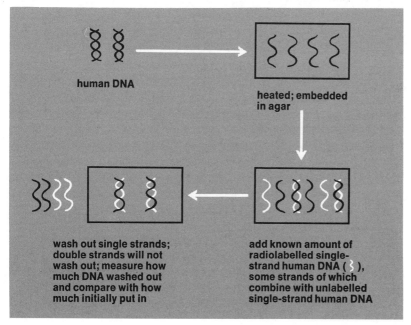

human DNA

heated; embedded in agar

add known amount of radiolabelled single-strand human DNA ( ), some strands of which combine with unlabelled single-strand human DNA

wash out single strands; double strands will not wash out; measure how much DNA washed out and compare with how much initially put in

Nucleic Acid
Sequence
Comparisons

Further information about the genetic makeup of species can be gathered via use of the enzymes known as restriction endonucleases and recombinant DNA techniques (Chapter 2). If a gene or cluster of genes is isolated by recombinant DNA methods, restriction enzymes can provide a preliminary measure of the similarity between comparable stretches of DNA, while other procedures can provide even more details.

More on Globins Here again globins have been widely studied. In Chapter 2 it was noted that adult human hemoglobin is composed of two different subunits known as α (alpha) and β (beta) chains. The production of each is controlled by a separate gene; the α on chromosome 16, β on chromosome 11. The chains produced by these genes are assembled in units of four so that a complete adult human hemoglobin (Hb) molecule, that is, the protein, has 2 α chains bonded to 2 β chains: $\alpha_2\beta_2$. Analysis of human blood indicates that adults have a minor protein called HbA_2 which also has 2 α chains but, instead of 2 β chains, has 2 δ (delta) chains: $HbA_2 = \alpha_2\delta_2$. The amino acid sequence of δ chains shows them to be very similar to β chains. Fetal hemoglobin, the hemoglobin we make from about two months after conception to roughly the time of birth, is called HbF and is composed of 2 α chains and 2 γ (gamma) chains. The first hemoglobin we make during development is called embryonic hemoglobin and can have the structure $\alpha_2\epsilon_2$ (ϵ = epsilon). Looking at the makeup of the protein subunits, studies of the amino acid sequences have shown that ϵ, δ, γ, and β form a family of related molecules. These are collectively known as the β-like globin family. (In fact, there is an α chain family, too.)

When recombinant DNA techniques were used for further study of

Figure 5.17. *Branching order of the higher Primates based on DNA hybridization.*

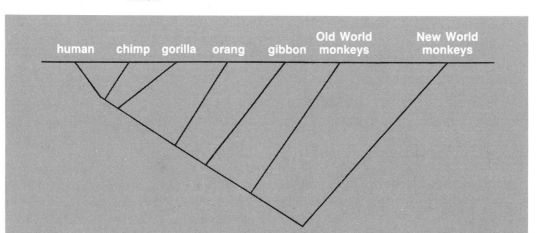

this group of genes, several new features were uncovered. As noted in Chapter 2, the genes were seen to be interrupted. The sequence of bases coding for each chain was not continuous as had always been supposed, but was broken into parts called exons and introns.

Additionally, the γ gene of humans was found to be present twice on each chromosome. That is, the gene has been duplicated and the two copies are arranged back to back on the chromosome. The copy on the 5' side is called $^G\gamma$ as it causes the amino acid glycine to be inserted at position 136 of the γ sub-unit. The 3' gene is called $^A\gamma$ for it puts alanine, a different amino acid, at this position.

Surprisingly, it was also determined that the "gene" to the 3' side of $^A\gamma$ was not a functional gene at all. At this position, people have a pseudogene, called $\psi\beta1$ (ψ=psi, and stands for pseudo or false). This is a sequence of DNA which bears an obvious relationship to the other β-like genes. Yet, upon looking at its complete DNA sequence, it is apparent that it possesses mutations which make it incapable of directing the production of a protein subunit (see pages 34–38 on mutation). Remembering that the DNA has a 5' end (written to the left) and a 3' end, the organization of the human β-like globin genes is as a cluster about 40,000 bases long (40 KB where KB = kilobase or 1000 bases). The sequence arrangement of genes is:

$$5' \; \epsilon-^G\gamma-^A\gamma-\psi\beta1-\delta-\beta \; 3'$$

β-like globin clusters of other species have been plotted. Those of the chimp and gorilla have exactly the same organization; the genes that are expressed early in development are 5' (to the right) to the ones expressed later. The Old World monkeys, typified by the baboon in Figure 7.2 are slightly different in that the δ gene, though present, is a pseudogene, incapable of being expressed. Moving further from humans, the New World monkeys have a shorter cluster with fewer genes. Old World higher primates all seem to have two γ genes, while those of the Americas have one. As prosimians too have only one γ gene, it seems reasonable to conclude that the γ gene duplicated in the Old World after the divergence of New and Old World higher primates.

The prosimians have a yet smaller β-like gene cluster, being only about 20 KB long. The lemurs have the cluster organization:

$$5' \; \epsilon \; \gamma \; \psi\beta \; \beta \; 3'$$

The $\psi\beta$ gene of the lemur is in fact a hybrid gene. As shown in Figure 5.18, it was produced by the loss of part of $\psi\beta1$, part of δ, and all the DNA in between. All this information, together with other data, suggests the tree of evolution for this gene family as pictured in Figure 5.18.

The size and organization of the cluster are not the only useful indices of similarities between species. In Chapter 2, we noted that many known enzymes can recognize specific sequences of DNA. These are called re-

Restriction Enzyme Maps

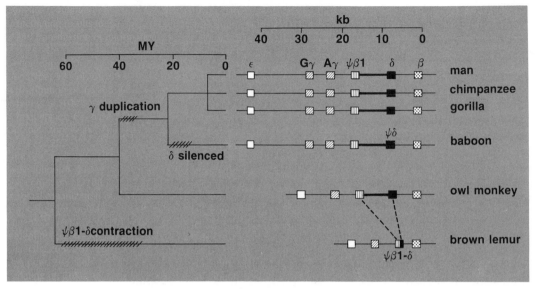

Figure 5.18. *The size, arrangement, and evolution of β-like globin gene clusters in the primates.*

striction enzymes. After the gene clusters (or parts of it) are isolated, a next reasonable step is to use a battery of these enzymes to approximate the similarities between comparable stretches of DNA in different species. For instance, if the β-globin genes of a baboon, gorilla, and human are treated with Bam HI, we see that identical six-base sequences (GGATCC) are recognized near the exon 1-intron/1 boundary in all three species. The enzyme Hind III cuts human and gorilla DNA at a site (AAGCTT) 5′ to the gene. The DNA sequence of the baboon is different in this region and Hind III cuts the DNA at a different site (Figure 5.19). Certainly the enzymes are sampling only a small percentage of the total DNA for any of these genes. Yet, one can argue that the number of identical restriction sites approximates the overall similarity between the genes of different species.

Using such approaches Paul Barrie of Leicester University in England found a small amount of divergence between the restriction enzyme maps of the gorilla, human, and baboon. As noted, the brown lemur gene cluster is quite short and remarkably similar to that of the rabbit (see also Goodman's protein tree, Figure 5.15).

DNA Sequencing   Now that we are in a position to isolate specific genes from particular organisms we can couple this ability with rapid techniques for the determination of the base sequence of a gene. We no longer need to estimate gene similarities via immunological or biochemical approaches; we can actually compare, base by base, the makeup of genes in different

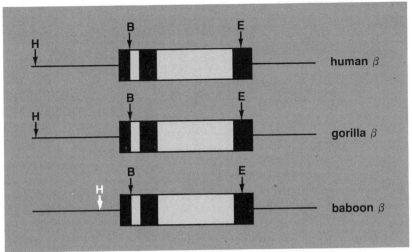

Figure 5.19. β-globin genes of human, gorilla, and baboon. B indicates sites cut by Bam H1; H, Hind III; E, Eco RI. This is a very abridged restriction map of this region. The dark boxed regions are exons, the light boxed areas are introns.

species. Now several such techniques exist which can tell us the makeup of any piece of isolated DNA in the matter of a few days.

Homologous genes are ones which correspond in structure and are of common evolutionary origin; the genes for β-globin chains in human and gorilla are homologous. If we isolate and sequence the β-chain genes from different species, we are in a position to accurately total the number of similar or different bases between all such sequenced genes. Just as with data derived from the preceding techniques, the numbers expressing the differences between all the compared sequences can be arranged into a matrix — or chart — which shows the number of genetic differences between each pair of sequences. For instance, looking at Figure 5.20, we see that the difference between comparable parts of the β-globin sequence of human and rabbit is one substitution, while rabbit and goat differ by six, and human/goat by seven.

Many computer programs can be used to order data such as that in Figure 5.20. Based on somewhat different underlying assumptions, the programs can be used to generate trees which reflect the amount of similarity or difference between species. For instance, in the small amount of data shown, the human/rabbit pair shows the least difference. These then are linked most closely in the tree. The computer then can generate a *likely* sequence for the human/rabbit ancestor. The modern human and rabbit sequences are discarded; the matrix is reformed, now including the presumed ancestral gene sequence, scanned, and the two most similar genes are united. In this clustering fashion, all sequences are paired and built into a "tree," that often is a reasonable reflection of genetic relationships.

Figure 5.20. First nine bases of exon one of the β-globin genes in human, goat, and rabbit. Vertical lines indicate differences between adjacent sequences. Underlined bases in goat sequence indicate differences from human sequence.

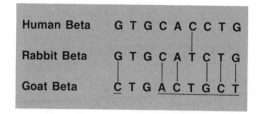

Human Beta	G T G C A C C T G
Rabbit Beta	G T G C A T C T G
Goat Beta	C T G A C T G C T

Why isn't this matrix a perfect reflection of evolution? For one, we are here looking at a very small component of an organism. The β-globin gene is one out of the thousands of genes each of us has. If the amount of difference between two homologous sequences was only the result of random neutral mutations undergoing drift (Chapter 3) then even one gene might provide a perfect record of evolutionary relationships. But we know that other factors are involved; for example, natural selection might be making the structure of some sequences more similar and causing others to diverge.

When comparing very distantly related genes, we run into other problems. For instance, the β-globins of humans and chickens have been evolving independently for about 300 million years or more (that is, roughly since the separation of mammals and birds). The β-globin gene has been undergoing independent mutations on both lines. We can be certain that at least some mutations on one line by chance also happened on the other line (Figure 5.21a and d). When comparing the sequences of the living species, we will underestimate the number of mutations which occurred on each lineage. Likewise, again by chance, some base positions will have changed more than once in a gene's history (Figure 5.21a, b, and c). Though a particular base in a gene of humans and chickens may appear identical today, the actual route may resemble the routes shown in parts a, c, or d of Figure 5.21. This would also lead us to underestimate the amount of genetic change. Though we can minimize the misleading effects of these features by statistical methods, the comparison of gene sequences is not without pitfalls.

At this time, the most intensively studied set of genes are those for the β-globin chains. Sequences are known for a sizable variety of these genes in a cross-section of different mammals, though our knowledge is still much more wide-ranging at the amino acid sequence level.

Summary

The Primates is a taxonomic order of the class Mammalia, containing the prosimians, the Old and New World monkeys, and apes and humans. Although there is general agreement on which living animals are primates, defining the order and assigning fossil animals to it are sometimes not easy tasks. Definitions range from those based on morphology to those based on evolutionary trends.

Modern nonhuman primates are distributed throughout the world. In the New World they extend from South America to the Yucatan Peninsula in North America. In Asia the primates have spread as far as Wal-

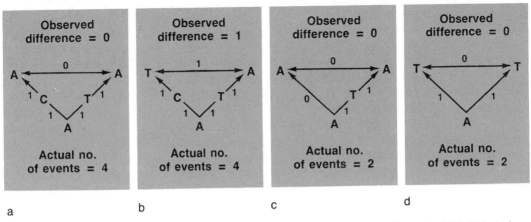

Figure 5.21. *Various routes by which amounts of change can be underestimated: a) Multiple independent mutations to identical bases; b) Multiple independent mutations along different lines of evolution, producing one observable difference; c) Multiple mutations along one line of evolution yet producing observed identity; d) Independent single mutations leading to observed identity.*

lace's line, which separates the animals typical of Australia from those of the Asian continent. They live as far north as the northern Japanese islands, where the winters can be rather severe. Elsewhere, climate has limited them and they normally live in temperate and tropical areas. The ability of humans to spread into habitats not colonized by other primates suggests one large selective advantage of our unique behavioral adaptation.

That the primates are closely related to us seems obvious; the proof can be found by dissecting dead animals. This anatomical relationship was known a long time ago. Today molecular anthropologists are classifying primates by comparing them genetically. Comparisons of immunological reactions, amino acid sequences, restriction enzyme maps, and the sequences of the bases of DNA itself give us a measure of the genetic difference between two living species; the greater the difference, the longer the time is assumed to be since the two species had a common ancestor. The molecular evidence confirms the anatomical: humans are very closely related to chimpanzees and gorillas.

Molecular studies are used in conjunction with the evidence from anatomy, behavior, and the fossils to provide a more accurate picture of the relationships among living primates. Although they also tell us a lot about the biological history of the primate order, molecular studies give us only an indirect picture of primate evolution. To clarify and understand the complete evolutionary development of our order, we must continue to rely on the direct evidence of primate evolution, the fossils. The next chapter will describe the fossil evidence and then show how molecular studies can help resolve some of the questions that fossil evidence fails to answer.

In the next two chapters, we will consider the evolutionary biology and behavior of the nonhuman primates and how this information can help place the biology and behavior of humans in a more understandable perspective.

Chapter 6

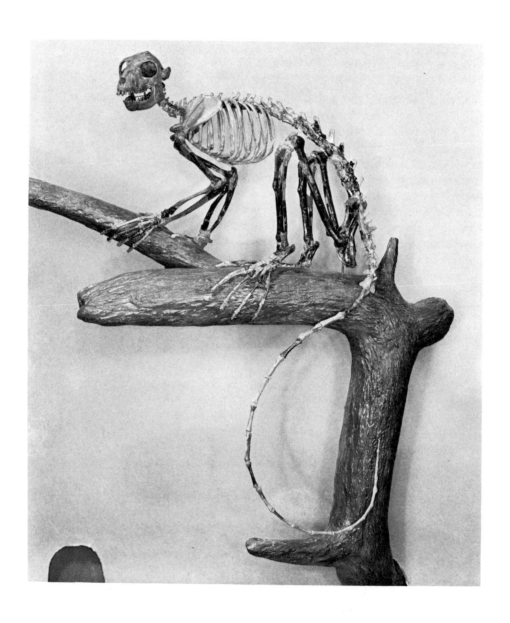

The Biological History of the Primates

The primates are one of the most ancient of the living mammal orders, with a long and rich biological history that extends over at least the last 65 to 70 million years. In this chapter we will trace this evolutionary record and document its major trends.

To understand fully the biological history of the primates would require a complete collection of fossils from every geological period. We do not have such a collection, and we may never piece together the exact biological path the primates took in their long evolutionary history. Our alternative, and a reasonable one, is to put together a history of the major adaptations, the major trends, and the background for the origin of the major groups of primates, including humans.

The Primate Fossil Record

We have a variety of materials to work with. The first and most important is the fossil evidence — the remains of living animals — which supply the direct evidence of primate evolution. The fossils give us a framework for reconstructing primate history. But the primate fossil record is very incomplete in many places, especially in the southern hemisphere, and in several epochs, above all the Paleocene, Oligocene, and Pliocene (Table 6.1). In those time periods and geographic areas where the fossil evidence is scanty, we fall back on indirect evidence of several types: comparative anatomy, comparative genetics and biochemistry, and comparisons with the behavior of living animals. These are useful because often the fossils are difficult to interpret; different scientists come up with a variety of explanations, even when looking at the same fossil material. This is especially true when we consider ancestor-descendant relationships: which earlier primates are the direct ancestors of later forms, and when did the later animals split off from the ancestral group? Comparative biochemistry and genetics can be of enormous help in resolving issues of this kind, just as they have helped in sorting out relationships among living primates. Fossils, however, remain the foundation of any examination of primate evolution. Various methods have been developed for analyzing the fossils and extracting information about the animals.

Table 6.1. Geologic time scale of the Mesozoic and Cenozoic eras, illustrating the relative abundance of the birds and mammals. The primate and human lines have been added to illustrate their presence during this time, but they are not drawn to the same scale as the mammal and bird groups, which were much more abundant.

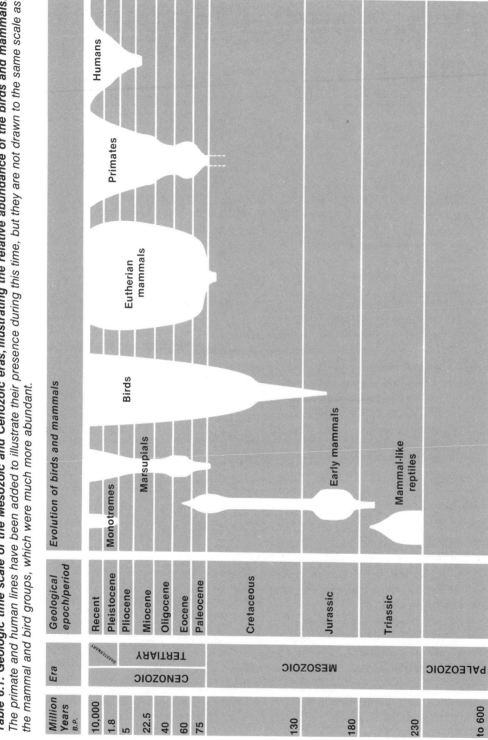

Million Years B.P.	Era		Geological epoch/period	Evolution of birds and mammals
10,000	CENOZOIC	QUATERNARY	Recent	
1.8			Pleistocene	
5		TERTIARY	Pliocene	Monotremes
22.5			Miocene	Marsupials
40			Oligocene	
60			Eocene	Birds
75			Paleocene	
130	MESOZOIC		Cretaceous	Early mammals
180			Jurassic	
230			Triassic	Mammal-like reptiles
to 600	PALEOZOIC			

Humans, Primates, Eutherian mammals

Fossils are the inorganic remains of living animals. Fossilization is a process which occurs largely through chemical substitution or change whereby a bone or tooth reaches a state of equilibrium with its environment, and no further disintegration occurs. Because fossilization is a relatively rare occurrence, the fossil record does not contain representatives of all animal species that once lived; it is estimated that we have found representative bones and teeth of less than 1 percent of all the mammals that roamed the earth during the Cenozoic era. After an animal dies, destruction of the body is usually very rapid, and unless the carcass falls into a deposit that quickly covers it and thus removes it from destructive agents such as scavengers and insects, nothing will be left to fossilize. Streams and lakes are good places for fossilization to occur, because an animal falling into the water can be covered by sediment, and the bones and teeth preserved. Because soft tissue parts are only very rarely preserved, the work of reconstructing the biological history of the primates is overwhelmingly a matter of understanding the significance of bones and (the much more commonly found) teeth. The task is made more difficult because it is unusual to find the complete skeletons of extinct animals, and rarer still to find two or more complete skeletons of animals of the same species. Thus reconstructing the primate past involves the minute examination of fragmentary and incomplete fossil bones and teeth.

*Determining
Structure and
Function*

Several levels of analysis can be applied to fossil remains. Initially, we examine and describe the form of the fossil and compare this description with similar structures in other fossil bones and in living animals. Our comparisons have two important aims at this level. One goal is to relate the fossil remains to other known fossil samples and to living animals, in order to reconstruct the evolutionary relationships of these forms, and in conjunction with the various molecular techniques discussed in the last chapter, to determine the biological history of living animal groups. The other aim is to use the structural description of the fossil bone in a comparison with living animals where the association between structure and function is known. In this way, we are able to draw inferences about the ways biological structures in extinct animals functioned, and we can use this extremely important information as a base for the next level of analysis, reconstructing patterns of behavior.

Successful behavior is the key to adaptive success. We arrive at behavioral inferences about fossil remains by studying and understanding the bones' functions when they were parts of living animals. If, in a fossil-bearing geologic deposit, we find the lower limb bones of a primate, our preliminary examination will be aimed at the structure of the bones, their shape, where the muscles were attached, and their nerve and blood supplies. We compare the fossil bones with equivalent bones in living animals, whose function we know. We may learn from these comparisons how the bones worked in the extinct animal.

Our examination will also give us an idea of which other living or extinct animals possessed bones that are most like the fossil limb bones. Except in the unusual circumstance in which two unrelated animals evolve similar structures as a response to adapting to similar environmental needs (a pattern termed by paleontologists a "convergence"), similar structures in two animals imply evolutionary relationships; the more specific the structural similarity, the closer the relationship is. If the fossil limb bones seem to be those of a higher primate and to have much in common with the modern apes and humans, we can relate them evolutionarily to these modern hominoids and use them in the comparative anatomical studies. Thus, on the level of comparative anatomy, we may learn something about the evolutionary relationships of the fossil bones, and using their close living relatives as a comparison, learn how they worked in the living animal.

Reconstructing
Behavior

Reconstructing behavior is the next step in our analysis. If the fossil limb bones come from a hominoid and resemble the lower-limb skeleton of modern humans, we may infer from our functional analysis that this form moved much as we do: as an erect biped, fully supported by the rear limbs, using only the legs in locomotion, with the hands free for other functions. Our behavioral studies will focus on the implications of this locomotor pattern for the successful adaptation of the living forms, as part of a population, in the particular environment in which it lived. A bipedal animal has to be mainly terrestrial, because this kind of movement would not be very adaptive in the trees. Does the geologic evidence from the deposit in which the fossils were found tell us anything about the environment in which these animals lived? Were tools or other evidence of complex behavior found in the deposit? Answers to these questions help us decide if our functional and behavioral analyses are correct. If the limb bones belong to a bipedal hominoid, what do they imply about the adaptation of the species?

Many primates, such as baboons, chimpanzees, and gorillas, have successfully adapted to life on the ground. But these are not bipedal animals, and the fact that our hominoid specimen was bipedal raises significant questions about the importance of this locomotor pattern. Evolutionary selection must have led to its development; one possible explanation (though not the only one) is that the hands were freed for fashioning and using implements. Chimpanzees make and use tools, yet they are not bipedal. Modern humans make and use tools, and this behavior has assumed crucial importance among the hominids.

Current fossil evidence indicates that hominids were bipedal almost 4 million years ago, but stone tools begin to show up at about 2.5 million years ago. Perhaps hominids used bone, wood, or other perishable substances for tools before they used stone. There may be other, more appropriate explanations for the orgin of bipedalism; perhaps the hands were used for transporting food, or carrying helpless infants over long distances. Still other explanations can be advanced. But the evidence that hominids evolved bipedalism early in their evolutionary history provides the starting point for reconstructing their adaptation and behavior.

In the end, the important questions are those concerned with how extinct animals realized, through natural selection, a long-term adaptation to their environment. We can answer these questions only by understanding how the animals' anatomy provided a basis for adaptive behavior.

Problems in Fossil Analysis

Comparisons of extinct animals with living ones are difficult when few closely related forms are still with us. In these cases we need complete skeletons to understand the total morphological pattern and to reach correct conclusions. Reconstructions can be wildly inaccurate if they are based on only a scrap of information about an extinct form of life. One interesting example of this problem occurred in the nineteenth-century studies of the dinosaurs.

In 1822, Gideon Mantell, an English physician, discovered some bones and teeth of a fossil reptile in the Tilgate Forest. An amateur naturalist, Mantell took his specimens to the Royal College of Surgeons in London to compare them with the collections of living reptile bones. The teeth were remarkably like those of the living iguana, a small quadrupedal lizard native to the Americas. Their only difference was in size; the fossil teeth were much larger. Nevertheless, Mantell felt justified in using the iguana in his studies. He coined the name *Iguanodon* for his fossil reptile (*iguana* = lizard; *don* = tooth), and he modeled his reconstruction of the skeleton on the iguana (Figure 6.1). Today we know that his analysis of the skeletal system was fundamentally incorrect. *Iguanodon* was a bipedal reptile, like many other Mesozoic reptiles (Figure 6.2); Mantell treated *Iguanodon* as a quadrupedal animal, following the comparisons he had drawn with the living animal.

Richard Owen, one of Britain's most famous anatomists and paleon-

Figure 6.1. *Mantell's reconstruction of* Iguanodon. *The bone on the tip of the nose was placed incorrectly in this reconstruction and is actually that of the claw-like thumb.*

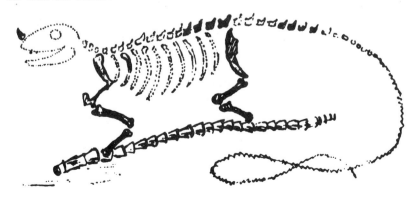

Figure 6.2. Modern reconstruction of Iguanodon *as a bipedal dinosaur, drawn by Margaret Matthew Colbert.*

tologists, introduced the word "Dinosauria" in 1841. No complete skeletons of dinosaurs were found until the 1870s, in Belgian coal deposits. Working many years earlier, Mantell had no clear idea of what a dinosaur was, and he did not know that bipedal reptiles had been commonplace for more than 150 million years. Comparative anatomy has come a long way since the early nineteenth century, making mistakes like Mantell's very unlikely today. Still, through almost the whole primate fossil record, we have only scattered fragments of fossils and few complete skeletons from one individual. The implication is clear: until we have adequate samples of primate fossil bones on which to base our investigations, many conclusions about primate adaptations must remain tentative. Fragmentary evidence also leads to alternative hypotheses in the reconstruction of primate and especially hominid biological history, as will be apparent in the discussions to follow in this and succeeding chapters.

The study of primate and hominid evolution has achieved important results in sketching the general course taken by the primates. However, many details still have to be worked out, with little hope of clear-cut answers from the fossil evidence we now have. The discovery of new fossils and the reevaluation of known material may solve many of these problems. Differences of opinion reflect the continuous nature of the study and demonstrate its vitality.

As we saw in Chapter 4, the mammals evolved at some time in the Mesozoic era, probably in the Triassic period, with the more advanced placental group, to which the primates belong, first appearing in the Cretaceous (Table 6.1). Toward the end of this period (70 to 80 million years ago), an animal that has been identified as a primate lived in a place in Montana called Purgatory Hill. The only evidence of its existence is a single, tiny molar tooth. Named *Purgatorius ceratops* (the species named *ceratops* because horned dinosaur bones were found nearby in the deposit), it has been placed in the same genus as a number of Paleocene epoch teeth found at the same site. The Paleocene *Purgatorius* teeth probably did come from a primate, but the one Cretaceous tooth may not have.[1]* At that time, of course, the differentiation so apparent today in mammalian teeth had not been fully developed. We have, then, very early but also very tentative evidence that the primates appeared during the last days of the dinosaurs. Most primate paleontologists would maintain that the primates did evolve then, but better evidence will be needed before we can be sure.

Early Mammals and the Environment

The primates share more biological characteristics with the mammalian order Insectivora, a group that includes the shrews, moles, and hedgehogs, than with any other animals still alive (Figure 6.3). This suggests that the primates evolved from insectivore ancestors. The insectivores seem to have been one of the earliest placental mammal groups to evolve. Until relatively recently there was little agreement among primatologists as to whether the primates sprang from a single ancestral animal or from different ancestral species. It is generally agreed now that the primates are a *monophyletic* order: all primates are ultimately related back to a single ancestral species. The presence of numerous primitive vertebrate anatomical features, like the collarbone (clavicle), found in all primates, but lost in most other later evolving mammal groups, also suggests that the primates appeared early in mammal evolution.

What was the environment like when the primates split from the insectivores? The deciduous trees, the flowering plants, and the grasses, all members of the last major vegetative class to evolve (the angiosperms), began to expand in number and distribution during the Cretaceous; this had a dramatic effect on the earth's ecological systems. It was during the Cretaceous that the familiar forest, bush, and grassland habitats started to predominate, and the basis was developed for the establishment of the modern food chain, with its dependence on the sun for energy to produce enough angiosperm plants; these plants would

*See page 564 for notes to Chapter 6.

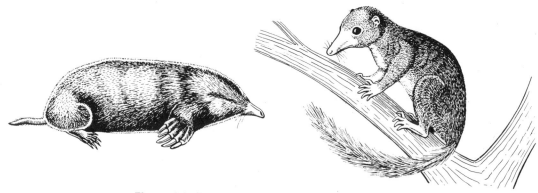

Figure 6.3. *Two living insectivores, the common mole (left) and the tree shrew. It has been suggested that the primates evolved from the Mesozoic ancestors of these living, specialized insectivores.*

support a wide array of mammalian, bird, and insect herbivores, which were preyed upon in turn by carnivores.

During the Cretaceous, the continental land masses were arranged somewhat differently than they are today (Figure 4.2, part d), and they were also apparently far to the south. Because of the northward drift of the continents, the climate changed during the course of the Cenozoic, and temperatures gradually declined. During the Paleocene and the earlier parts of the Eocene epochs, for example, tropical forests were widespread in the western United States — in Wyoming, Colorado, Utah, and the Dakotas — with plants like palms and cypress that today are found in the continental United States only in southernmost Florida. The current fossil evidence suggests that the primates probably originated in the Laurasian continental land mass, for the earliest primates have been found only in North America and Europe. Asia was separated from Europe through much of the early Cenozoic by a wide sea, the Turgai Strait.

Early Primate Adaptations Lacking fossil evidence of the earliest primates, it has been very difficult for scientists to develop reasonable models of the origin of the primates and the adaptations of the earliest members of the order. One suggestion has been to look at the earliest primates as mammals that were adapting to exploit omnivorous and herbivorous niches. Because they consumed some animal protein and many fruits, berries, leaves, buds, and flowers, the easiest place for them to live was in the trees, where the food was. To exploit these food resources, the primates evolved as arboreal animals.[2] Many Mesozoic mammals seem to have evolved to fill an arboreal, nocturnal, insect-eating niche, and there have been suggestions to consider the earliest primates as being adapted to this niche as well.

Matt Cartmill argues that the earliest primates shared a niche with many of the other early mammals; they, too, were eating insects. With the development of the angiosperms, the number of adaptive niches open to insects would have increased tremendously and their numbers risen dramatically. According to Cartmill, many of the primates' biological features, such as manipulative hands and better vision, evolved to provide the earliest primates with the adaptive equipment for becoming efficient nocturnal insect predators; many of the early primate fossils possess teeth with the same sharp cusps as the insectivores'. The primates probably became at least partly arboreal in order to reach the many insects living on the fruit and flowers of trees and shrubs.[3]

These proposals, which are educated guesses, appear reasonable and in accord with evolutionary processes. They provide reasons for the early primates' evolution as arboreal animals. In 1916 the British anatomist Frederick Wood-Jones suggested in his book, *Arboreal Man*, that the modern primates look the way they do because very early in their evolution many became tree-dwellers. Wood-Jones called this the *arboreal adaptation*. Many modern primatologists continue to believe that numerous characteristic features of the primates, especially those used by Le Gros Clark in his list of trends (page 151), evolved as a part of an arboreal adaptation.

Trends in Primate Evolution

An animal that lives in trees, a three-dimensional environment, needs to perceive depth (Figure 6.4). An arboreal creature not only has to move in one plane, like a terrestrial animal, but also has to be aware of the planes above and below. Thus, in the course of their evolution, primates developed stereoscopic vision, or depth perception, by a rotation of their eye orbits from the sides to the front of the skull. Safe movement in the trees also calls for acute perception of shades and color, which is probably important also for recognizing food; all living primates are equipped with color vision. The abundance of open space in the trees would disperse smells quickly; smell therefore became less important as the primates evolved.

The system of locomotion must be specially developed, because moving in the trees forces an animal to traverse supports of many different shapes. One branch may be very small in diameter and has to be grasped; another's surface may be as broad and flat as a path on the ground. The flexibility of the locomotor system that this environment demands seems to have been well satisfied by the primates' retention of the primitive vertebrate limb pattern, with, in the fore- and hindlimb, the single upper limb bone, two lower limb bones, wrist or ankle complex, and a five-digit hand and foot. Most living orders of mammals are thoroughly specialized in their niches and have lost this pattern; the horse, for example, by evolutionary change for life in a terrestrial environment, has evolved a limb pattern with only one of the two lower limb bones, and retaining only one of the five digits; the remaining toe is now expanded for use in body support and movement (Figure 6.5).

The primates have kept the general vertebrate pattern of two bones

Figure 6.4. *The arboreal habitat of the howler monkey. This provides a good illustration of the complex environment an arboreal animal, like a primate, must successfully move through.*

in the lower part of the limb because these elements are responsible for the rotatability of the wrists and ankles. The outside bone rotates around the fixed inner bone and thus permits the palms of the hand and soles of the feet of primates to be mobile enough to adjust to a wide variety of tree branches (Figure 6.5).

Most primates have a high degree of finger *opposability*, the ability to touch with the thumb the tip of each of the other fingers. Some primates do without opposable thumbs because they have a mobile enough hand and foot to grasp supports in the trees. The New World spider monkey has no thumb, yet can move in the trees by grasping branches between fingertips and palms; it also has a prehensile tail.

Most of the nonhuman primates, including the apes and the monkeys, are very agile in moving through the trees. They do fall, though, much more often than we might think, hurting and sometimes even killing themselves. A number of gibbons were collected in Sumatra for examination; 30 percent of these apes had long bones previously broken and healed.

Locomotion in an arboreal environment requires not only a mobile limb system capable of grasping but also coordination between the limb system and the eyes. For this and perhaps other reasons, the brains of primates, living and extinct, have become much larger in proportion to

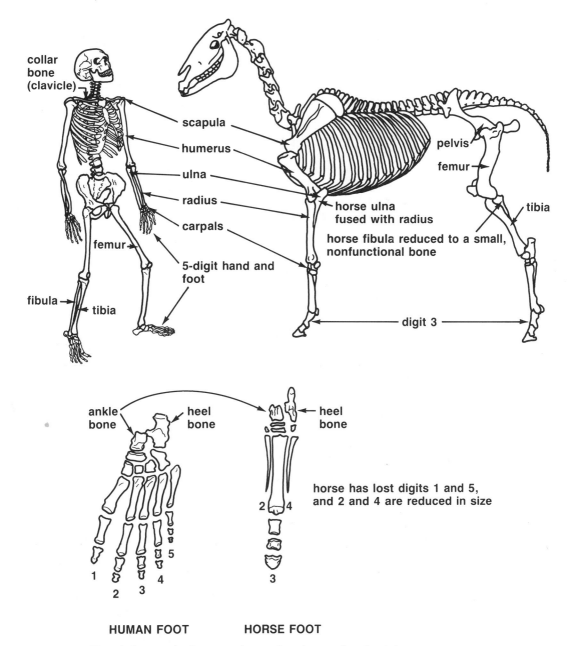

Figure 6.5. *The skeletons of a horse and a modern human (a primate), showing the specialized nature of the horse's limbs, which is a response to the needs of the animal in its terrestrial, open country adaptation. Note that one of the major changes in the limbs of the horse, as in many other ground dwelling mammals, is the loss of one or more of the digits, and the lengthening and modification of the lower parts of the limb system. The human skeleton, like those of all primates, has retained most of the primitive elements of the earliest vertebrates (compare with Figure 4.5), like all five digits and the collar bone.*

body size. This enlargement affected many areas of the brain, but especially the cerebral cortex and those areas of the cortex that are involved with motor control of the limbs and with vision. In contrast, those areas of the brain devoted to the sense of smell (olfaction) began to decrease in size.

We have described these aspects of primate biology as a consequence of a life in the trees because most primatologists believe that the arboreal adaptation has exerted the greatest adaptive pressure on the evolution of these primate traits. This is not, however, an opinion held by all who study the evolution of the primates. Matt Cartmill, for example, argues that the patterns in the vision and locomotor systems developed as a result of the need in early primates to effectively see and grasp insect prey. Regardless of the reasons for their initial evolution, modern primates do not all inhabit arboreal niches, nor, it is certain, were all extinct primates arboreal. As an order, they may have evolved as arboreal animals, but many primates subsequently adapted to life on the ground and developed specialized biological features of those niches. One of the best examples is humans and the evolution of bipedalism.

It is important to keep in mind that the evolution of these traits is brought about by successful behavior in a feedback relationship between behavior and morphology (biological features). *Morphological variability* in any population leaves some animals better able to perform some of their behaviors. An example is the collection of Sumatran gibbons that revealed a significant percentage of healed broken bones. This suggests that in using their characteristic locomotion, an under-the-branch swing called *brachiation,* some gibbons have the physical equipment to make the swing successfully more often than others; they will fall less often. Their genetic variation will remain in the population; natural selection preserves the morphological patterns that are responsible for the successful behavior. The range of variation eventually shifts toward the more successful pattern. This shift in turn feeds back to behavior as part of the range of morphological variability in the population, which is reflected in the behavior patterns, and so on. In other words, the changes to be observed in the evolution of the primates including humans are founded in the mechanisms of evolution.

Early Primates The earliest evidence of animals that are recognized as primates comes from the Paleocene epoch, 65 million years ago. These animals did not look like modern primates; they had claws, their eye orbits were located on the sides of their skulls and were not protected with a bony bar as in later primates; their long snouts indicate a continued reliance on the sense of smell (Figure 6.6). Because of these differences, these Paleocene animals have been placed in their own major category, the *Plesiadapiformes,* of equal status with the prosimians and anthropoids in the Primate order. Plesiadapiformes are identified as primates because dentally they look like the primates of the Eocene. Apparently, however, they were adapted to an arboreal environment. A study of the Paleocene primate

Plesiadapis

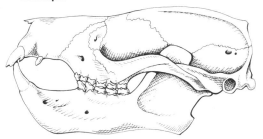

Adapis

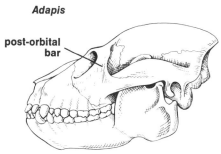

post-orbital
bar

Figure 6.6. *The skulls (partially restored) of the Paleocene fossil* Plesiadapis *and the Eocene primate* Adapis *(two-thirds actual size). Although their names suggest a close evolutionary relationship, there is no evidence that the earlier* Plesiadapis *evolved into* Adapis. *Notice in the* Plesiadapis *skull the lack of the postorbital bar and the rather rodentlike teeth.* Adapis *is much more primatelike and has many features similar to those of living prosimians.*

Plesiadapis (from whose name the larger taxonomic group derives) by Szalay and Decker shows that modifications in the limbs of these animals permitted them to turn their wrists and ankles toward each other so that they could climb a tree. Other Paleocene mammals lack this development; their limbs are directed downward in the posture of a typical four-legged terrestrial animal.[4]

In the Paleocene and into the Eocene, more of the characteristic primate traits developed. The evolution and radiation of these primitive animals continued from the Upper Paleocene to around the beginning of the Upper Eocene. Fossil primate remains from these periods turn up in North America and Europe; in many geologic strata they are exceedingly common. This radiation included not only arboreal animals but probably also terrestrial primates.

In this early Tertiary time the primates appeared in the greatest number of forms. Many Eocene geologic formations in the western United States can be identified by the kinds of primates found in them. Morphologically, the primates' evolution in the Paleocene and into the Eocene reveals important changes, with most Eocene primates possessing biological features like those of modern prosimians; they are classified as members of the prosimian category, presumably evolving from some member of the Plesiadapiform group. In particular, the morphological developments include orbits which have gradually rotated forward, providing the basis for depth-perceiving vision; the *postorbital bar* (a piece of bone separating the orbit from the back part of the skull) is completed; a bony layer begins filling in the back of the orbit; the snout is smaller, possibly reflecting a decreased emphasis on the sense of smell; and claws are replaced by nails. Like modern prosimians, many seem to have been hoppers and leapers (Figures 6.6 and 6.7).

Toward the Middle and Upper Eocene, climatic and biological conditions were changing, and the optimal environment for these early primates was disappearing. In the Lower Eocene and early part of the Middle Eocene, primates are most common in geologic formations in Utah, Colorado, the Dakotas, and Wyoming. In Upper Eocene times the primates disappeared from these areas, and they were limited to southern parts of North America. Changes in climate caused at least part of this shift in primate distribution. Colorado, Utah, and the Dakotas during the Lower and Middle Eocene were probably rather congenial to prosimian survival with the warm, damp environment they provided. In the Upper Eocene, as North America drifted northward, the climate became colder and drier, destroying the primates' best niches. Then, too, other mammals were evolving. The rodents, for example, would have been highly competitive for many primate niches. It seems reasonable that these events in the Eocene also had an important bearing on the adaptation and distribution of the living prosimians, which, apart from the Malagasy lemurs and indriids, are found today only in very specialized, arboreal niches. The modern prosimians — lorises, galagos, lemurs, and tarsiers —all live in the Old World; none survived in the New World. Living prosimians are directly related to the ancestral prosimians of the Eocene, but they are not the same species that lived at that time.

The lorises, the galagos, and the tarsiers that live today in East Asia and Africa are completely arboreal and nocturnal. It is significant that

Figure 6.7. *Skeleton (left) and flesh reconstruction (right) of an Eocene prosimian. Eocene prosimians, like their living descendants, probably exploited a wide range of food sources, including fruit and other vegetable foods; and also insects, birds, birds' eggs and perhaps other smaller vertebrates.*

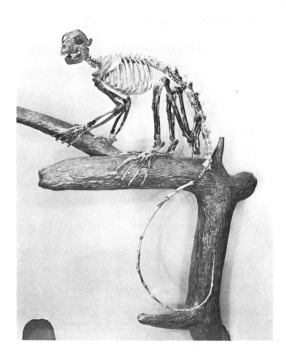

no Old World monkeys are nocturnal. Probably there were primates inhabiting every niche during the Eocene — arboreal, terrestrial, nocturnal, and diurnal — but the only prosimians who survived were the very specialized few who were both nocturnal and arboreal. Their descendants are the living prosimians. The lemurs are the exception, living on the island of Madagascar, now called the Malagasy Republic, in the southern Indian Ocean (see Table 5.3). Since the island has been separated from the mainland of Africa from at least the end of the Mesozoic, the ancestors of the aye-aye, lemurs, and indriids must have drifted across the Mozambique channel to Madagascar from the mainland of Africa on large clumps of river bank broken off and sent down river during the rainy season (zoologically, this pattern is known as "rafting").

It has been suggested that each of the three major groups of living Malagasy prosimians had separate ancestors rafting to Madagascar, although these animals are the only large mammals on the island. It may be that the Malagasy primates offer us a picture of what the primate world was like before the Upper Eocene began: prosimians living in a variety of adaptive niches, on the ground, in the trees, active at night or during the day.[5]

The Evolution of the Higher Primates

By Upper Eocene times, signs of primates are few and far between. Our knowledge and evidence of higher primates (members of the Anthropoid suborder) at this time are also very scanty, but fragmentary evidence (jaw fragments from the Upper Eocene of Burma) suggests that the higher primates (the group to which the monkeys, apes, and humans belong) began their evolution in the latter part of the Eocene. These jaw fragments are simply too scanty to make any but the most preliminary identifications, and we are therefore in the dark about the reasons for the evolutionary appearance of the higher primates, or even which Eocene prosimian was the ancestor of the anthropoids.[6]

The climatic changes that shifted the prosimians southward in the latter stages of the Eocene seem to have contributed to the major geographic distinctions found in the higher primates. Until that time the Eurasian continent and the North American continent were connected. Continental drift studies indicate that northeastern North America and the European parts of Eurasia were tied by a bridge of land. In the Upper Eocene, because of the climatic shifts, probably no primates could live in this colder, drier northern area, and the faunal connection between the New World and the Old World was broken. Continental drift ultimately completed the break by severing the land bridge. Until the climate changed, primates very similar to one another lived both in Europe and in North America. Several Paleocene and Eocene species are the only primates, besides *Homo sapiens*, known from both the Old and New Worlds. By early in the following geologic period, the Oligocene, there is evidence of a very primitive New World monkey in deposits in Bolivia, in South America, and thus the pattern of subsequent separate Old and New World primate evolution was established.

The later Eocene climatic conditions seem to have continued into the Oligocene; primate fossils are completely absent from Europe, and they are rarely found in North America. Our knowledge of Old World Oligocene higher primates comes from a fossil-rich area one hundred kilometers outside Cairo, Egypt, called the *Fayum Beds*. There is thus a profound change in the pattern of primate distribution. Early in their evolution, during the Paleocene and Eocene, primates are known only from the Laurasian continents, and it is reasonable to believe that this is where the primates probably originated. By the beginning of the Oligocene, however, the focus of primate evolution has shifted southward to the Gondwanaland continents of Africa and South America.

During the Oligocene the Fayum area of North Africa was lush tropical gallery forest, an ideal environment for arboreal primates. The Fayum primates may reflect very accurately the higher primates' evolution during this time, but keep in mind that this is the only fossil evidence we currently possess of Old World Oligocene primates; this area could also be a "backwater" of primate evolution. Important trends in their evolution may have gone on elsewhere, in places that have as yet given up no evidence.

The Fayum fossils are remains of higher primates related ancestrally to the monkeys, apes, and humans. They are not apes, Old World monkeys, or humans, but the primitive ancestors of these living forms, and they are therefore troublesome to characterize taxonomically. Modern apes and monkeys are distinguished by biological features such as the locomotor system and dentition.

Locomotion The anatomy related to locomotion differs significantly in the monkeys and apes. Old World monkeys (of the Superfamily Cercopithecoidea; see Table 5.1) are basically quadrupedal in the trees and on the ground. When moving in the trees, they walk on top of the branches, using their grasping hands and feet to hold on, and they jump or leap from branch to branch. On the ground, their palms and soles are flat on the surface. Their skeleton reflects this pattern of movement: the front and back limbs are about equal in length; the rib cage is narrow from side to side, with a relatively small collarbone or clavicle; and the position of the shoulder blade, or scapula, is on the side of the rib cage, with the shoulder joint itself facing front, or downward, when the animal is in its normal walking position (Figures 6.8 and 5.2). The shoulder joint surface is curved so that the joint can act effectively in quadrupedal movement; this gives monkeys stable but relatively immobile shoulder joints. Old World monkeys have tails, which though not prehensile (only some New World monkeys have prehensile tails) are used for balance in the trees. Old World monkeys also possess *ischial callosities,* flattened areas on the buttocks covered by insensitive connective tissue having few nerve or arterial connections. They serve as padding on which the animal can rest or sleep in the trees for long periods without undue discomfort.

The living apes (of the Superfamily Hominoidea) have a much more

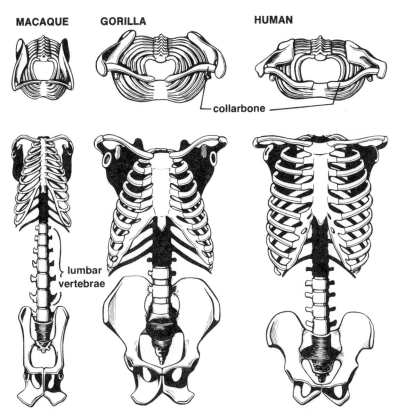

MACAQUE   **GORILLA**   **HUMAN**

collarbone

lumbar
vertebrae

Figure 6.8. *Three major differences in skeletal structure among monkeys, gorillas, and humans are in the shoulder, the lumbar region of the spine, and the pelvis. The shoulder blades of a monkey (here a macaque) are almost parallel to each other on opposite sides of its rib cage, as is seen from the drawing of the skeleton (top) as viewed from above; the human's are on the upper back, and a gorilla's extend up with a large bony collar. Notice the enlargement of the clavicle (collar bone) in the gorilla and human skeletons. The transversely enlarged chest in both humans and gorillas, associated with the large collar bone, is part of the anatomical equipment of an animal with a highly mobile shoulder. Monkeys usually have six or seven lumbar vertebrae (ones with no ribs attached), most apes have three, and humans normally have five. The monkey's tilted pelvis provides an anchor for the leg muscles of the quadrupedal animal. The gorilla pelvis gives anchorage for the muscles that support the animal in its normal quadrupedal knuckle-walking posture. The human pelvis not only supports the upper part of the body but also gives a base for strong walking muscles.*

specialized anatomical system related to locomotion. None of the living apes possess tails, and, except for the gibbon, none have an ischial callosity. In all living apes, the front limbs and supporting structures have a number of rather distinctive elements. The rib cage is broadened from side to side, which places the shoulder blades on the back of the rib cage, with the shoulder joint facing outward, rather than downward as in monkeys. The collarbone is larger and more strongly developed in the apes. The shoulder joint in apes is flatter, with less bony contact be-

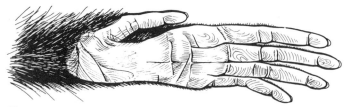

Figure 6.9. *A gibbon's hand. Notice how elongated the fingers are in proportion to the thumb.*

tween the shoulder blade and the ball of the upper arm bone, resulting in a much more mobile but less stable joint. Ape front limbs tend to be longer than the rear limbs, and the hands are equipped with a thumb about human length, but with fingers that are very long in proportion to the thumb (Figure 6.9). It is clear that these anatomical features are part of an adaptation in the apes for using the front limbs to hang suspended from underneath branches (Figure 6.10), which would require both a mobile shoulder joint and reinforcement from an enlarged collarbone. Additional strengthening comes from the enlarged ape breastbone, or sternum, and additional limb mobility comes from the arrangement of bones in the wrist joint (Figure 6.11).

This *suspensory hanging* adaptation may have initially evolved to permit these hominoid primates to exploit food items efficiently. An an-

Figure 6.10. *A brachiating gibbon and a gibbon skeleton. Compare with Figure 5.2. Notice the difference in limb proportion, especially the length of the front limbs.*

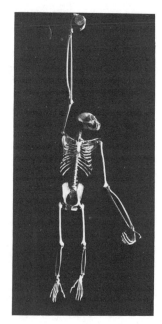

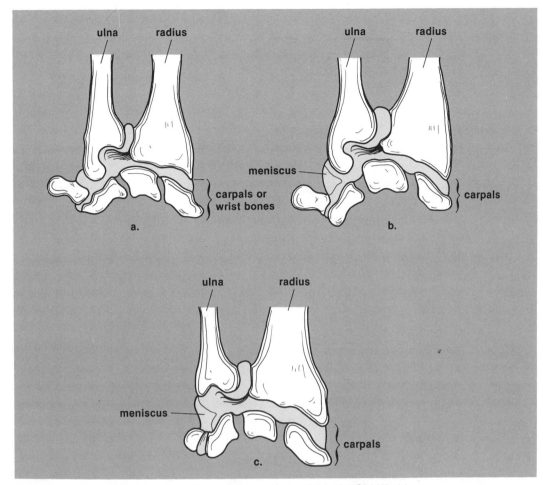

Figure 6.11. *The wrist joint of (a)* Cercopithecus *(a quadrupedal Old World monkey), (b) chimpanzee (a knuckle-walker), and (c)* Homo sapiens. *The suspensory hanging adaptation of the ancestors of the apes and humans can be seen in certain anatomical features of the wrist joint. In the chimp and human a disc of cartilage or meniscus is present between the ulna (a bone of the lower arm) and the carpal or wrist bones. The position of this disc makes for less bone-to-bone contact in the joint and therefore allows a greater degree of rotary movement in that joint. This range of movement is very important for suspensory hangers and their descendants. The quadrupedal monkey wrist, on the other hand, does not have this meniscus so that movement in this joint is more restricted.*

imal hanging from a branch by one hand and able to use its grasping feet to provide additional support from other branches would be better able to reach fruit and other vegetable foods growing at the ends of branches than a monkey which would have to move quadrupedally along the top of an increasingly thinner and unstable branch to reach the same foods. This anatomical specialization has led to the development in the lesser apes, the gibbons and siamang, of _brachiation_, an under-the-branch, swinging locomotion (Figure 6.10).

The great apes — the gorilla, chimpanzee, and orang — are not brachiators, although occasionally younger animals do swing in the trees. Chimpanzees and gorillas spend most of their time on the ground, where they move by knuckle-walking, in which their weight is supported on the knuckles, not the palms of their hands (Figure 7.14). A number of additional features have evolved in the hands of the knuckle-walkers to permit this kind of locomotion (Figure 6.12).

Because many of the anatomical features in the front limbs of the apes are also found in modern humans, it is clear that our ancestors shared this suspensory adaptation. The question is still open as to whether the ancestors of the living great apes and humans were once brachiators like the gibbons, or whether this locomotor behavior is limited only to the lesser apes and their ancestors. Fossils do not provide clear evidence either way, but it is likely that it would have been difficult for large-bodied apes like gorillas and orangs to be efficient brachiators. Despite the uncertainties involving a common brachiating ancestor the significant differences in the anatomy of the monkeys and the apes provide an important basis for distinguishing the two groups in the fossil record.

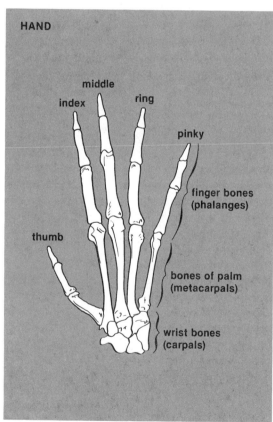

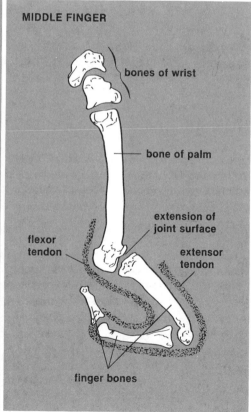

Another major difference between the monkeys and apes is their dentition. Mammals' teeth are specialized for several functions, and the number of their teeth depends on the kind of adaptation. We think that the
original dental formula for early mammals was 3.1.5.3, or three incisors,
one canine, five premolars, and three molars, totaling forty-eight teeth.
Most prosimians have a dental formula of 2.1.3.3, as do New World
monkeys of the family Cebidae. The New World marmoset family has a
formula of 2.1.3.2. Among the higher primates, Old World monkeys, apes,
and humans have lost one more premolar, making their formula 2.1.2.3.
The molar cusp patterns of Old World monkeys are distinctly different
from those of apes and humans (Figure 6.13). The occlusal or working
surface of an Old World monkey molar is divided roughly into two halves
with a deep groove between them. Each part of the tooth has two high
cusps with a transverse ridge between them. Each half, with the two cusps,
is called a loph, giving the pattern its name: *bilophodont* (two-loph tooth).
Dentition with bilophodont molars is characteristic of the upper and lower
molars of all the Old World monkeys.

The hominoids (apes and humans) have more complicated molar
patterns. The upper molars have four cusps, like those of the Old World
monkeys, but in a different arrangement. Instead of two sets of two cusps,
with transverse ridges connecting them, the cusps on hominoid upper
molars have an oblique ridge between the inside front cusp and the back
outside one; no deep groove separates front and back halves of the tooth.

Unlike Old World monkeys, whose lower molars are the same as
the upper teeth, hominoids have lower molars with different configura-
tions. The basic pattern in apes and humans is five cusps (Figure 6.13).

When we view a lower molar tooth from the tongue side outward,
the arrangement of grooves separating the cusps looks like a Y. These
molars have five cusps, so they are known as the Y-5 pattern. This distinctive Y-5 pattern shows up in all living and extinct ape lower molars.
But in humans, though the first lower molars usually follow this configuration, evolutionary selection has reduced the size of the second and
third molars. This decrease has been accomplished by losing one cusp,
so that modern human back molars usually have four cusps, arranged in
a simple + pattern.

A number of studies have attempted to provide a functional interpretation of the differences between the molar teeth of monkeys and apes,

Figure 6.12 (opposite). *The hand of a chimpanzee, with the third or middle
finger shown enlarged from the side. Note the backward extension of the
joint surface of the end of the palm bone (metacarpal), which permits the
finger bones to be bent back considerably farther than is possible in modern humans (try it yourself). This allows the chimpanzee to place its fingers
in the typical knuckle-walking posture. (see Figure 7.14). The flexor tendons
attach to the muscles which close the hand (making a fist) while the exten-
sor tendons attach to muscles that open the hand. Because of the stresses
involved in maintaining the hand bones in the knuckle-walking position, the
flexor muscles in chimpanzees are prominently developed.*

The Evolution of the Higher Primates 197

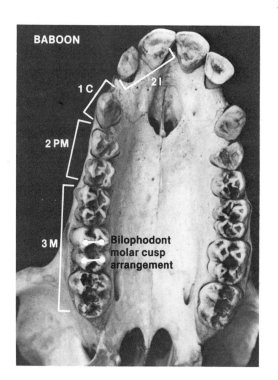

BABOON

1 C

2 I

2 PM

3 M Bilophodont
molar cusp
arrangement

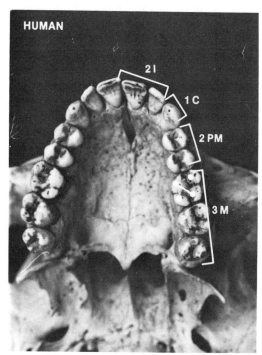

HUMAN

2 I

1 C

2 PM

3 M

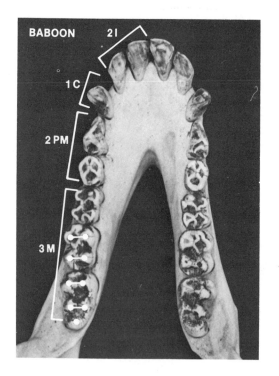

BABOON 2 I

1 C

2 PM

3 M

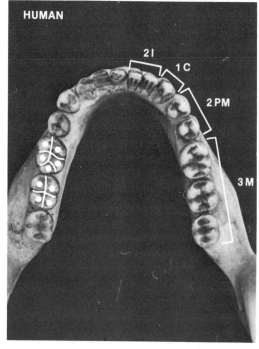

HUMAN

2 I

1 C

2 PM

3 M

thus far with only limited success. One suggestion, which appears reasonable, is that the bilophodont molars are a specialized development that evolved to permit the monkeys to more effectively chop up into small pieces various kinds of cellulose based leaves, grasses, and other vegetation, and therefore increase the ability of these animals to exploit herbivorous dietary niches.[7] It is apparent that the hominoid upper and lower molars represent a more generalized mammalian pattern, and it is likely that bilophodont molars evolved from a pattern like that of the hominoids.

Primates of the Oligocene

These two major differences — in the locomotor system and in the dentition — are the basic features distinguishing Old World monkeys and hominoids. The Oligocene fossils discovered in the Fayum Beds possess features that identify them as anthropoid primates, and several of them possess molar patterns similar to those of the hominoids, but they apparently had none of the distinctive locomotor characteristics of the ape superfamily.

Although the Fayum Beds have been searched for fossil bones since early in the century, in more recent explorations over the past twenty years Elwyn Simons and his associates have discovered a large number of fossil bones of the skeleton, skull, and jaws, along with lots of teeth. These fossils have been placed in at least three different genera, all higher primates, but differing in dental and jaw details. Early work on the Fayum fossils had led to the suggestion that these primates represented the direct ancestors of specific living Old World monkeys and apes. The new fossil discoveries have modified this view, and now point to these North African fossils as primitive higher primates who lived at a time before the lines leading to specific monkeys and apes had separated.[8]

The number and variety of higher primates at the Fayum indicate that they were important and successful parts of the North African fauna in the Oligocene. Of all these animals we have found more parts of Aegyptopithecus, including skulls, skeletal parts, and numerous jaws and teeth. Aegyptopithecus's skull is that of a higher primate, but the snout is more pronounced than in most living anthropoids, suggesting that smell was still important (Figure 6.14). From impressions left on the inside of the braincase, it appears that the sense of smell was emphasized. The

Figure 6.13. (opposite). Upper and lower jaws of a female baboon (left) and a modern human, showing the bilophodont molars found on the upper and lower jaws of Old World monkeys and the molar patterns found in the hominoids: the apes and humans. Notice, too, the relatively small size of the canine teeth in the female baboon, as compared to the much larger canine teeth of the male (Figure 7.7). Human canine teeth are not enlarged and the wear on these teeth is at the tips, rather than along the back edges. In the lower jaw molars of the baboon, the first two possess the standard bilophodont pattern, but the third has an additional (fifth) cusp in the back, which is sometimes found in the larger Old World monkeys.

Filled in orbit

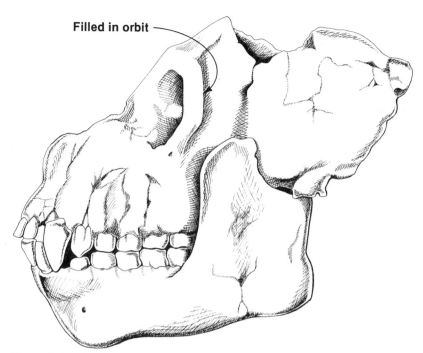

Figure 6.14. *A partially restored skull of* Aegyptopithecus zeuxis *found in the Fayum. The lower jaw restoration is based on fragments not found with the cranium. The upper incisors are also restorations.* Aegyptopithecus *dates to the Oligocene and is probably ancestral to the apes of the African early Miocene.*

eye orbits are filled in with bone like those of later higher primates, but their size is intermediate between the large orbits of nocturnal primates and the smaller ones of daylight active animals. The dental formula is 2.1.2.3, as in other Old World higher primates, and the upper and lower molars are much like those of the hominoids. The recent discoveries in the Fayum indicate that there was a considerable amount of *sexual dimorphism* in the canine teeth and perhaps in body size as well. Sexual dimorphism refers to differences in the size of biological features in the males and females of the same species; in sexually dimorphic primate species, it is always the males who will be larger. Larger size of the canine teeth and perhaps body size, too, suggest that *Aegyptopithecus* lived in social groups, since it is rare for solitary living primates, like many prosimians, to show any difference in size between males and females. Finally, analysis of the skeletal bones reveals a generalized quadrupedal limb system, lacking any of the suspensory hanging adaptations of the hominoids; and it had a tail. John Fleagle, who studied the skeletal bones, believes that *Aegyptopithecus*'s bones are most similar to those of the South American howler monkey, though lacking that animal's prehensile tail, and thus indicative of a relatively primitive arboreal primate.[10]

Thus, the evidence of *Aegyptopithecus*, the most well-known of the North African Oligocene primates, tells us that by this time, a social, arboreal higher primate had evolved; whether this early anthropoid was active at night or during the day is not clear from present evidence. The Fayum evidence is representative of primitive higher primates, but none of the Oligocene primates can be identified with living forms, because the lineages leading to living forms were apparently not yet distinct. The most reasonable evolutionary connection is that *Aegyptopithecus* evolved into the early Miocene hominoids of Africa.

Miocene Primates

Unlike the Oligocene fossil evidence, which is very limited, fossil primates of Miocene age are much more abundant and widespread. Fossil evidence of Old World higher primates in the Miocene is known from East Africa, many parts of Europe, the Middle East, China, India, and Pakistan (Figure 6.15). Brian Patterson called the Eocene the "Golden

Figure 6.15. *Fossil bones of Miocene primates have been found in many parts of the Old World, the first discovered in France in the nineteenth century. The most important and complete collections have come from East Africa, Pakistan, and India.*

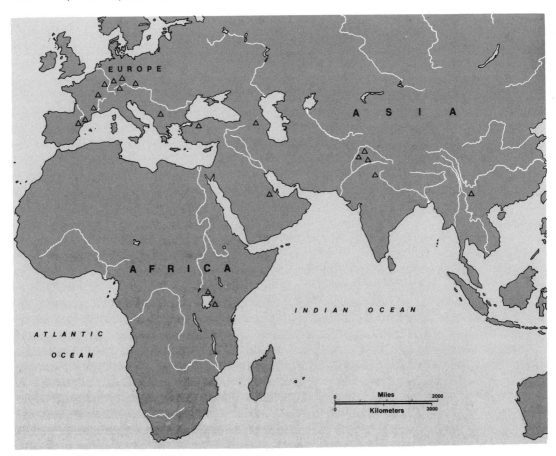

Age of Prosimians''; the Miocene might be considered the golden age of the hominoids.

We have much fossil material, several hundred specimens in all, of postcranial (skeletal) and cranial (skull) bones and teeth, placed in a number of different taxonomic categories.[11] But paleontologists have come to little agreement about what the fossil evidence means, and very recently discovered material has resulted in the need for still further consideration of the evolutionary patterns during the Miocene. Comparative biochemistry complicates the issue with evidence of another sort, which does not always agree with the fossil data.

The Miocene is very important for humans: by the end of the period, the human family, the Hominidae, had evolved as a distinct lineage, and the major lineages of the modern Old World primates had appeared.

Miocene Hominoid Evolution: An Overview Miocene hominoid fossils have been classified into more than ten genera, based primarily on geographic distribution, dating, size, and general morphology. Table 6.2 groups the major Miocene genera according to geographic area and time. The earliest material comes from East Africa; later Miocene fossils are more widely distributed. This suggests that the Miocene hominoids had their origins in Africa, presumably evolving from earlier forms, such as *Aegyptopithecus,* and that with the early Miocene continental contact established between Eurasia and Africa, these hominoids and other African mammals began to spread to the Eurasian continent.

The major hominoids of the Miocene have been divided into two families, the *Dryopithecidae* and the *Sivapithecidae.* Differentiated primarily on the basis of a number of details of the dentition, both families now appear to have a long and complicated evolutionary history throughout much of the Miocene; both seem to make their first appearance in the early Miocene of East Africa, later spreading from there to Eurasia. Both families disappear by the end of the period. Their biological traits suggest that from one of them, probably the Sivapithecidae, arose the lines leading to the modern great apes — chimpanzee, gorilla, and orangutan — as well as that leading to the hominids.[12]

While the fossil evidence is very suggestive, it does not provide answers to the questions as to when the lines leading to the specific living hominoids diverged, where this occurred, the evolutionary reasons for the splits, and who the immediate ancestors of the hominids were. We will return to these questions after considering the Miocene fossil evidence.

Early Miocene Hominoid Evolution

PROCONSUL The first hominoid fossils found in Africa were uncovered by Louis Leakey and A. T. Hopwood in the 1930s at Rusinga Island in Lake Victoria. Later finds of similar fossils have been made at a number of sites in western Kenya along the shores of Lake Victoria and in Uganda.

Table 6.2. Miocene hominoids, grouped according to time and geographic area.

Millions of years B.P.	Geological Epoch	East Africa	Europe and Middle East	Asia (China, India, Pakistan)
5	Pliocene			
10	Late Miocene		Pliopithecus Sivapithecus Dryopithecus	Sivapithecus Gigantopithecus
15	Middle Miocene	Kenyapithecus	Dryopithecus Sivapithecus	Sivapithecus
22	Early Miocene	Sivapithecus Proconsul		
	Oligocene			

Hopwood, impressed by the resemblances between these African fossils and living apes, coined the name *Proconsul* for them (after Consul, an ape then living in the Regents Park Zoo in London). A considerable number of *Proconsul* fossil bones have been found, including portions of several skulls (Figures 6.16, 6.17), and much of the skeleton of a single animal. The age of the East African deposits has been determined by the potassium-argon dating method (K-Ar dating; see Chapter 8), which places them in the early Miocene, some 17 to 21 million years ago, making these the earliest of the Miocene hominoid fossils.

Examination of the upper and lower molar teeth of *Proconsul* shows the distinctive traits of the hominoids, although they also possess some primitive features found in *Aegyptopithecus*. The skull of *Proconsul* is

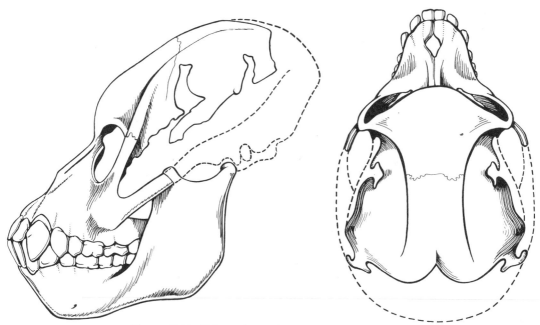

Figure 6.16. *Side and top views of a reconstructed skull of* Proconsul
africanus *(two-thirds actual size).*

that of a higher primate, with a brain somewhat smaller and more primitive than that of living nonhuman hominoids, but essentially similar to
later forms. Like the bones of *Aegyptopithecus*, *Proconsul*'s skeletal system appears to be that of a generalized, primitive arboreal primate, without
a tail, and with no adaptations toward suspensory hanging.[13] The fossil
bones and teeth of *Proconsul* have been divided into three species, primarily on the basis of size: a large, a medium-sized, and a small form.
Because of the primitive elements in the bones and teeth, it is unlikely
that these early Miocene hominoids represent direct lineal ancestors of
living apes, and indeed *Proconsul* appears to share as many features with
the earlier Oligocene *Aegyptopithecus* as with later Miocene hominoids. *Proconsul* has been classified in the hominoid family Dryopithecidae along with later-in-time fossil hominoids from Eurasia.

AFRICAN SIVAPITHECUS In the fall of 1983, Alan Walker uncovered
fragmentary pieces of several hominoid jaws at a locale in Kenya known
as Buluk. Dated to about 17 million years B.P., the Buluk fossils resemble the jaws of hominoid specimens found in India and Pakistan, and
dated much later in time. We will consider the further implications of
the Buluk finds after describing the other major Miocene hominoid fossils.

KENYAPITHECUS WICKERI Hominoid bones and teeth discovered at a
place called Fort Ternan in western Kenya have been dated by the K-Ar
dating technique to about 14.5 million years B.P. Called by Louis Leakey
Kenyapithecus wickeri (the species name after the owner of the farm where

PROCONSUL JAW   **GORILLA JAW**

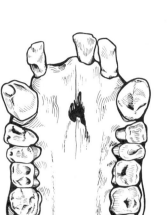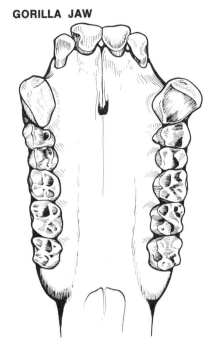

Figure 6.17. *A comparison of the upper jaws of an East African* Proconsul *fossil (left), drawn from a cast made by the Wenner-Gren Foundation, and a modern gorilla.*

the site is located, Mr. Wicker), they share some similarities with later-in-time fossils from India and Pakistan, and they have been suggested by some as possibly representative of the line leading toward the hominid family.

Thus, the earliest hominoid fossil material has been found in Africa, and seems to represent a number of different hominoid groups. Some time after the beginning of the Middle Miocene, which began some 15 million years ago, hominoids begin appearing in Eurasia, apparently having spread there from Africa.

Middle and Late Miocene Hominoid Evolution By the middle of the Miocene, fossil evidence of hominoids has become more widespread, and also more diversified.

DRYOPITHECUS In Europe, hominoid fossils dated to the Middle and Late Miocene have been placed in the genus *Dryopithecus* (*Dryo* = forest; *pithecus* = ape). *Dryopithecus* fossils are widely distributed in Europe, having been found in France, Spain, Germany, Austria, Hungary, and perhaps in other countries as well, and they have been divided into a number of species. The teeth of *Dryopithecus* are similar to those of the other hominoids, with four-cusped upper molars with the oblique ridge, and lower molars with the Y-shaped grooves between the cusps.

The few cranial and jaw specimens of *Dryopithecus* are somewhat different from those of the living apes, while the very few skeletal bones suggest the beginning adaptation for suspensory hanging. *Dryopithecus* shares dental features with the earlier *Proconsul* finds from East Africa, and it has been suggested that the *Dryopithecus* group represents an evolutionary development from the *Proconsul* early Miocene forms.

SIVAPITHECUS AND GIGANTOPITHECUS In Asia, Miocene hominoids have been discovered in parts of south China, but the bulk of the evidence comes from northern India and Pakistan, in a range of hills, the Siwaliks, which forms part of the western foothills of the Himalayas. Here, at a number of sites, an imposing array of fossil bones and teeth have been found which seem to represent a number of different hominoid species. These specimens, which range in date from about 11 to 12 million years ago to the latest, about 7 to 8 million years ago, differ as a group from the *Proconsul* and *Dryopithecus* fossils in several ways;[14] they appear to be more related to the Buluk and Fort Ternan fossils.

The hominoid fossils from India and Pakistan have been divided into two genera: *Sivapithecus* (after the Indian deity Siva), and *Gigantopithecus* (because of the huge size of the molar teeth and jaws). The distinctive traits of these Asian forms are apparently related to dietary adaptations. *Sivapithecus* and *Gigantopithecus* have molars whose chewing, or occlusal, surfaces are covered with thick layers of enamel. The teeth of *Dryopithecus*, *Proconsul*, and the living African apes, the chimpanzee and gorilla (but not the orang), in contrast, have much thinner layers of enamel. In addition, although *Sivapithecus* is similar to *Proconsul*, *Dryopithecus*, and living ape groups in having large projecting canine teeth while *Gigantopithecus* has relatively smaller canine teeth, the Asian Miocene forms are similar to one another in the kinds of dental wear on the canines. Because the canine teeth project beyond the level of the other teeth, they do not meet tip to tip, but rather slide past each other; thus, canine wear in these forms is on the front and back sides of the tooth (see pages 313–315 for a more detailed discussion of the canines). In addition to this sort of wear, *Gigantopithecus* and *Sivapithecus* have canine wear on the tips, suggesting some sort of tip-to-tip biting of tough food items (Figure 6.18). Finally, there appears to be a tendency in these Asian hominoids to have back chewing teeth that are, in proportion to the size of the front teeth, relatively larger in size (Figure 6.18). The combination of thick enamel on the chewing surfaces of the molar teeth, the wear on the tips of the canines, and the proportionally larger size of the back teeth seems to indicate that *Sivapithecus* and *Gigantopithecus* were adapted to a different niche than other Miocene hominoids; therefore they have been placed in a separate family, the Sivapithecidae.[15]

Gigantopithecus was probably the largest hominoid that ever lived (Figure 6.18). In addition to the Indian and Pakistani Miocene specimens, a number of jaws and several hundred teeth of this creature have been discovered in south China. These Chinese specimens are dated to the early Pleistocene, a time when hominid fossils are found in various parts of the Old World.

Sivapithecus was smaller than *Gigantopithecus,* and shows similar sexual dimorphism in tooth size. Into the genus *Sivapithecus* has recently been incorporated the genus "Ramapithecus," which for a considerable time was thought to represent the ancestor of the hominids. Newly discovered fossils from a part of the Siwaliks in Pakistan known as the Potwar plateau showed that "Ramapithecus" was a smaller version of *Sivapithecus,* perhaps representing females of a dimorphic species. As it became increasingly difficult to distinguish a large "Ramapithecus" jaw from a small *Sivapithecus* jaw, it was realized that the two groups were in reality parts of a single species.[16]

In addition to the Indian and Pakistani *Sivapithecus* fossils, and the East African Buluk specimens, jaws and teeth belonging to this genus have been uncovered in Miocene deposits in Turkey, perhaps in Hungary, and recently a major portion of skull was found at the site of *Lufeng* in south China where a number of jaws had previously been discovered.

PLIOPITHECUS Fossils of the genus *Pliopithecus* have been found in Upper Miocene deposits in a number of sites in central and eastern Eu-

Figure 6.18. *Casts of the jaws of two members of the Sivapithecidae,* Gigantopithecus *(left) and* Sivapithecus *(right). (*Sivapithecus, *GSP 15000, is shown from the side in Figure 6.20). Note the relatively large size of the back teeth compared to the front teeth, and the wear on the tips of the canine teeth.*

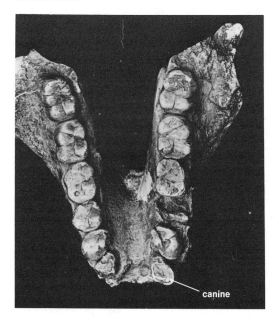
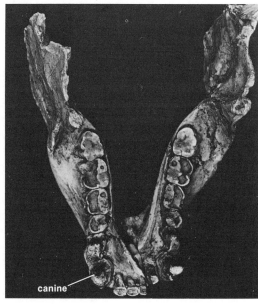

canine

canine

rope. *Pliopithecus* is the smallest in size of the hominoid fossil groups we have been reviewing, and its jaws and teeth look in many ways like the living lesser ape, the gibbon, whose ancestor it may be. However, complicating this evolutionary assignment is the fact that *Pliopithecus* postcranial bones reveal a generalized, quadrupedal anatomy, a tail, and a decided lack of the brachiator's specializations.[17]

Miocene Evolution: Biochemical Evidence Before examining some of the hypotheses about the evolution and adaptation of the Miocene hominoids, the evidence from comparative biochemical studies must be described.

In the last chapter we saw how the study of comparative biochemical and genetic traits can help solve problems of primate classification, and therefore provide insight into the evolutionary relationships of living forms. Figure 6.19 graphically summarizes the pattern of hominoid evolutionary divergence as developed by the variety of biochemical and genetic systems discussed in Chapter 5. It shows that modern humans group together with the African apes, the chimpanzee, and the gorilla; that between the three members of this group, it is difficult to determine more precise associations since most tests indicate that humans and chimps are more closely related; several show humans closer to gorillas, and some suggest chimps and gorillas are closest. This human/chimp/gorilla group is separated from its nearest living form, the orangutan, and that animal, in turn, is separated from the lesser apes, the gibbon and the siamang. This latter group seems to be in some ways intermediate between the human/chimp/gorilla group, and the orang, on one side, and the Old World monkeys on the other.

While these results are in general supported by most scientists working on this question, and the relationships in fact seem to be in basic agreement with comparative anatomical studies, some anthropologists, such as Vincent Sarich, believe that this data can be carried even further. They suggest that the amount of genetic divergence between species can be used to tell us how long it has been since the species last had a common ancestor. Sarich thus views the biochemical and genetic comparisons as having the potential for a *"molecular clock"* to compute the dates when the ancestors of living species diverged to follow different evolutionary pathways.

Sarich has focused his attention on serum albumin. He believes that his data on the evolution of this blood protein show a constant rate of evolution for this molecule, so that *phylogeny* (evolutionary history) can be reconstructed essentially without reference to the fossil record.[18] Basing his studies on the assumption of constancy of molecular change in serum albumin in many different lines of primates, Sarich compared immunologically (see pages 165–166) a number of living animals, and has computed the times of divergence of the higher primates. These data are included in Figure 6.19. Sarich's work has provoked numerous criticisms:

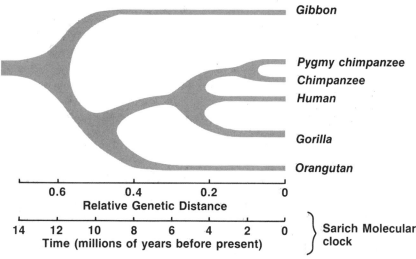

Figure 6.19. A molecular phylogeny of the Hominoidea based on nucleic acid, immunological, and electrophoretic data. (Goodman and Cronin, 1982). No molecular data have been conclusive in determining if any pair of the lineages Homo, Pan, and Gorilla share a common ancestor to the exclusion of the third species.

the results are based on only one protein; the technique is immunological and is less sensitive than DNA hybridization or studies of amino acid sequences (discussed in the last chapter); and the method he uses to relate immunological difference to time may not be correct.

In addition, Morris Goodman, using both immunological and sequence data, believes that the computation of specific dates of divergence is not in keeping with the results of his own research, which show evolution slowing down in the higher primates. On the basis of his work Goodman "attributes divergent evolution in proteins to selectively neutral mutations but also implies that more mutations were neutral in primitive organisms than in descendant species." According to Goodman, as an animal becomes more complex biochemically, fewer mutations will be selectively tolerated; that is, growing biochemical complexity increases the probability that mutation will harm the interaction between the gene product and other molecules, lowering the individual's fitness. It is still to be proven, however, that the higher primates are biochemically more complex than other animals.

Goodman also points out that because of the intimate contact between maternal and fetal blood supplies in higher primates, a female can reject a fetus that is making a substance she recognizes as foreign. This phenomenon does occur in modern humans, as we shall see in regard to some blood group systems (see pages 410–413). Because most prosimian primates have a different type of placenta they are less likely to reject a fetus because of antigenic differences. This difference would slow the rate at which new mutations would enter the gene pool of higher primates.[19]

The data from Sarich's serum albumin studies indicate rather late times of divergence for the hominoids (Figure 6.19). Can the results of these studies be reconciled with the evidence from the fossil record? In other words, do we have fossils that might be representative of the common ancestors of the different living hominoids, and dated in accord with the protein evolution data? There is considerable difference between the times of divergence shown in Figure 6.19 and the fossil material; the latter indicates consistently earlier times for the evolutionary origin of living hominoid groups. Recent fossil discoveries have emphasized the differences between the fossil and molecular clock dates of divergence, and indeed, have led to suggestions that the close evolutionary relationships between chimps, gorillas, and humans might also have to be re-evaluated.

Views of Miocene Hominoid Evolution A number of hypotheses have been developed about the relationships of the Miocene hominoids to the origin and evolution of the living hominoids. However, the very recent discovery of the Buluk *Sivapithecus* material has led to the need to re-evaluate some of these ideas.

Schemes of Miocene hominoid evolution generally focused on the evolutionary radiation of these forms from the early Miocene *Proconsul,* which was viewed as the most likely common ancestor from which much of subsequent hominoid evolution stemmed. According to this model, when the hominoids began to spread from Africa into Eurasia, sometime after 15 million years B.P., an evolutionary divergence occurred, with forms similar in adaptation and biology to the earlier *Proconsul* evolving into the *Dryopithecus* group, and the Sivapithecidae developing as a separate family as a result of the exploitation of new niches. This model views *Dryopithecus* becoming extinct without issue, and the family Sivapithecidae ultimately leading to the living hominoids, including humans (Table 6.3, Part B).

David Pilbeam, who with his associates has been responsible for many of the new discoveries in Pakistan, developed a model of Miocene hominoid evolution that relates the differences between the Dryopithecidae and Sivapithecidae to differing environmental adaptations. Identification of the animal bones found with *Proconsul* at sites in East Africa suggests that this hominoid was living in the deep forest. Analysis of the animal bones found with members of Sivapithecidae in Pakistan, in contrast, suggests an environmental mosaic of grassland, bush, and woodland. According to Pilbeam, the Sivapithecidae may have been adapting to more open country conditions, and their distinctive dental traits may reflect the need to exploit new food items, such as hard-shelled seeds or tough-skinned fruit, that require heavy chewing and the use of the canines to cut through a hard outer covering.

Table 6.3. Views of Miocene hominoid evolution.
Part A sketches in the possible evolutionary relationships of living and extinct hominoids on the basis of the recently discovered Buluk material. Part B pictures a more traditional view of hominoid evolution, with late divergence times for ape and hominoid groups. Part C is a scheme which would be considered fanciful by most anthropologists. Here, orangs and hominids are closely related, as Schwartz has suggested, and the chimp and gorilla lines stem from the Dryopithecus group, with which they share some dental and jaw features. Note that the heavy white lines in the three parts that illustrate divergences are here drawn to generally portray the various views.

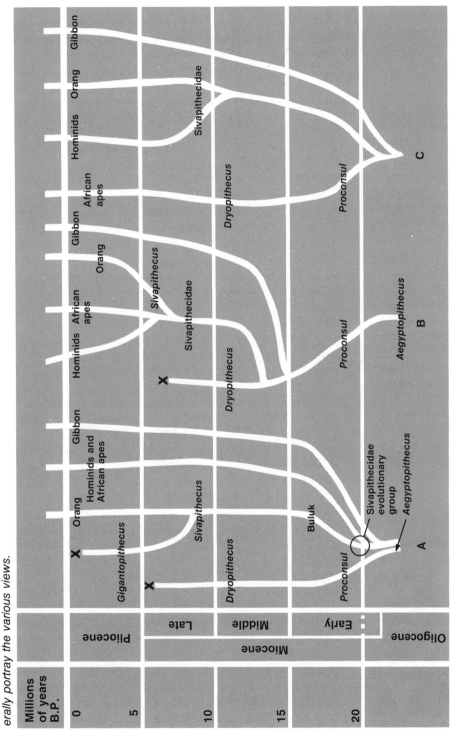

One of Pilbeam's discoveries in late Miocene deposits in Pakistan's Potwar Plateau was truly spectacular. Known by its catalog number, GSP 15000, it is one of the most complete later Miocene fossils ever found, parts of the jaws and face of a *Sivapithecus* (Figure 6.20). The jaws and teeth identify it as *Sivapithecus*, but the upper part of the face, until now completely unknown, shows a remarkable similarity to the distinctive facial regions of the living orangutan (Figure 6.20). Orangs, alone among the great apes, have thick layers of enamel on the chewing surfaces of their teeth, which is one of the distinctive features of the Sivapithecidae. The similarity of facial structures between the orang and this late Miocene *Sivapithecus* strongly argues for its placement as the direct ancestor of the living orang. The fact that it is from Pakistan, in South Asia, and near to the modern orang distribution, makes the case even stronger. Thus, it appears likely that *Sivapithecus* represents the direct ancestor of the orang.[20]

The recognition of the evolutionary connections of the *Sivapithecus* face, and the established patterns of relationship within the living Hominoidea, linking chimp, gorilla, and human, argued that the ancestors of these animals had to be sought elsewhere. Since chimpanzees, gorillas, and the earliest of our hominid ancestors are all from Africa, it was logical to think of the common ancestor of this group as an African member of the Sivapithecidae, probably living during the late Miocene, because Sarich's albumin results (Figure 6.19) had given a late date for the evolutionary divergence of this group. This was the general view of Miocene hominoid evolution prior to the discovery in the fall of 1983 of the Buluk material.

The Buluk specimens appear to represent pieces of the jaw of a hominoid very similar to the late Miocene *Sivapithecus* fossils from India and Pakistan which are now directly on the line leading to the orangutan. The Buluk material, however, is dated to about 17 million years ago, about 10 million years earlier than the South Asian fossils!

At the present time, it would seem reasonable to link this African *Sivapithecus* with the Asian material in the ancestry of the orang, as in Table 6.3, Part A. This means that *Proconsul*, as a contemporary of the Buluk *Sivapithecus*, but with more generalized morphological features, can no longer be placed as the common ancestor of later hominoids, for it is now clear that this ancestor must have lived much earlier. It also means that the line leading to the orang has been distinct for at least 17 million years, and therefore the evolutionary separation of the great apes and humans on the one hand, and the gibbon and siamang on the other, must be greater than 20, and closer perhaps to 25 million years ago. Sarich's albumin work resulted in a split-off time of about 12 million years (Table 6.4), so the Buluk discovery clearly makes the "molecular clock" dates off, in this case, by about 100 percent.

Prior to the Buluk discovery, the "molecular clock" dates showing a very late divergence of the human line from those leading to the African apes had generally been accepted (Table 6.4). Since the earliest definite

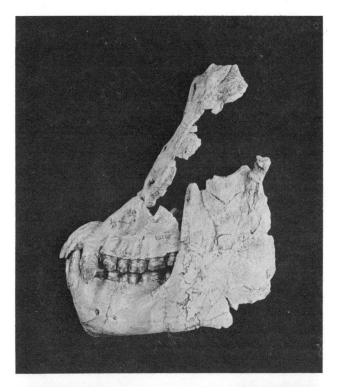

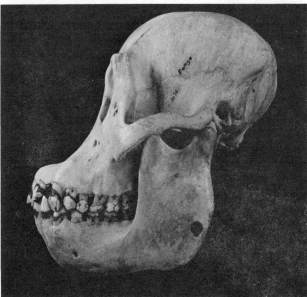

Figure 6.20. (top) *A cast of the late Miocene GSP 15000* Sivapithecus *face from the Potwar Plateau compared with a modern orangutan* (bottom). *Note the similarities in the shape and orientation of the facial region.*

Table 6.4. Sarich's estimated times of evolutionary divergence between several anthropoids and humans.

Species	Time of divergence based on immunological studies (in millions of years)
Human – Chimpanzee	4 – 5
Human – Orangutan	9 – 11
Human – Gibbon	11 – 13
Human – Old World Monkeys	20 – 22
Human – New World Monkeys	35 – 38

From Vincent M. Sarich and John E. Cronin, "Generation lengths and rates of hominoid molecular evolution," *Nature* 269:354 (September 22, 1977).

evidence of fossil hominids is about 6 million years ago (see Chapter 9), it was believed these early fossil hominids represented the very beginnings of human evolution and that no earlier hominid fossils would be found. Given the very early date for the Buluk material, and the implication of the long separate orang evolution that it provides, our views of hominid evolution must now be revised to include the possibility that the human line may have begun its evolution earlier than was generally thought.

Miocene Hominoid Evolution and Living Hominoids Where then does this leave all of the questions we posed earlier that relate the Miocene hominoids to living forms? Perhaps the most reasonable way to deal with the questions is to examine each of the major living hominoids in the context of Miocene evolution.

GIBBON AND SIAMANG It is apparent that the lesser apes (gibbon and siamang) diverged from the main hominoid line early, certainly before the split between African and Asian great apes. With the Buluk evidence, this would have to place the split back into the Oligocene at a time greater than 22 million years ago. There are no recognizable gibbon fossils that early, and in any case, accepting even the Middle Miocene *Pliopithecus* as an ancestral gibbon raises significant problems, the most important being the anatomy of suspensory hanging. Without exception, all of the hominoids possess these structures of the upper trunk and shoulder. It is unreasonable to believe these structures evolved independently in different lines, and thus the anatomical features associated with suspensory hanging evolved in the common ancestor of the hominoids before any of the lines leading to living forms had diverged. Therefore, a direct ancestor of any living hominoid must possess the anatomical traits of suspensory hanging, and *Pliopithecus,* with its generalized skeleton, does not qualify. Evidence from other Miocene hominoids would suggest that the line leading to the lesser apes has had a long separate evolutionary existence, but at present there are no acceptable fossils documenting this development.

ORANGUTAN As we have seen, the fossil history of the orang is the best documented line in the nonhuman hominoids. The few pieces of skeletal bones of the Sivapithecidae that have been discovered, primarily in Pakistan, do not provide any diagnostic details of the shoulder or frontlimb region.

CHIMPANZEE AND GORILLA One of the major problems in evaluating hominoid evolution is the lack of any fossil evidence of the African pongids. Until this gap in our knowledge is filled, it is very difficult to place these animals in the context of primate evolution.

HUMANS We know somewhat more about the human line in this context because we have a fossil record of hominid evolution beginning some 6 million years ago. Dentally, these early hominids possess traits, thick occlusal enamel, and large back teeth, which are also found among the members of the Sivapithecidae. It is reasonable to suggest that the hominids may have had a Miocene ancestor similar dentally to the already known Sivapithecidae, perhaps even a member of this taxonomic family.

Of the known fossil material, perhaps the best current candidate for placement as an ancestor to the Hominidae are the *Kenyapithecus wickeri* fossils from Fort Ternan.[21] Composed of dental and fragmentary jaw bones, they share many features with the *Sivapithecus* fossils from Asia, but they also have traits, like a relatively smaller canine tooth, that might relate them to the hominids. Until more fossil material of this creature is discovered, however, it is very premature to make any but the most tentative suggestions about its evolutionary relationships.

However, this raises a difficulty in our relationships with the African apes. Both the chimp and the gorilla differ in these dental details, whereas the orang seems closest to us with its thick enamel. Recently, Jeffrey Schwartz has suggested that this dental similarity, and a number of other, very subtle, shared biological traits may indicate that in spite of all the other comparisons, humans may be evolutionarily more closely related to orangs than to chimps and gorillas[22] (Table 6.3, Part C). Most primatologists have rejected this notion, pointing out that it is much more reasonable that hominids and orangs have retained the thick enamel on their molars' chewing surfaces from their common ancestor, while chimps and gorillas, becoming more specialized, have developed thinner layers.

Old World Monkey Evolution in the Miocene

At the early Miocene site of Napak, in Uganda, a tooth and a fragment of a skull were discovered. The tooth, a bilophodont molar, documents the first appearance of this distinctive molar cusp pattern of the Old World monkeys in the fossil record. The Napak fossils have not as yet been assigned to a taxonomic category, but they demonstrate the presence of Old World monkeys in the African early Miocene.[23] Numbers of fossil teeth from the middle Miocene, including bilophodont molars, have been found in Kenya (Figure 6.21). The late G.H.R. von Koenigswald, who

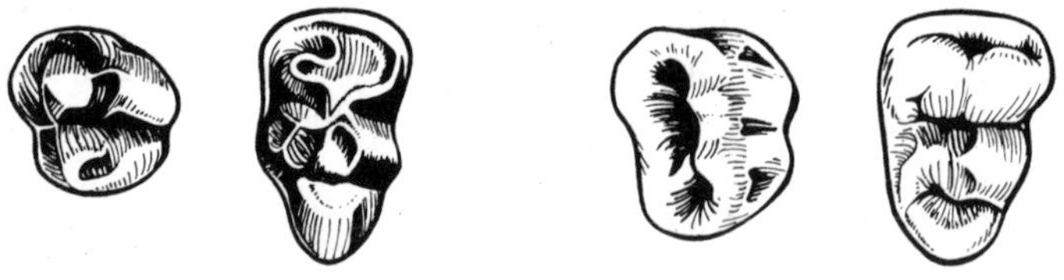

VICTORIAPITHECUS   MONKEY

upper   lower   upper   lower

Figure 6.21. The last upper and lower molars (one and one-third actual size) of the fossil Victoriapithecus, an Old World monkey of Miocene East Africa, compared with the last upper and lower bilophodont molars of a living monkey (about one-half actual size).

studied these teeth, placed in the genus *Victoriapithecus,* has noted that the bilophodont molars look as if they had evolved from the hominoid molar pattern.[24]

From this time on, increasing numbers of Old World monkeys are found in the fossil record, and by the late Miocene it appears that the two major groups of Old World monkeys, the cercopithecines and colobines, had diverged. Eric Delson, who has studied these fossils in detail, suggests that the reason for this evolutionary development was that, in a deciduous forest environment, the eating of leaves as well as fruits would prolong the time during which food was plentiful. Early Old World monkeys, then, became increasingly specialized, with the colobines emphasizing leaves and the cercopithecines fruit and more open country foods.[25]

Also by the late Miocene, Old World monkeys had expanded their distribution to include northern India and Pakistan and many parts of Europe.

It is interesting that the monkeys become more numerous in the fossil record at about the time when the hominoids are becoming less common, and it may be that increasing competition from the highly successful Old World monkeys played an important role in the extinction of many of the Miocene hominoids.

Evolution in the New World

The primates of the Eocene were widely distributed in the northern hemisphere of the Old and New Worlds. Toward the end of the Eocene epoch, they became scarce in the northern parts of North America, and in the succeeding Oligocene they were rarer still. These Eocene primates were morphologically not New World monkeys, and one major problem in understanding primate evolution in the New World has been to document the evolutionary transition from the prosimian primates of the Eocene and early Oligocene to the New World monkeys, which first make their appearance in the fossil record in early Oligocene strata of Bolivia.

Until very recently, it was thought that after the middle Eocene, Old and New World primates evolved independently. Because of their similar environmental adaptations, the evolution of Old and New World monkeys was often cited as one of the best examples in paleontology of parallel evolution (in which two independent evolutionary lines adapt to similar niches, are selected for similar attributes, and evolve along similar paths). Richard Hoffstetter has suggested an alternative explanation. During the Eocene and Oligocene, South America and Africa were much closer together than they are today; South America had yet to join with North America, and Africa did not become connected with Eurasia until the beginning of the Miocene (Figure 6.22). Hoffstetter views the similarities between Old and New World monkeys, and some Old and New World rodents, as indications that early in the Oligocene evolution of the anthropoids in Africa, some of these primitive higher primates, perhaps related to Fayum anthropoids, rafted across the narrow ocean barrier between Old World and New. According to Hoffstetter, Old and New World monkeys are similar in appearance because they have a common higher primate ancestor.[26] Other ideas concerning New World monkey origins suggest that the ancestors of these forms ought to be sought among the widespread and successful Eocene prosimian groups of North America; that it is more reasonable to postulate rafting from North to South America than from Africa to South America.[27]

Whatever their origins turn out to be, the New World monkeys subsequently evolved into two rather different groups of animals, the Cebidae and the Callithricidae. The Callithricidae, whose principal living representatives are the marmosets and tamarins, retain a larger number of more primitive characteristics than the Cebidae, whose representatives today are monkeys such as the spider, howler, and capuchin. Marmosets, for example, possess claws on all digits but the big toe, whereas the other New World monkeys, like the Old World variety, have nails. With a dental formula of 2.1.3.2, the Callithricidae are the only higher primates with less than three molars. The cebids' dental formula, 2.1.3.3, is like that of many prosimians, but in some other respects the cebids appear to be very like the Old World monkeys with a dental formula of 2.1.2.3).

We can identify other differences that reflect the two evolutionary histories. While New World monkeys show a rather wide variety of molar shapes, including in some species a form similar to those of the hominoids, they do not possess bilophodont molars. Other features distinguish these primate groups. Also, many, but not all, New World monkeys have prehensile tails that can be used as a fifth appendage. No Old World monkey has a prehensile tail; its tail may be used for balance, but not for grasping objects. Finally, Old World monkeys have that very special adaptation, an ischial callosity (see page 236).

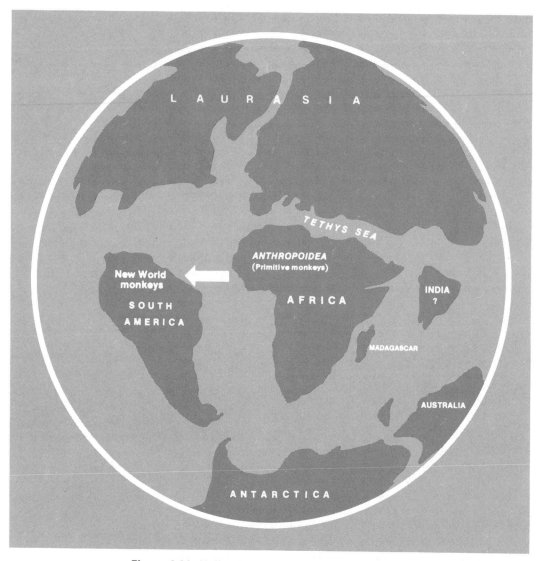

Figure 6.22. *Hoffstetter's view of the relationship between Old World and New World higher primates, suggesting that during the Oligocene, Africa and South America were closer than they are today and that primitive Old World higher primates rafted from Africa to South America.*

Summary   This chapter has reviewed the fossil evidence documenting the evolution of the mammalian order Primates. Fossil bones represent the only direct evidence of the evolution of an animal group, although comparative anatomy, biochemistry, and genetics can also provide important supporting data. The analysis of fossil bones is carried out through a logical series of steps which aim to establish the extinct animal's evolutionary relationships with other animals and to furnish information on how the fossil bones and teeth functioned when they were a part of a living animal. The final step in a fossil analysis, and the most difficult, is the reconstruction of behavior. This step provides the link between fossil animal bones and the ways by which animals whose parts they were achieved a successful adaptation to their environment.

Primates share more biological features with the members of the mammalian order of insectivores than with any other, and this order is one of the most primitive of living placental mammals. This relationship, and the numerous general vertebrate features that are still a part of primate biology but are lost or modified in most other living mammal orders, suggest that the primates evolved early in placental mammal history, probably sometime at the end of the age of the dinosaurs, in the Cretaceous period of the Mesozoic era. Fossil evidence of the very earliest primates is extremely scanty, and although the notion that many of the most distinctive primate features evolved because early in their history the primates became tree-dwelling (arboreal) animals continues to be held by most primatologists, there is little direct evidence in support.

Early in the Cenozoic era, during the Paleocene, primitive primates, with features in many ways different from later-in-time members of the order, are a common part of the then-tropical forests of the western United States and Europe. In the succeeding Eocene epoch, primates with a biology similar to living prosimians were extremely successful, with large numbers of different species occupying the tropical forest habitats of many parts of the northern hemisphere.

In the latter part of the Eocene, changing climatic, and perhaps zoological, conditions led to extinction of most of these early primates. The only members that survived were those adapted to highly specialized niches, mainly arboreal and nocturnal, and those isolated on the island of Madagascar (the Malagasy Republic) from the great trends in mammalian evolution.

Several fragmentary jaws from Burma offer evidence that at some time in the Eocene epoch, the suborder Anthropoidea arose from the prosimians. In the following Oligocene, primates disappeared virtually entirely from Europe and North America, where they were found in such great abundance during the Eocene, and the only fossil information we have for the evolution of the primates during this time comes exclusively from the Fayum Beds in Egypt. A number of higher primates have been identified in the Fayum. Although they are recognizable members of the Anthropoidea, they do not have the important distinguishing features of living higher primates: the distinctive molar crown patterns of the Old World monkeys and the anatomical evidence of suspensory hanging, a feature of apes and humans. The fossil evidence for the direct ancestry of modern Old World higher primates, including the human family, is first found in Miocene times, apparently arising from the generalized anthropoid primates of the Oligocene.

The Miocene witnessed the evolutionary development of a number of higher primate groups; in this epoch occurs the first evidence of the distinctive molars of the Old World monkeys. Miocene hominoids, appearing earliest in Africa, spread to Eurasia by the Middle Miocene, becoming more widespread and diversified during the course of this epoch. Recent analysis of the major fossil hominoids has separated them into a number of groups, including the extinct families Dryopithecidae and Sivapithecidae. By the end of the Miocene, evidence of hominoids becomes very rare, although it is clear from subsequent fossil evidence and comparative studies that the lines leading to the living pongids and the hominids diverged prior to this and were already in existence when the Pliocene begins some 5 million years B.P. On the basis of morphological features they share in common with the earliest hominids, one or another member of the family Sivapithecidae would seem to be the most reasonable candidate as immediate hominoid ancestor to the human family Hominidae.

This and the preceeding chapter have dealt with primate evolution and biology. Important though these aspects are in furnishing information crucial to an understanding of the primates and their relationships to humans, they are of limited value without an appreciation of primate behavior. Primates do not live in a vacuum, and their biological features cannot be understood without reference to the environmental adaptation and social systems that form the context for primate success. It is also becoming increasingly clear that if we wish to more fully understand the patterns of human behavior and adaptation, reference to these complexes in our closest living relatives is essential.

Chapter 7

Primate Behavior

Living primates are very successful animals whose behavior and anatomy have permitted them to adapt to a wide variety of environments throughout much of the tropical and subtropical Old and New Worlds. In this chapter, we will explore some of the behavioral characteristics common to all social higher primates, and then describe some examples of their social behavior within an environmental context.

A central theme of this book is the relationship between biology and behavior. Scientists generally agree that physical characteristics which are part of the biological equipment of a species are directly related to the successful patterns of behavior an animal employs in coping with the demands of its environment. Some relationships are easily recognized such as that between toolmaking and the enlarged areas of the motor cortex in the human brain devoted to hand and finger control; other ties between the biological and the behavioral are not so clear, especially when we try to relate biology to the diverse adaptive patterns of higher primates.

Behavior, Biology, and Adaptation

Many animal behaviorists have become concerned with the relationships between evolutionary biology and behavior, and their research is directed toward the construction of hypotheses that examine the connections between primate behavior and natural selection. This approach is termed *sociobiology*, and its proponents seek to explain why certain primate behaviors have appeared in particular environmental contexts. For example, it is apparent that primate species have evolved behavioral mechanisms permitting them to interact successfully in social groups and to exploit their environment efficiently. But how have these behaviors evolved: What is the relationship between behavior and biology?

Primate Sociobiology

As we have seen in earlier chapters, evolution operates through the mechanism of natural selection, in which individuals who possess traits of greater fitness within a particular environment have a better chance of reaching reproductive maturity and passing on their genes to the next generation. In this interaction, it is successful behavior that accounts for the ability of certain individuals to reach reproductive maturity and produce offspring carrying their genetic materials. But how does one account for the appearance of behaviors, such as acts of *altruism* (self-sacrifice), which seem to act against the survival of an individual and its continued ability to reproduce? In other words, when a female primate defends her infant from a predator and is killed or wounded in the process, how can this act be understood as successful if it results in limiting the female's reproductive potential? It would seem that behaviors of this sort would be weeded out of the behavioral repertoire, and that each animal would strive to maximize its own reproductive future.

According to sociobiologists, acts of altruism must be seen in relation not only to the individual, but also to the consequences of the act for others who share the genetic material of the individual performing the selfless behavior. In social species like the nonhuman primates, group members are likely to possess many of the same genetic materials. Indeed, a number of studies have demonstrated that a high degree of relatedness exists in many primate social groups. This is partly the result of the very common pattern in higher primates of females remaining in the group they were born in for their whole lives; male primates commonly switch social groups. In a study where it was possible to follow the subsequent movements of male monkeys after they had left the natal group, something that is extremely difficult to observe in most studies of wild primates, there appeared to be a tendency for these animals to join a group that already contained an older brother.[1]* Therefore, altruistic behavior, while quite possibly resulting in the death or injury to the animal performing the behavior, also results in other animals in the group increasing their reproductive potential and insuring that particular genetic materials will be well represented in succeeding generations. This aspect of natural selection has been called *kin selection* by sociobiologists, who argue that the evolution of primate behaviors may represent not only traditional individual selection, but also, as in this case, selection operating on a number of individuals; therefore it can be considered *group selection*.

Over the past few years, an increasing number of studies of primates have focused not on a description of the patterns of behavior and adaptation of a particular primate species, which was the major feature of earlier work, but rather on analyses to test possible explanations of how these patterns may have evolved. Several examples of the sociobiological perspective in primate studies have focused on behaviors that were difficult to understand in the context of an individual primate's reproductive potential.

A recent study by Sarah Blaffer Hrdy of the langur monkeys of India has revealed a pattern of behavior in male monkeys that seems to maximize their genetic contribution to the next generation. The stable langur social group is composed of females and young, who are joined by one and sometimes more adult males. Although female langurs remain in their

*See page 566 for notes to Chapter 7.

natal group for their entire life, males usually leave (or are forced out of) the group of their birth and join other males in all-male groups. According to Blaffer Hrdy, once every twenty-seven months, on average, in the study area, the all-male group will attack a female-male group, which results in the usurping of the resident male by another male from the all-male group. On several occasions, after the takeover, the new male was observed killing the unweaned infants in the group. Female langurs whose infants were killed almost immediately began sexual cycling and had sexual relations with the usurper. Since the new male has only a little more than two years before he himself will be supplanted, Blaffer Hrdy argues that infant-killing behaviors can be most reasonably understood as examples of individual selection operating to insure that the new male's offspring, and thus his genetic materials, will be represented in the succeeding generation.[2]

A variety of other explanations might account for this behavior, including one offered by Phyllis Dolhinow, a primatologist who also worked with the Indian langurs. According to Dolhinow, the number of observed infanticide cases is small, and the locations where they occurred were areas of high monkey population density. For Dolhinow, a more plausible, though not an adaptive or sociobiological, explanation, would ascribe this behavior to a social pathology brought on by overcrowding.[3]

Many problems in primate sociobiology remain, and convincing evolutionary explanations will have to await the collection of more detailed information on primates living under natural conditions. In a recent survey of primate sociobiological research, Alison Richard and S.R. Schulman listed a number of the most important, including long-term (several generations at least) data on population size and structure, biological relatedness, and long-term use of the environment.[4]

Patterns of Primate Social Behavior

All higher primates except the orangutan have one pattern in common: they live in a social group. It is not clear when this system evolved, but the presence of sexually dimorphic features in the Oligocene higher primate, *Aegyptopithecus*, indicates that it is at least 35 million years old. All mammals are social, if only for reproduction, but of the prosimians, only some of those in the Malagasy Republic live in social groups. At the present time, it seems more likely that sociality evolved independently in the Malagasy prosimians and the higher primates, although it is possible that the common ancestor of all these forms lived in social groups and is therefore part of the common heritage of lemurs and higher primates.

As we would expect, there seems to be a direct relationship between the environment and the size and type of social organization, though the connection is very complicated. For example, a recent sociobiological model of mammal group size by Wittenberger suggested that while the size of a primate group will be limited by crucial resources, there will be different evolutionary selection pressures on the number of females and the number of males in a group. This is because it is more important to the species to have an optimal distribution of females, who give birth to and care for the young, throughout the environment, than males, whose contribution to the continuation of the species is more limited.[5]

Population size and social groupings are limited not only by the amount of food and water and their seasonal availability, but also probably by the number of sleeping places: even the primates who spend their day on the ground move to relative safety in the trees or on rock faces at night to escape predators.

A higher primate is born into a social group, is nurtured by its mother, and plays with its peers; throughout its life the animal functions and interacts with other members of a group. Males of many species often leave the natal group, become solitary, join another social group, or return to the original group. Only in a few species have females been observed leaving the group of their birth. These are variations on the theme of social living; in large measure, the environment determines the characteristics of a particular social system: whether there is a dominance network (a rank ordering of adult animals in a social group, usually with each sex having a separate ranking); whether there are lasting relationships between the males of the group or nonreproductive relationships between the males and females; even the group's size and composition, including the ratio of adult males to females.

Generalizations about the nonhuman primates' behavior should be approached cautiously. Some primates still have not been studied in their natural environment. In addition, many primate species that have been observed have not been systematically studied in all the environments they inhabit. As data on their behavior accumulate, it becomes strikingly clear how variable the patterns are. In 1932 Sir Solly Zuckerman, a British zoologist and anatomist, watched Old World monkeys, hamadryas baboons, in the London Zoo. He saw that these baboons had a "harem" type of social organization; that is, one large adult male corralled and controlled one or more adult females. At that time, it was thought all nonhuman primates had this kind of social organization. It took further research to show that this was a very specialized kind of organization found only in some primate groups.

Higher primates live in groups of many kinds, ranging in size from one adult female orangutan and her offspring, through small groups with an adult male and female and their immature offspring, up to large groups which include adult males, adult females, and the young. Within this range there are many types and sizes of social groupings. Despite variation, some behaviors are common to almost all higher primates, though modified by each species in response to a specific environment.

The first pattern common in all higher primates but the orangutan is the existence of social groups containing at least one male, one female, and their immature offspring. Second is the close mother-offspring rela-

Figure 7.1. *A young chimpanzee nursing. Like most mammals, chimpanzees undergo a prolonged dependency period, but the attachment of the chimpanzee offspring to their mothers is an especially long one. Even in adulthood, offspring maintain a special relationship with their mothers.*

tionship that accompanies the period of childhood dependency (Figure 7.1). Third is a period of offspring dependency, in which the young primate learns by observing and imitating other animals' behavior, picking up appropriate skills and behaviors in relationships with other members of the group, either in the one-to-one relationship of mother and infant or in interactions with the peer play group. Fourth is communication between animals by vocal and nonvocal signals. Fifth are stereotyped, discrete behaviors, learned during maturation, which are shared by members of the group and ensure its continued existence. Finally, primate groups occupy a *home range*, a specific geographic area from which most female members do not roam. These important primate patterns deserve a more detailed look.

Social Organization

The primate social group has been observed in nature in many shapes and sizes. Social groups are more or less permanent aggregations of animals living in a specific area. The small group (adult male, adult female, and immature young) typical of the human nuclear family is found among one of the Asian apes, the gibbon, and several New World monkeys, including the titi monkey (genus *Callicebus*), marmosets (genus *Callithrix*), tamarins (genus *Saguinus*), and the night monkey (genus *Aotus*), the only nocturnal higher primate. These monogamous pair-bonded groups, however, are extremely rare in Old World monkeys.

Another type of social organization is a large, rather amorphous group of animals that can be considered a "community." It is not a distinct group; the animals are normally found in smaller, unstable subgroups that may occasionally coalesce to form the larger social entity. They may come together at night to sleep, or during the day to move on the ground across an especially dangerous open space. Ordinarily, however, the subgroups will move about more or less independent of one another. These subgroups are generally not stable but reflect a situation in which different individual animals come into and depart from the group at irregular intervals. This pattern is found in at least one New World monkey, the spider monkey (genus *Ateles*), and one great ape, the chimpanzee.

There is also the single-male group, or harem, with one adult male and one or more adult or young females (the group often includes sexually immature female monkeys and the young). These harem groups may also be part of a community, coalescing at night to sleep in the same area and separating during the day to forage on their own. A number of Old World monkeys share this type of social system: the hamadryas baboon (genus *Papio*) of Ethiopia, the patas monkey (genus *Erythrocebus*) of the savannas of Central Africa, the gelada (genus *Theropithecus*) of highland East Africa, some arboreal African monkeys, and some langurs, the colobine monkeys of Asia. Although some gorilla groups are multi-male units, most are led by one mature male, identifiable by lighter colored fur on the back and called a silver-backed male.

The pattern that seems most prevalent among social primates is a multi-male group of adult males, adult females, and their offspring; it is found among all the Asian macaques, all the baboons except the hamadryas, most vervet monkeys of Africa (genus *Cercopithecus*), many of the langurs (genus *Presbytis*), two social-living lemurs, and at least some New World howler monkeys (genus *Alouatta*).

Social Learning   Higher primates share with other mammals the mother-offspring bond, including a fairly long childhood dependency. Social living, an efficient way of maintaining the species, is also important because it provides the opportunity to pass information from one generation to the next. All higher primates, including humans, have this basic system for learning, which begins with the relationship between mother and offspring (Figure 7.2). By observing the mother, a young animal learns a great deal about its immediate environment, including what food to eat and what not to eat. The mother also gives the offspring a sense of security. In several famous and important experiments, Harry and Margaret Harlow demonstrated that two early relationships are crucial for the growth and development of a normal, functioning social primate: the mother-offspring relationship and peer associations of the young animal with others of its own age. The Harlows raised young macaque monkeys in isolation, depriving them of these relationships, and found that when the animals reached adulthood they were incapable of normal interaction with other monkeys and even lacked the ability for sexual relations, although the females eventually learned to participate successfully in sexual behavior. The monkeys were asocial, a deadly handicap for an animal that depends on sociality for survival. The early associations, therefore, were vital in the development of healthy, normal adult social animals.[6]

Figure 7.2. A baboon mother and infant. The bond between mother and offspring in higher primate social groups is perhaps the most intense relationship within the social unit, and may continue into adulthood.

The peer relationship in most primate species takes the form of the play group, young animals close in age who associate informally. There the young primates learn the behaviors they will use as adults. Primate groups do not do any formal teaching; instead, the young watch adult animals behave, imitating and practicing this behavior in play groups. When they become adults they will possess a set of behaviors that permits successful interactions with other adult members of the group. Play takes up more and more of the young primate's waking time after it begins moving away from its mother and until it becomes a fully adult member of the group. S. L. Washburn has pointed out how important play is to primates.[7] Playing is fun and, being enjoyable, reinforces learning behaviors. Human beings lose much by no longer looking at learning as play; learning has become work — we play only when school is over for the day. Yet primate studies suggest that when learning is enjoyable, the animal can assimilate things much more rapidly.

Thus, primate sociality is founded on a prolonged early maturation period, during which the young animals learn the behaviors characteristic of their social group, and which permits successful behavioral interactions as adults. They learn by observing the behavior of other animals and imitating these actions in the play groups. The biological basis of this ability in the primates is a large brain, with a complex cerebrum capable of assimilating a great deal of learned behavior during maturation.

Communication

Higher primates, like most other mammals, have vocal and nonvocal communicative signals. Part of the system of behavior that primates learn is discrete vocal signals, fixed in number, with most apparently limited in comprehensibility to members of the same species. Primate vocalizations may be directed toward a single individual, several individuals, or the group as a whole. A male baboon, for example, in an antagonistic encounter with another male, may combine vocal and nonvocal signals directly toward the other male. In other contexts, such as when a predator threatens, an alarm call will be directed toward the whole group.

In nonhuman primates, vocalizations are a closed system; the limited number of sounds are the whole repertoire. The human communications system is open. Human language depends on the speaker and the listener understanding the rules that govern the construction of grammatically correct sentences. Once the human speaker masters these rules and learns the vocabulary, it is possible to generate an infinite number of communications comprehensible to other speakers of that language. The fixed, limited vocalizations of nonhuman primates have no flexibility.

In addition to vocalizations, many interactions between members of a primate group are communicated by nonvocal signals using the body, and especially the head and face. Nonvocal gestures are stereotyped and discrete. They communicate feelings from one animal to another, providing for smooth interactions between members of the group. Like vocal behaviors, the young animal learns these signals during socialization, so that they form part of the repertoire of the animals in a group. Figure 7.3 illustrates primate nonvocal communication. A male baboon uses closed eyes, which provide a contrast to his light eyelids surrounded by the darker face, and the yawn, which exposes the large canine teeth, to communicate his state of high tension to others in the group. As with all behaviors that are performed by members of species other than our own, identification of this behavior, and thus our understanding of its significance, may be incomplete. However, within the context of the baboon social group, the signal is recognized, and other group members can react appropriately.

Most nonhuman primates possess distinctive features of the face and head, as well as fine-muscle control of the facial muscles that permit a wide range of facial movement and expressions. In this, modern humans, who also possess this muscle control, reflect the common higher primate evolutionary background.

Figure 7.3. A male baboon making what has been interpreted as a tension canine display.

Nonhuman Primates and Language Over the past fifteen years, a number of researchers have worked with captive apes, primarily chimpanzees but also gorillas and orangs, in an attempt to teach these primates to communicate by using human-created signaling devices. Apes do not possess the anatomical structures in the throat, the fine-muscle control of the tongue and lips, or certain specialized neurological structures in the brain that permit humans to speak. But are these the only differences that prevent chimpanzees from employing an open communications system? Several long-term studies of chimpanzees suggest that these animals are capable of learning what a limited variety of symbols mean, including symbols for concrete objects, such as foods, and symbols for actions or verbs. In one experiment David Premack and his associates taught a chimpanzee named Sarah to recognize and identify over 200 chips whose color and shape stood for different objects and actions. Sarah was able to understand what was "said" when the researcher arranged the chips in a particular order, and to respond appropriately. She was also able to request favorite foods or actions (such as to have her back scratched) by arranging the chips to communicate these wishes.[8] A review of these studies has challenged the notion that they demonstrate true language abilities and suggests instead that they reflect the ability of the apes to learn the meaning of particular words, but not the rules that govern the correct ordering of words into sentences, and thus are not indicative of the human capacity for language.[9] The question of the communicative abilities of the apes will remain an open one for a long time.

All the learned behavioral attributes that are basic among the higher primates form a functioning system of social behavior. This system includes not only vocal and nonvocal communicative signals, but also features that promote peaceful interactions among members of the group. Grooming is one of these; most primates spend several hours a day at it. Normally two or more animals sit together quietly, one combing and picking through the hair of the other, pulling out dirt, parasites, and insects. After a while they may reverse roles and the passive animal will begin grooming the other one.

Social Behavior Within the Environment

Taken together, behaviors of this sort are essential to the maintenance of the social group, because its existence depends on the primates' ability to live together in their environment. The individuals must be able to interact in a way that is not harmful to the group. During growth and development they learn how to get along with any other member of the social group: male-female, female-infant, male-infant, male-male, female-female, or any other type of interaction will conform to an acceptable and expected pattern. Because the behaviors toward any individual are stereotyped and predictable, the animals know exactly what an action means to them, and they can respond with an appropriate behavior. The word appropriate is important, because the continued functioning of the primate group is based on the sharing of a common but limited set of behaviors. This provides for a stable group organization with peaceful interactions between members.

An equally important role of the social group is the transmittal of information about the environment from one generation to the next. A social group lives within a particular environment, an area that is never uniformly rich in foods throughout the year. Effective exploitation of the environment is based on knowledge of where and when foods will be available. Observations of primate groups indicate that male primates are much more likely than females to switch social groups and it is therefore the female members who carry this environmental information, exerting considerable influence in directing group movements in search of food. As a young female primate matures, she travels through the yearly round and learns from the female adults where the group has found sources of food in the past; the adults have acquired this information by traveling with the group when they were maturing. Thus, the members of the social unit passively transmit vital information about the environment; the "traditions" of the primates that have lived in that area are carried down through the generations.

These mechanisms provide for the continuation of the social group (and the species) in their environment through time. We can think of the social group as an organized entity greater than the sum of its parts — the individual animals. Before an animal is born, an effective structure is already in existence; a primate grows and develops within the social system, learning the actions it needs to be a part of the system and to survive in its environmental context. It becomes an adult and a functioning part of the structure, contributing genes to the next generation of animals. That generation in turn will grow into integrated adulthood by learning the appropriate social behaviors from the present adults.

A primate group's behavior is very conservative, changing little as time passes. This stability is necessary, for if behavior were modified rapidly, the group would not have its limited collection of stereotyped behaviors, known by every member of the group. Individual members of the group would find themselves not understanding actions of others, and the group's cohesiveness would ultimately be upset. Because the behaviors are learned, however, they do have the potential for being modified quickly in response to the environment's demands.

An example of how new behaviors can become part of the repertoire of a primate group comes from the study of the macaque monkeys (genus *Macaca*) native to the islands of Japan. These monkeys, which live in multi-male groups and spend much of their time on the ground, have been studied extensively over a number of years. To facilitate observations, these animals are provisioned by the Japanese researchers. The macaques continue to forage for food, but they are also given a variety of foods, such as wheat kernels and various fruits and vegetables, including potatoes. During a provisioning of a group of macaques that lived in a particularly open area, along the ocean on the island of Koshima, researchers noticed that one adolescent female took a potato and carefully dunked it in a freshwater stream. Later, the potatoes were washed in fresh or sea water. Over time, scientists noticed that other animals in this social group were also beginning to dunk their potatoes in the water, obviously learning by observing and imitating the young female. However, this behavior did not spread to all members of the group. First to pick it up were the young animals, the peers, and especially the close female relatives of the innovative female; later, other young animals picked the behavior up; and after 3½ years, when these animals had grown to adulthood, it had become a behavior typical of most members of this social group. It never became part of the repertoire of most animals older than the female who began the activity. It seems relatively clear that the adult animals, having grown and learned within a social situation that lacked potato-dunking activities, found it difficult to learn an innovative behavior of this sort.[10]

Primate Behavior: Some Examples

Because of the appearance of innovative behaviors in response to specific environments, social groups of a particular primate species exhibit variations in behavior. Each primate species has a "core" of behaviors common to all members of that species; different parts of the core are stressed in different environments. A good example of this flexibility is the terrestrial monkeys of the subfamily Cercopithecinae, who have been able to exploit successfully wide areas of sub-Saharan Africa (Table 7.1). The adaptation of these monkeys to their environment will provide us with important perspectives in understanding the pattern and evolution of primate behavior.

Monkeys adapted to ground living are found only in the Old World. Baboons, the most widespread and abundant nonhuman primates on the African continent, are found almost everywhere south of the Sahara. Terrestrial monkeys that are generally accepted as baboons include members of the taxonomic genus *Papio* and the mandrills and drills, found in West Africa, which are sometimes placed in the genus *Mandrillus*.

Table 7.1. Terrestrial monkeys of sub-Saharan Africa.

Monkey	Vegetation zone	Location
Mandrill and drill	Tropical wet forest	West Africa
Savanna baboon	Tropical wet forest savanna, and thorn savanna	Sub-Saharan Africa
Vervet	Savanna	South, Central, and East Africa
Patas	Savanna	Central and East Africa
Hamadryas baboon	Thorn savanna	East Africa
Gelada	Thorn savanna	East Africa

The heavily mantled hamadryas baboons *(Papio hamadryas)*, once the sacred baboons of dynastic Egypt, live in East Africa and a small portion of the Arabian Peninsula and are considered a different species from the savanna baboons, although they are known to interbreed successfully. The gelada, superficially like the baboons but placed in its own genus, *Theropithecus* (Figure 7.4), lives in the highlands of Ethiopia. The much more gracefully built patas monkeys (genus *Erythrocebus*) of the savannas of East and Central Africa are also adapted to a terrestrial niche, but in a pattern different from that of these other monkeys. The vervet monkeys (genus *Cercopithecus*), widely scattered through sub-Saharan Africa, also spend a good deal of time on the ground (Figure 7.5). The one factor common to all these animals is adjustment to life on the ground. Evolutionarily, the members of the genus *Papio* and the drill and mandrill seem closely related. On the other hand, the gelada *(Theropithecus)* has been distinct from the members of *Papio* since the late Miocene or Pliocene. The separate evolutionary development of the patas and vervet is longer, for they are closely related to the arboreal monkeys of Africa. Several daylight-active prosimians spend time on the ground, principally the ring-tailed lemur *(Lemur catta)* of Madagascar; all the African and Asian prosimians and the nocturnal prosimians of the Malagasy Republic are arboreal.

Figure 7.4. *A gelada* (Theropithecus) *male (left) grooming a female.*

Figure 7.5. *A vervet monkey (Cercopithecus aethiops). Like other monkeys of Africa, the vervets often spend considerable time on the ground.*

Other terrestrial monkeys, the macaques (genus *Macaca*), are limited mainly to Asia (Japanese macaques are one of about twelve species of the genus *Macaca*), though macaques are found also north of the Sahara in northern Africa and on Gibraltar in Europe. The African baboons and the Asian macaques are so similar in behavior and morphology that a number of primatologists have grouped them in a single genus. In Asia, the langurs (genus *Presbytis*), also leave the trees. Two great apes, the chimpanzee and the gorilla, both spend much of their time out of the trees. The gorilla is too heavy to travel in the trees and has little to fear from predators; the chimpanzee makes use of terrestrial pathways. Both of them exploit many ground foods. Orangutans also spend time on the ground.

With the notable exception of the gorilla, the terrestrial existence of all these primates lasts only as long as their active hours during the day. At dusk the risk from predators increases, and all ground-living monkeys and the chimpanzees retire to relative safety, spending the night and the dangerous early dawn hours in places high above the ground (Figure 7.6). In forested regions or in the savanna along watercourses, the animals settle in trees for the night. Each night, chimpanzees construct a sleeping nest composed of branches that have been bent into a supporting structure; monkeys, in contrast, generally rest on their "sleeping pads," the ischial callosities that cover their buttock region. In the Ethiopian home of the gelada, mostly arid, open, bush country at elevations above 2100 meters, and in other parts of Africa that offer few convenient sleeping trees, the monkeys spend the night on rockfaces.

Being so widely distributed, the ground-living monkeys must adapt to a variety of environments, and their behavioral attributes are consequently distinct. The social group's size will depend directly on the environment's ability to support it; baboons, for example, are found in

Figure 7.6. *A baboon group has escaped from a lion by moving into a tree. Although baboons spend most of their daylight hours foraging on the ground, they will move into the safety of trees or other high places at dusk or when danger threatens.*

multi-male as well as single-male groups. Much of their other behavior is determined by the environment's lushness or sterility. All terrestrial monkeys are basically vegetarians, eating fruits, grass, leaves, tree sap, blossoms, seeds, seedpods, rhizomes, and stems, along with occasional insects and bird eggs. Some groups occasionally kill and eat a small mammal or bird. Some species have specialized to exploit particular food sources; for others, diversification ensures survival. Despite seasonal fluctuation, for example, even in the harsh Ethiopian highlands, the variety and amount of their foods allow the geladas and baboons to co-exist in the same habitat.

Let us examine the behavioral patterns of the most common of all ba- *Savanna* boons, the savanna baboon of the genus *Papio*. Although most of these *Baboons* animals are found in savanna areas, they are also adapted to other habitats, including forested regions, high, open bush country, and combinations of these environments. Savanna baboons live in multi-male groups ranging in size from two to almost two hundred, with an average of about forty. They are diurnal, like all Old World higher primates, and spend their days moving across the savanna searching for food: grass, roots, seeds, seedpods, and blossoms. Studies in East Africa by Robert Harding and Shirley Strum have shown that some baboons at least occasionally hunt and kill small animals and birds.[11] They also consume insects if they are available. Grasshoppers are devoured in vast quantities when the opportunity presents itself, as in East Africa during the great locust (grasshopper) plague of 1968. Fruit, too, is eaten in season.

At dusk, when predators (leopards, hyenas, and lions) are most active, the baboons move into sleeping trees and settle in for the night, spending the hours of darkness in the trees and returning to the ground soon after daylight to begin their daily round. Baboons exploit their environment efficiently. The distance a troop will travel in a day depends on how rich the environment is, how big the group, and the season of the year; most groups average about five kilometers per day. In the dry season a troop may move as far as ten kilometers a day. But during the rainy season, when fruit ripens (figs are a favorite) the troop may spend days in the same groves of trees, gorging themselves and not moving at all.

In their daily rounds of leaving the sleeping trees, foraging in the forest or savanna, and returning to the trees in the evenings, the baboons move as a group. In fairly open spaces on the savanna, where the grass is low and the animals can see long distances, the group may be dispersed over several hundred meters. But when they enter heavy undergrowth where observation is difficult, or when a predator threatens, the group will close up into a compact mass. During group movements, females with young appear to stay near the large males. Although some have reported that savanna baboons progress in a somewhat military formation, with subadult and low-dominance males in the dangerous positions at the front and back and the high-dominance males and the females at the center, this pattern has not been observed in most baboon groups.[12]

Terrestrial monkeys, especially savanna baboons that spend most of their time in open country away from trees, are much more liable to predator attack than arboreal primates or baboons found in more forested habitats. It may be for this reason that baboons are strongly sexually dimorphic. Many nonhuman primates exhibit marked sexual dimorphism; the gorilla male may be a hundred kilograms heavier than the female. Other primates are not as markedly dimorphic: there is only a minor difference in size between male and female chimpanzees. Still other primates, including many arboreal African monkeys and the small ape, the gibbon, show no sexual dimorphism at all: body size and canine size are similar in males and females.

A male savanna baboon weighs between 22 and 30 kilograms, a female between 11 and 15. Males also have very large canine teeth; the female's canines are visibly smaller. The male's big canines are associated with a much larger face, because large roots are needed to secure the teeth in the jaw, requiring an enlarged facial structure to house the roots (Figure 7.7). An enlarged face needs larger muscles. Both the temporal and the masseter muscles, two of the most important in chewing, are enlarged to work a large jaw equipped with large canines. The male's other teeth, too, are larger than the female's, and the greater muscle strength works them efficiently. A large face also needs heavier neck musculature. The larger the face, the greater the *prognathism* (jutting-out of the face), and the greater the need for strong neck muscles (the nuchal muscles) attaching from the back of the head to the vertebral column to keep the larger head balanced. The male baboon's large canines fit into a whole system of characteristics.

Sexual dimorphism in baboons appears to be related to differences in roles in the social group and to mating behavior. Male baboons are said to be mean-tempered and aggressive; their large bodies and great canines suggest that their role is to defend the group from predators. Several observations of male baboons making threats toward predators seem to provide evidence that the sexually dimorphic differences may be a partial reflection of this protective role. Other observations, however, reveal that in some instances, when a predator attacks a baboon group, the whole group, including the males, runs for the safety of trees. This variation in behavior has led to the formulation of alternative hypotheses to account for the presence of sexual dimorphism.

In savanna baboon groups, adult males are organized, at least sometimes, into dominance hierarchies, with a number one (alpha) male, a number two (beta) male, a number three (gamma) male, and down to the lowliest male. The hierarchy provides some stability to the relationships between males, and it is maintained by occasional fights and threat gestures (Figure 7.8). Part of the behavioral repertoire is a system of stereotyped threat and response gestures, known and understood by all members of the group. These predictable and limited behaviors give the

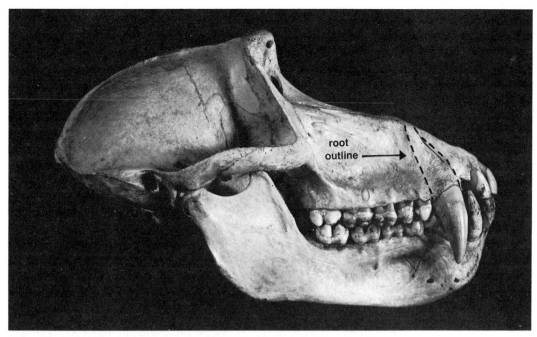

Figure 7.7. *The skull of a male hamadryas baboon (Papio hamadryas). Notice the huge canine teeth, which necessitate very large roots. The female baboons generally possess canine teeth much smaller than the males' (see Figure 6.13 for views of a female baboon dentition). The large male canine tooth and long root occupy a large portion of the face, as the root outline shows in this photograph.*

Figure 7.8. *Two male baboons fight in a dominance interaction. The baboon males' large canine teeth may be related to their defense against predators; the teeth are also related to the establishment of a strongly marked dominance network among the males. Although fights, as a general rule, seldom cause damage, the huge canines are capable of inflicting deep wounds.*

individual a number of appropriate actions to use in interacting with those both above and below it in the hierarchy. Although the dominance hierarchy enables the larger, highly aggressive, well-equipped adult males to interact without continuous fights and injuries, the arrangement is neither permanent nor stable, but appears to reflect changing patterns of behavior within the group and the fact that male baboons tend not to be permanent members of a group. This has led to the development of a sociobiological model which suggests that a male baboon high in the dominance hierarchy will have greater access to limited resources such as food or sexually receptive females.

Baboons' sexual relations are promiscuous, but male-female consort pairs may be formed for two or three days when the female is going through the *estrus cycle*. Estrus, the monthy reproductive cycle a female goes through unless pregnant or lactating, has both anatomical and behavioral effects (Table 7.2). Ovulation occurs in the middle of the cycle; it is then that the female is most likely to conceive. Like most primates, the female baboon also goes through other, more obvious anatomical changes, which make sexual receptiveness evident to the males. The skin around the buttocks and sexual organs swells and becomes deeply pigmented and red (Figure 7.9); the female also secretes odorous substances that are signals. In the first part of estrus the female is receptive to males, and subadult or low-dominance males may mount the female. As the cycle progresses toward ovulation and the time when conception is most likely to occur, the female becomes involved with dominant males and may form a temporary consort relationship, mating and remaining with one male. Although high-dominance males do not seem to have greater access to reproductively active females, they are able to concentrate their activities during those times when conception is most likely. The dominant male baboons therefore have the best chance of fathering the next generation; by providing their genetic material, they reinforce and select for the large body size and aggressive behavior that led to

Table 7.2. Female baboon monthly reproductive cycle (estrus).
Accompanying the anatomical and behavioral changes listed are several physiological changes, including ovulation, the release of the egg, usually about midway in the cycle.

Days in the estrus cycle	Anatomical change	Behavioral change
1 to 10	Gradual enlargement of sexual skin and change in coloration.	Female initiates sexual behavior by approaching and presenting to males; mates with juveniles and less dominant males; forms permissive associations; becomes more active and excitable.
11 to 19	Maximum enlargement of sexual skin, bright red in color.	Female forms consort relationship with dominant males; increased tension and excitement in the group.
20 to 35	Sexual skin decreases, becomes flabby, wrinkled, and finally flat.	Female becomes less active and unresponsive; interacts infrequently with males in the group.

their dominance. After ovulation, toward the end of the estrus cycle, the female baboon reduces sexual activity until, at the end of the cycle, it reaches zero. If pregnancy has not resulted, the estrus cycle begins again.

Baboons breed all year, but births may reach a peak at certain times of the year. Some monkeys breed only at one time of the year and have births at only one time of the year; the rest of the time they have no sexual relationships.[13]

In contrast to the unstable dominance network of male baboons, the ranking of females tends to be far more stable, with relationships in the hierarchy lasting for long periods of time. This stability is related to the crucial roles of the female in the group and to the absence of group switching by these animals in most primate species. Females are responsible for looking after their offspring and probably also for directing group movement, since adult male baboons are likely to switch social groups, leaving the females to carry on the traditions of the social group. Obviously, the female role is more important, since the group's continued successful adaptation depends on the continual birth and socialization of young animals who can pick up the necessary behaviors to survive in that social group in that environment. The importance of the stable female component in most primate species is reinforced by the recent recognition that one of the basic organizing foundations of a primate social group may well be the fact that most animals in the group are genetically related. Females therefore are usually more numerous in a group, since a smaller number of adult males is adequate to protect the group, fertilize the females, and furnish role models for young males. Also, everything else being equal, a small female uses fewer of the resources in the environment and therefore seems more efficient. Thus, females maintain the long-term stability of a group within an environment.[14]

Figure 7.9. Sexual swelling of a female baboon during the estrus cycle.

Primate dominance systems are exceedingly complex, and even in primates who do show dominance, like the baboons, their intensity and frequency can be quite variable, and may also be related to environmental factors. Baboons studied in the forest regions of Uganda by Thelma Rowell showed much less dominance activity than the same species living in the savannas of Kenya studied by Irven DeVore, S. L. Washburn, and K. R. L. Hall.[15] This difference in dominance between forest and savanna baboons may in part be a reflection of the higher level of stress imposed by life on the open savanna. The ground-living macaques of Asia and North Africa seem to have dominance hierarchies like those of the baboons; but some macaques, apparently under fewer population and environmental pressures, exhibit much less dominance than the savanna baboons.

Dominance, and probably aggressive behavior in general, seem to be directly related to environmental circumstances, such as predators, overpopulation, scarce food, and lack of sleeping trees, in addition to mating behavior and other factors we have yet to identify. Several studies have demonstrated this relationship. Charles Southwick and S. D. Singh observed macaque groups living in three Indian environments.[16] One was forest, a "natural" environment for the monkeys. Another was along a road, where the monkeys lived in contact with humans but could also retreat into the woods. The third group were the animals that lived in the city, dependent on humans for food and good treatment. Aggressive interaction, fights, and wounds were much more frequent in the city animals than in the other groups. One explanation is the higher density of macaques per square mile in the city; the larger numbers in a smaller area faced greater competition for resources and sleeping areas. The observers reported that the city animals seemed more tense, more ready to fight. This psychological state was less apparent in the other macaque groups.

Donald Sade has made an interesting study of the macaque's dominance network.[17] Like the baboons, these Asian ground-living monkeys have a strong network, and as one might expect, the dominance varies with the habitat. Sade observed these monkeys on Cayo Santiago Island, off the coast of Puerto Rico in the Caribbean, where they were placed in the 1930s to provide a reservoir of rhesus macaques for use in medical research. The 37-acre island is not large enough to support all the rhesus macaques, and they are given food once a day. Over the years they have been observed by many scientists, so we have a fairly complete history of the macaque groups on the island, comparable to the information gathered by Japanese researchers on their native macaques.

On Cayo Santiago all the animals are tattooed with an identifying sign so that they can be recognized by observers. Relying on these identifying marks in studying the dominance networks, Sade concluded that the offspring of high-dominance females are usually of high dominance themselves. That is, a male monkey whose mother was of high dominance (in the female hierarchy) had a much better chance of being of high dominance (in the male hierarchy) than an animal whose mother did not rank as high. Similarily, a female will be higher in the dominance network than all those females her mother outranks, and is subordinate to all those who rank higher than her mother.[18] Position in the dominance hierarchy probably results from both biological and behavioral factors. A young monkey, watching and learning the behaviors it will need as an adult, observes the kind of actions its mother takes part in, and perhaps learns to be a dominant animal.

A number of observational studies have focused on the terrestrial monkeys of the semiarid highlands of Ethiopia in East Africa. Geladas, hamadryas baboons, savanna baboons, and vervet monkeys all inhabit this region, and although it might seem difficult to conceive of four species of terrestrial monkeys coexisting in the same area, differences in the kinds of foods most often eaten and the specific environments utilized by the various monkeys permit each species to coexist with the others. There are also differences in social organization that are related to the adaptive needs of the monkeys in different environments.

In areas where geladas, savanna baboons, and vervets are all found, such as the Bole Valley of Ethiopia, where the Dunbars observed their behavior, the animals utilized somewhat different parts of the habitat, and exploited slightly different food resources.[19] In this valley both the baboons and the vervets were organized into multi-male groups, although the latter has been observed in other parts of Africa in single-male groups. The geladas were formed into single-male foraging groups as in other areas, but in the Bole Valley, these harem groups seldom clustered into larger aggregations, or herds, which John Crook has observed in areas where the environment is richer.[20] In the Bole Valley the vervets preferred the forested zones near the river; the geladas stayed mainly in the open grassland; and the baboons, though found in all the areas, seemed to be more populous in the forested zones.

Geladas in the Bole Valley are almost exclusively grass eaters, while vervets and baboons eat a much wider variety of foods. Geladas proved to be extremely efficient feeders, sitting back on their haunches and using both hands to harvest grass blades and roots. Baboons also feed on grasses, but with only one hand, so that geladas would appear to be able to eat a greater amount of food in a given time than the baboons. Similarly, vervets and baboons appear to utilize many of the same foods, including fruits, leaves, flowers, and bark, but the smaller vervet monkeys tended to harvest their foods from a higher layer of the trees.

Thus, differences in food choice permit coexistence among three different species living in the same area. Baboons tend to move a greater distance each day in foraging, which would be expected given their less efficient methods of harvesting grasses and their larger body size. The Dunbars concluded that actual competition between specific social groups of the different species would be minimal in most seasons because the baboons, whose use of the habitat overlapped the other two, moved about twice as far each day as the vervets and geladas, and thus were in contact with the others for only a short time.

In the Awash Valley of Ethiopia, near the Bole Valley, savanna and hamadryas baboons live in the same area but utilize different parts of the environment.[21] Hamadryas baboons, like geladas, are organized into single-male groups. Hans Kummer believes that this organization is the result of the need to adapt to an open country habitat not rich enough to support large groups of vegetarian, foraging baboons. During the day, the single-male hamadryas groups move about with their adult females and their young searching for food. In the evening these small groups come together at sleeping cliffs, and form large groups, sometimes of several hundred animals. Lack of suitable sleeping trees and cliffs seems to be the reason for these large aggregations. During the night hours, the single-male groups remain close but do not intermingle. Adult males are very possessive of the females in their groups, and forcibly prevent them from interacting with other males or even with other females. The males watch the females closely, asserting their dominance and encouraging them to follow by judicious bites on the neck. Fights between males are rare.

As with the geladas in the Bole Valley, hamadryas baboons in the

Awash Valley seem to be more efficient than the multi-male savanna baboons in exploiting the resources of the open, semiarid grassland environment. The single-male group appears to reflect a pattern of adaptation in a harsh environment that limits the number of baboons that can stay together as a group. Whether the single-male group is an evolutionary outgrowth of the savanna baboon multi-male organization is disputed. But the important point is that the biological basis of social behavior permits varied responses to different environments. Kummer demonstrated the level of learning flexibility in baboons in a series of experiments. Although female hamadryas and savanna baboons live in different kinds of social groups, with different sorts of relationships with males, when female hamadryas and savanna baboons were captured and then released near social groups of the other species, they both learned quickly to interact successfully within the new social circumstances. Hamadryas females soon learned not to follow a particular male and to adopt a more independent life, while the savanna "females learned, within one hour on the average, to follow the one hamadryas male who would threaten and attack them, and to interact with no other male."[22]

The Patas Monkey

The patas monkey has developed a different adaptation to the demands of terrestrial life. It lives in a single-male group, like the hamadryas and gelada, and is sexually dimorphic; the males are twice as large as the females. Patas monkeys are long-limbed and slender compared with the much heavier, stockier baboons (male patas: 13 kilograms; male baboons: 22–30 kilograms). This body build is well suited to rapid running; the patas are without doubt the swiftest of living primates, running with a bouncing movement like that of the cheetah.

Male patas monkeys are distinctively marked, especially around the rump and the rear of the hind legs, where they are conspicuously pure white. K. R. L. Hall, who studied the patas on the Uganda savanna, wrote: "The rear view of the adult male in the wild, when he is standing or moving, contrasts very strikingly with that of the other much smaller animals of the group, for the white expanse shows up very vividly against the grass and bare ground. No white is visible in the other animals as they move across country."[23] When faced by a predator, the single-male patas group responds very differently from other African terrestrial monkeys. The brown females and young freeze in the grass and blend into the background. The adult male begins a bouncy, very conspicuous run across the savanna, drawing the predator's attention from the rest of the group. With its great speed, the male outdistances the predator, which is led away from the females and young. This pattern permits the patas monkeys to roam farther out onto the savanna than the baboons, and thus to utilize environmental zones not open to other monkeys.

The African monkeys adapt to terrestrial life in many ways. All are successful in their habitats and cope with predators and the need for food and sleeping places. The monkeys are successful because the basic higher primate system gives them flexibility in their behavioral repertoire. Thus it is very difficult to generalize about primates: no terrestrial monkey behavior is typical, just as no human behavior is typical; individual groups suit their activities to their environmental requirements by modifying their behaviors. However, it must be kept in mind that these animals are limited biologically in their behaviors; they are not little humans dressed up in monkeys' suits. Like modern humans, part of their success is founded on their ability to use learned behaviors in adapting to the environment; unlike modern humans and many of our immediate extinct ancestors, their behavioral repertoire is limited and not completely flexible.

The terrestrial monkeys are not really representative of the monkeys in general, because most monkeys are arboreal. To place their behavior in perspective, let us examine the South American howler monkeys.

The New World arboreal monkeys' behavior is quite different from that of the African terrestrial monkeys. But they share some attributes that make it clear we are dealing with a higher primate. As we have seen, the fossil evidence suggests that the Old World and New World monkeys have been evolving independently since the Upper Eocene or Oligocene, perhaps 40 to 50 million years ago.

New World Monkey Behavior

Howler monkeys (genus *Alouatta*) are among the most widely distributed New World monkeys (Figure 7.10). There are at least six species scattered from the Yucatan Peninsula in southern Mexico through Central and South America to northern Argentina. They were first studied under natural conditions in 1932 by C. R. Carpenter, the great pioneer in the study of wild primates, on Barro Colorado Island, formed when the Panama Canal was flooded.[24] It is owned by the Smithsonian Institution, which uses it for the study of animal and plant life.

Although there is a difference in body size, the howler monkeys have little sexual dimorphism in canine size. Many such characteristics that are obvious in terrestrially adapted forms are not found at all in the howlers. Their dominance network is very subtle and the males do little intragroup fighting; instead, intragroup behaviors are mild and placid. Unusual among New World monkeys, juvenile female howler monkeys leave the group of their birth just before reaching maturity, and join a new one. It is difficult to explain the adaptive reasons for this behavior within the overall context of howler adaptation.[25]

Unlike the baboons, howler monkeys defend a *territory*. Territoriality is not part of the behavioral system in most primates. The geographic area in which a primate social group lives is called its home range, which is not the same as a territory. Different social groups may sometimes have overlapping home ranges, especially at rare but essential places such as waterholes (Figure 7.11). Those parts of a group's home range which — for reasons of richness of resources, or presence of sleeping trees, or other factors — are most heavily exploited and where the group spends most of its time are known as the *core area*. A group may occupy a home range of three square kilometers, but the core area may be only about

Figure 7.10. A howler monkey (Alouatta).

one square kilometer. A *territory* is a home range that is physically or vocally defended against incursions by members of the same species. Baboons, like most primates, are not territorial. Howlers, along with the gibbon and a number of other monogamous pair bonded monkeys, like the marmosets, are.

Like other primates, the howler monkey's social group size and pattern are related to the environment. On Barro Colorado Island, howler monkeys live in multi-male groups ranging in size from two to thirty-one, with an average of about twenty. Howlers in other areas, however, live in single-male groups of an adult male, adult females, and dependent young.

Like the terrestrial monkeys of Africa, the howlers share their environment with other monkeys. Lewis and Dorothy Klein observed the ways by which four different species of monkeys were able to coexist in the same trees in a national park in Colombia, South America.[26] Along with the howler monkeys, they observed groups of spider monkeys (genus *Ateles*), capuchin monkeys (genus *Cebus*) and squirrel monkeys (genus *Saimiri*). The howler monkeys in this area were organized mostly into single-male groups of three to six animals. Their diet was similar to that of the Barro Colorado howlers: leaves, immature and mature figs, and smaller quantities of other ripe fruit, decaying wood, and leaf stems. Spider monkeys, in contrast, although they ate more than fifty different kinds of fruit during the study period, including figs, consumed large quantities of palm fruit, which howler monkeys were never observed eating. Moreover, spider monkeys concentrated on ripe fruit with only a very small amount of unripe fruit in the diet.

The Kleins suggest that this feeding adaptation may be responsible for the specialized social organization of the spider monkeys. These animals are organized into social units whose members interact peacefully with one another. The social unit, however, is not a cohesive group, but is composed of animals who at times are isolated and at other times are members of subgroups of different sizes and compositions. The subgroups, ranging in size from two to twenty-two spider monkeys, are unstable: they share a common home range as part of the larger social unit, but travel and forage independently of other subgroups. It appears likely that the spider monkeys' reliance on ripe palm fruit, a relatively abundant but scattered forest resource, requires them to form small foraging groups to exploit this food source efficiently.

Squirrel monkeys are basically insectivores who live in multi-male groups ranging in size from twenty-five to more than thirty-five animals. Although squirrel monkeys occasionally eat vegetable materials, they are primarily adapted to capturing and eating insects, such as katydids, grasshoppers, caterpillars, spiders (not spider monkeys), and cicadas. The comparatively large size of their groups may be an advantage; their dis-

Figure 7.11. *A hypothetical map depicting the primate group's core area, home range, and territory.*

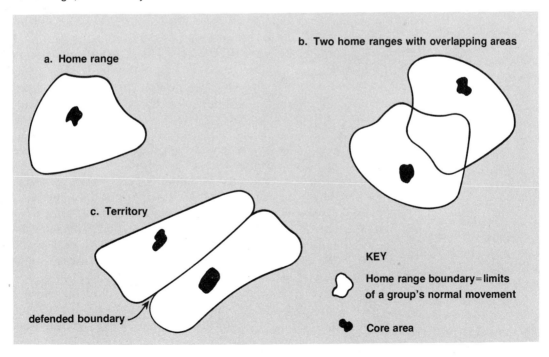

a. Home range

b. Two home ranges with overlapping areas

c. Territory

defended boundary

KEY

Home range boundary=limits of a group's normal movement

Core area

turbance of the branches and leaves as they move through a tree enables them to flush out and capture their prey.

Capuchin monkeys, like the squirrel monkeys, live in multi-male groups, though of a smaller size (from one to twelve; several capuchins were solitary). As feeders, they are the most diversified of the monkeys, eating fruit, flowers, leaf buds and stems, insects, and small vertebrates. To the extent that capuchin monkeys eat insects and palm fruit, they would appear to compete with both squirrel monkeys and spider monkeys for food. Capuchins, however, specialize in insects that must be dug out of dead bark and branches, an important difference from the squirrel monkeys, and their more diversified diet leaves them out of serious competition with spider monkeys. This diet is probably also the reason capuchin monkeys are not organized into unstable subgroups as spiders are.

The behavior of these New World monkeys illustrates the complexity of their adaptation and the difficulties involved in generalizing about the nonhuman primates. Differences in diet permit several species of monkeys to coexist in the same environment and account for differences in the social organization of, for example, spider and howler monkeys.

To return to the howler groups, daily activity for the howlers begins about dawn, when the animals begin moving about in their sleeping trees; once awake, but before the group moves, they start howling. Their larynx and *hyoid bone* are massively developed, making a large resonating chamber (Figure 7.12). The howls can be heard for several miles. These vocalizations, which gave the howler its name, are said to be a memorable sound. The morning howling seems to be a spacing mechanism, ensuring that the howlers are aware of the location of other groups. The gibbon, another territorial primate, also uses vocalizations (hoots) to announce the position of the family groups, as does the orangutan. After the morning howl, the group moves through the trees, eating mainly leaves but also blossoms, fruit, and seeds. A morning of feeding is followed by a late morning and early afternoon of sleeping, grooming, and sexual relations, with the young engaged in play; in the late afternoon they return to eating. Before dark, the group moves into sleeping trees for the night.

A howler group moving through the trees may come to the edge of its range and into visual contact with a howler group coming from another direction. Both groups start a territorial display. The males shake branches and howl; the females scream; the juveniles and the young become excited, running up and down branches. Each group remains in its own area, perhaps ten or fifteen meters apart. After ten or fifteen minutes of this, the troops slowly retreat into their own areas, occasionally looking back and giving a parting gesture. These displays rarely lead to physical contact or combat. Behaviors like this, and the localizing vocalizations these animals, and other primates, make, probably evolved as a way to permit the effective spacing of social groups of a species through an environment, and thereby ensure that the species could exploit resources throughout a range.

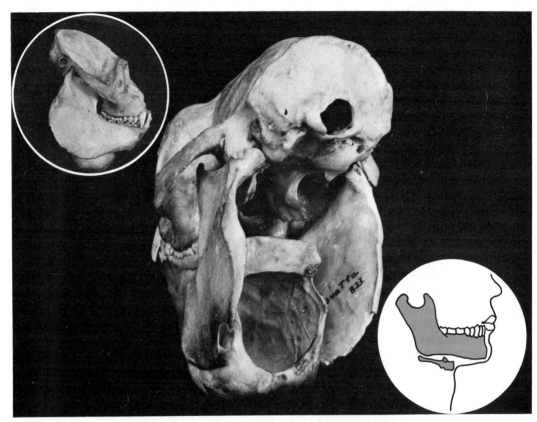

Figure 7.12. *A howler monkey skull with its hyoid bone in place between the two halves of the lower jaw. In main picture and side view, note the inflated, bulbous chamber of the howler hyoid, which provides the resonating chamber that permits the characteristic vocalizations. The lower inset illustrates the much more usual appearance of the hyoid bone in a primate, in this case, a modern human, and the bone's position beneath the lower jaw.*

The howlers, being primarily arboreal, rarely are found on the ground except during the height of the dry season, when their normal diet of leaves, fruit, and other arboreal vegetation is difficult to find. Even minor interruptions in the forest limit their distribution. Species and subspecies limits correspond with geographic barriers, such as rivers. Baboons, ground-living monkeys, are more widely distributed; geographic barriers do not limit terrestrial monkeys as tightly as they do an arboreal species.

Howlers almost never venture out of the trees. In the branches, they move cautiously, holding on with their hands and feet. Their distinctive grip is between the thumb and index finger and the other three digits. The prehensile tail is used as a fifth limb for an added grip on the branch. In some ways, the howler skeletal and muscular system (not including the manipulative tail which is a specialized, later development) reflects a more primitive quadrupedal pattern than either of the major Old World higher primate groups. The limb bones of the early higher primate from the Oligocene Fayum, *Aegyptopithecus,* share a number of similarities with howler anatomy. This does not imply close evolutionary relations, but rather aspects of common primate heritage.

The howler monkeys of the New World and the terrestrial monkeys of the Old are variations on a theme, similar in some features, differing in others. All are based on the adjustments that allow the species to survive within its environment.

The Behavior of the Hominoids

Chimpanzees, like baboons, are limited to Africa, and are distributed in a wide band across the central part of the continent, from Sierra Leone in the west to Uganda and Tanzania in the east (Figure 7.13). They are generally found in forest habitats, although they also live at the edge of the forest and in the adjoining open grassland or savanna. Chimpanzees, like the other members of the superfamily Hominoidea (gorillas, orangutans, gibbons, and humans), differ anatomically from the Old World monkeys. As we have seen, these differences include: distinctive molar

Figure 7.13. Distribution of chimpanzees in Africa (after Yerkes).

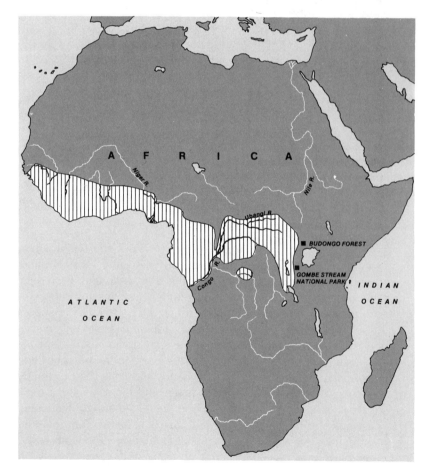

cusp patterns, an enlarged brain, no tail, and anatomical specializations in the shoulders and arms that permit greater arm mobility and allow the animals to hang suspended below branches. Both of the African apes, the chimpanzee and gorilla, are mainly terrestrial, though chimpanzees build nests in the trees at night to sleep. The African apes' mode of movement on the ground is termed knuckle-walking: both the front and rear limbs are used for locomotion, and the fingers of the hands are curled or flexed, with the animal's weight resting on the knuckles of the second joint (Figure 7.14)

The most famous study of chimpanzees in the wild was conducted by Jane Goodall and her associates in the Gombe National Park, a wildlife preserve on the shores of Lake Tanganyika, in Tanzania.[27] These chimpanzees live in a savanna-woodland environment. Chimpanzees have also been observed in a variety of other forest and woodland habitats in Uganda and Tanzania in East Africa, and Guinea in West Africa.[28]

Chimpanzees are organized into bisexual, somewhat amorphous social groups ranging in size from twenty to sixty animals, but these groups are rarely together. Instead, they are normally found in smaller, impermanent bands with an average size at the Gombe of about 4.2 chimps. They are most commonly composed of females and their offspring, or are made up of all males; less common are groups of male and female adults, and these are ordinarily based on the presence of one or more estrus females (Figure 7.15). Membership in these bands fluctuates regularly, as the animals move about in their habitat; indeed, Gombe chimps spend about one-fifth of their time foraging for food on their own. This social organization is similar to that of the spider monkeys of South America, and perhaps occurs for the same reason: to permit maximal exploitation of a scattered food resource.

Chimpanzee social organization is distinct among hominoids. The other African ape, the gorilla, has a social organization with more group cohesion that that of the chimpanzees. Gorilla groups studied in the Virunga Volcanos area, in Zaire and Rwanda, by George Schaller, Dian Fossey, and their associates are composed of fully mature (silver-backed) males, females, immature males, and young.[29] Although some groups have two or more silver-backed males, the usual pattern is for only one. Group size mostly ranges from about six to sixteen animals. When they reach maturity, male gorillas leave the group in which they were born and become solitary animals. Females, too, have been observed leaving the natal social group. Female gorillas leave their group only to transfer to another; males remain solitary until they form a new social group with emigrant females. Nearly all gorilla females appear to leave the group of their birth, usually before they become mothers. Females who have given birth to living offspring do not leave the groups they are in.

Figure 7.14. A sequence of steps showing the knuckle-walking locomotion in a chimpanzee. Notice that in the front limbs the chimp's weight is resting on the knuckles of the flexed second finger joint.

The two Asian apes, the gibbon and the orangutan, also differ fundamentally from the chimp pattern. The gibbon's group consists of an adult male and female and their immature offspring. The gibbon's social group is territorial and will not coalesce with other groups. The social

Figure 7.15. *Chimpanzee social interactions are normally peaceable and close. Here, a mother and her young offspring sit close together on a branch, feeding.*

organization of the orangutan (Malay: *orang* = man; *hutan* = forest) appears to be unique among higher primates, and seems to consist of a female and immature offspring. Occasionally they meet with other mother-offspring groups, and the young play together. This gathering is not permanent, and after only a short time, the mothers and their offspring will move apart. Adult male orangs are solitary animals that seem to meet with others only for reproduction. This pattern may be another kind of response to a lack of concentrated food resources, the orang pattern having evolved to permit this species to efficiently exploit widely scattered foods.

Like the orang, the chimpanzee's specialized social organization is related to its adaptive niche. Chimpanzees make use of a very varied diet. Although their primary source is fruit, they also eat leaves, blossoms, seeds, stems, bark, resin, honey, insects, eggs, and meat. In contrast, the gorilla is a vegetarian, including in its diet leaves, bark, stems, and fruit. George Schaller writes that he did not see gorillas eating any animal foods. Chimpanzees have been observed eating a variety of insects, including termites, ants, caterpillars, grubs, and bee larvae. They also hunt larger animals, and are known to have caught and eaten some fifteen species of mammals, including young baboons (Figure 7.16). Goodall reports that the chimp group she was observing hunted and killed twenty mammals (as well as birds, eggs, and smaller animals) in one year. She recorded a specific hunting incident involving two adult chimpanzees. A red colobus (a small leaf-eating monkey) was sitting on a branch when the chimpanzees spotted it. With no obvious communication between them, the two chimpanzees separated, one climbing the tree to the monkey and attracting its attention, and the other, much more quietly, approaching the animal from a different direction. While the first chimp occupied the monkey, the second quickly ran along the branch, grabbed the monkey, and wrung its neck. Both chimpanzees pulled the carcass apart and ate it.

Geza Teleki, who worked for a number of years at the Gombe Na-

Figure 7.16. *Chimpanzees do hunt animals and eat meat. Here a male chimp sits in a tree and eats his prey, a baboon, while another chimp watches.*

tional Park, is impressed with the variety of the chimpanzee diet, comparing it with the diets of a number of modern human gatherers and hunters (those human groups, such as the Australian aborigines and the San, formerly known as the Bushman, of southern Africa who until very recently did not practice agriculture, but gathered wild foods and hunted animals).[30] Teleki refers to the pattern of chimpanzee subsistence as that of a collector/predator, emphasizing by this term the wide range of chimpanzee foods. Collector/predators differ from the human gatherer/hunters, according to Teleki, in that humans are able to hunt animals larger than themselves. Although chimpanzees do hunt a variety of animals, including a number of primates, their prey is always smaller than themselves.

Chimpanzee social organization, like that of spider monkeys, apparently evolved to deal with this sort of dietary pattern. Although chimpanzees utilize a wide array of foods and will often at least sample from all the major food categories each day, fruit is a basic chimpanzee staple, and appears to make up more than half of the diet. Fruit is a widely scattered resource in a forest, and different kinds of fruit mature at different times of the year. The open social organization of the chimpanzees is efficient because it permits them to exploit this scarce resource in small groups. Orangs are also omnivorous in that they consume large numbers of invertebrates (but they have not been observed killing vertebrate animals, as have chimps), and like chimps their main food resource is fruit. One reason why orangs are solitary living animals may be related to the greater distance between clumps of fruit trees in their island habitats.[31]

Chimpanzees have been seen using sticks and their fists to beat on the bases of trees, making loud, hollow sounds that attract chimps from other parts of the forest to an area where food is concentrated. In crossing from one forested region to another, vulnerable to predators, they make similar noises, cross the open area in a group, and disperse on the other side. The large social group apparently serves a limited purpose, at least for the chimpanzees that have been observed, and this large group has never been seen to come together at the Gombe Stream during the thousands of hours of observation on these animals. However, the chimpanzees in the community are generally aware of which animals belong and which do not, and small bands of males often "patrol" the community boundary to ensure that chimpanzees from neighboring communities, male or female, do not intrude into their community area. Several observed episodes of males attacking strange females with infants resulted in the female receiving wounds and being chased from the area, but having her infant pulled from her grasp by the males, who then killed the young chimp, and partially ate it as they would a prey animal. The carcass was groomed and touched by several chimpanzees, usually not the animals responsible for the killing, as if they were aware of the nature of the creature prior to its death. Although a number of theories have been advanced to account for the adaptive or evolutionary nature of these incidents, they are not compelling, and it remains a difficult behavior to comprehend within the context of primate adaptive systems.[32]

Many years of experiments with caged chimpanzees have demonstrated that with incentives, these animals can perform many tasks, such as building crude shelters, making tools, and solving simple problems to get food or some other reward. Captive monkeys, such as the rhesus and the South American squirrel monkey, can also perform most of these tasks, although they do not usually learn as rapidly.

These experiments were conducted under artificial (manmade) conditions; the one real test of an animal's intelligence is how it performs in its natural environment. It is interesting to find that caged chimpanzees can put two pieces of bamboo pole together, making an implement long enough to reach some bananas suspended from the ceiling. But they would hardly go to such trouble in their natural habitat, where they would simply climb the tree to reach the fruit. Many anthropologists had concluded that humans are the only primate that, in natural conditions, deliberately fabricates and uses tools. Some were therefore more than a little shaken when Goodall and others reported observing chimpanzees making and using a variety of simple tools.

At times the Gombe Park is loaded with insects — termites, ants, caterpillars — and the chimpanzees will eat huge numbers of them. The chimpanzees' really remarkable behavior appears when they gather termites. According to Suzuki and Goodall, when chimpanzees see that termites have pushed open their tunnels on the surface, they will go off to find a suitable termiting tool (Figure 7.17). A foot-long, rather thin, straight twig is best, and it may take quite a while to choose a suitable one; then extraneous side branches and leaves must be carefully stripped off. The ape may even select and prepare several twigs at a time, carrying them all back to the termiting hill firmly cupped in a closed palm while it knuckle walks. The chimpanzee will lie down on its side, next to the termite hill, and, with skill and care, stick the twig into one of the open tunnels. The animal wiggles the stick, then slowly pulls it out; if the stick has termites adhering to it, the chimp licks them off the tool and does it again. The job may look simple, but it takes, skill and practice to maneuver the stick through the twisting termite corridors. This is a complex, learned behavior, based on the manufacture of an implement. The collecting of termites and ants is done primarily by females. This is in contrast to the hunting of vertebrates, which is, in the Gombe study area, a male behavior, although in other areas females have also been observed hunting vertebrates. Orangutans also do a considerable amount of insect collecting, oftentimes on the ground, but this differs from the behaviors seen in chimps in two ways. No tools are used, and both males and females are equally involved in gathering these foods.

Goodall has watched chimpanzees using other objects, modifying some, leaving most others as they are. They chew leaves and cup them in the hand to sponge water for drinking or to sponge out the brains of a hunted baboon.

Figure 7.17. *Chimpanzees have been observed making and using tools. In this picture, a chimpanzee has inserted a grass stem into a termite hole, and is withdrawing the stem with the termites clinging to it. Skill is attached to this learned behavior, since it takes careful effort to wiggle the tool into the curved corridors of the termite hill.*

The emerging picture of chimpanzee life in the natural environment strongly suggests that we may have been overemphasizing the extent of our differences from the rest of the animal world. Chimpanzees make and use tools. Their diet is a diverse one, based on vegetable foods, but with an appreciable amount of animal foods. In addition, the pattern of their social organization, with small groups existing as parts of a larger social community, has many similarities to the social organization of living human gatherer/hunters. This leaves us with a sticky question: Exactly how do humans differ from other primates? Many traditional ideas about our uniqueness may have to be modified because of the information primatologists are gathering about monkeys and apes in their natural environment.

Previous chapters have examined the biology, genetic and biochemical **Summary** similarities, taxonomy and distribution of the nonhuman primates, and their biological history. This chapter provides a look at modern primate behavior, focusing in particular on the social living higher primates.

Sociobiology, a field concerned with understanding the reasons particular primate behaviors have evolved in specific environmental and social contexts, has become an important research tool in primate behavior studies, and much current research uses this focus as a way to explain primate behavior, rather than just observe and record it.

Life in social groups permits primates to accumulate a large repertoire of learned behavior that in turn gives these animals their indispensable flexibility in responding to environmental demands. The primates' social organization seems to reflect the necessities of their differing environments, and it is not unusual to find different social groups of the same species emphasizing diverse behaviors, although it is sometimes very difficult to fully comprehend all the environmental factors that might influence primate social systems. There is no typical primate behavior or typical primate social group. Where resources and other environmental limitations allow large numbers of animals to live together, the social groups will be large. In other areas with scattered, specialized, or minimal resources, smaller social groups are the rule.

Field studies of higher primates in the New and Old World have revealed the wide array of dietary resources that these animals consume in the wild, and the variations in social organization and behavior that are also found. Typically, New World monkeys, among whom is found the only nocturnal higher primate, the night monkey, live almost entirely in the trees, with many living in single pair-bonded male and female groups with their young. However, also found in New World monkeys are larger multi-male groupings that are the usual pattern among the terrestrial Old World monkeys, the baboons and macaques. Other Old World monkeys, including terrestrial ones like the patas and mantled or hamadryas baboons, live in single-male, many female groups, while the numerous arboreal Old World monkeys exhibit a variety of social systems. The pattern common in the New World of a monogamous pair bond is extremely rare among Old World monkeys; it is found in the apes only among the highly arboreal gibbon and siamang, lesser apes.

Among the pongids, the orangutan is unique in that alone among the higher primates, it is a solitary animal, spending only a very small percentage of its time with other orangs. The African apes, the chimpanzee and gorilla, closely related genetically and anatomically, nevertheless have different behavioral and social systems. The large-bodied gorillas live normally in single-male groups, while chimpanzees have apparently evolved a rather amorphous community-like system to deal with the scattered fruit resources that are their major dietary items. Chimpanzees are omnivores in that they consume a variety of invertebrates, mainly ants and termites, collected by the females, and hunted mammal meat, usually killed by the males, but sometimes shared with females as well. Chimpanzees have also been observed making and using simple tools, which is often discussed in the context of their close anatomical and genetic relations to those supreme toolmakers, humans.

Much primate behavior research is used to demonstrate behavioral affinities between humans and other primates. Yet we are still not far enough along to understand the connections between primate and human actions. How far can we go in attributing human behavior to some common primate background? Just how much of the primate (and human) behavior pattern is fixed in the neurological structure of brain and nervous system? Sociobiologists have often suggested that a whole series of human behaviors have strong biological bases, and they compare these with similar behaviors in nonhuman primates, other mammals, and even other vertebrates. It is startling to see, in a film on the chimpanzees, how these animals greet each other: by shaking hands! But when a male chimpanzee, in a group with other males, attacks a strange female, forcibly takes her young infant and proceeds with the others to kill and eat the infant, are we justified in relating this action to human conduct as well?

To understand the relationships between humans and the nonhuman primates we have to examine not only the primates' anatomy and behavior but our own. We must prepare ourselves for this by examining human biological history. If there really is continuity in behavior and anatomy — if by studying the nonhuman primates we can more fully understand ourselves — then an examination of human evolution should provide insight into how close this connection is.

Chapter 8

The Hominidae

The information we have reviewed on the biological history and behavior of the nonhuman primates, including the mechanisms that result in evolutionary change, provides the background necessary to explore the origin of modern humans and the evolutionary development of our immediate ancestors. Unraveling the story of the human biological family, the Hominidae, has taken on increasing importance as we come to appreciate more and more how much of modern human anatomy, and perhaps behavior, had its origins in the adaptations of our ancestors. Greater knowledge of our evolutionary history is essential to a fuller understanding of why we look and act the way we do. But first, we must investigate the basic material, the hominid fossil record. From there we can evaluate with more confidence the theories of human development.

Neither morphological nor strictly behavioral definitions of the hominids have met with general acceptance. Scientists have viewed the evolution of the hominids in a variety of ways, and their definitions reflect this diversity of opinion. Let us set the definitions aside until we have explored some of the family's morphological and behavioral attributes.

Ideally, we should treat hominid biological history as we would that of any other animal family. Unfortunately, in dealing with our own ancestors this proves to be very difficult. The hominids, however, are subject to the same evolutionary mechanisms as other animal groups. As we look at their evolution through time, we see changes in physical features, as the genetic characteristics responsible for their appearance increase or decrease in frequency in response to the various factors that affect gene frequencies. But as in the study of other animal species, this picture of human evolution is in many places foggy and difficult to interpret, mainly because the fossil record documenting this biological history is an incomplete one, based on scarce, scattered, and usually broken and distorted fossil bones.

Furthermore, each time we unearth a fossil, we retrieve a slightly different part of the hominid chronology. The specimens come from different parts of the world and reflect the morphological variation inherent in and among all populations. One of the results of this situation is that it is often very difficult to decide whether two fossil specimens discovered in different places, and from somewhat different times, are similar

Table 8.1. Members of the human zoological family, the Hominidae.
All but the last, Homo sapiens, *are extinct. The locations indicate where fossils and/or other evidence of hominid presence have been found.*

The Family Hominidae		
Genus	*Species*	*Location*
Australopithecus	*A. afarensis*[a]	Ethiopia, Tanzania
	A. africanus[a]	South Africa, Kenya, Ethiopia
	A. robustus[a]	South Africa
	A. boisei[a]	Tanzania, Kenya, Ethiopia
Homo	*Homo*[a] (no species yet given)	Kenya, Ethiopia, South Africa
	H. habilis[a]	Tanzania
	H. erectus	Europe (?), Africa, and Asia
	H. sapiens (modern humans)	worldwide

[a]These categories are grouped in this book as the "australopithecines," a purely descriptive term for all hominid fossils dating from 5.5 million to about 1.5 million years B.P.

enough to be considered members of one species, perhaps larger male and smaller female of a sexually dimorphic species, or different enough to be parts of two distinct species.

This is not the only problem we face in the analysis of the pattern of human evolution. In the past, when evolution and population variability were not as well understood, the morphological variation of the fossils resulted in the invention of many unwarranted taxonomic names. Although literally hundreds of taxonomic names were given to various hominid fossils as they were discovered, most anthropologists today agree that all may be grouped into two genera, one of them extinct (Table 8.1).

The earliest fossils of the family Hominidae are members of the genus *Australopithecus,* whose fossils have been dated from more than 4 million years ago to about 1.5 million years ago. Discovered at a number of sites in East and South Africa, this fossil genus currently represents the first appearance of the hominids in the fossil record. The australopithecines apparently evolved into the surviving genus of the hominid family, *Homo,* about 2 to 1.5 million years ago.

Hominid Geology and Evolution

Like the study of the fossil record, our perspective of geologic time is very much a product of recent work. Research in the geologic and physical sciences has tended to increase the time depth of the geologic epochs and periods. For example, Sir Arthur Keith, a British anatomist, in 1930 published a major work on the hominid fossils, *New Discoveries Relating to the Antiquity of Man,* analyzing the fossil record in terms of a length of about 200,000 years for the Pleistocene. Today we continue to recognize the Pleistocene epoch as a crucial time for hominid evolution, yet sophisticated methods of determining age, unknown when Keith wrote, have extended the epoch back to about 1.8 million years, a ninefold increase since 1930.

Darwin speculated in his 1871 book, *The Descent of Man*, that the human family might perhaps extend as far back in time as the Eocene. We have since limited the possible time span of the hominids to more recent geologic periods, in particular the Miocene, Pliocene, Pleistocene, and into the Holocene, or Recent, epoch (Table 8.2). We are particularly interested in analyzing Eurasian and, especially during the earliest phases of human evolution, African geologic events, because the major phases of hominid evolution took place in the Old World, and the earliest seem to be limited to Africa.

The Miocene

Recent studies of continental drift suggest that the African plate did not make a final land connection with Eurasia until the beginning of the Miocene, about 20 million years ago. Large interchanges of animals between the two continents probably did not begin until then. Perhaps as a result of the continental collision between the African plate and the Eurasian plate during the Miocene, geologic instabilities were created

Table 8.2. The hominids: dates and distribution.

Date (B.P.)	Geological epochs	Africa	Asia	Europe	North America and South America
10,000	RECENT	*Homo sapiens*			
1,800,000	PLEISTOCENE	*Homo erectus*			
	PLIOCENE	australo-pithecines			
5,000,000					
	MIOCENE				
22,500,000	OLIGOCENE				

that caused the beginning of the Rift system of East Africa and the Middle East. Stretching today from Mount Carmel in northern Israel down the Jordan River Valley to the Red Sea, the Rift continues south along the East African coast to central Ethiopia, where it turns south and west, cutting through Ethiopia, Kenya, and Tanzania, finally ending in southern Africa. Formation of many of the East African sites, where the earliest hominid fossils have been found, is directly linked with Rift Valley geologic activity.

Another result of this continental collision was the development of the Mediterranean Sea. Prior to Africa's contact with Eurasia, there was an open waterway, called the Tethys Sea, between the Atlantic Ocean on the west and the Indian Ocean on the east. It has been suggested that the closing off of the Tethys at its eastern end, and the formation of the Mediterranean, resulted in the changing of wind directions, and thus rainfall patterns. A variety of analyses of the beginning Miocene epoch suggest that in East Africa, east of the developing Rift system, conditions were slowly giving way to a more open country environment.[1]* It is possible that climatic changes caused by the geologic changes were responsible for the development of these new habitats; as it has often been suggested that the hominids originated on the open savannas, it may be that these changes were the basis for the appearance of our family. The Miocene period merges without apparent break into the Pliocene about 5 million years ago. During the Pliocene, the patterns established in the Miocene continued, with the extensive east African forests diminishing at the expense of grassland and more mosaic habitats (combinations of grassland, bush, and small stands of forest).

The Pleistocene   Sometime around 1.8 million years ago, the transition between the Pliocene and the Pleistocene is marked. At one time this stratigraphic zone was defined by a number of characteristic fossils found in southern Europe, including the first appearance of the genus of cattle *(Bos),* the Indian elephant *(Elephas),* and the modern horse *(Equus),* all of them part of a larger animal sample called the *Villafranchian* fauna, which were thought to identify the Pleistocene's beginning. Later, research on marine microfauna, which are far more sensitive to climatic changes than are large, terrestrial animals, suggested that the period was very complex, and that the European Villafranchian consisted of alternating warm and cold periods.

Today it is recognized that any definite break between the Pliocene and Pleistocene will have to be an arbitrary one. Recently the reversals in the earth's magnetic field have been used as a boundary marker. Frequently in the planet's history, the polarity of the earth has completely turned around, and has remained reversed for a time. During these intervals, a compass needle would point south instead of north. Iron-bearing rocks formed during these times can be "read" for reversed polarity

*See page 568 for notes to Chapter 8.

by means of sensitive techniques, and earth scientists have found that one of these *paleomagnetic reversals* occurred about 1.8 million years ago. A great advantage in this type of boundary marking is that the reversals are usually worldwide; therefore they can be used to correlate geologic activity in different areas, unlike the use of the Villafranchian fauna, which is limited to parts of southern Europe.

More than a million and a half years ago the climate changed drastically in the northern hemisphere, breaking the rest of the Pleistocene into alternating *glacial* and *interglacial* periods. During the glacial advances, large parts of the northern hemisphere were covered by very slowly expanding ice sheets. Interglacial times were marked by climatic warming and the retreat of the glaciers. Not including the ice-bound Antarctic continent, Pleistocene glaciers may have occupied an area thirteen times greater than the glaciers of today, most of which are confined to high mountain areas and Greenland. Because so much water was trapped in the glaciers, sea levels dropped, and previously independent land masses came into contact. For example, a land bridge between Siberia and Alaska was formed by the glacier-caused drop in sea level. Hominids crossed the bridge into the New World, but only 20,000 to 50,000 years ago, when they were already fully modern in physical features.

The Glaciers

The classic studies of Pleistocene glaciation were carried out on geologic deposits in the central European Alpine region early in this century. This research suggested that there were four glacial advances (from the earliest to the latest): Günz, Mindel, Riss, and Würm, named for the locale where each was identified. Interposed between these glacials were three interglacials, when the climate warmed and the glaciers retreated. Later, a pre-Günz glacial, the Donau, was proposed. It was also recognized that the glacial advances were more complex, and that within a glacial, the climate briefly warmed at times; these warm periods are termed *interstadials*. Recent research in Europe has indicated that the pattern of glacial advances and retreats is extremely complicated, and that glacial activity cannot be neatly divided into four or five glacial advances; there is now evidence for seventeen climatic fluctuations in central Europe during the Pleistocene, and more than twenty over the last 800,000 years have been identified from the analysis of sea cores.[2] Because of the complexity of these fluctuations, and the fact that subsequent glacial advances tend to scour away the marks of previous ice sheets, correlations between glacial systems in different parts of the northern hemisphere, or even within limited areas, have been very difficult. In Europe, two great glacial systems have been identified. At its maximum, the Alpine glacial system covered almost all of Switzerland, north into southern Germany, west into France, east into eastern and central Europe, and south into much of northern Italy. The other, the Fenno-Scandinavian system, at its maximum covered the areas that are now Scandinavia — Denmark, Norway, Sweden, and Finland — and spread south and east into parts of northern Germany, the Low Countries, and the Baltic re-

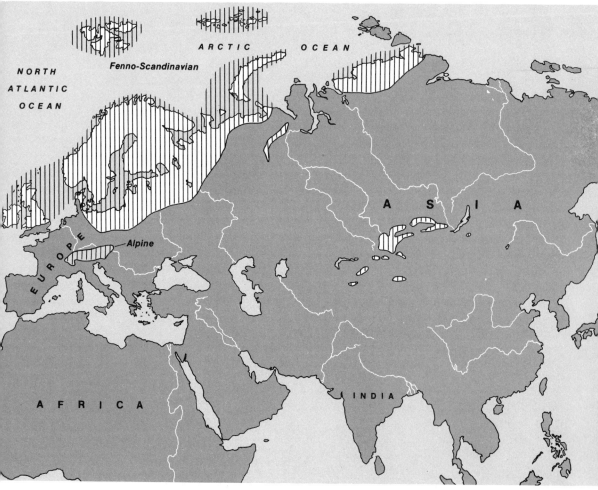

Figure 8.1. *The extent of the Weichsel and the Würm glacials during the last glacial advance in Europe.*

gions. Correlations between these two glacial systems have not been completely satisfactory, except for the last glacial advance, called the Weichsel in Scandinavia, which correlated with the Würm (Figure 8.1).

Asia, too, had ice sheets, the most important in the Himalayas, which at their maximum extended to the north, east, west, and south, and prevented animals and people from moving between northern and southern Asia and Europe. Other glacials were localized in the Ural Mountains between Asian and European Russia, and on many other mountain chains in Europe and Asia.

The glacial-interglacial sequence occurred only in the northern hemisphere. There is some evidence that glacial advances seem to have affected rainfall in the southern hemisphere, giving many areas less rainfall than they get today. There is also evidence in the southern hemisphere for glacials, but only at very high altitudes. Mount Kilimanjaro in East Africa, at about 7,000 meters, had a glacier, as did the high Andes of western South America. These local phenomena extended only short distances and were nothing like the northern hemisphere's glacial advances, which entombed huge parts of North America and Eurasia.

Glacial advances and retreats profoundly affected the life zones: although hominids did not live on the ice, its spread nevertheless had a strong influence on the environments exploited by hominids. As the northern latitudes got colder, all fauna and flora were forced southward. Hominids, too, had to shift with the environment, probably moving as the climate changed. In addition, the hominids had to adapt to these severe climatic conditions. Both cultural and biological adaptations were at work to make survival possible in these harsh environments. Modern humans subjected to extremes of temperature have evolved biological ways of dealing with chronic cold (see pages 485–488). These adaptations evolved by natural selection over thousands of years. In addition, growing up in a cold climate can increase an individual's tolerance to cold; this is a developmental response that can occur rapidly, but cannot be passed on across generations. Cultural and behavioral adaptations (such as warm clothing, fire, and ingeniously constructed shelters like the igloo) are a third, and much swifter response to environmental changes than strictly genetic adaptations, which must rely mostly on natural selection and chance mutations. Human evolution is much more complex than that of other animals because hominids have employed artifacts and other manifestations of cultural behavior to adapt to inhospitable environments. This interaction of the biological and the cultural, which has made it possible for humans to exploit greatly varied environments, has made humans unique among living creatures.

Glacial Ecology and Hominid Evolution

The cultural complexity or efficiency that enabled hominids to survive in severe cold took several million years to evolve. The biological bases for these cultural behaviors, such as large, complex brains, skill in using the hands, and numberless others, were developed in milder climates before our ancestors eventually spread to all parts of the world. Much of the early history of the Hominidae took place in the temperate zones of the Old World, mostly in Africa, and it is only relatively late in human evolution that we find evidence of hominid occupation of the cold areas of central Europe and north China.

The complexity of Pleistocene glacial activity, and the absence of ice sheets in Africa and parts of Asia, like Java, where crucially important hominid fossils have been found, makes the use of the northern hemisphere glacial sequence as a framework for dating hominid fossils rather impractical. A more reasonable approach to provide a general framework for the hominid fossil record is to divide the Pleistocene into Lower, Middle, and Upper segments.

Dating Hominid Evolution in the Pleistocene

An understanding of the basis for these divisions requires a brief re-

Table 8.3. Paleomagnetic history chart.
Here the last five million years of the earth's paleomagnetic history are divided into epochs of long duration, with shorter intervals of polarity change within them (events).

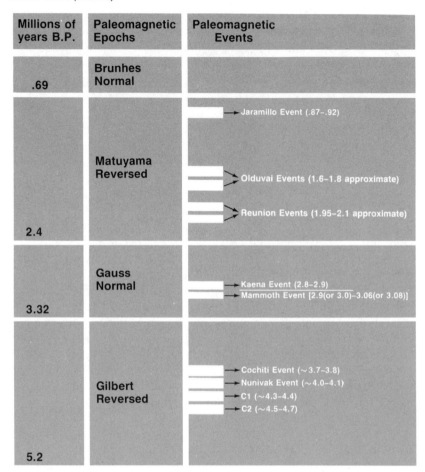

Millions of years B.P.	Paleomagnetic Epochs	Paleomagnetic Events
.69	Brunhes Normal	
2.4	Matuyama Reversed	→ Jaramillo Event (.87–.92) → Olduvai Events (1.6–1.8 approximate) → Reunion Events (1.95–2.1 approximate)
3.32	Gauss Normal	→ Kaena Event (2.8–2.9) → Mammoth Event [2.9(or 3.0)–3.06(or 3.08)]
5.2	Gilbert Reversed	→ Cochiti Event (~3.7–3.8) → Nunivak Event (~4.0–4.1) → C1 (~4.3–4.4) → C2 (~4.5–4.7)

view of the earth's recent paleomagnetic history (Table 8.3). In the past, as has been noted, the polarity of the earth's magnetic field has reversed. The prolonged periods of reversed polarity are termed *paleomagnetic epochs*. During the times of prolonged magnetic reversal, there have also been shorter intervals when the polarity switched again; these are called *paleomagnetic events*. The present epoch of the earth's polarity, which began about 690,000 years ago, is called the *Bruhnes Normal Epoch* ("normal" because this is the way it is for us). Before the onset of the Bruhnes Normal, there was an epoch of reversed polarity of long duration, from about 2.4 million to 690,000 years ago, called the *Matuyama Reversed* Epoch. Prior to that was another epoch of normal polarity *(Gauss Normal)*, and so on. Within the long Matuyama Reversed Epoch were a number of events of normal polarity, several of them occurring between about 1.6 and 1.8 million years ago, called the *Ol-*

duvai Events (named after Olduvai Gorge, an early hominid site in Tanzania, East Africa). By convention, the 1.8 m.y. Olduvai Event is taken as the Pliocene/Pleistocene boundary. Similarly, the Bruhnes/Matuyama boundary, at 690,000 years B.P., is used as the border between the Lower and Middle Pleistocene. Finally, a more limited marker, the beginning of the last interglacial in Europe, at about 125,000 years B.P., is used to separate the Middle and Upper Pleistocene. By convention, the Pleistocene is said to have ended, and the Holocene or Recent to have begun, about 10,000 years ago, when the last glaciers retreated and the climate began to warm. However, many geologists believe that we are currently living in an interglacial period, and that glacial advances will recur in the future; how modern industrialization and pollution (the "greenhouse effect") might interfere with these climatic changes is uncertain.

Dating Methods

Clearly, in order to understand the pattern of hominid evolution, to comprehend the changes over time which have affected the teeth, the braincase, or any other structure, it is essential that fossil discoveries be accurately placed within the hominid time continuum. Tracing the evolution of a particular complex necessitates the placement of a series of fossils in chronological order, so that we can follow the changes that have taken place over time. A variety of methods and techniques has been developed to date a fossil find precisely or generally.

Some fossils can never be dated, either because when they were found little attention was paid to their depositional context; because different dating techniques give different answers; or, most often, because difficulties in understanding the geology and the associated animal bones make dating impossible. We will encounter each of these difficulties in our discussion of the human fossil record.

For most fossil discoveries, however, some idea of their position in time can be achieved, either in terms of years before the present *(absolute dates)* or by reference to some event in earth history or the evolutionary history of a better known animal group *(relative dates)*.

Absolute Methods

One of the most important developments facilitating the study of human evolution is the use of techniques measuring the decay of radioactive isotopes to date geologic deposits and organic remains.[3]

Carbon-14 The pioneer work was done in the late 1940s by Willard Libby. He studied the decay of the radioactive isotope carbon-14 into the element nitrogen. Radioactive carbon-14 is formed naturally in the earth's atmosphere as it interacts with the sun's energy. In the upper atmosphere, free elements are bombarded by cosmic radiation. The earth's atmosphere is made up mainly of nitrogen in gaseous form; when it is struck by the sun's radiation, part of this gas is transformed into radioactive carbon-14 (by the addition of one atomic particle). This conversion takes place continuously in the atmosphere, so that carbon-14 makes up a minute percentage of the planet's air. Every plant, taking in carbon dioxide, also absorbs trace portions of carbon-14 into its system. Plants are eaten by animals, which in turn are eaten by other animals; thus, carbon-14 is incorporated in small but constant amounts into the bodies of all living things. When a plant or animal dies, carbon-14 stops being replenished, and the unstable isotope begins to break down into nitrogen again. Reducing the carbon-14 to half its original amount takes about 5,730 years; the other half becomes nitrogen. This reduction is called the *half-life*, and it continues, after the next 5,730 years leaving a quarter of the original amount, and so on. A living being has a constant proportion of carbon-14 to the common, stable element carbon-12. By analyzing the changed proportion in organic remains, we get some idea of when an animal or plant died: that is, when it stopped taking in carbon-14. Thus, the C^{14} technique can only be employed on organic remains, such as bone, wood, charcoal, and shell, materials which have had the C^{12}-C^{14} relationship.

This technique is extremely valuable in dating many hominid fossil bones and archaeological deposits, but it has a serious drawback: the time span of its usefulness. If the organic material to be dated is older than about 70,000 years, the amount of C^{14} remaining is so small that it cannot be measured. As much of the human evolutionary record extends far beyond 70,000 years this procedure cannot be used in dating the earlier phases of human evolution. Carbon-14 dates are normally given with plus and minus numbers of years, to cover the statistical error inherent in this technique. Carbon-14 is one of the small but growing number of dating methods whose results are expressed in years before the present, and are therefore called absolute dating methods.[4]

Potassium-Argon Another absolute dating method, which covers the distant time periods beyond the range of carbon-14, is the potassium-argon (K-Ar) method. It does not rely on organic material but is applied to rocks that contain the radioactive isotope potassium-40. This unstable element breaks down into the gas argon much more slowly than C^{14} does into nitrogen: its half-life is 1.3 billion years. With sensitive reading instruments, dates earlier than about 200,000 B.P. can be determined. In a rock, the isotope breaks down and the resulting argon accumulates. If the rock is heated to a high temperature, the argon gas will escape; when the rock cools, the argon will begin accumulating again. In many rocks of volcanic origin, such as lavas or obsidian, the proportion of potassium-40 to argon can reveal when the rock was last heated and the argon began to build up. This dating technique has been used in dating many primate fossils. It has proven invaluable in placing many of the early hominid fossils in time, especially those from East Africa, where lavas and other material resulting from volcanic activity in the area can be used to date the geologic strata.[5]

It should be remembered that this technique is not performed directly on the fossils, but rather on the rocks that contain the datable material. Except for the unusual circumstance of a fossil found directly in a deposit of volcanic origin, a K-Ar date will derive from a level either above or below the fossil and thus will give a date that is somewhat younger or older than the fossil.

C^{14} and K-Ar are the two most valuable and widely used absolute dating techniques. Unfortunately, their time spans do not overlap, and there is a gap of over 100,000 years (between about 100,000 and 200,000 years) in which neither can provide dates. In order to overcome this problem, a number of other absolute dating procedures have been or are under development.

Amino-acid Racemization This technique may prove to be extremely important in dating fossil finds that fall between the time ranges of C^{14} and K-Ar, or those that cannot be otherwise placed in time because of complex geologic contexts or poor associations with animal bones. The amino-acid racemization method is performed directly on the fossil bones themselves. Every bone is made up of long strands of a protein called *collagen*, onto which the mineral, or inorganic, component of bone is arranged. Although collagen is a protein, and therefore organic, it is an extremely stable molecule and can remain in a fossil bone with relatively minor changes for a very long time; it has been found in fossil bones from the Paleozoic. One of the changes that collagen undergoes over time is the basis for its usefulness in dating. As we have seen in Chapter 2, proteins are made up of long chains of animo acids. Every amino acid has two forms of its chemical structure, the "normal" and its reversed, or mirror image, form. After an animal dies, the amino acids making up collagen gradually change from the normal to the mirror image; this process is called *racemization*. Amino acids racemize at different rates; some change quite rapidly, others very slowly. By examining the amino acids in the collagen of a fossil bone, and determining which have and which have not changed form, it is possible to date the bone to the time when the animal died.

There is a serious problem with this technique. Because racemization is a chemical change, temperature will affect the rate of change of amino acids to their mirror image forms; unless this can be controlled for, as in a cave deposit where temperature has been relatively constant, inconsistent dates can sometimes result.[6]

Other Absolute Methods There are a number of other absolute dating methods, less extensively used than C^{14} and K-Ar, including fission track, electron spin resonance, and uranium series. *Fission track dating* can be employed on minerals containing uranium traces, and it is based on the counting of the radiation damage tracks left in the mineral crystals. Fission track has a time range encompassing the entire Pleistocene. *Electron spin resonance* is currently in the experimental stage but promises to provide dates to about one million years ago when used on the calcium portion of bones, shell, and some rocks. *Uranium series* is based on the radioactive decay of uranium into almost a dozen isotopes that are found in a variety of rocks, shells, some bones, and ocean floor sediments. Although its time span covers virtually the entire last 1 million years, contamination of the material to be dated by environmental uranium is a serious limitation.

These dating techniques, along with others yet to be developed, when used together as part of a cross-checking system, promise to provide a firm basis for understanding the chronology of events in the hominid fossil record. Paleomagnetic reversals, though not in themselves a dating technique, can be used with absolute dating methods like K-Ar to gain knowledge of a particular fossil's place in time.

Relative Dating Before absolute dating was possible, geologic deposits and most archaeological sites were given relative ages based on the relationship of the deposit or site to other geologic contexts or to the associated bones; a find could then be said to be older than, younger than, or the same age as another. The relative time at which a geologic deposit was laid down might be identified by the strata above and below it. The stratum might be recognizable as one in a long sequence of geologic deposits laid down over eons. Placing the deposit within the sequence gave some idea of its relative position in time. Similarly, by identifying the fossil bones and relating them to other, closely related fossils found elsewhere, a relative age determination was possible.

Under these conditions, only a very approximate age can be worked out; errors in correlating geologic deposits over wide geographic areas and in cross-referencing fossil bones are common. It is extremely difficult, for example, to correlate the geologic traces of glacial activity in various parts of Europe; thus, two hominid fossils found in glacial deposits, one in eastern Europe and the other in western Europe, will be hard to relate to each other. Nevertheless, because many geologic deposits containing hominid fossil bones cannot be dated by any of the absolute dating methods, the geologic contexts as well as the faunal correlations retain great importance.

Identifying the Hominids

We know that sometime after the beginning of the Miocene, there was a series of speciations in an ancestral hominoid population and that eventually these led to the independent lines of the African and Asian pongids (chimpanzee, gorilla, and orang) and the hominids (see Figure 6.19 for a representation of this). Resolving when and how this occurred is one of the thorniest problems in human evolutionary studies. During the Miocene, as we have seen, there were several families of hominoid primates, including the Dryopithecidae and the Sivapithecidae. Members of the sivapithecine group, *Gigantopithecus* and *Sivapithecus,* share a number of features — such as thick enamel on the chewing surfaces of the teeth, short faces, and relatively large back chewing teeth in relation to the size of the front teeth — that are similar to features found in the early hominid, *Australopithecus,* and this has led to suggestions that the hominoid ancestry of the hominids was among the members of the Sivapithecidae family. However, at the present time, there are no definite fossil candidates to fill the role of hominoid ancestor to the hominids, and indeed, there is considerable debate about the possible time when the hominid family became a separately evolving line. Comparative biochemical data suggest a very late divergence between the lines that lead to the apes and to the hominids, perhaps 5 to 7 million years ago, while the fossil evidence of Miocene hominoid evolution suggests a date of greater than 10 million years.

Complicating the issue of hominid origins is the lack of agreement among anthropologists as to which morphological or behavioral features will identify hominids and separate them from pongids. In dealing with modern human beings, we recognize a host of features that are unique to humans: language, bipedalism, complex toolmaking, large brain, small nonprojecting canine teeth. We do not know, however, when each of these features appeared, so although they are useful in examining modern humans, it is difficult to use them in defining all hominids.

Bipedalism

Modern humans possess physical attributes in the upper trunk region — such as a broadened rib cage, and an outwardly directed and very mobile shoulder joint — which suggest that our ancestors at one time shared with the apes an ability to hang suspended by the arms. It is in the lower trunk and legs that the unique hominid form of locomotion is most marked. It has long been thought that the evolution of bipedalism in hominid evolution was directly related to the need to free the hands for toolmaking, but the fossil evidence (to be related in the next chapter) now indicates that early hominids were bipedal 1½ million years before definite signs of toolmaking turn up in the hominid record. It therefore seems likely that the ability to stand erect and walk on the back limbs is one of the earliest profound changes to have occurred in human evolution. Thus, evidence for the evolutionary appearance of bipedalism appears to be the best marker in identifying a hominid, and bipedalism itself the most definitive trait of the family Hominidae.

Culture

Another uniquely human characteristic often helpful in separating humans from other animals is culture. It has long been used in cultural anthropology to study behavior and habits in modern human societies, but because of the complexity of modern human behavior, there is considerable disagreement as to how one may define and describe culture. Some early anthropologists saw it as embodying all of a society's material goods: tools, pottery, dwellings, boats, clothing, weapons. Other anthropologists thought of culture as the way in which human groups are organized. Many anthropologists would agree with Ward Goodenough, who has defined culture as acceptable standards of behavior learned and understood by all members of a society. During socialization, the individual learns standards of behavior enabling him or her to interact successfully with other members of the society.[7] These behaviors include learning the spoken language, as well as all the subtle gestures and movements that communicate so much to members of the same group and nothing to outsiders. Technological skills and economic pursuits are included in the repertoire of acceptable behaviors: how to make and use a tool; what crops to farm and where to farm them. Modern human groups are complex in their social organization, and individuals have to master the governing rules and regulations as they learn to be members of their particular society: whom one may marry; which relatives one can go to for help; who one's close relatives are; which clan or club one is assigned to or born into. All these behaviors are internalized by the young as they grow to maturity in their society.

This definition of culture is troublesome when we are searching for uniquely hominid attributes, for it is very similar to our way of describing the nonhuman primates' behavior. The higher primates, too, must learn, while they grow up, standards of behavior appropriate to their social group. Human and nonhuman primate behaviors differ in complexity, but the nonhuman higher primates also have a form of cultural behavior.

One possible way of differentiating humans from other primates has been offered by Ralph Holloway.[8] Emphasizing the crucial relationships between the social group's standards of behavior and their translation into reality, Holloway focuses on the manufacture of a tool. Holloway stresses that a tool does not have to have a particular shape in order to be effective; rather, its final form is dictated by what the toolmaker thinks its right shape should be when beginning to make the tool. Consider the wood saws in Figure 8.2: they perform the same function, yet they look different. This is because the toolmaker, during socialization, has observed adults making and using tools and has learned what the society believes an appropriate tool should look like. This is the image the toolmaker has when beginning the fabrication of the implement. Thus toolmakers from different societies can produce tools of similar function yet different form. For Holloway, the human ability to translate this mental image of a tool onto the raw material represents the foundation of uniquely human behavior. In short, social rules governing what constitutes the shape of a tool are internalized by the toolmaker, and this standard of what is appropriate is then the image for the tool that will be made.

From the time of the first appearance of stone tools in the fossil record, about 2.5 million years B.P., there is a discernible pattern to the tools; they group into types, suggesting that they reflect the ability of the toolmaker to replicate what the society believes tools should look like. Holloway believes there were important changes in the cerebral cortex and cerebellum of the hominid brain to permit this kind of behavior, thus that this development can be considered uniquely hominid.

Toolmaking Although bipedalism precedes evidence for stone toolmaking in the fossil record by over 1 million years, it is possible that prior to the use of

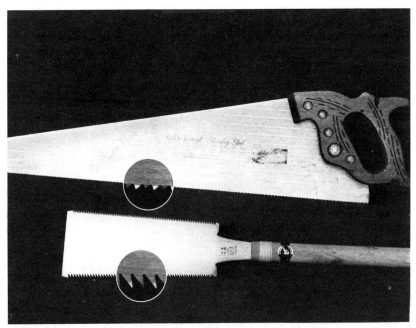

Figure 8.2. *Japanese (bottom) and American wood saws. The Japanese saw is designed to cut on the pull stroke, while the American saw cuts on the push stroke. Note the orientation of the teeth in each saw. Both tools will cut wood, but they differ in their design, reflecting the ways by which each society visualizes a wood-cutting tool.*

stone as a raw material, other, more perishable materials, such as wood, were employed in toolmaking. Jane Goodall's discoveries in Tanzania of chimpanzee toolmaking proclivities have shown that these close relatives are also capable of this behavior, but Holloway's views of the nature of toolmaking may represent a pattern unique to the hominids. Many authors point out that toolmaking is useful to the chimpanzee only in a few food-gathering activities, but it is of crucial value for the hominids; they suggest that the hominids depend on tools for their very survival. The origin of the hominids may lie in the shift from the chimpanzee pattern of behavior in part-time toolmaking to the later hominid pattern of full dependence on toolmaking. We shall present a hypothetical reconstruction of this shift.

For a new line to evolve, there must first be reproductive isolation. The first step in the divergence of the hominids from their apelike ancestors, then, was the prevention of interbreeding between populations. This isolation could have been realized either by a geographic barrier between the two populations, such as a river or mountain range, or simply by distance. Because the living apes are adapted to the forest or its fringe, the common ancestors of both apes and humans might have been forest

Hominid Origins: Some Hypotheses

Tools and Adaptation

forms. During the early Miocene, changes in climate appear to have led to a shrinkage of the extensive East African forests, with an increase of mosaic and open country habitats intervening between the now limited forested areas. Populations of these ancestral apes would have been isolated in different forested areas, with the result that interbreeding would be prevented even though the distance between the groups was not great. If, in the now-isolated population that was to lead to the hominids, the usual foods were harder to find, perhaps because of changes in climate, toolmaking might have become more important as a way of gathering new food resources. Toolmaking, until then of minor importance, would now be vital to the groups' adaptation. There is not much difference between the termiting stick used by modern chimpanzees in getting at termites (see page 255) and the digging stick, a longer, more robust, wooden stick that many modern human groups still use to dig up eatable tubers, roots, small burrowing animals, insects, and insect grubs. If this change in the behavioral emphasis occurred and was successful, natural selection would modify the physical features of the population to use the behavior more suitably. Thus, one hypothesis for the origin of the hominids involves a shift in the food-gathering behavior of an ancestral ape population to one based on tools.[9] The proposal seems reasonable enough, but there is little definite evidence to support it. Furthermore, no one knows how much like the modern chimpanzee this ancestral ape population was; modern chimps may have changed as much as the hominids have in the millions of years since the human and ape lines diverged.

A Diet of Seeds   Another suggestion for hominid origins is offered by Clifford Jolly.[10] He is impressed by the morphological resemblances, especially in dentition, between early hominid fossils and the gelada, the baboonlike terrestrial monkey of the Ethiopian highlands. The geladas feed on small objects, such as grass, tubers, and seeds. As an adaptation to this kind of feeding, the geladas have hands with great manipulative ability. Jolly suggests that the hominids originated as small-object feeders, and that this basic adaptation opened the way for the later development of toolmaking and for other hominid morphological and behavioral traits. In this view, tools would have little to do with the origin of the hominids.

Hunting   One of the later complexes Jolly thinks evolved from an early seed-eating adaptation is hunting. Many feel that hunting is one of the hominid's most important features and that it deeply influenced human evolution. Raymond Dart and, later, the dramatist Robert Ardrey, in his book, *African Genesis,* have suggested a "predatory transition between ape and man"; the hominids began as carnivorous apes, and the earliest tools were tools of a very select form — weapons. Their suggestions were made before Goodall and others demonstrated that chimpanzees, too, hunt other animals. How important hunting was to the earliest hominids is far from settled.

Another hypothesis concerning hominid origins focuses on the importance of the evolution of bipedalism. A number of anthropologists, including G. H. R. von Koenigswald, Russell Tuttle, and J. T. Robinson, suggest that the need of an increasingly savanna-adapted primate for a more efficient type of locomotion was the initial impetus for the appearance of the hominids. In their view, bipedalism evolved as an adaptation to savanna life, and from this, later hominid traits, such as tool use, followed.[11]

The Savanna and Bipedalism

Finally, Owen Lovejoy views hominid beginnings as taking place not on the savanna, but in the forest. Lovejoy believes that a pattern of decreased time between births was crucial to hominid development because it meant that females spent more time with their dependent offspring. As a result the males were required to forage for food for their mates. This behavior in turn necessitated the development of a pattern of locomotion — bipedalism — that would permit males to carry food back to the females.[12]

A Male Foraging Model

These different views of hominid origins are based on the varieties of habitats and food resources that are thought to have influenced the earliest hominids' pattern of adaptation. The major difficulty, as Jane Lancaster has pointed out, is that the forms representing the evolutionary transition from an ancestral ape population to the earliest hominids are all extinct, and so are their life ways. It is probable that these earliest hominids were unique in many ways, which leaves us with a serious practical problem: lacking fossil evidence, what living animals, and what parts of their total adaptations, are we to use as a model in reconstructing the adaptive patterns of the earliest hominids? Are we to consider the chimpanzee, whom many believe to be our closest living relative, as the best approximation of what the earliest hominids were like? Or, if the suggestions of Jeffery Schwartz are correct, ought we to substitute the orangutan as our closest living relative? Or, if the needs of a savanna adaptation were most important to the earliest hominids, perhaps the savanna baboons of the genus *Papio* are the most appropriate model of hominid origins. Or maybe the gelada represents a better model, as Jolly suggests. It has also been suggested that because some aspects of hominid social behavior are similar to that of the social carnivores, such as wolves and African hunting dogs, the hominids' origin and early evolution ought to be viewed in terms of cooperative hunting.

Also to be considered is the adaptation of living humans who do not practice agriculture, the gatherer/hunters, such as the *San* of southern Africa. It is interesting to note that both chimpanzees and the gatherer/hunters that have been studied seem able to exploit a number of different environments by eating a great variety of plant and animal foods.

Seen in the context of human evolution, this similarity between chimpanzees and human gatherer/hunters would suggest that the earliest hominids moved through a variety of different habitats in a yearly round, and ate a wide variety of seasonally available plant foods, but also some animal foods, including insects and small vertebrates like amphibians, reptiles, birds, and small mammals.

Major Trends in Hominid Evolution

Future discoveries may invalidate all of these hypotheses, and another explanation, not yet proposed, may well fit the new facts more closely. Whatever the ultimate solution to the problem of hominid origins, examination of the known fossil evidence for human evolution has revealed a number of morphological and behavioral trends. The major changes in physical appearance from the earliest hominids to living humans are the development of bipedalism, a decrease in size of the face and teeth, and an increase in size of the brain. These changes did not come all at the same time or proceed at the same rate. They are general trends in hominid biological history, spread over millions of years.

Behavioral Changes

These anatomical changes are associated with modifications in behavior. To reconstruct the behavior of our ancestors, we use the fossil bones themselves and the archaeologist's analyses of the traces that past human activity has left. Usually, the further back in time we travel, the less we find. There are two reasons for this. The recent archaeological record is well supplied with the evidence of our hominid ancestor's complex behaviors, including tools made of stone, bone, wood, and other material (Figure 8.3); bits of skin clothing; evidence of dwellings; and ornaments. Burials yield clues to ideological and social systems; animal bones, plant pollen, and other food debris provide data for reconstructing economic patterns. Further back, many of these remains have disintegrated without leaving the slightest trace. The only evidence of the behavior of our ancestors that far back are items hardy enough to survive, such as stone tools and animal bones. In addition, the behavioral abilities of our more remote hominid ancestors were much more limited so less is left for us to study. This leaves us with sometimes difficult decisions to make regarding the significance of the lack of archaeological evidence: were the tools, and other traces of behavioral activities, present but destroyed? Or is the lack of any tools or other clear indication of complex behavior a sign that early hominids were incapable of these activities? For example, although a rich sample of hominid fossil bones has been found in Middle Pleistocene deposits on the island of Java, in Indonesia, no stone tools have been found. Recent interpretations of this evidence (or lack of it) have been directed toward the idea that these peoples were using other raw materials for their tools and weapons, such as easily available and easily worked bamboo.

The archaeological record of hominid activity shows a pattern of increasing complexity and sophistication over time. However, this trend

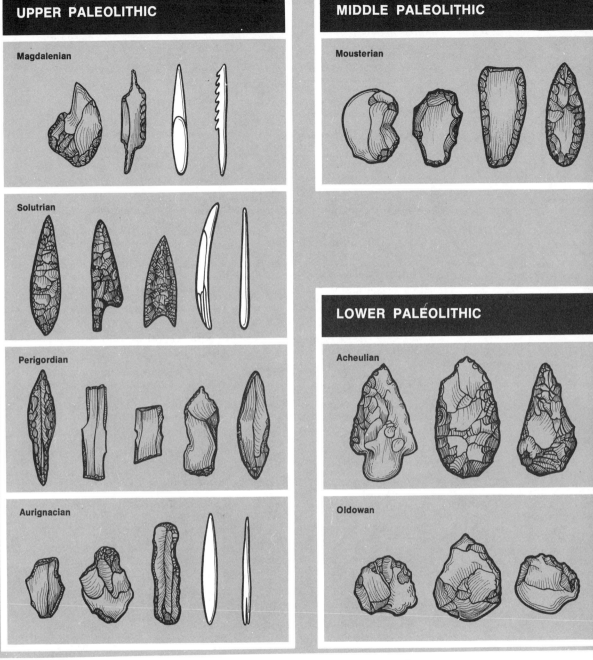

Figure 8.3. *The evolution of stone and bone tools. These drawings (bone artifacts are in white) show the general changes that occurred in tool technology during hominid evolution. Many — but not all — of the same styles of tools, however, are found in more than one culture and time period.*

begins with a very long period at the start when almost no change can be recognized. Later the tempo of increasing complexity speeds up so that by the development of agriculture some 10,000 years ago, cultural change was occurring at a rate many times swifter than at the beginning of the archaeological record some 2.5 million years ago.[13]

This pattern is clearly reflected in the stone tool technology. The earliest evidence is the cobble tools of the australopithecines (Oldowan), which are crude and have few marks of delicate workmanship (Figure 8.3). These Oldowan tools appear first about 2.5 million years ago, and they seem to remain more or less similar for over a million years. At about 1.5 million years ago, the hand axe traditions (Acheulian) evolve, and they exhibit better-made tools in greater variety, suggesting specialization for individual tasks. Both of these early tool industries are known as Lower Paleolithic (paleo = old; lithic = stone: old stone age), and can be contrasted with later stone tool traditions of the Middle and Upper Paleolithic, which show the makers' greater skill and the growing complexity of the artifacts. Middle Paleolithic industries, like the Mousterian of Europe and the Middle East, first appear after about 125,000 years ago, and these industries are in turn replaced by the more complex and finely made Upper Paleolithic industries about 30,000–40,000 years ago.

Biological and Cultural Changes

The major changes in the brain, face, teeth, and locomotion in hominid physical evolution are closely interrelated with changes in behavior. Whatever the reason for its initial development, bipedalism frees the hands for using tools and other implements. Perhaps the face and teeth became smaller as tools took over tasks once performed by the teeth, such as holding objects. It is more likely, however, that the interrelationships are far more complex; we are only now beginning to understand the complicated patterns of interaction between different biological systems in a single individual. The hints we currently possess suggest that changes in the size of the brain, for example, which lead to modification. in the shape of the braincase, influence the positioning of the face in relation to the braincase, and this in turn may end up modifying the shape and size of the dental arch, leaving less room for the teeth. The ultimate result of all this is that an increase in the size of the brain may also lead to reduction in the size of the teeth, but through a complex series of steps.

The increasing size of the brain can be related to changes in behavior. If successful behavior is one of the keys to a successful adaptation, and if in the hominids a successful adaptation is based on the use of tools, individuals who are better able to make and use tools will be selected for. In a variable population, individuals whose nervous system gives them a stronger basis for this behavior would be better able to survive and reproduce; evolution would select for more complex brains. The changes in the brain would include increasing size and complexity of the motor cortex and other parts of the cerebrum, and expansion of the cerebellum. Thus, the hominid brain's organization and complexity would eventually shift toward providing better ability in making and using tools. The shift would also feed back into the behavior, providing for still more complex activities. Once this system began operating, the two parts, brain and behavior, would reinforce each other, providing the impetus for further change.

We may treat the physical and behavioral complexes as separate, but very clearly the components are strongly entwined. As one system evolves it directly affects the others; for this reason, it is not easy to examine any one system, physical or behavioral, without reference to the others.

Summary

This chapter deals with a number of general issues related to the study of the evolution of the family Hominidae, modern humans and our immediate direct ancestors. Like all animals, the hominids have evolved through time via the mechanisms of natural selection, in response to the demands of the environment. The direct evidence for hominid evolution, the fossil bones and teeth, has been divided into two genera: *Australopithecus,* all of whose members are now extinct; and one genus, *Homo,* of which modern humans are the living representatives.

Although there are difficulties in precisely defining the family Hominidae, the fossil evidence now suggests that one of the earliest of the important evolutionary changes, the development of bipedalism, is the most appropriate way of defining the family.

Various methods have been developed to date hominid evolution. An important development is the use of techniques measuring the decay of radioactive deposits and organic remains. The carbon-14 and potassium-argon methods allow absolute dating. Where these, and other absolute dating techniques cannot be used, relative dating provides a rough approximation of the fossil's age by determining the relative position of the site or the remains in the context of geologic strata.

Hominid evolution has been dated to the Miocene, Pliocene, Pleistocene, and Holocene epochs. The most important stages occurred in the Old World, probably beginning in the Miocene epoch. Recent studies of continental drift suggest that the African and Eurasian continents became joined at the beginning of this epoch. The geologic changes that ensued perhaps caused climatic changes that resulted in the development of a more open, less forested environment in East Africa. Some researchers believe that the hominids originated in such open country, although this is merely an educated guess since no fossil evidence of the earliest hominids has been found. The early phases of hominid evolution — when biological changes such as bipedalism developed — occurred in the temperate zones of the Old World, probably in Africa. By the time hominids first appear in the northern hemisphere of the Old World, their biological development was sufficiently advanced to permit cultural adaptations to severe climatic conditions.

In the course of hominid evolution, a number of major morphological and behavioral changes have occurred. These changes did not all happen at once, nor did they proceed at the same rate; they include evolution of bipedalism, expansion of the brain, and decrease in the size of face and teeth. An associated behavioral change is the increase in cultural complexity as seen in the stone tool industries and other archaeological remains. These biological and behavioral trends are probably interrelated: changes in one have influenced others.

Thus, we can now discern the general outline of hominid evolution. Anthropologists have not agreed on when these behavioral and physical trends began; as we shall see in the next chapter, estimates range from 15 or more million years B.P. to 5 to 7 million years B.P. Nor is there any general agreement as to the factors responsible for the origin of the hominid family: changes in the environment, in the diet, or the beginning of tool or weaponmaking. Only the discovery of new fossil evidence may eventually solve these problems. Nevertheless, we do know a great deal about hominid evolution through our analysis of the fossil material already discovered, and this material will form the topic of discussion in the following two chapters.

Chapter 9

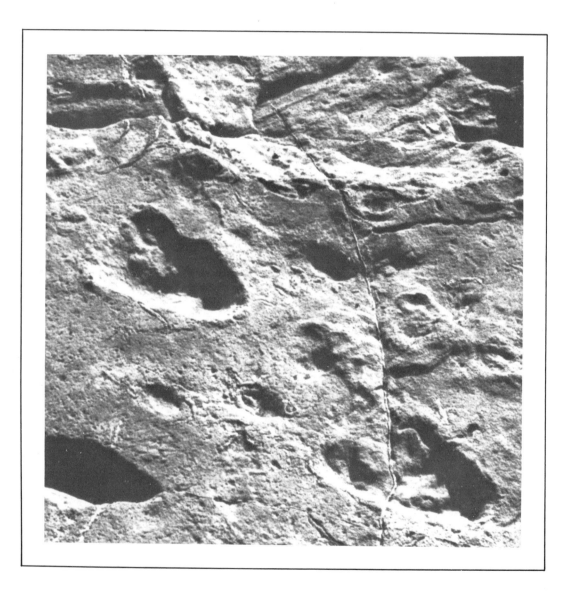

Human Evolution I: The Early Hominids

The fossil specimens discussed in this and the following chapter were unearthed in many areas of the world and outline the general path that our hominid ancestors followed over the past few million years.

As we have seen in earlier chapters, there continues to be much debate about the exact time of the origin of the hominid family, and which fossils are its earliest true representatives. Biochemical evidence suggests that the hominids did not become a separately evolving group until about 5 to 8 million years ago. If we accept this date, no hominids could have been around earlier and our presently known fossil evidence just about reaches back to the beginnings of our line. Vincent Sarich, whose work on comparative albumin proteins led to this date, has remarked "That one no longer has the option of considering a fossil specimen older than about 8 million years as a hominid, no matter what it looks like."[1]* On the other hand, many paleontologists view the Miocene hominoid family Sivapithecidae as sharing important dental and jaw features with the early hominids: smaller, less jutting faces, thick layers of enamel on the molar teeth, and relatively large molar teeth. Out of the sivapith group may have evolved the earliest members of the hominid family, perhaps as early as 15 million years ago. We do not yet have fossil evidence documenting this connection of the hominids with the sivapiths, but it is often suggested that the sivapiths are representative of the general group from whom the direct hominid ancestor sprang.

Only the discovery of additional fossil material can resolve the issue of the timing of hominid origins. At the present time, the fossil evidence of the hominids begins at about 4 million years, with the *australopithecines*.

The Beginning of the Hominid Line

Australopithecine fossils dated from the end of the Miocene, the Pliocene, and from the early part of the Pleistocene have been found at sites scattered throughout South and East Africa (Figure 9.1).

Australopithecines in South Africa

*See page 569 for notes to Chapter 9.

285

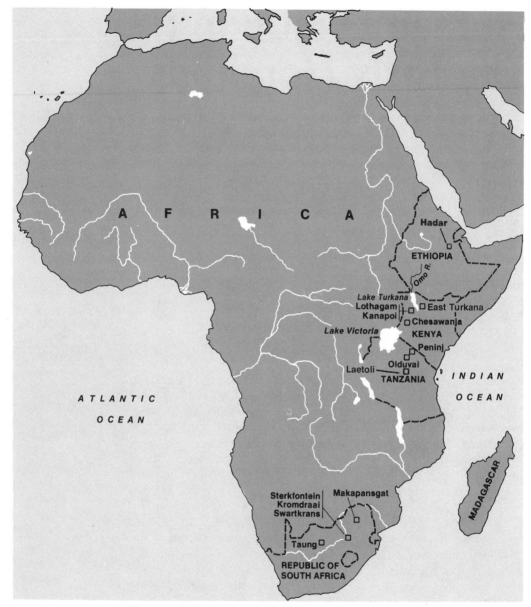

Figure 9.1. Major australopithecine sites.

The Taung Fossil: In 1924, Raymond Dart, a young South African anatomy professor, was
Australopithecus given some fossil bones from a limestone quarry at Taung in the Cape
Africanus Province (Figure 9.2). It was the skull of a young primate child, with the
first permanent molars just erupted (in modern human children this would
occur at about six years of age). Its molar teeth were larger than modern
molars, but the milk canines were small and nonprojecting, the whole
dentition had a human shape, and the dental arch was human. Only the

size of the brain, comparable to that of a chimpanzee, distinguished it from other hominids. Since the brain of a fossil has long since disintegrated, its measurement is based either on the volume (expressed in milliliters, or ml.; for comparison: 1,000 ml = 1 liter = 1.1 quarts) of the inside of the skull, or (as with the Taung child) on that of a fossilized cast of the inside of the braincase. Modern human brains vary greatly in size, from about 1,000 to more than 2,000 ml; most, however, are between 1,350 and 1,450 ml. Chimpanzee brains are usually between 350 and 450 ml, and gorillas about 500 to 600 ml.

The Taung child's brain is about 440 ml. Professor Dart decided it may have been a hominid or perhaps an intermediate step between the apes and humans, gave it a scientific name, and described it in the journal *Nature* in 1925.[2] Dart called his creature *Australopithecus africanus,* or the southern ape of Africa. Most of Dart's professional colleagues disagreed vehemently, believing instead that the Taung child was a young anthropoid ape. At the time, they had valid reasons, one of them being the very small sample—the remains of one individual. But there were other reasons for not classifying *Australopithecus* as a hominid or even

Figure 9.2. *A drawing of the Taung fossil, the first australopithecine specimen found (four-fifths actual size; right side reversed). The shaded area at the back of the skull delineates the size of the braincase, which can be accurately restored from the cast of the inside of the braincase also found with the fossil.*

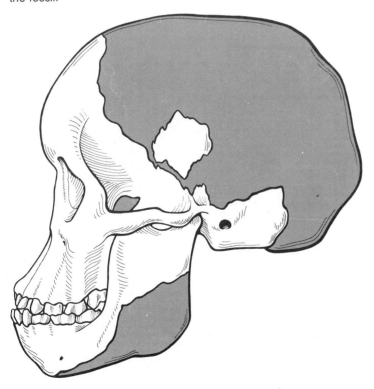

a near-hominid. It was believed that the human line had originated in Asia, and not much attention was paid to Africa. Darwin had suggested in *The Descent of Man* (1871) that Africa was the hominid homeland, mainly because the chimpanzee and the gorilla, our closest living relatives, were natives there; but by 1924 emphasis had shifted from Africa to Asia. Another reason was that a human child and a young chimpanzee look more alike than an adult chimpanzee and an adult human. Many of the features that strongly distinguish chimpanzees from modern humans only develop during the adolescent growth spurt. The Taung fossil was that of a young child; Dart's critics suggested that had it grown to maturity, it would have developed clearly apelike features.

The Piltdown Hoax

Perhaps the most important objection to considering *Australopithecus* a hominid was the existence of known fossils whose morphological characteristics contradicted those of the Taung child. *Australopithecus*'s jaws and teeth were hominid-like, but its brain was the size of an ape's. Fossils of two individuals had been found in a gravel deposit near the river Thames in Piltdown, Kent County, England, between 1912 and 1915. The features they showed were exactly the reverse: the Piltdown fragments had a brain as big as that of a modern human being, but the jaws

Figure 9.3. *Excavation at the Piltdown site. Charles Dawson, the most likely perpetrator of the Piltdown hoax, is seen on the left, holding the screen, while Sir Arthur Smith-Woodward searches for more of the Piltdown "fossils." The workman on the right stands in the pit where Dawson said the original "fossils" were found.*

and teeth were those of an ape. The Piltdown story is one of the more interesting, not to say embarrassing, stories in the hundred-year search for the remains of human ancestors.

In 1912 at a meeting of the Royal Geological Society an amateur naturalist named Charles Dawson announced he had discovered parts of a darkly patined skull and lower jaw, along with flint tools and worked animal bones, in early Pleistocene deposits (Figure 9.3). The fossils were given the scientific name "*Eoanthropus* dawsoni" (eo = dawn: Dawson's dawn man). Their physical features are remarkable from our perspective today, but from the point of view of early twentieth-century evolutionary theory there was nothing strange about them. Here was a creature that had a modern human braincase, with about the same cranial capacity, 1,450 ml; yet its lower jaw could not be distinguished from those of the living apes except by the modern human wear patterns on the teeth (Figure 9.4). The lower canine tooth was missing and so was the whole facial portion of the skull. One of the outstanding paleontologists of the time, Sir Arthur Smith-Woodward, tried to reconstruct the important missing canine, building from the size and appearance of the

Figure 9.4. *Side view of the fraudulent Piltdown skull; the dark areas of the skull are the preserved parts, along with the back portion of the lower jaw. Notice that the knob which attaches the lower jaw to the skull was not found, but was reconstructed for this model. (The dotted lines show the break between the part of the jaw that was "found" and the restored part.) The skull mirrored early views of hominid evolution, possessing a modern human braincase and the large jaws and projecting canine teeth of an ape.*

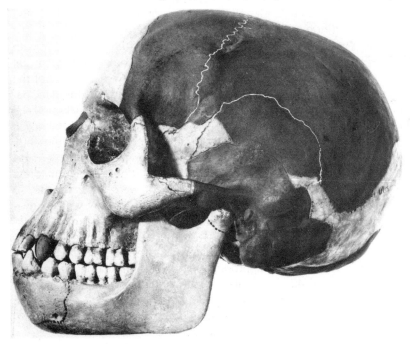

preserved canine tooth socket. His carved chalk model, similar to the canines of chimpanzees, was exhibited at another meeting of the Geological Society. Several months later, further excavation in the Piltdown gravels uncovered the missing canine tooth, almost an exact duplicate of the model Smith-Woodward had carved. No one suspected a connection between the shape of the Piltdown canine and the model Sir Arthur had made.

Among the pieces of the skull, apart from the other cranial pieces, were the nasal bones, extremely thin bones that cover the upper part of the nasal aperture. Having apparently lain in a deposit of gravel for hundreds of thousands of years, they were in perfect condition. Again, no suspicions were aroused. In 1915, pieces of another individual, Piltdown II, were discovered at a gravel pit some distance from the first.

The remains, it turned out, were a carefully assembled fraud, perpetrated with full knowledge of the theories and expectations of early twentieth-century evolutionary scientists. At that time it was believed that the enlarged human brain had evolved before the teeth and jaws. A very early hominid, then, should have a modern-human-sized brain and ape-sized dentition; the Piltdown fossils had just that. Later a great number of authentic hominid fossils proved that human evolution had not taken that route. Even at the time of discovery some scientists did not believe that the skull, so apparently human, and the jaw, totally apelike, had ever been together in one animal. An American doubter, Geritt Miller, curator of mammals at the Smithsonian Institution in Washington, D.C., was struck by the incongruity of the two pieces. Miller proposed that the jaw belonged to an extinct chimpanzee, even though no fossil ape has ever been found in England, and the chances of one being found cheek-by-jowl with a hominid fossil would have to be close to nil.

It was not until 1953 that the Piltdown remains were looked at with any suspicion of a deliberate hoax. They had become an enigma that could no longer be shoved aside. A careful look revealed traces of the forger's hand. A small hole drilled in the jaw showed that the dark patina was only on the surface; the drill came up with fresh bone. The skull seems to be that of a Roman age British burial, probably chosen for its unusually thick cranial bones, which helped convince the early investigators of its great antiquity; the jaw belonged to a modern orangutan. The perpetrator of the fraud knew a great deal about anatomy: the jaw would not articulate with the skull if it were left complete, so the articulating knobs or condyles at the back of the jaw were conveniently broken off; the large ape canines would prevent the rotary chewing characteristic of modern humans, so the teeth were filed down to simulate a human wear pattern. The site was shrewdly salted with these "human fossils," and with appropriate worked animal bones, unworked animal bones, and flint tools, all probably authentic artifacts except for a club made from an elephant bone. Finally the pieces were stained to give them the dark color typical of some fossil material. J. S. Weiner recounts the detective work in *The Piltdown Forgery*. Although in the years since its unmasking, practically every scientist who was ever associated in any way with the Piltdown material has been identified by someone as the guilty party, most of the available evidence points to the original discoverer, Charles Dawson, as the most likely culprit.[3] Dawson died in 1916, well before the truth came out. Yet in 1925, Piltdown was still a recognized member of the hominid lineage and proved a stumbling block to the acceptance of *Australopithecus africanus*.

Sterkfontein One man not deterred by Piltdown, and convinced that Dart's ideas were correct, was Robert Broom. Born in Scotland, trained as a physician, Broom had lived in Australia prior to his arrival in South Africa. His earlier paleontological research had resulted in the discovery of the therapsids, the mammal-like reptiles that helped bridge the evolutionary gap between the reptiles and the mammals. Broom was convinced that more fossils, especially those of adults, were needed to bolster Dart's claims for the hominid status of *Australopithecus*. Helped by some of Dart's students, he began looking into limestone quarrying sites in and around Pretoria. On a visit to the Sterkfontein Valley, thirty miles west of Johannesburg in the Transvaal, he asked the quarry manager if he ever saw fossils, and he was handed some remarkable pieces, several of which he saw immediately might be hominids. Back at the Transvaal Museum in Pretoria, where he worked, Broom felt confident he had discovered adult individuals of an extinct hominid similar to Dart's *Australopithecus africanus*. Broom eventually named his find *"Plesianthropus transvaalensis"* (near-man of the Transvaal) because he believed the fossils from Sterkfontein were different enough to be put into a new genus. It was recognized later that the Sterkfontein fossils, as well as those from another site in the northern Transvaal, Makapansgat, were much like the child from Taung and all are now called *Australopithecus africanus*.

Kromdraai and Swartkrans About a kilometer from the Sterkfontein site, also in the Sterkfontein Valley, Broom discovered another hominid fossil deposit in 1937. This site was Kromdraai, situated atop a small hill east of the limestone quarry of Sterkfontein; here Broom found fossils with interesting differences from the fossils now called *Australopithecus africanus*. The Kromdraai fossils had bigger molars and premolars than *Australopithecus africanus*, as well as more robust faces and chewing muscles. Broom felt justified in naming these finds *"Paranthropus robustus"* (robust near-man). In 1948, on the other side of the Sterkfontein Valley, quarrying in a small hill on the Swartkrans farm uncovered a third australopithecine fossil site. The finds from Swartkrans are much like those from Kromdraai, and have been placed in *Paranthropus*. Many, but not all anthropologists today would place the *Paranthropus* fossils in the genus *Australopithecus*, but retained in a separate species: *A. robustus*.

Makapansgat Dart began work in 1948 at the last of the South African early hominid sites, about 320 kilometers north of Johannesburg, in a valley with a historic past. In the mid-nineteenth century, when the Boers, European settlers of Dutch descent, were moving into the Transvaal, they fought a number of wars with the Bantu-speaking peoples of southern Africa for control of the land. In one skirmish a large group of Bantu were caught in a valley, taking refuge in a large cave from which few escaped alive. The valley was named for the Bantu chieftain who perished with his people: Makapan. The Makapansgat (*gat* = Afrikaans "valley": Makapan valley) hominids were found not in that cave, but in another in the valley where limestone was being quarried. The five South African sites of Sterkfontein, Kromdraai, Swartkrans, Makapansgat, and Taung have yielded 130 to 150 hominids.

The South African sites Taung, Sterkfontein, and Makapansgat, where *Australopithecus africanus* have been discovered, and Kromdraai and Swartkrans, where *Australopithecus robustus* have been found, are geologically similar (Figure 9.5). The sites are the remains of caverns deep in the limestone hills. The hominids never lived in these caves, but perhaps on the surface of the hills, which have long since eroded away. The caverns were connected with the surface by vertical shafts; animal bones, hominid bones, and other debris accumulating on the surface were swept down the shaft and became incorporated into the deposit. The geologic history of these sites is somewhat more complicated because it now seems likely that during their long history, these sites may have had different vertical shafts connecting them with the surface at different times. This means that each cave had material added to the deposit a number of times; at two of the sites, Sterkfontein and Swartkrans, there is evidence in upper and therefore presumably later cave fillings of a hominid more advanced than *Australopithecus*.

At the present time, it is not possible to use absolute dating methods to determine the precise age of these deposits. However, analysis of animal bones found with the hominid fossils suggests that the two *A. africanus* sites of Sterkfontein and Makapansgat are earlier than the *A. robustus* sites of Kromdraai and Swartkrans, with Makapansgat the earliest at 3 or more million years B.P., Sterkfontein somewhat later, and Kromdraai and Swartkrans perhaps a million or more years later than Makapansgat.

Australopithecines in East Africa

Olduvai Gorge, Tanzania

The dramatist Robert Ardrey, deeply interested in early hominid studies, talked about the three "wild men of Africa" who were responsible for finding much of the early hominid fossil material. These men had great measures of imagination and a strong fascination with our early ancestors. Dart and Broom are two of these. The third was Louis S. B. Leakey,

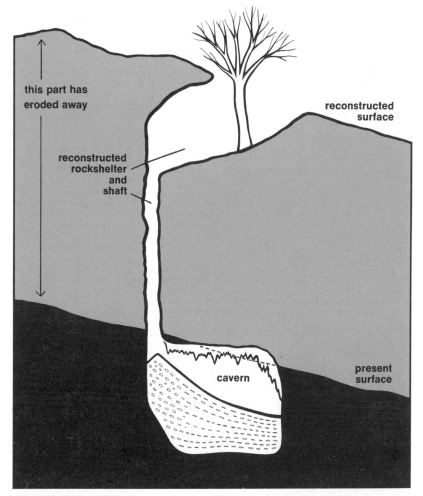

Figure 9.5. *Reconstruction of the Swartkrans site. Most australopithecine fossils found in South Africa accumulated in caverns. At Swartkrans there was apparently a shaft from the cavern to the surface, down which dirt, bones, and other matter tumbled and eventually became consolidated with limestone to become the rock-hard, fossil-bearing matrix called* breccia. *At the surface, there may have been a crevice or a depression in which trees would probably be found. This location offered trees shelter from the wind of the open grassland. This situation may provide a clue to why many bones entered the shaft to the cavern: some predators, such as leopards, eat their prey in trees to escape scavengers, and leftover bones could drop into the crevice and down the shaft. Possibly some australopithecine remains were deposited in this way. Erosion of the hillside occurred after the cavern filled.*

who concentrated on East Africa. Born in Kenya of missionary parents, Leakey went to school at Cambridge, England, and in the late 1920s returned to Kenya to begin a long and renowned career. With his wife, Mary, he explored many areas in East Africa, discovering fossils of the

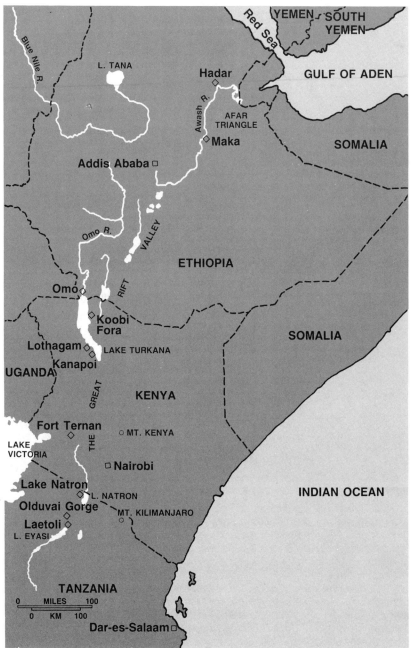

Figure 9.6. *The distribution of early hominid sites in East Africa, showing their locations in relation to the Rift Valley System.* p.264

Miocene higher primate, *Proconsul,* at sites on the shores and islands of Lake Victoria. They also explored one of the more interesting geologic formations in East Africa: Olduvai Gorge, located in northern Tanzania (Figure 9.6).

In 1959, Mary Leakey discovered major parts of a hominid skull in a deposit deep in the gorge, at a site called FLK (Frida Leakey Korongo, named after a relative; *korongo* is Swahili for gully). The skull, when excavated and cleaned, looked very much like the *Australopithecus robustus* specimens Broom had collected from Kromdraai and Swartkrans in South Africa, but possessed back teeth and a face even larger than these forms (Figure 9.7). Louis Leakey decided the fossil was different enough for him to establish a new taxonomic category: "*Zinjanthropus boisei*" (*Zinj* = an old Arabic word for East Africa; *boisei* commemorated the Boise Fund, which provided funds for Leakey's scientific work). Today, the "Zinj" fossil is usually placed in *Australopithecus*, but retains the species name, becoming *A. boisei.*[4]

After this discovery, the Leakeys uncovered many hominid fossils at Olduvai, at different sites up and down the gorge. Some of these hominid fossils, including parts of upper and lower jaws, almost complete skulls, and postcranial bones, seemed to possess features, such as smaller teeth and larger brains, that were more advanced than either the "Zinj" fossil or the South African hominids. These fossils were given the name *Homo habilis*, placed in the same genus as modern humans.[5]

Geologically, Olduvai Gorge is an erosion gully. Since the time when the early hominids lived in the area, there has been a slow accumulation of material so that the lower layers containing the hominid fossils have been covered by several hundred feet of rock. Without erosion of the material above, there would be no way of reaching the fossils or

Figure 9.7. *Casts of the face of* Australopithecus robustus *from Swartkrans (right) and* A. boisei *(Zinj) from Olduvai (left). Note that both possess the robust chewing muscle attachment areas of the top and sides of the skull, but that the East African specimen has a much larger facial region.*

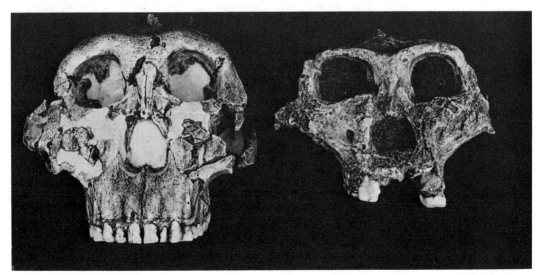

even knowing they were there. Thus, the development of the gorge has exposed the ancient fossil-bearing strata. The stratigraphy, or layers, through which the gorge cut is divided into four major beds, from I up through II, III, and IV, with several later beds on top (Table 9.1). Because of past volcanic activity, some of the rocks in Olduvai Gorge can be dated by the potassium-argon (K-Ar) process. The bottom of Bed I is dated to a little more than 1.8 million years ago; the change from Bed I to Bed II occurred about 1.7 million years ago. The "Zinj" fossil (*Australopithecus boisei*) was found in Bed I, and dated to about 1.75 million years B.P., but other "Zinj"-like fossils, and the *Homo habilis* fossils, have been found scattered from the bottom of Bed I to the middle of Bed II.

Omo River Basin, Ethiopia   At sites along the Omo River, which flows southward through southern Ethiopia, a large number of hominid fossils, mostly teeth but also a few jaws and other bones, have been found in geologic contexts that have been particularly well dated by potassium-argon (K-Ar) and confirmed by paleomagnetic determinations. The leaders of the expedition, F. C.

Table 9.1. Highly schematic diagram of Olduvai Gorge and the fossils discovered there.
After the time of Upper Bed I, volcanism in the Olduvai Gorge area ceased and K-Ar cannot be employed. The Bed IV date is extrapolated from a paleomagnetic reversal.

Date (B.P.)	Geological beds	Hominid fossils	
	Later beds	Homo sapiens	
c.400,000–500,000	Bed IV	Homo erectus	
	Bed III	Homo erectus	
	Bed II (Upper)	Homo erectus	
c.1,700,000	Bed II (Lower)	Homo habilis	
		Homo habilis	Australopithecus boisei
	Bed I	Homo habilis	Australopithecus boisei
c.1,800,000		Homo habilis	Australopithecus boisei

Howell and Yves Coppens, have reported at Omo forms similar to the South African *Australopithecus africanus* from contexts between 2 and 3 million years B.P.; forms like *Australopithecus boisei* first appear in the sequence about 2 million years B.P. These dates seem to confirm the South African evidence that *A. africanus* appeared earlier than its more robust relatives *A. robustus* and *A. boisei.*[6] The Omo River flows into Lake Turkana on the Ethiopia-Kenya border; here, along the eastern shores of the lake, are hominid fossil sites of incredible richness (Figure 9.8).

East Turkana, Northern Kenya

Richard Leakey, son of Louis and Mary, had been hunting fossils along the Omo River when on a flight back to Nairobi, Kenya, he passed over the eastern shores of Lake Turkana (then known as Lake Rudolf) and noticed that this wind-eroded and mostly desolate place might prove to be a rich fossil area. In 1968 he visited the area and quickly found a number of animal fossils, and soon after, some hominids. Since that time, Richard Leakey and his associates have discovered hominid fossils representing well over a hundred individuals.[7] The fossil-bearing locales are numerous, and contain many hominid skulls, jaws, and skeletal bones. Volcanic activity has resulted in the presence of rocks in the East Turkana deposits that can be dated by the potassium-argon (K-Ar) process, but these volcanic ashes were laid down in exceedingly complex ways, requiring very careful preparation of the rock samples to be dated if consistent dates are to result. A small number of fossils date to a period earlier than 3 million years B.P., but the vast majority of hominid fossil bones from the East Turkana sites are dated between about 2 and about 1.4 million years B.P. The East Turkana hominids possess a wide variety of features, some with attributes similar to *A. boisei,* a few suggesting *A. africanus,* several undoubtedly members of the genus *Homo,* and others whose features are very difficult to assign to one or another category. We will consider in detail the morphological features of all these forms after reviewing the fossil sites themselves.

Hadar, Ethiopia

At Hadar, in the Afar region of north-central Ethiopia, 1,600 kilometers north of Lake Turkana, a joint French-American expedition, headed by Donald Johanson and Maurice Taieb, has been looking for fossils since 1972. Like the locales of East Turkana, Hadar is an extremely rich fossil area, and many hominid and animal fossil bones have been collected, including the most complete early hominid skeleton yet found: approximately 40 percent of the bones were preserved (Figure 9.9). Potassium-argon dating has placed the hominid levels between 2.9 and more than 3.2 million years B.P. The hominid bones from Hadar seem to differ in a number of ways from the others we have so far described; their closest affinities appear to lie with the fossils discovered in Tanzania, at the site of Laetoli.[8]

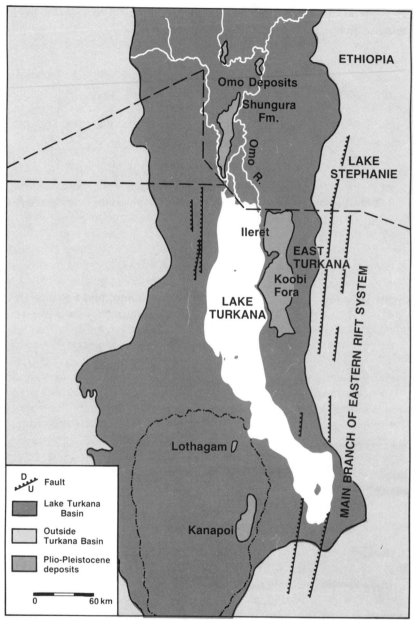

Figure 9.8. Lake Turkana and the Omo River, areas where large numbers of early hominid fossils have been found. In the East Turkana area, the Koobi Fora peninsula region has been the richest area to date; along the Omo, the Shungura Formation has provided the overwhelming bulk of fossils. To the south and west of the Lake are Lothagam and Kanapoi where only scraps of hominid fossils have been found. Current fossil hunting work is focusing on the areas to the west of Lake Turkana, where there are numerous fossil-bearing deposits.

The Laetoli site was first worked in the late 1930s by a German paleon- *Laetoli, Tanzania*
tologist, Kohl-Larson, who discovered several early hominid fossils. But
it was in 1975 when Mary Leakey and later Tim White returned that
significant numbers of fossils were found and the hominid levels dated.
Laetoli is an important site for a number of reasons: its date, about 3.7
million years B.P., makes it the earliest site with an appreciable number
of fossils; the hominids are in some ways similar to those from Hadar;
and finally, hominid footprints have been discovered there. The footprints provide direct evidence that hominid bipedalism had evolved at
this early date, for they are unquestionably those of an animal that walked
much as we do (Figure 9.10).[9]

According to Johanson and White, the hominid fossil specimens from
Hadar and Laetoli, dated earlier than other australopithecines, possess a
number of distinctive features, which led to the establishment of a new
taxonomic species *Australopithecus afarensis*.[10]

Just south of the Kenya-Tanzania border lies Lake Natron; near its shore *Other East*
is the site of Peninj, which has yielded a large lower jaw comparable in *African Sites*
many ways to *A. boisei* fossils from Olduvai, Omo, and East Turkana.
The Peninj jaw has been dated to about 1.5 million years B.P. In western Kenya, the site of Chesowanja has yielded a broken *A. boisei* skull.

Figures 9.9 and 9.10. (Left) A. afarensis *skeleton found at Hadar, Ethiopia.*
Approximately 40 percent of this one individual, named "Lucy," was pre-
served. (Right) *Footprints of the bipedal hominid* A. afarensis *found at the*
site of Laetoli. Notice that the big toe is aligned with the other toes and that
the footprints in general are characteristically human in shape.

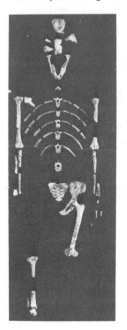

Several fossils have been found in deposits between about 4 and 5 million years B.P., but their fragmentary nature does not currently permit us to exactly identify them. At Maka, in the Awash Valley, near Hadar in north-central Ethiopia, a fragment of the front of a skull was found; and at Belohdelie, a piece of the upper part of an immature thighbone, in contexts dated to about 4 million years B.P. The thighbone's internal structure is like that of bipedal hominids and differs from the form found in the apes; this bone is the earliest dated evidence for hominid bipedality. At two sites south and west of Lake Turkana, Kenya, fossil bones were found: at Kanapoi, the elbow joint end of an upper arm bone, dated to about 4.5 million years B.P.; and at Lothagam Hill, a small piece of a lower jaw, in contexts that may be dated to more than 5 million years B.P. In the Baringo Basin, Kenya, portions of a jaw were dated to about 5 million years. If confirmed as hominid, these fossil specimens would be the earliest australopithecines. More fossils and firmer dating are necessary, however, before they can be accepted.

Summary of Early Hominid Sites

Before discussing the physical features of the early hominid fossils, it is useful to summarize the location of the discoveries and their dating. Table 9.2 summarizes the geographic distribution and dating of the early hominid sites. The more robust forms, *Australopithecus robustus* from South Africa and *A. boisei* from East Africa, are more limited in time than the others, and show up later. *A. afarensis* is earlier than other fossil groups, while evidence of the genus *Homo* seems limited to a period later than 2 million years B.P.

The geographic range of early hominid finds in Africa suggests that they were distributed continuously from South Africa north to Ethiopia. Were they also living in other parts of Africa or the Old World? Drawing conclusions from this kind of evidence, or the lack of it, is very difficult. Other parts of the Old World have been searched for traces of early hominids, but with no luck thus far. All that can be said at the present time is that the early hominids appear to be limited to eastern and southern Africa, but the question must remain an open one.

Fossils from the Lower Pleistocene Djetis Beds on the island of Java, Indonesia, represent the earliest known occurrence of the hominids outside of Africa. These fossils seem to possess a number of similarities to the *Homo habilis* fossils from Olduvai Gorge. This may indicate that, sometime before 1.5 million years B.P., the early hominids began to spread from Africa to other parts of the Old World.[11]

The fossil evidence for human evolution from about 4 million to about 1.5 million years B.P. has been placed in five different taxonomic categories: *A. afarensis, A. africanus, A. boisei, A. robustus,* and *Homo.* The term "australopithecine" is often used as a descriptive name for all of these early hominids. Because most of these australopithecine fossil specimens are very fragmentary and incomplete, there is continuing debate about the placement of some of the fossil samples in particular

Table 9.2. The australopithecines, grouped by date and location.
Most of these fossils have been K-Ar dated, but Lothagam Hill is relatively dated, and the South African sites are only tentatively placed in time.

Millions of years B.P.	Geological epoch	African Australopithecines						Not further identified
		A. afarensis	A. africanus	A. robustus	A. boisei	Homo[b]		
1	PLEISTOCENE							
			East Turkana[a]	Kromdraai	Chesowanja Peninj ←Olduvai Gorge East Turkana	←Omo East Turkana Olduvai Gorge		
2			Omo →Sterkfontein Makapansgat	Swartkrans	Omo			
	PLIOCENE							
3		Hadar Laetoli ←						
4								Maka
5	MIOCENE							Kanapoi
6								Lothagam Hill

[a]The presence of A. africanus forms at East Turkana is uncertain.
[b]Includes Homo habilis.

groups. After considering the morphological features of each category we will look at these differing views, as well as how the various australopithecines might be ordered in an evolutionary sequence.

General Australopithecine Morphology

There is considerable variation within the australopithecine fossil collection, in brain size, tooth size, body size, and the development of some muscles, but all of these fossils share a number of morphological features that permit us to place them in the hominid family and to assess their evolutionary position in relation both to later hominids and to each other. These general morphological traits include the skeletal bones relating to bipedalism, the general structure of the teeth, and the size of the brain.

Bipedalism

One of the australopithecine's most important sets of physical characteristics is related to bipedalism. Prior to the discovery at Laetoli of hominid footprints indicating a bipedal animal, postcranial bones indicating bipedalism formed the most convincing evidence for calling the australopithecines hominids. Habitual bipedalism and the anatomical structures responsible for it are unique to hominids. Chimpanzees and other primates occasionally move with their body weight completely on their rear limbs, but this is not their usual method of locomotion. Bipedalism, which frees the hands from the requirements of locomotion, has drastically changed the postcranial skeleton, especially the lower part of the vertebral column, the pelvis, the thighbone, the knee joint, the ankle joint, and the foot. The bone modifications are accompanied by changes in the muscles, in particular those of the lower back, which help hold the trunk upright; in the thigh and buttocks; and in the foot.

In modern humans these skeletal and muscular elements operate together to permit a kind of bipedal locomotion called the *striding gait* (Figure 9.11). In stride, the legs move through alternate phases, *stance* and *swing*, which are basic to solving the built-in problems of bipedal locomotion. First, all the body's weight is transmitted to the ground through the lower limbs, so that the lower back, pelvis, and the legs must be stout enough to handle the additional weight, even when the individual is running, adding stress from the bouncing and jarring footfalls. Second, movement itself is a problem. In quadrupedal animals, such as dogs, cats, and monkeys, the four limbs work as a unit, usually with at least two of the limbs on the ground at a time when the animal is walking. If bipedalism is to be efficient, each foot in turn must leave the ground as a step forward is taken; when one of a hominid's feet leaves the ground only one is left for support, and all the body's weight is transferred to the ground through one limb.

Human beings progress by alternating the two limbs through stance and swing phases. First, from a stationary position, one leg flexes at the knee and is bent forward, taking the whole foot off the ground. Swing

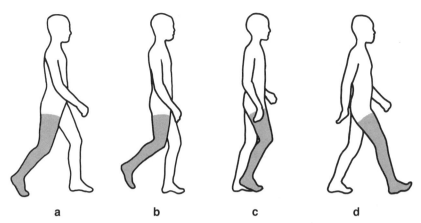

Figure 9.11. *The human stride. (a) The right leg (shaded) is about to begin the swing phase of the stride which starts with toe off. (b) The right leg has begun swing phase, while the left leg, in stance phase, furnishes support to the body. (c) The right leg's swing phase is at its midpoint and (d) moves toward heel strike and the end of swing phase. At this stage the left leg is about to begin its swing phase as it moves toward toe off.*

phase begins here for this limb, with the other leg in the stance phase furnishing the sole support for the whole body. The leg in the swing phase is swung ahead of the body, the knee begins to straighten, and the foot regains the ground, the heel touching first with *heel strike*. While this leg is moving forward, the trunk has been carried forward too, and after heel strike, body weight is gradually transferred to this forward foot as the trunk moves over the leg. Heel strike is the end of a leg's swing phase and the start of the stance or support phase. The other leg, which has been in the stance phase, begins swing phase as body weight is gradually transferred from it, the knee begins to flex, and the foot begins to leave the ground. The last part of the foot to leave the ground is the end of the big toe, which pushes off the ground with some muscular force, giving the leg a propulsive push as it begins its swing phase. *Toe off* marks the end of stance phase and the beginning of swing phase.

The skeletal modifications that make this form of locomotion possible contrast obviously with the skeletal parts of the apes, our closest living relatives and quadrupedal animals. In the human vertebral column, the lower bones of the spine form a characteristic curve, the *lumbar curve*, which provides a more efficient way of transmitting the upper body's weight to the pelvis (Figure 9.12). The human pelvis is also distinctive. The mammalian pelvis has three bony elements: the two pelvic bones *(innominate bones)* make up the sides of the pelvis and are joined at the front; the *sacrum,* the last major bone of the vertebral column, fits like a keystone between the two pelvic bones at the back of the pelvis (Fig-

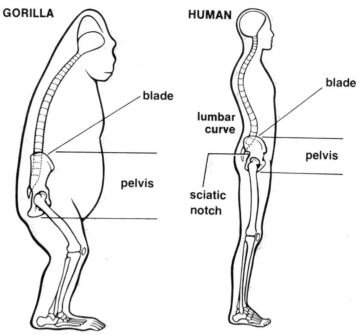

Figure 9.12. *Spinal columns of a gorilla and a modern human compared. The curves in the human spinal column are part of the anatomical system of bipedalism, especially the lower back, or lumbar, curve.*

ure 9.13). On each side of the pelvis is the hip joint socket, where the ball of the thigh bone articulates with the pelvis. Many muscles attach to the pelvic bones, some directed downward to the legs, where they assist in movements of the leg; and some directed upward, helping maintain upright posture.

The modern human pelvis is shorter than that of the chimpanzee, and has a larger area for the attachment of the sacrum (the sacroiliac joint). Human pelvic bones are foreshortened because the upper body's weight has to be transmitted to the ground through the pelvis. The shortened human pelvic bones reduce the distance between the sacral-pelvic bone joint, through which the upper body's weight is transmitted, and the hip joint, which transmits it to the legs. The large sacral-pelvic bone joint provides additional strength at a point subject to more weight. The upper parts of the pelvic bones, the blades (the *ilia;* plural of ilium), are much broader than in the chimpanzee. This broadening puts several important muscles of the front of the thigh, which attach on the blade, in a more advantageous position for lifting the thigh as the swing phase begins. In addition, the expansion of the pelvic blades has repositioned two muscles (*gluteus medius* and *gluteus minimus*) extremely important for bipedalism to the sides of the hip joint rather than behind, where they are located in the apes (Figure 9.14). These muscles contract when the opposite leg is lifted off the ground during swing phase; by attaching

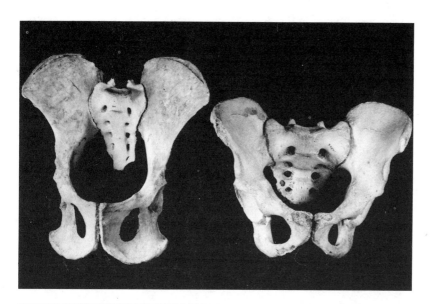

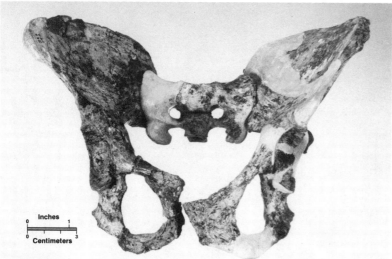

Figure 9.13. The pelves of a chimpanzee (top left), a human, and STS-14 (A. africanus *from Sterkfontein*) (below) compared. Notice the similarities between the human and the australopithecine bones, especially in the foreshortening of the pelvis and the broadening of the blades. (Not to scale.)

from the pelvic blade to the top of the thigh-bone (femur), they maintain the stability of the pelvis when the body is being supported by only one leg. This broadening of the blades of the pelvis has led to the development of a strongly angulated notch at the back of the pelvis, the *sciatic notch.*

Parts of the pelvis and virtually complete pelves have been recovered from a number of sites in South and East Africa (Figures 9.9 and

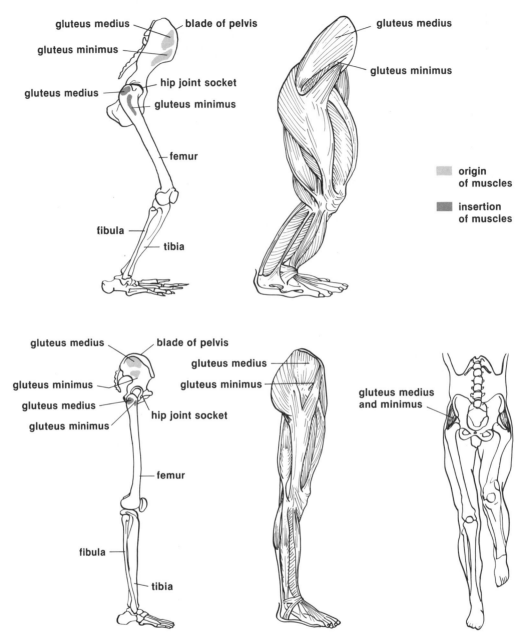

Figure 9.14. Lower limbs of a gorilla (top) and a modern human (bottom) compared. In the drawings of the bones, the two attachment areas (the origin and insertion) of each of the gluteal muscles are indicated. In apes, the gluteus medius *and* gluteus minimus *lie behind the hip joint socket because the blade of the pelvis does not curve around the animal's side. In humans, the blade of the pelvis has expanded around to the side, and these muscles are located to the outside of the hip joint. Therefore, as the drawing on the lower right illustrates,* gluteus medius *and* gluteus minimus *serve in humans to maintain the stability of the pelvis during stride when the opposing leg is lifted off the ground.*

9.13); all show that the australopithecine pelvis is remarkably like that of modern humans: the pelvis is foreshortened, and the blades are expanded; it has an enlarged area for the sacral-pelvic bone joint; and there is a marked sciatic notch. The several australopithecine fossils vary in size, and the most complete specimens, from Sterkfontein and Hadar, are smaller than skeletons of most modern humans. The fossils also differ morphologically from modern human bones, but the australopithecine pelvic material is clearly closer to modern humans than to the pongids; the vertebral column also seems to have the lower back curve characteristic of humans.

Added to the distinctive bipedal features of the pelvis are important characteristics in the knee, ankle, and foot. The human knee joint is underneath the body, giving it maximum support during stride (Figure 9.15); the hip joint is at the side of the pelvis. For the knee joints to be in an efficient position, the thighbone (femur) must angle in from its upper joint at the hip to its lower joint at the knee. Thus, modern humans are characterized by thighbones that are directed, not more or less straight down as in the chimpanzee, but at an angle, to bring the knee joints much closer together than the hip joints. The knee joint itself, which must be able to transmit body weight to the lower part of the leg, has three bones: the lower end of the thighbone (femur) and the upper part of the shinbone (tibia) meeting, and the kneecap (patella) sitting in front of the articulation and with its muscles and ligaments maintaining the integrity of the front of the joint. The thighbone and shinbone are joined by two concave surfaces on the shinbone, into which fit two condyles, or rounded projections, of the thighbone. If the angle the thighbone makes from hip to knee were to be continued down the shinbone, the legs would cross, making bipedal locomotion somewhat difficult, if not impossible. To compensate for the thighbone angle, the inside condyle of the thighbone is larger than the outside one, thus allowing the shinbone to drop straight down from the knee to the ankle. Fossil thighbones can be examined and the size of the inner condyle at the lower end of the thighbone can be used to determine whether the thighbone angled in, and whether the knee joints were beneath the body's weight. We have quite a few fossil australopithecine thighbones, and they show the enlarged inner condyle typical of modern human skeletons. A complete knee joint discovered at Hadar also confirms the bipedal nature of the australopithecine locomotor system. Analyses indicate that the bones of this joint were capable of the same range of movement that is found in modern humans, and much greater than that characteristic of ape knee joints.

Because the human anklebone *(talus)* must support body weight, it is more robust than in the pongids. Australopithecine anklebones differ from those of both modern humans and the chimpanzee, but they are closer to the hominids.

The modern human foot is specialized for supporting body weight. The foot's complex arch has developed, and the last bone of the big toe is enlarged and flattened to provide the push off at the beginning of swing

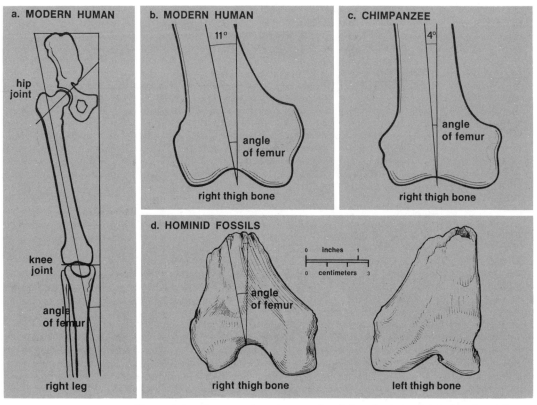

Figure 9.15. *Because humans need to bring the knee joint directly under their body weight, (a) the shaft of the thighbone (femur) angles in from the hip to the knee joint. This angle is reflected in the relative sizes of the knobs, or condyles, at the ends of the thighbone. (In b, c, and d, the inner condyle is on the right in all but the lower right illustration.) In modern human thighbones (b), the inner condyle is larger than the outer, but the two are more equal (c) in the chimpanzee. (d) Two fossils (from different individuals) from the Sterkfontein site in South Africa show that in these hominid fossils, the inner condyles are larger than the outer, emphasizing the hominid nature of the australopithecine knee joint.*

phase (Figure 9.16). Unlike the ape's opposable big toe, the modern human digit is set against the other toes and cannot be opposed. Another fortunate find, this time at Olduvai Gorge, was the greater portion of an australopithecine foot. Like all the other structures, there are some differences between these bones and those in modern humans; the fossil foot, nevertheless, is meant to support weight. The big toe is not opposable, and the arch seems to have had some development. At another site at Olduvai Gorge, the last bone of the big toe was found. It shows the flattening and enlargement typical of modern human bones.

Recent examination of australopithecine fossil foot bones by Randall Susman and Jack Stern have focused on the shape of the bones of the toes. While they do not deny that when on the ground, the early hominids were bipedal, these authors suggest that the somewhat curved shafts of the toe bones, and several other features of the lower limb, indicate that the australopithecines may have spent a considerable amount of time in the trees.[12] This assertion has become a hotly debated issue, and at the present time, no clean-cut answers to the question of australopithecines' arborealty are possible.

In reviewing modern human locomotor abilities and the known fossil evidence of the australopithecines, we have ignored other structures related to bipedalism and known from fossil evidence. Human locomotion, too, has been treated in less than full detail. The points raised, however, demonstrate that the australopithecines were bipedal animals.

The discovery in 1976 of australopithecine footprint trails at the Lae-

Figure 9.16. Human and gorilla foot bones compared with those of an australopithecine from Olduvai Gorge, Bed I. This fossil foot is incomplete, but its big toe was placed up against the other four toes, and was not an opposable digit, as is the big toe of the pongids. Notice the differences between the last bones in the pongid and the human big toes. The strongly developed last bone in the modern human big toe is related to the push off in walking. A last big toe bone was discovered in Bed I, Olduvai Gorge, but not from the same individual as the rest of the foot; this bone is very similar to that in modern humans. (Not to scale.)

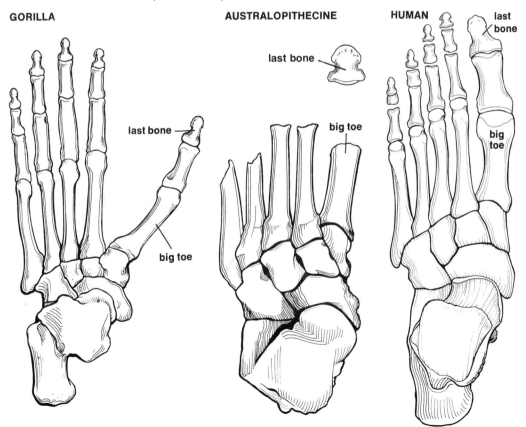

GORILLA

last bone

big toe

AUSTRALOPITHECINE

last bone

big toe

HUMAN

last bone

big toe

toli site in Tanzania (Figure 9.10) confirmed the evidence of the fossil bones. The footprints are those of an animal with a smaller foot and with a shorter distance between footprints; they suggest a hominid of smaller stature, but with certainty an animal that moved with the striding gait.

The major morphological difference between the postcranial bones of the australopithecines and those of modern humans is in the upper part of the thighbone, or femur; many australopithecine bones show a longer neck and smaller head (the ball of the hip joint) than are found in modern humans (Figure 9.17). The fossil evidence from East Turkana in north Kenya suggests that femurs much like those of modern humans, with larger heads and shorter necks, first appear in the fossil record between about 2 and 1.5 million years B.P., toward the end of australopithecine evolution. Although some have interpreted these differences as an indication that the australopithecines may have moved in a some-

Figure 9.17. *The upper part of a thighbone of a modern human compared with a fossil thighbone of an australopithecine from Swartkrans. The main difference between the two is the longer, narrower neck and smaller head (which fits into the hip socket) of the australopithecine bone. Other australopithecine thighbones, especially some from East Turkana, are more like those of modern humans.*

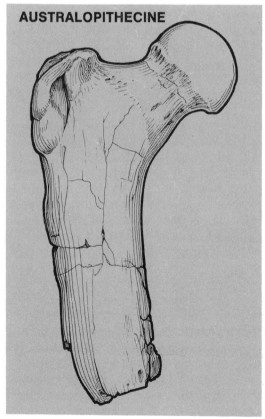
AUSTRALOPITHECINE

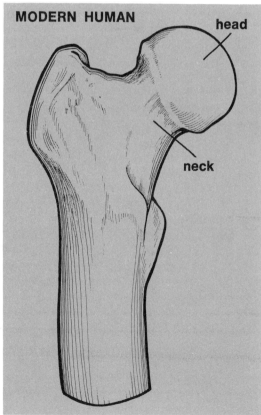
MODERN HUMAN

head

neck

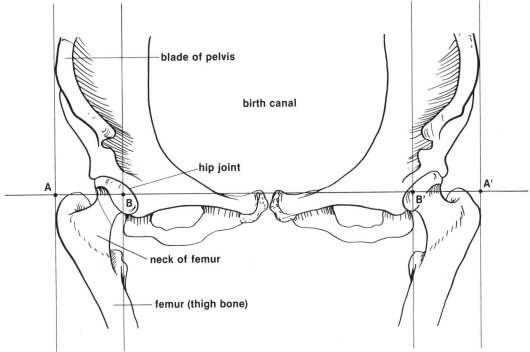

Figure 9.18. *In an early hominid, with a small brain, the distance B-B' can be smaller because of the small size of the infant brain. Thus distance A-B (and A'-B') can be greater. In the course of human evolution, as brain size increases, the size of the birth canal also increases and this results in a greater distance between B-B'. Since the total pelvic breadth (A-A') must remain the same to permit efficient stride, A-B (and A'-B') must decrease in length, which is reflected in the shortening of the neck of the femur or thighbone.*

what different fashion than modern humans, Owen Lovejoy has suggested that the differences in the head and neck of the australopithecine femurs are more closely related to brain and body size than to any fundamental differences in their patterns of movement. Lovejoy suggests that during the course of later australopithecine evolution, when brain size was increasing, there was a need to provide a larger birth canal for a larger-brained infant. This created evolutionary pressure to increase the distance between the hip joint sockets (Figure 9.18), resulting in a shorter-necked femur in those australopithecine species with larger brains. Lovejoy points out that these changes in the shape and size of the thighbone neck and pelvis appear in the fossil record at about the same time as hominids with larger brain sizes.[13]

Similarly, the size of the femur head is related to body size; Lovejoy suggests that as body size increases, there is evolutionary selection for the development of larger hip balljoints to support increased body weight more efficiently.

Skull, Teeth, and Jaws

Complete and nearly complete australopithecine skulls have been found in both East and South Africa. In general the volume of the braincases ranges from about 400 to almost 800 ml, with those dated earlier tending to be smaller.

Skull The australopithecine skull differs in its general form from that of modern humans, especially in the relationship of the facial portion to the braincase (Figure 9.19). In the australopithecines, the facial area is large and juts out in front of the braincase; its position is similar to an ape's. In modern humans, the face is smaller relative to the total size of the skull, and the enlarged braincase is positioned above the face. The differences in the australopithecine and modern human skulls reflect the evolutionary changes that occurred between the time of the australopi-

Figure 9.19. *Skulls of two australopithecines — (a)* Australopithecus africanus *and (b)* Australopithecus robustus, *both from South Africa (c) a modern human, and (d) an orangutan. Notice the difference in size between the braincases of the australopithecines and that of the modern human, as well as the difference in position of the faces in relation to the braincases.*

a. *A. AFRICANUS*

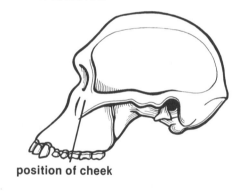

position of cheek

b. *A. ROBUSTUS*

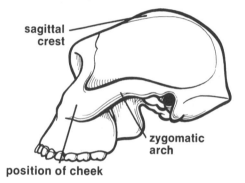

c. HUMAN

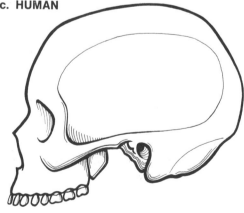

d. ORANGUTAN

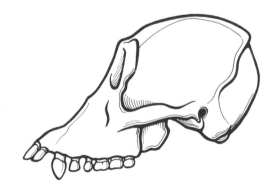

thecines and the emergence of modern humans: the increase in the size of the brain and the decrease in the size of the face and teeth (trends that were discussed in Chapter 8).

Jaws and Teeth Because there is a great deal of variation in the teeth of australopithecines, differences in details of dentition are the most important features (along with brain size) used to identify and distinguish the various species of early hominids. The australopithecines, like all hominids, have a dental formula of 2.1.2.3, with the upper and lower molar cusps in an arrangement typical of hominoids. Other features of the australopithecine dentition, and its relationships to ape and human jaws and teeth, can be better understood from a comparison of a human jaw with an ape jaw (Figure 9.20).

Two of the major changes in human evolution are the reduction of the face and teeth and the enlargement of the braincase. Both have contributed to the differences in the jaws of modern humans and apes. The pongids' dental arcade has two long, parallel rows of back teeth, the premolars and molars, occasionally with the last molars converging (Figure 9.20a). The human tooth row is shorter because the teeth are smaller, especially the canines (Figure 9.20b and c). The human dental arch forms a diverging, parabolic shape. The size of the teeth accounts only partially for this difference in shape. The evolutionary expansion of the brain has positioned the human face and jaws beneath the braincase, rather than in the front as in the apes (Figure 9.21). The position on the base of the skull where the knobs of the lower jaw attach remains constant in apes and humans. Thus, the jaw changes dimensions: as it becomes shorter, the relationship of width to length changes (compare jaw width to length in Figure 9.20a and 9.20b). The relatively shorter and wider human jaws are parabolic in order to remain functional as the brain expands and facial size decreases. One measure of this change is the position of the origin of the cheek (Figure 9.21): in humans, it usually lies above or slightly behind the first molar, reflecting the decreased amount of face and jaw jutting out in front. In contrast, in chimpanzees it is above the third molar, and sometimes even behind that.

Ape canines are long and tusklike, projecting above the other teeth; wear is on the sides, not the tips (Figure 9.20d). Human canines are much smaller and do not project beyond the other teeth; they are not pointed or tusklike and the wear is on the tips. Two other features are functionally related to the large canines in the apes (and the monkeys). Ape canines are so big that if the upper and lower ones met tip to tip, the rest of the teeth could not occlude, and chewing would be impossible. The canines therefore slide together, with the back of the lower canine rubbing against the front of the upper canine. In addition, the back of the upper canine, which fits between the lower canine and the first lower premolar, rubs against a long shoulder on the latter tooth. The interdigitation of these three teeth provides for honing on the back surfaces of

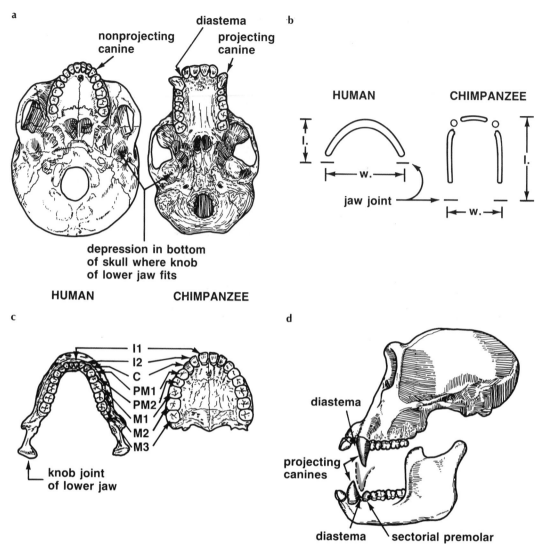

Figure 9.20. *Comparison of the jaws and teeth of a modern human and chimpanzee. (a) The bottom of the skulls of a human (left) and chimp (right), showing the differences in the size and dimensions of the face and teeth; (b) illustrating the relative differences in the proportions of a human and chimp jaw; (c) illustrating the human upper and lower dentitions. Note the small size of the canine teeth, the wear on their tips, the lack of a diastema, and the first lower premolar's shape and similarity to the second lower premolar. (d) A skull and jaw of a chimpanzee showing the relationships of upper and lower canines and first lower (sectorial) premolar, and the resultant wear patterns on the teeth.*

the canines, giving them sharp edges on this border. The space between the teeth, the *diastema*, lets these pointed canines fit together and the jaws close. The first lower premolar with the elongated shoulder is un-

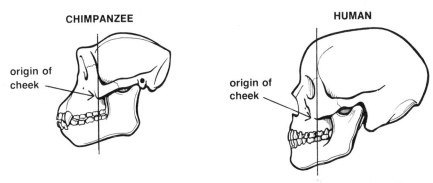

CHIMPANZEE

origin of
cheek

HUMAN

origin of
cheek

Figure 9.21. The skulls of a modern chimpanzee and a modern human. Notice the differences in size of the braincases in relation to the faces. The
modern human face is positioned more underneath the braincase than the
chimpanzee's. The chimp's large canine teeth are also clearly visible.

like the other lower premolar and the two upper premolars in that it has
only one cusp; it is called a *sectorial premolar.* The large canine, diastema, and sectorial premolar form a functional unit found in all the apes.
Modern humans lack the large canine, a diastema, and a sectorial premolar. In humans, the first lower premolar, like the second, has two cusps
(bicuspid) and none of the functional relationships with the canine that
characterize the pongid dentition.

All of the australopithecine teeth are larger than those in modern humans, although there is considerable variation among early hominid taxa.
However, with the notable exception of the canines and first lower premolars of some *Australopithecus afarensis* fossil specimens, all australopithecine teeth are completely hominid in form.

The jaws of the australopithecines are large, with a thick lower jawbone to house the large teeth securely and an arch shape different from
both apes and humans (Figure 9.22; see also Fig. 9.28). Large muscle
attachment areas for large chewing muscles are a feature of all the early
hominids, with some species possessing huge jaw closing muscles.

Although this general description of features can be applied to all
australopithecines—bipedal, with small brains and large teeth—there is
enough variation among these structures to justify a number of different
taxonomic categories.

Fossil specimens of *A. robustus* from the South African sites of Swartkrans and Kromdraai and *A. boisei* fossils from the East African sites of
Olduvai Gorge, East Turkana, the Omo, Peninj, and Chesowanja, possess features that are more robust and larger than those of other australopithecines (Figures 9.7, 9.19, 9.23, 9.24, and 9.25). The robust specimens have very large premolars and molars; larger facial areas,
presumably to house the larger teeth; and larger chewing muscles. As in

Australopithecine Varieties

Australopithecus
Robustus *and*
Australopithecus
Boisei

other hominids, there are two primary sets of chewing muscles, *temporalis* and *masseter*. *Temporalis* is at the side of the skull, attaching to the side of the braincase and to the back part of the lower jaw (Figure 9.23). *Masseter* lies outside *temporalis* and attaches from a bony bridge between the face and side of the skull (the *zygomatic arch*) to the lower part of the back of the jaw. Both muscles are greatly developed in the robust australopithecines; the temporal muscle is so big that a bony ridge or crest, the *sagittal crest*, on the top of the skull, has developed to provide more space for attaching the muscle fibers. Many male gorillas and some male chimpanzees also have such a crest. This development of the muscles and face appears directly related to the large back teeth in a functional complex, perhaps for chewing rough, fibrous foods. The need to place the action of the *masseter* muscle over the back teeth has apparently led, in the robust australopithecines, to the forward projection of the zygomatic arch and its connection to the face in the upper cheek region. In side view, the projecting cheek region completely hides the nasal cavity; note, in the comparison of *A. robustus* with *A. africanus* in Figure 9.19, the position of the zygomatic arch, and the projection of the arch and cheek regions in the robust form. It is primarily this complex of features relating to the very large back teeth that separates the robust forms from other australopithecines.

Within the group of robust australopithecines, those from East Africa, *Australopithecus boisei*, possess larger teeth and larger and more massive faces and jaws than the *Australopithecus robustus* forms from South Africa. Most interpretations of australopithecine evolution associate the South and East African robust australopithecines together as part of a

Figure 9.22. *The upper jaw of a robust australopithecine from the Swartkrans site in South Africa. Note the shape of the dental arcade which differs from both the chimp and the human upper jaws pictured in 9.20a. During the time between the death of this individual and the preservation of the jaw as a fossil, the left second molar was pushed out of its socket, and the front teeth were lost.*

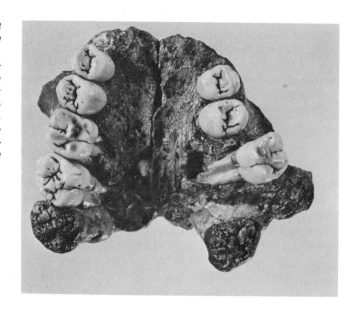

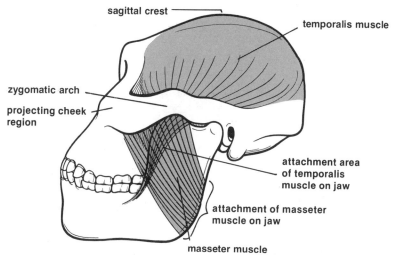

Figure 9.23. *A robust australopithecine showing the attachment of the main chewing muscles,* temporalis *and* masseter. *The muscles are drawn on a composite skull and jaw, the skull being the same one figured in 9.24 and the lower jaw illustrated in Figure 9.25. These fossils represent two different individuals, but have been combined here to demonstrate muscle attachments. If they were from the same individual, and were not distorted or broken during their long burial, the knob or condyle of the lower jaw would fit into a depression (the* glenoid fossa) *on the base of the skull.*

Figure 9.24. *A robust australopithecine skull from the Swartkrans site in South Africa. This specimen has been considerably damaged; the back portion of the skull, in addition to bits and pieces on the side and front, is missing. Notice the large zygomatic arch and sagittal crest, along with the projecting face and low forehead.*

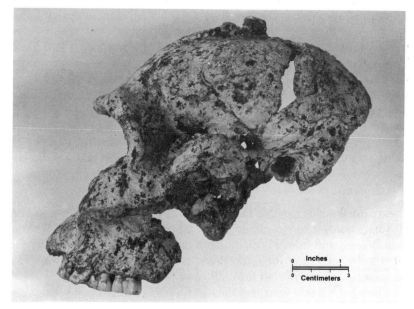

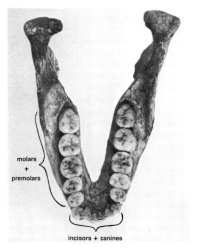

molars
+
premolars

incisors + canines

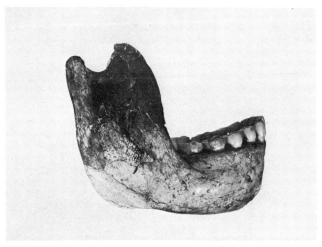

Figure 9.25. *Two views of the lower jaw of one of the most complete robust australopithecine jaws found at the Swartkrans site. After the death of the individual, the jaw was broken at the middle and the two halves were pushed together, so that the fossil now has the right and left sides too close together; in life, the jaw would have been wider. Notice the larger size of premolars and molars in comparison with the front teeth.*

specialized side branch of human evolution. Because the South African forms may be earlier and are not as extreme as the East African forms, the evolutionary sequence seems to be from the earlier, more generalized *A. robustus* to the later, more specialized *A. boisei*. Both south and east African forms have the same size brain, about 500 ml.

The few bones of the skeleton that can be assigned to the robust australopithecines suggest that these early hominids were somewhat larger in body size than the other forms, perhaps 40 kg in weight, and 1.5 m tall.[14] The whole issue of australopithecine body size is made difficult by the small number of skeletal bones that have been recovered and by the question of sexual dimorphism: were there large-bodied males and small-bodied females, similar to the differences seen in baboons and gorillas? And if so, are the skeletal bones we have found those of males or females? Further complicating the issue is that apart from the "Lucy" *A. afarensis* partial skeleton, and one or two other specimens, virtually all of the skeletal bones have been discovered in isolation and not directly associated with skull pieces or teeth.

Australopithecus Africanus

These australopithecines are known primarily from the South African sites of Taung (only one specimen, the original *A. africanus* child), from Sterkfontein, and from Makapansgat (Figures 9.26 and 9.27). They also seem to be present at the Omo River, and several specimens from East Turkana have been placed in *A. africanus*.

Their back teeth, the premolars and molars, though large compared

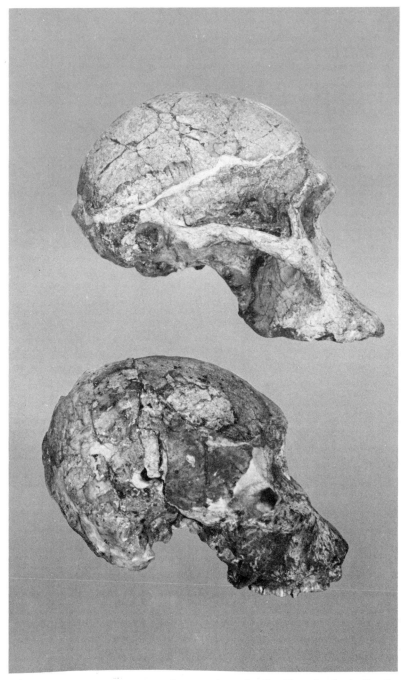

Figure 9.26. *Two skulls of* A. africanus *from the Sterkfontein site in South Africa.*

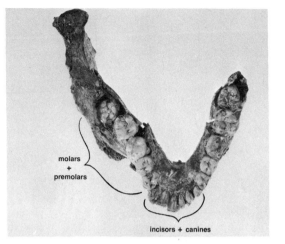
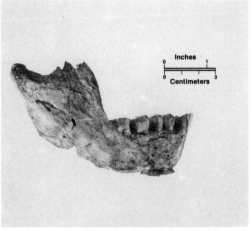

Figure 9.27. *Two views of the broken and distorted lower jaw of* A. africanus *from the Sterkfontein site in South Africa. Most of the back portion of the left side has been destroyed, and the back part of the right side has been distorted outward. Notice, however, that the jaw is smaller than the robust specimen in Figure 9.25 and that the front and back teeth are more in proportion with each other.*

with those of the genus *Homo,* tend to be somewhat smaller than those of the South African robust australopithecines (Figure 9.28). As Milford Wolpoff has pointed out, within the range of back tooth sizes of South African robusts and *A. africanus* there is some overlap; some teeth from Sterkfontein, for example, are as large as those from Swartkrans *A. robustus.* Although the sum of their morphological features makes *A. africanus* look more like later hominids, the size of their teeth has caused debate about their precise position in hominid evolution. In brain size *A. africanus* is similar to the east and south African robust australopithecines: from about 440 to a little less than 500 ml.

Australopithecus africanus appears to be somewhat smaller in body size than *A. robustus,* but this is based primarily on the fossil bones of one individual, for which we have recovered many of the bones of the spinal column and lower limbs. However, this individual was probably a female, and it is difficult to determine just how different the male was (if there was a sexual dimorphic difference).

Australopithecus Afarensis

The fossils from Hadar and Laetoli have features somewhat different from those of the other australopithecines. These differences and the early dates from these sites—from about 2.9 to 3.2 million years B.P. at Hadar to about 3.7 million years B.P. at Laetoli—led Donald Johanson and Tim White to establish the taxon *Australopithecus afarensis* (named after the Afar region of Ethiopia, where the Hadar site is located) in 1978. Although these fossils are dated earlier than other australopithecines, the size of their back teeth is generally smaller than in the robust australopithecines and *A. africanus;* their brains tend to be smaller, too, with

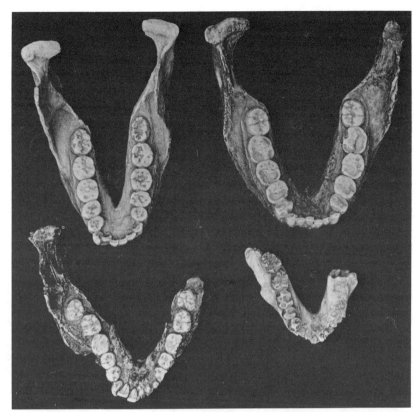

Figure 9.28. *Four australopithecine lower jaws:* A. robustus *(upper left),* A. boisei *(upper right),* A. africanus *(lower left), and* A. afarensis *(lower right). Note the differences in the size of the jaw bones, and the back teeth among the four and the relative proportions of back to front teeth in the robust and hyper-robust* A. boisei. *The* A. africanus *jaw in this picture has back teeth that are smaller than the* A. robustus *just above it, but the total range of sizes of the two groups do overlap. All of the jaws are typical of most hom- inid fossils in their being broken and incomplete or distorted. (For example, the two sides of the* A. robustus *jaw have been pushed together).*

one around 400 ml. The "Lucy" skeleton is virtually the same size as the female *A. africanus* skeleton, and has been reconstructed to about 23 kg and about 1.1 m in height. The presence in the Hadar deposits of skeletal bones larger than those of "Lucy" suggests a dimorphic species with larger males, but these bones have also been viewed by some an- thropologists as evidence for the presence at Hadar of another hominid species.

What is really distinctive about *A. afarensis* is the size and morphol- ogy of some of the canines and first lower premolars (Figures 9.29 and 9.30). First, there seems to be some sexual dimorphism in canine size. In most pongids, male canines are larger and more strongly developed than those of the females. The canines of modern humans and other australopithecines show no sexual dimorphism. The apparently male

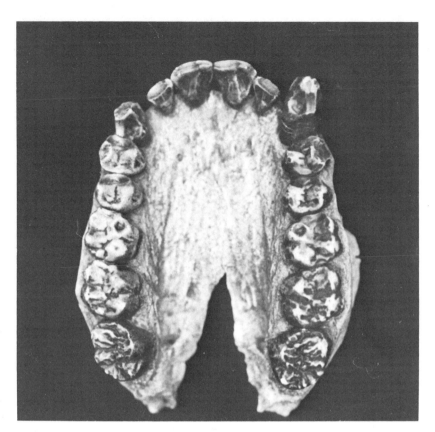

Figure 9.29. *A cast of an upper jaw of* A. afarensis *from Hadar. The left (on the right side in this picture) canine has been pushed up out of its socket.*

Australopithecus afarensis canines are similar in shape to those of the hominids but larger, sticking out slightly above the level of the other teeth, while presumed female canines are somewhat smaller.

Second, in some fossil specimens, the shape of the first lower premolars is different from that of other australopithecines. Figure 9.30 shows the first lower premolars of the famous skeleton from Hadar, "Lucy," and the same tooth from the jaw of a Sterkfontein *A. africanus*. The *A. afarensis* tooth has cusps of unequal size, the outer cusp being larger, the inside quite a bit smaller. The *A. africanus* tooth, like that of modern humans, has two more or less equal-sized cusps. The "Lucy" premolar is somewhat similar to that in the apes (compare with the ape premolar in Figure 9.20d) where it serves a honing function against the back of the upper canine. There is evidence that the first lower premolar in *A. afarensis* did serve this function, though to a much more limited extent than in the apes. This canine/premolar complex in *Australopithecus afarensis* is associated with a completely bipedal animal, as the skeletal and footprint evidence demonstrate.

Dated early, *A. afarensis* may represent beginning evolutionary trends toward later hominids, and is thus representative of the earliest true

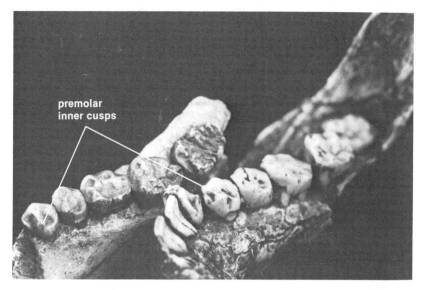

premolar
inner cusps

Figure 9.30. Casts of the Lucy A. afarensis *lower jaw (left) and* A. africanus *from Sterkfontein. Note the difference in the sizes of the first premolar cusps, with the* A. afarensis *inner cusp smaller, and those of* A. africanus *more equal in size.*

hominids. However, much debate still focuses on the status of *A. afarensis,* with many arguing that there are valid reasons for doing away with it altogether. For example, Phillip Tobias has suggested that there are not enough distinguishing features of the *A. afarensis* material to warrant its separation from *Australopithecus africanus.* According to Tobias, all of the attributes used by Johanson and White to establish *A. afarensis* can be found among the *A. africanus* fossils.[15]

Several European and American anthropologists have separated the *A. afarensis* material into two, or more, different species. Some view the *A. afarensis* fossils as belonging to *A. africanus* and *A. robustus,* but others also see a third group, early members of the genus *Homo,* in the sample as well.[16] Finally, there is considerable debate over the lumping of the Hadar (Ethiopia) and Laetoli (Tanzania) fossil material together into one species. Many anthropologists believe that the significant time difference between the two sites (almost half a million years) argues against their membership in the same species; that the earlier-in-time Laetoli fossils show more primitive features than the Hadar pieces. The very recently discovered, but very fragmentary, fossil hominids from the site of Maka in the Awash Valley, near Hadar, in Ethiopia, dated to about 4 million years B.P., or from the 6-million-year locality in the Baringo Basin of Keyna, offer the promise of eventually ending this debate. Discovery of additional fossils from these sites will tell us more about the hominids of this early time, and will allow us to evaluate the features and the justification of *A. afarensis.*

A number of fossils from Bed I and the lower part of Bed II at Olduvai Gorge have cranial capacities ranging from about 600 to 670 ml, larger than other australopithecines. The teeth, especially the back teeth, are

Australopithecines Placed in the Genus Homo

smaller and the dental arcade more similar to that of later hominids (Figure 9.31). Louis Leakey, Phillip Tobias, and John Napier gave these fossils the name *Homo habilis,* suggesting they are more advanced than other australopithecines and deserve to be placed in the genus *Homo.*

This idea did not escape comment. John Robinson suggests that the taxon *Homo habilis* ought to be divided into two groups: the earlier fossils, from Bed I, share affinities with other australopithecines, such as *A. africanus* and *A. afarensis;* those from later deposits, in Bed II, should be placed with members of the later hominid group, *Homo erectus.* According to Robinson, all fossils now assigned to *Homo habilis* may be part of the evolutionary transition between the australopithecines and later hominids.[17]

In addition to the *Homo habilis* fossils from Olduvai Gorge, a number of other fossils from East Africa, East Turkana, and the upper part of the Omo sequence have also been placed in the genus *Homo.* There is also a fragmentary skull from a deposit above the *A. africanus* levels at Sterkfontein that has been called *Homo.* The most complete and important of these fossils come from East Turkana and date from about 1.5 to 2 million years B.P. They possess several different combinations of features. Some, like the fossil KMN–ER 3733 (Kenya National Museum East

Figure 9.31. *Pieces of a skull and jaws from Olduvai Gorge, found in the Lower Bed II level. With a braincase larger than those of* A. africanus *and* robustus *australopithecines, as well as some teeth smaller than in other australopithecines, this specimen and others led L. S. B. Leakey, Tobias, and Napier to propose the term* Homo habilis *for these creatures, suggesting that they are more advanced than the other australopithecines.*

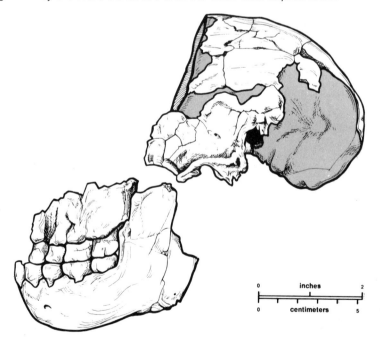

inches
0   2

centimeters
0   5

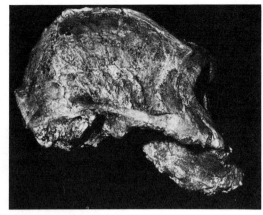

Figure 9.32. KNM-ER 3733 (left) compared with a cast of KNM-ER 406. The latter, a robust australopithecine with a sagittal crest, a flaring cheek region, large chewing muscles, and other attributes of this group, is only slightly older than KNM-ER 3733, which, with its higher forehead, smaller face, smaller chewing muscles, and much larger brain, is clearly a member of the genus Homo, *perhaps* Homo erectus.

Rudolf, the former name of Lake Turkana) in Figure 9.32 are unquestionably members of the genus *Homo*, probably *Homo erectus* (see Chapter 10). They have large brains—over 800 ml—small teeth, and morphological features that link them to these later hominids. The fossil

Figure 9.33. Two views of KNM-ER 1470, a relatively complete early hominid skull from the Koobi Fora area east of Lake Turkana. The skull was found in many pieces, and there is no good bony connection between the facial portion and the braincase. Since this photograph was taken, a later restoration has moved the face into a more projecting position, giving it more of the appearance of other australopithecines. It does, however, possess a cranial capacity of 775 ml.

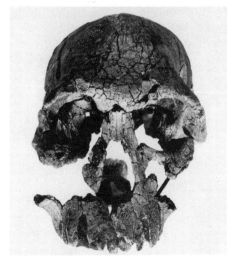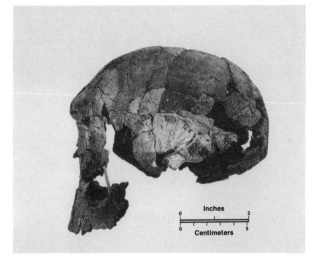

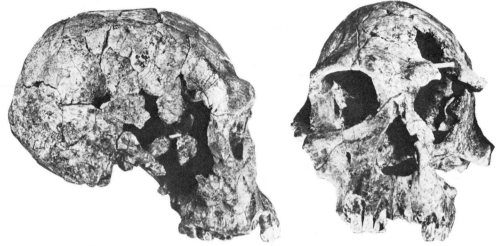

Figure 9.34. *Two views of the skull of KNM-ER 1813, from East Turkana. Note that the forehead rises more steeply than in the* A. africanus *specimens from Sterkfontein (see Figure 9.26), and in this as well as in the size of the teeth, which are small, this specimen is like members of the genus* Homo. *It does, however, possess a small cranial capacity, just a little over 500 ml.*

dates from about 1.5 to 1.6 million years B.P. Other, somewhat earlier East Turkana fossils are not so straightforward. KMN–ER 1470 (Figure 9.33), for example, and another like it, KMN–ER 1590, possess large brains, almost 800 ml, but the teeth are also large, *Australopithecus africanus*-sized. Still others, such as KMN–ER 1813 (Figure 9.34), have small brains (this one about 520 ml) and small *Homo erectus*-sized teeth. What criteria can be used to define a fossil as a member of the genus *Homo*? All these creatures were bipedal, so this attribute is not of help. We must focus on the other major trends in hominid evolution: the reduction in size of the face and teeth and the expansion of the brain. Some of the East Turkana fossils possess *Homo*-sized brains and *Australopithecus*-sized teeth, and others the reverse. Depending on which criteria we use, the fossils can be sorted in different ways, and this influences the view of australopithecine evolution.

Theories of Australopithecine Evolution

Table 9.3 summarizes the various australopithecine groups, their morphological features, and their placement in time. There is presently no agreement about how all these categories ought to be arranged in an evolutionary sequence, or even about whether all the currently recognized species are really necessary, or justified.

Several years ago a theory was proposed, termed the "single species hypothesis," which suggested that all early hominids belonged to one variable species and that differences in morphology between the specimens could be accounted for by their separation in time and space, as

Table 9.3. Suggested groupings of East and South African early hominids.

	A. afarensis	Robust group	A. africanus	Homo group
Brain size	400–500 ml	500–550 ml	450–500 ml	650–775 ml
Dentition	Back teeth generally smaller than *A. africanus*, larger canines, unequal cusps on first pm.	Very large back teeth; relatively small front teeth	Large front and back teeth	Variable; generally smaller than robust and gracile forms
Species and location	*Australopithecus afarensis* East Africa: Hadar, Ethiopia Laetoli, Tanzania	*Australopithecus robustus* South Africa: Swartkrans, Kromdraai *Australopithecus boisei* East Africa: Olduvai, Peninj, East Turkana, Chesowanja, Omo	*Australopithecus africanus* South Africa: Taung, Sterkfontein, Makapansgat East Africa: Omo, East Turkana	*Homo habilis* East Africa: Olduvai Gorge *Homo* South Africa: Sterkfontein East Africa: East Turkana, Omo
Dating	Hadar: 2.9 million to 3.2 million B.P. Laetoli: 3.7 million B.P.	East Africa: 2 million to c. 1.5 million B.P. South Africa: relative placement =2.5 million to 1.5 million B.P.	East Africa: 3 million to c. 1.5 million B.P. South Africa: relative placement = >3 million to 2.5 million B.P.	East Africa: c. 2 million to c. 1.5 million B.P.

well as by the variability normal in any species. This idea can be rejected on the basis of recent fossil discoveries. The skull KMN–ER 3733, from a time 1.5 to 1.6 million years B.P., is a member of *Homo erectus*, for it is similar to specimens in that taxonomic category. Yet, at the same level at East Turkana, or just a little earlier, are *Australopithecus boisei* specimens like the skull KMN–ER 406. The differences between these two skulls are too great to be encompassed within one species (Figure 9.32).

Thus, it is clear that there were at least two different early hominid species living at the same time. But how many? Some paleoanthropologists suggest that three species were coexisting (Table 9.4, part A). This view, supported by Richard Leakey and others, holds that the genus *Homo* has a greater antiquity than current estimates or fossils allow, and that these early *Homo* forms coexisted with members of *A. africanus* and robust australopithecines. This theory does not recognize *Australopithecus afarensis* as a separate category, but suggests that some of the forms called *A. afarensis* may in fact be members of *Homo*. In the period between 2 and 1.5 million years B.P., when there are a number of East Turkana fossils with different combinations of features—large brains with small teeth and small brains with large teeth—this theory proposes a division of the fossils on the basis of brain size, with the larger-brained specimens (like KNM–ER 1470) considered part of the *Homo* line and the smaller-brained forms (like KNM–ER 1813) part of the *Australopithecus africanus* line, which becomes extinct around 1.5 million years ago.

The two other major views of australopithecine evolution differ only in their placement of *Australopithecus africanus*. In their article establishing *A. afarensis*, Johanson and White consider a number of possible evolutionary sequences, concluding that the arrangement pictured in Table 9.4, part B, is the most reasonable. In this view, *Australopithecus afarensis* is the earliest of the australopithecines, perhaps very close to the split between hominids and pongids, and is the common ancestor for all later australopithecines. After the time of *A. afarensis*, presumably in the period 2 to 3 million years B.P., the hominid line split, with one line evolving toward *Homo* and the other culminating in the appearance of the robust australopithecines. According to Johanson and White, the teeth of *A. africanus* are too large for them to be placed as intermediate forms between *A. afarensis* and early members of the genus *Homo*. This takes into consideration the overlap in the tooth sizes of *A. africanus* and South African *A. robustus* forms. Thus, this view presents the *A. africanus* forms as the beginning of the line leading to the robust australopithecines, and off the line of hominid evolution leading to modern humans.

According to the third theory of australopithecine evolution (Table 9.4, part C), the earliest of the australopithecines, *A. afarensis*, evolves into *A. africanus*, and about 2.5 million years B.P. the robust line begins to speciate. It is suggested that the South African *A. robustus*, because it is less extreme than the East African *A. boisei*, represents this early speciation, with the East African forms representing the later, continued

Table 9.4. Theories of early hominid evolution.

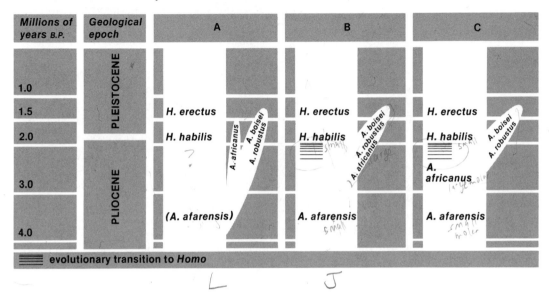

evolutionary transition to *Homo*

evolution of the group. After the robusts speciate, *A. africanus* continues, beginning to evolve into members of the genus *Homo* sometime after 2 million years ago. According to this idea, the difficulties in distinguishing members of the genus *Homo* from those of *Australopithecus africanus* in the period between 2 and 1.5 million years B.P. arise from the fact that the species at this time contains individuals with features reminiscent of both kinds. Robinson's claim, that the *Homo habilis* material represents the evolutionary transition between *Australopithecus* and *Homo*, meshes with this situation.

Whether any of these theories, or yet another one, most adequately describes early hominid evolution will depend on future fossil discoveries. All the current theories assume the presence of at least two coexisting hominid lines during the late Pliocene/early Pleistocene. How two hominids were able to coexist is an interesting and important question that requires examination of the evidence for australopithecine adaptation.

Australopithecine Adaptations

Australopithecine Environments

Through the study of plant pollen, and the identification of the animal bones found in the early hominid deposits, as well as sophisticated geologic analyses, a general picture of the environments in which the australopithecine sites were located has been developed. This picture is at variance with the traditional notions that early hominid evolution took place in open country and that the australopithecines were savanna-adapted hominids. These new investigations reveal a more complicated situation. In East Africa, most of the australopithecine bones come from places that were on the margin of lakes or beside a stream. A variety of habitats were close by: open-country savanna, woodland, and forest. It is not clear whether one or the other australopithecine line was limited to any one of these zones, or was able to seasonably exploit the resources in all of them.

At Olduvai Gorge, thanks to the work of the geologist Richard Hay, we have a rather complete picture of the environment during Bed I times when *A. boisei* and *H. habilis* lived in the area. According to Hay, beneath the shadow of the then active volcano of Ngorongoro, there was a perennial lake which varied in size from season to season. Feeding the lake were a number of streams that ran down from the highlands. Contrasting with the well-watered, forested volcanic highlands were open country and woodland around the lake shore. Early hominid sites are almost always located either by the side of one of the feeder streams, or along the lake edge.[18]

In South Africa, the evidence seems to show much the same situation: a variety of habitats located in the immediate vicinity of the cave deposits.

The Evidence of Archaeology The description of a fossil's morphological features is the first step in an analysis. Our goal is to understand the ways by which a population maintained a long-term successful adaptation within its environment. The evidence indicates that the australopithecines were a successful animal group, surviving for at least 4 million years, much longer than their modern human descendants have thus far been around. Unfortunately, archaeological materials, which furnish a great deal of information for later periods, are very scarce for this time. The very limited data that have been recovered have proved to be exceedingly difficult to interpret. The South African australopithecine sites consist of accumulations of debris that fell down a shaft and were incorporated into the deposit. Animal bones, australopithecine bones, and, at one or two of the sites, stone and bone tools are all found. Clearly early hominids were in the vicinity of the caverns, but whether they had any responsibility for the animal bone accumulations is a very difficult question to answer. A recent detailed assessment of the South African cave fillings by C. K. Brain suggests that most of the animal bones in the deposits are the result of carnivore activity, and this may also apply to the australopithecine bones (Figure 9.35).[19]

The East African sites are more rewarding. At Olduvai Gorge and East Turkana several living floor areas have been excavated, surfaces on which the australopithecines lived. These sites have stone tools, broken animal bones, and sometimes broken australopithecine bones. At one site east of Lake Turkana, known as the Hippo Artifact Site (HAS), the remains of a partially dismembered hippopotamus were found in a dry streambed, with a few stone tools around the carcass. It is not likely that the australopithecines were capable of dispatching a tough creature like a hippo;

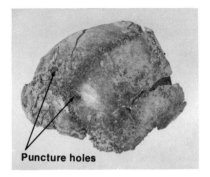

Puncture holes

inches
0   1
0   3
Centimeters

Figure 9.35. *Evidence indicating that some South African australopithecine fossils were victims of predators' attacks, and a hypothetical reconstruction. The photographs are exterior and interior views of the back of a young robust australopithecine skull from the Swartkrans site. Notice the presence of two puncture holes. C. K. Brain believes that these holes resulted from a bite by a carnivore's canine teeth, possibly a leopard's. Brain has a fossil leopard jaw whose canines fit these holes exactly, and has suggested such a kill in this drawing.*

the context probably reflects the fortunate discovery of a dead or dying animal. At a site in Bed I, Olduvai Gorge, stone tools were found on a living floor with the remains of many different animals, including pigs, frogs, chameleons, rodents, birds, fish, and small and medium-sized antelopes. At another site at Olduvai, where the first *Homo habilis* fossils were found, the hominid bones were discovered scattered over the living floor, intermixed with a variety of animal bones.

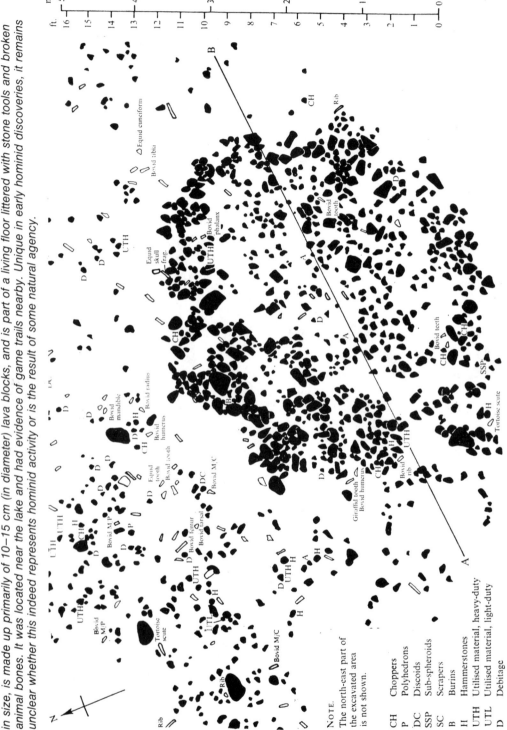

Figure 9.36. *Part of the plan of the site of DK, in Bed I, Olduvai Gorge, prepared by Mary Leakey. The stone ring, some 4 by 5 meters in size, is made up primarily of 10–15 cm (in diameter) lava blocks, and is part of a living floor littered with stone tools and broken animal bones. It was located near the lake and had evidence of game trails nearby. Unique in early hominid discoveries, it remains unclear whether this indeed represents hominid activity or is the result of some natural agency.*

NOTE.
The north-east part of the excavated area is not shown.

CH   Choppers
P   Polyhedrons
DC   Discoids
SSP   Sub-spheroids
SC   Scrapers
B   Burins
H   Hammerstones
UTH   Utilised material, heavy-duty
UTL   Utilised material, light-duty
D   Debitage

At the site of DK, low in Bed I, the fragmentary skull of a *Homo habilis* was found with a curious ring of stones (Figure 9.36). First identified by the Leakeys as the remains of a dwelling, it is now being viewed as the remains of a hunting blind, a place located near to the lake margin, and close to animal trails that would be used by animals coming down to drink.

The stone tools are crudely chipped from pebbles, or cobbles, which accounts for the term "cobble tools"; they are called the Oldowan industry (Figure 9.37). We cannot reconstruct how the australopithecines used these tools, but they were not suitable for delicate tasks. Occasionally a variety of worked animal bones are also found. These stone and bone implements may have been used for digging plants, animals, and insects out of the ground, or for pounding tough vegetable foods, such as tubers, or for cracking open animal bones to reach the marrow.

Reconstructing Behavior

The archaeological and environmental data, along with the australopithecine fossils themselves, do not provide enough information for any firm conclusions to be drawn about their behavior and adaptation.

We do not know if the australopithecines hunted the animals whose bones we find with them, or if they scavenged the remains of animals killed by predators. The animal bones may also come from old or sick animals that would be relatively easy for australopithecines to kill. Nothing

Figure 9.37. *Cobble tools of the Oldowan industry from Bed I, Olduvai Gorge, Tanzania (one-third actual size).*

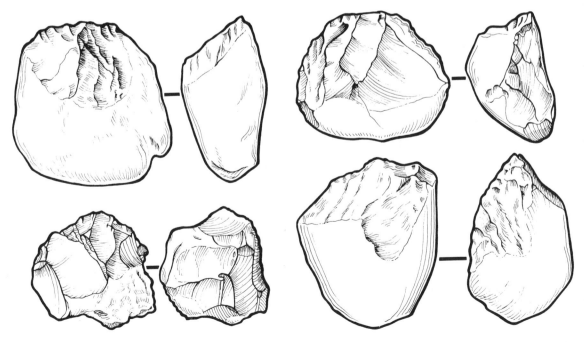

is left of vegetable or insect foods, so that we have no way of determining how much of the diet was hunted meat (if any) and how much gathered vegetable foods, insects, insect grubs, birds, birds' eggs, amphibians, small reptiles, and mammals.

While the earliest stone tools have come from deposits above the *A. afarensis*-bearing rocks at Hadar in Ethiopia, and dated to about 2.5 million years B.P., stone tools do not become a common element in the hominid record until after 2 million years B.P. It is possible that prior to this, other, perishable materials, such as wood, were employed for tools, but the evidence for this is lacking. We do not know if all the early hominids were capable of toolmaking behaviors. The lack of associated tools with *A. afarensis* and *A. africanus* would argue against viewing them as toolmakers, but were these behaviors limited to the more advanced-appearing australopithecines of the kind represented by the *Homo* group? Or were robust australopithecines also capable of these behaviors? Unfortunately, there have been no discoveries of hominid bones and tools that would demonstrate beyond question that only one line of early hominids were toolmakers.

On the basis of similarities in dental development between the australopithecines and modern humans, we believe that the australopithecines had a prolonged childhood dependency period. The modern human's prolonged childhood provides time for transmitting learned behavior from one generation to the next; the young learn the skills needed to survive in their environment. Childhood is longer for us than for the apes because we have more to learn.[20]

Like all higher primates, the australopithecines lived in social groups. The group size is not known but it could not have been large. It may well be that the male-female bond characteristic of modern humans developed at this time, perhaps because they needed a way of caring for the young, which spent more time depending on their parents.

Given this limited data base of known information about the early hominids, it is not surprising that there is little agreement among anthropologists (we know how tired you must be to keep reading that!) in reconstructing the patterns of adaptation of the various australopithecines, with just about every kind of diet and habitat being suggested at one time or another.

Before discussing the various adaptive models that have been proposed for the australopihecines, it might be useful to briefly summarize what we do know about these early hominids.

The earliest australopithecines, those belonging to *A. afarensis* and *A. africanus*, have not been found with tools, or any other direct evidence of complex behavior. Tools first appear about 2.5 million years ago unassociated with any hominid. After about 2 million years B.P. stone tools and signs of meat eating appear in East Africa, on living floors with both the robust *A. boisei* and *Homo habilis* fossil bones. There are thus signs that behavior evolved during early hominid evolution.

One of the most widely accepted models of australopithecine adaptation was offered by J. T. Robinson, who suggested that the robust australopithecines were inhabiting different ecological niches from the others; the robust forms, with larger back teeth, faces, and chewing muscles, were forest-dwelling vegetarians, living on tough, fibrous vegetable materials that require much chewing. The other australopithecines were omnivores more adapted to open country, subsisting on animal tissue as well as plants.[21]

Models of Australopithecine Adaptation

This view of the two early hominid lines being adapted to different habitats and diets has been a favored concept for many because it provides a way to explain how two biologically similar hominid species could coexist in the same area, for example, at Olduvai Gorge. Many models of early hominid adaptation utilize this same basic concept, but modify the diet or the habitats involved.

Raymond Dart proposed that *Australopithecus africanus* and the members of the hominid line leading to *Homo* were adapted to the open savanna, and that they were basically predatory hunters. In contrast, others, like Noel Boaz and Charles Peters, view *A. africanus* as essentially opportunistic foragers subsisting mainly on vegetation. Peters has actually gathered eatable vegetable materials in the Makapan Valley of South Africa in order to demonstrate the likelihood of his ideas.[22]

Other suggestions have focused on the kinds of habitats that the early hominids were exploiting, arguing that since social groups of chimps and baboons routinely exploit a number of different environments during the course of their yearly round, it is simplistic to believe that the early hominids were not at least as complex. These models must then provide an explanation of how the robust line and the line leading to *Homo* were able to coexist, since this model does away with any environmental limitations on the hominids.

One such model views all australopithecines as adapted to the environment in much the same way, as generalized feeders of plants, insects, and small vertebrate foods. After the robust australopithecines speciate, both lines continue to live in the same environments and to compete for the same resources. Both lines react to this competition biologically, but in different ways. The robust line evolves increasingly large back teeth to facilitate more efficient chewing. Large back teeth are an ancient part of the hominid adaptation and perhaps extend back to the hominoid ancestors of the hominid family. The robust line thus elaborates a trait that has been an important part of the basic adaptation of the hominids for a long time, perhaps as a way to increase food processing efficiency in what proved to be a futile change: the robust line disappears from the fossil record after about 1.5 million years B.P. Robust australopithecine brain size does not increase; the only change we can note in the robust line is an increase in the size of the back teeth and the supporting structures of muscle and bone.

In the line leading to *Homo*, in contrast, competition leads to more

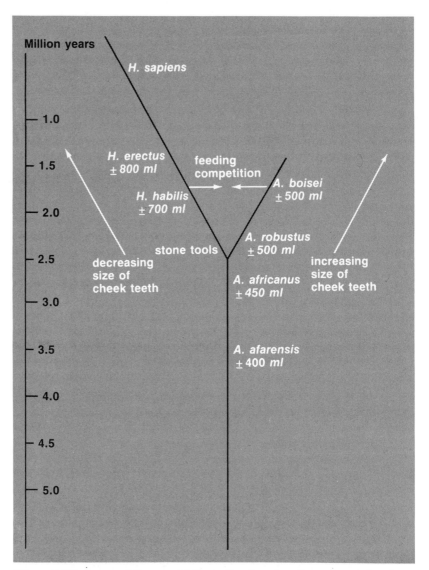

Figure 9.38. *A speculative model illustrating how two lines of early hominids, both adapted to the environment in the same way, might have interacted, and the biological and behavioral changes that may have resulted.*

efficient ways of procuring food by more adept toolmaking. This model thus attempts to explain the evolutionary origins of the genus *Homo* in the time period from 2 to 1.5 million years B.P.; that as a result of competition with the robust line there was evolutionary selection for more complex behavior which led to increasing brain sizes in the line leading to *Homo* (Figure 9.38). This is an attractive model because it is able to fit the known fossil information into a pattern which also explains the extinction of the robust australopithecines, and the sudden increase in brain size in the line leading to *Homo* as well as the flowering of tool technology. It provides a way of understanding the subsequent evolutionary events that were to lead to the appearance of modern humans, and indeed, develops a reason for these events. Finally, this model highlights the differences between australopithecines and later hominids.[23]

Attractive though it is, this idea, and others like it, are unverifiable at present. Excavations are continuing at a number of sites in South Africa and East Africa, and new fossil and archaeological materials are being discovered regularly. We can hope that the additional evidence will help to clarify the still very murky picture of early hominid evolution, and its relationships to the appearance of later hominids.

The discovery from East Turkana of KNM-ER 3733 demonstrates that by about 1.5 to 1.6 million years ago, members of the genus *Homo* were present in East Africa. As we have seen, they evolved probably during the period between 2 and 1.5 million years B.P. From 1.5 million years ago, we are dealing with the biological history of our own genus and one of the important parts of this story is the appearance of the hominids in other parts of the Old World.

Summary

This chapter has examined the fossil evidence for the early phases of hominid evolution, up until about 1.3 million years ago when hominids of the genus *Homo* begin to appear outside Africa.

The earliest known members of the family Hominidae belong to the genus *Australopithecus*, who are grouped for convenience in this chapter with an early representative of the genus *Homo*, *Homo habilis*, as the australopithecines. These hominids, from the period from about 4 to 1.5 million years B.P., are known from a number of sites in South and East Africa. They share with later hominids a bipedal mode of locomotion, and, except for the earliest of the australopithecines, possess essentially hominid-like, though larger-in-size, dentitions in a large projecting face. The brain size of these early hominids is generally small, though some general increase in size can be noted from the earliest to the latest. On the basis of differences in the teeth, jaws, and skull, five species of australopithecines have been named, including two species of larger, more robust forms that seem to represent an extinct side branch of hominid evolution that disappeared from the fossil record after about 1.5 million years ago. Members of our own genus, *Homo*, seem to appear in the fossil record between 2 and 1.5 million years B.P. From that time to the emergence of modern humans, the story of human evolution extends to other parts of the Old World, and the archaeological traces of our ancestors' behavior increase dramatically.

A more elaborate summary including the material covered in this chapter will be found at the end of Chapter 10.

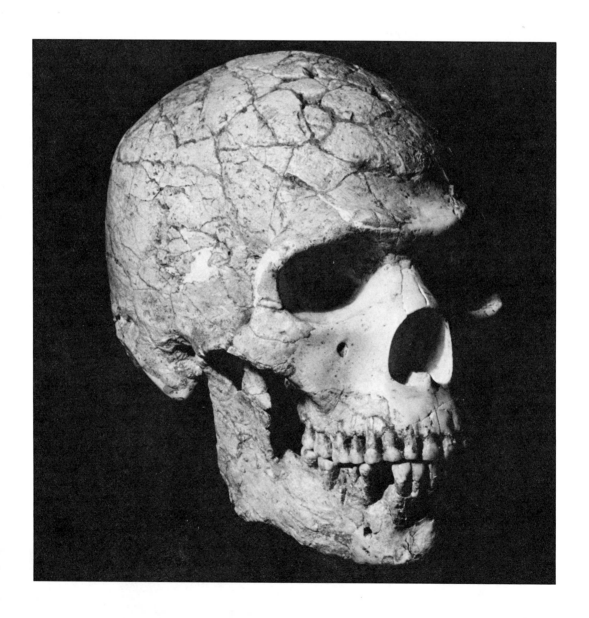

Chapter 10

Human Evolution II: The Emergence of Modern Humans

In the last chapter we traced the development of the family Hominidae from its rather shadowy beginnings, and described the extensive australopithecine fossil collections from South and East Africa, dated to the period from about 6 million to about 1.5 million years ago. By this time, fossil hominids of the category *Homo erectus,* such as KNM-ER 3733 from East Turkana (see Figure 9.32), are on the scene, to remain as the sole hominid until evolving into early members of *Homo sapiens* some 300,000 to 400,000 years B.P. Thus, *Homo erectus* is the hominid taxon between the earlier australopithecines and later *Homo sapiens,* from the early part of the Pleistocene, about 1.5 million years B.P., to the latter stages of the Middle Pleistocene, around 300,000 to 400,000 years ago.

The evolutionary development of *Homo erectus* also coincides with the gradual geographic expansion of the hominids (Figure 10.1). Earliest *Homo erectus* appears to have been limited to the temperate and tropical parts of the Old World, while later *Homo erectus* is found in the colder parts of Asia, like north China, and perhaps the central parts of Europe as well. By the time of the earliest *H. sapiens* fossil evidence, hominids are to be found in most parts of the Old World. Much of the rest of the world, however, remained uncolonized by hominids until very late in human evolution, when anatomically modern peoples moved into Siberia, and from there into North and South America; by boat they occupied the islands of the Pacific, including Australia and New Guinea.

It is reasonable to speculate that the expansion of the hominids out of Africa was based on the continued elaboration of complex behavior, especially tool making and using skills. This permitted the hominids to exploit environments that would not have been open to them without these abilities. The last chapter described a model of competition between the two hominid lines, with the line leading to *Homo erectus* reacting to the competition from the robust australopithecines by developing more complex tool-making behaviors. In this imaginative model, the competition between the two early hominid lines literally sets the stage for subsequent events in human evolution, including the reason why the hominids, at this point in their biological history, move into new areas.[1]*

*See page 570 for notes to Chapter 10.

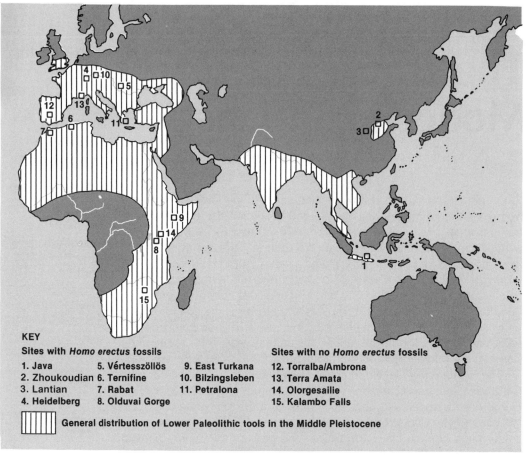

KEY

Sites with *Homo erectus* fossils

1. Java	5. Vértesszöllös
2. Zhoukoudian	6. Ternifine
3. Lantian	7. Rabat
4. Heidelberg	8. Olduvai Gorge

9. East Turkana
10. Bilzingsleben
11. Petralona

Sites with no *Homo erectus* fossils

12. Torralba/Ambrona
13. Terra Amata
14. Olorgesailie
15. Kalambo Falls

|||||| General distribution of Lower Paleolithic tools in the Middle Pleistocene

Figure 10.1. *Distribution of* Homo erectus *fossils and archaeological sites. The European fossils, Heidelberg, Bilzingsleben, Petralona, and Vértesszöllös, may be early representatives of* H. sapiens.

Homo Erectus

Discoveries in Java

In the late nineteenth century, more than thirty years before Dart described *Australopithecus,* Eugene Dubois, a Dutch physician, became interested in human evolution. This was a time of great controversy about our origins. Some still hoped that an intermediate form, a "missing link" between humans and the apes, would be found. Dubois, determined to find traces of this creature, joined the colonial service and sailed to the Dutch East Indies in 1887.

In 1891, after several years of fruitless searching, Dubois found a skull cap, and later a thighbone (femur), and a few other fragments washed out of a river bank at *Trinil,* on the Solo River, in the central part of Java, now part of the country of Indonesia. The skull cap and the thighbone contrasted remarkably. The leg bone was indistinguishable from those of living humans but the skull cap's forehead was much lower and more sloping than those of living humans (Figure 10.2). The total height of the braincase was significantly lower than those of modern people, and because of this the greatest width across the skull, when viewed from the back, was low on the skull, just behind and above the ear holes. Above the eye orbits were large, projecting brow ridges and directly behind the orbits was a "waisting," a narrowing or constriction in the braincase not found in modern human skulls because of their larger brain. Dubois's Trinil skull had a cranial volume of about 775 ml, larger than almost all australopithecine skulls but smaller than the 1,350 to 1,450 ml capacity normally found in modern human skulls. The Trinil specimen also had very thick skull bones.

Dubois decided that these physical features might mean he had found the long sought missing link. A few years before Dubois's discovery, Ernst Haeckel, a German scientist, suggested that if a link between apes and humans were found, it would be logical to call it "Pithecanthropus" (*pithec* = ape; *anthropos* = man: apeman). Dubois was impressed by the modern human look of the thighbone, which indicated this fossil had in life assumed erect posture, and he gave the Java fossil the taxonomic name *"Pithecanthropus erectus,"* or erect apeman. This taxonomic category was changed in the 1960s to *Homo erectus.*

Like many other discoveries of fossil hominids, Dubois's conclusions were strongly criticized by some scientists, who particularly objected to his association of the primitive-looking skull and the modern thighbone.

Figure 10.2. *Cast of the skull cap discovered by Dubois in Java (right) and a modern human skull (left) are compared. The Trinil skull cap shows the low sloping forehead, large brow ridges, and marked constriction behind the brow ridges which are found on many members of* Homo erectus.

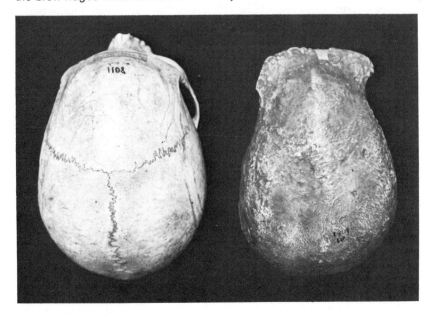

They suggested that the skull cap belonged to an extinct giant gibbon; the thighbone could have belonged to a modern human skeleton accidentally washed into the geologic deposit with the skull cap. The controversy burned on for several decades, and was not to be settled until the discovery of new fossil material enabled paleoanthropologists to place Dubois's Trinil finds in perspective.

As we have seen, Dart announced the discovery of Australopithecus in 1925. An increased understanding of the implications of australopithecine morphology ended many of the debates over "Pithecanthropus erectus." The australopithecines' morphological characteristics were more primitive than those of Dubois's find, yet they appeared to be hominid. In comparison with the australopithecines, "Pithecanthropus erectus," looked more like modern humans. "Pithecanthropus erectus," then, was evolutionarily intermediate between modern humans and the australopithecines. Additional hominid fossils, in appearance like that of "Pithecanthropus," and dated to the Lower and Middle Pleistocene, supported this conclusion.

At a number of sites in central Java, near the locale of the original Trinil find, many fossil skull pieces, and some jaws and teeth, have been found. The richest site is Sangiran, where over thirty fossil specimens have been recovered. The hominid-bearing geologic deposits have been examined carefully, and based on the identification of the animals' bones, they are divided into three Beds. Lowest of these deposits, and therefore oldest, are the Djetis Beds, whose hominid bones have been likened to some of the later-in-time Bed II Homo habilis fossils from Olduvai Gorge. Above this bed is the Trinil Bed, in which Dubois discovered the original "Pithecanthropus" skull cap, and which has subsequently yielded a number of additional fossil bones. Situated above the Trinil faunal beds, and therefore later than both the Trinil and Djetis Beds, are the Ngandong Beds, in which the German paleontologist G. H. R. von Koenigswald discovered a series of skull caps and several shinbones, all known as the Solo sample because they were found along the banks of the Solo River, in central Java.

Many fossils from both the Trinil and Djetis Beds have features similar to those in Dubois's original find: strong brow ridges with a waisting behind the orbits; low, sloping foreheads and low, flat braincases with low maximum width of the braincase; and thick cranial bones. A recently discovered Homo erectus skull from relatively high up in the Trinil Bed possesses an exceedingly rare feature for Homo erectus fossils: facial bones (Figure 10.3). Except for this specimen, and one or two others, Homo erectus fossil skulls are discovered without their faces, and usually without the skull bases as well. The Homo erectus face apparently was very large, with big eye orbits below the brow ridges, a large nasal structure separating the orbits, and a large and expanded cheek region above the teeth.

The later-in-time Solo skull series possesses features, such as larger braincases, that have made them more difficult to classify; some would

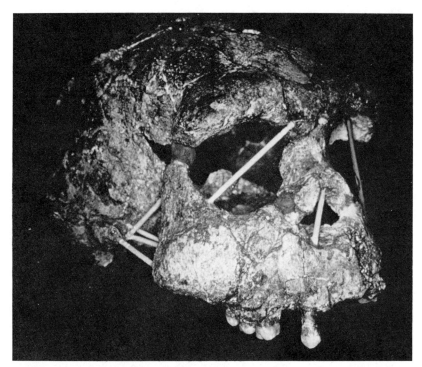

Figure 10.3. *A* Homo erectus *skull from the Trinil beds at Sangiran, Java, one of the few* H. erectus *specimens found with a face.*

identify them as late *Homo erectus,* while others suggest they are early representatives of *Homo sapiens.* The fact that the Ngandong Beds have not been well dated is an added problem. We will return to the complex situation surrounding the evolutionary appearance of *Homo sapiens* presently.

A number of K-Ar absolute dates have been made on the Djetis and Trinil Beds at various sites in Java. For a variety of reasons, these dates have proved to be difficult to interpret. It is currently estimated that the earliest hominids in Java, in the Djetis layer, are about 1.3 million years old, with the Trinil Bed perhaps extending from about 1.0 million to about 600,000 years B.P. There are no reliable dates for the Ngandong Bed, but it most probably represents a late Middle Pleistocene deposit (the Middle Pleistocene ends at about 125,000 years B.P.; see Chapter 8).

Paleontologists had long known that the Chinese believed fossil bones ("dragon" bones, they were called) had great curative powers when crushed with other ingredients in many medicines. A tooth bought in a Chinese drugstore seemed to come from a hominid; this eventually led, in 1921, to the discovery of a large cave site located on a hill, known locally as Dragon Bone Hill, just outside the village of *Zhoukoudian,* 40

Discoveries in China

km southwest of Beijing. Initiated by a Swedish team, the excavations were continued by a Canadian anatomist, Davidson Black, who was working at the Beijing Union Medical College. In 1927 a clearly hominid tooth was discovered. On this discovery alone, Black established a new fossil taxon: "Sinanthropus pekinensis," meaning the Chinese man of Peking (now Beijing). Work continued at Zhoukoudian almost until World War II under Black and other scientists, including a Chinese anthropologist, Wu Rukang, and a German anthropologist, Franz Weidenreich.

By 1937 this great cave site had given up the skulls, teeth, and other fossil bones of about forty-five hominid individuals, along with stone tools, bones from thousands of animals, and evidence of fire. At the end of 1941, as World War II began and the Japanese moved on Beijing, it was feared that the fossils might be damaged; they were packed and sent by train to a seaport for shipment to the United States for safekeeping. Sometime after they left Beijing, the fossils disappeared. Although in the years since their loss many theories have been advanced to account for their whereabouts, no trace of these precious bones has been found.[2] Fortunately, Weidenreich had published a complete description of the bones, and accurate casts, like those pictured in Figures 10.4 and 10.10 (page 354), were made, so that the loss is not total. After the war the People's Republic of China reopened the Zhoukoudian excavation, and several new hominid fossils have been found. The Beijing skulls do not differ greatly from Trinil layer Java fossils, except that there is a wide range of variation in their cranial capacities, with some as great as 1,225 ml. These larger braincases support the geologic and dating evidence

Figure 10.4. *Two views of the cast of a skull of a Beijing person ("Sinanthropus pekinensis") from Zhoukoudian. Most of the face and the bottom of the skull have been restored.*

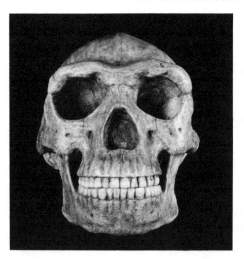
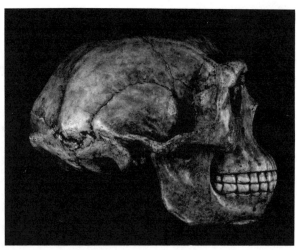

that the Zhoukoudian hominids (now also placed in *Homo erectus*) lived later than the Trinil layer Javanese *Homo erectus* group. Relative dating of these Chinese cave deposits suggests that most of the hominids lived between 400,000 and 600,000 years ago.

Additional fossil material has been uncovered in the People's Republic of China. At *Lantian*, in central China, a hominid skull and lower jaw that look like the Trinil Javanese material have been excavated. This fossil material is probably somewhat earlier than the Zhoukoudian fossils, in the time range of the Trinil specimens, and like the Trinil material, it has large projecting brow ridges, a low forehead, and low braincase height. At *Hexian*, in central China, another *Homo erectus* skull cap was excavated in 1982. This fossil is much like the Zhoukoudian skulls in appearance, and like them, seems to date from a time later than Lantian, probably around 400,000.[3]

Hominid fossils similar in appearance to the Eurasian *Homo erectus* fossils have been found in East, South, and North Africa. At East Turkana, in northern Kenya, Richard Leakey's discovery of the KMN-ER 3733 skull confirmed the existence of two separate hominid lines living at the same time (see pages 324–328). The ER3733 skull (Figure 9.32) shares many features of the braincase with Asian *Homo erectus*, especially with the much later-in-time Zhoukoudian fossils, but its volume of 800 ml also relates it to the Early Pleistocene Java specimens. At Olduvai Gorge in Tanzania, fossils from Bed I and Lower Bed II look somewhat like both the australopithecines and *Homo erectus*, which led to their placement in the transitional taxon, *Homo habilis*. A distinct geologic break divides Lower Bed II from Upper Bed II. In Upper Bed II, at the site of LLK (Louis Leakey Korongo), a large skull cap was found that has many similarities with the Asian *Homo erectus* skulls: low braincase combined with a low, sloping forehead, large brow ridge, and defined waisting behind the orbits (Figure 10.5); the cranial capacity is about the same as some of the larger Chinese fossils. *Homo erectus* fossils have also been found in Bed IV at Olduvai Gorge. Included is a piece of the pelvis which, like the thighbone Dubois discovered, confirms that *Homo erectus* was an erect, bipedal hominid. Mary Leakey suggests a date of about 500,000 years for this find. There are other *Homo erectus* fossil materials from Beds III and IV, including a portion of a lower jaw remarkably similar to those found at Zhoukoudian.

The Sterkfontein Valley in South Africa has yielded many australopithecine fossils. At the site of Swartkrans, there is some evidence of *Homo erectus*, a part of the skull and face. The complex geology suggests this fossil was deposited in the Swartkrans breccia a considerable time after the robust australopithecine specimens were accumulated.

On the Mediterranean side of the Atlas Mountains in North Africa, *Homo erectus* fossils have been discovered. *Rabat* and *Sidi Abderrahman* in Morocco have yielded fragmentary lower jaws in some ways like those from Zhoukoudian. And from *Ternifine*, in Algeria, the French pa-

African Hominids

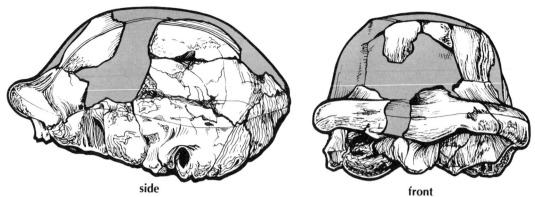

side   front

Figure 10.5. *Views of the restored skull cap of a hominid (OH 9) found at Olduvai Gorge, drawn from a Wenner-Gren Foundation cast.*

leontologist, C. Arambourg, discovered three almost complete lower jaws and a piece of the skull cap. These, too, are like the fossils from China.

European Fossils   Some fossil bones found in Europe have been called *Homo erectus,* but their morphological features are in some ways more advanced than the *H. erectus* fossils from other parts of the Old World. One of these was found in 1907 in a little town called *Mauer,* outside of Heidelberg, Germany. A lower jaw of a mature individual, the Mauer or Heidelberg jaw is difficult to interpret because its massive jawbone, with no chin, is combined with relatively small, modern-looking teeth (Figure 10.6). The geologic and faunal context places the fossil in the earlier part of the Middle Pleistocene. Opinion is divided as to whether the Heidelberg jaw is a European representative of *Homo erectus* or an early member of *Homo sapiens.*

Figure 10.6. *The Mauer jaw. It differs from jaws of other Middle Pleistocene hominids found in China and Africa.*

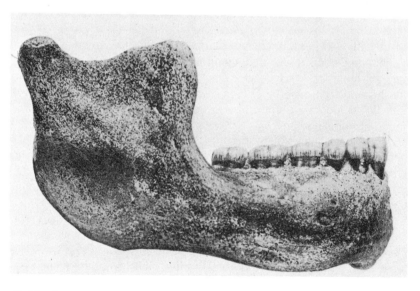

Like the Mauer or Heidelberg jaw, the back of the skull (occipital bone) found at *Vértesszöllös,* Hungary, in 1965 has inspired differing views. Milford Wolpoff has suggested that the relatively high position of the attachment areas for the neck muscles on the bone identify it as *Homo erectus,* while the Hungarian scientist Andor Thoma believes the bone comes from a skull larger than those usually attributed to *H. erectus,* and feels it belongs in the taxon *Homo sapiens.*[4]

At Bilzingsleben, in East Germany, fragments of the front and back of several hominid skulls have been discovered in Middle Pleistocene deposits. The front part of the skull has massive brow ridges, and the back part a large ridge for attachment of the neck muscles. However, both *Homo erectus* and early *Homo sapiens* possess such features and the Bilzingsleben fossils are too incomplete to provide a definite answer to the question of their status.

Similarly, the skull found in the Petralona cave, Greece, in 1960 has been subject to a variety of interpretations (Figure 10.7). The Petralona skull is the most complete of the early European fossils, and probably is about 300,000 to 400,000 years old, somewhat later than the African and Asian *Homo erectus* specimens just described. Christopher Stringer, Clark Howell, and John Melentis assessed its evolutionary position.[5] They found that the skull height is not as low as the Zhoukoudian or African *H. erectus* fossils, and it possesses a cranial capacity of at least 1200 ml, which is matched only by the largest of the Zhoukoudian Beijing skulls.

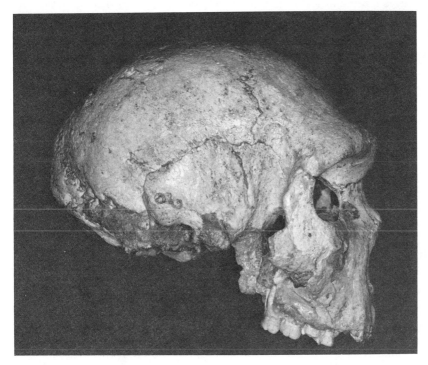

Figure 10.7. *The Petralona skull.*

They could not agree whether the Petralona skull was a late *H. erectus* or an early *H. sapiens;* thus, even the most complete of the European fossils poses problems of identification as do the Mauer, Vértesszöllös, and Bilzingsleben bones. All the European fossils are difficult to interpret, and it remains unclear whether *H. erectus* lived in Europe or whether the earliest hominids to populate this area were members of *Homo sapiens*. This is the same sort of problem that the Solo skull series from Java presented: how can representatives of *Homo erectus* be distinguished from those included in *Homo sapiens?* If the fossils possess features similar to both these taxonomic categories, does this not suggest a gradual evolutionary change from *H. erectus* to *H. sapiens,* in contrast to the model of punctuation presented in Chapter 3? These are important questions, crucial to our understanding of human evolution and the emergence of modern humans; they will be dealt with after we have examined more fully the adaptation of *Homo erectus.*

Tool Industries   If fossil bones were the only remnants, we could conclude that *Homo erectus* walked upright, had a brain larger than that of the australopithecines but smaller than that of modern humans, and had a face and teeth larger than those in modern humans. These morphological attributes would help us understand the biology of these fossil hominids and would tell us how *Homo erectus* was related evolutionarily to other hominids. They would not, however, give us an adequate understanding of the behavior patterns of these hominids. Fortunately, we have found traces of the culture along with the bones of *Homo erectus,* including tools, fire, and cooking debris. At archaeological sites that have not yielded hominid fossils but have been dated to the time of *Homo erectus* we have evidence of living structures and signs of other complex behaviors.

The tools found with *Homo erectus* fossils belong to the lower Paleolithic. They exhibit a diversity of types, perhaps reflecting the specialized tool kits required for the different environments in which *Homo erectus* was living. The later australopithecines, too, as we have seen, have been occasionally found with stone tools made from cobbles, the Oldowan industry.

The Oldowan tools are simple and unspecialized. We find it hard to understand just what they were used for, but they surely were not suitable for delicate tasks. From the Oldowan industry developed a more complex tool tradition, the evolved Oldowan industry. These tools are better made and are of more types, perhaps to equip their makers to perform a greater range of tasks. Evolved Oldowan tools were found at Olduvai Gorge, as well as at the Swartkrans site in South Africa. The fossils from North Africa have been associated with tools rather different from those of the evolved Oldowan tradition.

In the nineteenth century, with controversy raging about human evolution, those who were building the modern science of prehistoric archaeology uncovered deposits of great antiquity including stones intentionally chipped by humans. As part of this search, French scientists had investigated a site in a small French village called St. Acheul, where stones of a particular shape came to light. They were large, measuring about 9 centimeters wide by 12 to 15 centimeters long, and were in teardrop form, with one end pointed and the other rounded. The makers of the implements were skilled, for the tools were finely flaked. The tools were called hand axes, but we do not know their actual function. This tool tradition took its name from the village of St. Acheul, and is called the *Acheulian* industry (Figure 10.8). Acheulian hand axes have been found virtually all over the Old World, from Africa and Europe in the west to Asia in the east. Most of these were not found with hominid fossils, though the *Homo erectus* fossils from Ternifine, in Algeria, were found with Acheulian tools, suggesting that hand axes, as well as the evolved Oldowan tools, were being manufactured by different *Homo erectus* groups.

There are no simple, clear associations between tool types and varieties of fossil hominids. The Acheulian industry may have lasted for more than a million years and is associated with both *Homo erectus* and, later in time, with *Homo sapiens* populations. Cultures, like animals, evolve; the Acheulian industry in the Lower Pleistocene is different from that found in deposits dated to the end of the Middle Pleistocene. Later tools are more competently made in greater variety; they include stone tools that became part of later prehistoric cultures.

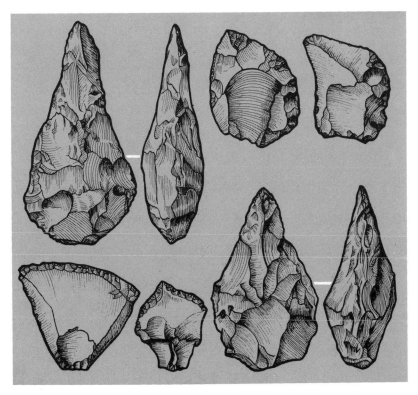

Figure 10.8. Acheulian tools (one-half actual size). The tools in the upper left and lower right corners are hand axes; the others are mainly scrapers designed to perform a number of tasks.

Both the evolved Oldowan industry and the Acheulian are found with different *Homo erectus* fossils. A third stone tool industry, found with the Zhoukoudian fossils, was named the *Chopping Tool* tradition. These were made from large pieces of stone, sometimes flaked on one side only, sometimes on both sides. The three stone tool industries suggest that these Middle Pleistocene hominids manufactured regionally specialized tools in response to the requirements of their particular environments, or that perhaps different activities required the use of different sorts of tools. The virtually complete absence of stone tools in *Homo erectus* deposits on the island of Java has suggested to some archaeologists that perhaps the picture is even more complicated. G. J. Bartstra maintains that these hominids may have been making tools from bamboo and other local woods; these would have been excellent, useful tools entirely comparable to those made of stone, but with one major difference: they would not be preserved and thus they left no record for us.[6]

Gatherers and Hunters   The stone tools and the fossils tell us something about *Homo erectus*. But if we want to learn more about how these hominids successfully adapted to their environment, we must examine archaeological sites that have no hominid fossils associated with them but are dated to the Middle Pleistocene. Some of these sites are *Ambrona* and *Torralba* in central Spain, *Terra Amata* in the city of Nice in southern France, and *Kalambo Falls* and *Olorgesailie* in East Africa. Because of the problems in classifying the European fossils, it is difficult to know whether the European sites were occupied by *Homo erectus* or early *Homo sapiens* populations. However, the important point is not the nature of the exact hominid responsible, but rather what these archaeological sites can tell us about hominid adaptations in the Middle Pleistocene.

Terra Amata Terra Amata is an open-air site in Nice, France, discovered in 1965 when construction workers were digging the foundation of a building.[7] Henry de Lumley, a French archaeologist, had the construction stopped while he and his team excavated the site. According to de Lumley, the site was originally much closer to the Mediterranean shoreline than it is today, and the hominids probably used it for short times as a seasonal camp while they exploited the local plant, animal, and seashore resources. Many animal bones were found, including deer, wild boar, elephant, wild ox, smaller mammals, turtles, and birds. The larger mammals are usually young, probably because they were easier to bring down.

Along with these things and tools of the Acheulian tradition, de Lumley found clear evidence of fire. We think the hominid group that camped at Terra Amata were also erecting shelters (Figure 10.9). In Bed I at Olduvai Gorge, Leakey found a ring of stones that suggests the australopithecines had built a structure, windbreak, or hunting blind, but the evidence from Terra Amata is different. At Terra Amata, de Lumley found post holes, that is, the remains of supporting posts sunk into the ground,

Figure 10.9. Recon-
struction of the
probable appear-
ance of a hut at
Terra Amata.

after the wooden posts above the ground have completely disintegrated.
In an excavation they appear as filled-in circles on the ground, usually
of a different color from that of the surrounding soil. The post holes were
so arranged that they must have supported oval structures that were
probably covered with interlacing branches. Inside these hutlike dwellings were fireplaces, sunk into the ground or placed on raised stone
platforms. The Terra Amata site suggests that our ancestors of Middle
Pleistocene times occupied an environmental niche much like that of
modern human gatherers and hunters.

Few human groups today subsist entirely by gathering wild vegetable materials, small animals, and insects, and hunting larger mammals.

Most human societies now practice some agriculture. However, before the great changes that marked the introduction of agriculture and the domestication of plants and animals, which seem to have taken place independently at several places in the world about 10,000 years ago, all human groups lived by gathering and hunting. To understand the patterns of human life through most of our biological history, we have to know something about how the gatherer and hunter lived, for that way of life shaped hominid biology and behavior for much of our evolution.

Most modern human groups still living as gatherers and hunters are found in marginal environments, and it is difficult to reconstruct conditions for gatherers and hunters in richer environments. Early researchers in cultural anthropology overemphasized the importance of hunting to the group's survival, giving the impression that hunting provided most of their food, and stressing the male's vital role as hunter. More recently we have found that hunting may not have been that important; for most gatherers and hunters living in tropical and temperate climates, the fruits, vegetables, nuts, birds and birds' eggs, insects and insect grubs, frogs and other small vertebrates, and small mammals gathered were the main part of the diet.[8]

Human societies based on agriculture today are permanently settled in one area, using the land near their village for farming or herding. Gatherers and hunters do not lead a settled existence, because even the richest environments may not be rich enough to support a gathering and hunting group throughout the whole year. Modern groups at this economic level usually move about over a wide area. These movements are not, however, arbitrary, and gatherers and hunters generally do not roam out of known and defined terrain. Over the generations, the group has learned where to find food at different seasons. This lore is part of the group's tradition, as is intimate knowledge about how the plants and animals live in the area. Gatherers and hunters are superb natural historians; they need to have extensive knowledge of the flora and fauna in order to be able to exploit all the environment's resources.

The environment limits the group's size. At some times during the year, food and water are plentiful, and then the gatherers and hunters may form rather large groups, and may even have more or less settled camps. At other times, when food or water is scarce, the group may be small, perhaps no larger than the nuclear family, with a father, mother, and dependent children. Their social organization is not permanent, but flexible enough to break apart and re-form, depending on the resources. According to pollen studies, it appears that the Middle Pleistocene camp at Terra Amata may have been such a seasonal stop during the late spring and early summer, when the group exploited the food available locally for a time, and moved on when it was depleted. The group returned to the same site each year for a number of years.

Torralba and Ambrona Other archaeological sites are also helpful in reconstructing more of Middle Pleistocene hominid life. One extremely important human feature, the ability to cooperate, seems to be suggested in the archaeological material from the sites of Torralba and Ambrona, located about 2 kilometers apart along the margins of a swampy valley with permanent water some 150 kilometers northeast of Madrid, Spain. F. C. Howell and Leslie Freeman, who excavated the sites, suggest that Torralba and Ambrona were specialized "kill" sites, perhaps located along seasonal migration routes of large herd mammals.[9] The remains of many game animals were found at the sites, including deer, horse, aurochs (the wild ancestor of modern domesticated cattle), and elephants. Many of the bones of these animals had been smashed, and a few show slicing marks made by hominids cutting at the carcasses. Many of the skeletal elements, especially the limb bones and feet, are missing, suggesting that these were cut from the carcass and carried off to be eaten elsewhere or, as there is little meat on these parts, they were simply thrown away. Along with the animal bones were numbers of stone tools and evidence of pieces of wood, some with chisel-shaped or pointed ends. Burnt wood and charcoal are found all over the sites, but little evidence of hearths, which may indicate that the Middle Pleistocene hominids who hunted in this area used fire as a means of driving their prey into a place where they could be easily dispatched. Although the many dead elephants at Ambrona may mean that the hominids living in this area were, over the years, successful in hunting, records of modern groups suggest that hunting large animals is a consistently chancy business; a hunting group is unlikely to kill an animal each time it sets out. It is much more likely that the hominid group returned to the Ambrona site year after year, perhaps when the elephants and other animals were migrating through the area. This is another indication of the similarity between the reconstructed patterns of behavior of Middle Pleistocene hominids and those of modern gatherers and hunters.

Zhoukoudian The Zhoukoudian deposits outside of Beijing rewarded the searchers with the remains of about forty-five individuals, plus significant archaeological data. Zhoukoudian represents the earliest documented use of fire by hominids, and it is as well one of the most northerly sites of *Homo erectus* times. There may very well be a relationship between the presence of fire and the hominid's ability to survive in an environment that was probably subjected to rather severe winter conditions. Although the site was first excavated in the 1920s, its size is such that excavations continue today, and more material, including hominid fossils, can be expected. This large cave shows evidence of periodic short-term occupations by hominids, which stretched over perhaps 200,000 years. Like the reconstruction of Terra Amata, the Zhoukoudian cave seems to have been lived in by hominids for a short time, then abandoned as the hominid group depleted local resources and moved on. Interestingly, the original excavators reported that the lowest levels of the cave showed evidence that carnivores were inhabiting the site, signs that disappear later on when the hominids move in for their short stays.

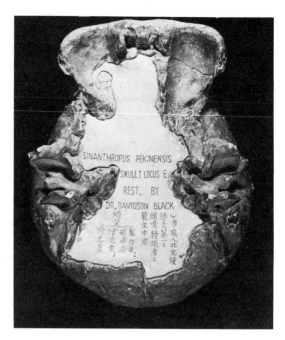

Figure 10.10 *The broken base of one of the Beijing* Homo erectus *skulls. Many* H. erectus *and later neandertal skulls possess broken-open skull bases, presumably for the brains to be removed. This is a photograph of one of the original plaster casts made by Chinese technicians under the direction of Franz Weidenreich. The original fossils were lost at the beginning of World War II.*

The resources in the area during *Homo erectus* times were varied. Excavators discovered huge numbers of the preserved seeds of the oriental hackberry, which is reported to be a rather tasty berry that ripens in the summer. In addition, the bones of many animals were found, including those of thousands of deer.

All of the hominid skulls lack facial bones, and many were broken open at the bottom (Figure 10.10). It has often been suggested that the skulls were damaged in this way to get at the brain, which is an excellent source of protein. Or this may suggest that these hominids had an ancestor cult, much in the fashion of some modern New Guinea peoples who place the skulls of deceased relatives in an honored location in their houses. Or these broken skulls could represent the attempt by the eater to gain something of the skill, magic, or memories of the dead individual. Or, most likely of all, the breakage may have been the result of the way the bones were incorporated into the deposit. Speculations are all we have, for we know nothing about their ideological patterns, or even if they had any. There is no evidence of intentional burial of *Homo erectus* individuals; all the fossil evidence comes from the bones that have been incorporated by chance into deposits, like the Zhoukoudian skull caps.

Homo Erectus Adaptations

The picture that emerges from the evidence of *Homo erectus* is very similar to that drawn by cultural anthropologists of modern nonagricultural gathering and hunting groups. The hominids of the Middle Pleistocene show us that the later hominids' basic economic pattern, gathering and hunting, has a long history. It is possible that its start lies back in australopithecine times, but archaeological evidence of their cultural behavior is still too meager to draw firm conclusions. Or it may be that the foundation for this adaptation lies in the 2 to 1.5 million year time range when the ancestors of *Homo erectus* were apparently in competition with the robust australopithecines and developed more complex tool-making behaviors. As a result, hominid behaviors during this time eventually reached a level of efficiency that permitted the hominids to expand gradually out of the mild environments of east and south Africa.

A total reconstruction of the life style of *Homo erectus* will never be possible; even with the greatest skill and the most sophisticated techniques, only a small portion of the cultural context can be recovered. Nevertheless, there are enough similarities between *Homo erectus* and modern gatherers and hunters for us to use these living peoples as a model. In this fashion, the time of *Homo erectus* can be seen as one marked by the increasing ability of hominids to exploit efficiently environments with harsher climates in many parts of the globe.

In all environments, the group's size would be limited by the resources. The social unit, we assume, never became smaller than the nuclear family. Modern gatherers and hunters, even in the most extreme environments, such as the Eskimos of the North American Arctic and Greenland (during their days as gatherers and hunters, which for the vast majority of them, are past), did not fragment into units smaller than that. An adult male and female Eskimo made up a complete economic unit; between them, they could manufacture, catch, cook, and build everything they needed for survival. This specialization in roles may have led to pair bonding of women and men during hominid evolution, but this is only one suggestion; the evolutionary development of the long childhood dependency may also have been responsible for this pattern.

Our archaeological evidence is not clear, but *Homo erectus* peoples, like their modern gatherer and hunter equivalents, may have depended for most of their subsistence on the gathering of plants, small animals, and insects, and the occasional hunting of large mammals. The similarity between these hominids of the genus *Homo* and modern peoples was one of the major reasons that the genus "Pithecanthropus" was dropped in favor of *Homo*. Because the pithecanthropines shared the same basic environmental adaptation as modern humans, they can reasonably be placed in the same genus but retained in a separate species.

The Transition to *Homo Sapiens*

As we have seen, fossil skulls, such as the Solo group, and European bones, such as the Mauer jaw, Vértesszöllös occipital, the Bilzingsleben fragments, and the Petralona fossil, all present difficulties in taxonomic identification. There is no generally agreed on definition of the genus and species *Homo sapiens*, although Stringer, Howell, and Melentis, in their description of the Petralona skull, suggest that changes in skull architecture and shape related to increasing brain size are the most important distinguishing features. In Figure 10.11 a Zhoukoudian *H. erectus* skull, the Petralona skull, a Solo skull cap, and that of a fossil *Homo sapiens* (a neandertal) from the Upper Pleistocene are compared. The major differences in these four skulls relate to increasing brain size, reflected in the increasing height of the skull and the smaller amount of constriction, or waisting, behind the orbits. Associated with this growth is the relative position of the ridges on which the neck muscles attach at the back of the skull. Because of the increased size of the brain, the ridges are positioned lower on the skull in the later hominids. These features, Stringer, Howell, and Melentis suggest, are the main ones differentiating *Homo erectus* from early *Homo sapiens*. The size of the facial area is still large on all the skulls, and the face is positioned relatively in front of the braincase. A decrease in the size of the facial region and its repositioning more underneath the braincase are changes important in

Figure 10.11. *Comparisons of a Zhoukoudian skull (reconstructed) (a), a Solo skull cap (b), Petralona (c), and an Upper Pleistocene* Homo sapiens *(a neandertal) (d). Note the difference in skull size and shape.*

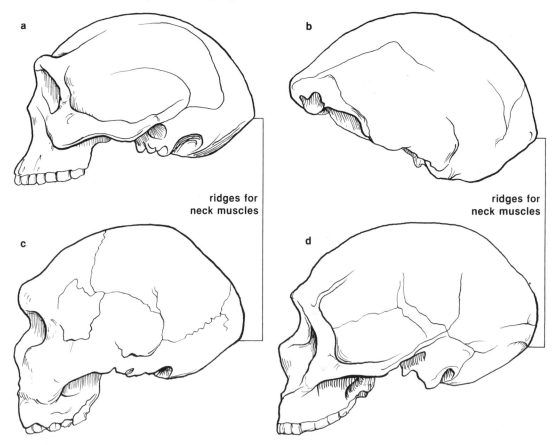

a

b

ridges for
neck muscles

ridges for
neck muscles

c

d

the later appearance of anatomically modern humans. It is clear from Figure 10.11 why the Solo skulls and the Petralona skull are so difficult to interpret.

Table 10.1 summarizes the hominid fossil evidence from about 1.5 million years ago to about 125,000 years ago, noting the geographic distribution and dating of the *Homo erectus* fossils from Africa and Asia, those from Europe that are difficult to classify, and a number of widely distributed fossils that seem to be early representatives of *Homo sapiens.* Most of these latter fossils are not well dated, but can be generally placed in the late Middle Pleistocene, from about 275,000 years to about 125,000 years B.P. From Europe, they include the *Swanscombe* skull fragments from England, the *Steinheim* skull from Germany, and the *Arago* fossils from southern France. From Africa, they include the *Kabwe* skull from Zambia, the *Saldanha Bay* skull cap from Elandsfontein, in South Africa, and the skull from *Bodo,* in the Afar region of north-central Ethiopia.

Swanscombe

This fossil was discovered in deposits along the river Thames, at Swanscombe in southern England, in the 1930s, along with tools of the Acheulian tradition. The geologic deposits in which the fossil was found place them in an interglacial of the Middle Pleistocene, most probably the next to the last one. Together with a piece of the skull found at the site after World War II, the Swanscombe fossil is composed of three bones of the braincase, the occipital and both parietals (paired bones making up the middle part of the braincase), all belonging to the same individual (Figure 10.12). The frontal bone, with forehead and brow ridge, and the face were not found. The fossil shows a mixture of physical features. The portions of the skull preserved show a rather high, rounded shape characteristic of *Homo sapiens,* and the ridges for the attachment of the neck muscles are situated rather low on the occipital bone. On the other hand, the cranial capacity, about 1100 ml, is not as large as that of other early sapiens, but is in the range of the Chinese *Homo erectus* fossils. The skull bone is thick like those of *Homo erectus.* The dating of the Swanscombe fossil and its morphological features suggest that it is a representative of early *Homo sapiens* but somewhat more advanced than the Petralona and Vértesszöllös fossils.

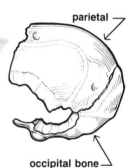

Figure 10.12. *The Swanscombe early sapiens skull pieces from southern England.*

Steinheim

The Steinheim fossil was discovered in 1933 in the village of Steinheim on the river Murr in Germany. The age of the fossil is probably the same as Swanscombe (next to the last interglacial), and there are a number of similarities between the two specimens (Figure 10.13). Steinheim is the more complete fossil, with most of the skull preserved. Unfortunately, it was badly crushed during its long interment in the ground, and its present distorted condition makes it somewhat difficult to assess accurately. The brow ridges are large, but they show the beginnings of separate rounded eminences over each eye orbit, similar to the condition in later *Homo sapiens,* and different from the more or less continuous bar of bone that marks the *Homo erectus* brow ridge. The height of the brain-

Table 10.1. Hominids from about 1.5 million years ago to the beginning of the Upper Pleistocene, about 125,000 years ago.

Some fossils whose time placement is unknown have been omitted from the chart, and some that have been included are only very generally placed in time.

Years B.P.	Geological epoch	European glacial sequence	Europe	Africa	Asia
100,000	UPPER PLEISTO-CENE	Würm	Neandertals		
125,000		Last interglacial			
200,000		Glacial	Arago Petralona	Kabwe	Solo
300,000	MIDDLE PLEISTOCENE		Steinheim Swanscombe	Bodo	
500,000			Vertesszöllös	Olduvai Bed IV	Zhoukoudian
600,000			Heidelberg		
700,000				Ternifine	Lantian
					Java: Trinil
1.1	LOWER PLEISTOCENE			Olduvai Hominid 9	
					Java: Djetis
1.5					
1.6				East Turkana ER 3733	
1.8					
	PLIOCENE				

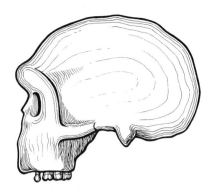

Figure 10.13. *The Steinheim early sapiens skull from Germany (right side reversed). More complete than the Swanscombe fragments, this fossil has been distorted during its long interment, and it is difficult to determine what it looked like before burial.*

case is a little higher than those of *Homo erectus* and the earlier European fossil from Petralona. The face, though large, is smaller than that of *Homo erectus*. The most reasonable interpretation of the Steinheim fossil is that, like the Swanscombe bones, it is representative of early *Homo sapiens*. It has been suggested that the earlier, though somewhat larger, Petralona fossil and the smaller Steinheim skull can be identified as male and female, and demonstrate the presence of sexual dimorphism in Middle Pleistocene Europe.

The cave of Arago in the village of Tautavel, in the Pyrenees Mountains of southern France, is being excavated by Henry de Lumley, who also excavated the Terra Amata site. A number of fossil hominids have been recovered at Arago, including the front part of a skull with most of a face (Figure 10.14), several lower jaws, and assorted other bones, including part of a pelvis. The Arago fossils seem to be dated toward the end of the Middle Pleistocene, perhaps contemporary with the Swanscombe and Steinheim specimens. Recently, at an international congress held in France, much debate was focused on the identification of the Arago material as either *Homo erectus* or early *Homo sapiens*. It was the overwhelming opinion of the assembled scientists that these fossils were representative of early *Homo sapiens,* and shared a number of morphological similarities with other early *Homo sapiens* such as Petralona.[10] The two lower jaws from Arago (Figure 10.15) show differences in size which would suggest, like the comparison of Petralona and Steinheim, that European Middle Pleistocene early *Homo sapiens* was sexually dimorphic.

Arago

These are similar looking fossils from southern Africa; the Kabwe skull, from the Broken Hill Mine in Zambia, is more complete than the Saldanha Bay specimen from the west coast of South Africa. The date of these fossils is not clear, but recent evidence suggests the Kabwe skull (Figure 10.16) may be close to 200,000 years old. It has a large face, a low, sloping forehead, and a relatively small cranial capacity, some 1100 ml. Along with Saldanha Bay it is similar in many ways to both the Petralona fossil from Europe and the recently discovered Bodo skull from

Kabwe and Saldanha Bay

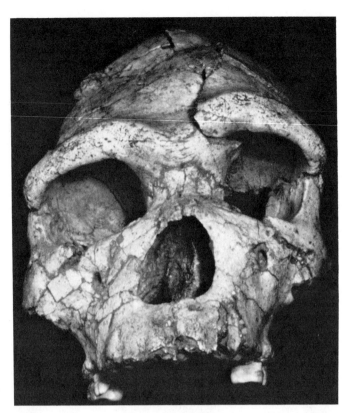

Figure 10.14. Front part of the skull with most of the face of a fossil hominid from Arago.

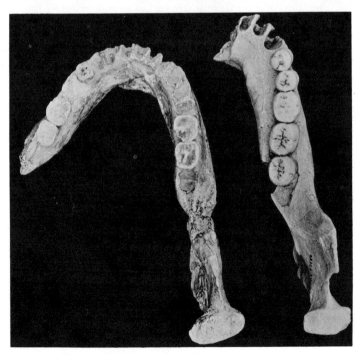

Figure 10.15. Casts of two lower jaws of early Homo sapiens from the Arago site in southern France. Note the larger size of the jaw on the right and its larger teeth. The different sizes suggest that this larger jaw belonged to a male, and the smaller jaw on the left to a female.

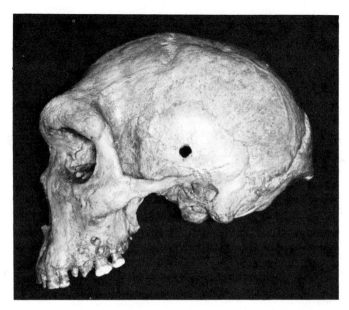

Figure 10.16 *Skull from Kabwe, Zambia.*

Ethiopia, suggesting either a late *Homo erectus* classification or, more probably, that these African fossils are representative of early *Homo sapiens.*

The fossil evidence from various parts of the Old World (China; Java; north, east, south Africa and Europe) — from a little earlier than 1.5 million years to the end of the Middle Pleistocene, about 125,000 years B.P. — seems to indicate the continued operation of evolutionary mechanisms on hominid populations. As we have seen in this and the preceding chapter, the fossil record appears to show slow, gradual evolutionary change, and it is difficult to determine exactly when, in the period between 2 and 1.5 million years B.P., the first members of the genus *Homo* appear. It is also difficult to determine accurately which fossils belong in *Homo erectus* and which in *Homo sapiens*. Does this mean that this part of the hominid evolutionary sequence is not marked by periods of relative equilibrium punctuated by short bursts of marked change, a model of evolution suggested in Chapter 3 as an alternative to phyletic gradualism? Although the fossil evidence for this period seems to indicate gradual change, the many problems of dating the fossils precisely indicate that we ought to maintain an open mind on this question until a better understanding of the exact relationships of one fossil group to another have been more fully worked out.

As we have seen, the earliest fossils of *Homo sapiens* are dated to the end of the Middle Pleistocene. Though placed in the taxon *H. sapiens,* they are not yet anatomically modern humans. Somewhat later than these Middle Pleistocene early *Homo sapiens,* but not yet anatomically mod-

Homo Sapiens of the Upper Pleistocene

ern either, are the *Homo sapiens* fossils that date to the early part of the Upper Pleistocene, about 125,000 to about 35,000 to 40,000 years ago. These hominids possess a number of distinctive anatomical features. A variety of names and taxonomic categories have been used to identify this group of fossils, but problems in interpretation have again resulted in rather complicated schemes. One group, limited to a part of the Upper Pleistocene in Europe, the Middle East, and North Africa, have been called the *neandertals,* and have usually been placed in the subspecies *Homo sapiens neanderthalensis,* in contrast to modern humans, *Homo sapiens sapiens.* Other groups of Upper Pleistocene hominids have been placed in their own subspecies. For the early *Homo sapiens* fossils from the end of the Middle Pleistocene, such as Steinheim, Swanscombe, Petralona, and Kabwe, however, there is no generally recognized subspecies; and the use of these labels presents problems when fossils from different geographic areas are placed in the same subspecies. Perhaps the most reasonable solution is to call all the *Homo sapiens* fossils dated prior to the appearance of anatomically modern humans about 35,000 to 40,000 years ago early, or archaic, sapiens. Table 10.2 lists the various fossils from different parts of the Old World who have been grouped into the descriptive category of early or archaic sapiens.

Table 10.2. Early or Archaic Sapiens.
This lists the major finds (and there are numerous additional fossils that could be included), especially in Europe. Many problems in the dating of these finds have yet to be worked out, and therefore the fossils are arranged generally in terms of Middle and Upper Pleistocene.

		Europe	Middle East	Asia	Africa
PLEISTOCENE	UPPER (125,000)	(Saint Césaire) Neandertals (Neandertal) (Monte Circeo) (Teshik Tash)	(Shanidar) (Wadi Amud) (Tabūn)	Wadjak	Olduvai Gorge Omo (Kibish Fm.) Florisbad
	MIDDLE	Steinheim Arago Swanscombe Petralona Bilzingsleben Vértesszöllös Heidelberg		Maba Solo(?)	Bodo Kabwe Saldanha Bay

Neandertal fossils were the first bones of a fossil hominid to be discovered. In the seventeenth century, a composer of hymns named Joachim Neumann, of some local fame, lived in Düsseldorf. Taking a cue from many individuals of his time, he hellenized his name to Neander ("new man"). When Neumann/Neander died, a valley where he had spent much of his free time was named the Neander Valley (Neander Tal) in his honor. In 1856, workman quarrying in a cave in the valley came upon a skull cap and some postcranial bones.

Discoveries of Neandertals

Because this was the first recognized fossil of a "primitive" human, scientists of the day differed as to its identity. Some, like Thomas Henry Huxley, recognized it as an extinct human ancestor; others were not so sure. One anatomist wrote: "It may have been one of those wild men, half-crazed, half-idiotic, cruel and strong, who are always more or less to be found living on the outskirts of barbarous tribes, and who now and then appear in civilized communities to be consigned perhaps to the penitentiary or the gallows, when their murderous propensities manifest themselves."[11] Reasonable anatomical judgment won out, and neandertal took its place in the human lineage.

Since the neandertal discovery, many early sapiens fossils similar in appearance have been found in France, Germany, Belgium, Spain, Yugoslavia, Italy, Gibraltar, Russia, Czechoslovakia, Hungary, Israel, Lebanon, Iraq, and Morocco (Figure 10.17). As a group, they are called neandertals, *H. sapiens* who inhabited Europe, North Africa, and the Middle East from the beginning of the Upper Pleistocene until the end of the first glacial advance of the Würm, or last glaciation, 30,000 to 40,000 years ago, when they disappear from the fossil record.

In addition to the Upper Pleistocene *Homo sapiens* from Europe, North Africa, and the Middle East—the neandertals—hominids of this time period have also been discovered in other parts of the Old World. These specimens possess features generally similar to those of the neandertal group, though there seem to be some distinctive attributes found among different geographically limited groups, suggesting that regional evolutionary trends were developing, a point we will return to when we consider the origins of modern human population differences.

Other Upper Pleistocene Early Sapiens

These Upper Pleistocene fossils include specimens such as the partial skull from *Maba,* in China. From *Wadjak,* in Java, have come several individuals, including a virtually complete skull. Australia has yielded several groups of fossil specimens, from *Kow Swamp* and from *Willandra Lakes.* Finally from Africa, Upper Pleistocene discoveries include the *Florisbad* and *Border Cave* fossils from South Africa, two skulls from the uppermost beds at Olduvai Gorge, Tanzania, a number of specimens from west of Lake Turkana in Kenya, and three individuals from the Upper Pleistocene Kibish Formation in the Omo River Basin of Ethiopia.

Most of these fossil samples from parts of the Old World share some general physical similarities: low, flat braincases with low, sloping foreheads; large brow ridges usually with some curvature over each eye

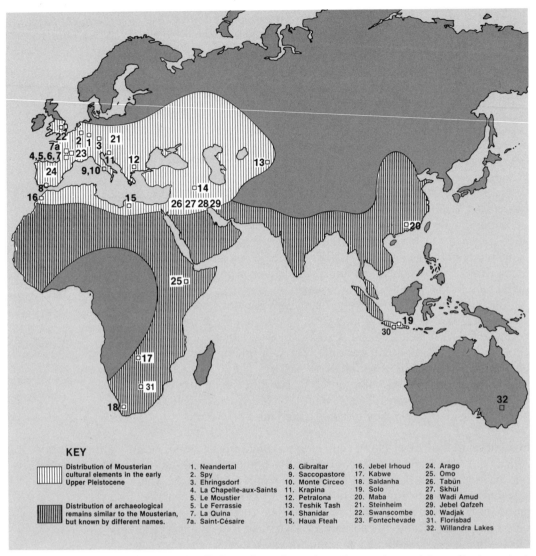

KEY

▥ Distribution of Mousterian cultural elements in the early Upper Pleistocene	1. Neandertal 2. Spy 3. Ehringsdorf 4. La Chapelle-aux-Saints 5. Le Moustier 5. Le Ferrassie 7. La Quina 7a. Saint-Césaire	8. Gibraltar 9. Saccopastore 10. Monte Circeo 11. Krapina 12. Petralona 13. Teshik Tash 14. Shanidar 15. Haua Fteah	16. Jebel Irhoud 17. Kabwe 18. Saldanha 19. Solo 20. Maba 21. Steinheim 22. Swanscombe 23. Fontechevade	24. Arago 25. Omo 26. Tabūn 27. Skhūl 28. Wadi Amud 29. Jebel Qafzeh 30. Wadjak 31. Florisbad 32. Willandra Lakes
▦ Distribution of archaeological remains similar to the Mousterian, but known by different names.				

Figure 10.17. *Early sapiens sites where the most complete and/or important specimens have been found.*

orbit; facial areas that project markedly and are more in front of the braincase than in modern humans; sometimes an inflated cheek area, without the depression just above the canine tooth (called the *canine fossa*) in modern humans; and a weak chin (Figure 10.18). Generally, these Upper Pleistocene fossils differ from the earlier Middle Pleistocene *H. sapiens* sample (Steinheim, Petralona, for example) by having larger braincases; in other features, their physical traits are similar to those of the earlier dated *Homo sapiens*. This fossil evidence suggests a trend in

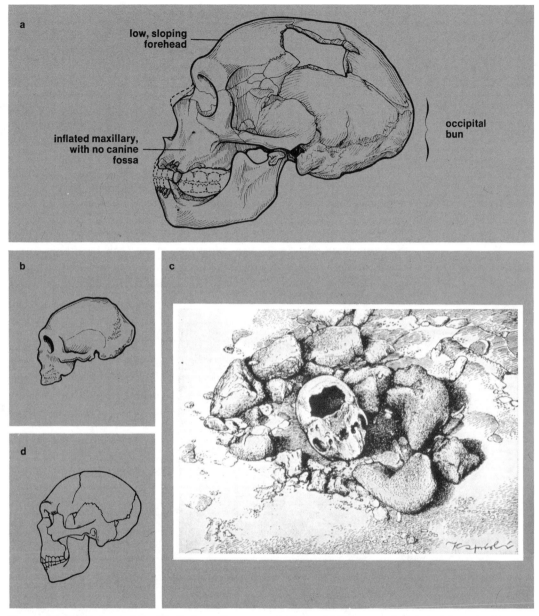

Figure 10.18. *Early sapiens fossils from Europe and Africa. (a) The neandertal skull from La Cha-pelle-aux-Saints in France. Before death, this individual had lost almost all his teeth (reconstructed here, as is the upper part of the nasal area); he had a large face, poorly developed chin, and an occipital bun. (b) A skull from Monte Circeo in Italy, similar to (a). (c) The Monte Circeo skull as it was discovered lying on the floor of a cave whose entrance had been sealed. It was found in a ring of stones, with its mutilated base turned upward. (d) The skull from Wadi Amud in Israel, with features similar to western European forms, but lacking some of their specializations, such as the occipital bun.*

early *Homo sapiens* evolution of enlarging brain sizes, which is, of course, part of the long-term general hominid trend of increasing brain size.

Morphological Features of Neandertals Some morphological features of the early sapiens fossils are more strongly developed in the neandertal sample dated to the early part of the last, or Würm, glacial advance (from about 75,000 to about 40,000 years B.P.). These features include a large brain size, with some over 1,700 ml, and most larger than those of modern humans; the average brain size of a large sample of neandertals was recently computed to be about 1,650 ml. The cheek region tends to be inflated and lacks the canine fossa. There are also special features found only in the western European sample. One is a rounded projection on the back of the braincase, resembling the hair style known as a chignon (or bun); it is called an occipital *chignon*. Another feature of this particular neandertal group are large, robustly developed limb bones, with larger than usual articular ends. These features, along with limb bones with curved shafts, have been interpreted as indicating the neandertals habitually used their limbs in very strenuous muscular exertions, and were capable of physical feats beyond our abilities.

The Mousterian Industry The European, Middle Eastern, and North African neandertal finds are almost always associated with stone tools of a particular kind. This tool tradition has been named the *Mousterian industry* after a village in France, Le Moustier, where an adolescent neandertal skeleton and the stone tools were found (Figure 10.19). The Middle Paleolithic Mousterian industry has been termed a "flake tool" tradition because many of its imple-

Figure 10.19. *Stone tools from the Mousterian (Middle Paleolithic, Europe) and Upper Paleolithic (Middle East). The Mousterian point is a typical artifact of the Middle Paleolithic culture. (All one-half actual size.)*

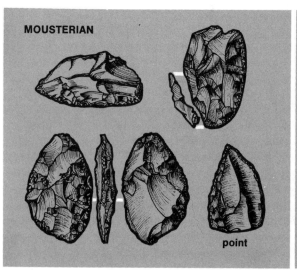
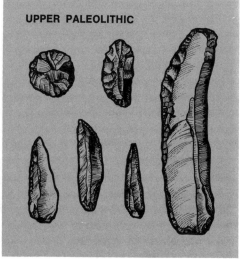

MOUSTERIAN

UPPER PALEOLITHIC

point

ments are shaped from flakes of stone chipped off a core. The Lower Paleolithic Acheulian industry is called a "core tool" industry because its characteristic hand axes are made on the cores themselves. Although these cultures may be termed core or flake traditions, actually there are core and flake tools in both the Acheulian and Mousterian industries. Despite numerous examples of flake tools in the Acheulian tradition, the hand axe has come to represent the most important identifying artifact, or "type fossil," of the Acheulian industry.

The Mousterian's typical tools are the point, perhaps to be hafted onto the end of a spear; a variety of "scrapers," stone tools with a sharp, working edge along the long side ("side scrapers") or at the end of the flake ("end scrapers"); and tools manufactured in a specialized way, using the *Levallois technique* (Figure 10.20). This method prepares a core by flaking chips from the top, bottom, and sides, with very strong vertical chipping on one end giving the core a rather straight edge, called a faceted butt. Once the core is ready, one flake, called a Levallois flake, is taken off the top by the toolmaker striking the core from the faceted butt end. The characteristically shaped flake is then worked further to produce different kinds of tools, such as points and also scrapers, perhaps used for cutting or scraping hides, bone, antler, wood, tubers, and other tough-skinned vegetables.

Mousterian Tool Kits For a long time, archaeologists used the typical artifacts to identify whole stone tool industries. After World War II, these tool industries were recognized as much more complicated, each having an assortment of tools that could be found in other traditions, either earlier or later. François Bordes, a French archaeologist, developed a method for identifying a stone tool industry by its total assemblage of tools. Bordes felt that a culture could be identified as Mousterian, even if Acheulian hand axes were found, if the relative percentage of hand axes was low and the relative percentage of Mousterian points, Levallois flakes, and other characteristic tools of the Mousterian was high. The entire tool kit has to be taken into account, and both the number and kind of tools found are important in determining which culture is present.

Bordes found by analyzing the Mousterian collections from a number of sites in France that the Mousterian really consists of numerous subtraditions, all recognizably Mousterian but differing in the percentages of tools.[12] He identified five of these, each with generally the same kinds of tools, but different in their percentages. These subtraditions are not the result of change through time, one being earlier than another: at some sites one subtradition will be found at a low level; on top of this, another subtradition will be discovered; then over this the first subtradition is found again. Sally and Lewis Binford, American archaeologists working on this problem, suggested that the subtraditions represent specialized tool kits that the neandertals used for specific jobs and perhaps at different times of the year.[13] One subtradition might be the tool kit used for work around the camp: preparing food for cooking, cleaning

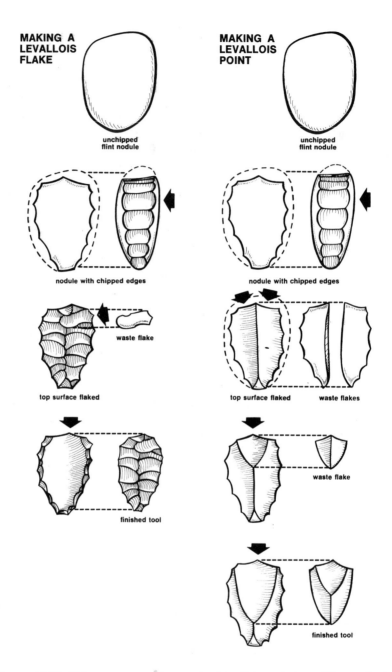

Figure 10.20. *Using a prepared core: the Levallois technique. The methods of shaping either a flake or a point start with the same prepared core. The Levallois flake (left): The flint nodule is trimmed by chipping both side and top surfaces. A final blow at one end detaches the finished flake, which has sharp edges. The Levallois point (right): The nodule is trimmed on the sides. Then two parallel flakes are struck off the top surface, leaving a ridge in the center. A light blow detaches a small flake from one end, and a final blow strikes off the point.*

animal carcasses, chopping up tubers and roots, cleaning skins, and keeping the fire going; another tool kit might be used for rough butchering of animals; and still another might be used on seasonal foods, such as fish or small mammals and vertebrates. The subtraditions would be part of the Mousterian industry; each neandertal social group would be able to manufacture any of the subtraditions, but each had its definite use in the neandertal economy. The cultural complexity that these subtraditions reveal indicates that the neandertals had a highly developed set of behaviors for dealing effectively with the demands of their environment.

Mousterian and Other Stone Tool Industries One subtradition in the Mousterian, called the Mousterian of Acheulian tradition, has a fairly high percentage of hand axes. Bordes suggested that this subtradition may be the link between the Acheulian industry of the Lower Paleolithic and the Mousterian of the Middle Paleolithic. He believed the Acheulian industry evolved into the Mousterian by slowly replacing typically Acheulian tools with those of the Mousterian, and that the transition was so gradual that, even if we had a complete record of the stone tool industries, it would be hard to tell just where the Acheulian left off and the Mousterian began. On the basis of the tools, Bordes suggested the in-place development of a culture from the one before it, without resorting to any significant outside influences. The transition from Lower Paleolithic Acheulian to the Middle Paleolithic Mousterian seems to have occurred in the early part of the Upper Pleistocene, during the last interglacial, between 125,000 and 75,000 years ago, when the Würm glacial advance began.

Throughout Europe, the Middle East, and North Africa, the Mousterian industry also slowly evolved, with its makers learning new techniques and introducing new tools. At about 30,000 to 35,000 years ago, the Mousterian seems to have passed into a new cultural tradition, the *Perigordian,* named after the district Le Perigord in southern France. The Perigordian is part of the Upper Paleolithic cultural sequence in which blade tools are predominant. The difference between a blade and a flake is shape: flakes usually are short and wide; blades are longer and thinner. The blade is also manufactured differently; it, too, is removed from a core, but the core is longer and usually cylindrical in shape, which means more blades of a similar size can be chipped from the core.

Throughout the Mousterian industry there was a small percentage of blades, but this percentage appears to increase in the latter stages of the Middle Paleolithic, and it may have slowly evolved into the Upper Paleolithic Perigordian culture. Only a few sites in Europe document the evolution of Mousterian into Perigordian; in the Middle East there appears to be better evidence for this transition to Upper Paleolithic.

The archaeological data therefore suggest a long development for the tool traditions in Europe and the Middle East, from Acheulian to Mousterian to Upper Paleolithic. This portrait of the Middle Paleolithic has emphasized the European and Middle Eastern tool industries because more is known about the flake tool industries of this region than any other. Flake tool industries are known from sub-Saharan Africa and Asia; in general these industries show similarities with the Mousterian traditions, but with numerous variations indicative of hominids living in a wide array of environments and having different adaptive requirements. These also show evidence of the transition from Middle to Upper Paleolithic industries.

Archaic Sapiens and Modern Humans

When we try to understand the evolutionary relationships between Upper Pleistocene hominids and the anatomically modern humans who come after them, the situation is extremely complicated. In Europe and the Middle East, Upper Paleolithic industries, like the French Perigordian, are usually (but not always) found with skeletal material not significantly different from that of modern humans. When compared with Upper Pleistocene archaic *Homo sapiens* skulls, the fossils generally associated with Upper Paleolithic industries possess a skull with a greater height, with the maximum width of the skull now located relatively high on the braincase; there is a more vertical forehead, generally with no occipital chignon, and smaller or no brow ridges (Figure 10.21). The face and nasal cavity are smaller, and the distance between the eye orbits is reduced. The base of the braincase, a plane that separates the facial portion of the skull from the brain portion, shows a flexion (bending) in comparison to early sapiens skulls. This bending is related to the relative positioning of the face more directly underneath the braincase, resulting in changes in the cheek region above the tooth row, where a fossa, or depression, the canine fossa, has formed above the canine teeth on the cheek (Figure 10.22). The lower jaw has a chin, a specialization that is

Figure 10.21. *Front and side views of the Cro-Magnon skull, one of the earliest anatomically modern human fossils found in Europe. Skulls similar to those of modern humans first appear in the European archaeological record about 35,000 years ago.*

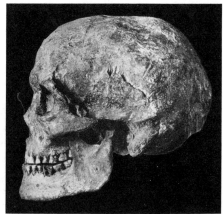

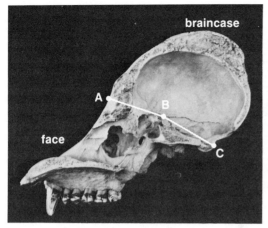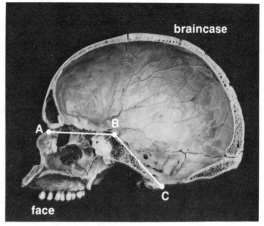

Figure 10.22. *Skulls of a modern human (right) and orang (left), sectioned down the middle. A line drawn from a point just below the browridge (A), to the front of the large opening at the base of the braincase where the spinal cord joins the brain (foramen magnum) (C), through the cup for the pituitary gland (B), divides the braincase part of the skull from the face. Note the angle this line makes at (B); in modern humans, this is the flexing of the skull base to accommodate the shifting of the face underneath the braincase. Modern humans have angles that range from 125–150 degrees (the orang is closer to 180 degrees), and while neandertals are generally within the human range, they are at the high end — 135 to 150 degrees.*

usually (but not always) lacking on neandertal fossils. These physical features appear on fossils discovered in western Europe and dated to after about 30,000 years ago, including the French cave site at Cro-Magnon; Chancelade, also in France; and Grimaldi in Italy. Two sites in Israel, Skhūl and Jebel Qafzeh, have also produced finds that appear to be representative of modern humans, but the dating of these Middle Eastern fossils is somewhat earlier than the European finds, indeed when neandertals were still alive in western Europe. Possibly still older yet is the fossil hominid from Border Cave, in South Africa, which may be evidence that anatomically modern humans had appeared in southern Africa while neandertals were still around in both Europe and the Middle East.

Theories of Modern Human Origins

How the neandertals and other Upper Pleistocene early or archaic sapiens fit into the origin and development of anatomically modern humans is a most difficult problem. Stated briefly, the question concerns the relationship of early sapiens populations to the modern human populations that succeeded them in particular geographic areas. Were neandertals and other early sapiens living in different geographic areas the direct ancestors of modern humans, or is there a more complex evolutionary sequence? The question is complicated because the placement in time of various fossils seems to suggest that anatomically modern humans were already on the scene in some areas when early sapiens were still around in other places. If, as current evidence suggests, modern humans and early sapiens were contemporaries, how can the relationships between the two groups be satisfactorily worked out?

Further, the question of early sapiens/modern human relationships cannot be examined without also considering the development of living human populations ("races"). Later chapters will look at modern human differences and the adaptive significance of many of these differences. Chapter 14 will specifically deal with human races and their complex nature. In the context of hominid evolution, two alternative views of racial origins have been developed. W. W. Howells has summarized these competing ideas as evolutionist versus migrationist.[14] The migrationist position is that only after the evolution of modern humans did groups spread (or migrate) to all parts of the world and begin evolving distinctive biological features; this view, then, suggests a relatively recent origin of modern human races. In contrast is the evolutionist idea that these differences are of very great antiquity: that from the time of the spread of *Homo erectus* to many parts of the Old World, hominid populations have been adapting to local environmental conditions. This view sees the later phases of hominid evolution as a general continuum, with modern human populations representing the spatial evolution of groups in particular environments.

These questions about the antiquity of modern human populations, along with the attempts to describe the place of neandertals and other early sapiens in the context of human evolution, have formed the basis of several theories (Table 10.3).

Neandertal Phase of Human Evolution

An American physical anthropologist, Ales Hrdlička, summed up one theory as the *"neandertal phase of man."*[15] He and his supporters give the name neandertal to all hominids throughout the Old World from the appearance of *Homo sapiens* in the Middle Pleistocene to the end of the early Würm. They call this a *grade* or "phase" of evolution between *Homo erectus* and anatomically modern humans. This view emphasizes variability in populations, and suggests that all the early sapiens fossils are similar enough to be part of one variable group, distributed both in time and geographically. The early sapiens from Africa and Asia can be integrated into the same theory.[16]

The neandertal phase hypothesis traces an evolutionary trend from *Homo erectus* through the neandertals and other early sapiens into modern *Homo sapiens sapiens*. This evolutionary sequence would have occurred all over the Old World, including western Europe; in all areas these early sapiens are the immediate ancestors of modern humans.

Several fossil discoveries in eastern Europe and the Middle East have been used to support this hypothesis. Among the most important are the cave finds at *Mount Carmel,* just outside Haifa in Israel (Figure 10.23). At Mount Carmel, Dorothy Garrod, T. D. McCown, and their coworkers uncovered many archaeological levels, from the Acheulian through the Mousterian and into the Upper Paleolithic. Two Mount Carmel caves,

Table 10.3. *Theories of neandertal evolution.*

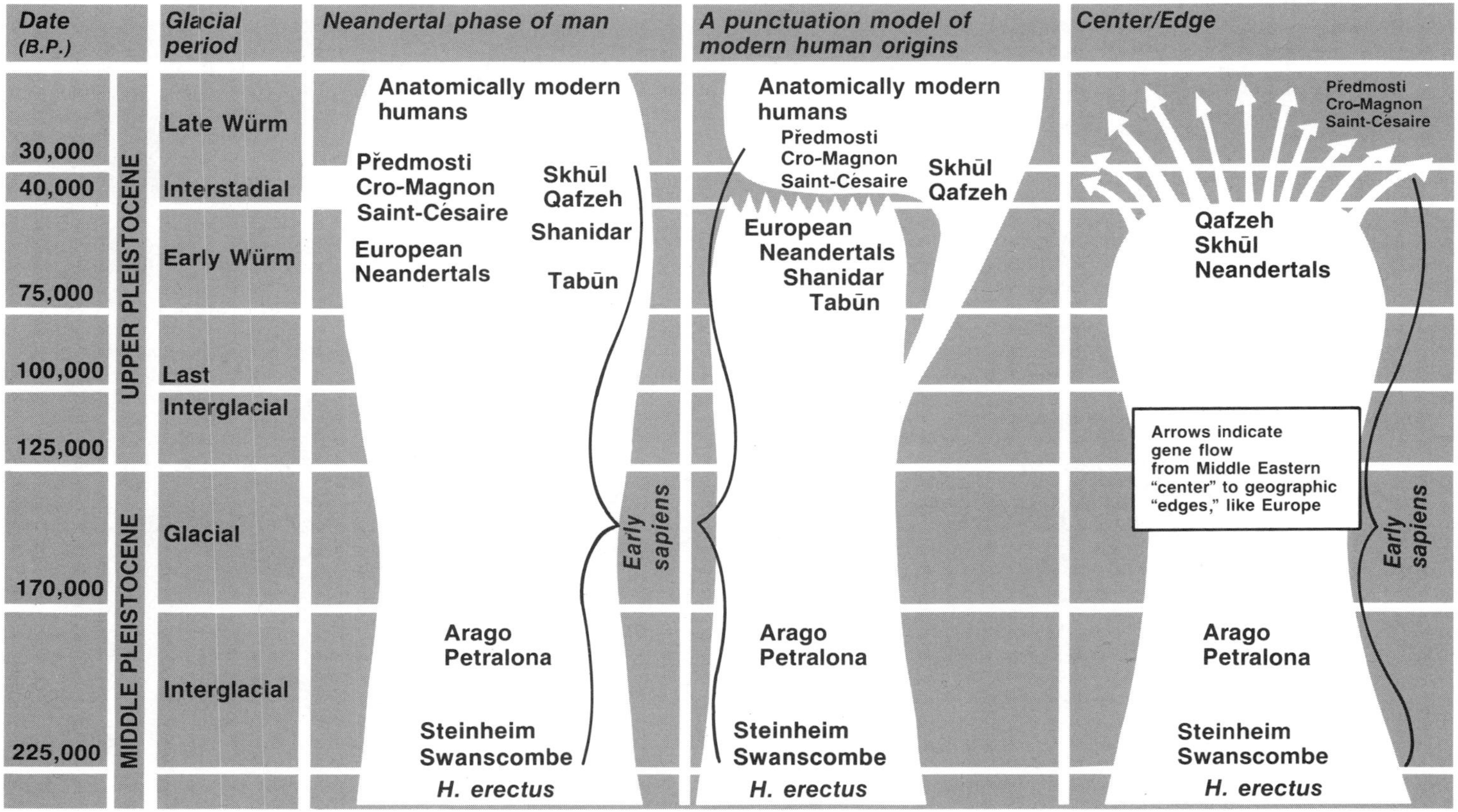

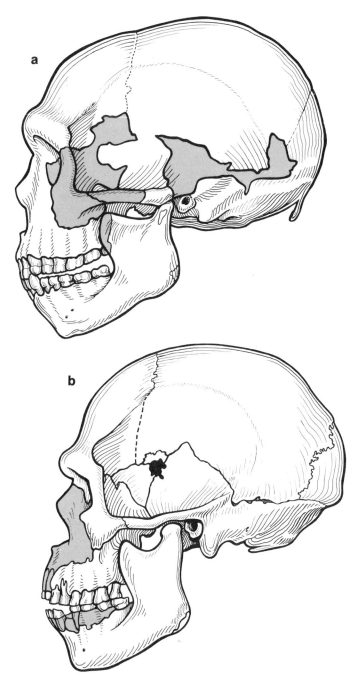

Figure 10.23. *Two skulls from the Mount Carmel caves, (a) from Tabūn and (b) from Skhūl, one of the more modern appearing skulls from this cave (right side reversed). Compare to Figures 10.18 and 10.21.*

es-Skhūl (cave of the kids [young goats]) and et-Tabūn (cave of ovens), yielded fragments and complete skeletons of more than twelve individuals, all associated with Mousterian tools. The two individuals in the Mousterian layers of Tabūn are like other Middle Eastern neandertals in many morphological features. Fossils discovered in *Shanidar Cave,* Iraq, and the *Wadi Amud,* Israel, are similar to the Tabūn specimens. The ten individuals from Skhūl have varied anatomical characteristics; some appear essentially like modern humans.[17]

At another cave site in Israel, in the Galilee, *Jebel Qafzeh,* a number of hominid skeletons have been discovered in association with Mousterian artifacts (Figure 10.24). The Qafzeh fossils are similar to the Skhūl fossils and share with these finds higher braincases; higher, more vertical foreheads; smaller brow ridges; smaller, less projecting faces located more underneath the braincase; and a chin. In sum, as F. C. Howell notes, they look "in all respects like a proto-Cro-Magnon"; in other words, like anatomically modern humans. Unfortunately, the precise dating of many of these fossils is uncertain. Recent estimates place the Tabūn fossils as early as 70,000 years ago, and although the Skhūl and Qafzeh fossils are later, just how much later is not certain, although they are probably 35,000 to 40,000 years old. The proponents of the neandertal phase theory suggest that the Middle Eastern fossil evidence may document the evolutionary transition from neandertals like Tabūn, Shanidar, and Wadi Amud to anatomically modern human-appearing forms like Jebel Qafzeh and Skhūl.

In addition to the fossils from the Middle East, there is a series of fossils from eastern Europe, several of which seem to possess features similar to both the neandertals and modern humans.[18] One of these was dredged out of the Vah River in the town of *Šala* in Czechoslovakia. The Šala fossil (of which only the frontal bone was found; see Figure 10.25) possesses brow ridges, but they are reduced in size, and the forehead is higher than those typical of neandertals. The nature of the discovery, however, precludes good dating.

The theory of the neandertal phase of humans also emphasizes that early anatomically modern humans, found with Upper Paleolithic tools, sometimes show considerable variability. One group of specimens often used to illustrate this point are the *Předmosti* skeletons. The site of Předmosti, in what is now Czechoslovakia, was excavated in the nineteenth century. Underneath a covering of limestone slabs and mammoth shoulder blades, the remains of forty-six individuals were discovered in a common grave. All but scraps of this material was destroyed during World War II, but photographs and casts of the fossils reveal an interesting range of variation in the individuals, with some possessing rather large brow ridges, and even a chignon, but others with a stronger resemblance to modern humans (Figure 10.26).

Although the neandertal phase of human evolution theory has been widely supported over the past fifty years, a recent discovery would seem

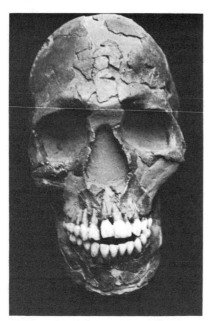

Figure 10.24. *Cast of a skull from Qafzeh.*

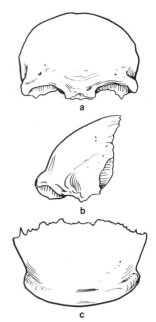

Figure 10.25. *Three views of the frontal bone from Šala: front (a); side (b), and top (c).*

Figure 10.26. *Two of the skulls from the site of Předmostí, in Czechoslovakia, found with Upper Paleolithic tools at the end of the last century. Note the large brow ridge development of the skull on the right, and the pronounced areas in the back of both skulls.*

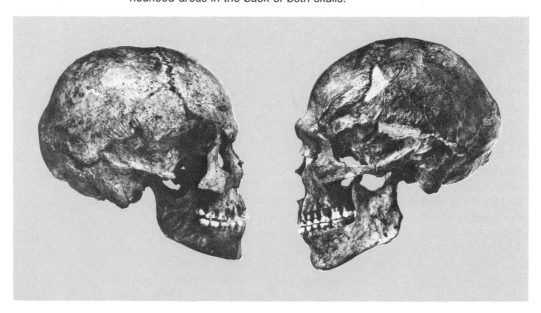

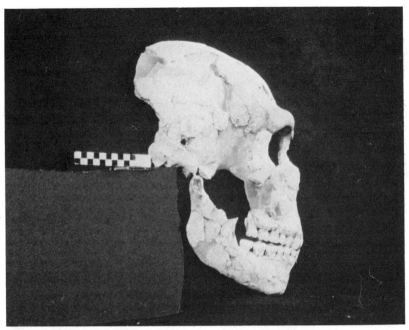

Figure 10.27. The partially reconstructed skull of the neandertal from Saint Césaire in southern France.

to destroy its credibility, at least in its present form. In 1981, French anthropologist Bernard Vandermeersch excavated a hominid skeleton from the site of *Saint-Césaire,* in southern France, close to the area where many neandertal and early modern human fossils have been discovered in the past 100 years.[19] The Saint-Césaire skeleton was badly crushed, and it has not yet been completely reconstructed. However, much of the front of the skull has been restored (Figure 10.27), and it is clear that this is a neandertal possessing a low forehead, large projecting face, and other features of this group. What makes the Saint-Césaire discovery so important is that this neandertal was found with Upper Paleolithic tools of the Perigordian industry, which up until now was always associated with modern human fossils. Perigordian tools are not known before about 32,000 years ago, at the earliest, so that even if the Saint-Césaire find were that old, it becomes difficult to accept the theory of the neandertal phase of human evolution, for by this time forms similar to anatomically modern humans, such as Skhūl and Qafzeh, are presumably already present in the Middle East. There are alternative models to account for the origin of modern humans.

Over the past few years, a number of highly sophisticated statistical studies have been performed on the neandertal fossil collections from Europe and the Middle East. Christopher Stringer, whose analysis is the most

An Evolutionary Population Model

elaborate, has concluded that although there is some variability in skull and jaw features among the different neandertal fossils, they seem to form a distinct group that can be distinguished both from anatomically modern humans and from fossils such as Skhūl and Qafzeh.[20] This can also be seen in some features of the postcranial skeleton.[21] According to Stringer and other scholars, such as William Howells and Erik Trinkaus, who also support this position, Qafzeh and Skhūl group with, and should be identified as, anatomically modern humans. Yet both were found with Mousterian tools, and seem to date earlier than the disappearance of neandertals like Saint-Césaire. This suggests that all neandertals did not evolve into modern humans, and that to view the relationships of Upper Pleistocene *Homo sapiens* to anatomically modern humans as a straight line from one into the other is probably simplistic and not in accordance with our understanding of how evolutionary changes occur. Over the past few years, a number of concepts have been introduced to explain what is beginning to look like an exceedingly complex evolutionary pattern.

A Punctuation Model

One recently developed concept emphasizes a punctuation model and suggests that the transition from archaic sapiens to modern humans may have occurred very rapidly and in particular locales; for the neandertal/modern human evolutionary change, for example, probably somewhere in the Middle East or perhaps eastern Europe. In a recent article dealing with the evolution of the neandertals, Howells and Trinkaus argue that a punctuation model of evolutionary change provides the most satisfactory account of the origin of modern humans.[22] They reason that the neandertals, having evolved from the early sapiens populations of the Middle Pleistocene, were distributed widely throughout the nonglaciated areas of Europe and the Middle East. Sometime during the Upper Pleistocene, probably after 100,000 years B.P., one population of neandertals, perhaps having moved into a marginal environment, underwent rapid evolutionary change, developing features like those of Skhūl and Qafzeh. This population gradually expanded out of its original environment, replacing local neandertal groups, or in some cases interbreeding with neandertals. In this view, the neandertals of western Europe were replaced by modern human populations that had evolved elsewhere.

The Center-Edge Model

Australian Alan Thorne, Chinese Wu Xin Zhi, and American Milford Wolpoff have jointly proposed a concept of Upper Pleistocene hominid evolution that stresses gene flow and morphological variation to explain the relationships between archaic sapiens and modern humans.[23] According to these anthropologists, after the hominids expanded their geographic range during *Homo erectus* times, hominid groups found themselves in a wide variety of environments, some rich and some poor. They reason that genetic contact (via gene flow) between and across these hominid groups was always maintained so that the hominids remained a single species over time. Hominid populations in rich environments would show a greater amount of variation; groups in a poor area would be under stronger natural selection and would have less variation.

These authors argue that evolutionary change in the hominids would occur in the areas of greatest morphological variation, in the richer areas, the "center," while the "edges," the poorer environments on the periphery of the hominid distributions, would be the recipient of genetic changes from the "center." One such "center," but only one among numerous rich environments occupied by the hominids during the Pleistocene, was the Middle East. Like the punctuation model just considered, Thorne, Wu, and Wolpoff suggest that archaic sapiens evolved into anatomically modern humans in the Middle East, probably sometime after 100,000 years B.P., and that gene flow from this "center" resulted in the change of neandertals into modern humans at later and later times as one moves away from the Middle East "center." Thus, this model explains why Saint-Césaire in western Europe, at an "edge" far removed from the "center," can have lived later than Skhūl and Qafzeh and still be a neandertal. This model would suggest that the origins of all modern humans can be viewed within this *center-edge* model.

Many problems remain to be worked out before a clear picture of the evolutionary appearance of modern humans can be formulated. It does seem clear that some archaic sapiens did evolve into modern humans, but whether all these early sapiens are the direct ancestors of the modern humans who succeeded them is not certain. When we broaden our perspective to Africa and Asia, early sapiens populations seem to be found just before the appearance of modern human groups, but things get more complicated. For example, at the site of Border Cave in South Africa, fragmentary pieces of what looks like an anatomically modern human were discovered in a context dated to about 75,000 years ago. If the dating is confirmed, and the fossil really is that of a modern human, this would suggest that the earliest appearance of *Homo sapiens sapiens* is in southern Africa, and that perhaps early modern humans, or their genes, spread northward from there.[24]

Further, the model of the neandertal phase of humans, suggesting continuous evolution between all early sapiens and anatomically modern humans, supports the notion that human races have a great antiquity, and that they represent the long-term, in-place, evolution of hominid populations in particular environments,[25] a notion also supported by the "center-edge" model of Thorne, Wu and Wolpoff. In contrast, the punctuation model, suggesting a rapid development of modern humans from one isolated population, may confirm a more recent origin of human races; modern human population differentiation may have resulted from the spread of anatomically modern humans after their evolutionary appearance, replacing early sapiens in various parts of the Old World[26] (Table 10.3). We will deal with this question again in Chapter 14 when we discuss the differences in modern human populations.

Early Sapiens Adaptations

In spite of differences of opinion about the place of archaic sapiens in hominid evolution, a great deal is known about their cultures and adaptations. They continued in the basic hominid niche, gathering and hunting. The Mousterian and other Middle Paleolithic flake tool industries are more complex and sophisticated than the preceding Acheulian; they have a greater variety of artifacts, many of them apparently made for specific tasks.

In Europe most neandertal sites are found in caves, probably chosen for their protection from the cold. During the short summer the neandertals inhabited open-air sites, and they had tentlike structures for dwellings. The archaeological evidence shows that, like earlier hominids, they moved in a seasonal cycle, exploiting one area and then traveling to another. They were certainly as skilled in hunting as *Homo erectus,* especially during the Würm glacial in Europe, when long winters kept them from finding much in the way of vegetable foods.

Here we see our first glimmering of an ideological system. Many neandertals were intentionally buried; occasionally there are grave offerings with the body. On the South Russian steppes, at *Teshik Tash,* the burial of a neandertal youngster was found. Around the body were wild goat skulls, with the horns pointing toward the burial. Another neandertal fossil indicating concern for the dead is the skull found in a cave in Circe's Mountain *(Monte Circeo)* in Italy (Figure 10.18). This skull was discovered in a large cavern, lying on its top in a ring of stones. The base of the skull had been broken off, presumably to clean the brains out. We cannot really hope to understand what these actions were intended to symbolize. The *Teshik Tash* burial might suggest deep feelings about death, or about the loss of a loved child.

Ralph Solecki discovered nine neandertals in the Mousterian levels in Shanidar Cave, in the Zagros Mountains of Iraq.[27] The cave's roof was not stable, and periodically fell in, burying the people caught inside. One of the skeletons, Shanidar I, was that of a forty-year-old male who had been crushed and killed by a cave-in. T. D. Stewart found that this individual was crippled, with an underdeveloped right shoulder blade, collarbone, and upper right arm bone, and he had lost the lower part of the right arm just above the elbow joint long before death. If the arm was not lost via an accident but was amputated surgically, the techniques and (stone) tools that were used, and how the individual stood the pain, will never be known. It does reveal that neandertal groups had a strong social bond, capable of supporting a member with a useless arm. In addition, healed scars on the top of the skull testify to the fact that prior to being killed by a cave roof collapse, this individual had received several nasty bumps on the head from small pieces of falling cave roof. Many neandertal skulls show similar injuries. Finally, the Shanidar I skull, along with another from the same cave, shows evidence of being artificially deformed. Many modern human societies either accidentally or intentionally deform the skulls of their infants, by binding cloths around the head, or simply by tightly wrapping an infant on a flat board so that it can be easily carried.

Another discovery at Shanidar Cave was an intentional burial. This neandertal, Shanidar IV, was found in a niche surrounded by stones; the body was lying on its side with the legs drawn up almost against the chest. Around the head was pollen from several kinds of flowers. Shanidar IV probably was buried in late May to early June, and many brightly colored wildflowers were placed in the grave with the body.

This elaboration of cultural behavior reflects the evolution of the biological bases that are a part of hominid evolution. Although early sapiens' faces and teeth are only slightly smaller than those of *Homo erectus*, their brains are significantly larger. Their average cranial capacity is a little larger than that of modern humans, and the overall structure of their brains, from the limited evidence of endocranial casts, does not appear to differ in any meaningful way from those of modern humans.

In spite of these similarities, there is debate as to whether early sapiens were capable of modern spoken language. Based on the analysis of a neandertal skull base, Philip Lieberman and E. S. Crelin reconstructed the entire soft tissue voice tract, and concluded that early sapiens were incapable of articulating a full range of modern human language sounds.[28] This idea has not been accepted by most paleoanthropologists. For one thing, the neandertals and even *Homo erectus* are associated with archaeological evidence indicating a rather complex technology, as well as suggestions of a very complex environmental adaptation. It is difficult to reconcile these indications of a sophisticated way of life to the notion that these hominids were incapable of speech. In addition, there is Ralph Holloway's analysis of the ways by which a hominid neurological system develops a mental image of a tool, and then translates this image to the raw material in tool manufacture. Holloway's ideas were presented in Chapter 8 as part of the discussion of the origin of hominid toolmaking; Holloway believes that the brain's structures responsible for toolmaking would also serve as the neurological foundation for speech. According to Holloway, then, even early hominids like australopithecines would have been capable of speech.

Anatomically Modern Humans

The earliest documented evidence of anatomically modern humans comes from around 30,000 to 35,000 years ago. Apart from the Jebel Qafzeh and Skhūl materials, the fossils are associated with Upper Paleolithic tools, and with both open-air and cave sites; the gathering and hunting tradition was continuing. In most respects, Upper Paleolithic hominids are morphologically similar to modern humans. Some specimens, such as those from Předmosti, possess features similar to the neandertals. However, Upper Paleolithic hominids also differed from modern humans in several features: they were shorter in stature and, like the neandertals, capable of much more strenuous muscular activity. Increased height is a well-documented part of recent human evolution, and may be due in part to changes in diet (see Chapter 12 for additional discussion). The greater strength of the Upper Paleolithic hominids may be related to the need of hominids in a gathering/hunting economic system to be able to deal with the environment in a more direct manner than those of us who possess a more sophisticated culture.

Final Expansion of Range During the Upper Paleolithic the hominids expanded to their current distribution. The evidence suggests that Siberia was first colonized then; from there the hominids migrated across the Bering Strait into North America, and soon after into South America. The New World was peopled not by a purposeful migration, but probably by human groups following herds of large game animals. The earliest, well documented archaeological evidence in North and South America is about 15,000 years old. The human bones occasionally found with the early evidence reveal a modern human form, with clear physical relationships to northern Asians. By about 10,000 years ago, hominids had spread to all of the Americas.[29]

Recently discovered evidence from the site of Willandra Lakes, near Canberra, Australia, suggests that hominids had developed the sophisticated technology necessary to cross the water barrier between Australia and New Guinea and the islands associated with mainland Asia by 60,000 years ago (Figure 10.28). Only by the use of boats could hominids have reached Australia, and the discoveries at Willandra Lakes suggest that this was accomplished much earlier than was previously thought. Much later, humans from both Australia and New Guinea and from mainland Asia began the island-hopping by boat that was to result in the peopling of virtually the entire Pacific island area.

Thus, the range of the hominids increased, but their basic adaptation, gathering and hunting, continued. The tools and the rest of their culture became more complex, the whole becoming more efficient, capable of providing the basic materials for human groups to successfully exploit almost every environment on the planet. The basic pattern, however, remained unchanged.

Agriculture Sometime around 10,000 years ago, plants were domesticated in both the Old and New Worlds. Shortly after mastering the flora, humans also domesticated animals, two shifts in the economic base that profoundly changed hominid history. Gathering and hunting limits the size of the social group and prevents it from developing a settled life; agriculture and a stable supply of food allow aggregations of large numbers at permanent sites. Only part of the group is needed to raise enough food for all, and roles can be specialized. Biologically, however, hominids are gatherers and hunters; they have passed most of their recent biological history as small-group foragers. Like our primate relatives, who also live in small groups, the hominids probably evolved many of their

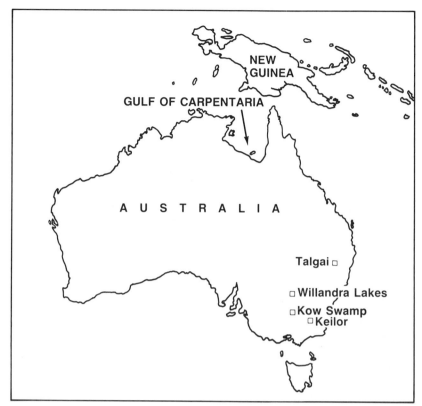

Figure 10.28. *Map of Australia showing the location of the most important early sites. Evidence from a variety of sources suggests that the first peoples to reach Australia came across from New Guinea and landed in the Gulf of Carpentaria area, perhaps as early as 60,000 years ago.*

attributes in response to the demands of this kind of life. It may be that we are not adapted to life in large social aggregations, a question we will return to in the last chapter.

The dating and the place of origin of the human zoological family Hominidae is still very uncertain (see Table 10.4 for a summary chart). So too is the identity of the immediate hominoid ancestors of the hominids. The earliest documented evidence of hominid evolution is the australopithecines, who appear in the record at the end of the Miocene, about 4 million years ago. The australopithecines have been found in some numbers at various sites in East and South Africa from this time to about 1.5 million years ago. During most of their evolution, they apparently were confined to the African continent — at least we have not found them elsewhere — and there is no evidence of hominids in other parts of the

Summary

Table 10.4. Summary of the evidence for human evolution.
Only the major sites, especially those with reasonable dating, have been included. The chart has not been drawn to scale, but reflects the important times in hominid evolution.

Years B.P.	Geological epoch	Hominid groups	Africa	Asia	Europe	Some important fossils	Brain Size	Evidence of culture
10,000	HOLOCENE	Anatomically modern humans						Agriculture
40,000	PLEISTOCENE — UPPER			Skhūl Qafzeh	Predmosti, Cro-Magnon, Saint-Cesaire, La Quina		1350–1450 ml	Upper Paleolithic tools
70,000		Neandertals		Shanidar, Tabūn	Neandertal		1300–1700 ml	Mousterian tools
125,000		H. sapiens						
.2 MY	PLEISTOCENE — MIDDLE	Early sapiens			Arago, Petralona, Steinheim, Swanscombe, Vértesszöllös	Solo Skulls	1200–1300 ml	
.3		} Transition from H. erectus to H. sapiens	Kabwe	Solo			900–1300 ml	
.4								
.5				Zhoukoudian	Heidelberg		800–950 ml	
.6		Homo		Java: Trinil				
690,000		H. erectus	Ternifine			Olduvai Hominid 9	1000 ml	
1.0	PLEISTOCENE — LOWER	H. habilis		Java: Djetis		ER 3733, 406		
1.2						ER 1813	800 ml	
1.5		A. boisei	East Turkana			ER 1470, 1590	500–775 ml	Acheulian tools
1.8		A. robustus	Olduvai					
2.0		Australopithecus — A. africanus	Omo, Swartkrans, Sterkfontein					Oldowan tools / First evidence of stone tools
3.0	PLIOCENE	A. afarensis	Makapansgat, Hadar, Laetoli, Maka			A. afarensis skeleton, jaws, footprints	440–500 ml (First evidence of bipedalism)	
4.0			Kanapoi					
5								
10	MIOCENE		Lothagam			Lothagam jaw		
15								

Old World until about 1.3 million years ago. Discoveries in the Djetis Beds of Java, Indonesia, suggest that late australopithecines or early *Homo erectus* were able to expand out of the African continent, having evolved a culture effective enough to permit expansion into many environmental zones.

The australopithecines are unquestionably hominids; they were bipedal, and later forms are found with tools. There is some dispute concerning the number of different australopithecine taxonomic categories living at the same time during this period. On the basis of morphological differences, there may have been as many as five different species of australopithecines.

One, known from sites in Tanzania and Ethiopia in East Africa, is *Australopithecus afarensis*. This species is the earliest of the australopithecines, having been dated to between about 2.9 and 3.7 million years B.P. *A. afarensis* was bipedal; but its front teeth, canines, and first lower premolars were different in some ways from those in the other australopithecines and reminiscent of pongid teeth.

Another australopithecine, known from rather large fossil samples from South Africa, and perhaps also from East Africa, is *Australopithecus africanus*. Still another, known from large numbers from South Africa, has been termed *Australopithecus robustus,* the robust australopithecine. In East Africa, fossils similar to the South African robust group are placed in the taxon *A. boisei*. Although both these groups generally differ from the other australopithecines in having larger back teeth and chewing muscles, the East African sample possessed chewing teeth and musculature that were generally even larger than those characteristic of the South African robust forms.

Finally, there are fossils known primarily from East Africa that differ in a number of ways from those already described. They possessed larger brains and their teeth were smaller. First identified at Olduvai Gorge, they were placed in the taxon *Homo habilis,* suggesting they were sufficiently different from other australopithecines to warrant placement in the same genus as modern humans. Discoveries at sites east of Lake Turkana have produced fossil specimens dated to between 1.5 and 2 million years B.P. Some of these, such as the fossil skull KNM-ER 3733, dated to about 1.5 to 1.6 million years B.P., can be placed in *Homo erectus*. Others, dated somewhat earlier, possess a variety of features, some indicative of *Homo* and others of *Australopithecus*.

It seems reasonable that australopithecines evolved during this period into early members of the genus *Homo*. Unresolved is whether *A. africanus,* an evolutionary development from the earlier *A. afarensis,* represents the immediate ancestor of early members of *Homo,* or whether it is already on the separate lineage to robust australopithecines.

The period between 2 and 1.5 million years B.P. provides a reasonable point of transition from some of the australopithecines to *Homo*. Yet at about the same time the skulls and jaws of robust australopithecines are found, demonstrating that the robust australopithecines continued to exist after the evolutionary appearance of *Homo erectus*. The robust australopithecines represent a limited evolutionary specialization from the main hominid line. They apparently became extinct sometime after 1.5 million years B.P., leaving no descendants.

Homo erectus fossils have been discovered in many parts of the Old World, including Java, China, and North, East, and South Africa. They possessed larger brains than the australopithecines and smaller faces and teeth. The postcranial skeleton, apart from minor differences, is identical to that of modern humans. *Homo erectus* may be represented in Europe, but the known fossil evidence has features that make it difficult to determine whether these fossils are *Homo erectus* or early *Homo sapiens*.

Sometime in the latter part of the Middle Pleistocene, *Homo erectus* evolved into *Homo sapiens*. These early members of *Homo sapiens* differ from the preceding hominid groups in possessing larger brains and related changes in skull form.

Early *Homo sapiens* from the Middle Pleistocene generally have smaller brains than the early sapiens fossils of the Upper Pleistocene. One group of Upper Pleistocene hominids, from Europe, North Africa, and the Middle East, are called neandertals. There are also numbers of other Upper Pleistocene early or archaic sapiens from other parts of the Old World. There are several models to account for the relationship of Upper Pleistocene early sapiens to anatomically modern humans. These theories differ basically on whether all early sapiens are the immediate ancestors to modern humans, or whether the latter evolved rapidly in one place, and then quickly spread, replacing early sapiens populations in various parts of the Old World.

Although present evidence suggests that hominids similar in appearance to modern humans appear on the scene about 30,000 to 40,000 years ago, these do not represent humans identical to modern populations. Along with robust skeletons indicative of extraordinary muscular exertion were smaller stature and other differences. The changes that have characterized the evolution of human populations from then to the present are not as profound as those changes characteristic of the evolution from the australopithecines to modern humans; yet they illustrate the continuing nature of human evolution, and represent the action of natural selection on the evolving hominid gene pool.

The detailed catalog of hominid fossils presented in Chapters 9 and 10 provides a basic outline of the evolutionary pathways followed by our ancestors. Many questions about that evolution are unsolved or clouded by differing interpretations. Only newly uncovered fossil remains will help resolve these problems. More fossils dated from about 5 to 15 million years ago would be extremely important in identifying the time of hominid origins and the physical features of the immediate hominoid ancestors. Additional fossils from East Africa of 2 to 5 million years ago would be of great assistance in unraveling the relationships between the various kinds of australopithecines: how did the robust types speciate? What environmental or other factors led to their speciation? The exact dating of the South African australopithecine fossils would be very useful in sorting out the connections between the South and East African early hominids: were South and East African *A. africanus* the ancestors of the early *Homo* forms from East Africa? Finally, well-dated fossils from 35,000 to 70,000 years ago would be extremely helpful in deciding what happened to the early sapiens and their relationships to the modern humans who appear on the scene after them.

Despite problems, we know the basic outlines of hominid evolution. The family Hominidae seems to have been associated with a behavioral complex based on tools for at least the last 2.5 million years. The family Hominidae and the origins of this dependence on tools for survival may have been simultaneous evolutionary events. Without the fossils, we cannot document the beginning with any certainty. The hominids' complex learned behavior evolved along with other biological features. The major evolutionary trends in their biological history were bipedalism, smaller face and teeth, and larger brain. These are thought to be closely related to complex cultural behavior. They, and especially the brain, are connected in a feedback system with culture, each impelling the other toward further elaboration. These biological trends ultimately come from the genetic material carried by the population and new genetic material introduced by mutation and gene flow.

Subsequent chapters will analyze modern human evolution and variation. In the final chapter we will return to the questions raised by the study of the evidence of our evolution and explore some of its implications.

Chapter 11

Human Polymorphisms

The last several chapters have outlined the past several million years of human evolution. Traits that are found throughout our species, toolmaking and use of language, can be accounted for in evolutionary terms. These capabilities have evolved and been refined all over the world, for they are advantageous to people wherever they may live.

All people are alike in many ways; it is equally true that populations of people differ in various ways. Why does variation exist? This is a problem which physical anthropologists look to resolve in terms of a group's history. Oftentimes the variations are adaptations to environmental stresses. In the next few chapters, we will consider several traits on which populations differ as a result of adaptation to different surroundings. We will look first at the traits themselves, from blood to skin, and then at the mechanisms of adaptation: how people deal with stresses, from climatic to psychological.

These investigations will sometimes overlap with and draw upon those made in other, often medically related, fields; but they will retain the anthropological perspective, with its focus on biological history and adaptation. We are interested in knowing why traits appear when and where they do, and if they help a population tolerate stress. Many adaptations have evolved in a population over the generations and are genetic; others, such as sweating or shivering, are alterations made by an individual to accommodate to stresses encountered during one lifetime. In either case the anthropologist asks why these adaptations exist. How did they come into being? Why here and not there? The physician is more interested in the health-related responses of an individual and not so much in why a particular trait is common in certain populations. Generally anthropologists are not interested in the variant that pops up in one out of every 50,000 people; they are concerned instead with traits where variation is common, polymorphisms. In Chapter 3 polymorphisms were discussed as genetic traits for which two or more forms (*morph* = form) exist at appreciable frequencies within human populations.

Sometimes variation may result from migration and subsequent interbreeding or gene flow. This is a particularly relevant factor to consider in seeking answers to questions about the biology of migrant populations. In the last several years, some microevolutionists have come to believe that a significant fraction of the variation between groups of people results from random processes, that is, genetic drift. For much of our evolution, we lived in relatively small groups. Under such conditions, it is not difficult to imagine that accidents and chance could affect the structure of human gene pools.

This chapter will focus on the evolution and distribution of several variable traits: those for which the mechanism of inheritance is well understood, which are easy to measure, which are subject to minimal environmental modification, and for which we have some fairly well developed and documented explanations. Subsequently we will look at some that are not as simple.

Nature and Nurture

The old dichotomy between "nature and nurture" is a poor way of viewing human variation. It is no longer acceptable to hold that people differ because of either genes or environment; rather it is an interaction of genes *and* environment. Genes, even those for such a straightforward trait as hemoglobin type (page 50), do not work in a vacuum, nor does the environment shape a geneless organism. Each of us has a singular combination of genes functioning in a unique environment, making an individual that has never existed until now and will never exist again.

Inheriting Genetic Disorders

Schizophrenia illustrates this interplay between environment and genetics. This mental disorder appears in all human sociocultural settings and populations. Varying extremely in its severity, it shows up as a loss of contact with the environment and a disintegrating personality. By comparing the concordance rate (the frequency with which members of a pair of people suffer from the same disorder) of monozygotic (identical) twins with that of dizygotic (fraternal) twins, Franz Kallman, among others, was able to clarify in part what causes this disorder. Monozygotic (MZ) twins are genetically identical; dizygotic (DZ) twins and other full siblings share 50 percent of their genes; half-siblings share 25 percent, and so on. If genetics influences the disease, we would expect that the closer the genetic link between individuals, the greater the concordance. Kallman's results indicate that genetics does have something to do with the disease. Imagine picking unrelated people from the general population in groups of two. If the first in a group is schizophrenic, the chances are one in a hundred that the second will also be schizophrenic. But if we are dealing with MZ twinships, not the general population, and we know that one member is schizophrenic, the chance is 80 percent that the twin will be schizophrenic. For DZ twins and other full sibships, the rate of concordance is only about 14 percent. It seems that the greater the relatedness the higher the concordance for schizophrenia.

Not all twin pairs, though, are concordant for schizophrenia. They inherit a genetic predisposition to the disorder, not the disease itself. In an environment full of stress and high anxiety, schizophrenia alleles will often express themselves. That MZ twins are not 100 percent concordant proves that environmental factors can modify genetic traits. Even though MZ twins very often dress alike and are treated similarly, their environments are not exactly the same (Figure 11.1). Other diseases, diet, and psychological and physiological stress can all affect them; the same set of genes in two different environments can yield very different outcomes. For one, it seems that the amount of vitamin C in the diet and how efficiently the body uses it helps determine the mental health of people predisposed to schizophrenia. Concordance studies such as these can be criticized on some grounds, but their overall significance cannot be neglected. Schizophrenia, like most other traits, is not caused by either genes *or* environment, but by genes *and* environment.

Figure 11.1. *Genetic identity does not imply that two people will be phenotypically identical. These identical twins, for example, differ in height.*

That a strong genetic influence can be environmentally modified is also well demonstrated by a disease known as phenylketonuria, or PKU. This inborn error in the body's biochemical machinery results in the lack of the enzyme needed to convert the amino acid phenylalanine into tyrosine (see page 60), leading to high levels of phenylalanine in the blood. When toxic levels are reached, brain damage and mental retardation result. This trait might be used, incorrectly, to exemplify a purely genetic trait. In fact, by detecting children with this condition shortly after birth and prescribing a phenylalanine-free diet, the phenylalanine buildup can be avoided, and the retardation prevented.

Although schizophrenia and PKU are abnormalties, many nonpathological traits are also subject to both genetic and environmental influences. Stature is one. People do not inherit genes specifying an adult height of 171.653 cm; instead, they inherit genes that influence their development. The interaction of their environment — disease, exercise, sunlight, psychological state — with their genes determines the final phenotype: they inherit a range of possible responses. The maximum adult height in Japanese children born and brought up in Hawaii clearly indicates this range: the males were, on the average, 4.1 cm taller than their parents born in Japan. It is not likely that their genetic constitution differed markedly from that of their parents, but we know that their environment, in terms of diet and medical care, certainly did.

Normal Variation, Genes, and Environment

Stature is one of many continuous, or quantitative, traits, for which our genes set broad phenotypic limits but with which the environment interacts quite noticeably. Continuous traits are those in which people differ along a continuum, for which there are no discrete categories. Such traits are largely under the influence of several sets of genes as well as the environment. People also possess discontinuous, or qualitative, traits: these are ones where people fall into discrete categories. Every person falls into one or another class for MN blood groups (page 63). No one is a fraction more (or less) type M than someone else. As with pregnancy, wherein a woman can't be a little pregnant, you can't be a little type M blood — you either have it or you don't. Genetic control of these qualitative traits is usually relatively simple and the effects of the environment on them may be subtle.

The Environment

The word environment conjures up images of climatic conditions and geography; however, its application is much broader. A group's culture, for example, affects and is part of the environment. As a group's subsistence practices change, changes in diet can affect the people biologically.

There are dental defects which serve as mirrors of environmental stress. Dental hypoplasia is the term used to describe a condition of pitted teeth with discolored enamel (Figure 11.2). The study of hypoplasia in early Native American agricultural populations shows them to have been more vulnerable to stress than previous groups with broader based economies. Anthropologists have not confined their studies to long-past groups. The decreasing incidence of hypoplasia noted by El-Najjar and colleagues in Cleveland may indicate an improving environment for modern, urban Americans.

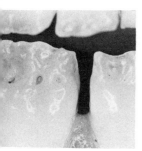

Figure 11.2. *Dental hypoplasia is more common in groups encountering the stresses of disease and malnutrition.*

The effects of disease and malnutrition can show up clearly in longitudinal sections of long bones from human populations (Figure 11.3). The transverse dense areas at the ends of the bone, called *Harris lines,* reflect periods of arrested bone growth during childhood. Had the environment been better, final stature might have been greater. Henry McHenry found that the frequency of Harris lines diminished in California Indians as their subsistence economy expanded from hunting to include fishing and seed and acorn collecting; as the diet improved, Harris lines diminished in frequency.

We tend to think of the environment in terms of diet, climate, and the like, but we also have an internal environment. Although cells may have the same DNA content, in one tissue some of the DNA may be actively producing protein, but in another the same DNA is "turned off." Different environmental conditions, such as oxygen supply and acid-base balance, in different parts of the body may be partly responsible for this phenomenon.

Genetic factors may also be involved: the environment of one gene can include other genes present in the person. The enzyme deficiency PKU, for example, can significantly affect the expression of other genes that are related to brain function. Interactions between gene products are not uncommon. Environment, then, is not an easily defined, nor an easily regulated, factor.

A Well-Adapted Gene Pool

Evolution is starting to look less and less simple. Not only must a gene produce a functioning protein; it must also work well in its external and internal environments and not interfere with the functioning of other gene products. Theodosius Dobzhansky described this as evolution producing a well-adapted gene pool complex, with the genes working well together to turn out viable individuals. Selection will work against the gene that by itself seems superior in adaptive value but upsets the effects of

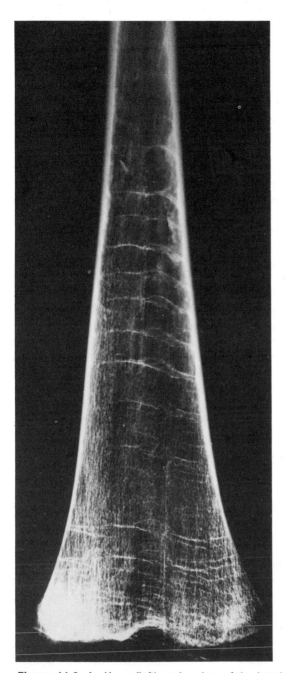

Figure 11.3. *An X ray (left) and a view of the interior of a thighbone from a young California Indian. The horizontal plates of bone, Harris lines, are clearly visible. These lines are thought to mark periods during which growth slowed down due to environmental causes, such as poor diet. Thus, Harris lines portray how the environment modifies the genes' expression.*

other genes. Dobzhansky said, "A genetic good mixer becomes superior to a genetic rugged individualist."[1]*

Then, too, within a species, meiosis is a mixed blessing. On the one hand, by reshuffling or recombining genes and producing new genotypes for each generation, it can yield variation by associating different combinations of genes. Theory and a great deal of experimental work have shown that much variability can be produced simply by associating different alleles. By no means does all variation depend on new mutations (see page 86). But the price paid for meiosis is that well-adapted genotypes are broken up in each generation. In a sexually reproducing organism, only half the genes can come from one parent, no matter how well adapted that parent's genes may be. The compromise is that the benefits and costs make for a gene pool in which many individuals will be reasonably well adapted, while a few will have above average and a few below average selective worth.

Evolution has ways of making sure that such well organized systems of genes continue and keep their integrity. The most obvious are the barriers to interspecies crosses (Chapter 3).

Population Structure

Dobzhansky's vision places a tremendous emphasis on natural selection as the force of evolution most responsible for the constitution of gene pools. As has been noted, there are now anthropologists and evolutionary theorists who say that people like Dobzhansky are overemphasizing the role of selection. Certainly, they say, selection can be important, but it is not vastly more responsible for the genetic organization of today's populations than other forces. This challenge to the primacy of selection ascribes much of a group's evolution to its population structure: its mating practices such as inbreeding (page 95) and assortative mating (see below), its size and subdivisions, if any, and migrations.

We've already noted in Chapter 2 that deviations from random breeding can alter the distribution of genotypes in a population. If people practice inbreeding, there will be a decrease in heterozygotes; likewise, if people marry others to whom they are similar for a trait. If type M people always married type M and type N always married N, no heterozygotes would be formed. This is known as *positive assortative mating.* When people who are dissimilar for a genetic trait marry *(negative assortative mating),* the immediate effect is to increase heterozygosity.

If a population is small in size, the opportunity for genetic drift is clearly enhanced. Drift will cause gene frequencies to change in a random fashion, ultimately causing the frequency of an allele to hit 0 percent or 100 percent. On page 74, it was shown that drift is more likely in small populations or in large groups which do not freely interbreed. India, for instance, has a tremendous population, but its complex social rules severely limit some mate choices. The effective size of the subgroups is much smaller than one might first imagine.

*See page 572 for notes to Chapter 11.

The size of a population may also vary dramatically over time and this too can allow genetic drift to effect the structure of a gene pool. A large population might be drastically reduced in size due to a calamity such as an epidemic or natural disaster. Though survivors can repopulate the area, the subsequent generations are all descendants of the few survivors. If survival is purely a result of chance, then the array of genes which go on through time has been altered by genetic drift. This is known as a *genetic bottleneck*.

Migrations are often affected by cultural and geographic factors. The Greek island of Tinos is subdivided into several local populations. D. F. Roberts and colleagues were able to show that to some degree, choice of marriage partners was simply a reflection of geographic location. If two towns were connected by a donkey track, there was a tendency to exchange mates. Yet, some potential migration routes were not used. Two villages a half-mile apart and connected along a track shared very few mates. Presumably, this lack of migration was the result of some cultural barrier.

While Dobzhansky and many others believe that most of the makeup of a population's gene pool is the end product of selection and reflects an adaptive solution to some problem, others say that population structure can be equally, if not more, important in molding the gene pool. According to the latter thinking, the allele frequencies reflect the workings of drift, population size (both present and past), non-random mating, and migration. This debate is reminiscent of the question (in Chapter 3) of whether all features need be explained in terms of adaptation.

Measuring and Appreciating Variability

In this chapter, we will look at several of the more commonly studied human polymorphisms. Where we have some clues as to the forces producing the variation within a population or the differences between populations we will point them out. The theory we have studied gives us a basis for interesting conjectures about human evolution. Now we must apply these theories to problems in the real world. To do this, we need ways of measuring variability.

Sampling a Population

In order to describe variation in a population, do we have to measure every member? The answer, clearly, is no. In testing people, we eventually reach a point of diminishing returns beyond which further testing does not give us enough information to justify spending the time and effort. When we try to tell if a coin is loaded, we know that flipping it two or three times will not accurately assess its fairness. Six heads out of ten tosses does not tell us if the coin favors heads or if the variation from the expected five heads is simply due to chance. A hundred tosses should give us a closer approximation to a 50:50 distribution if it is a fair coin, though 1,000 tosses would give us a still more nearly accurate answer. On the other hand, our assessment of its honesty would not be improved by making 20,000 rather than 10,000 tosses.

When we study human variations, we need a large, yet manageable, sample of the population. How many people must be tested for a large enough sample without wasting energy by oversampling? It all depends on the problem and what we want to do with the results. Sometimes we can make educated guesses about the size of the sample by looking up previous studies. Some statistical tests require larger samples than others in order to reward us with valid conclusions. Pilot projects, dry runs for larger projects, make use of smaller samples. Biostatisticians can give us rough approximations of the necessary sample sizes. It is impossible arbitrarily to specify an adequate sample size; it depends on the problem we are thinking about and such mundane factors as the amount of time and money the researcher has.

Along with the sample's size, we must consider its appropriateness. If we wanted to find the frequencies of normal and sickle-cell hemoglobin alleles in a population, would we use as our sample the people who report to a hospital? The idea is attractive because the hospital would have a list of patients and their blood types, but our sample would be badly biased if some types are more susceptible to disease than others. Would we want to test only females, cutting our work in half? No, because the genes might be unevenly distributed between the sexes. How about testing everyone on a selected street? Our results would be very different if we chose a street in Fairbanks rather than a street in Harlem: the samples would come from two very different biological populations. If we tested members of the same family, we might count the same gene twice, once in the parent and once in the children. A fairer method might be to assign each individual in the population a number, throw the numbers into a hat, mix well, and draw out a sample of suitable size. This might work well if we could get all the members of the sample to cooperate, willingly or unwillingly, as the Internal Revenue Service does. But this would assume that we know the boundaries of the population we want to study. And we now know that it is often extremely difficult to delimit groups with a biological reality, and at times the sample should cut across biological lines. If we were interested in the blood types of hospital patients, we might well utilize hospital records.

Blood and Blood Groups

Physical anthropologists have a reputation for having rather morbid tastes because of the attention they pay to blood. Actually there are some very good reasons for this fascination. For one, several milliliters of blood can be tested for dozens of genetic traits to provide information on variation. Blood is easy to collect; people are much more willing to part with blood than with muscle. For our purposes, environmental effects on blood type are minimal: if we know a person's phenotype we have a very good indication of his or her genetic composition, unlike the situation with continuous traits. This results in a greater ability to focus on the causes of evolutionary change.

All the traits referred to as blood group systems deal with classes of molecules on the surface of the red blood cell; they have nothing to do with the molecules found inside the red cells. Hemoglobin is not a blood group system. Dozens of blood group systems are known and each of us has a genotype and phenotype for every system. For MN everyone has M and/or N molecules, depending on the genotype; for Rh, Rh + and/or Rh −; for ABO, some combination of A, B, and/or O molecules. The surface of red blood cells, or erythrocytes, is pictured schematically in Figure 11.4.

Classification or typing of a person according to which molecular forms are present on the red cells depends on antigen-antibody reactions. The antigen and antibody are mutually defining: an antigenic molecule is recognized by an animal's immunological system as a foreign substance, to which it reacts by producing an antibody. Antibodies are the substances produced to counteract antigens (see page 165).

Although the mechanics of antigen recognition and antibody production are not completely understood or controllable, much research is going on in immunology. In early life the individual's immune system is programmed to recognize "self." The substances in the fetus are locked into its immunological memory as normal. Other substances, such as some bacteria, viruses, and foods, come to be recognized as "not self," and upon exposure to these foreign substances later in life, antibodies are produced to banish them from the body. In MN blood groups, the M and N substances are antigenic: an M substance introduced into someone who is not type M will cause anti-M antibodies to be made, and an N substance will cause the production of anti-N antibodies in non-N individuals. Isolation and use of these antibodies gives us a method for distinguishing among people according to MN type.

In a test tube of blood revolved at high speed, the denser materials are forced to the outside of the circle of revolution (to the bottom of the test tube) and lighter materials move closer to the axis of revolution. Three noticeable layers are formed. At the bottom of the tube are the heavy red blood cells. Next are white blood cells, important in preventing dis-

Figure 11.4. *Two phenotypes of red blood cells. The various blood types result from the attachment of different molecules to the surface of red blood cells. Each of the many blood group systems (ABO, Rh, MN, etc.) represents a series of related molecular forms.*

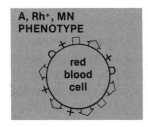

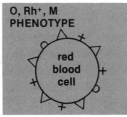

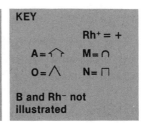

Blood type	Reaction with	
	Anti-M	Anti-N
M	+	–
N	–	+
MN	+	+

Figure 11.5. *Typing blood for MN blood groups. Two drops of a person's blood were placed on a slide. To one drop, antibody to M was added; to the other, anti-N. The anti-M reacted with the blood, causing clumping or agglutination of the red blood cells (left), while the anti-N did not react with it (right). In other words, the anti-M recognized M substance on these cells, while anti-N did not find any N substance with which to react. Therefore, this person has type M blood.*

ease. Uppermost is the fluid portion, which we can call the *serum*. Floating in the serum are many types of molecules, such as antibodies, hormones, and molecules that transport iron. When we take some serum from a person of known blood type and add it to a drop of blood to be tested, one of two things will happen. The serum may mix freely with the red cells with no noticeable change; or the mixture may result in agglutination, clumping together of the red blood cells. If we run this test with serum from a type M person, who is making antibodies to N (simpy called anti-N), and then repeat it using serum from a type N person making anti-M, we can correctly type the blood of any other person for the MN trait. If the sample is agglutinated by anti-M but not by anti-N, it is type M: the molecules on the red blood cells reacted with the anti-M antibodies. Figure 11.5 lists the possible reactions. Tests for other blood group systems may differ slightly because antibodies are a highly heterogenous group of molecules and act in several ways. For example, some, instead of causing agglutination, make the red blood cells break open; others operate best at specific temperatures. Remember, in these tests we are looking for the presence or absence of the antigen on the person's red cells; we are not testing for which antibodies the person has.

Variable characteristics such as blood groups have been used in many studies of human variation because they are easy to test. Furthermore, they are completely genetic, and thus we can explain variability for them because it is not compounded by the effects of the environment.

Dozens of blood group systems are known (Kell, Duffy, Lutheran, to name just three) but we will deal with only a few anthropologically important ones.

The ABO Group   This most widely discussed blood group was discovered in 1900 by Karl Landsteiner, but the mode of inheritance was not explained until 1924. This trait is controlled by three alleles, A, B, and O, of which each of us has two. The A and B alleles are codominant; that is, they do not mask each other's expression. Because both are dominant over O, there are six genotypes and four phenotypes (Table 11.1).

The ABO alleles produce proteins that result in the attachment of different sugar molecules to a blood group "core" molecule. What we refer to as A, B, or O substances are not the direct product of the genes (genes produce only proteins), but the result of the gene product's action (Figure 11.6).

Typing for ABO is a little more complex than for MN, for there are three alleles (A, B, O) but only two antigens (A and B substances) and thus two antibodies. O substance is not antigenic: it is not recognized as a foreign substance by the immune system of anybody, even those who do not have the O allele. Hence there is no anti-O. Antibodies to type A substance cause type A cells to clump together. If a blood sample is clumped only by anti-A, the antibody was able to combine with a molecule (A substance) present on the red cells. Having A molecules, the person is type A. Likewise, anti-B clumps type B cells, and AB cells are clumped by either antibody. Type O cells are not affected by either

Table 11.1. ABO genotypes and phenotypes.

Genotype	Phenotype
AA	A
AO	
BB	B
BO	
AB	AB
OO	O

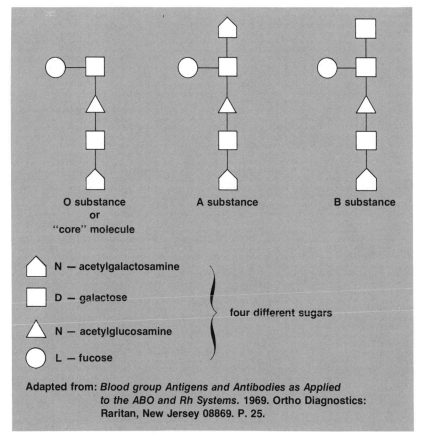

Figure 11.6. Schematic representation of the ABO molecules.

O substance
or
"core" molecule

A substance

B substance

N — acetylgalactosamine

D — galactose

N — acetylglucosamine

L — fucose

} four different sugars

Adapted from: *Blood group Antigens and Antibodies as Applied to the ABO and Rh Systems.* 1969. Ortho Diagnostics: Raritan, New Jersey 08869. P. 25.

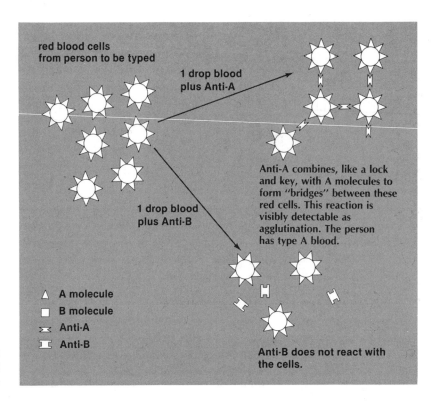

red blood cells
from person to be typed

1 drop blood
plus Anti-A

1 drop blood
plus Anti-B

Anti-A combines, like a lock
and key, with A molecules to
form "bridges" between these
red cells. This reaction is
visibly detectable as
agglutination. The person
has type A blood.

△ A molecule
□ B molecule
☒ Anti-A
☐ Anti-B

Anti-B does not react with
the cells.

Figure 11.7. Typing viewed at a molecular level.

antibody (Figure 11.7). People who are type A will normally have anti-B in their blood as a defense against B substance, which does not belong in them. They will not make anti-A, which would make their own cells clump. The characteristics of the other ABO blood types are set forth in Table 11.2.

At this time, we cannot routinely distinguish AA from AO or BB from BO individuals except possibly by analyzing the blood types of the person's genetic relatives. A person who is AO has just as many A sugar molecules as one who is AA.

One feature in the ABO system may have very important evolutionary implications: most of us have antibodies against the antigens we lack. Besides their clinical importance, the natural occurrence of ABO antibodies may determine differential susceptibility to disease. If, as some research has indicated, the structure of A substance is like that of a substance found on the syphilis disease organism, people of blood types A and AB cannot produce antibodies to syphilis as readily as type B and O individuals. Moreover, the latter have circulating anti-A antibodies that can attack the syphilis microbe almost immediately after exposure. In fact, we all have antibodies to the A or B antigens we lack because we are exposed to A- and B-like substances on bacteria, viruses, or foods we all encounter.

Computing ABO gene frequencies is slightly more complex than for

Table 11.2. ABO blood typing.

A person's ABO blood type is determined by combining one drop of blood with anti-A and one drop with anti-B. Noting which of the antibodies causes clumping or agglutination (±) and which does not (−) tells us that person's ABO type. The antibodies normally present in the blood stream, as a defense mechanism, are also noted.

Blood Type	Antibody Normally in Blood	Reaction with Anti-A	Reaction with Anti-B
A	Anti-B	+	−
B	Anti-A	−	+
AB	None	+	+
O	Anti-A Anti-B	−	−

a two-allele trait. We cannot simply count the alleles as we did with the MN system (see page 64). But we do have ways of computing the ABO gene frequencies from the phenotype frequencies. The frequencies of the alleles are highly variable from population to population.

The maps in Figures 11.8–11.10 show the general frequency distribution of genes around the world, though it is not at all uncommon to find neighboring populations with significantly different frequencies. Most Native American populations have very high frequencies of type O blood, low frequencies of A, and almost no B. But the Blackfoot Indians have the world's highest frequency of A, little O, and no B.

The Rh Group

Another blood group system familiar to most people is the Rhesus, or Rh, system. First discovered in 1939, it is one of the most complexly inherited and clinically important blood group systems.

The system was first studied when a woman, after a stillbirth, developed a severe reaction to a transfusion of her husband's ABO-compatible blood. That is, the blood she was receiving contained an antigen against which she had previously produced antibodies. Because she and her husband had the same ABO type, she could not have been reacting to the ABO antigens. Her immune system had found some other substance on her husband's red blood cells foreign and reacted by producing antibodies against it. Because this agglutination was not correlated with any known blood system, a new blood group system was hypothesized and later named Rh.

Even today we are not certain about the details of the genetics of Rh. One view holds that the Rh antigens are controlled by three closely linked sets of genes, each with two or more alleles. The most common alleles, known as C, c, D, d, E, and e, are inherited in blocks such as cde, CDE, and CdE, so that each individual has two such complexes. The common

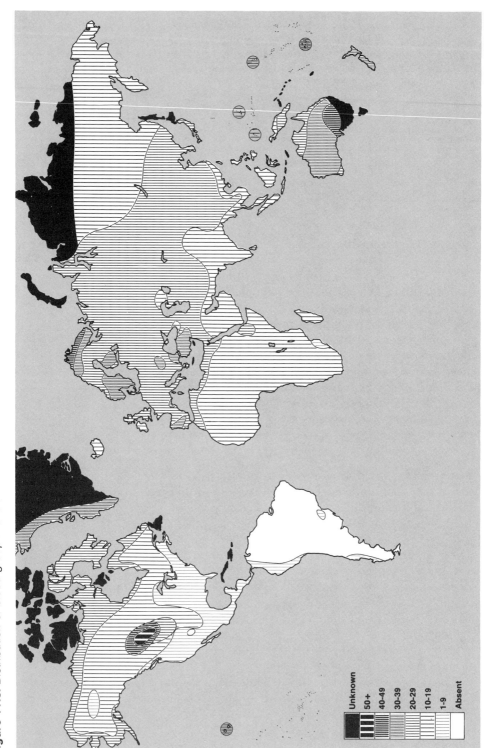

Figure 11.8. Distribution of blood group A allele.

Unknown	
50+	
40–49	
30–39	
20–29	
10–19	
1–9	
Absent	

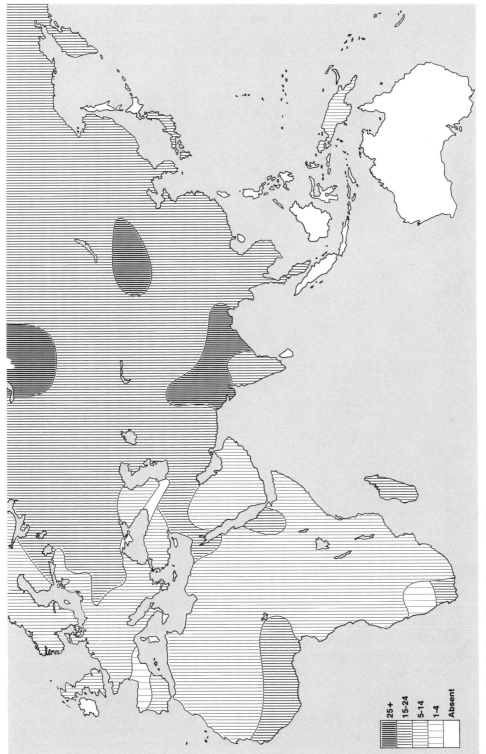

Figure 11.9. Distribution of blood group B allele.

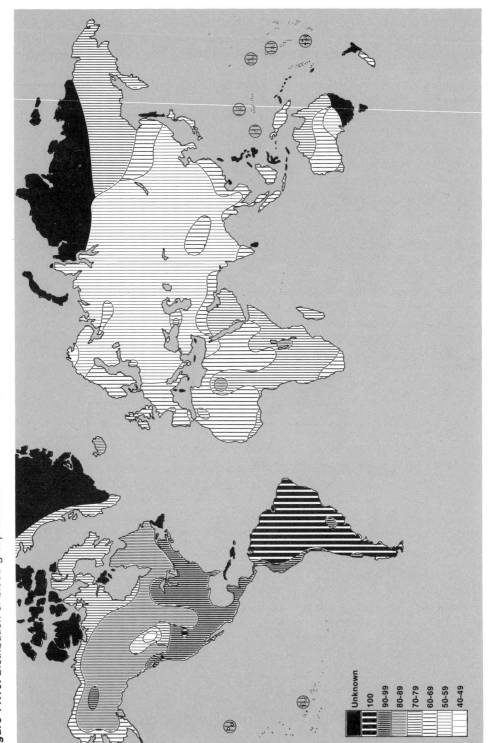

Figure 11.10. Distribution of blood group O allele.

Unknown
100
90-99
80-89
70-79
60-69
50-59
40-49

concept of Rh positive and Rh negative is a function of the D and d alleles only. Those with at least one D allele are Rh +; those who are homozygous recessives, dd, are Rh −. When blood is referred to as positive or negative, the terms relate to Rh type; as with type O blood, there is no antibody against Rh −.

Unlike ABO, we do not produce antibodies to the Rh antigens we do not possess until we are directly exposed to the antigens by blood transfusion or pregnancy. Evidently, the Rh molecules are much rarer in nature than antigens A and B.

In the maps in Figures 11.11 and 11.12, the frequencies of several of the more common chromosome complexes are shown. CDe reaches very high frequencies in Europe and hits its lowest levels in sub-Saharan Africa. It is also very common in Asiatics and Native Americans. cDe reverses the pattern, being most common south of the Sahara and rare elsewhere. The complex cde reaches its highest frequencies in Europe, is uncommon in Africa, and is absent in Asia and the Americas.

The MNS Group

In the examples used for figuring gene frequencies (see page 64), we referred to a seemingly simple system, MN. After the complexities of Rh and ABO, this seems a pleasantly understandable system. Life is not so simple, however. One major modification to the two-allele, codominant situation mentioned is the presence of a second linked trait called S. Here, too, are two alleles, S and s, which are codominant. Thus, instead of two alleles (M and N), there are four complexes, analogous to those of Rh: MS, Ms, NS, Ns. Chemical studies of M and N substances seem to show that they, like ABO, involve sugars bound to amino acids. It also seems that, as with ABO, the difference between M and N antigens results from the attachment of different sugars to a blood group "core." Several chemists have shown that type M cells react weakly with anti-N. Thus, our knowledge of how the MN genes work is incomplete.

The worldwide frequencies of M and N are highly variable, making this trait most useful in characterizing peoples from different parts of the world. The frequency of M ranges from less than 30 percent in Australian Aborigines to more than 90 percent in some Native American groups (Figures 11.13 and 11.14).

Less Important Groups

Many other blood groups are known to exist. These systems are not generally considered very important for several reasons. Some are not well understood genetically. Others have been ignored primarily because they have not much medical significance. ABO and Rh are of great clinical importance not only for blood transfusions, but also because of their correlations with diseases. Most of the lesser systems are rarely important in transfusions and, as far as we know, are not associated with susceptibility to disease. Many of these blood groups also have a common allele found in most people and are therefore of little use in describing or measuring population characteristics or affinities.

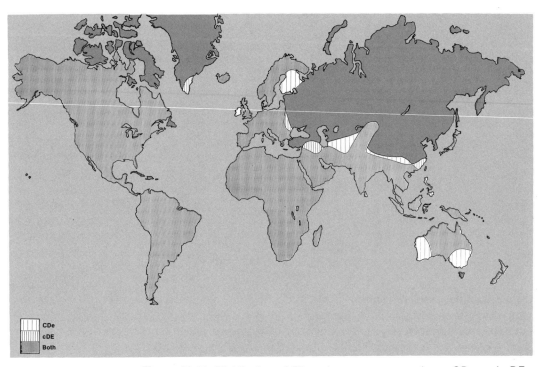

Figure 11.11. Distribution of Rh+ chromosome complexes CDe and cDE.

Figure 11.12. Distribution of Rh+ chromosome complex cDe and the Rh− chromosome complex cde.

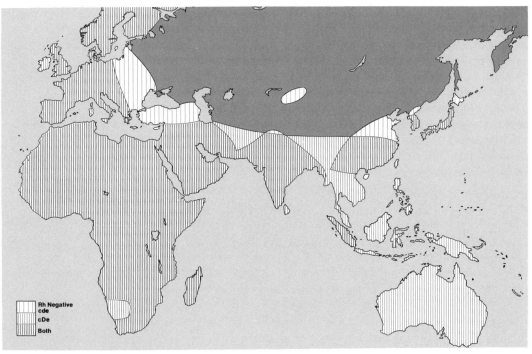

Figure 11.13. Distribution of the MS and Ms complexes.

Figure 11.14. Distribution of the NS and Ns complexes.

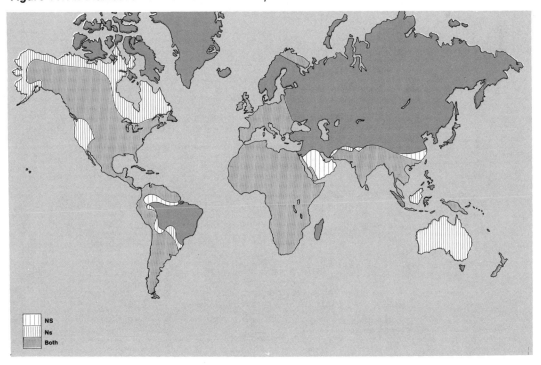

The Diego and Sutter Groups The Diego antigen, Di^a, has a unique worldwide distribution: it is found at appreciable frequencies in the blood of native New World inhabitants and Asians. In this way its distribution agrees well with the postulated Asian derivation of Native Americans. Its absence in Eskimos may be due to genetic drift. Diego seems to be genetically controlled by two alleles, resulting in Di(a+) and Di(a−) phenotypes. The former corresponds to the homozygous Di^a and heterozygous genotypes, and the latter is the homozygote for Di^b.

The Sutter blood group system also has a unique distribution: the resulting antigen is found mostly in sub-Saharan Africans, especially those from West Africa. Blood types with such limited distributions can serve as useful markers to trace migrations and biological relationships between populations.

The Xg Group This is the only blood group system known to be sex-linked in humans. As with hemophilia and color blindness, males have only one Xg allele; females have two. Like many other less-publicized systems, it was first discovered in a person who had received many Rh-, MNS-, and ABO-compatible transfusions, yet produced antibodies against something in some units of transfused blood. All known blood groups could be ruled out as the cause of the reaction, leading to a successful search for a new antigen.

The antigen discovered in this case, now called Xg^a, was found to have the complicated distribution of a sex-linked trait: unequal representation in the sexes. The "silent" or, so far as we know, recessive allele of Xg^a is signified as Xg.

Linkage Maps Several attempts have been made to locate the blood group traits on specific chromosomes or to determine which other traits they are close to on a chromosome. The easiest to place is Xg (on the X chromosome) because of its peculiar distribution between the sexes. It is also possible to find the position of Xg in relation to other sex-linked traits, such as hemophilia, color blindness, an enzyme deficiency disorder, and a pigment disorder of the eye. We build linkage maps by seeking *recombinants,* or offspring that show recombinations of traits. We can tell whether the alleles for hemophilia and color blindness are on the same X chromosome or on different members of the pair in the daughter (Figure 11.15). If the father showed both of these disorders, the alleles are on the same chromosome; if he had only one of the abnormal alleles, the other must have been derived from the daughter's mother; therefore, one variant is carried on each X.

Once this information is gathered, we can measure the distance between the two traits by other techniques. If the daughter's genetic structure is like that shown in possibility 1 of Figure 11.15, most of her sons will inherit either the fully normal or the doubly abnormal X. Some-

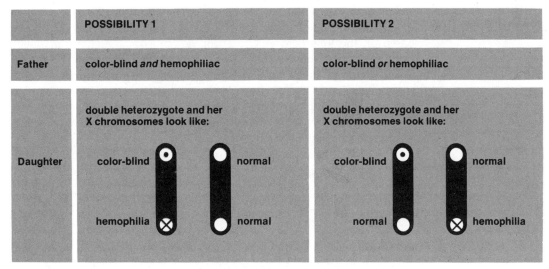

	POSSIBILITY 1	POSSIBILITY 2
Father	color-blind *and* hemophiliac	color-blind *or* hemophiliac
Daughter	double heterozygote and her X chromosomes look like: color-blind — hemophilia / normal — normal	double heterozygote and her X chromosomes look like: color-blind — normal / normal — hemophilia

Figure 11.15. The inheritance pattern for two traits (hemophilia and color blindness) depends on whether the alleles are on the same member of a pair of chromosomes (left) or different members (right).

times, however, there will be a son who exhibits only one of the traits. This change is caused by a breakage of both members of a chromosome pair and crossreunion, or crossover, between the X chromosomes during meiosis in the woman. We expect the frequency of occurrence of such recombinants to be proportional to the distance separating the traits. The farther from each other two traits are, the more likely it is that the chromosome will break in the intervening space. Chromosomes can be broken and reunited by a variety of factors, including temperature, nutrition, and the age of the parents.

Mapping the nonsex chromosomes is far more difficult. Several linkage groups have been uncovered, however, which involve blood groups. ABO alleles are located on chromosome 9 and are linked to a gene causing an abnormality of the fingernails and kneecaps. Rh alleles are on chromosome 1 and are linked to genes which cause deformed red blood cells.

Knowing about these linkage groups can be very important clinically. If it is known that the allele for a blood type is on the same chromosome as a harmful allele in a specific mating, the fetus can be blood typed while it is still in the uterus to determine if it, too, is suffering from the disorder. We cannot always detect fetal defects in this way, but when it is possible, preparation can be made for treatment at birth, or, if the defect is severe, abortion may be chosen. From an anthropological point of view, medical techniques like this one exemplify cultural adaptations to biological problems. Selective mechanisms are culturally modified to reduce the occurrence of genetic defects.

Blood Groups and Evolution

Documenting evolutionary change for the blood group alleles and trying to explain why allele frequencies differ is a seemingly unending task. Based on the long-held view that all variability is somehow adaptive, many researchers have worked hard to understand why blood group allele frequencies are so variable. While selection is certainly involved to some degree, it is also apparent that population structure has played a role as well. Trying to decide whether the allele frequencies in a population are primarily a reflection of natural selection, other forces, or some combination is exceptionally difficult.

In looking for the operation of selection, scientists have used several approaches. First are the studies that try to show a correlation between a blood group allele, say A, and an increased or decreased susceptibility to a disease, such as smallpox. These studies rely on statistical analysis, but are based on laboratory demonstrations of structural similarities between blood group substances and the antigens on disease organisms.

Another technique demonstrates by elaborate statistical analysis that blood group alleles and phenotypes are not randomly distributed according to some variable, such as month of birth, other genetic traits, or birth weight. If the results are significant, the relationship of the variable to the blood group still has to be explained in biological terms.

The third kind of analysis uses a computer to simulate evolution. This requires making some assumptions about the populations and the fitnesses and frequencies of the genotypes.

The associations found in the studies that have been done are not always repeatable. Some experts say that all would-be selective forces are invalid except for one well-documented, incompletely understood example. This one universally accepted selective agent is known as Rh maternal-fetal incompatibility.

Rh Incompatibility and Natural Selection

A person can produce high *titer,* or high-strength, antibodies against foreign blood group substances. This immunological response is usually desirable, as when bacteria are carrying foreign blood-group-like molecules but it can have unfortunate consequences when a mother is carrying a fetus of unlike blood type.

Rh incompatibility appears when an Rh− mother (dd) carries an Rh+ (Dd) fetus. The anti-D antibodies of the mother can cross the placental barrier and attack the red blood cells of the fetus, causing a disorder known as erythroblastosis foetalis, or hemolytic anemia of the newborn. This anemia, a reduction in red blood cells, comes about because the mother's antibodies break open the newborn's red blood cells (hemolysis). It can range from a mild to a fatal form; when fatal, it usually kills shortly before or after birth.

Although no blood flows directly between mother and fetus, the placenta provides for a very close apposition of blood supplies; fetal red cells can leak into the mother's system around the time of birth. Assuming the Rh− mother has never received an improper blood transfusion of Rh+ blood, she is initially sensitized at the time her first Rh+ child is born. As it takes some time for the newborn's Rh+ red blood cells to stimulate the mother to produce anti-D antibodies, this first incompatible baby is safe from hemolytic disease; it is out of the uterus by the time the mother is making anti-D. Now the problem has started, for the woman's immune system has learned how to make anti-D and the antibody will be circulating in her blood stream. This antibody consists of small molecules that can cross the placenta from mother to fetus. By her second or third incompatible pregnancy enough antibody is present to cross the placental barrier and harm the fetal red blood cells. This sort of reaction does not occur in the reverse incompatible type (Rh+ mother, Rh− infant) because there does not seem to be an anti-Rh− antibody, or if it does exist it is very weak or cannot cross the placenta.

Every incompatible pregnancy involves a heterozygous fetus. The mother is Rh− and therefore can give only d to the fetus. To be incompatible is to say the fetus is Rh+: it has a D allele from the father. The genotype is Dd. Thus, each time a fetus or a newborn dies one D and one d allele are selected out of the population. The net outcome should eventually be fixation of the allele initially present at the highest frequency at 100 percent, and the rarer allele at zero. Because the alleles are being lost in equal numbers, the rarer one disappears first. This result, however, does not seem to have occurred (Figure 11.12). Although Native American, East Asian, and Oceania populations, before European contact, lacked the Rh− allele, many other populations are maintaining both D and d. We therefore have to ask why our theory does not fit reality. Selection should be reducing the frequency of d to zero in low-d areas such as sub-Saharan Africa, but d is still around. The reply that d is decreasing but at a very slow rate, that it is a transient polymorphism, does not make much sense, for this polymorphism has undoubtedly been with us for a very long time. Are there any factors that would retard the rate at which d is eliminated, or support it as part of a balanced polymorphism?

We do have some further tentative clues on the Rh polymorphism, which we owe to the pioneering work of Philip Levene and A. S. Wiener, and more recently Bernice Cohen. It has been known for some time that an hemolytic anemia can be caused by ABO incompatibility when, for example, a type O mother carries an A fetus. All ABO phenotype combinations are incompatible when the fetus carries an antigen absent in the mother (Table 11.3). The causes behind the disorder are generally much the same as in Rh incompatibility, except that (1) usually the mother will already be producing antibodies to the antigen she lacks, and (2) ABO incompatibility usually produces abortion early in fetal life. Rh incompatibility, on the other hand, affects developed fetuses and the newborn.

As long ago as 1943, Levene postulated that maternal-fetal pairs doubly incompatible for ABO and Rh ran less risk of fetal death than those incompatible for only one system. Recent research by Cohen has supported this hypothesis. Immunologically it appears that the normally

A Selective Interaction: Rh and ABO

Table 11.3. Maternal-fetal pairs that can result in incompatibility for ABO and/or Rh.

Mother's phenotype	Incompatible fetal phenotypes. The blood group involved in the incompatibility is shown in white.
AB+	None
AB−	A+, B+, AB+ Rh
A+	B+, AB+, B−, AB− ABO
A−	B−, AB−, B+, AB+, O+, A+ ABO Rh
B+	A+, AB+, A−, AB− ABO
B−	A−, AB−, A+, AB+, B+, O+ ABO Rh
O+	A+, B+, A−, B− ABO
O−	A−, B−, A+, B+, O+ ABO Rh

circulating antibodies to A or B attack the fetal red blood cells that escape into the mother's system. The early destruction in the mother's body of the doubly incompatible fetal red blood cells prevents the mother from producing anti-Rh+ antibodies. Thus, ABO- and Rh- incompatible maternal-fetal phenotypes do not often allow for the chain of events that follows Rh incompatibility. The ABO- and Rh-incompatible cells are eliminated from the maternal bloodstream before the mother's immune system becomes aware of the Rh+ cells. The mother's antibodies to ABO antigens are already present and destroy any fetal cells that get into her system before her body can recognize that the cells are also Rh+. The mother never gets a chance to make antibodies to Rh+ substance. ABO antibodies are protecting against subsequent fetal rejection caused by Rh incompatibility. Why double incompatibility also ameliorates the ABO effects is more puzzling. The most prevalent theory is that the double incompatibility somehow suppresses the maternal immune system and prevents it from synthesizing large quantities of antibody directed against A or B, but we are still far from a complete answer.

Table 11.4 lists a ranking of the risk of fetal death for women who

Table 11.4. The likelihood that various types of maternal-fetal incompatibilities will result in fetal death, judged from available data.

Incompatibilities	Likelihood of fetal death
Neither ABO nor Rh incompatible	Least likely to result in fetal death
Rh incompatible and ABO incompatible	
ABO incompatible	
Rh incompatible	Most likely to result in fetal death

were incompatible only for Rh and women who were incompatible with their fetus for both Rh and ABO. The data clearly indicate that double incompatibility is less likely to result in fetal death than Rh incompatibility alone. Other data indicate the same trend for double incompatibles compared with those who were just ABO incompatible. These results, if correct, do not negate the predicted, but unfulfilled, movement toward fixation for Rh+ or Rh− alleles. They do illustrate that selection on this trait is not as simple as we might like to think. More generally it proves that we cannot consider an allele's selective worth in isolation. The benefits of one ABO blood type over another depend at least partly on a person's Rh blood type.

In fact Rh maternal-fetal incompatibilities that become medically significant appear to be confined to people of European ancestry, while medically noted ABO incompatibilities are more common in Africans; these phenomena indicate further genetic complications. Far from operating in isolation, gene products interact with one another as Wright and Dobzhansky note. The overall reproductive ability of one's alleles can be quite different from what we might expect simply by looking at each set of alleles as an isolated factor.

Noninfectious Disorders

Besides the well-established maternal-fetal incompatibilities for both Rh and ABO, little is known about blood groups and selection. Several other possibilities relate Rh and disease; these are joined by a huge number of preliminary correlations of ABO types and disease. Many researchers feel that natural selection must be maintaining the ABO allele frequencies in human populations. It is a long jump, though, from intuition to proof.

Several studies have shown that people of different ABO phenotypes are unequally susceptible to noninfectious disorders. Type O people are up to 40 percent more likely to develop duodenal ulcers than other people. They also more commonly have gastric ulcers, at least in the Western societies studied. Type O women taking birth control pills appear less likely to develop blood clots as a side effect of the pill than women of other blood types. Group A individuals, on the other hand, seem predisposed to cancer of the stomach and cervix, ovarian tumors, and pernicious anemia. Many of the associations are related to either the gastrointestinal tract or the female reproductive organs; also, large quantities of A or B substances are found in the stomach lining and ovarian cysts of some people, as well as in saliva. The significance of this association is not yet apparent.

These disorders seem to have no evolutionary significance, for most of them strike relatively late in life, after the reproductive years.

ABO and Infectious Diseases The more promising approach seems to be demonstrating antigenic similarities between A or B substances and molecules found on bacteria, viruses, and parasites. In 1959 two doctors at Walter Reed Army Hospital demonstrated that the bacteria *Escherichia coli 086* reacted strongly with anti-B. Anti-B antibodies can kill this bacterium because it has on its surface a sugar molecule very similar to the B sugar molecule. Type B and AB people infected with it cannot make antibodies against this part of the bacterium because they would also destroy their own red blood cells. A and O people, on the other hand, already have or are able to make antibodies against this sugar on the bacterium's surface. Because *E. coli 086* is one of the organisms that cause diarrhea in the newborn, a potentially lethal disease, this selection might favor blood types O and A. But the problem is not that simple. Bacteria do not have just one surface molecule that can stimulate the host's immune system. We have to ask, therefore, whether the ability to produce anti-B affects the newborn's ability to survive diarrhea. Let us assume that this bacterium has ten molecules that a type A person's immune system can recognize and produce antibodies against. Type B and AB people can react to all except the one that is like B substance. How important is it to be able to react to the B antigen? One thing we can do is test the efficiency of antibodies directed against all ten molecules and compare their ability to kill the bacterium with that of antibodies directed against all but the B-like substance. When this was done, the researchers found that the drop in bactericidal (bacteria-killing) effect was slight but noticeable (Figure 11.16). Type B individuals may be slightly more susceptible to infantile diarrhea, but the ability to react to B-like antigens on *E. coli* is only a small part of a person's ability to kill this bacterium.

A follow-up study was made later at a New York hospital. Instead of looking only for antigenic similarity between *E. coli* and blood group substances, researchers analyzed all young patients with serious infections admitted to the hospital during a one-year period. They blood typed each and cultured the disease organisms for proper identification. They found that the risk of *E. coli* infections among type B and AB individuals really was higher than in type A or O people. Type B and AB people also ran a higher risk of infection with another genus of bacteria that

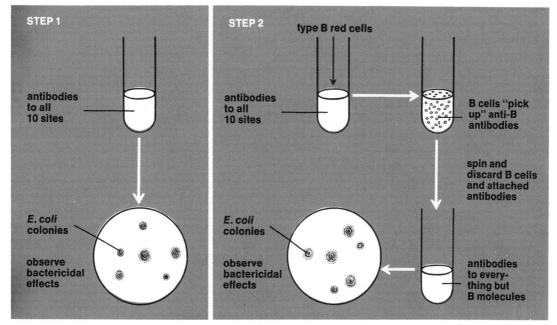

Figure 11.16. *A method to estimate the bactericidal effects of an ABO anti-body.*

Step 1: The bacteria-killing effect of whole serum from a type A person is observed.

Step 2: The bacteria-killing effect of whole serum from a type A person minus anti-B is noted. Anti-B is removed by incubating the whole serum with type B red blood cells. Then the two results are compared.

causes typhoid fever and other intestinal disorders. These results must, however, be tempered by the realization that the researchers could identify the causative bacteria in only 36 percent of the patients. If for some reason it is more difficult to detect the bacterium in A and O people, these conclusions would be misleading.

This kind of statistical problem has plagued those who try to demonstrate differential susceptibility to disease. The real world is so full of variables which cannot be controlled that we are constantly tempted by intriguing results; but we are never quite sure that they are correct.

Smallpox and ABO Until a vaccine was developed, smallpox was a major killer in many parts of the world. In groups such as the Native Americans, which had never been exposed to the disease, smallpox killed up to 90 percent of the population at the first exposure. This fact was not lost on early British and American adversaries of the Native Americans. One British lord queried an army officer, "Could it not be contrived to send the small pox among (the) Indians? We must . . . use every stratagem in our power to reduce them."

In 1960 two German researchers claimed they had discovered an A-like antigen on the cowpox virus, a close relative of the agent that causes smallpox. This finding was disputed by others who felt it came simply from experimental error.

Others tried to clarify the results by studying the incidence of the disease in people of the various blood groups. One set of data, gathered in India where smallpox still existed, supports the hypothesized similarity of A antigen and a structure on the smallpox virus. In a rural unvaccinated population in India the researchers found a much higher incidence of smallpox among type A and AB people than in O and B individuals. Not only was the disease more common in the A/AB group, it was more often severe or fatal in people with the A antigen. Poor medical care raised the mortality rate in the A/AB group to 50 percent.

More on ABO and Infectious Disease Other experimenters, too, have claimed associations between blood group antigens and antigens on pathogens (disease-causing agents). Although none of the associations is unanimously accepted, it is very likely that the ability to produce antibodies directed at A or B molecules has helped determine the world's distribution of ABO alleles. Theoretically it makes sense that populations will have evolved to tolerate diseases in their homeland and, if antibodies to A and B help determine resistance to a disease, ABO allele frequencies will, in part, be affected by indigenous diseases; different populations will have attained different adaptive complexes, or peaks, for ABO alleles.

A complexity introduced several hundred years ago was the rapidity with which humans and their diseases can travel. As the Native Americans found with smallpox, a population may learn to handle its own diseases, only to fall before new evolutionary problems introduced by a foreign disease. Going back to Wright's idea, we can say that Native Americans fell from their adaptive peak when Europeans introduced them to smallpox.

Computer Simulation: Recapitulating Evolution When we try to decide on the ABO system's overall evolution, computer simulations are a great help. To recreate the trait's evolution we program the computer with educated guesses about a population's past (the input): population sizes, fitness values, admixture rates, and the rest. The computer races through thousands of years of evolution, reaching the present in short order, and prints out the gene frequencies. The computer's output is then compared with what we see in the real world. If agreement between the two is poor, the evolutionary information is juggled, the computer is turned on, and again the output and the real world are compared. When the two agree, we can conclude that the evolutionary information we fed into the computer is reasonably close to the evolutionary factors that actually prevailed. Computer simulations test possible evolutionary circumstances to see which might account for today's distribution of a trait. One conclusion reached by all computer simulations of ABO is that heterozygote advantage, a balanced polymorphism, must have existed to maintain variability; whether it still exists is another question.

Now we have a problem. If we still have (or ever did have) heterozygote advantage, is selection operating on the genotype and not the phenotype? Just because we cannot distinguish between AA and AO does not mean that selective agents cannot. Might not some of our problems in associating infectious diseases with ABO blood type be caused by differences in susceptibility of homozygotes (AA, BB) and heterozygotes (AO, BO) necessarily lumped together in the studies?

Alice Brues, trying to determine the relative fitness of the ABO genotypes, used a computer simulation routine. After the computer was given initial gene frequencies, population sizes, and selective pressures related to maternal-fetal incompatibility, it simulated the evolutionary changes that might come about during 500 years (roughly twenty generations). Starting from the populations Brues created, the computer "gave birth" about 100 times a second by picking out gene pairs (newborns) at random from the gene pool, and "threw out" a percentage of the offspring, those who died because they had ABO incompatibilities. The gene frequencies were also subjected to drift by a random component in the computer's way of picking genotypes in each generation. The resulting distribution of frequencies closest to the observed showed that AB was the most fit, followed by AO, BO, OO, AA, and finally BB (Figure 11.17; notice that the smallest populations drifted most).

It is doubtful that we will soon come up with a final answer on selection and ABO. Anthropologists and serologists have written hundreds of papers on this topic and have designed clever techniques to detect selection, but the problem's inherent complexities have defied a full answer. We may eventually find that bacterial, viral, and parasitic disorders as well as dietary differences, maternal-fetal incompatibility, and interactions with other genes have all helped determine ABO distribution.

Several evolutionary processes have been suggested as being responsible for the maintenance of MN polymorphism. Because people normally do not carry antibodies to the MN antigen they lack, most theories have been built on factors other than selection by infectious disease. Some researchers found that MN heterozygotes were produced more often than chance would account for. In MN male × MN female matings they found, instead of 50 percent MN offspring, about 55 percent. The explanation offered was that the MN genotype was more fit and had a better chance of surviving. If that is true, MN is a balanced polymorphism.

Other hypotheses have tried to account for these results. One is that M and N sperm are produced in equal numbers but do not have equal probabilities of fertilizing the egg: in some conditions, the probability of M fertilization is higher; in others, N sperm have a better chance of winning the race. This theory, too, has been used on ABO, and is appealing

MN Polymorphism

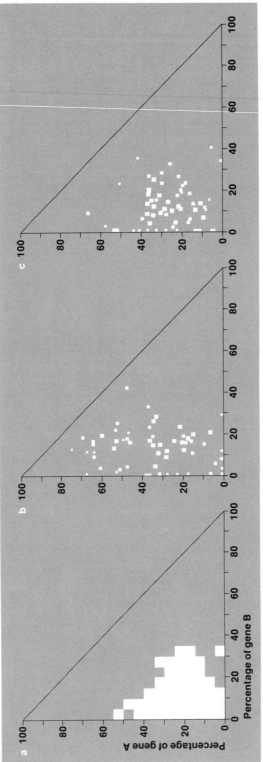

Figure 11.17. The actual distribution of ABO allele frequencies and two simulated distributions using different fitness values.

(a) A graphic representation of the worldwide ABO alleles from 350 representative populations. The axes of the graph correspond to the frequencies of A and B; O can be computed by subtracting the A and B frequencies from 100 percent. Most populations are clustered toward the high O, low (10–30%) A, and low (10–20%) B region.

(b) The expected distribution if fitness values for the genotypes were ranked from most fit to least fit as follows: $AB > AA = AO = BO > OO > BB$.

(c) The expected distribution given another set of fitness values: $AB > AO > BO > OO > AA > BB$. Based on the comparisons of observed and expected distributions, it seems reasonable that the fitness values in (c) more closely approximate reality.

because cervical mucus can contain antibodies to A or B and thus could select out sperm carrying the unlike antigen. The only problem here is that we are not yet sure if sperm carrying the A or B allele have the corresponding antigen on the membrane. That we can apply this idea to the MN system is even more uncertain. All these hypotheses are more equivocal than disease associations and we have very little empirical evidence to support them.

More recently, it has been shown that the parasite which causes a very dangerous form of malaria invades a person's blood cells by first attaching to the MN antigens on the cells' surface. Cells with reduced numbers of MN antigens on their surface are resistant to invasion. Whether this has affected the evolution of the MN trait must be determined.

Other Genetic Traits in Blood

Along with the blood group systems we can find many other genetic traits in the blood. Blood groups result from the attachment of molecules to the surface of the red blood cells, but genetically controlled molecules are inside the red cells, on the white blood cells, and in the fluid portion of the blood, the serum.

Variant forms of these proteins can often be detected by electrophoresis. This technique relies on the fact that proteins are positively or negatively charged, and will migrate in an electrical field. The greater the negative charge, the farther the protein will move to the positive pole, and vice versa. Differential migration coupled with appropriate use of dyes can yield results such as those seen in Figure 11.18.

Figure 11.18. *Electrophoresis of monkey serum. These monkeys display a great deal of variation for some serum proteins, particularly transferrin, whereas other proteins, such as albumin, exhibit no variation.*

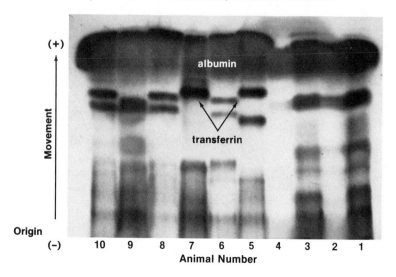

The Structure of Hemoglobin Hemoglobin is the most intensively studied protein inside the red blood cell; it makes up more than 90 percent of the cell's protein content. Briefly reviewing the discussion on pages 170–174, we find that at different times in our life we make different forms of hemoglobin. All of these forms use the α chains made by the α gene. During embryonic life two α chains combine with two ϵ chains ($\alpha_2 \epsilon_2$) and during fetal life with two γ chains ($\alpha_2 \gamma_2$). After birth, we make a major hemoglobin called HbA with the

Figure 11.19. *The oxyhemoglobin (hemoglobin combined with oxygen) molecule, composed of two identical α and two identical β chains. The iron-containing heme groups bind to oxygen for transport to the body's tissues. Hemoglobin A_2 contains two types of chains also but has δ chains. In sickle-cell anemia there are again two normal α chains, but the β chains differ from the normal form by one amino acid.*

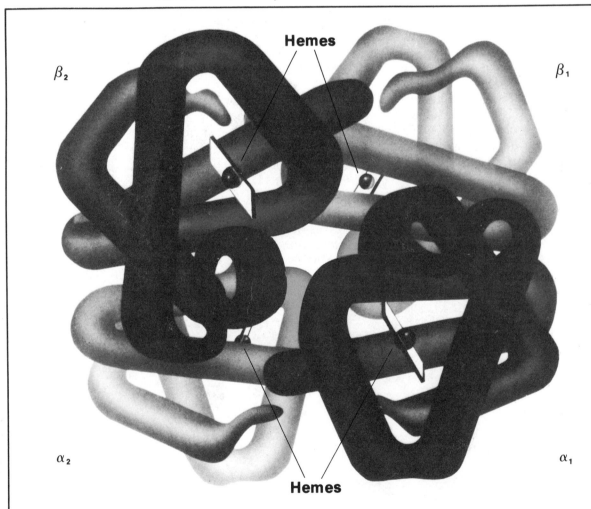

composition $\alpha_2 \beta_2$, as well as a minor hemoglobin, HbA_2 ($\alpha_2 \delta_2$) (see Figure 11.19).

There are many hemoglobin variants known, but most are very rare. Those most interesting to anthropologists are hemoglobins S, C, and thalassemia, as they reach rather high frequencies in some parts of the world.

Of these three variants, the one we know most about is hemoglobin S. The allele for this form occurs in high frequencies, up to about 20 percent, in populations from malarial areas in sub-Saharan Africa, and at lower frequencies in India and parts of the Mediterranean (Figures 11.20 and 11.21). Several explanations have been offered for the high frequencies of this allele in malarial areas. All come from the observation that people who are heterozygous for the sickle-cell allele are better able to survive and reproduce in a malarial region.

The Sickle-Cell Variant and Malaria

Malaria is really several diseases caused by different species of parasites of the genus *Plasmodium*. The parasite enters the human body through the bite of an infected mosquito. Once inside, it sets up residence inside red blood cells and goes through a development that eventually destroys the red cell (Figure 11.22). If the parasite is able to reproduce easily inside the body, it will infect many red cells; when these cells are destroyed, the malaria victim will die.

Cells containing sickle-cell hemoglobin are not conducive to the

Figure 11.20. *Distribution of the sickle-cell allele.*

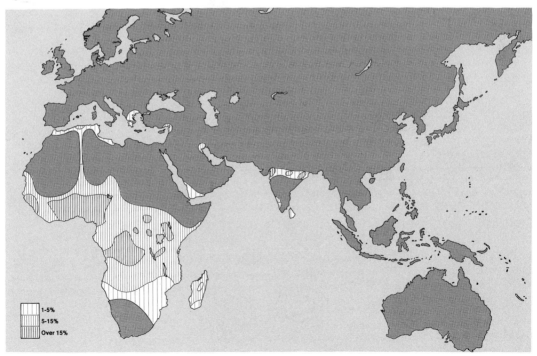

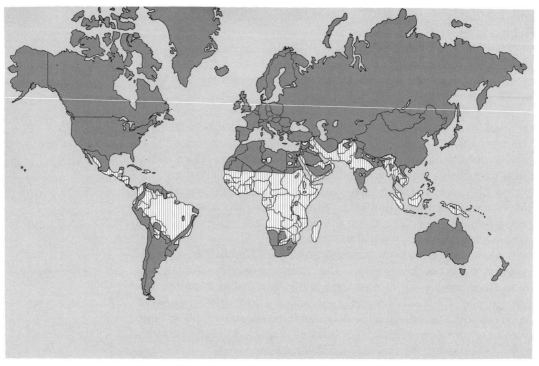

Figure 11.21. *Areas where malaria is commonly encountered today.*

Figure 11.22. *Uninfected red blood cells and some parasitized by malaria. Eventually parasites cause the cells' destruction.*

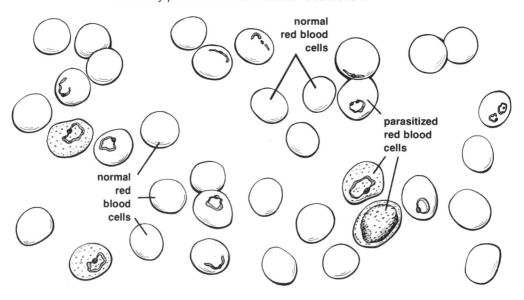

parasite's proper development, making heterozygotes for this form of hemoglobin less susceptible to severe malarial infection. Recent research demonstrates that the parasite infects the red cells of heterozygotes, but when the cell sickles, the potassium level drops and the parasite dies. Though the parasite can survive in the heterozygote's non-sickled cells, the resistance provided by sickling is sufficient to allow the person to mobilize other protective mechanisms and survive the disease. Because roughly half the hemoglobin in the heterozygote's red blood cells is normal, many of the red cells do not sickle and thus these people do not develop sickle-cell anemia. Data from malarial areas show clearly that heterozygosity for normal and sickle-cell β chains does protect against death by malaria. Of 104 malaria-caused deaths considered in one study, only one occurred in a sickle-cell heterozygote, though 23 deaths would be expected by chance association.

Besides greater resistance to malaria, the AS heterozygote may have other advantages in malarial regions. Some research indicates that female heterozygotes have greater fertility than AA homozygotes. A possible explanation is that parasite levels in the heterozygote's placenta are lower than in the placenta of AA homozygotes; the fetus therefore is not deprived of oxygen by the parasite. Heterozygous males, too, may have greater fertility in malarial areas. Abnormally high body temperature for a brief period can suppress sperm production for weeks; thus, reduced susceptibility to malarial fevers might increase fertility.

For any or all of these reasons, sickle-cell hemoglobin has been maintained as a balanced polymorphism for some time in malarial areas; some have tried to estimate how long. We can assume that the S allele was not selected for before malaria became a common disease in humans. By observing the malaria-carrying mosquito's ecology we can estimate when that happened.

Before the advent of agriculture in Africa it is unlikely that humans often contracted malaria. But by clearing the land for agriculture, they blundered into playing the host for the *Plasmodium* parasite. The mosquito that carries the parasite has little chance of breeding in a tropical rain forest; although its breeding sites are highly diversified, it cannot reproduce in shaded, salty, or polluted water.

Several scientists demonstrated decades ago that the malaria-carrying mosquito spreads as land is cleared. To establish a rubber plantation in Liberia, the Firestone Company cleared huge swaths of forest. Shortly afterward, scientists found that the malaria mosquito accounted for 46 percent of the mosquito population. Several years later it reached 100 percent. In areas not used the jungle cover was restored, removing this form of mosquito almost completely.

Looking at the incidence of malaria in human populations, we find that hunting groups living in rain forests, such as the Pygmies of the Congo, are almost completely free of malaria. Many other peoples of Central Africa depend on agriculture, subsisting on yams, bananas, coconuts, and cereals. To make arable land the natives burn over an area of rain forest, greatly transforming its ecology. The shade cover is removed and the continued cultivation removes the humus, making the ground impervious to water and establishing perfect malarial mosquito breeding grounds.

We conclude, then, that the clearing of land for agriculture brought about the selective advantage for the sickle-cell allele. Some of Frank Livingstone's work, which draws on linguistic, cultural, and archaeological data, indicates that an African mutation probably originated in East Africa, in the area of Sudan, and spread from there along with slash-and-burn agriculture. This is an impressive example of our often unwitting disruption of many ecological niches, our propensity for altering the environment, and therefore the course of evolution, in many unforeseen ways.

More information on the sickle-cell allele has come to light by use of recombinant DNA techniques (page 38). If one uses the restriction enzyme Hpa I to digest the human β-globin genes of a normal individual, several fragments are produced (Figure 11.23). A fragment 7.6 kb long is the one which contains the β gene. Two scientists at the University of California, San Francisco, noted that the pattern of digestion was somewhat different in many American Blacks with the sickle-cell allele. In eleven of fifteen people with sickle-cell anemia (SS), the 7.6 kb fragment was absent. In its place was a 13 kb fragment. This was interpreted to mean that a mutation had changed the Hpa I site noted in Figure 11.23 so that it no longer could be cut by this enzyme. When treated with Hpa I, the mutated DNA was cut into a 13 kb fragment containing the β gene instead of a 7.6 kb β-containing fragment. This is called a restriction site polymorphism.

Although this change in the Hpa I site has no functional relationship to the mutation which causes the sickle-cell β gene, the two are linked

Figure 11.23. 1. Indicates sites at which the enzyme Hpa 1 cuts the DNA in the vicinity of the normal human β gene (kb = Kilobase or 1000 bases). 2. Hpa 1 sites found in association with the sickle-cell hemoglobin gene. The site labeled * is abolished, yielding a 13 kb fragment.

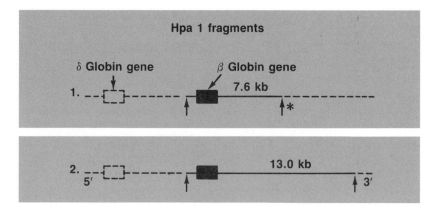

(page 54). Thus, chromosomes with the sickle-cell gene coincidentally usually also lack a Hpa I site. This discovery can allow for early detection of fetuses with sickle-cell anemia. By looking in fetal DNA for the presence or absence of a 13 kb fragment containing the β-globin gene, the occurrence of this disease can be predicted. DNA with the 13 kb fragment is likely to also have the S allele. More recently, direct identification of the sickle-cell gene in fetuses has been possible through use of restriction enzymes.

Earlier, it was mentioned that the S allele exists in the Middle East and parts of India. Analysis of the sickle-cell genes by restriction enzyme digestions suggests that the sickle-cell genes in different parts of the world are not identical. This is actually not too surprising. Though some Saudi Arabians and Indians are said to have sickle-cell anemia, they rarely die from the disorder. This is very different from the situation in West Africans and their descendants in America who have sickle-cell anemia. These may be two different mutations that only share the ability to cause red cells to sickle.

Hemoglobin C versus Hemoglobin S

The C form of hemoglobin is produced by a third hemoglobin allele, so that it, too, produces an abnormal β chain. People who are homozygous for C suffer from an anemia, but it is not as severe as that suffered by sickle-cell homozygotes. We think some selective advantage must be attached to being genotypically AC; otherwise this allele should not be so common in some populations.

As with the other hemoglobin variant we have considered, this allele's distribution coincides with that of malaria in Africa (Figure 11.24). There is therefore a sizable overlap in the ranges of C and S alleles, but it seems that the higher the frequency of one of these alleles in a population, the lower the frequency of the other: they are alleles of each other and thus are in competition. Because the SC heterozygote has a very low fitness, one of these alleles should drive the other out of the population, which can be proven mathematically. Nonetheless, both of these alleles are present in many populations, and Livingstone has tried to explain the phenomenon.

Besides the *Plasmodium* parasite associated with hemoglobin S, called *P. falciparum,* the genus has several other members, *P. malariae, P. ovale,* and *P. vivax.* All are carried by members of the same mosquito genus but each has a different life cycle and ecology. It is Livingstone's contention that AS heterozygosity is a defense against falciparum malaria, but is of no benefit in counteracting the other malarias. That does seem to be true, because AS individuals often have higher *P. malariae* parasite levels than AA individuals. AC people, Livingstone contends, have an inherently lower susceptibility to *P. malariae,* and possibly the other malarias, than people with other sorts of β chains (except AS people and *P. falciparum).* Because populations may play host to both *P. falciparum* and *P. malariae* at the same time, selection must balance several factors: resistance to the two malarias and frequency of the anemias. In parts of

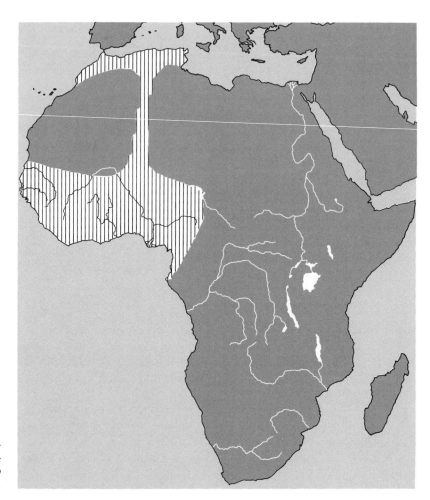

Figure 11.24. Distribution of hemoglobin C is confined to Africa.

West Africa, the distribution of the malarias and β-chain variants fits this theory nicely. Going north through Ghana, the incidence of *P. falciparum* decreases as *P. malariae* rises; likewise, the frequency of S drops from about 10 percent to 5 percent as C attains its highest frequency. In North Africa, too, *P. malariae* is predominant as is hemoglobin C. Some areas do not fit this theory, but the deviations may be explained by migrations and gene flow.

It is exceedingly hard to analyze how such a complex system of interactions evolved. It would not be too perplexing if we were dealing with only one variable, the hemoglobin β chains. But we have another complication, in that the fitness also depends on the type of malaria.

Thalassemia, Major and Minor   In several parts of the Old World another genetically caused anemia is found in sizable frequencies (Figure 11.25). This type of anemia, known as thalassemia (*thalassa* = sea; *haima* = blood), results in a peculiar hematological picture. While sickle-cell anemia can be traced to an ab-

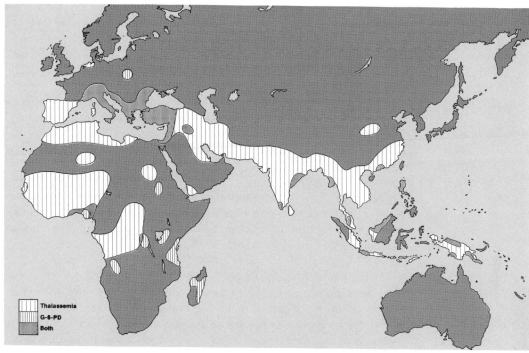

Figure 11.25. *Distribution of both thalassemia (in the Old World) and G-6-PD deficiency.*

normal hemoglobin, thalassemia is characterized by virtually no hemoglobin A, abnormally high levels of hemoglobin A_2, the normal minor component, as well as high levels of fetal hemoglobin. No abnormal hemoglobin is present however. For a long time it was thought that thalassemia was caused by an allele which prevented production of β chains. People thought to be homozygotes for this allele were said to have thalassemia major, with heterozygotes having thalassemia minor.

The disease manifests itself at birth when β-chain synthesis normally begins. The body compensates for the stress from partial or complete deficiency of adult hemoglobin by continuing to make fetal hemoglobin and also large amounts of hemoglobin A_2. In the homozygote, the body's compensatory action usually is not enough to support life; most thalassemia major victims die before reproductive age. In thalassemia minor cases, normal adult hemoglobin production is enough to support life and the elevated levels of fetal and minor-component hemoglobin do not appear.

Again, we find that newer techniques of molecular biology provide insights into the origin of this disorder. To start, thalassemia is in fact a result of many different genetic events. In different parts of the world, it results from one or more different mutations. Some cases are due to deletions, where various sized pieces of DNA encompassing part or all of the β gene are lost. Other thalassemias come about because of alterations in the switches that are meant to turn the β gene on at the time of birth. Some people with thalassemia have several different defects. As with sickle-cell hemoglobin, it appears that different mutations can cause the same phenotype. In fact, there are also thalassemias caused by lack of α chains. These α thalassemias are also highly heterogeneous at the genetic level, as might be expected.

Comparing Figures 11.21 and 11.25 we again see a correspondence between the distributions of a hemoglobin abnormality, thalassemia, and malaria. As yet we have little direct evidence to link thalassemia to malarial resistance except for (1) the similarities in distribution, and (2) the assumption that thalassemia minor must be advantageous in some respect or it would not be present at such high frequencies. Peter Brown has proposed that the distribution of thalassemia in Sardinia can be explained, in part, by the pattern of migration into the area by Carthagians and Romans two thousand years ago. His data do not support the idea that thalassemia provides resistance to malaria.

Variation in Red Cell Enzymes: G-6-PD Deficiency

Inside the red blood cells are many genetically controlled molecules besides hemoglobin. One class of these is the red cell enzymes, molecules that speed up biochemical reactions. Not nearly as plentiful as hemoglobin, the red cell enzymes are relatively simple to detect, and because there are many, they give us much information about a person's genotype and a population's gene frequencies.

Of the variable red cell enzymes, probably the one that most interests physical anthropologists is glucose-6-phosphate dehydrogenase (G-6-PD), which aids in the reduction of glucose-6-phosphate, a sugar, to another sugar and also produces an energy-rich molecule.

It was found in the early 1950s that a drug, primaquine, precipitated an anemia in many blacks. Investigators showed that primaquine-sensitive people were deficient in red cell G-6-PD, and that their red cells could be broken down by other drugs or foods, too. It has also been found that many other populations of the world have an allele that produces G-6-PD deficiency. As is now becoming a common story, the deficiency in southern Europeans is caused by an allele (B−) different from the one causing the deficiency in sub-Saharan Africans (A−). In other words, the same phenotype, an enzyme deficiency, is caused by different genotypes. In all cases, however, the genes are inherited as a sex-linked characteristic; males have only one gene for the trait, while females have two.

Plotting the distribution of the variant alleles A− and B−, we see again a large overlap with the distribution of malaria (Figures 11.21 and 11.25). We have ample reason to expect a deficiency in this protein to affect the parasite's viability. When it is in a red blood cell, the parasite relies on the cell's biochemical machinery for its energy; if it cannot get energy in this way it will not develop properly. People affected by the deficiency are usually fully fit, for their cells can produce energy by a route not involving G-6-PD, which the parasite cannot use. Unless anemia is precipitated by food or drugs, those with the enzyme deficiency do not suffer repercussions.

Besides the correspondence in the distributions of G-6-PD deficiencies and malaria, direct support for the malaria hypothesis has come from the laboratory. Researchers have shown that cells with normal levels of G-6-PD are more prone to malaria infection than deficient red cells. This results from the shorter life span of G-6-PD-deficient red blood cells. Normal erythrocytes have a life span of about four months, and the parasite has evolved to develop properly within this time. Because the deficient cells have a quicker turnover, the parasite does not have time to grow and multiply. Another suggestion is that it is the female heterozygote alone who is at a selective advantage. In these women there are enough red cells with G-6-PD to allow for normal oxygen transport, but enough cells are enzyme deficient to prevent large scale growth of the parasite.

Figure 11.25 shows the frequency of the G-6-PD deficiency alleles in several populations. Only the more common variants are incorporated, though many rare variants are known. It has a wide frequency range from population to population, which can be explained in several ways. In small, isolated populations, the frequency may be distorted from equilibrium because of inbreeding and genetic drift. The fitnesses may also vary depending on the severity and type of malaria. Furthermore, it seems that G-6-PD deficiency interacts with the hemoglobin alleles that provide resistance to malaria. For unknown reasons a female who is heterozygous for G-6-PD and also heterozygous for thalassemia has more resistance to the parasite than one would predict simply by multiplying the resistances based on the individual traits. Evidently the G-6-PD-variants are good mixers with the hemoglobin variants, but the hemoglobin alleles do not mix well with each other.

We cannot yet tell how old this enzymatic disorder is, but it is curious that many Greek philosophers and Egyptian priests warned against eating fava beans, one of the agents that cause anemia in deficient individuals. The reason is not clear, but it might have been a cultural adaptation to a biological factor. The widespread occurrence of G-6-PD variants also suggests that this disorder has a long history.

Blood groups and the other systems mentioned pertain to the constitution of red blood cells. Over the last thirty years it has become known that white blood cells, or leukocytes, contain on their surface a series of antigens that are markers of our individuality: to a great degree these are molecules that our immune system learns to recognize as "self." Tissues with a different molecular structure are "not self" and are rejected, as can happen in organ transplants. From this we get the name histocompatibility antigens (*histo* = tissue). These antigens are present on most body cells, but as they are most often studied in reference to leukocytes, the system is often referred to as HLA (human leukocyte antigens).

This system is analogous to the Rh system, for both have many al-

Histocompatibility Antigens

leles occupying closely linked, but distinct regions, or *loci* (singular, *locus*). The HLA loci are known to be on chromosome pair 6, and are called A, B, C, D (the commonality of C and D with Rh is coincidental). The potential variability is remarkable; locus B, for example, has over twenty alleles. Computations show that there are more than 100,000 possible human HLA genotypes based on the known variation, and more alleles are still being identified. This is why it is so difficult to match organ donors and recipients.

Not all the alleles are equally common (Table 11.5), nor are the allele frequencies the same in different populations. Because of the population differences, this system is particularly useful in tracing genetic relationships among populations. The A locus allele, W24, is found at frequencies of roughly 34 percent in Oriental populations and 25 percent in Native Americans, but at less than 5 percent in Africans and less than 10 percent in European groups, again indicating the Asian origin of Native Americans.

Because these antigens are so important in separating self from foreign, it is not surprising that many alleles appear to be associated with disease susceptibilities. Many of these are with noninfectious disorders, such as arthritic conditions, allergies, diabetes and malignancies. Allele B27, for example, which occurs normally in roughly 5 to 10 percent of American whites, is found in 90 percent of those suffering from a crippling condition of the spine called ankylosing spondylitis. This does not mean that those with B27 will develop the disorder; the vast majority do not, nor do all people with the condition have this allele. The allele does not cause the disease, but it does predispose people to develop ankylosing spondylitis under certain environmental conditions.

The laws of probability state that within any one population the frequencies of various combinations of alleles for the different loci should be predictable — in the absence of evolution. If we know the frequency of, say, an A locus allele and a B locus allele, the frequency with which

Table 11.5. Some representative HLA allele frequencies for the A, B, and C loci.[a]

Locus allele	A				B					C			
	A1	A2	A3	Aw24	B5	B7	B8	B12	B27	Cw1	Cw2	Cw3	Cw4
Europeans	16	27	13	9	6	10	9	17	5	5	5	10	13
Zambians	2	15	5	1	2	9	4	12	0	0	11	10	16
Japanese	1	25	1	34	21	7	1	7	1	11	1	26	4
Native Americans[b]	3	45	1	25	14	1	2	2	6	10	5	17	23

[a] Because new, more specific antibodies are constantly being discovered, these data are only approximate. Not all alleles are included. There is not sufficient information on the D locus to warrant its inclusion.
[b] The group tested was of mixed ancestry.

Modified from V. C. Joysey, and E. Wolf, "HLA-A, -B and -C Antigens, Their Serology and Cross-Reaction," *British Medical Bulletin* 34(1978):220.

they appear together should be the frequency of one times the frequency of the other. If, in Europeans, the frequency of A1 is 16 percent and B8 is 9 percent, we would expect to find them together on the same chromosome with a frequency of 1.4 percent (0.16×0.09). In fact this combination is found 6.7 percent of the time, evidence that these two alleles are genetic good mixers. This distortion of expectation, known as linkage disequilibrium, along with the known disease associations, are proof that the allele frequencies have been molded by evolutionary forces.

Serum Proteins: Haptoglobin, the Transporter

The serum proteins are the last genetically controlled traits of the blood that we will consider. These proteins have several functions, but the one we will deal with works as a transporting agent, carrying other molecules to the body tissues. Like the enzymes inside the red blood cells, many proteins in the fluid portion of the blood, the serum, are variable from person to person and in frequency from population to population. The reasons for much of this genetic variation are poorly understood, but for the serum protein haptoglobin we do have some hints.

For our purposes, this serum protein is controlled by two common alleles, known as Hp^1 and Hp^2. Most people, then, are either homozygous Hp1–1, Hp2–2, or heterozygous Hp2–1. The protein is very important as a scavenger, picking up hemoglobin liberated into the serum when a red cell breaks open. It transports the hemoglobin to a place where the constituent parts of the hemoglobin can be recycled.

It has been shown recently that haptoglobin 1–1 is better able than 2–1 or 2–2 to bind with free hemoglobin and may be advantageous because it conserves this valuable molecule. A team of scientists at the University of Texas has also demonstrated that people who are haptoglobin 2–2 are superior in the ability to survive infection with typhoid bacteria, because they are more effective in producing antibodies against the bacteria. The heterozygous condition Hp2–1 may in time prove to be most helpful in environments containing typhoid and a factor that breaks down red blood cells, such as G-6-PD deficiency. That is, the balance between Hp^1 and Hp^2 alleles may be maintained as a balanced polymorphism.

The distribution of Hp^1 does not coincide well, however, with that of factors that break down red cells (Table 11.6). In Africa, where anemia caused by breakage of red blood cells (from malaria, G-6-PD deficiency, etc.) is common, the Hp^1 allele is also common. But in Asia, which also has a high rate of anemia, the Hp^2 allele is the most common. The association is not necessarily disproved, however, because other factors may be at work in Asia.

Other Genetic Variations

Tasters and Nontasters

In 1931 a laboratory researcher accidentally dropped a sample of a synthetic compound called phenylthiocarbamide. As the cloud of powder spread through the air, some fellow researchers complained about the bitter taste and others insisted it was completely tasteless. Subsequent research proved that the ability to taste PTC (or its close chemical rela-

Table 11.6. The approximate frequency of the Hp¹ allele in some representative populations.[a]

Populations, by country/tribe/group	Frequency of Hp¹	Populations, by country/tribe/group	Frequency of Hp¹
North Africa		**South Africa (cont.)**	
Egypt	.21	Hottentot	.51
		Zulu	.53
Europe		**Asia**	
England	.41	North India	.15
Gypsies (Sweden)	.12	Thailand	.24
Norway	.36	Japan	.28
South Italy	.32	Hong Kong (China)	.39
United States		**North America**	
(European descent)	.38	Eskimos (Alaska)	.30
United States		Navajo	.45
(African descent)	.55		
West Africa		**South America**	
Liberia	.70	Alacaluf (Chile)	.48
Nigeria	.50–.90	Quechua (Ecuador)	.78
		Xavante (Brazil)	.46
East Africa		**Pacific**	
Kenya	.48	Australia (central)	.20
Uganda	.63	New Guinea	.66
South Africa		Philippines	.39
Bushmen	.29	Melanesians	.48
		Polynesians	.54

[a] Arranged to illustrate broadly some genetic relationships.

Adapted from Eloise R. Giblett, *Genetic Markers in Human Blood* (Oxford: Blackwell Scientific Publications, and Philadelphia: F. A. Davis, 1969), pp. 94–98, and from Moses, R. Schanfield, "HLA and Immunoglobulin Allotypes," in James H. Mielke and Michael H. Crawford (eds.), *Current Developments in Anthropological Genetics*, vol 1. (New York: Plenum, 1980), pp. 65–85.

tives, such as phenylthiourea, that occur in nature) is a genetic trait inherited as a simple dominant Mendelian gene.

As with genetic markers in the blood, many populations have been screened by standardized techniques to find the frequency of tasters (T T and Tt) and nontasters (tt). The percentage of nontasters varies from a high of more than 40 percent in India to a low of less than 5 percent in sub-Saharan Africa, but we have not been able to give a full evolutionary explanation for this polymorphism (Table 11.7). We do have several intriguing leads, however.

Harry Harris and his associates were the first to show that nontasters are more susceptible to a thyroid gland disorder known as nonendemic nodular goiter, which can cause weakness, severe weight loss, and neurological disorders; it could be a selective mechanism. Physiologically this association makes sense, because compounds like PTC that occur in cabbage, brussels sprouts, kale, and other members of the mustard family are known to upset thyroid function and produce goiters. Several researchers have reasoned that those who cannot taste PTC-like chemicals are more likely to ingest the compound, and therefore stand a greater risk of developing a thyroid dysfunction. In fact an outbreak of goiter in Tasmania was tied to such an agent in milk from cows fed on kale.

Over the years many other studies have borne out the original findings, but the taster polymorphism appears to be complex. It may well be that the ability to taste PTC is just one part of the biochemical effect of the taster allele. Several anthropologists suggested that the ability to taste PTC may affect body size, because thyroid function is important in regulating growth. Nontasters might be smaller because, theoretically, they ingest more thyroid-depressing foods. On the other hand, it appears that tasters may be more susceptible to another form of goiter, toxic diffuse. Tasters are also more likely to suffer severely from tuberculosis and leprosy.

Restriction Enzyme Polymorphisms

In Chapter 2, we looked at a class of enzymes known as restriction enzymes. These are produced by a species of bacteria after which each enzyme is named. As a class, restriction enzymes recognize specific sequences of bases and cut DNA wherever the particular sequence appears (page 39).

Several research groups have demonstrated that human DNA can be polymorphic for restriction sites. That is to say, there are chromosome sites which in some people have a DNA sequence that can be cut by a restriction enzyme; in other people the same site is slightly different. Due to this difference, the enzyme will not cut the DNA. Thus, within a population, we find that peoples' DNA may react differently to a particular restriction enzyme. The variability need not be within a known gene; it can, for instance, be a site that lies between two genes. This is just the sort of situation that was described in relation to the sickle-cell gene and a polymorphic Hpa I site. Some people had the site, some didn't.

Why would anyone want to identify variation in what may be totally nonfunctional DNA? One answer is a very practical one. As in the sickle-cell case, the restriction site may act as an easily detectable marker for the presence or absence of an associated, important gene. At the Uni-

Table 11.7. The approximate frequency of the nontaster (t) allele in some populations.

Populations, by country/group	Frequency of t	Populations, by country/group	Frequency of t
West Africa	.16	Europe	
		Denmark	.56
Asia		Lapland	.25
Japan	.26	Spain	.50
Malay	.40		
China	.14	South America	
		Indians (Brazil)	.11

Adapted from G. A. Harrison, J. S. Weiner, J. M. Tanner, and N. A. Barnicot, *Human Biology: An Introduction to Human Evolution, Variation, Growth, and Ecology*, 2nd ed. (New York: Oxford University Press, 1977), p. 286.

versity of Utah, Ray White is directing a project to find many more polymorphic restriction sites. He is not particularly concerned with knowing anything about these sites except if they are polymorphic — that some people have them (either as homozygotes or heterozygotes) and some people don't. He hopes to detect a few hundred such polymorphic sites scattered throughout the human chromosomes. Then one could establish linkages between one or another of these restriction sites and the genes which are involved in producing diseases. For instance, if a site variant was found to be associated with the gene causing cystic fibrosis, fetuses could be tested early in a pregnancy for the presence of this very dangerous condition. Parents would then be able to make better informed decisions about continuing the pregnancy. This would be particularly important to couples who had already produced a child with CF and were worried about the health of future children. There are many other genetic diseases which cannot be tested for directly at the moment. Linkage to a restriction site variant could be a major medical aid.

In order to establish such associations, White's team is making use of pedigree records kept by the Mormon Church. This information allows the researchers to follow genes through several generations of people. If they find that a particular site variant (judged by testing the DNA) appears in the same people who inherit a disease, an association is strongly suspected.

Restriction polymorphisms can also be used as markers of the genetic relatedness of groups. If two populations are seen to share variants for some restriction site, it is a good bet that the groups have genetic ties. The odds that identical variants would appear independently in separate groups would seem to be very low. At this point, however, so little data have been generated on population variability that this is very much an open issue.

Summary   The variations covered in this chapter barely scratch the surface of genetically determined human variation (Figure 11.26). People and populations differ in many other characteristics, such as patterns of hair growth, earlobe shape (Figure 2.18), and ability to roll the tongue. Genes even determine whether a person's ear wax is dry or wet and sticky. Many of these are easily determined genetic markers that we can use to judge relationships of populations and to study the operation of the evolutionary forces. Many other such variants may yet be discovered.

In this chapter we have looked at the traits of simple inheritance, ones for which variation within and among populations is determined primarily by alleles. The discussion of the genetics of the various blood group systems was followed by a consideration of the evolutionary forces causing the present-day distribution of the blood group alleles. Various forms of investigation provide clues as to why populations vary with re-

Figure 11.26. *The protrusion of the lower lip and jaw, known as the Hapsburg lip, results from a dominant allele. This trait was passed through many generations of European rulers, including Maximilian I (top) and Charles V (bottom).*

spect to these traits. Laboratory studies have shown similarities between ABO substances and molecules present in disease-producing organisms. Field studies likewise have shown that people of certain blood types are more or less susceptible to various infectious diseases. Correlations have also been found between some noninfectious disorders and specific blood types. Computer simulations have helped clarify which combinations of evolutionary forces might be necessary to produce the observed distribution of blood group alleles. Many studies set out to prove that natural selection is in back of much of the observed variability. Sometimes, as with sickle-cell hemoglobin, this is indisputably true and documented. Other cases present hints of the operation of selection, as with ABO, but the ground is shakier. Yet, further traits have yielded little, if any, evidence for an important role for selection and adaptation. Here we can reasonably expect that population structure has been of great importance in molding the distribution of traits seen today.

The discussion also dealt with several other allelic variations observable in blood: hemoglobin, G-6-PD, HLA, and haptoglobin. Last, a few nonblood-related variations were discussed. We now know more about genetic variation in the blood than in any other tissue, but in time our knowledge will expand.

Several general principles of evolution have been introduced. The ABO-Rh, the G-6-PD deficiency-thalassemia, the hemoglobin S and C interactions show that the adaptiveness of a genotype depends very much on the other genes present. The Rh group illustrated that selection does not depend on "survival of the fittest" but on reproduction. By considering the known variability in modern humans, and the causes of it, we can better appreciate the ways evolution operates.

These discontinuous traits, strongly influenced by genes, are capable of a limited range of responses. There are relatively few phenotypes that a particular genotype can produce, and the phenotypes are relatively inflexible. It would be nice if one made hemoglobin S only when threatened with malaria, making normal hemoglobin at all other times. Such flexible responses are not a feature of the traits discussed. More flexible adjustments can be made in features discussed in the next two chapters.

Chapter 12

Human Variation: Morphological Traits

Analysis of human polymorphisms hinted at the tremendous potential for human variation and evolutionary change. The traits considered were manifestations of the action of variant forms of a gene, and it is generally thought that much of the difference noted is due to the operation of natural selection. Genetic change requires long periods of time because once conceived, a person cannot alter genes.

The traits we will now consider, including some of the most obviously variable ones, have phenotypes that are markedly open to environmental modification. Except for intelligence, the features discussed are morphological: visible anatomical characteristics. From an anthropological perspective, the malleability in phenotypes for morphological traits is adaptive. Unlike the polymorphisms, however, the change can take place within a person; we see the phenotype change as it is fine-tuned to match the prevailing environment. As sunlight increases in the summer, many people increase pigment production (tanning) as a way of preventing the penetration of harmful parts of sunlight deep into the skin: an adaptive response, though not a genetic change. Such changes can occur quickly within an individual, and they provide a flexibility of response to accommodate the person to specific environmental circumstances.

We will also deal with an invisible, hardly an ignored, behavioral characteristic, intelligence. For this human attribute we will need a slightly different approach. First, we know very little about its inheritance; we are not even sure what intelligence is. Second, because so many people think of this trait as having something to do with "racial differences," we will focus especially on this aspect. But first let us consider some of the better understood and less sensitive characteristics of complex inheritance.

Visible Morphological Traits

Analysis of morphological traits can often indicate the degree to which people have adapted to their environment; hence they can be quite useful as general indicators of health status: height and weight are two of the first features a physician notes during a physical.

Like the simply inherited traits, morphological differences among populations are numerous, but the visible traits are often socially important as well. Each of us has an idea about what the "perfect" male or female looks like, and one's mate is often chosen mostly by external appearance. Societal values, then, limit our choices of acceptable mates, which in turn can affect a population's gene pool; skin color is an example. Americans do not marry at random with respect to skin color, and this behavior affects the biological composition of American gene pools. Although simply inherited characteristics, such as blood type, are pleasant to work with, a mate is rarely chosen with blood type in mind. For this reason alone external traits would interest students of human microevolution.

Skin Color   Of all the ways in which people differ, the most obvious and socially important is skin color. For that reason, variation in skin color is one of the physical anthropologist's deeper interests, but progress in the field has been slow. Until recently, the greatest stumbling block was the lack of an effective, repeatable, objective method for measuring skin color. One of the earliest techniques involved a set of about thirty coded tiles that the investigator could match to a subject's skin. Gertrude and Charles Davenport later modified this technique; they devised a top that holds cards composed of areas bearing different colors. By varying the proportion of the card devoted to each of the colors and rapidly spinning the top to merge the colors, they could match a person's skin color to a specific card. Skin color could then be expressed in terms of the proportions of the card's area that contained black, white, red, and yellow.

These devices were replaced by an instrument that measures the amount of light reflected by the skin at different wavelengths compared with a pure white standard. Pure white reflects equally at all wavelengths; skin gets its color by unequally absorbing light because of pigments in the skin. Skin reflectance can then be plotted as in Figure 12.1. These graphs do not give a name to the color, which is a visual phenomenon; they are an objective measure of pigmentation.

Measuring skin color in this way is a great advance over previous methods. Because all the older methods required matching some standard with a patch of skin, there was much variation among experimenters due to different perceptual abilities, differences in light sources, and other factors. In addition, skin color is a continuously variable trait, and having to match a person's skin with one or another colored tile or spinning disk is bound to be inexact. Reflectometry has resolved many of these problems, although some still remain. It is undeniably more accurate than verbal description.

To make data on skin color gathered by different researchers comparable, techniques have been somewhat standardized. Usually the readings are taken on the inside surface of the upper arm to minimize the effects of tanning and hair; the area must be cleaned and the reddening caused by rubbing must be allowed to disappear before readings are taken.

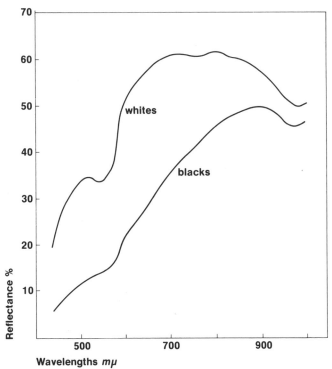

Figure 12.1. *Developments in instrumentation have led to more accurate ways of describing skin color. The reflectance spectrophotometer measures the amount of light of a specific wavelength reflected by a person's skin. This graph records the percentage of light reflected at each of a number of wavelengths, and shows the average reflectance of light for a sample of American whites and blacks. The two plots are similar in shape, except that at each wavelength, light skin reflects more light. The depression in the reflectance curve for whites at about 550 mµ results from the strong absorbance of blue light by the pigment in blood — hemoglobin; darkly pigmented skin prevents the blood from influencing the curve for blacks.*

Human skin gets its color mostly from two pigments, melanin and hemoglobin. Melanin is a complex combination of biochemical compounds that have proved very difficult to analyze. In the body it is even more complicated because the melanin is combined with other molecules. We do know that melanin is formed in specialized cells, melanocytes, that are in the lower level of the epidermis; each melanocyte has branches or dendrites that extend toward the skin's surface. The dark-colored melanin granules secreted by melanocytes are conveyed into another cell-type, the Malpighian cells, by the dendrites (Figure 12.2). Although melanocytes vary in number in different parts of the body, the average number of melanocytes per unit of skin area does not change for the same body region between sub-Saharan Africans and Europeans. The difference in color comes from the varying number and size of granules formed in the melanocytes.

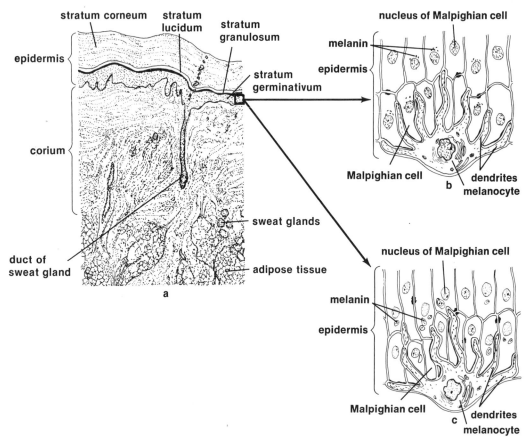

Figure 12.2. *Human skin has two layers, the outer epidermis and the deeper dermis, or corium. (a) The epidermis is subdivided into several anatomically distinct strata; the dermis is dense connective tissue. Melanin is produced by melanocytes within the lowest stratum of the epidermis. The melanin-producing cell transports the pigment to the Malpighian cells of the stratum germinativum via branches known as dendrites. (b) In sub-Saharan Africans and Australians the melanin granules are more plentiful and form a cap over the Malpighian cells' nuclei. (c) In Europeans and Asiatics the melanin granules form clusters, but not necessarily over the top of the nuclei.*

In people who produce little melanin, much of the skin's coloration is produced by reflection from hemoglobin, giving the skin its pinkish cast. The color can be affected by the number of small blood vessels under the skin as well as by whether the hemoglobin is carrying oxygen.

Skin Color and Selection It is clear that skin color varies gradually, or clinally, in Africa and Europe (Figure 12.3); that is, there is no one place at which darkly pigmented skin abruptly gives way to light pigmenta-

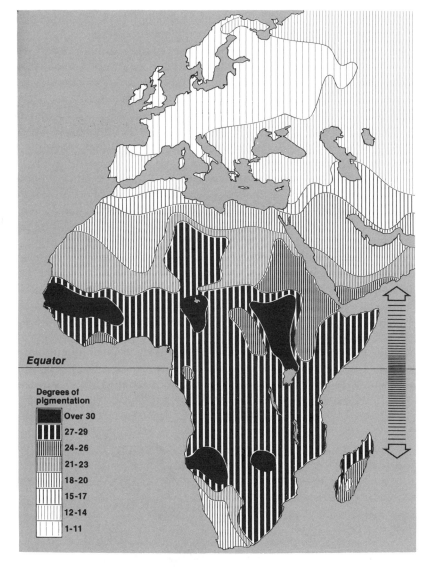

Figure 12.3. *Clinal variation for skin color. Going northward (and to a lesser degree southward) from equatorial Africa, the degree of pigmentation decreases in a relatively even fashion, as shown by the arrow.*

Degrees of pigmentation

- Over 30
- 27-29
- 24-26
- 21-23
- 18-20
- 15-17
- 12-14
- 1-11

Equator

tion. Rather, populations progressively farther from the equator average lesser and lesser amounts of melanin.

What follows is a discussion of several of the ways in which natural selection might have produced the population differences seen today. Virtually all look to sunlight as the ultimate cause of the variation. This idea starts with the fact that the average amount of sunlight, as well as the average amount of melanin, decreases as one moves away from the equator. Some have said that large amounts of melanin protect against sunburn, and that in equatorial regions where the burning rays of the ultraviolet part of the spectrum are strong year-round, dark skin is favored. Away from the equator, seasonal variation is greater; ultraviolet light falls to very low levels in winter and climbs as high as those at the equator in summer. Although the outer layer of dark skin absorbs fewer of the sun's ultraviolet rays, avoiding sunburn, one must ask whether susceptibility to sunburn could actually function as a selective agent. People with light skin pigmentation who visit equatorial regions may suffer sunburn, but after a while many of them tan by producing more melanin and become acclimated. Others, however, never tan enough to avoid sunburn; the infections that can appear in badly sunburned areas could reduce reproductive abilities.

Another biological factor that has been discussed is susceptibility to skin cancer. Here, too, ultraviolet light is the troublemaker, for it can precipitate cancerous changes in cells. Skin cancer, though, has a rather low incidence even in Europeans and usually occurs late in, or after, the reproductive years.

W. F. Loomis, a biochemist, has revived another theory. Ultraviolet light is important because it stimulates production of vitamin D in the deep layers of the skin. If this vitamin is not plentiful, either because of lack of exposure to sunlight or because dietary intake of the vitamin is low, not enough calcium is absorbed in the intestines. Calcium keeps the nervous system functioning properly and is a structural support for bone. When a calcium deficiency arises, the body ensures proper functioning of the nervous system by drawing the mineral out of the bones. That can cause the symptoms of rickets: deformed legs, spine, and pelvis, and, if it is severe enough, death from a malfunctioning nervous system (Figure 12.4). The changes in pelvic shape can also be dangerous

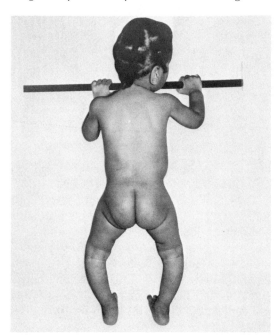

Figure 12.4. Rickets can be a severely debilitating disorder, as this child's deformed legs indicate.

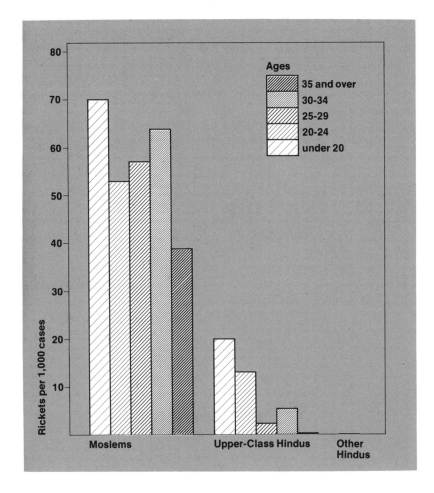

Figure 12.5. *In India, wealthy Moslems tend to stay indoors more than upper-class Hindus, who in turn are indoors more than poorly fed, lower-class Hindus. Accordingly, the Moslems have the highest frequency of rickets, and the poor Hindus the lowest.*

for women who have not finished reproducing. Too much vitamin D, on the other hand, causes *hypervitaminosis,* which forms calcium deposits in soft tissues. It can lead to fatal kidney dysfunction.

Loomis contends that proper vitamin D maintenance in the body comes from the skin's ability to accept the right amount of ultraviolet rays. Dark skin evolved in tropical climes to filter out ultraviolet light and prevent hypervitaminosis. When the hominids migrated out of the warm regions, selection favored those with less pigmentation, which would help prevent rickets. Being able to tan helps the European prevent hypervitaminosis during the summer months when ultraviolet light can be as strong as in the tropics.

However, cultural developments in Europe may have had disadvantageous health effects. By building very narrow streets and polluting the air, Europeans cut down the ultraviolet light reaching the ground; even with pale skin, many eighteenth- and nineteenth-century children and adults were crippled by rickets. Living indoors can powerfully affect the frequency of rickets, as seen in Figure 12.5.

Inviting as this theory is, it remains untested. Many natural situations could be used to test this theory: do blacks in the northern United States and Canada who have poor diets suffer from rickets more than whites on the same diet? It is probably fair to say that vitamin D synthesis may affect the evolution of skin color, but how great that effect might be is open to question.

Lately it has been suggested that melanin may serve an adaptive role relative to other nutrients. Folate is one of several vitamins that are light sensitive. Sunlight causes decomposition of these nutrients, even when the light is filtered through lightly pigmented skin. Branda and Eaton have shown that blood levels of folate are noticeably lowered in light-skinned people who have been exposed to a lot of ultraviolet light (Figure 12.6). They suggest that heavily melanized skin has evolved to prevent the photodestruction of vitamins in tropical peoples. The selective effect is quite reasonable, for folate deficiency is very dangerous, causing anemia, spontaneous abortions, and infertility, and thus is capable of preventing reproduction by those with little melanin where sunlight is intense. Other nutrients, such as vitamin E and riboflavin, are also known to be damaged by exposure to light. Photodestruction of these substances would add more weight to Branda and Eaton's hypothesis.

Other theories have been tested to relate skin color and the ability to tolerate climatic conditions. Because white skin reflects more light, we would expect it to be better adapted to hot climates than heat-absorbing dark skin. That would bring about a distribution in skin color the reverse of the one we see.

Paul Baker has run several research projects on this problem. So far he has found that a swarthy complexion is best adapted to a hot, dry climate. This medium pigmentation averts severe sunburn and does not absorb the heat that could lead to heat stress and death. It has also been noted by Peter Post that darkly pigmented skin is more susceptible to frostbite, partially explaining the presence of light skin colors in cold areas. However, many other factors enter the picture, such as heat loss by sweating, ionizing radiation, amount of body fat, stature, and cultural factors. Although many desert populations have medium pigmentation (San Bushmen and the Papago Indians), wide variation, from Negroes in the South Sahara to Berbers in North Africa, indicates that skin color is not the only factor providing adaptation for a climatic zone.

N. A. Barnicot says that the genes controlling melanin production may have more evolutionary importance for some unknown pleiotropic effect than for pigmentation itself; that is, selection may favor the genes that produce dark pigmentation in equatorial regions not because dark pigmentation is important but because some other effect of the same genes is beneficial there. This would fit with a proposal by Wasserman that heavy pigmentation is a secondary effect of genes which provide increased resistance to disease. As the tropics are conducive to growth of microbes, selection, he says, would favor genes which provide resis-

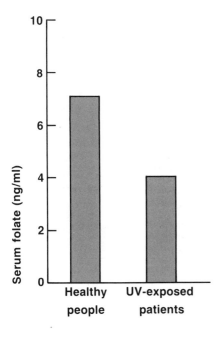

Figure 12.6. *The concentration of folate in the blood serum of 10 healthy people is compared to that in ten patients who had been exposed to ultraviolet light for at least 3 months. The level is significantly lower in those exposed to the UV light.*

tance to disease. Besides providing for a powerful immune system, these genes also cause production of a lot of melanin.

We now have several intriguing selective possibilities and an accurate measuring device. Only further research will tell which of the selective agents are important in maintaining differences in skin color.

Mating by Color Natural selection is by no means the only force affecting skin color. Aspects of population structure can also be of significance. Earlier it was noted that the tendency to mate with someone with similar attributes is called positive assortative mating. In America, this certainly holds true for pigmentation. We are not, however, the only people so influenced. In traditional Japanese society, too, skin color has caused assortative mating patterns. To the Japanese, fair skin has been much more desirable and sexually attractive than darkly pigmented skin. A lightly pigmented, middle-class Japanese woman has been able to move up the social ladder; dark pigmentation has led to downward mobility. Figure 12.7 shows the difference in skin color between upper- and lower-class women in traditional Japanese society. While the pictured difference in skin color is caused by upper-class women's powdering their skin, Frederick Hulse was able to demonstrate an actual biological difference with a reflectance spectrophotometer. The upper class is the lightest in pigmentation, the lower class the darkest, and the middle class is intermediate. Positive assortative mating is concentrating the genes for light and dark pigmentation in different social strata.

Figure 12.7. *In traditional Japanese society, light pigmentation was favored and cosmetically produced (right) but even without cosmetics the skin color of the upper classes was lighter. The Japanese peasant girl has noticeably darker skin.*

Hair: Color, Form, and Distribution

The color of hair, too, can be objectively described by reflectance spectrophotometry. So far we know that blond, brunette, and black hair are colored by the increasing number and size of melanin granules in the hair shaft's cortex, as we see in the similar shape of their reflectance curves (Figure 12.8). Red hair yields a curve of different shape with a sharp inflection at 520 mμ, probably meaning that red hair has an extra pigment.

Little is known about the genetics of hair color, except that redness is controlled by variation for a gene different from that controlling the black-blond continuum. Red hair also seems to express the homozygous recessive condition. Black hair can result from homozygosity for the red hair genes combined with alleles for dark hair. Very red hair appears in those homozygous for red and light hair.

Red hair is most common in western European populations, although it occurs sporadically in most other groups. N. A. Barnicot has found red hair in Nigerians with no European ancestry. The skin color of these people is light with a copper tinge, and their eye color, too, is lightened.

Blond hair has two centers, one in the Baltic and Alpine regions of Europe and the other in Australia among aborigines. In both groups children are more likely to have it than adults, showing that age as well as genes determines pigmentation. Clinal variation is also known, as in Italy, where the frequency of blonds decreases toward the south.

The effects of age on hair color are obvious to most of us, and hair care companies have not ignored the incidence of graying, a loss in hair melanin; in some populations, however, these companies might go broke.

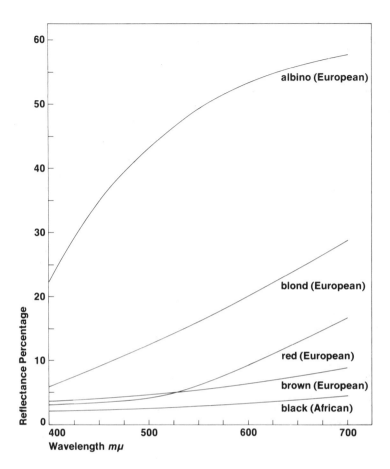

Figure 12.8. Reflectance curves of human hair colors. Like skin pigmentation, hair colors can be studied by using a reflectance spectrophotometer. Except for red hair, the normal hair colors form a graded series from blond to brown to black: each color reflects less light at each wavelength, indicating increasing amounts of the same pigment. The shape of the red hair curve probably indicates the presence of a pigment other than melanin.

Many Native Americans have so much melanin in their hair that any that is lost with age is not noticeable. Other people, though, may be gray by the age of thirty; this phenomenon is widespread throughout the mammals.

Hair form is also partly controlled by the genes. Fine, straight hair is characteristic of Europeans, and coarse, straight hair is predominant among Asiatics and Native Americans. Sub-Saharan Africans and Melanesians are described as having woolly hair. Most Australian Aborigines have hair varying from straight to wavy. Some scientists have hypothesized that woolly hair is advantageous for insulation; others feel that much of the variation may be caused by sexual selection. Because of the emphasis on hair as a sexual characteristic in our own culture and others, those with socially favored hair form are more likely to mate and reproduce.

We can find population, age, and sex differences in facial and body hairiness, which is most evident in Europeans and least so in Native Americans, Asiatics, and Africans. Baldness is most frequent in Europeans and Indians; less so among Africans, Australians, and some East Asians; and very rare among Native Americans.

Eye Color   The beautiful variations in human eye color that so interest poets, lovers, and physical anthropologists rely partly on the concentration of melanin and partly on optical effects. The pigmented part of the eye, the iris, regulates how much light enters the eye much as the diaphragm regulates the aperture on a camera (Figure 12.9). Partly composed of muscle fibers, the iris has several layers. The deepest is pigmented in all normal individuals. People who have pigment only in this layer have blue eyes; the melanin is not blue, but the light reflected back to the observer is. Individuals who have extra pigment in the more superficial layers of the iris have one of the other eye colors. These range from very dark brown to green; the less pigment, the lighter the color.

Eye color is genetically controlled, and that control is extremely complex. Several genes affect the phenotype in a way that we understand poorly. Generally, dark eyes are dominant over light colors, but only if we use gross phenotypic categories. Looking closely at the iris, we can see differences in the patterns of pigment deposition and in the thickness of various layers of the iris, both of which affect eye color. Other factors, such as hormones, several steps removed from the genes, can influence eye color, too. Several investigators have reported that male Britons generally have lighter eye colors than the females, but in other parts of the world the reverse is true. Eye color also darkens progressively after birth and lightens again in old age.

Because the iris's contraction and the amount of pigment in it limit the amount of light that reaches the light-sensing nerves of the retina, the varying degrees of pigmentation may be selectively advantageous in different conditions. What the relationship might be is debatable. Albinos have little pigment in the iris and are extremely sensitive to strong light. To suppose that tropical regions receive more sunlight and therefore favor dark eyes would be oversimplifying drastically. Many other things enter the picture, such as cloud cover, vegetation cover, and glare off snow or water. It seems, too, that a population must adapt to tolerate the strongest lighting it faces during the year, not simply the average amount of light. Simply correlating decreasing pigmentation with increasing latitude explains not much at all.

The areas of Europe where light eyes are common overlap with, but are larger than, the regions where blond hair is found. Much of northwest Europe has greater than a 65 percent frequency of light eyes. Eye

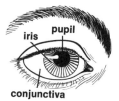

Figure 12.9. The human eye's major superficial features.

iris   pupil

conjunctiva

and hair pigmentation may be caused at least partly by pleiotropic effects of the same genes.

Humans differ for a wide variety of traits relating to growth and development, such as stature, weight, proportions, and composition. Anthropologists are interested in documenting the range of variation for these and other dimensions and in understanding the role of genes, nutrition, disease, and climate in producing differences between individuals and populations. In many respects we grow in accord with our environment; the study of growth and development can help elucidate human adaptability for environmental variation.

Although psychologists also study growth and development, anthropologists are more interested in the physical changes, and associated variability, noted throughout the life cycle. Anthropometrists, people who take body measurements, have evolved a series of standardized techniques for gathering data. Stature is one of the most obvious aspects of growth and serves well to illustrate the techniques and information of growth and development studies. Stature is determined with the person standing at attention, heels together; the back is pressed firmly against the vertical measuring rod, as is the head, so that the eyes are aimed straight ahead. The instruments are quite sophisticated to allow for precise and repeatable measurements.

Data can be expressed in terms of the amount of growth: how tall X is, in centimeters, at age A. This is referred to as distance; a typical distance curve is shown in Figure 12.10. If we are interested in the dynamics of the growth process, stature and other measures can be expressed in terms of velocity: how much X's stature has increased over a specified time. Velocity is commonly expressed in terms of centimeters per year, as in Figure 12.11.

Gathering data on growth in stature or any of several other anthropometric measurements is a major problem because of the time scale of human growth. It is desirable but often unrealistic to plot the growth of individuals over several decades: the investigator would have a long wait before obtaining the final data; also, it is very difficult to enlist subjects' attention and cooperation for years on end. The expense of this sort of study is also prohibitive. Thus, longitudinal studies, ones that remeasure the same individuals at fixed intervals over long periods, are rare.

One alternative is a cross-sectional approach; groups of children of different age classes are each measured once, and an average measure is computed for each age group. Although cross-sectional studies need measure the child only once and can be quite useful for some purposes, they are unsuitable for studying rates of growth. Averaging works to obliterate individual variation; the curve of average increase in stature is a poor reflection of the growth curve of an individual child (Figure 12.12).

A third alternative is a mixed longitudinal study, which though not a

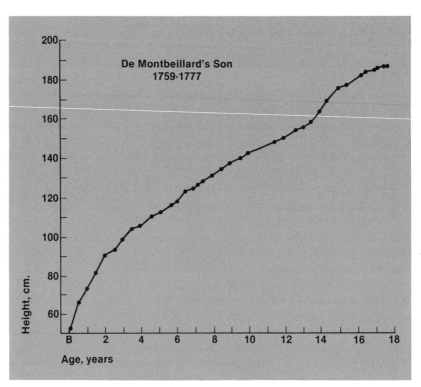

Figure 12.10. A distance curve, showing growth in height to age 18. Count de Montbeillard was the first to do a longitudinal growth study.

From J. M. Tanner, *Foetus into Man: Physical Growth from Conception to Maturity* (Cambridge, Mass.: Harvard University Press, 1978), p. 7. Published originally in J. M. Tanner, *Growth at Adolescence*, 2d ed. (Oxford: Blackwell Scientific Publications, 1962).

perfect solution, does help ease the problems noted. Children are followed over a period of years, but new subjects may enter and others leave the sample; some are measured often and some only once. In order to decrease the number of years required, children may be divided into several overlapping age categories, say 0–6, 5–11, 10–15, and 14–20. By following all groups for a period of five years, estimates of the growth rate can be computed for the entire age range.

From birth through early adulthood children, of course, gain in stature (Figure 12.10); however, the rate at which growth takes place is by no means constant (Figure 12.11). The classic description of normal growth is that from birth through the first four years, we grow less than the year before; but we grow slower. Then there is a plateau in growth rate for several years; each year the amount grown is about the same. There follows a further slowing, then the adolescent growth spurt during which the rate of growth picks up. Finally, the rate decreases until at roughly 18, we grow very little.

A graph such as Figure 12.11 leaves the impression that growth is a smooth, gradual process. Michelle Lampl and Robert Emde have recently questioned the gradual nature of growth. Growth curves are generated by measuring height (or other anthropometric features) at yearly

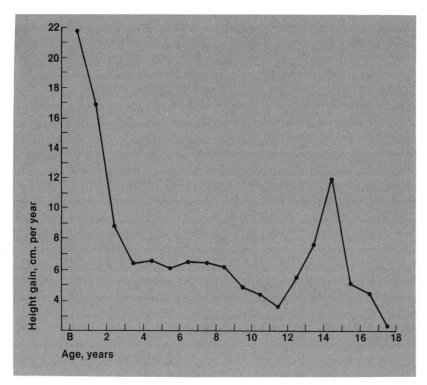

Figure 12.11. *A velocity curve, showing number of centimeters grown per year to age 18. The adolescent growth spurt is clearly visible from roughly age 12 to 15.*

From J. M. Tanner, *Foetus into Man: Physical Growth from Conception to Maturity* (Cambridge, Mass.: Harvard University Press, 1978), p. 7, fig. 1. Published originally in J. M. Tanner, *Growth at Adolescence*, 2d ed. (Oxford: Blackwell Scientific Publications, 1962).

or twice yearly intervals. A longitudinal study, for instance, may involve measuring the child on his or her birthday every year. The measurements are plotted on a graph and a *straight line drawn* between the yearly points. Lampl and Emde questioned the appropriateness of this procedure. Why, they asked, assume that during the year's time growth has occurred on a constant basis? Maybe some days (or weeks or months) a child grows a lot and other times barely at all. To test this theory, they measured twenty-eight infants once or twice a week for up to a year. What they found was a very uneven rate of infant growth. Infants grow in spurts, a finding that many parents have already realized. In a matter of days an infant may grow a significant amount and then not grow at all for weeks.

Information which better defines normal growth can be quite important for health practitioners as well as being of academic interest. There also was evidence in Lampl and Emde's study that the spurts in infant growth (especially the size of the head) correspond in time to the onset of new behaviors, an observation of great interest to psychologists.

Although many first think of growth in terms of the skeletal system, it is also possible to plot growth curves for other body systems (Figure 12.13). Different systems are under different sets of controls; while stat-

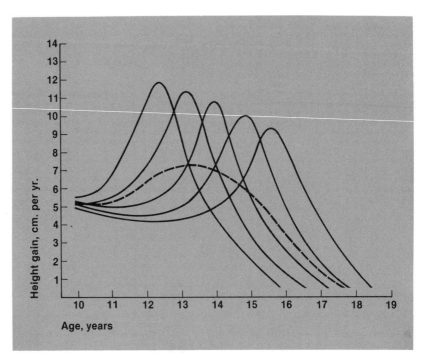

Figure 12.12. *A curve (broken line) averaging the growth of individual children (solid lines) of the same chronological age does not reflect the growth pattern of any child.*

From J. M. Tanner, *Foetus into Man: Physical Growth from Conception to Maturity* (Cambridge, Mass.: Harvard University Press, 1978), p. 12, fig. 3. Published originally in J. M. Tanner, R. H. Whitehouse, and M. Takaishi, "Standards from Birth to Maturity for Height, Weight, Height Velocity, and Weight Velocity: British Children, 1965," *Archives of Disease in Childhood* 41 (1966): 454–471; 613–635.

ure follows the "general curve," lymphoid tissue, such as tonsils and lymph nodes, grows quite large during adolescence and then decreases in size. The brain attains a large percentage of its maximum growth quite early (80 percent by age five) and then slowly completes its climb to full growth. Evidently the genes, hormones, and other features controlling the brain's growth rate differ from those controlling the tissue of the immune system. In Chapter 3 we noted that much of the shift from ape to human may have involved alterations in the mechanisms that control development of different parts of the body.

Size is not the only important aspect of growth; body composition also changes. The layer of fat immediately under the skin, the subcutaneous fat, is one aspect of body composition that changes over time. Subcutaneous fat can be measured in a variety of ways, most simply by measuring skin folds. With skin fold calipers, the thickness of a double fold of skin and the underlying fat can be ascertained at a number of sites. Most commonly this measure is taken on the back of the upper arm, the triceps skin fold. If the circumference of the upper arm is also obtained, the contribution of fat and muscle to limb circumference can be computed by geometric principles. One of the experts on body composition, William Mueller, says it is important to start measuring fat de-

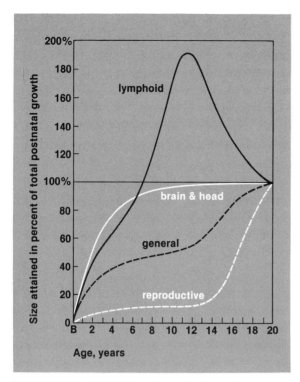

Figure 12.13.
Growth curves for different body parts and tissues. All are distance curves, plotted as a percentage of the size of that part or tissue at age 20.

From J. M. Tanner, *Foetus into Man: Physical Growth from Conception to Maturity* (Cambridge, Mass.: Harvard University Press, 1978), p. 16, fig. 6. Published originally in J. M. Tanner, *Growth at Adolescence*, 2d ed. (Oxford: Blackwell Scientific Publications, 1962).

posits at several points on the body as individuals and populations develop different locations for their fat stores. Being able to subdivide weight gain in a growing child into its component parts, fat and lean body mass, is very important in assessing the child's health (lean body mass + fat = body weight).

Later in life, body composition is important too. It should not be news to anyone that fatness is not healthy. Obesity is often noted as a risk factor in cardiovascular kidney diseases and hypertension (high blood pressure). Yet, things may not be so straightforward. There are indications that it is *change* in amount of fat which is the danger. People who as children are relatively thin and become obese adults have a much higher incidence of these disorders than people who have been obese since childhood.

Women are a particularly interesting group for study of body composition as it may well effect their reproductive life. Some researchers have proposed that the end of adolescent growth and the onset of menses is triggered in girls by the accumulation of a threshold amount of fat. Continued menstruation is said to rely on the maintenance of a critical ratio of fat to total mass.

By studying body composition, we can gain some knowledge of the general health of a group. Linda Adair and colleagues studied changes in maternal weight and amounts of body fat in rural Taiwanese women during pregnancy and lactation. Although the number of calories these women take in per day is low enough to qualify as malnourished, the fact that they increase weight and body fat during pregnancy and lactation argues that they are well adapted.

Variation in stature and other body measurements reflects the outcome of genotype-environment interactions to produce the phenotype. Nutrition is a key environmental factor influencing growth; as the diet's adequacy is altered, children grow accordingly. In 1978, Lampl showed that addition of protein to the diet of New Guinea children noticeably affected their height, weight, and rate of maturation. Within the limits of this study, growth speeds up in proportion to increasing degrees of protein supplementation.

It appears that we are programmed to follow, at least roughly, a particular growth curve. After periods of deprivation or ill health, when conditions permit we speed up the growth process to get back to where we should be (Figure 12.14). This is called catch-up growth and illustrates a phenomenon known as canalization; that is, the growth process has a target toward which it will move whenever possible; if prevented from reaching the goal at one time it will try to catch up later.

Besides nutrition, disease and climatic variables influence the growth process. These environmental components are in turn strongly affected by political, economic, and other social institutions and cultural variables. Culturally prescribed responses to infection can have significant impact. In the United States many people switch to a bland diet, such as tea and toast, when ill. A normally well-fed American child faced with scant food intake for a few days has large stores of nutrients to fall back upon. Many children, because of poverty and urbanization, do not have these stores, and at best, growth may be retarded; at worst they die.

In some parts of the world children account for more than half of all deaths. In the southern Mexican highlands, for example, where R. Malina and J. Himes found evidence of widespread malnutrition, 59 percent of all deaths occurred before the age of 15: in the United States about 950 of every 1,000 live children born will survive to at least the age of 20. The Mexican data illustrate a significant opportunity for selection to favor the reproduction of people who are genetically most suited to survive under poor nutritional conditions. If such selection has been occurring, people may well differ in terms of what kind of diet is biologically best for them.

Growth data and anthropometric measures can vividly indicate social inequalities. In Poland, Pielicki and Welon note a clear relationship between the income, occupation, and education of parents and the growth of their children. Individuals with better educated, wealthier parents are taller and grow at a faster rate than less advantaged children.

In the United States, Robert Malina and colleagues have docu-

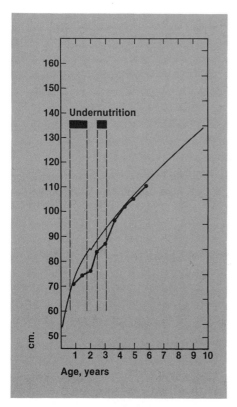

Figure 12.14. Catch-up growth in the height of a child that encountered two periods of retarded growth due to undernutrition. The line with dots plots growth of the child to age 7; the solid line is the average for children of the same sex in this population.

From J. M. Tanner, *Foetus into Man: Physical Growth from Conception to Maturity* (Cambridge, Mass.: Harvard University Press, 1978), p. 155, fig. 50. Published originally in A. Prader, J. M. Tanner, and G. A. von Harnack, "Catch-up Growth Following Illness or Starvation," *Journal of Paediatrics* 62 (1963): 646–659.

mented similar trends in the Mexican American community of San Antonio, Texas. Stature increases with income for Mexican American men and women. The women are also heavier in the lower class urban ghetto and lighter in the upper income suburbs. Comparison with the Anglos of similar social class indicates that there may be genetic differences in the pattern of fat deposition; that is, people of different ethnic backgrounds may be geared to store fat in different sites on the body. In considering "normal" growth, then, it is important to consider ethnicity as well as other variables.

Stanley Garn has also noted that poor women are generally heavier than the more affluent. Surprisingly, however, he also notes that during childhood, the opposite holds: poor *girls* are leaner than better-off *girls*. As he concludes, "childhood obesity (is) not so closely related to adult fatness as one might expect."[1]*

*See page 573 for notes to Chapter 12.

Certainly today there are variations in social and genetic factors which affect growth in different populations. Over time too, society has changed in various ways which affect growth. The nutritious diet of Westerners, the advances of Western medicine, smaller family size, better sanitation, and child labor laws have all contributed to a noticeable increase in both the rate at which we grow and the distance grown at any particular age (Figure 12.15), called the *secular trend*. As a population, our stature (and weight) has increased dramatically. An average fifteen-year-old white American boy in 1960 was more than 12 cm (5 inches) taller and 13 kg (30 pounds) heavier than his counterpart in 1880. Our legs in particular have lengthened over the last century, disproportionately contributing to the increase in height. Comparable secular trends are seen in other

Figure 12.15. The secular trend for height. Curves showing mean height for North American white males in 1880 and 1960. The insert shows differences between the curves at selected ages.

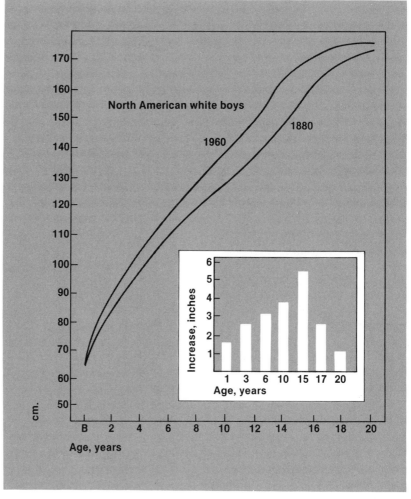

After Robert M. Malina, *Growth and Development: The First Twenty Years* (Minneapolis: Burgess, 1975), p. 50, fig. 14.

Westernized countries. During wars, the secular trend can be reversed. It is even suspected that our concern for dieting when applied to children and the increasing cost of food may reverse the U.S. secular trend.

Sexual maturation has speeded up too. Girls attain menarche, the onset of menstruation, at about 12.5 years in the United States; in 1900, menarche was at 14. This trend is seen on a worldwide basis. For instance, between 1935 and 1980, the age at menarche dropped almost 1.5 years for Greek girls in Athens. However, data indicate that the secular trend has slowed dramatically in Western countries, if not stopped altogether. This may be for the best, for rapid growth is not necessarily beneficial; there is some evidence, for example, that dysmenorrhea, or incapacitating pain at the time of menstruation, is associated with an early menarche in conjunction with a delayed age of first pregnancy. There are indications too that women who began menstruating very early (under twelve) have a greater rate of spontaneous abortions than women who achieved menarche at twelve to thirteen years of age. It may be that a later maturation age allows a woman to build up a bigger fat store which serves as an energy reserve during pregnancy.

Chapter 4 pointed out that the skeletons of mammals grow in a characteristic fashion. Each bone starts out as cartilage which over time ossifies, or turns to bone. Each bone has at least one ossification center which appears in the child at a standard stage of development. For long bones, these centers are divided into diaphyses, present in the shaft, and the terminal ones or epiphyses. The two are separated by an area of cartilage where growth in length occurs, the growth cartilage. Elongation takes place as the cartilage grows at its epiphyseal edge while turning to bone at its diaphyseal border. Ultimately, the whole cartilage turns to bone and at this point growth ceases (Figures 12.16a–12.16b). Anthropologists have compiled large amounts of data to discover the ages at which these events occur in human populations for different standards must be established for different populations. Japanese children, for instance, do not mature at the same rate as American blacks. This may be due to genetic and/or environmental factors. Additionally, boys and girls within a population adhere to different patterns of skeletal growth. Information must be gathered for a rather large number of normal children so that we can identify the boundaries of normal individual variation. Once in hand, such information is quite useful in several contexts. First, as we have seen, growth is a good indicator of health. Many disease states can be detected and monitored by following skeletal maturation via X-rays (Figure 12.17). This can be of importance both in assessing the health of an individual or that of an entire population.

Though any appropriate epiphysis can serve to estimate skeletal age, those of the hand and wrist are quite commonly used on living people. This part of the body can be X-rayed with minimal radiation exposure and contains a large number of epiphyses. Since some people mature a

The Skeleton

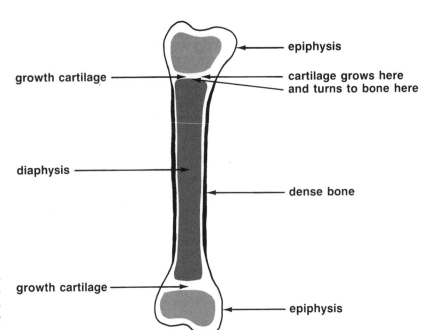

epiphysis

growth cartilage — cartilage grows here
and turns to bone here

diaphysis — dense bone

growth cartilage —

epiphysis

Figure 12.16a. Dia-
grammatic repre-
sentation of a grow-
ing human long
bone.

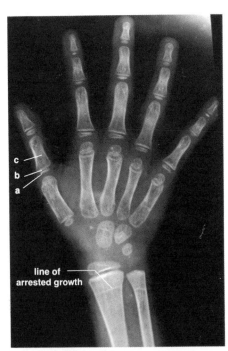

c
b
a

line of
arrested growth

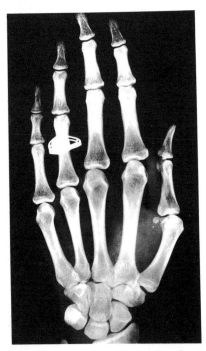

Figure 12.16b. *The epiphyses and diaphyses can be seen quite clearly on radiographs. On this radiograph (left) of the hand of an 8-year-old Japanese boy (a) is an epiphysis, (b) a growth cartilage, and (c) a diaphysis. The line of arrested growth (page 393) seen on the arm bone is attributed to injuries incurred from exposure to the atomic bomb dropped on Hiroshima. Ultimately,
the growth cartilage turns to bone and the epiphysis and diaphysis fuse, as seen in the hand of an
18-year-old female (right).*

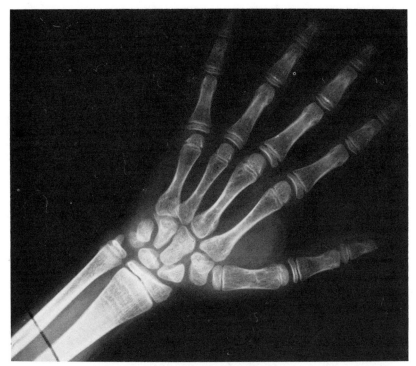

Figure 12.17. *Variation in rates of skeletal maturation comes about as a result of population and individual factors. Disease states also can cause a person to deviate from the norms. This is the hand of a 20-year-old zinc-deficient individual. His skeleton looks to be that of a child of about eleven.*

bit faster or slower than average, a person's skeletal age — as judged from the skeleton — might not exactly reflect the person's chronological age (Figure 12.18).

Many times archaeological deposits are sufficiently rich so as to provide information on the demographics of past populations. Aging of skeletal remains can help establish the frequency of infant death, sex differences in age at death, and other such aspects of a group's vital statistics.

Then, too, skeletal analysis can have invaluable legal applications. A growing field within physical anthropology, but one with a long history, this area is called forensic anthropology. It is of obvious practical importance in solving crimes, identifying remains, and so forth.

In all these applications, it is important to know that the standards being used are truly applicable to the individual or population in question. American black children, for instance, are born more mature skeletally than American whites, thus requiring different sets of standards.

Generally, children mature in a consistent fashion throughout the growth years. That is, those who are advanced (or retarded) in skeletal

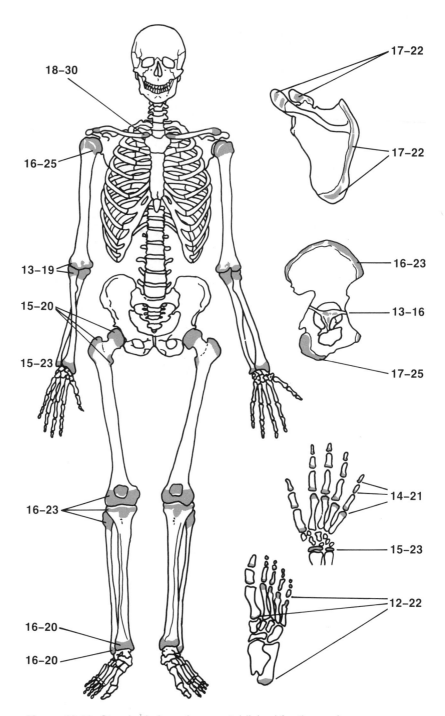

Figure 12.18. *Standards have been established for times of appearance and disappearance, through fusion, of epiphyses. Numbers on this chart refer to the ages, in years, when the various epiphyses fuse with the diaphyses.*

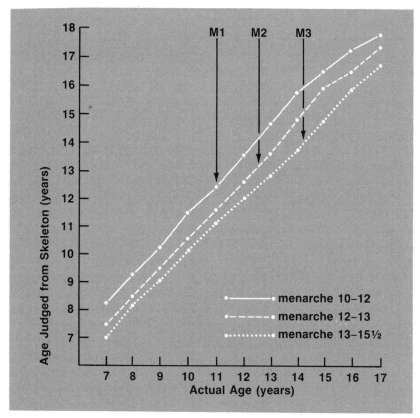

Figure 12.19. *On the average, girls who show early skeletal maturation also achieve menarche early. Late maturers as judged from the skeleton also achieve menarche late.*

maturation at one age will be so at other times. Figure 12.19 shows that girls who attain menarche early are skeletally more mature not only at this time but from seven to seventeen years of age. Conversely, girls who reach menarche later than average also have skeletons that mature more slowly than average throughout the growth period.

For aging skeletal remains, the epiphyseal fusions are quite accurate. However, as most epiphyses are fused by eighteen years of age or are simply not available for analysis, other techniques are utilized. The age at which specific teeth erupt through the gums is quite constant within a population (Figure 12.20), even more so than the epiphyses. Again, children who have one tooth erupt early are likely to have all of their maturation speeded up. Tooth eruption is less affected by nutritional and disease factors than skeletal maturation. Looking at the teeth can help to estimate age in populations which do not keep track of time. For forensic and archaeological purposes, teeth, being very hard, are likely to last in the ground. The drawback is that once all the teeth have erupted, there is little to base an age estimate upon. All one can say when faced with

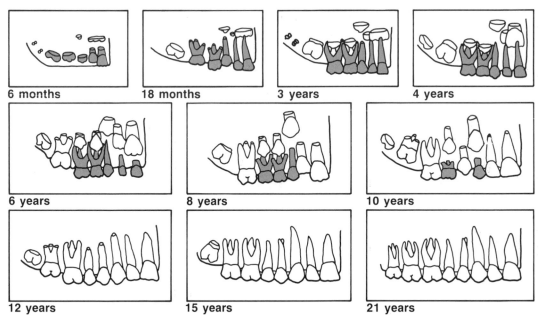

6 months **18 months** **3 years** **4 years**

6 years **8 years** **10 years**

12 years **15 years** **21 years**

Figure 12.20. *Average pattern of eruption of deciduous (baby) and permanent teeth. Dotted teeth are deciduous.*

a fully erupted set of teeth is that the person is more than eighteen years old.

During the Korean War, another method of aging was developed based on changes in the shape of the bones of the pubic symphysis. A symphysis is a rigid joint; the pubic symphysis is the joint where the two pelvic bones meet at the front of the body. This area undergoes age changes, becoming smoother and more worn over time. Though only usable on the dead, this feature can be applied to those who died well after their last teeth erupted. A trained forensic anthropologist can compute a person's age at death well into the fifth decade using the pubic symphysis.

The skeleton can provide information other than age or maturity. In the archaeological and forensic contexts, it can be very useful for sex typing of skeletal materials. A variety of aspects can be looked at in this regard, but the most diagnostic, not surprisingly, are in the pelvis. Most of these features of course, relate to the fact that women need a bigger pelvic outlet to allow for births. Hence, on the average, their sciatic notch and pelvic angles are bigger than in men of the same population. The brim of the pelvis is more circular in women as well. Further differences are noted in Table 12.1. A well-trained anthropologist can correctly assign the sex to a pelvis about 95 percent of the time. With a whole skeleton, the right sex can be deduced in about 99 percent of the cases.

Aspects of the skeleton such as its rate of maturation are certainly

Table 12.1. Sex differences in pelvic morphology.

Trait	Male	Female
Pelvis as a whole	Massive, rugged, marked muscle sites	Less massive, gracile, smoother
Symphysis	Higher	Lower
Subpubic angle	V-shaped, angle	U-shaped, rounded; broader divergent obtuse angle
Obturator foramen	Large, often ovoid	Smaller, triangular
Acetabulum	Large, tends to be directed laterally	Small, tends to be directed anterolaterally
Greater sciatic notch	Smaller, close, deep	Larger, wider, shallower
Ischiopubic rami	Slightly everted	Strongly everted
Sacro-iliac articulation	Large	Small, oblique
Preauricular sulcus	Not frequent	More frequent, better developed
Ilium	High, tends to be vertical	Lower, laterally divergent
Sacrum	Longer, narrower, with more evenly distributed curvature; often 5+ segments	Shorter, broader, with tendency to marked curve at S1-2 and S3-5; 5 segments the rule
Pelvic brim, or inlet	Heart-shaped	Circular, elliptical
True pelvis, or cavity	Relatively smaller	Oblique, shallow, spacious

Source: From W. M. Krogman, *The Human Skeleton in Forensic Medicine* (Springfield, Ill.: Charles C Thomas, 1962).

influenced by both genes and environment. Reference has been made to some environmental components that exert control on growth. Likewise, we know that identical twin sisters reach menarche at very similar ages while dizygotic twin sisters average ten-month differences in the age of menarche. Skeletal and dental features also mature at very similar times in identical twins. The fact that different populations have somewhat different standards for maturation, even when living in similar environments, argues for genetic effects.

Anthropometrists have devised many other measures of the human frame. Though originally devised so as to distinguish "racial types" of people, that is, to establish typologies, many of these measures have new uses today. Human engineers need to make many measurements so as to fit machinery and clothing to the average person. Automotive companies, for one, use such information to place steering wheels, rear view mirrors, seat backs, and so on in positions that will best suit most potential users.

Measurements may also be used to track secular trends. Earlier, we mentioned that over the last century, elongation of our legs has accounted for a large percentage of the increase in stature. This can be studied by looking at "sitting height." The subject is seated at attention, legs dangling over the side of a table, and is measured from the vertex of the head to the table top. By forming a proportion of sitting height to total stature, we can compare how much the torso and head add to stature as opposed to the legs.

A well-known combined measurement is the cephalic index (not, as one student wrote on an exam, "the phallic index"). The cephalic index has little to do with brain size and nothing to do with intelligence. It is an easy-to-derive estimate of head shape (Figure 12.21). The length of the head is measured from the slight bulge just above the nose and between the eyebrows (a location known as glabella) to the point (opisthocranion) farthest from glabella in the midline of the occipital bone. Breadth of the head is measured in a plane perpendicular to length and is the maximum width above and behind the ears. The cephalic index is breadth/length × 100.

Commonly, the range of variation is divided into:

a. Those below 75 — dolichocephalic
b. Those from 75–80 — mesocephalic
c. Those above 80 — brachycephalic
(dolicho = long, meso = middle, and brachy = short)

An average cephalic index can be generated for a population of people. Asiatics, Native Americans, and Europeans are generally in the mesocephalic or brachycephalic range, while Africans and Australian aborig-

Figure 12.21. *Landmarks on the human skull. Measurements involving these can be useful in describing human variability.*

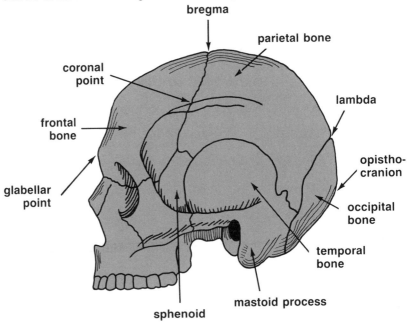

ines are either dolichocephalic or mesocephalic. Over time, many populations seem to become more brachycephalic, a change most likely due to nutritional factors.

Judging relationships between groups can also be attempted using anthropometric measures of living people or similar measurements on skeletons. Dean Falk and Robert Corruccini used a variety of skull measures to see if they could distinguish remains known to be from five different human populations. The cranial measurements included some which span several bones: maximum length, maximum breadth, height of face, nasion-basion distance, nasal breadth, and bizygomatic breadth. Other measures, such as breadth of foramen magnum, involved only one bone. The researchers found that the traditional measures spanning several bones were far better at distinguishing the skulls of different populations.

Everyone's skin or hair has color, but there are several traits that are typical of certain peoples. One trait with limited distribution is the shovel-shaped incisor tooth. Looking down at the biting surface of an incisor from a European or African we see an oval outline. In Asiatics and Native Americans the outline is often bent into a U (Figure 12.22). This shape may make the tooth last longer, and thus would be valuable in cultures that depend on great amounts of chewing. Eskimos soften animal hides by chewing on them, which might put selective pressure on teeth that can take the constant friction.

Another morphological trait, common among Asiatics and less so among Native Americans and several other groups, is the epicanthic fold, the extra flap of skin on the eyelid that gives the Oriental eye its slanted appearance (Figure 12.23). Undoubtedly it has a genetic component, but we know that hormones, too, influence it, because it is most common in females.

Cultural alternatives to chewing and reduced frequency of shoveling seem to be related; where shoveling is uncommon today, fossil populations often had appreciable frequencies. About 10 percent of the neandertals from Krapina, Yugoslavia, showed this trait. We cannot explain why shovel-shaped incisors are uncommon in groups that no longer rely on their incisors.

Steatopygia is a curious characteristic of the San Bushmen and Hottentot people of Africa. The female buttocks protrude because fat is stored there, much as it is in the camel's hump (Figure 12.24). This may be an adaptation to a hot climate, because the insulative fat is concentrated in one place and is not spread all over the body, which would increase heat stress. This trait may be coupled with positive selection for ability to store energy for times when food is scarce, a seasonal fact of life for the San Bushmen, or when extra energy is needed, as during pregnancy. The trait might also have been present in fossil populations from Europe. Statuettes such as the Venus of Willendorf from prehistoric Germany

Traits of Limited Distribution

shovel-shaped

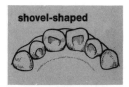

no shovelling

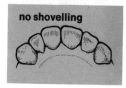

Figure 12.22.
Shovel-shaped incisors (top) compared with incisors lacking the trait. Notice the buttressing on the sides of the shovel-shaped teeth.

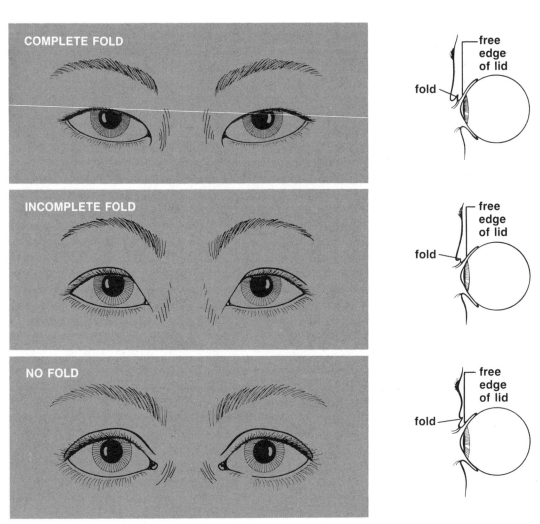

Figure 12.23. *The Oriental eye results from an extra fold (epicanthic fold) of skin that covers part or all of the upper eyelid's free edge.*

certainly look steatopygous (Figure 12.24). Alternatively, these small statues may suggest that obesity was not unknown in Paleolithic Germany.

Theories of Intelligence

Intelligence is the most emotionally charged trait we will consider. Not only do we recognize individual differences, but many feel that population differences exist, too. For most Americans this opinion is put in terms of blacks versus whites, but depending on one's geographic location, the discussion of intellectual inferiority and superiority may be phrased in terms of Native Americans, Hispanics, or any one of a number of other minority groups.

Before we begin to study the inheritance of intelligence, and before we can consider whether populations differ in intelligence, we must consider just what intelligence is. Most people might say that intelligence is being smart. But what is smartness and how do we measure it? Is the ability to remember facts and figures a sign of intelligence? To a degree, yes, but memory is not the whole story. Is the ability to solve problems a good sign of intelligence? Yes; in fact, intelligence is often defined in terms of problem-solving ability: this capability is dependent on the ability to think logically. But imagination and abstract thought play a role, too. How about the ability to synthesize theories and facts? And certainly motivation is of import. All these features, and many others, determine whether a person is deemed intelligent, average, or otherwise in our society. Then, too, someone can be brilliant in one sphere and average in others; Albert Einstein could deal with abstract physical concepts but he had difficulty spelling.

Intelligence is an ability or capacity. It is not something that can be taught or practiced. Intelligence is not knowledge, for someone can be highly intelligent but untutored, and vice versa.

In order to deal with intelligence on a scientific basis, psychologists have tried to devise a scale for measuring it: the intelligence quotient (IQ). The one most commonly used is the Stanford-Binet, for which average intelligence is defined as a score between 90 and 110. These tests have been developed over the course of decades and standardized so

Figure 12.24. Steatopygia (left) is a trait generally encountered among Bushmen and Hottentots of Africa. Some pieces of prehistoric art, such as the Venus of Willendorf (below), from an Upper Paleolithic site in Austria, indicate that steatopygia may once have been present in European populations.

that the average for middle-class American whites is 100. Basically, an IQ score reflects how well a child performs on these standard tests relative to other children of the same age. If results on all the subtests are precisely average, the child's IQ is 100; better-than-average performance for age is reflected in a higher score. If a six-year-old does as well as the average child of eight — that is, as well as children 33 percent older than he or she is — then the six-year-old's IQ is 133.

Although tests of IQ have their uses, few would argue that they accurately measure such a diffuse phenomenon as intelligence. There are several reasons to believe that IQ does not equal intelligence. For one, anybody can learn how to take tests; memorizing vocabulary lists or practicing mathematical skills can increase a person's IQ, but it doesn't make that person more intelligent.

Second, in order to answer a test question, the question must make sense; it must fit into our perception of the world. An apocryphal tale of a poverty-level child illustrates this nicely. The child was performing poorly on the exam. The teacher, knowing the boy could do better, asked him: "If you had 50 cents and gave half to your friend, how much would you have left?" No answer. "I know you can figure this out. Why won't you answer?" The boy replied, "If I had 50 cents, I wouldn't give half to anyone." In white, middle-class American society, the question makes perfect sense, but in a culture built on poverty it is irrational. As the exams are actually multiple-choice and computer-graded, the only acceptable answer is 25 cents; the perfectly logical nature of the child's answer would be ignored and his IQ score would suffer. The poor do not perform well on an examination designed for middle-class society; they are from another subculture. Likewise, using a test based on American black vocabulary and the general culture of poverty, middle-class American whites have a lower IQ than blacks.

Questions should also deal with persons, places, concepts, and things with which one is familiar. Historically, urban Americans scored higher than rural residents on IQ tests when asked standard questions such as, "Who is President of the United States?" or "How can banks afford to pay you interest?" When a new test was composed asking "Of what is butter made?" and "About how often do we have a full moon?" the rural children scored better.

No one has yet devised a culture-free IQ test, one in which the ability to answer the questions is independent of one's culture. For these sorts of reasons, a person's (or a population's) IQ measures the ability to take IQ tests; it does not measure intelligence. Thus, it is not, nor should it be, particularly surprising that American blacks and whites differ in average IQ; blacks average about 85 while whites average 100.

Do genes affect intelligence? Most definitely. Few behavioral scientists would maintain that intellectual differences among individuals within a population are unrelated to genes. The old idea that anyone could be taught to be a genius if only given the proper rearing is passé. In terms of population comparisons, the question is not whether IQ differences exist; they certainly do. Rather, the question is, what are the causes of the IQ differences? Do these differences indicate any difference among populations in the forms or frequencies of genes related to intelligence, or do they reflect different environmental effects on separate groups taking the same IQ test? At this point, one should probably abandon the whole question of population differences, for if we cannot decide on a definition of intelligence, and therefore cannot decide on how to measure intelligence, it would seem very unintelligent to discuss the topic of how we can tell if two populations are the same or different. Yet, we will go on to consider some data on the population differences in IQ, for this is a terribly important social question about which many half-truths have been written.

IQ and Heritability

In back of this concern about IQ and genes is usually a desire to deal specifically with American blacks and whites. As of this date, we have large bodies of data showing that the average IQ of blacks is about 15 points below the white average. What is the cause of this difference? Though some would maintain that genes account for part of the difference, there is not valid evidence to back up this point. One large body of data developed over the years by an eminent British psychologist, Cyril Burt, is supposed to demonstrate a genetic basis for IQ. In the late 1970s, it was undisputably shown that much of Burt's data were fabricated.

Heritability estimates are a second data set used by some to demonstrate a genetically based population difference. Though heritability or h^2 is a useful statistic, one must be aware of what it actually measures. What many are not (or choose not to be) aware of is that heritability as a statistic tells us absolutely nothing about the reasons why two groups differ in some way. The statistic has a very precise definition: the ratio of genetically caused variation (here, in IQ scores) to the total variation *in one population at one point in time.*

If we firmly knew the heritability of IQ scores to be, say, 50 percent in American whites, we could say that 50 percent of the variation among whites is due to genetic differences between members of the group. This tells us absolutely nothing about the causes of IQ differences between different groups. In fact, we don't even have reliable heritability estimates for IQ scores.

Other research has been conducted, not utilizing heritability estimates, to investigate the role of genetic factors in IQ performance. Several tested the hypothesis that the more European ancestors a particular American black has, the higher will be that person's IQ. Because it is possible to estimate admixture, several researchers divided American blacks into those with high European admixture and those who were minimally admixed. The IQs of the two groups were then compared. The hypothesis being tested was that if whites are genetically smarter than blacks, those blacks with a high degree of admixture should do better on IQ tests than the relatively unmixed blacks. None of the studies found a significant effect of admixture on IQ scores. Others have reversed the hypothesis and looked to see if high-IQ blacks had more admixture. Again the results were negative. There is no good evidence, then, that genes play a role in the black-white IQ difference.

Environment and IQ

What about the environmental factors that contribute to a person's IQ score? We have two ways of avoiding genetic effects on IQ to see environmental causes of variation directly. Either we can test one person several times or test genetically identical twins who have grown up in different environments. Only the environment can have made their IQs vary. It is not uncommon for a person's IQ to change as much as 20 to 30 points over many years, partly because as we grow older, we learn how to take tests. Interestingly enough, this change is greater than the difference between the average IQs of blacks and whites. The average IQ difference between twins reared apart after birth is about 8 to 10 points, with some differences of more than 20 points.

Many other lines of evidence show how important environment is to intelligence. Several decades ago, studies of performance on the United States Army's IQ examination showed that blacks from some northern areas surpassed whites from some southern areas (Table 12.2). Does this mean that southern whites are genetically inferior to northern blacks? No; it simply reflects the well-known difference in quality of education at that time. It also illustrates again the culture-bound nature of the exams themselves.

IQ scores are also entwined with the complex relationship between child and parents. Jerome Kagan studied the role of maternal behavior on child development. Kagan noted that for a multitude of reasons mothers in the lower socioeconomic strata are less likely to pay attention to their daughters', and presumably their sons', vocalizations. Upper-middle-class women, on the average, respond more immediately and via more modes: vocally, tactilely, and visually. Because everyone must learn to communicate, it is not surprising that the more practice one has with the use of language, the better the linguistic development. Kagan concludes that a person is more likely to do well on a test of language facility if one has used the language longer and more often.

Other research relating development and maternal behavior has pointed to the same conclusion. In Milwaukee, a project involved the study of two groups of children who differed only in the amount of attention they received. Those who received a lot of attention, if not from the mother then from a specially trained teacher, showed a markedly higher IQ than the children who received little attention. Another study involving two-year-old children in an institution showed the same trend. One group of children was well cared for but received little tenderness. In the second group there was a nurse assigned to each child, so that

Table 12.2. IQ of blacks and whites scored on a scale from A (highest) through E (lowest), as determined by the United States Army's alpha test used during World War I.

	A & B	C	D & E
The overall results obtained by testing tens of thousands of whites and blacks are:			
whites	12%	64%	24%
blacks	1	20	79
Much of the apparent difference disappears when literate northern blacks are compared with literate southern whites:			
Alabama whites	9	72	19
New York blacks	7	72	21
The superiority of the whites disappears completely if illiterate southern whites are compared with illiterate northern blacks:			
Alabama whites	0	20	80
New York blacks	0	28	72

this group received a lot of affection as well as physical care. After as little as six months, it was possible to demonstrate developmental differences between the groups.

Diet will be a major topic in the next chapter, but one study is worth considering here. It is widely acknowledged that diet affects the development of the central nervous system, and it is equally clear that the diets of whites and blacks are not comparable. A team from Columbia University, in order to judge the effects of vitamins on IQ performance, gave a variety of vitamin supplements to a group of poor blacks in Norfolk, Virginia. They found that with a vitamin B complex supplement, the IQ increased an average of 8 points.

Dietary changes may have been particularly important in the secular trend in Japanese IQ scores. For Japanese born between 1910 and 1945, the average IQ is 102–105 on tests for which American average 100. Japanese born in 1959 average 107, and those born in the 1960s about 111. It is hard to imagine that a rise of this magnitude could be due to genetic change. The indications are that it is probably due to higher nutritional standards in Japan, which have also caused higher birth weights and taller and earlier maturing adults.

All this evidence does not guarantee that blacks, if they had equal opportunity, would perform as well as whites on standard IQ tests (or Americans as well as Japanese), but the data do show that environmental factors could easily account for the difference. Given the nature of our society and the complexity of the trait, we may never be able to invent a test that would resolve the problem. Many wonder whether it is even worth the effort to try to get an answer. Two geneticists wrote:

> Perhaps the only practical argument in favor of research on the race IQ difference is that since the question has been raised, an attempt should be made to answer it. Otherwise, those who now believe — we think on quite inadequate evidence — that the difference is genetic will be left to continue their campaigns for an adjustment of our educational and economic systems to take account of "innate" racial differences.[2]

If this is a question worth investigating, the evidence on the effects of the environment may indicate that the question should be rephrased to compare rich and poor rather than black and white.

Summary   In Chapter 11 we investigated some human polymorphisms. Here we have looked at some traits for which variation is environmental as well as genetic. Difficulties in segregating the causes of variation are compounded by difficulties in measuring and data gathering. Yet many of these traits are of great social and biological significance. Many of us choose a mate on the basis of some of these complexly determined traits, and the social significance of IQ studies needs no elaboration. Monitoring of traits such as stature can be important in assessing the health and development of children. Though at times frustrating, attention to these traits can be exceptionally rewarding.

In addition to the visible traits, we discussed variation in IQ performance, stressing the important distinction between intelligence and IQ; though we know that populations differ in IQ scores, we have no evidence that they differ in intelligence. The misapplication and misinterpretation of a statistical measure, heritability, has confused the distinction between them. The relative contribution of environmental and genetic factors to IQ test success was stressed.

Variability for skin color, stature, and other visible anatomical traits is known to help populations survive under particular environmental conditions. One aspect of being human that is of importance in all places and at all times is the ability to function within and utilize a culture. Thus, while it may be reasonable to expect populations to differ in the ability to adapt to nutritional deficiencies or varying amounts of ultraviolet radiation, it is also reasonable to expect human intelligence to have been selectively favored all over the world.

In the next chapter we will look at some more environmental stresses and how human groups deal with them.

Chapter 13

Human Adaptability

So far in our study of human variation, we have looked mostly at the ways genetic differences between populations can come into being. Human variation has been discussed on a trait-by-trait basis, such as skin color and ABO blood types. We will consider here some complex interactions that involve a series of traits as adaptations are made, or attempted, in response to several stresses.

We know that humans have ways other than genes for adapting to varying conditions: one is biological, one is behavioral, or cultural. In addition to genetic adaptation, humans can adjust to the environment by physiological and anatomical alterations (physiology being the study of the functioning of living organisms). If it is hot, we sweat; hardly a genetic change, but certainly an adaptive, physiological one. We can also try to deal with heat by turning on the air conditioner, a technological, cultural adaptation.

Sometimes the division of adaptations into three neat categories is pleasingly simple but not totally accurate. In a sense the ability to utilize a culture is a genetically based, evolved capacity that allows us to avoid having to make many other, genetic, adaptations. If we need to fly, we invent airplanes; we don't have to evolve wings. Categorizing adaptations as genetic, physiological, and cultural may thus be an oversimplification. Still, this approach is useful as an introduction to the subject.

What is an adaptation? The answer may seem apparent at first: it is an advantageous change, some alteration that benefits the person or people involved. Often changes are adaptive in that they help maintain an equilibrium. As air temperature rises, we sweat, which cools the body; by changing we try to stay the same. Premature babies need more protein than full-term ones; the milk of mothers who have given birth prematurely has a higher than normal protein content: an adaptive response to ensure normal growth by the newborn. At a genetic level, the alterations in gene frequencies resulting from selection also are responses to environmental demands in an attempt to survive. Likewise, many cultural adaptations, such as clothing, are attempts to maintain the status quo.

Several qualifications to this definition must be considered. For one, genetic adaptations occur over generations; physiological and cultural ones can happen much more rapidly. Some physiological adjustments occur almost instantly; others may take days or weeks. Culture, too, can change quite quickly, depending on such factors as the effectiveness and social status of the initiator. Second, genetic adaptations often are not as flexible as the other forms. As individuals, we cannot change blood type in order to adapt to the latest disease in our environment; for better or worse, we have a given blood type from conception to death. But adapting culturally to a new disease is possible: if penicillin won't work, we develop tetracycline in a very flexible response. Exposure to a new disease also triggers physiological alterations that help fight the microbe: raising body temperature, or a fever, helps kill off many disease organisms in a comparatively swift response that returns us to a healthy state. Some physiological or anatomical adaptations are not totally flexible; once made they cannot be undone. These irreversible physiological adaptations are often related to growth; short stature as a childhood adaptation to limited food cannot be changed should food become plentiful at age twenty-five.

The level at which adaptations are made — population or individual — is also variable. Although a gene or genes may help an individual survive and reproduce, genetic adaptation is a population phenomenon: people cannot change their own genes, but the genetic composition of the population can be realigned. A culture, too, characterizes a population, though the use of a particular cultural adaptation may be by a particular person. Physiological changes occur at the individual level.

Because adaptation involves change and all parts of an organism and population are complexly interrelated, we encounter a paradox: sometimes response to one stress becomes a stress itself. Sweating, an effective way of dissipating heat, can itself lead to dehydration (water loss) if a water supply is not available. Drinking alcohol may be a culturally acceptable means of tolerating cold, as at a football game, but if too vigorously pursued on too many occasions it may become a problem itself, interfering with proper nutrition and liver function. Thus, alterations may be adaptations from one perspective yet quite harmful from another.

Also because of the interaction of body systems, it is sometimes difficult to understand how a trait is adaptive at all. Some genetic traits may be common simply because they are linked (page 54) to other, beneficial genes, as is the case of restriction site polymorphisms. Sometimes, in fact, an alteration may not be adaptive at all. It would be rather silly to refer to death due to dehydration as an adaptive response to heat. Earlier (Chapter 3) we noted that there is a movement away from interpreting all features as necessarily being adaptations. Even when we know a trait is helpful, we don't always fully understand how. The vast number of small blood vessels in the muscles of people living at high altitude may be an adaptation to lower oxygen pressure or low air temperature. People and populations must deal with more than one stress at a time. Assigning the adaptations to just one of these stresses can be very difficult.

To avoid confusion in discussing genetic, physiological, and cultural responses, we will use the word *adaptation* as a general term to apply to any and all of these three mechanisms. The terms *acclimatization* and *adjustment* are reserved for adaptive physiological alterations made during an individual's lifetime. As we look at a wide range of stresses in this chapter, we will consider the ways in which the human body attempts to maintain a steady state by alterations in its functioning. The underlying assumption is that many of the adjustments — whether involving response to infections, high altitude, or any other stress — represent an attempt to survive under less than ideal conditions.

Sometimes the problems faced by a population may mimic problems caused by disease. High altitude makes the body deal with reduced availability of oxygen. Cystic fibrosis (page 53) is a genetic disease affecting the lungs. People with CF also have the problem of reduced oxygen supply to tissues. By understanding the adaptations made by residents in mountainous areas we may better be able to help CF children. Let us further consider high altitude as a stress.

Altitude Stress

The Quechua Indians of highland Peru have lived at high altitudes for a long time. Their home, the Andean plateau, rises about 2,500 meters (8,200 feet) above sea level, and Indians have also lived farther up in the Andes (Figure 13.1); some Quechua settlements are as high as 5,200 meters (17,000 feet) and some male Quechuas work for short periods as miners at the 6,100-meter (20,000-foot) level. The Incas, the Quechuas' ancestors, also lived on this plateau.

Living at high altitudes causes stresses different from those imposed by lowlands. People have to adjust to lower oxygen pressure in the air they breathe; that is, the percentage of oxygen in the air at 15,000 feet is the same as at sea level, but the pressure or force pushing oxygen across the lung membranes and into the blood vessels is decreased. Temperatures, too, are lower at high elevations than in lowlands at the same latitude; so the natives of the high Andes are subject to cold stress as well.

Paul Baker has long investigated the Quechuas' ability to tolerate hypoxia, or oxygen deprivation. One measure of their adjustment to this stress is aerobic capacity, the body's ability to use available oxygen, which affects a person's capacity for work. Quechuas born and brought up at about 4,000 meters (13,000 feet) have been tested for this capacity and the results compared with those of Quechuas who have spent only a month at high altitude. The values for the two groups are quite different: the high-altitude group was much better able to perform work as tested in the laboratory. Because both the highland and lowland Quechuas are drawn from the same or very similar gene pools, the difference in oxy-

Figure 13.1. A Quechua town, situated on an eastern slope of the Andes more than 3,000 meters (10,000 feet) above sea level.

gen consumption must not be genetic in origin. Yet if a lowland-born Quechua moves to high altitude, his aerobic capacity can eventually approach that of highland Quechuas; the younger the person at the move, the more similar the work capacity as adults. Evidently, a developmental process must be involved.

During development, the body can be molded anatomically by its responses to the environment. Although genetic factors may influence the final morphology, environmental demands can guide the developmental outcome. If the oxygen supply is low during the growth years, the chest cavity and possibly the lungs are bigger. Children in a Quechua highland village have larger chests at all ages than do lowlanders. After growth is complete, a lowlander brought to high altitude cannot greatly enlarge the respiratory apparatus and thus can never attain the lung capacity of his or her highland-reared counterpart. The body adjusts itself during development to suit the prevalent oxygen conditions.

The effects of altitude stress are not necessarily the same in different populations. According to Cynthia Beall, the chest dimensions seen in the Quechua are not fully mirrored in Tibetans living at high elevations in Nepal. The width of the chest starts out lower in young Quechuas but by the time growth is complete, the Quechuas have wider chests (Figure 13.2). For chest depth, the Tibetans are smaller through most of the growth

Figure 13.2. *Chest dimensions for height in two populations of boys from high altitude areas.*

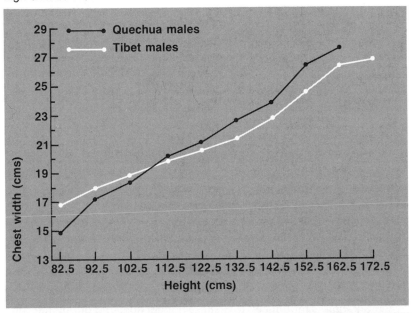

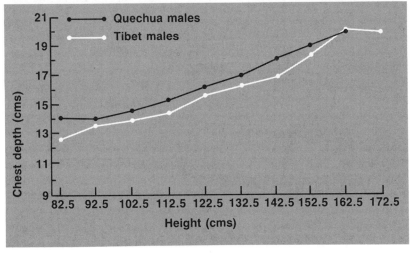

period and, at the last moment, catch up to the Quechua. Sherpas, renowned for their mountaineering skill, have significantly smaller chest circumferences than Tibetan neighbors. Such variation might have a genetic basis or it may reflect differences in environment such as nutrition and general health.

Many of the adaptations made to high altitude are built into the anatomy during the growth years and it is not surprising that the growth process is altered at high altitude. As with the chest cavity of the Quechua, specific parts of the body may grow more or less than in lowlanders. The heart's right ventricle in highlanders is enlarged to help push blood to the lungs. Then, too, the timing of the growth process is changed. Roberto Frisancho and Baker showed that highland Quechuas of both sexes have a longer growth period and a much less marked adolescent growth spurt than sea-level Americans (Figure 13.3). Other highland populations are also known to grow quite slowly. Brooke Thomas feels that the slower growth and delayed maturation are actually an adaptation to limitations in food supply encountered by many high-altitude groups.

Weinstein and Haas looked at the weights of newborns delivered to women who had spent varying lengths of time at high altitudes. Birth weight is a prime indicator of the health of newborns; infants with low birth weights are much more at risk of death. The reproductive performance of women who moved to Leadville, Colorado (altitude: 3,200 m), before or during puberty was compared to those who moved there after puberty. Newborns of women who encountered high altitude early were larger, suggesting that exposure to hypoxia during but not after the critical period of reproductive maturation leads to adaptation. Curiously, a third group, women born and reared at high altitudes, had the smallest newborns.

Physiological Adjustments When an adult is introduced to a stress not encountered during the subadult years, two levels of physical response are generally possible: the initial, immediate response, which is generally not very efficient, and a secondary, more lasting acclimatization. A lowlander at first deals with the stress of hypoxia by increasing respiratory rate, pulse rate, blood pressure, and cardiac output, and by dilation (expansion) of the arteries. These are all rather inefficient attempts to get more oxygen to the tissues by working the heart harder. Later, secondary responses ease the demands on the heart by producing more red blood cells and hemoglobin; the blood can now carry more oxygen. The lungs also increase slightly in size and surface area, making it easier to get oxygen to, and carbon dioxide from, the red blood cells. The transfer of gases between blood and muscle is enhanced by expansion of the vascular network in the muscles. Acclimatization is a multistage, multifaceted response (Figure 13.4).

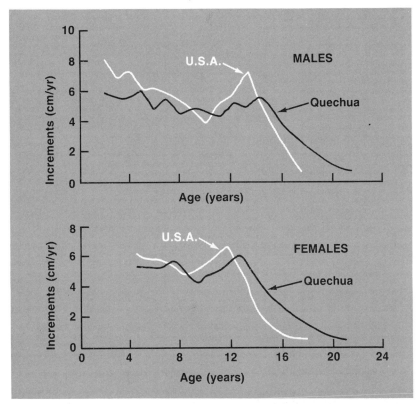

Figure 13.3. *The time and tempo of growth is different for highland children and children reared at sea level.*

Figure 13.4. *The fitness level increases at high altitude with time. The inefficient primary responses of a recent arrival to a high altitude area do not yield as high a fitness as the secondary responses that are developed after some time at high altitude.*

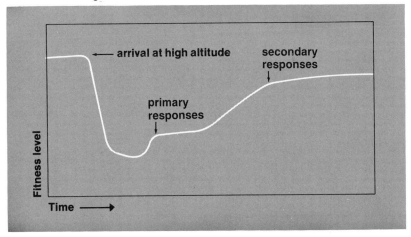

Generally the level of acclimatization to a stress, whether hypoxia, cold, heat, humidity, or any other, is referred to as fitness. This is not the same thing as genetic fitness. Physiological fitness covers health but not reproductive ability. Fitness at high altitude shows much variability. Some lowlanders feel fine at 3,700 meters (12,000 feet); others faint, are nauseated, and lose peripheral vision; still others may die unless returned within hours to lower elevations. Likewise, Quechuas born and reared at high altitude show a high incidence of respiratory infections, especially tuberculosis, when they move to lower elevations. Dutt and Baker note that this is a result of physiological adaptations to life at high altitude that subsequently become dysfunctional.

Genetic Adaptations

We have no doubt that much of the Quechuas' ability to live and work in a rarefied atmosphere comes from physiological acclimatization and plasticity. They may have some genetic adaptations, too, but the evidence we have is debatable. A comparison of two groups of Peruvian students, one Quechua and one "white" (possibly with some Quechua ancestry), both born and reared at about 3,700 meters, showed that, with similar environments, the Quechuas have a higher aerobic capacity and more efficiency in supplying oxygen to the tissues. Similarly, whereas aerobic capacity drops about 20 percent in Europeans brought to high altitudes, Quechuas born and raised close to sea level lose only about 10 percent of their ability to absorb oxygen when moved to high elevations.

C. Beall has noted that the birth weight associated with greatest infant survival, the optimum birth weight, is lower at high altitudes. She suggests that the lower birth weights seen in groups long resident at high elevations in part reflects a genetic adaptation. The genes for lower birth weight are selectively beneficial at high altitudes and, hence, have become common.

Cultural Adaptations

Along with developmental and physiological adjustments and genetic adaptations, the Quechuas seem to have made some culturally mediated adaptations to life at high altitudes. Vast amounts of data indicate that the frequency of miscarriages increases with altitude. Because this is well known to highland dwellers, the richer highlanders, primarily mestizos (hybrids of Europeans and Indians), send their pregnant women to lower elevations to ensure successful gestation. The highland Quechuas also marry at an earlier age and reproduce for a longer time than lowlanders, both cultural factors that maintain population size. Even though the age of menarche is rather late in the highlands, the average age at first pregnancy is earlier than among lowlanders. The number of childbearing years is great at high altitudes, but among lowlanders fertility drops off markedly after a few years of marriage. Both these culturally influenced factors help offset the high rate of fetal death brought about by hypoxia.

Another important variable at high altitudes is cold stress. In the United States, alcohol is one of the ways people have of trying to keep warm, and it seems to be common among the Quechuas, too. Just as the American football game is a socially accepted context for drinking to keep warm, so are Quechua outdoor activities such as weddings, markets, and soccer games. These Indians regularly consume sizable quantities of ethanol in the form of sugarcane alcohol (up to about 85 proof). Beer and sugarcane alcohol account for more than 20 percent of the trading in at least one highland town.

Michael Little conducted some experiments with Quechua males to see if alcohol consumption acclimates the Indian to cold. He gave the subjects fixed quantities of sugarcane alcohol at standardized temperatures while monitoring the Indians' foot temperatures. The foot temperatures were significantly higher when alcohol was ingested. But for acclimatization to cold, drinking alcohol is a mixed blessing. Alcohol causes greater blood flow to the extremities, raising skin temperature; the ears, for example, become hot. The increased flow of blood temporarily increases comfort out in the cold, but extending the habit over a long period can be dangerous. In the course of warming the skin, the body throws off heat to the external environment, lowering internal temperature. As Little says, "The consumption of alcohol . . . should give the Indian a thermal advantage during natural exposure to the cold. . . . Over short periods of time, the advantage in terms of comfort should outweigh the disadvantage of [heat loss.]."[1]*

Quechuas have many other cultural ways of surviving cold stress. The Indians commonly chew coca leaves mixed with lime, which releases several chemicals, one of which is cocaine. Although the narcotic does not appear to alleviate cold stress physically, many said they chewed coca leaves because it made them "feel warm." If nothing else, coca chewing may be giving them a psychological adaptation to cold.

Economics also enters the picture. In the higher reaches of the Andes, economic factors have encouraged many to shift their subsistence activity from agriculture to pastoralism. Because they must constantly move their herds of llama, alpaca, goats, and sheep to new pastures, few bother to build a permanent adobe home. Instead, they build rock-pile huts with straw roofs, which are very poor insulators. At lower (though still high altitude) elevations, Quechua farmers are more closely tied to the land, for it is privately owned. The homes they build are long-term investments and are better insulators. The farmers are exposed to less cold stress. The thermometer may fall to freezing during the coldest time of the night but the interior temperature averages 7° C (45° F). The Indians may also sleep in groups to share body heat.

The San Bushmen of the Kalahari Desert use a cultural technique to combat cold stress. During the winter, night temperatures drop to about freezing, and the San have cultural adaptations that, though they appear

*See page 573 for notes to Chapter 13.

Figure 13.5. A San Bushman camp.

crude to us, are very helpful in warding off cold stress. Early in the evening they split into three groups, each around its own campfire (Figure 13.5). At one are mothers and small children; a second is surrounded by young men and by husbands whose wives are nursing (and, therefore, taboo). A third group consists of family units in which the mother is not nursing, each family having its own fire. At each fire the people lie with skin cloaks tucked around their bodies and pulled over their heads, with feet toward the fire; often they will also huddle together to share their body heat and cloaks. Their feet seem to serve as thermostats, for when the fire dies down, they awaken and add more wood. By using only the cloak and fire, they keep the air next to their bodies at about 18°C (65°F). They do not sleep in the grass huts, but use them as windbreaks, also reducing cold stress.

One of the most important techniques used to deal with cold is clothing. The Eskimo use a variety of skins for making clothes but prefer those of the caribou. These provide a great degree of insulation which can actually become a problem itself. When exercising strenuously, the Eskimo may become overheated. The parkas have many vents which can be opened and closed with drawstrings to allow more or less ventilation.

Genetic Adaptations and Physiological Adjustments   Variation in response to cold, like response to hypoxia, may be brought about partly by genetically caused physiological differences. Populations may be able to generate heat (by burning calories) with differing efficiency; their bodies may also use the heat differently; and some may be better insulated than others. From the Andes, several researchers have reported tentative results that seem to show a genetic difference between Quechua Indians and whites in reaction to cold.

Paul Baker was able to estimate roughly the relative effects of genetic adaptation and physiological acclimatization to cold by comparing three groups: native Quechua Indians, university students of Quechua ancestry, and white Peruvian university students. All three groups lived at about the same altitude, but the two student groups had experienced less than lifelong exposure to cold. When the subjects' fingers were exposed to cold in the laboratory, the two Indian groups reacted in much the same way, and both differed from the whites' reaction. The fingers of both Indian groups did not cool as much as the whites' fingers, and the Indians' fingers rewarmed more rapidly. Baker concluded from the finger temperatures that "the difference between Indian and white genetic inheritance was of more significance than environmental exposure [and subsequent physiological acclimatization]."[2]

The warmer Quechua extremities appear to be caused by increased blood flow to the limbs, which seems to be adaptive in helping prevent cold stress. Because Quechuas do not wear gloves, this is a vital way of warming themselves. Heat is also needed in the extremities to keep the muscles working properly during physical activity. On the other hand, if heat flow to the limbs continues for hours on end, it can be (as with relying on alcohol) a very dangerous way of combating cold. As the warm blood reaches the limbs, the heat it carries warms the tissues, but the heat is also radiated away to the environment. This heat loss can cause a drop in internal body temperature. A prolonged drop in internal temperature can kill; therefore, the need for warm extremities and the heat loss that it causes must be balanced. If this balance is upset in either direction, injury or death can result.

To maintain this balance, humans exhibit cyclic constriction and expansion of the blood vessels in the extremities, what is called a "hunting" response. When a hand is exposed to the cold the vessels close down to help prevent heat loss. After about 15 minutes, the small vessels open up, allowing the warm blood to reheat the tissues of the hand; then they shut down again. This cycle can be very important to anyone who has to use his hands with dexterity in the cold. Though Eskimos may have very efficient gloves, they cannot tie knots, sew, etc., without removing their gloves. As their hands cool, they lose dexterity, but they regain it as a result of the hunting response. All people exhibit this response; however, the rapidity and strength of the response are greater in Eskimos (Figure 13.6).

The Eskimos seem to deal with cold by burning energy at a very high rate too. This is called their metabolic rate. It is not clear whether this high rate is a result of the composition of their diet, which is primarily protein and fat, or a result of some other, possibly genetic factor. It is known that when highland and lowland Quechuas and whites are exposed to overall body cooling, the lowland Quechuas' response is much

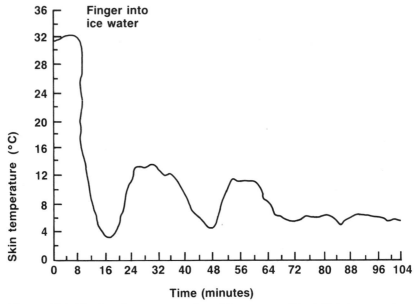

Figure 13.6. *The hunting response to cold exposure. The initial, large and long skin temperature changes are replaced by small, more rapid changes. This is due to changes in the cycle of blood vessel constriction and dilation.*

more similar to that of whites, indicating a physiological, nongenetic similarity.

We have done no more than touch the surface of responses to cold stress. We have not talked about how the different responses come about or discussed the relative importance of genes and acclimatization. Other kinds of adaptation may enter the picture, too. Living in an atmosphere deficient in oxygen increases the capillary bed in the muscles and causes greater heart output. The Quechuas' response could be in part anatomical and physiological accompaniments to hypoxic stress. Acclimatization to hypoxia, for example, could be partly responsible for their having warmer extremities. Yet the large lungs of the Quechua result in large heat loss via respiration. Thus, they need to replace this lost heat by burning food at a higher metabolic rate, which then means they need more food. Differences in skin color, age, amount of body fat, and other traits can also affect one's response to cold, too.

Heat Stress   Adapting to a hot climate involves interactions as complicated as adapting to cold or hypoxia. But heat by itself is not nearly as important as heat plus humidity. Heat stress and humidity interact because of one of the body's way of dissipating heat: evaporation. In a hot but dry environment it is easy for sweat to evaporate from the naked body, thereby removing heat; if the surrounding air is already moist, however, water will not evaporate, and sweating loses its efficiency.

Populations do not seem to differ in the number or distribution of sweat glands: each human being has roughly 2 million. However, different parts of an individual vary in sweat gland density, and a population may also have some person-to-person variability. But some populations do differ in the way their sweat glands work.

As in adapting to cold, in hot conditions the body must reach a compromise between opposing factors, in this case heat loss and water loss. In desert conditions the body can lose up to two liters of water an hour by sweating. If drinking water is scarce, sweating can be very dangerous; water loss that rapid can be fatal in a short time. If the body is not cooled, though, heat stress can bring death. Fortunately, the body has more than one way of cooling itself.

Another way the body can be cooled is by radiation, that is, transferring heat between two objects that are not directly in contact. If we sit by a window in a short-sleeved shirt on a cold day, our arms feel cool because we are radiating body heat to the outside, even though we are not in direct contact with the window. Radiation's efficiency in dispersing body heat is determined partly by the relative size and shape of the extremities and the body trunk.

Nineteenth-century ecologists who noticed the relationship between the size and shape of extremities and trunk, Bergmann and Allen, lent their names to two ecological rules.

Two Ecological Rules

Bergmann's Rule states that, of two bodies with similar shapes, the larger has less surface area per unit of volume, will hold heat better, and thus is better adapted to the cold. Let us assume that two bodies are spherical (Figure 13.7) and that the radius of one is twice that of the other. Geometry tells us that the surface areas of the spheres are proportional to the radii squared, but the volumes of the spheres are proportional to the radii cubed. Looking at the ratio of surface area to volume for A and B, we see that as the sphere gets bigger, the ratio of surface area to volume decreases. That is, for every unit of surface area in A there is one unit of volume, but in B for every unit of surface area there are two units of volume. Heat production is related to body volume, but heat loss occurs at the surface and therefore is related to surface area. A has one unit of surface area to radiate away the heat produced by one unit of volume, and B has one unit of surface area to dissipate the heat generated by twice as much volume. A is therefore better adapted for hot conditions because it loses heat more readily, and B is better adapted to conserve heat.

Generally, this rule holds true for individual species of mammals. Figure 13.8 shows that the body size of the American puma increases as the temperature of its habitat decreases.

Several research studies show that body weight in humans is lower in warmer areas and higher in colder areas. D. F. Roberts, using infor-

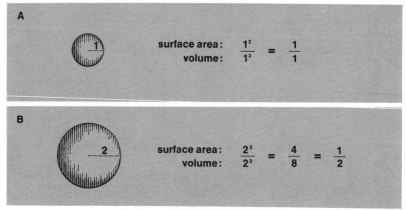

Figure 13.7. *An illustration of Bergmann's Rule: the surface area of a sphere is proportional to the radius squared, and the volume is proportional to the radius cubed. Thus, as the radius increases, the ratio of surface area to volume decreases and the body is better suited to retain heat.*

Figure 13.8. *The puma is a wide-ranging species that conforms to Bergmann's Rule. This cline of puma body size shows it to be large in cold areas and smaller in warm regions. The map is based on field estimates of E. A. Goldman.*

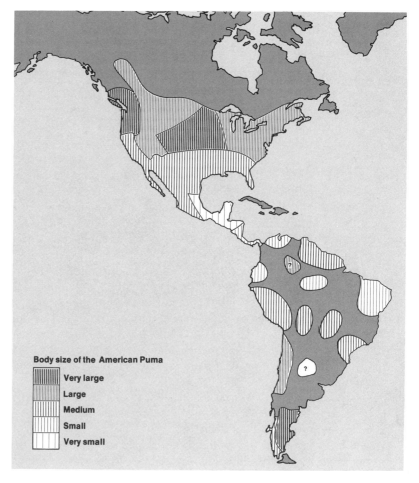

Body size of the American Puma

- Very large
- Large
- Medium
- Small
- Very small

mation on more than one hundred human populations, showed a strong inverse correlation between the average body weight of a population and the average temperature of its environment; that is, as temperature climbs, body weight falls (Figure 13.9). A French scientist, Eugene Schreider, has demonstrated the same trend. Marshall Newman, working with data on Native Americans, showed that much of the difference in body weight among tribes can be explained simply by differences in environmental temperature. It has also been shown that children of Americans living in the former Panama Canal Zone were lighter in weight than members of the same gene pool in the cooler United States. It seems that this rule reflects not genetic adaptation but physiological acclimatization.

In addition to predictions about body size, Bergmann's Rule states that body shape will vary with temperature. We can again demonstrate geometrically that a circle contains the maximum volume for a fixed surface area. Therefore, the best shape for dissipating heat is a long and slender one, because it has less volume per unit of surface area; and a compact, spherical body shape is best for conserving heat. Many human populations illustrate this difference: many sub-Saharan Africans are linear in build, while circumpolar people such as the Eskimos are very compactly built.

Allen's Rule describes regularities of the body's proportions; it states that in hot regions, extremities (in humans, the arms and legs) are long to provide maximum surface area for dissipating heat. In cold regions

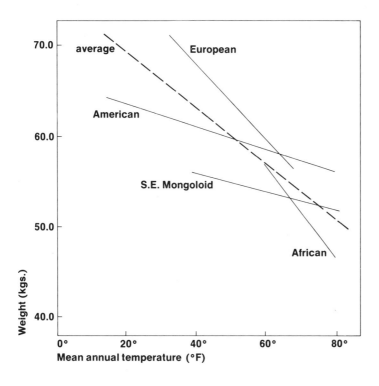

Figure 13.9. Relationships of body weight to temperature. Although the degree of relationship of body weight to environmental temperature varies from population to population, humans do show a marked conformity to Bergmann's Rule.

limbs are short to reduce surface area and therefore heat loss. Most sub-Saharan Africans fit both rules, having long limbs and slender trunks, while Eskimos have large-volume trunks and short limbs (Figure 13.10).

More Physiological Adaptations

These rules are not the only factors affecting body size and shape, and therefore exceptions exist. Another factor, as we shall see later in this chapter, is diet.

Ecological rules also are not the only biological adaptations to heat stress. One very important biological mechanism for throwing off excess heat is an increase in blood flow to the skin of the extremities. Bringing the excess heat to the surface radiates it away. Convection, heat transfer between the body and a moving fluid or gas, can also take place. Curiously, it appears that the genetic differences in heat adaptations are quite minimal. All human groups seem to have comparable limits in terms of dealing with heat. Maybe selection for modes of tolerating heat was very strong early in human evolution, when our ancestors lived in the tropics. Current research would indicate that only very minor differences have evolved in varied human populations.

Though there may not be major genetic differences, this is not to say that acclimatization does not occur. For it certainly does. Figure 13.11 shows the changes in sweating rate and body temperature which took place in twelve men as they acclimated to exercising in a hot-humid environment. Before acclimatizing their sweat rate was very high and very inefficient when they exercised for four hours. Repeating this re-

Figure 13.10. A Nilotic black and an Eskimo. Their body shapes conform to the ecological rules.

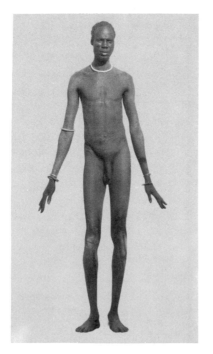

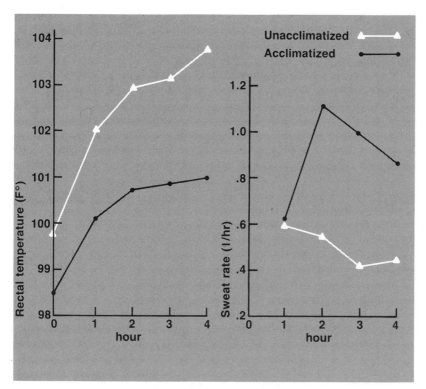

Figure 13.11. *Physiological changes during acclimatization to heat. As the men adapted to working four hours in a hot, humid environment, sweating increased and body temperature decreased. The acclimatized measurements were taken ten days after the unacclimatized.*

gime, for ten days, they adapted to the heat quite noticeably, and their sweat rate dropped. Likewise, their body temperature when exercising showed a major change over the ten days.

Depending on the humidity in an area, clothing can serve as a cultural adaptation to heat stress. In hot-dry conditions such as a desert, clothes can be quite helpful. By shielding the skin, clothing cuts down the heat gain due to solar radiation, much like sitting in the shade. Because less heat is gained, the need to perspire is reduced and the dangers of dehydration are avoided. When working hard and perspiring heavily, loose clothing is best, for it allows for more heat loss by evaporation. In a hot-humid climate, though, clothing is best forgotten — it doesn't help.

Cultural Adaptations

Housing can be varied to help tolerate heat. Adobe and stone were mentioned as adaptive to life in the cold; they are also good materials for housing in a hot, dry area. When the sun beats down on these materials, they absorb much of the heat before passing it to the interior, keeping the occupants cool in the day and warming them at night. Using few, well-placed, shaded windows, painting the home a light color, planting shade trees — all of these are adaptations used by people living in hot-dry areas. When the environment is hot and humid, as in a tropical jungle, there is already much shade, but there ventilation becomes important. Homes in these areas are made of light, porous materials like thatch. Sometimes the houses are raised off the ground to provide for greater air circulation.

Infectious Disease

So far we have emphasized how genetic variation copes with disease. Humans do, however, adapt to disease by means that are not genetic, and they also adapt to infectious and noninfectious diseases in rather different ways.

Physiological Defenses

Our physiological responses to infectious disease agents are multifaceted, like our ways of adjusting to altitude. The first line of defense is the skin, a strong barrier to microbial penetration. The inside of our respiratory passage is lined with mucous membranes whose sticky secretions trap many foreign particles. The tiny cilia, or hairs, of the cells in the respiratory system beat outward, sweeping foreign materials out of the body (Figure 13.12). We also have a subclass of antibodies, or immunoglobulins (IgA), that appear to be secreted by the cells lining most of our body openings, and help keep microorganisms out.

If a microorganism gets through these barriers, several other defenses are set in motion. We start rapidly producing another class of antibodies, IgM, somewhat different in structure from IgA, that appear to be effective against comparatively large particles, such as bacteria. IgM acts as an identification tag, attaching to the bacteria and helping the white blood cells identify and destroy the invaders.

The last defenders are the antibodies known as IgG, which counteract infection. They contribute to a reaction known as *immunological memory*. Antibodies specifically produced for an antigen may initially take some time to build; after the antigen disappears the antibody level drops until it can no longer be detected. Subsequent exposure to the antigen sets off very rapid production of specific antibodies: the immunological system "remembers" the kind of antibody to produce. Just how our immune system does this we do not know, but it definitely is observable (Figure 13.13). Our cells are geared to start rapid, specific antibody production upon subsequent exposure to an antigen. In this way individuals in a population build immunity to many of the diseases they normally encounter.

Infants get some immunity to disease by acquiring maternal antibodies, either by transfer across the placenta or by breast feeding. The mother's first milk (colostrum) is rich in IgA antibodies. Should infection occur, maternal antibodies help protect the infant until its own immune system becomes effective.

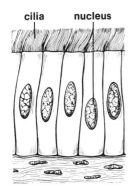

cilia   **nucleus**

Figure 13.12. Cells of the respiratory tract, with cilia. These fine, hairlike structures move constantly and help keep the air passage free of foreign substances.

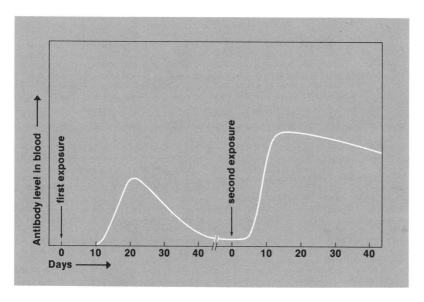

Figure 13.13. *The speed and quantity of antibody production upon first and subsequent exposure to an antigen. Upon exposure to a new antigen (at left arrow), antibody production is delayed for a week or more and then rises to moderate levels; the quantity of antibody subsequently falls off relatively rapidly. Upon injection of the same antigen a second or third time (right arrow), antibody production is more rapid and its level rises to greater heights and remains elevated longer.*

For physiological reasons an infection is often more severe in previously unexposed adults than in children. Cultural practices as well as physiology influence who will and who will not get sick — sometimes, too, who will be treated and thus who will survive. The natural history of poliomyelitis shows how interdependent biology and culture are. Polio, caused by a virus (see Figure 2.14), was often transmitted from child to child amid poor sanitary conditions, usually because of contact with feces as a result of not washing the hands. In many areas of the world, polio virus was quite common and most of the viruses were not too virulent. Usually a childhood infection produced only mild symptoms: headache, slight fever, and respiratory or gastrointestinal problems, followed by complete recovery and the production of antibodies. If a virulent strain came along later, the people rapidly produced effective antibodies and thus avoided paralysis and death. As our culture became more and more antiseptic, many people avoided this early, relatively safe exposure to the virus. When epidemics of highly virulent strains did hit, as in the early and middle 1950s, many young adults were severely crippled because they could not rapidly make antibodies to the virus. In less sanitary areas, the critical cases during an epidemic are mostly those under

Cultural Adaptations

Table 13.1. Paralytic polio in Detroit, by age and by race.

Age	1939				1946				1952 [a]			
	White		Nonwhite		White		Nonwhite		White		Nonwhite	
0–4	23%	(49) [b]	36%	(19)	24%	(41)	64%	(33)	32%	(144)	48%	(17)
5–14	71	(147)	60	(32)	47	(78)	24	(12)	42	(190)	46	(16)
15+	6	(13)	4	(2)	29	(48)	12	(6)	26	(120)	6	(2)
Total no. of cases		(209)		(53)		(167)		(51)		(454)		(35)

[a] The group with poorer sanitation, the nonwhites, usually had: (a) fewer cases; (b) a greater percentage of cases in the 0–4 age bracket, while among whites, the preponderance of cases were in the older age brackets.
[b] The number of cases appears in parentheses.

After Richard D. Leach, "Socioeconomic Status, Race, and Poliomyelitis in Detroit, Michigan: A Sociological Analysis" (Unpubl. MA thesis, Wayne State University, 1967), p. 73.

age five. Table 13.1 shows the attack rates of paralytic polio in a major United States city during several outbreaks.

Disease can strike a previously unexposed population with terrible violence. In 1949, when several Eskimo communities were first hit by polio, 14 percent of the population died and 40 percent were paralyzed. Paralysis rarely occurs in the very young, and here it did not affect any children less than three years old. The disease was spread even faster by the social disorganization and breakdown in nutrition and hygiene that followed the epidemic. Subsequent polio epidemics among the Eskimos have been more comparable to epidemics elsewhere; the Eskimos have adjusted physiologically, psychologically, and socially to the disease.

Social systems can determine the impact of an infectious disease. J. B. S. Haldane has postulated that epidemic diseases did not greatly affect human evolution until agriculture came along, and with it large population centers. In an epidemic not every susceptible person contracts the disease, nor does every infected individual pass the infection to someone else. In a small, scattered population, the probability that the disease will spread as an epidemic is quite low, but in a large, densely populated city the microorganism has a far easier time finding new hosts. Eventually, even in a large community, the rate of new infections slows down (Figure 13.14). By this time the disease has usually moved to another city, returning to the first city after several years, during which time more susceptible children have been born.

Epidemics need population centers and ways of getting to them. In the Western world today, an infection can easily travel great distances in a short time. Several hundred years ago, with longer travel times and fewer people traveling, epidemics were rather more limited around the world. Epidemics did, of course, scourge people in the past; the waves of bubonic plague that swept through Europe from the 1300s to the 1700s are estimated to have killed more than 25 million people, about a quarter

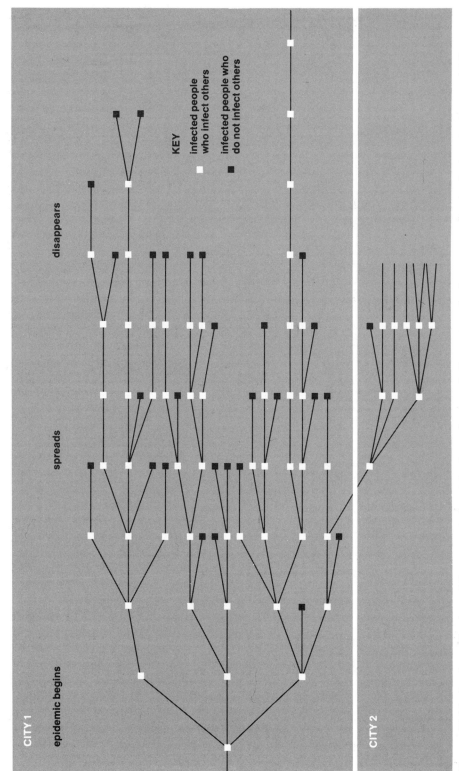

CITY 1

epidemic begins

spreads

disappears

KEY

□ infected people who infect others

■ infected people who do not infect others

CITY 2

Figure 13.14. A schematic view of the spread of an infectious disease. A disease rarely disappears completely, but continues ad infinitum; the final white square in one of the City 1 chains indicates that a few persons will continue to infect others. The final black square in the remaining chains means that the person does not pass on the disease.

Table 13.2. Paralytic polio rates in Detroit, by socioeconomic status and by race.

Socioeconomic status	1952 [a]		1958 [a]	
	Whites	Blacks	Whites	Blacks
Highest	42.5	0.0	1.4	0.0
Upper middle	39.1	10.9	3.7	45.1
Lower middle	17.9	12.5	10.0	52.6
Lowest	24.6	5.9	16.3	51.8

[a] Figures represent the number of cases per 100,000 population.

After Richard D. Leach, "Socioeconomic Status, Race, and Poliomyelitis in Detroit, Michigan: A Sociological Analysis" (Unpubl. MA thesis, Wayne State University, 1967), p. 47.

of the European population. Often it was spread as people panicked at its arrival, carrying it with them to new areas.

Socioeconomic status, too, often affects disease patterns; the first polio epidemics were confined almost entirely to the United States, Canada, Scandinavia, and Australia, all comparatively wealthy regions. Polio vaccines were heralded in the 1950s as a major step toward eradicating paralytic polio, but the disease was not eliminated without exposing the costs of social deprivation and racial discrimination. The 1952 Detroit epidemic affected mostly whites of high socioeconomic status because of their high hygiene standards and lack of childhood exposure. This group had seven times as many cases of paralytic polio per 100,000 members (of all ages) as did the poorest blacks; this is the classic distribution pattern for polio (Table 13.2). In 1955, the Salk vaccine was introduced, and the Detroit board of health was faced with a choice of vaccination programs: should the limited supply of vaccine be distributed by private physicians or public health clinics? They chose the first, spreading most of the vaccine among whites, who had easiest access to private doctors. When the 1958 epidemic hit, the incidence of paralytic polio was reversed. Now the richest group, almost 100 percent white, had 1.4 paralytic cases per 100,000 population, and the poorest blacks suffered about 52 cases per 100,000. In 1960, neighborhood immunization clinics were established in the inner city and paralytic polio finally became a rarity.

Noninfectious Disorders

As time goes on infectious disease rapidly shrinks as a cause of human deaths in Western nations; but deaths from noninfectious disorders rise at the same time. This shift is referred to as the epidemiologic transition, and its occurrence can be well documented. For instance, three anthropologists were able to use census and burial records to show that the town of Manti, Utah, went through such a transition in the early 1900s. At that time, as the dependence on a contaminated water supply declined and as modern medicine became available, the causes of death changed to degenerative diseases.

Countries like the United States annually suffer hundreds of thousands of deaths from cancer and heart disease, in part because medical science is making rapid advances. By not dying of infectious diseases, people can live long enough to develop the noninfectious disorders of adulthood. The average expected life span grew from forty-six years for an American white male born in 1900 to seventy-four years for one born in 1976, reflecting the reduction in contagious diseases. The incidence of the outstanding killers in modern America, cancer and heart disease, is shown in Table 13.3.

We know that many of the noninfectious diseases vary in incidence throughout the world, but the reasons for this variation are complex and poorly understood. The Australian Aborigines in native conditions rarely have cancerous growths or high blood pressure (hypertension). The low incidence of cancer could be partly genetic, because we do know that cancer tends to run in families. Among whites, anyway, people appear to inherit predispositions to develop some forms of cancer. But the scarcity of cancer-producing agents (cigarettes, pollutants, and others) among the Aborigines may be the major reason. Hypertension also may be missing because of environmental differences. Aborigines living in the big cities of Australia show hypertension rates much higher than unacculturated Aborigines, which seems to indicate that Western diets and the pressure of life in large cities are most responsible for hypertension. Although genetic factors may affect resistance to noninfectious disorders, environmental factors such as diet, pollution, and crowding are responsible too.

Table 13.3. Leading causes of death in the United States during 1900 and 1979.

1900		1979	
Cause of death	Number per 100,000	Cause of death	Number per 100,000
1. Diseases of the heart and blood vessels	345	1. Diseases of the heart and blood vessels	435
2. Influenza and pneumonia	202	2. Cancer	183
3. Tuberculosis	194	3. Accidents	48
4. Diseases of the stomach and intestines	143	4. Bronchitis, emphysema, and asthma	23
5. Accidents	72	5. Influenza and pneumonia	21
6. Cancer	64	6. Diabetes mellitus	15
7. Diphtheria	40	7. Cirrhosis of the liver	14
8. Typhoid and paratyphoid fever	31	8. Suicide	12
9. Measles	13	9. Certain diseases of early infancy	11
10. Cirrhosis of the liver	13	10. Homicide	10

Data for 1900 from U.S. Bureau of the Census *Historical Statistics of the United States Colonial Times to 1957*. Statistical Abstract Suppl. (Washington, D.C.: Government Printing Office, 1960), p. 26, and for 1979 from U.S. Bureau of the Census, *Statistical Abstract of the United States 1982–1983, 103 edition* (Washington, D.C.: Government Printing Office, 1982), p. 76.

Stress in Modern Life

The advances of modern civilization have eased the cost of some previous stresses. Our culture allows us to deal quite effectively with heat and cold stress. Likewise, infectious disease has declined as a cause of human suffering. Unfortunately, as the increase in noninfectious disease implies, we are not without stresses. Actually, as our culture solves one problem, we may be creating new ones. Burning fossil fuels may provide energy to run our air conditioners and furnaces, but it also creates air pollution.

Anthropologists have a reputation for being interested in the inhabitants of exotic lands. As Western cultures have expanded and native cultures disappeared, anthropologists have started to consider all peoples, including Westerners, appropriate for study. In this regard, the anthropological literature now contains information on some of the stresses encountered by the residents of Westernized regions.

Life-Style

Up to this point, we have used the word "stress" in a very general sense. In everyday life, though, we tend to use it in a more limited sense, referring to psychological problems encountered in daily living. G. A. Harrison, V. Reynolds, and their colleagues at Oxford University have been studying the biology of the people of some Oxfordshire villages for several years. One of the areas they have been looking at is the relationship of life style to biology.

In situations of stress humans secrete stress hormones or catecholamines; they are epinephrine (also called adrenaline), and norepinephrine (noradrenaline). Very simply stated, catecholamines are secreted into the blood under stressful conditions to gear the body for strenuous activity. This response is called the "fight or flight" reaction; these hormones pass into the urine for excretion. By collecting urine samples it is possible to judge the amount of catecholamines a person has recently produced.

There have been many studies in laboratories of volunteers who are put under stress, but the Oxford group wanted to learn about the hormonal responses of average people going about their daily lives. The basic data on life-style was obtained by questionnaires, asking people about happiness, boredom, frustration, and so on. Urine samples were gathered and catecholamine levels determined. A number of associations were found in the men and women of Oxfordshire. In the women, high epinephrine levels were related to a feeling of frustration and general dissatisfaction with life. Cigarette smoking and high coffee consumption were associated with high epinephrine levels in men as well as women. For men, a competitive personality, a need to meet self-established deadlines, and a feeling of being under pressure were also related to high epinephrine levels. High norepinephrine levels went along with a greater amount of physical activity. Low levels of catecholamines were found in men who felt bored. Thus, it seems that subnormal levels of stress hormones can be found in people who are understimulated. The authors wonder if too little catchecholamine might not be as undesirable as too much. Much evidence has accumulated to indicate that long-term elevation of catecholamines is associated with coronary heart disease. We have all heard that personality and life-style can be related to heart disease. In light of these results, the authors feel that coffee intake and cigarettes may well be related to coronary heart disease.

Members of bands or tribes living under aboriginal conditions do not have to worry about unemployment or the need to make money. The members of a band of pygmies cooperate with one another to provide food and shelter. This is not the case in the United States. Sidney Cobb and colleagues undertook a long-term study of men who knew they were about to lose their jobs as a result of a permanent plant shutdown.[3] During the course of the study they collected physiological, social, and psychological data in an attempt to see the interplay among these factors. *Unemployment*

The men studied were drawn from six companies: an urban area plant that was about to be closed, a similar plant in a rural area, and two urban and two rural companies (the controls) for which there was no threat of a shutdown. The men were visited at five different times; just before job loss (the anticipation stage), at the time of termination, and six, twelve, and twenty-four months after job loss. Controls were visited at the same time. The physiological variables that were measured included cholesterol levels and norepinephrine excretion rates.

One of the variables was that of social support, a measure of the degree to which close relatives and friends would buoy up the unemployed man in part as reflected by the frequency of his social activity outside the home. A second psychosocial variable measured, called "psychological defense," was the unemployed's ability not to blame himself for his situation.

The data show that norepinephrine excretion rates were considerably higher for those whose jobs were abolished, both before and for a year after job loss (Figure 13.15). As already mentioned, norepinephrine levels increase to help deal with short-term stress. If the stress — continued unemployment — doesn't go away, the prolonged norepinephrine elevation can be harmful to one's health. When the terminees are divided along urban-rural lines, it is apparent that social setting affects norepinephrine excretion rates. Rural men seemed much less stressed by unemployment than urban men (Figure 13.16). Those men with high psychological defense were significantly lower in excretion rates than those who blamed themselves for having lost their jobs (Figure 13.17).

The social and psychological factors are seen also to moderate the cholesterol and other chemical levels. Those with high social support had noticeably lower serum cholesterol levels than the unemployed with little support. Because cholesterol levels may be related to heart disease, it is entirely possible that those with high social support may live longer.

Thus we see that our biological functioning is affected by how we

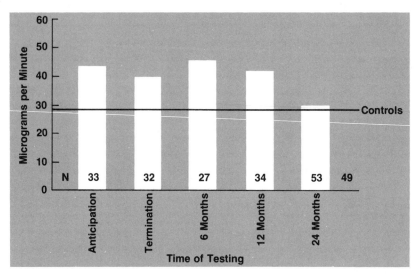

Figure 13.15. *Norepinephrine excretion rates in micrograms (millionths of a gram) per minute at five different times in the study. The line labeled "controls" indicates the average rate in the unstressed, employed man. "Anticipation" is the time after the men were informed they would lose their jobs but prior to job loss. Numbers in each bar indicate number of men tested.*

perceive our situation — whether or not we have friends with whom we can share emotions, whether we live in a city, and so on — and all these factors are influenced by the type of society we live in.

Comparable socioeconomic effects on health are being documented elsewhere. In Australia, a trend in deaths due to heart disease has been strongly linked to high unemployment and periods of economic recession.

Figure 13.16. *Norepinephrine excretion rates in micrograms per minute, by location of company and by time.*

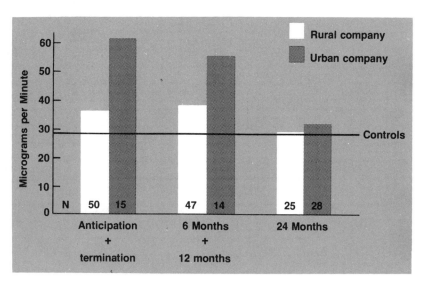

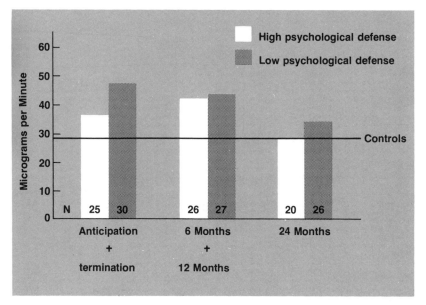

Figure 13.17. *Norepinephrine excretion rates in micrograms per minute, by time of analysis and by level of psychological defense.*

Light

Normally people think of light in terms of the requirements for vision. In Chapter 12 it was pointed out that different parts of the spectrum can have different effects on us; ultraviolet light is responsible for sunburn and vitamin D synthesis. When Edison devised the incandescent bulb he was concerned only with amount of light, not the relative proportions of light of different wavelengths. Figure 13.18 illustrates quite clearly that the spectra of both the incandescent bulb and the cool-white fluorescent lamp are different from that of sunlight. It is not that fluorescent lamps cannot be made to mimic the spectrum of sunlight, but until rather recently no one thought about the biological effects of different kinds of light. Construction of bulbs was based solely on economic and technological considerations.

A study carried out by Robert Neer, Richard Wurtman, and coworkers demonstrated clearly the physiological effects of exposure to different light sources on calcium absorption. In this work a series of elderly, healthy males in Boston were divided into two groups, all of whom agreed to stay indoors from the beginning of winter to mid-March. For the first seven weeks all members of both groups stayed inside, where they functioned in light provided by a mixture of incandescent and fluorescent bulbs. At the end of this time, members of both groups were equally poor in ability to absorb calcium through the gut. Although the diet was supplying an adequate amount of calcium, but little vitamin D, the subjects could absorb only about 40 percent of that present in the food, presumably due to a decreased production of vitamin D. After this initial period both groups continued to stay inside, but one of the groups was exposed to a special lamp designed to mimic the spectrum of sunlight.

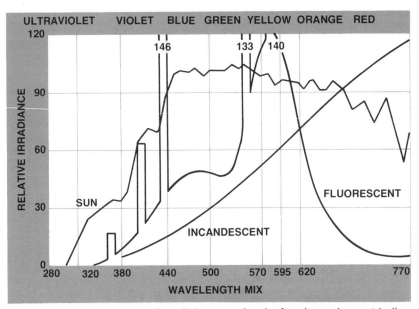

Figure 13.18. *The spectra of sunlight at sea level, of an incandescent bulb, and of a cool-white fluorescent bulb. The peak emissions of the curves are quite different.*

The amount of ultraviolet light this group received was comparable to what they would receive during a fifteen-minute walk on a sunny, summer day. Calcium absorption was remeasured at the end of this four-week period. The absorption in the unexposed group had dropped to 30 percent; the UV-exposed group increased its absorption of calcium to 50 percent (Figure 13.19). Given that many of us spend little time outdoors during the winter, it is reasonable to postulate that much of the American population, especially the very young and very old, is suffering from some degree of lowered calcium absorption. Low calcium absorption can lead to decalcification of bones and then to fractures. One solution in nursing homes might be to install fluorescent bulbs that have emission spectra similar to the sun's.

Light is also known to affect the maturation of the gonads in humans. Wurtman found that females who became blind in the first year of life had an earlier onset of puberty than did those with normal sight. We do not yet know the effects of electric lighting on sexual maturation.

Noise   One of the side effects of life in a modern society is the increased noise level. It has been well documented that living in a large urban center has a very direct effect on the auditory equipment itself. Residents of noisy areas and people who must work in noisy places such as factories suffer hearing loss (Figure 13.20).

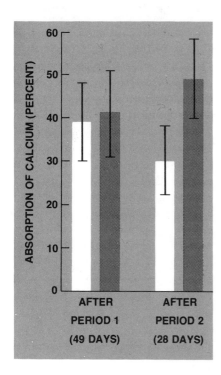

Figure 13.19. Effects of light exposure on calcium absorption. The control group (open bars) and experimental group (shaded bars) were initially exposed only to typical indoor lighting for seven weeks. This was continued four more weeks for controls, while the experimental group received exposure to special fluorescent lamps. The brackets indicate the range of variation within each group.

Noise has, it seems, less obvious sorts of effects as well. Noise can be quite disturbing psychologically. People living near a major London airport had a higher rate of admission to psychiatric units than a similar group living in a quieter area. In the laboratory, psychologists have shown that noise which is unpredictable and uncontrollable is very upsetting. If a person believes that he can make a bothersome noise stop (whether it is true does not matter) he can tolerate the noise much better. Though the psychologists were interested in mental and behavioral adjustments, it would be reasonable to look for biological effects in such experiments. The frustration of uncontrollable noise could well trigger hormonal shifts, which could then affect a person's health.

A recent report dealt with pregnant women who lived near a very noisy airport. Looking at more than 100 such women, Lawrence Schell found that their newborns' weights were lower than expected. This is in accord with other research in Japan which noted an increased incidence of prematurity and low birth weight in association with maternal exposure to a lot of noise. Some researchers have even found an increase in birth defects in the offspring of women exposed to high noise levels.

There may be harmful effects of too little noise as well. One researcher looked at the offspring of female rats exposed to various noise levels while pregnant. Females exposed to high levels had very small infants while females exposed to no noise had smaller babies than females exposed to moderate noise levels.

Figure 13.20. *The noise produced in modern society may have biological effects on us.*

Nutrition

Let us now consider the interrelationship of diet, biology, and behavior. The nutritional content of a group's diet can affect its health, and the existence of vitamin deficiency diseases is well known. Also, people are more likely to contract or to suffer greater damage from infectious disease when they are undernourished. Often the interdependence of biology and culture as mediated by nutrition is more complex and may have unexpected repercussions.

Diet and Variability

Average dietary requirements have been formulated for the "normal" American living in "normal" environmental conditions (Table 13.4). Variation in age, sex, and body size is allowed for; women need more iron but fewer calories each day than the average male. These figures provide a convenient standard for analyzing and comparing the nutritional status of individuals or populations, although some individuals in any population may need more or less of these nutrients. People with a predisposition to schizophrenia, for instance, may have an increased vitamin C requirement. It has also been shown recently that these people seem to metabolize the plant protein, gluten, in an abnormal fashion, again indicating individual variation regarding diet.

We do not know if the daily requirements of different populations differ significantly. Because body size partly determines nutritional needs and because this trait exhibits genetically influenced populational differences, some variation probably does exist. We know that many of the world's inhabitants do not approach, for at least part of the year, the levels recommended in the United States. Not all nonwestern peoples are malnourished, though; in fact, severe malnutrition usually becomes obvious only as a result of the cultural disruptions produced by industrialization. Yanamama Indians of the Amazon Basin take in more than adequate amounts of protein per day (75 grams per adult per day). The San of the Kalahari Desert of southern Africa evidence some mild undernutrition, but malnutrition is not present. Nor do they seem overly concerned about the source of their next meal: women, who are the chief suppliers of food (60 to 80 percent), need work only two or three days per week. Men spend about the same amount of time hunting.

Calories, Carbohydrates, Proteins, and Fats: An Adequate Diet

The one requirement most Americans are acutely aware of is caloric intake. A calorie is the unit of heat required to raise the temperature of one gram of water from 15° to 16° Celsius (centigrade); a diet's caloric value reflects its ability to produce energy. The calorie is actually a very small amount of heat and, for convenience, dieters and nutritionists talk of the large calorie (often with a capital C), or kilocalorie, which equals 1000 calories. When the caloric intake drops below that needed to perform basic body functions (muscular activity, growth, maintaining body temperature), energy reserves, such as fat deposits, are drawn on to make up the deficit.

The sources of calories vary widely around the world. In poorer agricultural regions the primary source is carbohydrates; hunters get much of their energy from fats and proteins. Beyond the provision of energy, however, the sources fill roles that are not interchangeable. Proteins are the only route by which we can get some amino acids. The eight essential amino acids are the ones we cannot synthesize; they must be present in the food we eat. We then use these amino acids to construct our own proteins (Chapter 2). Synthesizing and repairing tissues, not producing energy, are really the primary functions of proteins. Adequate carbohydrates and fats spare the proteins from having to make energy. We must also eat at least some fat to get fatty acids, which are important in structural parts of the tissues and in keeping the gonads working properly.

The major dietary sources of proteins are animal products: meat, milk, eggs, fish, and some plants, such as nuts. Although all plants have some protein, they are generally poorer in the essential amino acids than animal sources. Fats, too, generally come from animal foods, but plants also have them. Carbohydrates are supplied by cereals, fruits, starchy roots, and sugar. Fats are the most concentrated source of calories, providing 9 Calories per gram. Proteins and carbohydrates both provide about 4 Calories per gram.

Equally adequate diets can vary widely in the contribution protein, carbohydrates, and fat make to the caloric intake. Generally, we see the variation as a reflection of cultural differences. Nevertheless, we have a few indications that a member of one culture cannot adapt to the diet of another group (Figure 13.21). The high fatty acid content of the Es-

Table 13.4. Recommended Dietary Allowances[a] (RDAs), revised 1980, for selected age groups.

| | | Weight | | Height | | Energy[b] | Protein | Fat soluble vitamins | | |
| | | | | | | | | A | D | E |
	Age	kg	lbs.	cm	in.	kcal.	grams	μgR.E.*	μg†	mgαT.E.‡
Children	1–3	13	29	90	35	1,300	23	400	10	5
Girls	11–14	46	101	157	62	2,200	46	800	10	8
Boys	11–14	45	99	157	62	2,700	45	1,000	10	8
Women	23–50	55	120	163	64	2,000	46	800	5	8
Pregnant women						+300	+30	+200	+5	+2
Men	23–50	70	154	178	70	2,700	56	1,000	5	10

[a]Dietary allowances cover most normal, healthy persons living in the temperate United States.
[b]The number of kilocalories listed for each category refers to people engaged in some physical activity. College professors and other sedentary people need fewer calories. Body size, maturation rate, and climatic conditions can also alter the required number of calories.
*Retinol equivalents: 1 retinol equivalent = 1 μg. retinol
†As cholecalciferol: 10 μg. cholecalciferol = 400 I.U. vitamin D
‡α tocopherol equivalents: 1 mg. d-α-tocopherol = 1αT.E.
Reproduced from: Recommended Dietary Allowances. 9th rev. ed. (1980, in press), with the permission of the National Academy of Sciences, Washington, D.C.

kimo diet can produce disorders in people not used to such a diet. Most variation, though, is determined by culture and ecology. Yanamama Indians of South America get their protein by eating fried insects and raw lice. For most of the year, highland Quechua Indians get about 85 percent of their calories from carbohydrates, about 10 percent from protein, and 5 percent from fats. These proportions reflect their economic dependence on cultivating potatoes and several other plants. Potatoes account for well over half the food consumed daily by inhabitants of at least one Quechua village, meat and fat for less than 10 percent. From this diet, the people take in up to 3200 Calories per day. Eskimos take in each day an average of about 3100 Calories. The proportions of protein, fat, and carbohydrates are radically different from those in the Quechua diet, however. Eskimos are primarily hunters, and eat a lot of animal fat and protein. These substances provide about 47 percent each of the total calories, with carbohydrates contributing the remaining 6 percent. In Western societies just over half the total calories are, on the average, derived from carbohydrates, about a third from fat, and the rest from protein.

Humans are highly flexible in their ability to tolerate widely varied diets. Culture is generally acknowledged as the source of our great adaptability, but physiologically we are quite flexible, too. Many of the other primates are tightly limited in their food sources, for physiological and other reasons; humans, on the other hand, can eat and survive on food from many sources. Australian Aborigines get much of their protein by eating insects; Eskimos are almost exclusively carnivores; Hindus are vegetarians. Culture may dictate the choice of foods, but people can eat almost anything.

People do not flourish equally well on all the different diets. The large

Water soluble vitamins							Minerals					
Ascorbic Acid mg	Folacin μg	Niacin mg	Riboflavin mg	Thiamin mg	B_6 mg	B_{12} μg	Calcium mg	Phosphorus mg	Iodine μg	Iron mg	Magnesium mg	Zinc mg
45	100	9	0.8	0.7	0.9	2.0	800	800	70	15	150	10
50	400	15	1.3	1.1	1.8	3.0	1,200	1,200	150	18	300	15
50	400	18	1.6	1.4	1.8	3.0	1,200	1,200	150	18	350	15
60	400	13	1.2	1.0	2.0	3.0	800	800	150	18	300	15
+20	+400	+2	+0.3	+0.4	+0.6	+1.0	+400	+400	+25	+12–42	+150	+5
60	400	18	1.6	1.4	2.2	3.0	800	800	150	10	350	15

amount of sugar in the American diet (just under 100 pounds per capita per year in the 1970s) does much to decay teeth. Before European contact, gatherers and hunters such as Australian Aborigines rarely had tooth decay, as we see in skeletal remains, and they ate little sugar. Many who live in underdeveloped nations survive on a diet low in animal protein and calories, but they also suffer from disorders known as kwashiorkor (protein deficiency) and marasmus (calorie deficiency).

Although we will consider kwashiorkor and marasmus as protein-calorie malnutrition (PCM), the real picture is often more complex. Some show the swelling (edema) characteristic of a deficiency only in protein, while others, receiving sufficient protein but insufficient calories, show the wasting of marasmus (Figure 13.22). Many are deficient in both, hence PCM. The toll this disorder takes is enormous, being present in between 5 and 45 percent of the children in the developing countries. The Citizen's Board of Inquiry into Hunger and Malnutrition in the United States has also identified it in poor American families; it cuts across ethnic boundaries, being found in poor Hispanics, blacks, Native Americans, and whites. It may sometimes be caused by child neglect, but its primary direct or indirect cause is poverty, and the poor bear the mental and physical scars of PCM for years.

Protein-Calorie Malnutrition

The joint Food and Agriculture Organization-World Health Organization Expert Committee on Nutrition has described a typical sequence in the development of PCM. The breast-fed child develops normally until about the age of six months. Then the growing child's caloric and protein requirements outstrip the supply in the mother's milk. The mother, because the child is still nursing, fails to see that it is underfed, or else the parents cannot afford to supplement the child's diet. In some socie-

Figure 13.21. *A population's sources of nutrition can vary widely from place to place: (left) a wedding feast aboard a Hong Kong junk with a pan of the staple, rice, prominently displayed; a youngster with the Eskimo staple, fish.*

ties breast feeding is continued until the age of three or four. During this time the mother's milk remains high in protein but the supply dwindles. This postponement of weaning gives the child enough protein to maintain life, but not enough to support proper growth; in fact, the name *kwashiorkor* is a Ghanian word meaning "the disease affecting the child after it leaves the mother's breast." The short stature of adults in many underdeveloped areas and the greater height of first-generation immigrants to the United States (Chapter 12) is a definite reflection of dietary variables.

In many underdeveloped areas, the food source at weaning is shifted to a cereal gruel or simply water in which cereal has been cooked. Many groups find poor nutrition exacerbated by the cultural disruption that attends urbanization and changing dietary habits. In many urban areas where the mother must work, breast feeding is terminated early and overdiluted cow's milk and thick gruel are the only foods, providing a very low protein intake. The protein supply is now too low to produce enough antibodies, because the child is not getting enough amino acids for the cells to string together to form the proteins. Neither is the youngster receiving antibodies from the mother's milk. The child is now an

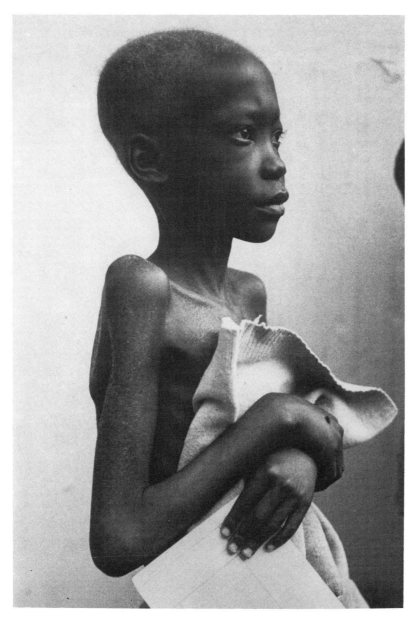

Figure 13.22. The effects of protein and calorie malnutrition are obvious in this photograph of a Zairian child.

easy target for many infectious diseases, particularly respiratory disorders. Because of the many related factors, mortality rates for PCM are underestimates; a child who died from pneumonia might well have survived the disease had he or she been well nourished. Table 13.5 shows the results of a study in Guatemala on the interplay of nutrition and infectious disease; the children who had lower weight gains, and thus poorer diets, were sick much longer than those on better diets.

We need not cross the borders of the United States to see evidence of this. The mortality rate for two- to twelve-month-old whites is 5.9 per

Table 13.5. Effect of infections on well-fed and poorly fed children.
A comparison of the number of attacks and days of illness per year in six children with greatest weight gain and six children with least weight gain, in Santa Maria Caugué, Guatemala, 1964–1966.

Disease	Children with greatest weight gain (6–12 mos. old)		Children with least weight gain (6–12 mos. old)	
	No. of attacks	Days ill	No. of attacks	Days ill
Diarrhea	12	100	11	170
Upper respiratory infections and conjunctivitis	24	155	23	209
Bronchitis and bronchopneumonia	1	7	2	24
Stomatitis and thrush	3	20	6	39
Totals	40	282	42	442

After L. J. Mata. J. J. Urrutia, and B. Garcia, "Effect of Infection and Diet on Child Growth: Experience in a Guatemalan Village," in G. E. W. Wolstenholme and M. O'Connor (eds.), *Nutrition and Infection: Ciba Foundation Study Group No. 31* (Boston: Little, Brown, 1967), p. 123.

thousand; in Navajo County, Arizona, it is 40.1 deaths per thousand. The statistic becomes even more striking when broken down by race. White infants die at a rate of 10.5 per thousand in this county, while 58.5 Native American infants are dying, and PCM has been diagnosed among Native Americans. In Rio Grande County, Colorado, the population is 99.7 percent white but more than 33 percent are poor; here the postneonatal mortality is 36 per thousand.

One of PCM's saddest consequences is the possibility of irreversible tissue damage, including brain damage. Although not completely substantiated, it appears that infants reared on a low-protein diet have retarded tissue growth. If the diet is later supplemented, the child may at least partially catch up with the norm by rapid growth spurts. A one-year-old child hospitalized in San Antonio, Texas, weighed eight pounds at admission, but gained three pounds in one month when properly fed.

For children born to undernourished mothers, the prognosis is not as good. Evidence is growing that chronic protein deficiency in the months before and after birth may cause irrevocable harm, for it is at this time that the brain is growing fastest. Figure 13.23 shows that rats that were undernourished because they were suckled in groups of fifteen by one female have lower brain weights than those suckled in groups of three per female. After weaning, at twenty-one days, all rats were given free access to high-protein food. The previously undernourished animals never caught up with the well-nourished animals in brain weight. Because the maximum growth rate for rat brain tissue is achieved just after birth, undernourishment at this time should be comparable with human *in utero* deprivation, for the maximum rate of growth for the brain in humans is reached just before birth. If the model is correct, prenatal protein deficiency in humans should be expected to produce permanent retardation

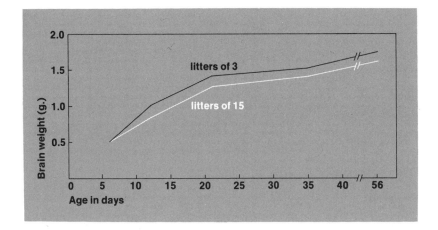

Figure 13.23. Malnutrition's effect on the development of the central nervous system in the rat.

in brain growth. In fact poor fetal nutrition and low birth weight have been linked to later intellectual decrements. One report on white newborns in Boston showed that those weighing more than 6.5 pounds later had IQs 13 points higher than those weighing less than 4.5 pounds at birth.

The consequences of PCM may be long-lived. Many animal studies show the existence of intergenerational effects on normal growth. Poor nutrition during critical growth periods can permanently retard the development of an organ system, such as that for reproduction. Should an affected animal become pregnant, its fetuses are malnourished because the mother's earlier growth problems prevent the formation of a normal placenta even if she is eating well now. The inadequate placenta in turn starves the fetus, producing a second malnourished generation.

Physiological and Genetic Adaptations The body can suffer a tremendous toll from malnutrition. What physiological and genetic adaptations might be made to a disorder such as PCM? We know little about them, but one interesting hypothesis states that the body contracts its "metabolic frontiers": absolutely essential proteins are synthesized at nearly normal rates but at the expense of luxuries such as muscle, skin, and brain. Several studies have shown that animals on a low-protein diet continue to manufacture liver, pancreatic, and intestinal proteins at more or less normal levels but the output of muscle and skin cells is curtailed. One disadvantage children in poor communities suffer is nutritional dwarfism; as with the brain, body weight and stature are much reduced, presumably to ensure that enough essential materials will be produced. We have many documented examples, even in the United States, of children four or five years old weighing only 20 pounds and of one-year-olds weighing less than they did at birth.

Children born of poorly nourished women also are typically below the normal birth weight. Infants of poor black South African mothers average about 6 ounces less at birth than infants of white South Africans.

Offspring of high-income black South Africans average the same weight at birth as South African white infants.

Stanley Garn and other researchers have proposed that small body size, and thus reduced protein and caloric requirements, would be a selective advantage when nutrition is inadequate. They have found that people with a genetic trait known as brachymesophalangia-5 (a short middle section of the little finger) also show a marked reduction in stature compared with unaffected members of the same population or family. We know that brachymesophalangia-5, a seemingly unimportant trait, is found at frequencies of 5 percent or more in many populations of Central and South America and Asia. Could it be, Garn asks, that this little symptom reflects a genetically influenced reduction in body size as an adaptation to chronically inadequate nutrition? (Figure 13.24)

Table 13.6 shows the caloric requirements for a 70 kg (154 lb) man and a 60 kg (132 lb) man. Assuming the smaller man is not suffering from retarded growth but is geared to be small, he can live and work well on a significantly lower number of calories per day. Imagine the reduction in required food resources for a large population, with each member needing hundreds fewer calories every day of the year.

Natural selection may have worked as Garn speculates. Genes for small body size may be best suited to areas where nutritional deprivation is common. Still we do know that many people in the world would have grown more if they were better fed. This is not simply a question of academic (or humanitarian) interest. Repercussions of suboptimal

Figure 13.24. Radiograph of a child with brachymesophalangia-5.

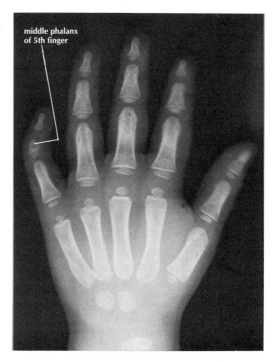

middle phalanx
of 5th finger

Table 13.6. Comparison of calorie requirements of a 70 kg U.S. male with those of a 60 kg Colombian male at similar activity levels.

	U.S.A.	Colombia
Mean Body Weight (kg)	70	60
Calorie Costs (kcal)		
Resting (8 hrs.)	570	480
Very Light Activity (6 hrs.)	630	540
Light Labor (8 hrs.)	1624	1392
Moderate Labor (2 hrs.)	602	516
Total	3462	2928

Source: From William A. Stini, "Human Adaptability to Nutritional Stress," in Paul B. Pearson and Richard Greenwell (eds.), *Nutrition, Food, and Man* (Tucson: University of Arizona Press, 1980).

growth can be seen in very concrete economic terms. The physical work capacity can be measured by the maximum oxygen consumption (VO_2). The maximum amount of oxygen capable of being consumed by a person measures the person's ability to do work. As undernutrition gets worse, the maximum oxygen consumption decreases markedly.

The productivity of Columbian sugar cane cutters was measured in one study by the number of tons of cane they cut each day. The best harvesters cut more than four tons per day, the worst less than three. The best workers weighed more, were taller, had more muscle and less body fat (Figure 13.25). The best harvesters also had higher VO_2 (Figure 13.26). Healthy people make better workers.

A Cultural Adaptation: Synthetic Foods The social causes of protein-calorie malnutrition are many, though poverty and lack of education are often at the root of the problem. In the past decade several foods have been developed that are designed to provide nutritious diets at a very

Figure 13.25. Physical characteristics of good, average, and poor sugar-cane cutters. The most productive cutters were the healthiest.

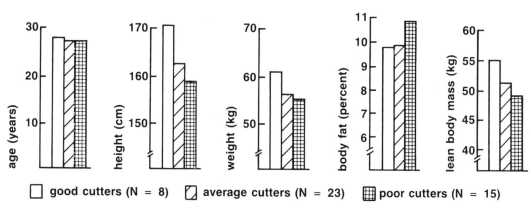

☐ good cutters (N = 8)　▨ average cutters (N = 23)　▦ poor cutters (N = 15)

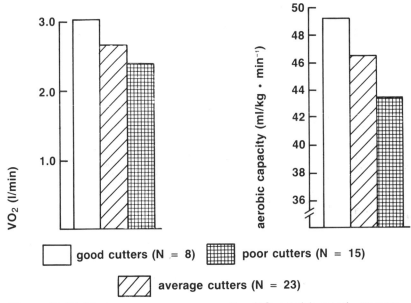

Figure 13.26. *Maximum oxygen consumption (VO₂ max) in good, average, and poor sugarcane cutters. The good cutters had a greater biological ability to do work.*

low price. The nutrient content of one, Incaparina, is compared in Table 13.7 with cow's milk and corn gruel, the latter being a common food in areas such as Guatemala. Many of the new foods are mixtures of locally available foods, for example, soybeans, cottonseed oil, and nut meal.

Such products have not been a great success. Peruvita, a nutrient-rich soft drink developed in Peru, failed because its taste was unacceptable; Incaparina was a success in Guatemala and Colombia because the people liked the taste. In Ghana, a soybean preparation failed even though its taste and appearance were not objectionable: the amount of fuel needed to cook the soybeans was almost as great as the family's total supply. When Pro-nutro, a South African preparation, was first marketed to black South Africans, it was advertised as a special food for poor people. It occurred to no one that the poor would assume it was food no one else wanted and, therefore, to be avoided. As one expert said, "the poor want . . . the things the non-poor have." In a second campaign Pro-nutro was named "Incumbe," the same as the corn gruel used to feed Zulu children. It was assumed the people would accept and use the fortified food because of its familiar name. This tactic also failed, because when mothers brought their malnourished children to the hospital and were asked what they were feeding the children, their answer was "Incumbe." The mothers meant corn gruel, but the doctors thought they meant the new food, giving rise to the mistaken idea that the special food was harmful to children. Some marketing success was finally

Table 13.7. Comparison of the nutritional content of corn gruel, incaparina, and milk.[a]

	Corn gruel[b]	Incaparina[b]	Cow's milk
Calories	86	138	141
Protein (gm.)	1.0	6.9	6.9
Fat (gm.)	0.4	1.0	7.6
Carbohydrates (gm.)	20.2	25.3	11.3
Calcium (mg.)	22.0	164.0	374.0
Phosphorus (mg.)	22.0	174.0	168.0
Iron (mg.)	0.0	2.1	1.0
Vitamin A (IU)	0	1,125	363
Vitamin B_1 (Thiamine; mg.)	0.02	0.58	0.08
Vitamin B_2 (Riboflavin; mg.)	0.0	0.28	0.50
Niacin (mg.)	0.19	1.95	0.10

[a] The amount compared was one glass of each.
[b] Prepared with 25 grams of corn "masa" or Incaparina in one glass of water, boiling and sweetening with 12 grams of sugar.

Hunger, U.S.A.: A Report by the Citizens Board of Inquiry into Hunger and Malnutrition in the United States (Boston: Beacon Press, 1968), p. 47.

achieved when Pro-nutro was advertised as a "food of athletes" (sounds familiar), desirable for people of all socioeconomic levels.

Culture and Malnutrition

In our country, malnutrition may affect poor people who move from one area to another. Many Puerto Ricans in New York are found to be malnourished, partly because they continue to eat the tropical foods with which they are familiar (bananas, sweet potatoes, beans) without substituting other nutritious foods for the ones they can no longer get.

Ignorance of simple health standards also perpetuates malnutrition. A child in Brooklyn, for example, was diagnosed as having rickets, which surprised the mother because she thought the child was simply bow-legged.

Old people also suffer from malnutrition, partly because of our social values. Mealtime for the lonely aged is a chore to be finished as soon as possible or completely avoided. It no longer means spending time with the family, but makes them remember they are alone. Restaurants seldom cater to the old because old people take a long time to eat and spend little money; shopping is difficult because it is hard to get around; and many old people live in rooms with no cooking facilities.

The economic sensitivity of the very poorest is particularly pathetic. The 1,000 members of a tarpaper-shack village near the New Orleans garbage dump had an upsurge in malnutrition when the cost of dumping garbage was raised, causing much of the edible garbage to be dumped elsewhere and depriving the residents of their primary food supply.

In many parts of this country people eat laundry starch or clay to avoid hunger pains. But laundry starch reduces the body's ability to absorb iron from other foods, leading to iron-deficiency anemia. Nutritional anemia in the United States is shockingly common, though its causes vary. More than 40 percent of one-year-old children in low-income families in New York City have abnormally low hemoglobin levels either because of iron-deficiency anemia (iron is one of hemoglobin's building blocks) or insufficient protein to build the hemoglobin chains. In Alabama, 550 of 709 poor children tested had anemia.

Agriculture and Malnutrition Elsewhere in the world, a changing economic base can result in a marked decline in a group's nutritional status. One case was beautifully documented by Daniel Gross and Barbara Underwood.[4] The peasants of northeastern Brazil had for some time been subsistence, self-sufficient agriculturalists, growing enough beans, corn, and manioc to feed themselves. In the early 1950s the Brazilian government attempted to bring these peasant farmers into a modern cash economy. The government felt that if these farmers grew a crop that could be sold, the peasants would be able to buy more food than they could grow for themselves, and their lives would be improved. The farmers were persuaded to grow sisal, an inedible plant used in the production of rope. This particular choice seemed wise, for sisal was selling for a very high price. By 1966, 300,000 Brazilians were directly dependent on sisal production. When the price dropped as a result of the increased supply of sisal, many people found themselves without homegrown food and without sufficient funds to buy food.

One of the representative families studied by Gross and Underwood showed that malnutrition did not fall equally on all members of the family. In order to continue working in the fields, the parents took a major share of the purchased food. The children received just over half the requirements for their age group; the three-year-old boy, with a daily requirement of 1300 Calories, received about 700 Calories per day. It is not that the parents were greedy and unfeeling; if the father had given the children some of his food, he would have been too weak to continue working and the family income would have dropped to zero. As a result of this change from growing their own food to working for money, the nutritional health of tens of thousands of Brazilians had suffered.

Food sources can affect health in other ways, too. Parasitic diseases like trichinosis may be caused by eating infected foods. A particularly curious example is a disease called *kuru*.

Kuru: Nutrition and Infection Kuru, found mostly among the 35,000 Fore speakers of New Guinea, causes total incapacitation, inability to swallow, and death by starvation, suffocation, or pneumonia. It affects women and the young of both sexes. Kuru has been known to Western medicine since 1957; from 1957 to 1970 it killed 2,100.

Because of its distinctive choice of victims, several research projects were carried out to determine if the disease might be genetically caused. Others thought kuru might be influenced by a cultural variable. It was found at last by D. C. Gajdusek that the cause is a virus passed from person to person by cannibalism, a discovery which helped earn him the Nobel Prize. The virus, which affects the brain, can take years to produce symptoms. Women were the primary practitioners of cannibalism before the government stopped the practice in the 1950s. Adult males generally would not use this source of food because they thought it would rob them of vitality or stunt their growth, and under no circumstances would they eat women. Thus, kuru was spread among women by their dietary custom. Some young males probably had kuru because the prohibition against cannibalism was not so strictly applied to male children. Since the habit was eradicated, kuru has become rarer; no children born after it was banned have developed the disease.

We may yet see that genetic variation has something to do with susceptibility to kuru. The disease was first spotted on the boundary separating the Fore from the Keiagana peoples. It spread poorly through the Keiagana, even though they too were cannibals. Kuru is more likely to appear in people homozygous for an allele that produces the serum protein Gc than in people with a different genotype. The disease is not genetic in origin, but susceptibility to it may be genetically influenced.

Iodine and Social Organization The people of the South American country of Ecuador are divided into the rich nonnative peoples (blancos) and poor natives (indígenas). Iodine deficiency is quite common among the poor, resulting in a high incidence of thyroid gland malfunction. This can cause an enlargement of the gland, a goiter (see Figure 13.27). People with very severe deficiency also suffer neurological retardation; they have a very low IQ and are often deaf and mute. The people who show such defects due to thyroid malfunction are called cretins. Cretinism is known in many parts of the world. In many areas the normal diet is naturally iodine deficient so iodine is added to salt to prevent goiter and cretinism. Because of poverty and the uncorrected dietary iodine deficiency, cretinism levels can approach 10 percent in Ecuadorian indígena populations.

Lawrence Greene has studied several aspects of this situation. For one, he tested the mental and motor skills of "normal" indígenas and found that about 20 percent are subnormal by our standards. He concluded that for some iodine deficiency is not severe enough to cause cretinism but may still produce neurological problems. Considering that 25 to 30 percent of an indígena population has some degree of defect, it is not surprising that the natives define "normal" as anyone who has more than minimal ability to use language.

A second result of a high frequency of neurologically deficient people in a group is that they are all integrated into the society. Each, including most deaf-mute cretins, has a functional role, usually in the agricultural sphere. They are not separated from the rest of the society.

Third, the blancos see the indígenas as being inferior and thus have no qualms about continuing to exploit them as a cheap labor source. The Ecuadorian society continues a pattern of high stratification, with a

Figure 13.27 *People with severe goiters. These are Dani people of Western New Guinea. (Plate #DCG59DNGII)*

large number of subnormal people. If it were desired, future cretinism could be cheaply and easily prevented by iodine supplementation.

Elsewhere, cultural definitions of normalcy can include people we would class as defective. In an iodine-deficient area of Java, a Dutch group noted that many "normal" people showed abnormalities of the central nervous system.

Nutrition and Adaptation

A group's nutritional status is the result of interplay between the members' food sources and their culturally determined ways of using them. The amount and type of food in turn determine population size and health standards, and possibly also the individual's physical shape and size. A group with a hunting economy cannot be large; and dense populations, as we have seen, affect epidemiology.

Body Build

Subsistence patterns may have provided the selective forces that caused some of the morphological differences we see today. Alice Brues suggests that different body builds are suited to using different weapons: "The determining factor in the efficiency of the spear is the velocity with which the weapon leaves the hand, and it is favored by linear build [long and slender]." For a less advanced weapon like the bludgeon, a stocky, powerful build is best: "The archer requires a power leverage in the arm, which is favored by short limb segments and relatively short and thick muscles; the exact opposite of the most favorable structure for throwing a spear. . . . The bow probably developed and spread most rapidly among peoples who were of short stature and relatively mesomorphic [having a strong, muscular build]."[5] As the bow succeeded the spear in a group's cultural evolution, selection favored the archer's body build.

Paul Baker has speculated that "the plainsman of the Argentine stalked and chased his food while the Quechua Indian dug the ground, cultivated, and harvested with a dawn-to-dusk tenacity. In each instance, a different combination of skills and physical characteristics would be favored, suggesting that the subsistence activity may act as a selective force."[6]

Two other researchers, Morton S. Adams and Jerry Niswander, have gathered data that may support a similar hypothesis. Going over Native American birth records for a two-year period in the 1960s, they found greatly varying average birth weights among tribes. This variation correlated closely with variation in adult stature, a trait that has a large genetic component. Both traits also correlate with methods of getting food: the cliff-dwelling agriculturalists are uniformly small, but descendants of the bison hunters are large. Migrating gatherers and hunters, the primitive agriculturalists of the Great Basin and eastern woodland tribes, are between the extremes.

Similarities in body build of tribes with similar subsistence patterns are not caused by close genetic ties; morphologically similar tribes are known to be linguistically and genetically distinct. Where are the cause and effect here? Are cliff-dwellers small because shortness adapts them to their subsistence activities or because their food supply and daily activities result in small offspring? It would seem this variation is adaptive.

Color Blindness

Methods of getting food may also affect the incidence of color blindness. Several researchers, including R. H. Post, have found that color blindness generally is less frequent in the gathering and hunting populations than in agricultural groups. The average frequency for males in twelve groups of gatherers and hunters (Eskimos, Australian Aborigines, and North and South Native Americans) is less than 2 percent; the range of variation for groups long removed from a gatherer-hunter existence is from about 5 to 10 percent.

Post has proposed (not without opposition) that agriculturalists have more color blindness because selection against color-blind males is relaxed. A color-blind hunter would be at a disadvantage in getting food: he would have trouble seeing his prey. Thus, in primitive groups the trait would be kept at low frequency. In an agricultural or industrial society the color-blind male would not be apt to die because of his affliction and the incidence of the trait could increase.

Enzyme Deficiency Another example of the interaction of a group's diet and biology involves the inability of most of the world's adults to break down lactose, the sugar found in milk. Until we are about three, our bodies can split lactose into smaller sugars, which we can then absorb through our intestinal wall, getting nutritional value from them. The substance that enables us to digest lactose is an enzyme called lactase.

Whether or not we continue to produce this enzyme as we enter late childhood or adulthood seems to be settled by alleles. The dominant allele keeps synthesis of the enzyme going; homozygous recessives stop producing the enzyme at some time during childhood. If a lactase-deficient child or adult ingests any lactose, flatulence, diarrhea, and cramps result, and the calcium of special importance to growing children is not efficiently used.

In most of the world's populations adults are lactase-deficient, but in several populations most adults are lactase-sufficient. The limited data indicate that the populations with many adults who can digest lactose have long depended on dairy herding and drinking fresh milk. Generally, populations with many lactase-deficient adults have not been herders or drinkers of milk. Before dairying began, one hypothesis states, almost all the adults in every population were lactase-deficient; when some populations started to herd mammals several thousand years ago they introduced lactose into their adult diet. Selection then worked toward the rare individual who was best able to use this new food source. As time went on, lactase-sufficiency in adults became more and more common in these populations. Selection, then, in the form of milk use, may have been at work in some human populations to increase the frequency of lactase-sufficient adults, while it has been absent in populations that did not rely on dairy herding.

The evidence seems to support this hypothesis. Lactase-sufficient adults are numerous in many European and white American populations, as well as in some populations in southern and northeastern Africa—the very groups that have long practiced dairying. Among American blacks there are many lactase-deficient adults, because most of the American blacks' African ancestors came from coastal West Africa, which even today has little dairy farming. Modern West African adults also show a high frequency of the deficiency. The hypothesis does not fit all populations, but the results are inviting.

In some groups with many enzyme-deficient adults, people get nutrition from milk products by allowing the milk to ferment into yogurt or similar substances, such as koumiss. Fermented milk products trouble the digestive systems of deficient adults less because during fermentation bacteria break lactose down into digestible sugars.

Even without proof on this trait's evolution, we should use our knowledge of it in dealing with other people. White doctors and government officials have often felt we could help the poor in the United States and other countries by giving them milk. Because milk is good for whites, it is assumed to be good for everyone. This assumption can be very far from the truth. One Peace Corps volunteer reported that West Africans felt the powdered milk provided by CARE contained evil spirits, a rumor that could easily have been started by the symptoms they saw when lactase-deficient adults drank the milk. In Colombia, attendance at school was high except just after a shipment of milk came from the United States. As soon as the milk had been disposed of, attendance returned to normal. On the island of Bali, milk is used as a laxative.

As we have seen, a group's economic base is related in many ways to its biology. Sometimes genetic factors may make people choose which sources of nutrition are acceptable. On the other hand, cultural practices may select for genetic traits, as may be happening in the case of kuru. If a nutritional component is scarce it may be compensated for by physiological, cultural, or genetic adaptation. Cultural practices and biology are related by no simple bonds.

Summary

Groups of people react to many kinds of stresses, including climate, disease, and diet. For each we have looked at the adaptations and adjustments a population makes in order to survive in less than ideal conditions. Cultural adaptation uses behaviors in order to ease stress; genetic adaptation uses natural selection. Physiological acclimatization changes the body's functioning.

After a general consideration of the concepts of adaptation and physiological fitness, this chapter reviewed a few of the stresses to which humans are subject and the varied adaptations made in one or another setting. The stresses discussed included classic aspects of the physical environment such as heat, cold, and high altitude. Also discussed was infectious disease as a stress and other stresses found in modern, urban environments. Lastly, nutrition was discussed in terms of the causes and incidence of malnutrition and the genetic, physiological, and cultural adaptations made. Of particular note here is the realization that food choices are an aspect of culture, and as such, subject to belief systems and cultural values. Biological variation in metabolic processes can also be of significance in determining the composition of a good diet for different groups of people. Thus a knowledge of anthropology can be of practical value in helping to assure adequate nutrition.

The specific stresses are not independent; diet influences disease; climate affects diet and disease. Human beings are integrated organisms that respond to their whole environment, making studies of stress very complex. Response to one stress may in turn originate a new problem. Many of the differences we see in people today come from adaptive reactions to stress. Visible traits, such as body build, skin color, and hair form, are probably related to environmental stresses. Blood type, disease resistance, and many other "invisible" characteristics also react to environmental differences. Human variability, then, is the result of dynamic interactions among human biology, culture, and the world around us.

Chapter 14

Biological History of Human Populations

Physical anthropology is a historical science. Whether we are looking at the fossil record and the long-term history of our species, the historical reasons why blood group frequencies vary from place to place, or a historical analysis of the forces affecting the growth of a child, we are trying to understand events within a time frame. In the last several chapters, we have concentrated on the recent history of biological traits within populations and how it is affected by genes, development, culture, and evolution.

Until recently, the framework within which physical anthropology studied modern human differences had to do with races; physical anthropology is identified in the public eye as dealing with fossils and races. Yet, we have nearly completed the discussion of modern human variability and we have barely used the word "race" at all.

There are two major reasons for the recent shift away from racial analysis. As we will see, while the reconstruction of the history of a group of people is an interesting and valid endeavor, the race concept turns out to be a very poor aid in pursuing this end. Second, to a degree, the sorts of questions asked by physical anthropologists have changed over time. As the understanding of evolutionary processes has progressed, we've seen some questions based on newer information. This is nothing unique to physical anthropology; all spheres of inquiry change over time as knowledge and assumptions change. Consider fifteenth-century Europe when it was reasonable and important to ask: "How far west can you sail before falling off the edge of the world?" As the assumed Flat Earth gave way to the globe in the sixteenth century, the important questions changed. A reasonable question of one time and place can be made obsolete by new information. So, too, the questions of race, racial purity, and so on have become the anthropological version of the flat earth.

Definitions and Concepts of Race

The concept of race originated in Western thought several hundred years ago, at roughly the same time as European colonialism, prior to any knowledge of modern evolutionary ideas (Chapter 1). Its origin resulted partly from the need of colonial powers to explain the diversity of people and to rationalize their exploitation. Because the concept has its roots in pre-Darwinian thought, it has proved difficult, if not impossible, to apply to a post-Darwinian view of humanity.

One of the most frequently used biological definitions was proposed by Theodosius Dobzhansky in *Mankind Evolving:* races are breeding populations that differ from other populations in their frequency of one or more genetic traits. The next step seems easy: listing the human groups within which breeding occurs. But this task is monumentally difficult; many physical anthropologists believe that races are larger aggregates of populations, synonymous with subspecies, as illustrated by units like sub-Saharan Africans and Europeans.

Most people think of race as large groups composed of many smaller subgroups. Few people off the street would call one population a race. If we were asked, "On what do you base a decision about someone's race?" most of us would say "skin color"; we tend to reduce all the ways in which people differ to one easily noticeable, socially important trait. We confuse sociological races (black, white), groups defined mainly by skin color or other obvious features, with biological races, which at least theoretically are based on breeding patterns. Compounding the problem, the word has also been used to differentiate people in terms of time; the neandertals are designated as a subspecies or race *(H. sapiens neanderthalensis)* of our species in contrast to all modern humans, who are called *H. sapiens sapiens.* The word means many different things to different people and often many things to even one person. It covers units from as small as a breeding population to large clusters of such groups; many people even refer to the "human race," implying we all belong to the same race.

For the time being, let us set aside the dimension of time; understanding the problem as it stands today is difficult enough.

Pure Races The idea of the "pure" race can be laid to rest at once. To meet the condition, humanity would have to consist of long-separated, genetically distinct groups, each group's members having specific features. The pure race would not be mixed with the genes of any other race. This kind of treatment of human variation is built on stereotypes and typologies and implies great homogeneity within a group and great differences between groups (Figure 14.1). Descriptions of a "typical" African or a "typical" Asian are based on this approach. No living individual exhibits all the ideal Nordic characteristics, but those who stereotype people explain this as being due to the mixing of pure races in that person's ancestry. In 1923, Jon Mjoen, a Norwegian anthropologist, in his article "Harmonic and Disharmonic Racecrossings," discussed the "undesirable" consequences of crossing races. He defined Nordic features as tall stature, long skull, narrow, high nose, light complexion, heavy beard, blond hair, blue or light brown eyes, "and above all, the Nordic features." Laplanders have short stature, round skull, broad, flat nose, yellow-gray skin, uneven small beard, black, straight hair, and mongo-

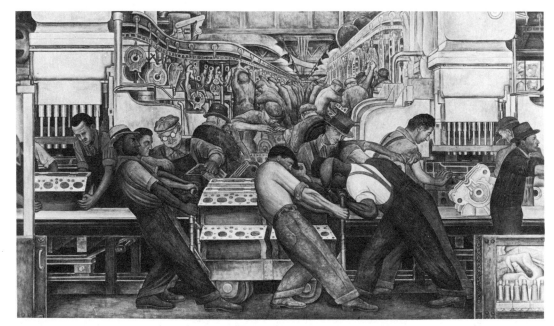

Figure 14.1. *People do not look the same — a fact obvious to us all. But do we want to call them members of different races? Mexican artist Diego Rivera sampled the variety of men in his V-8 Motor Block Machinery assembly fresco (a detail of which is shown here from his extensive work, the* Detroit Industry Murals*). Rivera used as his models actual workers from such diverse places as Bulgaria, England, and Mexico.*

loid features. Having already been unscientifically redundant by defining Nordics as having Nordic features, Mjoen tried to show that crosses between Nordics and Laplanders often resulted in feeblemindedness, drunkenness, and prostitution. After apologetically admitting that light brown eyes are common among Nordics, he attributed the discrepancy to the "mixture between two distant races, the one with blue, the other with black eye color."[1]*

If we could ignore the racism in such statements, we should not miss their completely antievolutionary feeling. Because of the ways in which genetics and evolution operate, it would be nearly impossible to have a completely homogeneous group of people. Mjoen considers all variation within a group to be caused by admixture and looks down on all who deviate from the ideal. Interbreeding does produce variability within a group, but it certainly is not the only source. Even if an invariant population were possible, it would have a very poor evolutionary prognosis, for variation allows populations to benefit by continued adaptation. An unmixed race is impossible because no group has ever gone very long without getting some genes from other populations.

*See page 574 for notes to Chapter 14.

The typologist's definition of race has now been rendered obsolete in biological anthropology, but it lingers on in the way most people think of human variation. We tend to think of an American white, black, Arab, or Jew as looking or behaving a certain way. When doing so, we are creating stereotypes. These stereotypes are based in part, on biological traits and in part on cultural traits. It should be needless to say that not all Jews are good at business dealings and not all blacks have broad lips. Neither cultural nor biological attributes are invariant. Stereotypes are created for a purpose. By classifying all members of a group as being greedy, or brilliant, we generally are supporting some economic or sociopolitical ideology, though we may try to support the stereotype with "science."

Stephen Gould has reported on the sorts of statements that often masquerade as science. One of the nineteenth century's most productive investigators of human variation in cranial capacity was Samuel Morton, a Philadelphia physician. To Morton, the size of a cranial case was a direct correlate of intelligence. Big brain equals smart. Cranial capacity is the internal volume of the braincase and generally approximates brain size. Today, there is no evidence that brain size reflects anything about ability or behavior. Size is more likely to say something about the sex of the skull's owner (women on the average have a smaller cranial capacity) than anything about intelligence. To Morton, however, size was everything and the aim of his work was to document the natural superiority of Western Europeans. Though Morton was purported to be a careful worker, Gould has uncovered many shoddy details in his research. Morton misreported information when it served him: small-brained Europeans were "forgotten." Big-brained non-Europeans were either ignored or became the victims of convenient errors in transcription. Because Morton's work supported a social status quo, it was lauded and went unchecked, to be reported over and over by later researchers. Social divisions along racial lines have often been supported by this type of "scientific" data, and the stereotypes we all have heard are no exceptions.

In physical anthropology, we are not dealing with the sociological view of race, based on stereotypes, but rather with a biological interpretation of populations. Biologically, we are interested in variation within as well as between groups; sociologically, only the variation between groups counts.

Biological and sociological ideas about race do not necessarily coincide, as Gabriel Lasker and Bernice Kaplan found in Peru. Racial names are used there to describe differences in class. The three major classifications are white, mestizo (mixed Spanish-Indian), and Indian. The researchers found little correlation between a person's sociological classification and biological ancestry. In the towns they studied, the European forms of a trait, such as wavy hair, seldom show up in people who consider themselves white.

Stanley Garn has tried to alleviate some of the semantic problems by tightening the definition of biological race. He proposed three specific terms: geographic race, local race, and microrace.

Geographic Race, Local Race, and Microrace

Geographic, or continental, races are the large groupings we usually think of: sub-Saharan Africans, Australian Aborigines, Native Americans. Local races are much like the breeding populations that Dobzhansky considered; Garn calls Eskimo, Ainu, Hawaiians, and East Africans local races. Most microraces are found in densely populated areas and are maintained as distinct units by geography or behavior. American blacks in Detroit are genetically different from blacks in Charleston, South Carolina, in spite of the genetic continuity between them. Microraces also refer to groups living in one area but not interbreeding because of cultural differences. That description generally fits blacks and whites in a large city.

Garn's three racial divisions are an appealing simplification, but some groups of people do not fit neatly into any one category. Native Americans are called a geographic race, like Asiatics, Europeans, and sub-Saharan Africans; yet they are genetically much closer to Asiatics than to the other groups. Garn's groupings do not reflect evolutionary relationships, for each geographic race is not equally different from all the other geographic races.

If the Crow and Navaho Indians are separate local races, how do we classify the Hidatsa Indians? These people constitute a separate tribe that often, but not always, interbreeds with the Crow. Because of mating, the Hidatsa are genetically more similar to the Crow than to the Navaho. If we call each of the three tribes a local race, we obscure the fact that two of the tribes commonly interbreed. Because the Crow and Hidatsa mate more often with each other than with the Navaho, these two groups should be placed closer together taxonomically.

This breakdown proves to be very artificial; similarities and differences between groupings of people do not fit into neat categories or levels of analysis. We can find myriad levels at which to study differences between groups. Garn established small, medium, and large races; we could just as easily set up tiny, small, medium, and large classes, or six classes, or twelve, or, as Dobzhansky did, only one.

In response to the Dobzhansky and Garn definitions that accord to a single population the status of a race, French anthropologist Jean Hiernaux asks, "Will we equate the concept of race with that of the breeding population?" and answers that "one word is enough for one thing."[2] Races to Hiernaux are groupings of populations.

The Individual Population — A Race?

Frank Livingstone partly agrees with Hiernaux. In his article "On the Nonexistence of Human Races," he says it is impossible to divide a single species into meaningful groups larger than populations. Since Livingstone does not consider populations to be races, races thus do not exist. He thinks the word "race" would have validity only if it could be applied to natural clusters of geographically and biologically distinct populations. It is not valid to apply the word to artificial groupings. As such, races of people do not exist, he believes. He would not call sub-Saharans a race, for instance, because the desert is not an effective barrier to gene flow; sub-Saharan Africans do not constitute a distinct, natural cluster of populations. "An analysis of the populations and/or genes in the Sahara Desert," he says, "certainly indicates that the desert is not a major reproductive barrier," and it was even less so in the past.[3]

Livingstone suggests that if races really exist, the variable traits should vary together: if a population is 10 percent "Negro" in one characteristic, it should be 10 percent "Negro" for all other traits. But Ethiopia, for example, has dark-skinned peoples without kinky hair and lighter-skinned populations with kinky hair. Peter Workman and others found that the frequency of the sickle-cell allele in American blacks is less similar to the frequency of that allele in Africa than are the frequencies of other genetic characteristics; the ABO allele frequencies are more alike in West Africans and American blacks than are the sickle-cell frequencies.

From these two examples it is apparent that the concept of race fails to fit biological reality.

Ethnic Group   Ashley Montagu says races are supposed to be "groups of human beings comprised of individuals each of whom possesses a certain aggregate of characters which individually and collectively serve to distinguish them from the individuals in all other groups."[4] Because there is always variability within human groups, human groups do not fit this definition and hence there are no races.

Montagu also feels the term "race" is artificial and burdened with false connotations. He substitutes genogroup and ethnic group. The former term comes out of scientific jargon and the latter from lay usage. Although Montagu acknowledges that ethnic refers to cultural rather than biological phenomena, he says that his is an intentional device to make the problem manageable. Everyone has an emotional reaction to the word, but nobody understands what a race is. Montagu believes that a neutral word helps clear the air of harmful connotations. He defines an ethnic group as "one of a number of populations . . . which individually maintain their differences, physical and cultural, by means of isolating mechanisms such as geographic and social barriers." Essentially, we are back where we started. Does changing a word change the way people view human differences? Would it matter to a bigot preaching hatred whether it is called a race or an ethnic group? And a statement like "races don't exist; only ethnic groups exist" is highly misleading when it turns out that ethnic group is a synonym for race.

Lack of   More definitions of race or denials of its existence are unnecessary, for
Agreement   our point is clear. Anthropologists agree that people live in populations

and that populations exhibit internal variation as well as differences among groups. Few anthropologists today would say that the layperson's view of race (Mongoloids, Caucasoids, and so on) has any biological reality. Species are the only true taxa (and even those are sometimes questionable). Theoretically we can decide that two animals are *conspecifics* if they are actively or potentially interbreeding. We have no such hard-and-fast test for determining membership in one or another race.

Racial ideas are a vestige of the typological approach to variation. Instead of studying human variation as ranges of variation and gradual geographic shifting in frequencies of traits, the classic racial approach emphasizes homogeneity within the group and heterogeneity among groups. Even the lay vocabulary (white, black) reflects this emphasis. We tend to see only what our culture teaches us to see (Figures 14.2–14.11). Many talk of sub-Saharan Africans as a race characterized by deeply

Figure 14.2. An Eskimo graduating class in Alaska.
   The photographs in this chapter show not only how different people look in different parts of the world, but also that within what is commonly called a race, many visible traits can vary greatly. Look carefully at the faces in group photos and decide for yourself whether a typological approach to human variation fits the real situation: do all the members of any group look the same? These photographs by no means capture all populational variability; many regions are not represented. Instead, these pictures highlight a small portion of humanity's variability.

Figure 14.3. A Sioux Indian woman and a Pueblo Indian girl.

pigmented skin; yet the skin color of some members of this group (San Bushmen and some Pygmies) is quite different, being yellowish.

The word "race" therefore arouses several objections: (1) populations are not the same as races; (2) race is a loaded word; (3) races have no biological reality; (4) races are often typological; and (5) race is a very vague word.

Ethics and Sociological Races

The sociological interpretation of race and the associated phenomenon of racism have exacted a terrible biological cost. The best-known example is the millions of lost lives during Adolf Hitler's rule. But the United States too has frightening, though more subtle, examples of how much racial discrimination costs.

A white child born in the United States in 1979 could expect to live to be about 74 years old; a black child born then could expect to live about 70 years. Four years does not sound like much of a difference unless they happen to come from your own life expectancy. Let us look at the statistics in another way. In 1979 this country had about 25 million blacks. On the average each will live 4 years less than if he or she were white. These people, and American society, will lose 100 million years of human life and productivity to discrimination based on an inaccurate view of human variability. Culture and biology do interact, sometimes with appalling results.

Figure 14.4. *Part of the group that was responsible for the discovery of the* Choukoutien Homo erectus *fossils (Chapter 10), including Franz Weidenreich, a female assistant, and several Chinese men.*

What alternative to race do we have for looking at human variation? One that has been used quite successfully is the cline. As mentioned in Chapter 11, a cline is regular variation in a trait over space shown by the alteration in the frequency of one or more traits from population to neighboring population. In Chapter 11 we saw that the frequencies of the ABO alleles form two clines through Europe and Asia: the frequency of A decreases as one travels east and at the same time the frequency of B rises.

In Chapter 12 we noted that a similar situation exists in Africa and Europe for skin color: there is no one place where dark skin abruptly gives way to lightly pigmented skin. For many other traits, too, anthropologists have shifted from a desire to form typologies to a desire to explain observed variation, and the clinal approach has come to be much more useful than a racial approach.

If one is interested in explaining why a particular trait varies in a certain way, as we have been in this book, it makes much more sense to look at the actual distribution of that particular trait. Rather than studying a whole series of traits at once and then trying to explain this complex, we have considered one trait at a time.

By noting changing environmental conditions over space (amount of sunlight, malaria, etc.) or by taking into account known population movements, it has proved possible to develop and test hypotheses about the causes of a clinal distribution. The clinal approach to human variation is preferable to a racial analysis in many ways, because it is closer

The Cline: An Alternative to Race

Figure 14.5. A group of Japanese men.

Figure 14.6. An Ainu group from Japan, photographed at the St. Louis Exposition.

to reality. Intentionally or not, the word "race" stresses similarities within groups and differences between groups. The word "cline," besides having no connotations, has the advantage of being based on the frequencies of specific traits, and implies acknowledgment that not everyone in a group exhibits a specific form of a trait. Clinal analysts look for trends, increases or decreases in frequency, from population to population. They account for several groups' sharing a characteristic, when the characteristic is more common in some groups than in others.

The clinal approach can be very useful for understanding the distribution of a trait over space. Anthropologists continue to be interested in the history of the population, not just in a trait. While such a desire was often seen in racial studies, it was directed toward the end of classifying people according to stereotypes. Now we seek to understand better the genetic and evolutionary forces at work on human groups.

Studying What Is

The unraveling of biological history has come into a new age as is well exemplified by work on a South American Indian tribe, the Yanomama (Figure 14.9). A large, multi-disciplinary crew of scientists has been trying to document the structure and functioning of this tribe for several decades, not only to understand these people in particular, but to understand the forces that may have shaped the evolution of many earlier human populations. For hundreds of generations the social organization of human populations roughly approximated aspects of life that are still seen in modern, pre-literate, pre-agricultural peoples. In large measure, the work on the Yanomama and other South American tribes is a salvage operation, for there are very few groups still untouched by Western culture. Studies of these people must go on now for soon there will no longer be the opportunity to learn from them.

Biological History of the Yanomama

The Yanomama are living in the Brazil-Venezuela border region. There are about 50 villages, each with a population of 50 to 200 people. Most villages are several days walk from the nearest neighbor. However, there are clusters of villages which regularly interact with each other. About every three to five years, each village must move as the soil becomes infertile or as a result of deteriorating relationships among the inhabitants. Living in an inaccessible tropical rain forest, they were first contacted by Westerners on a continuing basis in the 1950s.

That the Yanomama are isolated genetically can be seen by examining their gene pool and those of neighboring groups like the Guaymi. There are alleles present in the Yanomama gene pool which are lacking in neighboring tribes, and vice versa. Evidently, different mutations have appeared in different tribes. The concentration of these relatively newly arisen alleles in different tribes implies that gene flow between tribes is not very great.

Within the tribe, the story is different. The general rule is to marry a cousin living within the same village. These marriages are arranged so as to pay off much as in our society when a person wants to marry into the "right" family. As the Yanomama are polygynous — a male may have more than one wife — a complex web of social relations develops. Mar-

Figure 14.7. Aborigines from the Northern Territory, Australia.

riage usually involves people residing in the same village. However, one of the marriage partners may have recently migrated into the community. Thus, villages within a cluster are united in part by marriages.

Genetic relatedness between villages also exists because of the manner by which new villages appear. When struggles for leadership or

Figure 14.8. A Kikuyu (Bantu) group in Kenya.

women start to boil, the village splinters or "fissions." The loser in the power struggle and some of his relatives are forced to pack up and move out, forming a new settlement. Sometimes the offshoot group may rejoin the parent village, a case of village fusion. A similar sort of group splintering has been documented by James Hurd for a religious isolate, the Amish, living in central Pennsylvania. Here, when tensions rose within the group, fissioning took the form of a reorganization of church attendance. The end result, the formation of a new group within which people were related, was the same in Pennsylvania and in the Amazon.

The Yanomama are not a particularly peaceable people and one rather common activity is raiding for women. If a woman is taken from a nearby village, she is apt to be genetically related to her captor, at least to some degree as a result of past village fissioning. She may later be captured from her new home and moved to yet another village. There is also an appreciable level of raiding for women over long distances. This movement of women has great significance for the effect of migration on the genetic structure of the Yanomama.

Inbreeding is quite high among the Yanomama for several reasons.

Figure 14.9. *Several Yanomama Indians along with the anthropologist Napoleon Chagnon.*

For starters, the non-random nature of village fissioning leads to the formation of new settlements largely composed of genetic relatives. When marriage occurs between these people, inbreeding results (see page 95). Inbreeding is also very high among the Yanomama because of the uneven genetic contributions of different men to the next generation. Some powerful men produce many offspring because they have many wives. Those with lesser social standing have fewer wives and children. As much of one generation is sired by a small part of the previous generation, there is an increased likelihood of relatives mating with each other.

It has been speculated that if differences in social power are at all related to genetic differences — for instance, if men with genes for intellectual skills are those who manage to accumulate power and wives — this relationship would provide an opportunity for natural selection to work. Those with genes for intelligence would have more offspring and the frequency of these genes would increase. Whether this tie between intelligence and reproduction exists, however, is not demonstrated.

This sort of population data on the Yanomama provides a highly detailed view of the biological and cultural features which shaped the genetic structure of the tribe. With this sort of data, we are in a better position to assess the importance of the various evolutionary forces operating on the people. The degree to which cultural features like fissioning have been important in other tribal peoples may never be known. Yet, by carefully deciphering the history of the Yanomama, we at least get to see the sorts of factors that may have been operating on other human populations, and thereby may better understand the origins of variation within and between human populations.

Population Relations

Population dynamics and relationships on a larger scale were often dealt with in terms of race, but here again there are newer ways of looking at the degrees of similarity or difference between groups. In Chapter 5, comparative computer analysis of molecules in different species were described as a way of producing evolutionary trees. A similar approach can be taken in trying to assay the relationships between populations of humans. Rather than using amino acids or nucleotide sequences as data, the computer can analyze gene frequencies. Populations with similar frequencies of an allele are classed as being more closely related.

Newton Morton has lately reanalyzed the question of genetic kinship of Jewish populations in different parts of the world. The HLA system alleles can be particularly useful in judging group relations. As HLA has many different alleles, it can be reasonably assumed that two groups with similar arrays of alleles at similar frequencies share a recent common ancestor. It would be quite a coincidence to be very similar by accident.

Morton gathered information on HLA alleles in a variety of Jewish populations scattered around the world. Comparable data also were gathered for non-Jewish neighbors in each area. When the figures were

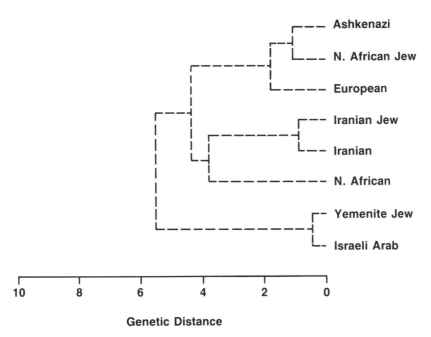

Figure 14.10. *A statistically derived tree, based on allele frequencies, showing the degrees of genetic similarity between eight populations.*

compared, it appeared that Jews in an area are more like their neighbors than they are like Jews elsewhere in the world. This indicates that the Jewish populations have had a significant degree of admixture with their neighbors for many years. Likewise, analysis of blood groups and polymorphic proteins points to the same conclusion. Figure 14.10 is a diagram of genetic similarity for four Jewish and four gentile populations. The Ashkenazim (Jews of northern Europe) cluster with North African Jews and European non-Jews. The two groups from Iran are most similar to each other, while the Yemeni Jews and Israeli Arabs are most alike. The genetic data are in accord with nonbiological information such as historical documents.

Molecules can be useful for comparing species or populations. So, too, with anatomical traits. Much of hominid evolution is analyzed by looking at teeth. Some prefer to try to judge genetic relations of populations by looking at teeth and the like. The size of teeth has clear adaptive significance, since bigger teeth are important where elaborate food preparation techniques are not present. Big teeth make up for the lack of cultural methods to process food.

C. Loring Brace and Robert Hinton used tooth size to measure the relatedness of people living in the Pacific Ocean. The first people to move into the Pacific were, they say, the big-toothed ancestors of modern, big-toothed native Australians and some New Guineans (see Figure 14.11a). Later, small-toothed peoples moved further out into the Pacific from Asia,

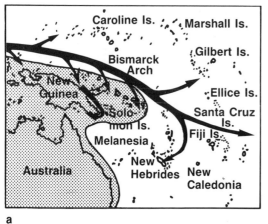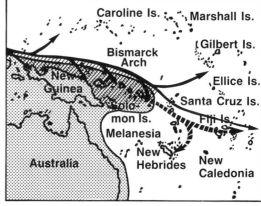

a   b

Figure 14.11. (a) The arrow indicates the proposed migration of small-toothed people into Melanesia and Polynesia. The stippled area had been previously populated by large-toothed people. (b) The diagonal line shaded region shows a cline today for tooth size. The broken arrow plots the presumed movement of hybrid populations into eastern Melanesia.

colonizing the islands of Melanesia and Polynesia whose modern inhabitants have small teeth. Where the two groups met and interbred, people with intermediate-sized teeth appeared. For this intermediate group, the size of the teeth reflects the amount of interbreeding. The map (Figure 14.11b) shows a cline today resulting from degrees of admixture. Small teeth in Melanesia and Polynesia grade into the big teeth of South New Guineans and Australians. The history which Brace and Hinton reconstruct agrees with cultural and linguistic evidence on population affinities in this area.

Again, we see an attempt to understand human variation in an evolutionary dynamic framework as opposed to the stereotypic, static view that goes with racial analysis.

Summary This chapter has dealt with several methods and concepts that are emphasized in trying to uncover biological history. One of the earliest and most debated concepts was race. We have considered some of the anthropological controversy over "race." As we've seen, anthropologists have offered an assortment of definitions, but there is no unanimity on the validity of any of these postures. Some say a race is a population, others say races should be larger groupings. Some say a race is a cluster of populations, others say such groupings have no biological reality. Some say the word is emotionally loaded and propose other words, but this does not affect the definitional problem. We now feel that biological races simply do not exist and that race is an arbitrary and biologically unrealistic way to consider human variability. It means many different things to different people and can even mean several things to one person.

Clouding the biological usage of the word are its sociological connotations. All physical anthropologists agree that (1) there are no pure races and (2) populations of people do vary a lot.

Whether we are looking at human variability today or in the past, it is more helpful to look at traits as they are actually distributed in the real world instead of at stereotypes that exist only in someone's mind. As Dobzhansky has said, "The only way to simplify nature is to study it as it is, not as we would have liked it to be." For this reason, the clinal approach has proved to be much more useful than the racial approach in answering questions about human variability.

For questions of relatedness between groups, we can now use rather sophisticated computer programs to generate trees showing genetic similarity from allele data. History can also be studied by reference to anatomical data and, of course, archaeology, written documents, and so on. The detailed knowledge of evolutionary force at work in small isolated groups like the Yanomama also proves invaluable in trying to understand the origins and maintenance of human variability.

Chapter 15

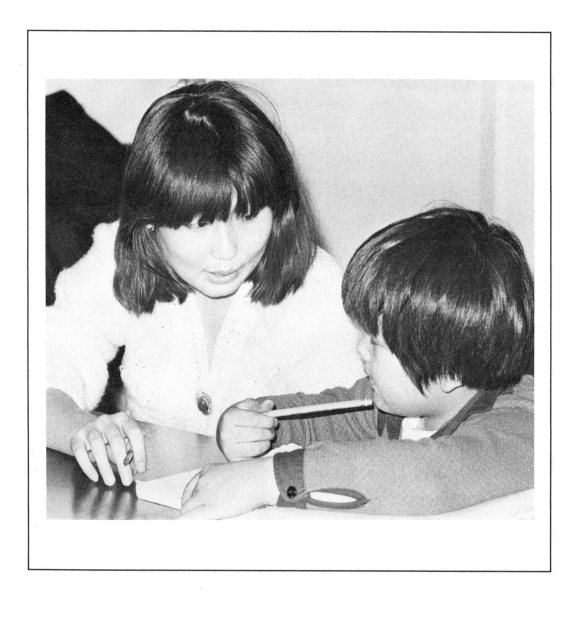

Prospects and Perspectives

This book has been devoted to one task: making human evolutionary history clear. How, why, when, and where did we evolve, and in what ways are we evolving today? These are not purely theoretical questions, to be regarded as merely an intellectual exercise. The better we understand our biochemical, anatomical, and behavioral evolution, the better equipped we will be to deal with problems in today's world.

We shall have to appreciate our present cultural and biological variability if we are to run health care and other social services effectively and make new environmental and foreign aid programs work; these must not be done without thorough knowledge of a people's biological and cultural heritage. Constantly coming into contact with people from other cultures or American subcultures other than our own, we need all the understanding we can get about how people function and behave.

Willingness to talk about human variation without assuming that differences imply inferiority or superiority is vital; knowing the facts covered in this book will help. Evolutionary theory tells us that the reasons for variation often can be found in adaptation. This truth, distorted by equating difference with inequality, has led to much needless misunderstanding, discrimination, and suffering.

We must be willing to admit too that humans are animals, evolving animals, and that all humans are like one another and like other living things. Not only are we not outside the web of nature, we are very much a part of it. The millions of years of genetic adaptation that lie behind us are the evolutionary legacy that affects how we look and act today. This past has made us able to modify the environment by cultural activity. Without our large brain, dexterous hands, and bipedalism human cultures would not exist. Although the relationships are exceedingly complex, it was selection for cultural capabilities that produced many of these anatomical traits.

This reasoning, circular though it is, still is not incorrect. The cultural and biological effects of using tools evolved in a mutually reinforcing relationship, a feedback loop. We can say the same about our linguistic abilities, too. At a microevolutionary level, evidence shows that gene pools are being altered by cultural activities. An example is the appearance of malaria in Africa, which is tied to the development of agriculture. The spreading of disease led to selection for the sickle-cell allele. In turn, a genetic change can produce cultural innovation. When sickle-cell anemia appeared, a search for a medical treatment was begun.

Human culture and biology are inextricably interwoven today as they have been for millions of years. The interacting system is so complex and old that a change in one sphere may tremendously affect the other.

Yet these ideas are by no means universally recognized. Many feel that human beings, the technologically sophisticated groups in particular, are not a part of nature. Because we know how to exploit the physical world for economic gain today, they think, we can blithely continue to do so, never paying for the consequences. This is, beyond all doubt, a disastrous way of looking at humans and nature. Animals, including humans, need a reasonably unpolluted air supply. Our food has to be nutritious, and cannot be contaminated with harmful additives and insecticides. We need clear water and adequate shelter, just like other animals.

Certainly human activities have affected the environment from our beginnings, and however simple or complex a culture's organization, it alters the environment as it adapts. After all, what we evolved to do best is to modify our surroundings. Complex technological societies undoubtedly affect the world in ways we have not even imagined, yet few of us would be willing to revert to gatherer and hunter economies to stop disrupting the environment. Even if we took such a major step, because the human is a biological organism we would probably not be better off. The return of disease and famine would undoubtedly offset much of the benefit of clean air. Modern medicine, insecticides, and power plants are cultural adaptations designed to make it easier to get along in our environment. Compare the life expectancy in parts of Asia (less than 30 years) with ours (close to 70), and you see that many Western cultural adaptations have their usefulness.

We will surely have to keep producing energy, pest controls, manufactured goods, and the rest to retain our standards of living and health. We cannot forget, though, that when fulfillment of these needs opposes our biological requirements, we will need great forbearance and much knowledge and wisdom. Nature will not allow humans to forget that we have biological as well as cultural requirements.

Behavior Patterns from Primates to Humans

The biological necessities that modern humans live with, the strong relationships that bind us to the rest of the living world and to the resources of the planet itself, all are clearly visible. In recent years, scholars have looked with great interest back into human evolution to find the reasons for modern human behavior. They have pointed to the small groups that are universal in primate societies, showing how that pattern carried through into hominid evolution and suggesting that it may have deeply marked modern human biology. Others have stressed hunting's importance in human evolution, and the selection for aggressiveness it may have caused.

Aggression, Hunting, and Killing

The anatomist Raymond Dart, who was responsible for describing the first australopithecine fossil, the Taung child, is convinced that the hominids' origin and early evolution came about when weapons for killing prey were invented. Dart argues for a "predatory transition between ape and man" — that the hominids were adapted mostly as carnivores. The dramatist Robert Ardrey later expanded on Dart's proposal, suggesting that hunting became integral in human behavior because evolutionary selection favored individuals better able to handle hunting activities. The most skilled hunters would be selected for, the behaviors of killing would become part of the neurological system, and in time every hominid male would be genetically endowed with the killing instinct.[1]*

The relationship of killing and aggression in modern humans to the evolution of hunting is hotly debated; there are no clear-cut answers. The archaeological evidence at Bed 1 at Olduvai Gorge holds many animal skeletons, including several large mammals. No one can tell whether the australopithecines hunted and killed these mammals or found them dead and butchered them. We also know nothing about how much hunted animal meat the early hominids included in their diet. The early hominids, like living nonagricultural peoples, may have lived on vegetable foods, gathered small animals, and filled out their diet by hunting larger animals. But we need more evidence to clarify such a hypothesis. Associating the hunting way of life with aggressive instincts in modern human beings is still an uncertain approach. There are other scientists who believe that human aggression is genetically based, but that something other than hunting may be responsible for this trait (Figure 15.1).

Aggression in Other Vertebrates

The Nobel Prize-winning ethologist Konrad Lorenz suggested in *On Aggression* that aggressive behavior is commonly found in many vertebrates, that among other things it efficiently spaces members of a species far enough from each other to exploit the environment or select mates. Lorenz considers aggressive behavior in these animals to be adaptive because it is ritualized and because there are ritualized behaviors that will stop an aggressive encounter. But human aggression, he thinks, is maladaptive, because hominids have not evolved ritualized terminating behaviors.

The American psychiatrist David Hamburg has examined aggressive behavior in other vertebrates, in particular the nonhuman primates. He suggests that aggressive behaviors in the savanna baboons and the chimpanzees are very similar to those in modern human beings. He believes that a male sex hormone, testosterone, may be at least partly re-

*See page 575 for notes to Chapter 15.

Figure 15.1. *To what degree, if any, is human aggression a function of our genes?*

sponsible for a high frequency of aggressive behavior in male baboons, chimpanzees, and humans.[2] Recent studies with ground-living monkeys demonstrate that males have more testosterone in their blood just after fighting than during other activities; this chemical may in some way trigger centers in the brain for aggressive behavior. The studies on testosterone levels in the blood of monkeys did not show whether the presence of this secretion in the blood initiated the aggression, or whether the fighting itself stimulated its production.[3] Some have suggested that male aggression is related to genes carried on the Y chromosome (see page 553).

Lorenz and Hamburg think of human aggression as part of a general pattern seen in other animals. It may have been emphasized in hominid evolution by reliance on hunting, but hunting is not its cause. Jane Goodall's observations of chimpanzees reveal that frustration is one of the major triggers for aggression in these animals. And many psychologists believe that frustration may be the most important cause of aggression in modern humans. They do question how much genetics has to do with this behavior. Some sociologists, cultural anthropologists, and psychologists feel that aggression in people is produced by social deprivation, childhood maladjustment, mental illness, or other social factors. It may be that all these proposals are valid, that human aggression is an exceedingly complex behavior with many roots. Certainly an understanding of this human behavior is one of the greatest problems facing the modern social and life sciences.

Seeking an explanation for the presence of a behavior such as aggression in modern humans leads to the consideration of many different lines of evidence. One promising area of study in our attempts to understand more fully the roots of many modern human behaviors and actions is sociobiology. As we have seen in Chapter 7, sociobiology relates behavior to the differential transmission of particular alleles from one generation to the next.

Sociobiology and the Evolution of Human Behavior

Sociobiologists argue that the evolution of many human behaviors can be understood only in the context of how they contributed to the successful transmission to succeeding generations of one allele over its alternatives. It has been suggested that human sociality, kinship and family ties, and sexuality, among many other behaviors, can be better understood and explained within a sociobiological context.

For example, a recent book by Donald Symons examines the evolution of human sexuality from a sociobiological perspective.[4] Symons suggests that in order to insure that their genes are represented in the next generation, human males and females employ different reproductive strategies. According to Symons, it is more successful for males to have as many children as possible, since their biological investment in each child is rather limited. Therefore, the male strategy is to attempt to have sexual relations with many different females, in this way insuring that the particular alleles they are carrying will be passed on to the succeeding generation. In contrast, females make a much greater biological investment when having children, not only during the prolonged pregnancy, but also during the early years of infant dependency. Thus, the way by which females insure that their alleles will be represented in the next generation is by devoting considerable energy and effort to each offspring. Symons notes that while it is in the best interests of the female to form an attachment with a male, in order to assist in child care, it is in the best interest of the male to maintain independence and be able to impregnate as many females as possible. In this view, the conflicting interests of male and female reproductive strategies have led to difficulties in male-female relationships and can explain, Symons believes, the differing notions about sexual behavior held by men and women in our society. In sum, Symons has proposed an idea which attempts to relate sociobiological concepts of differential transmission of particular alleles between generations to patterns of sexual behavior. Symons has been criticized by some anthropologists, who maintain that human sexual behavior is not only exceedingly complex, but that there are also considerable differences among human societies.[5] They argue that it is currently very difficult to demonstrate links between specific genes and particular behaviors, such as sexual activities, and that it is much more realistic to propose that the flexible behavioral patterns of humans are the result of social learning, rather than being biologically determined.

Whatever the outcome of this argument, it is clear that sociobiological explanations for human behavior will continue to be employed in our attempt to understand human activities.

Primate and Human Social Groups

All higher primates except the orang live in social groups. These aggregations vary greatly in their size and structure, but continual interaction with other members of the species is essential to the higher primates' existence, and may be necessary for their well-being. Our primate ancestors probably have been organized into social groups for at least 40 million years, long before the origin of the family Hominidae. But is group living genetically determined? All we can say is that all human beings known to us live in social groups, and although they are quite variable in composition and size, they are certainly a universal of human behavior.

How Primates Learn

In both nonhuman primate societies and human groups, the young learn how to be social animals in the same way. Young primates learn social behaviors by watching how adults in their group act (pages 228–230), and by imitating and practicing these behaviors in play groups among young animals of similar age and development. These peer play groups appear to be a subgroup within the larger primate social unit, where young animals can practice and perfect their developing muscular coordination and social skills. By learning from the behavior of adult animals, the young are socialized and thus can later successfully interact with other members of the group. Adult primates are rather lenient toward immature animals and will tolerate inappropriate behaviors (tail pulling, attempts at fighting) directed at them by young animals. If the youngsters persist, of course, the adult may reach the end of its patience and stop the nonsense by a judicious slap or bite.

Human Learning

In modern human groups there is a tendency for young children to form peer groups, and although the activities of these groups can be greatly varied, including rough-and-tumble play and solitary games, much of the behavior is directed toward developing adult skills and roles. N. G. Blurton

Jones, observing nursery school children in Britain, reports that "children in nursery school spend much time simulating adult occupations in their play ('Firemen,' 'Policemen,' 'Shops,' 'Offices,' 'Tea Parties').''[6] Anthropologists report similar behavior patterns in nonwestern societies. They find especially interesting the ways of transmitting important behavior from one generation to the next. The cultural anthropologist Gladys Reichard points out:

> One reason why it is difficult to study . . . education [in nonwestern societies] is that one method used to teach . . . is intangible. It is a method as old as the life of man but one which our self-conscious analysts often forget: simply that children do not do what adults *tell* them to do, but rather what they see adults *do*. [Nonwestern] people do not lay stress on telling. In many languages, the word for "teach" is the same as the word for "show," and the synonymity is literal. One of the things which amuses natives . . . is the habit . . . [anthropologists] have of asking questions: "What are you going to do next?" "What are you doing that for?" The craftsman or hunter always knows what he is going to do next, but he may not be able to give orally the reason for doing it . . . all these things . . . [a] child picks up by constant observation and by imitation.[7]

Human and Primate Learning in Childhood

This pattern of learning is quite similar to that of the nonhuman primates. In our complex technological society, much of the skill demanded in many professions is so complicated and known by so few people that we have to have specialists to tell the young how to perform these tasks. Even in modern Western society, however, children continue to learn patterns of behavior — roles, actions used in dealing with other people, standards of moral behavior, clan and family relationships — and general tasks like cooking, driving, and speech, by observation and imitation.

The ancient (in the evolutionary sense) primate patterns of learning are continued in modern human groups. They form one foundation holding together the social group: the children's ability to learn the behaviors of the adults in the society, and to become fully socialized members of their group, able to interact successfully with other members.

An important distinction between the hominids and other higher primates is the length of childhood. Many primates reach adulthood by the fifth or sixth year; it usually takes the hominids twice as long. We have evidence that even early hominids, the australopithecines, went through a long childhood dependency like that of modern human beings. This prolongation of childhood in the hominids seems to be related to the amount of learned behavior that must be communicated to the younger generation. Hominid evolution is closely related to toolmaking and other complex behaviors. Acquiring the skills needed to perform these tasks would take more time, extending childhood (Figure 15.2).

The primates' biological basis of learning, involving rates of growth and development of body and brain and muscular coordination, is so

Figure 15.2. *The long human childhood period provides many opportunities for learning.*

complex that we cannot tell just how much of it is genetically determined. When we do know the genetic determinants, we will probably find them built into an extremely complex system of genes.

The Small Group in Human Evolution

The hominids may have retained the basic higher primate patterns of learning because of their evolution as gatherers and hunters living in small groups.

How our long history as gatherers and hunters has affected us we have just begun to learn. Only 10,000 years ago, after the hominids had spent countless ages gathering and hunting, was this economic system radically changed by the invention and spread of agriculture and animal domestication. Some biological features may have evolved earlier than agriculture to adapt hominid groups to a small-group, nonsettled way of living. In a small group of gatherers and hunters, the primate learning system of observation, imitation, and practice would have been efficient. In the nonhuman primates and modern human beings, the young observe adults physically close to them; in small groups, every adult comes into visual contact with the young individual, and thus patterns of behavior of the whole group may be observed by the youngster. As an adult, the individual shares with all others in the group the behaviors necessary for getting along in the society. This pattern evolved in the higher primates and continued in hominid evolution because the economic limitations of gathering and hunting kept them from forming larger, more complex aggregations. Agriculture, however, established a new economic base, making way for larger human groups in settled, permanent locations. In larger groups, the young human being continues to learn by observation and imitation, but can no longer observe all the adults in the society. The young see only the behaviors of the adults with whom they are in immediate contact.

In most agricultural societies, behavioral differences have developed among the social, economic, religious, and professional subgroups within the larger society. Because a child raised in such a group will not learn the normative behaviors of all segments of the society, as an adult the individual will come into contact with other members of the society where patterns of interaction will not be completely successful. Sociologists have said much about the difficulties a person may have in establishing rapport with other members of the same society who have different social, economic, or other backgrounds. Human biologists have seen a pattern like this in the choice of marriage partners in the United States. The chances are high that a person in the United States will marry someone with very similar background. Some choices, of course, are made by conscious decisions. Others, however, reflect the fact that individuals with similar backgrounds will be more likely to establish an intimate, meaningful relationship; in a word, they will have more in common. Our evolutionary heritage as primates may influence our behavior even in choosing our marriage partners, and may be the reason for assortative mating (see Chapter 12), which helps maintain genetic diversity among subgroups.

Modern Society Versus Human Biology

Primate learning patterns raise a question that preoccupies many social and biological scientists. Is modern *Homo sapiens* adapted to the densely populated, specialized, technological environment in which most of us live? Many scientists believe that our complex society has placed serious stresses on modern humans. Because these may profoundly influence the future of our species, we should explore some of the proposals. Although these ideas have not been fully demonstrated, they show one more contribution that physical anthropology can make toward a more fundamental understanding of humans.

The feedback system that has related biology and culture through much of hominid evolution obviously reflects successful behavior (see page 278). *Homo erectus* was able to expand to many parts of the world, surviving in hostile environments by applying learned behavior to the problems these habitats presented. Later these abilities led to agriculture, specialization, and complex systems of communication and transportation. Now human beings can survive in large numbers in just about any part of the world.

One reason for a primate group's continued survival is the conservatism of their behaviors (see page 232). Innovation generates new behaviors, but not quickly. In a primate society, the behaviors of one generation are those of the next, the continuity providing for successful interaction between younger and older adults; the group maintains some stability. From the archaeological record we have indirect evidence that this conservatism continued through most of hominid evolution. In the past few hundred years, technological development has speeded up, accelerating markedly in the past seventy years.

Technological elaboration has profoundly changed the social system. Children still learn by observation and imitation, but soon realize that some behaviors they learn from adults are not appropriate to their experience. For generations, a female's role as housewife and mother has been considered a full-time occupation; few other jobs were considered socially acceptable: schoolteacher, secretary, stewardess, nurse. The traditional role was communicated during the child's socialization: acceptable play involved "house," "dolls," "nurse." Little girls observed and imitated their mothers' behaviors, and, by the age of three, nursery school children, asked what they wanted to be when they grew up, responded by naming the traditional occupations: mommy, dancer, nurse, teacher. These behaviors have been profoundly altered by two technological innovations: controlled fertility and labor-saving household machinery. Recent advances in contraception have permitted a woman to limit her family's size; the machinery has significantly reduced the time it takes to maintain a house. Women now have a freedom unknown one or two generations ago. Women see themselves differently and reevaluate the roles they learned were theirs in the society, roles still accepted by most of their mothers. These and other changes in behavior have made it hard for adults of one generation to interact successfully with adults of an older generation. The "generation gap" is not new to modern human societies, but it has increased in the past three or four generations.

Sex Roles   Additional questions about sex roles have emerged with great force over the past few years. Why do men and women behave differently? Why, in most societies, do men wield so much more public power than women? Must this state of affairs persist?

Many parallels can be drawn between these questions and the ones raised in Chapter 12 in reference to IQ and race. Some have looked for biological explanations, others have looked at environmental and cultural factors, while still others have considered biocultural phenomena. A complete consideration of the topic would require a book in itself;

thus, we will have to limit the discussion to but a glimpse of the subtleties involved.

Those who feel that the sex roles are not subject to alteration often look to the "nature" side of the picture. As in the IQ controversy, it is felt that if biology accounts for behavioral differences between males and females, nothing can be done to change things. Neither should anything be done, for to do so would be to go against nature. Within this perspective several different lines of evidence have been presented. One deals with a behavior that we generally presume to be a masculine trait — aggression — seeking to find its origin directly in the genes.

As we know, males have an X and a Y chromosome while women have two X's. If males are more aggressive, then the genetic underpinnings, it is reasoned, are on the Y chromosome. Thus, men who are XYY (pages 57–60) may be more aggressive than normal males. Many studies have been carried out to find whether this is in fact true. Most have been based on the argument that XYY males, if they are more aggressive, will commit antisocial acts more often than XY males. If this is true, then XYY's should be disproportionately common in special institutions, jails, and hospitals for the criminally insane. Some of the research has found this to be the case, especially for security hospitals. Adherents of this line have gone as far as saying "the urge to violence may be inborn — may be traced . . . to the Y chromosome."[8]

Such data require deeper examination. Does the extra Y chromosome cause antisocial, highly aggressive behavior? The answer seems to be "not necessarily." The association is not between XYY and aggression but between XYY and incarceration. Because confinement results from legal proceedings and because lawyers cost money, economic factors may be involved. It is estimated that much less than 10 percent of criminals are imprisoned; this results in an overrepresentation of the poor in penal settings. Other research has indicated that sex chromosome disorders are more common among the poor, due in part to lower nutritional and health care levels. Thus, one could hypothesize that the relatively large number of XYY men in security hospitals results from a high frequency of XYY among the poor and the overrepresentation of the poor in penal institutions. Furthermore, a study on a Danish population, though finding that a high proportion of the XYY males had criminal convictions, provides scant support for a Y chromosome-aggression link. The XYY criminals were, with one exception, convicted of nonaggressive crimes such as turning in false fire alarms. These lines of evidence are far from proving a chromosomal basis for increased aggressiveness in males.

Another biological argument is based on our primate relatives and is more general in approach. Selection, it states, has for millions of years favored sexual dimorphism in anatomy, physiology, and behavior. Males were selected to be larger, better hunters, and more aggressive. Females developed the anatomy and behaviors necessary for motherhood. Any attempt by women to adopt the behaviors normal to men, or vice versa, is thus contrary to our evolution and potentially dangerous. This idea is very tempting to some, but its simplicity is probably an indication of its inaccuracy.

Early field studies of primate behavior reinforced this view, for the species most commonly studied, baboons, is highly dimorphic. Once other primates were watched we saw the tremendous range of variation within the order (Chapter 7).

This argument is akin to saying: "If humans were meant to fly, we would be born with wings." Our large, complex brain is our key asset in adapting to new situations. To limit our behavioral options by saying we shouldn't construct airplanes, that women shouldn't pursue a career, or that men shouldn't take a more active role in child rearing is to take a very dim, limited view of our capabilities.

It is also important to keep in mind that there is a great deal of variation in the division of roles in cultures other than our own. Up until very recently, females in our society were responsible for the care of the house and child rearing, a practice that has begun to change very rapidly with more and more women now working full time. However, in other cultures men traditionally have had an important role in house care and child rearing.

Proponents of the idea that sex roles are learned behaviors also draw on several sorts of evidence (Figure 15.3). Drs. Money and Ehrhardt describe the rearing, as a female, of a normal male infant who traumatically lost his penis at the age of seven months.[9] As a result of the trauma, it was decided to perform surgically a sex reassignment. This particular case provides a good control in that this infant had a normal male identical twin. This rare situation provides a good insight into the effects of rearing and learned behavior on the development of sex roles.

At the age of seven there was a tremendous difference in the behavior of the two. The little girl likes to be dressed nicely, dislikes being dirty, loves to have her hair set, helps with the housework, plays with dolls, and wants to be a doctor or teacher when she grows up. Her brother plays in the dirt, helps his father fix things, and wants to be a policeman or fireman. These children, in spite of having exactly the same genes, conform perfectly to the traditional American sex roles. Learning is evidently of great importance.

Looking at male and female roles in other societies can be even more informative because trauma or pathologies are not involved. We have space to consider only a few general points. In most societies, females do have less control than males over important limited resources — trade, food, fuel, political positions, and so on. Where they do exert some control or power, it is often in the form of "the power behind the throne" or through kin ties to a male. Indira Gandhi followed her father, Nehru, as prime minister of India and Juan Perón's wife succeeded him as leader of Argentina.

As Ernestine Friedl notes, not all anthropologists are in agreement about the factors involved in this generalized lack of control by women.[10]

Figure 15.3. Sex roles appear to be largely a result of learned behavior.

Biological factors are probably partly responsible, though not as the direct result of gene action. The biological factors — a uterus, mammary glands, and different hormone levels — in turn have cultural ramifications. Although males, older people, and children assume much greater responsibilities for child care in some societies than in our own, only females in their reproductive years can bear the children. To some degree, then, adult females are more tied down than males of comparable age. Because they are limited to a degree by pregnancy, they do not have equal access to the things that mean power, such as control over the distribution of scarce, important resources. Among hunters like the Eskimos, females never have the primary responsibility for catching game. Possibly this is a consequence of the requirement that they carry the children, both during pregnancy and while the child is nursing, which would severely hinder a hunter's ability to track and attack game.

Possibly the social position of women is a cultural adaptation. Females are the limiting factor in the reproduction of a group. Theoretically, one adult male could father hundreds of offspring, so that any individual male is expendable. Maintenance of population size depends on the number of females in their reproductive years. Hunting is a dangerous occupation, and females may be too precious a commodity to risk in this way. In any case, female Eskimos have little control over the food supply and in turn do not achieve the power which comes with the distribution of food.

Patricia Draper has reported on the status and roles of another gathering-hunting society, the !Kung San of the Kalahari Desert in southern Africa.[11] Draper's study involved the observation of two different !Kung groups, one that was continuing the traditional non-settled gathering and hunting way of life, and the other which had become settled farmers, herdsmen, and laborers for nearby non-San Africans. Draper found considerable difference in the roles of the San women in the two groups, with relationships between the sexes much more egalitarian in the group continuing the traditional way of life. Here, the women had direct control over the gathered and collected foods, which made up a major part of their food supplies. Both men and women, because of the importance of their roles in providing food, were about equally absent from the camp, and Draper observed that men frequently performed tasks usually part of the women's work. Draper saw no evidence that women were excluded from sitting around the campfire, or any other gathering. In contrast, she reports that the San group that became settled agriculturists had modified their social patterns, the result being that the status of the women had declined, with their roles viewed as more inferior than those of the men. Women were now more limited to the camp, while the work of the men took them outside of the camp. This study suggests that it may have been the introduction of agriculture that resulted in the development of unequal female-male relationships.

Among agriculturalists, control over land becomes very important. As the population grows and new land is needed to grow more food, warfare becomes common. Warfare is again primarily an occupation engaged in by males; control of land by conquest again gives them control over the food supply and hence control over people.

In industrialized societies, at least until recently, the need to bear children kept women at home or in subservient occupations. To some degree, the advent of relatively safe contraception has freed women of this role and contributed to the feminist movement.

Thus, the place of women within society and the behaviors of the sexes would appear to rely on many factors. Biology, ecology, and the subsistence pattern of a culture play a part. Within societies with class structures, one's social status is important. The learning of the group's normative behaviors (Chapter 1) through socialization certainly plays a part. Once again we see that the old nature-nurture argument is a major and dangerous oversimplification.

Learning and Social Spacing

In addition to its part in reshaping women's roles, technological change has had still another effect. Rapid transportation and communication have deeply and permanently modified the amount of contact social groups have with one another. More and more, individuals from one society are meeting members of other societies. Yet human behavior still differs between societies and parts of a society. The difficulty of fully understanding the behaviors of a member of another society leaves many chances for misunderstanding and inappropriate behavior.

Edward Hall, an anthropologist who has been studying the human use of space, reports in *The Hidden Dimension* that people keep distances of varying sizes around them in interacting with others, or in trying to limit or cut off communication. Many animals, including the nonhuman primates, practice this spacing, and it probably has biological foundations in humans. The size of the space around an individual, and the social circumstances in which it may expand or shrink, are learned behaviors that vary from society to society. Hall defines patterns of distance used by middle-class, educated, eastern seaboard Americans in different social situations. One is social distance, which at its closest is between 4 and 7 feet; this is the distance that separates people in a group at a casual social gathering. These Americans feel uncomfortable when the distance is violated, and try to restore the appropriate spacing. Many foreigners visiting the United States have felt rejected and hurt, because their own social distance was closer than 4 to 7 feet, and conversing with Americans at a party, think the great distance is an attempt to minimize communication. This behavior, like many others we use in our interactions, is learned. As Hall points out, however, "concepts such as these are not always easy to grasp, because most of the distance-sensing process occurs outside awareness."[12]

Modern technology has brought us all into close contact, many times arousing conflicts in people who don't understand the behaviors of other individuals because they are used to doing things differently. Whether we will be able to solve the crucial problems created by these differences, which are based on a pattern of learning that evolved in small groups, may decide whether or not *Homo sapiens* will survive.

Our Future

These are some of the ways in which our evolutionary past may affect our present social situation, but what of the future? Biological evolution proceeds by natural selection, responding to environmental demands. No one can predict which direction our future adaptations might take. If we knew that air pollution would continue long into the future, we might evolve biological tolerances for it. But in many Western countries cultural agencies are already being utilized to try to clean the air —in England with notable success. Thus any speculations about how people might look thousands of years from now are just that — speculations based on assumptions about future environments and how we will adapt to these assumed conditions.

Another complication to bear in mind is that, however the environment may change, we can adapt to it through cultural means. Therefore many of the features that we might expect to be important in determining a person's reproductive success can be at least partially removed from the sphere of biological evolution. As technology advances, our biological ability to tolerate heat, cold, disease, and all the rest may well become less and less important.

Some have thought that this cultural "interference" in biological processes has polluted the gene pools of many human populations. Many people are born each year with genetic defects that in the past would have hampered their reproductive potential. Now, medical treatment enables them to survive, reproduce, and pass on the defective genes. Followers of this view, such as the Nobel Prize-winning geneticist H. J. Mueller, see this tampering with selection as a black cloud hanging over our future. Someday, Mueller says, all people will be born with one major genetic problem or another: diabetes, PKU, hemophilia.

Mueller suggests that we encourage some people to reproduce and discourage others. Is that biological good sense? Wright's topological view of evolution showed us that variability within and between populations is very advantageous. Reducing this variability might be temporarily beneficial, but then if the environment should change (and we can be reasonably certain it will), we may find ourselves in a bind. We cannot know that traits we select for today because they seem desirable will always be desirable. And variants that now seem disadvantageous may, because of changes in the environment, prove to be beneficial. Therefore, if we reduce our genetic variability we may find ourselves without the genetic alternatives that we need for survival in a changing environment.

Mueller also failed to realize, as many biologists do, that humans have tremendous potential for cultural change. If we have the cultural ability to prevent human suffering and yet allow for a relatively normal quality of life, why should we not use it? Mueller responds that our gene pool will become so polluted, so congested with deleterious genes, that some day all of a society's activities will be concentrated on keeping its members alive. Anthropologically, the fabric of Mueller's argument falls apart. One of the outstanding features of human cultural activity is that societal institutions strive to keep its members alive; culture evolved to fulfill just this end. If we are not going to use our brains and culture to ease the human condition, why did we evolve them? Then too, even if all 230 million Americans had diabetes or bad vision, would we really expend all of our resources and time producing insulin and eyeglasses? It is highly doubtful.

Mueller's concerns may now be short circuited by developments in bioengineering. Genetic therapy may be just around the corner as recombinant DNA technology holds the potential for relief of much human suffering. People with missing or defective genes may be infected with viruses engineered to carry the appropriate replacement gene. In fact, this has already been attempted in two cases of people with thalassemia. An ex-member of a major American medical school who was unable to get clearance to try out the procedure on humans went to Israel and Italy to perform this genetic surgery. Medically, the results were inconclusive, and ethically the treatment was highly suspect. Though the technique sounds straightforward, in reality it is not so simple. Some work suggests that inserting a new gene into a person's chromosomes can disrupt the function of neighboring genes. Without having a solid understanding of the possible or probable effects, most feel that it is wrong to experiment on humans. This is particularly true for experiments which are "shots in the dark," unlikely to provide information which will increase the success rate of future attempts.

In applying recombinant DNA technology to thalassemia, there is an attempt to treat or cure a pre-existing state. The new gene is being inserted into body cells but not the sex cells of the individual. Thus, if and when this approach does work, it will not alter the genes passed from parent to offspring, though it would affect the potential of a person to become a parent.

An even more dramatic application of these techniques would be in the cloning of whole individuals. Here, the full complement of genes from a cell of one person would be inserted into an enucleated cell (one which has the nucleus removed). This newly constituted cell would then be stimulated to start dividing, ultimately to become a genetic carbon copy of the DNA donor. This has been achieved already in mice and technically it would seem easy enough to replicate in humans. Whether society wants to allow this will be a hotly argued point.

It would even be possible to engineer chimeras, animals that have tissues of two (or more) distinct genetic types. British and German scientists have produced chimeras between two rather dissimilar mammals, a sheep and a goat. These chimeras have some tissues that are purely sheep and others purely goat. These are not hybrids wherein each cell would have some goat and some sheep genes. What reasons other than academic curiosity can justify such research? For one, chimeras are useful in studying immunological phenomena, information that can be very helpful in a wide variety of applications including cancer treatment, organ transplants, and the cure of infertility. Chimeras might even allow the preservation of species about to go extinct. Yet again, we must ask if the gains are worth the biological and ethical costs. Mary Shelley's vision of human pride creating a Frankenstein monster is no longer purely fiction.

A less fantastic use for recombinant DNA involves employing bacteria as pharmaceutical factories. If a gene producing a medically important protein such as insulin or growth hormone is inserted into bacteria, the microbes can be tricked into producing vast quantities of the desired product (one geneticist has now rephrased the key sequence of events in biochemical genetics as "DNA makes RNA, RNA makes proteins, and proteins make money"). Though this application would seem to be less questionable ethically, there are ramifications to be considered. Consider human growth hormone (hGH). This protein is used medically to treat children who do not grow normally. Presently the protein is obtained from the pituitary glands of cadavers and is quite expensive. With increased availability via recombinant DNA, it is reasonable to assume that pressures will be applied to pediatricians to "treat" short children with hGH. Corporations and parents might both be expected to apply this pressure, though for different reasons; the corporation for profits and parents because, in our society, stature is related to status and financial success. Yet, if a child is perfectly normal for his or her genes, healthy and growing at a normal rate, is it good parenting or doctoring to inject hGH? The shots are painful and not correcting a defect. It is one thing to treat a child with Turner's Syndrome (page 56) or other disorders that cause abnormally short stature and quite another to inject a child whose parents are anxious that he be 6 feet tall, not 5 and a half feet.

We have now reached a time when human beings can affect their own evolution in ways never envisaged. Such abilities might relieve much pain and suffering, but they could also be misused. Our society must decide on the ethics of genetic manipulation. What would cloning do to our feelings about individuality? Could a copy of Einstein choose his profession or, from the time of birth, would he be pushed into becoming a mathematician? From a biological point of view, could we even expect a twin of Einstein to be a genius? The twin would not grow up in the same environment as the original. Then too, who would decide which men and women should be cloned? These questions are crucial, and we have no pat answers. Yet all will require rational decisions by a well-informed public.

It is important to bear in mind, when considering this or other biological and social questions, that humans are not culture-bearing demigods free of biological features. Neither are we animals without cultural abilities. Human beings are not the product of nature or of nurture but of both. We must keep both our culture and our biology in mind when we make such vital decisions. G. G. Simpson wrote:

> Man is a glorious and unique species of animal. The species originated by evolution, it is actively evolving, and it will continue to evolve. Future evolution could raise man to superb heights as yet hardly glimpsed, but it will not automatically do so. As far as can now be foreseen, evolutionary degeneration is as likely in our future as is further progress. . . . Although much further knowledge is needed, it is unquestionably possible for man to guide his own evolution (within limits). . . . But the great weight of the most widespread current beliefs and institutions is against . . . attempting such guidance. If there is any hope, it is this: that there may be an increasing number of people who face the dilemma squarely and honestly seek a way out.[13]

Notes and Suggested Readings

Chapter 1   The Perspective of Physical Anthropology

Notes

1. Quoted in Thomas Jefferson, "On the Character and Capacities of the North American Indians," in *The Golden Age of American Anthropology*, ed. Margaret Mead and Ruth Bunzel (New York: George Braziller, 1960), pp. 75–76.
2. Cornelius Tacitus, *Germania*, in *Dialogus, Agricola, Germania*, trans. William Peterson and Maurice Hutton (Cambridge, Mass.: Harvard University Press, 1914), p. 331.
3. Quoted in Alan Moorehead, *Darwin and the Beagle* (New York: Harper & Row, 1969), p. 83.
4. David Lack, "Mr. Lawson of Charles," *American Scientist* 51(1963):12–13.
5. David Lack, "Darwin's Finches," *Scientific American* 188(1953):66–72.

Suggested Readings

Eiseley, Loren. 1961. *Darwin's Century*. New York: Doubleday Anchor Books.

Goerke, Heinz. 1973. *Linnaeus*. New York: Charles Scribner's Sons.

Goodenough, W. H. 1971. *Culture, Language, and Society*. McCaleb Module in Anthropology. Reading, Mass.: Addison-Wesley.

Gould, S. J. 1980. "Wallace's Fatal Flaw." *Natural History* 89:26–40.

Huxley, T. H. 1863. *Evidence as to Man's Place in Nature*. Reprinted as *Man's Place in Nature*. Ann Arbor: University of Michigan Press, 1959.

Kelso, A. J. 1966. "The Subdivisions of Physical Anthropology." *Current Anthropology* 7:315–319.

Moore, Ruth. 1971. *Evolution*. New York: Time-Life Nature Library.

Moorehead, Alan. 1969. *Darwin and the Beagle*. New York: Harper & Row.

Chapter 2   Genetics: The Study of Heredity

Notes

1. George Gaylord Simpson, "Principles of Classification and a Classification of Mammals," *Bulletin of the American Museum of Natural History* 85(1945):5.
2. Ernst Mayr, *Animal Species and Evolution* (Cambridge, Mass.: Harvard University Press, Belknap Press, 1963), p. 136.

Suggested Readings

Anderson, W. French, and Diacumakos, Elaine G. 1981. "Genetic Engineering in Mammalian Cells." *Scientific American* 245:106–121.

Ayala, Francisco J., and Kiger, John A., Jr. 1980. *Modern Genetics*. Menlo Park, Calif.: The Benjamin/Cummings Publishing Co.

Castle, W. M. 1977. Statistics in Small Doses. 2nd ed. Edinburgh: Churchill Livingstone.

Gilbert, Walter. 1978. "Why Genes in Pieces?" *Nature* 271:501.

Lewin, Benjamin. 1983. *Genes.* New York: John Wiley.

Schull, William J., Otake, Masanori, and Neel, James V. 1981. "Genetic Effects of the Atomic Bombs: A Reappraisal," *Science* 213:1220–1229.

Chapter 3 Evolution in Action

Notes

1. Sir MacFarlane Burnet and David O. White, *Natural History of Infectious Disease,* 4th ed. (Cambridge: Cambridge University Press, 1972), p. 140.
2. Ernst Mayr, *Principles of Systematic Zoology* (New York: McGraw-Hill, 1969), p. 26.
3. George Gaylord Simpson, *Principles of Animal Taxonomy* (New York: Columbia University Press, 1961), p. 153.
4. Theodosius Dobzhansky, *Genetics of the Evolutionary Process* (New York: Columbia University Press, 1970), p. 207.
5. Ernst Mayr, *Animal Species and Evolution* (Cambridge, Mass.: Harvard University Press, Belknap Press, 1963), p. 586.
6. S. J. Gould and R. C. Lewontin, "The Spandrels of San Marco and the Panglossian Paradigm: A Critique of the Adaptationist Programme," *Proceedings of the Royal Society of London, Series B* 205 (1979):581–598.

Suggested Readings

Bendall, D. S., ed. 1983. *Evolution from Molecules to Men.* Cambridge: Cambridge University Press.

Gould, Stephen Jay. 1980. *The Panda's Thumb: More Reflections in Natural History.* New York: W. W. Norton.

King, Mary C., and Wilson, A. 1975. "Evolution on Two Levels." *Science* 188:107–116.

Kitcher, Philip. 1982. *Abusing Science: The Case Against Creationism.* Cambridge, Mass.: MIT Press.

Mayr, Ernst. 1963. *Animal Species and Evolution.* Cambridge, Mass.: Harvard University Press.

Smith, John Maynard. 1978. *The Evolution of Sex.* Cambridge: Cambridge University Press.

Smith, John Maynard, ed. 1982. *Evolution Now: A Century after Darwin.* San Francisco: W. H. Freeman.

Sober, Elliott, ed. 1984. *Conceptual Issues in Evolutionary Biology: An Anthology.* Cambridge, Mass.: MIT Press.

Stanley, Steven M. 1979. *Macroevolution: Pattern and Process.* San Francisco: W. H. Freeman.

Chapter 4 The Evolution of the Vertebrates

Notes

1. D. H. Tarling and M. P. Tarling, *Continental Drift: A Study of the Earth's Moving Surface* (London: Bell, 1971).
2. L. W. Alvarez, Walter Alvarez, Frank Asaro, and H. V. Michel, "Extraterrestrial Cause for the Cretaceous-Tertiary Extinction," *Science* 208 (1980):1095–1108; Walter Alvarez, E. G. Kauffman, Finn Surlyk, L. W. Alvarez, Frank Asaro, and H. V. Michel, "Impact Theory of Mass Extinction and the Invertebrate Fossil Record," *Science* 223(1984):1135–1141.
3. H. J. Jerison, *Evolution of the Brain and Intelligence* (New York: Academic Press, 1973).

Suggested Readings

Colbert, E. H. 1961. *Evolution of the Vertebrates.* New York: Science Editions.

Desmond, A. J. 1977. *The Hot-Blooded Dinosaurs.* New York: Warner Books.

Halstead, L. B. 1968. *The Pattern of Vertebrate Evolution.* San Francisco: W. H. Freeman.

Miles, A. E. W. 1972. *Teeth and Their Origins.* New York: Oxford Biology Reader.

Miller, R. 1983. *Continents in Collision.* Alexandria, Virginia: Time-Life Books.

Olson, E. C. 1971. *Vertebrate Paleozoology.* New York: Wiley-Interscience.

Romer, A. S. 1966. *Vertebrate Paleontology.* Chicago: University of Chicago Press.

Sullivan, W. 1974. *Continents in Motion: The New Earth Debate.* New York: McGraw-Hill.

Tinbergen, N. 1951. *The Study of Instinct.* London: Oxford University Press.

Van Gelder, R. G. 1969. *Biology of Mammals.* New York: Charles Scribner's Sons.

Young, J. Z. 1950. *The Life of Vertebrates.* New York: Oxford University Press.

———. 1957. *The Life of Mammals.* New York: Oxford University Press.

Chapter 5   An Introduction to the Primates

Notes

1. F. S. Szalay, "Phylogeny of Primate Higher Taxa: The Basicranial Evidence," in *Phylogeny of the Primates,* eds. W. P. Luckett and F. S. Szalay (New York: Plenum Press, 1975), pp. 91–125.

2. W. E. Le Gros Clark, *The Antecedents of Man,* 3rd ed. (Chicago: Quadrangle Books, 1971).

3. J. H. Schwartz, "If *Tarsius* is not a prosimian, is it a Haplorhine?" in *Recent Advances in Primatology. Volume 3: Evolution,* eds. D. J. Chivers and K. A. Joysey (New York: Academic Press, 1978), pp. 195–204; Morris Goodman, D. Hewett-Emmett, and J. M. Beard, "Molecular Evidence on the Phylogenetic Relationships of *Tarsius,*" in *Recent Advances in Primatology. Volume 3: Evolution,* eds. D. J. Chivers and K. A. Joysey (New York: Academic Press, 1979), pp. 215–225.

4. F. S. Szalay and Eric Delson, *Evolutionary History of the Primates* (New York: Academic Press, 1979).

5. Matt Cartmill, "*Daubentonia, Dactylopsila,* woodpeckers and klinorhynchy," in *Prosimian Biology,* eds. R. D. Martin, G. A. Doyle, and A. C. Walker (London: Duckworth, 1974), pp. 655–670.

6. R. L. Ciochon and A. B. Chiarelli, eds. *Evolutionary Biology of the New World Monkeys and Continental Drift* (New York: Plenum Press, 1980).

Suggested Readings

Cartmill, Matt. 1982. "Basic Primatology and Prosimian Evolution." In *A History of American Physical Anthropology,* edited by Frank Spencer. New York: Academic Press, pp. 147–186.

Clark, W. E. Le Gros. 1963. *History of the Primates.* 4th ed. Chicago: The University of Chicago Press.

Dover, G. A., and Flavell, R. B., eds. 1982. *Genome Evolution.* London: Academic Press.

Hill, W. C. Osman. 1953. *Primates: Comparative Anatomy and Taxonomy. Volume I: Strepsirhini.* Edinburgh: The University Press.

———. 1955. *Primates: Comparative Anatomy and Taxonomy. Volume II: Haplorhini: Tarsoidea.* Edinburgh: The University Press.

———. 1957. *Primates: Comparative Anatomy and Taxonomy. Volume III: Hapalidae.* Edinburgh: The University Press.

———. 1960. *Primates: Comparative Anatomy and Taxonomy. Volume IV: Cebidae, Part A.* Edinburgh: The University Press.

———. 1962. *Primates: Comparative Anatomy and Taxonomy. Volume V: Cebidae, Part B.* Edinburgh: The University Press.

———. 1966. *Primates: Comparative Anatomy and Taxonomy. Volume VI: Cercopithecinae.* Edinburgh: The University Press.

———. 1970. *Primates: Comparative Anatomy and Taxonomy. Volume VIII: Cynopithecinae: Papio, Mandrillus, Theropithecus.* Edinburgh: The University Press.

————. 1974. *Primates: Comparative Anatomy and Taxonomy. Volume VII: Cynopithe-cinae.* Edinburgh: The University Press.

Luckett, W. P., and Szalay, F. S., eds. 1975. *Phylogeny of the Primates.* New York: Plenum Press.

Goodman, Morris, Weiss, Mark L., and Czelusniak, John. 1982, "Molecular Evolution above the Species Level: Branching Pattern, Rates, and Mechanisms." *Systematic Zoology* 31:376–399.

Napier, J. H., and Napier, P. H. 1967. *A Handbook of Living Primates.* New York: Academic Press.

Schultz, A. H. 1969. *The Life of Primates.* New York: Universe Books.

Chapter 6   The Biological History of the Primates

Notes

1. L. Van Valen and R. E. Sloan, "The Earliest Primates," *Science* 150(1965):743–745; G. G. Simpson, "Concluding Remarks: Mesozoic Mammals Revisited," in *Early Mammals,* eds. D. M. Kermack and K. A. Kermack (New York: Academic Press, 1971), pp. 181–198; and Z. Kielan-Jaworowska, T. M. Bown, and J. A. Lillegraven, "Eutheria," in *Mesozoic Mammals: The First Two-Thirds of Mammalian History,* eds. J. A. Lillegraven, Z. Kielan-Jaworowska, and W. A. Clemens (Berkeley: University of California Press, 1979), pp. 221–258.

2. F. S. Szalay, "The Beginnings of Primates," *Evolution* 22(1968):19–36.

3. M. Cartmill, "Rethinking Primate Origins," *Science* 184(1974):436–443.

4. F. S. Szalay and R. L. Decker, "Origins, Evolution, and Function of the Tarsus in Late Cretaceous Eutheria and Paleocene Primates," in *Primate Locomotion,* ed. F. A. Jenkins (New York: Academic Press, 1974), pp. 223–259.

5. I. Tattersall, "Of Lemurs and Men," *Natural History* March 1972:32–43.

6. U. Ba Maw, R. L. Ciochon, and D. E. Savage, "Late Eocene of Burma Yields Earliest Anthropoid Primate, *Pondaugia cotteri," Nature* 282:65–67.

7. P. Walker and P. Murray, "An Assessment of Masticatory Efficiency in a Series of Anthropoid Primates with Special Reference to the Colobinae and Cercopithecinae," in *Primate Functional Morphology and Evolution,* ed. R. Tuttle (The Hague: Mouton, 1975), pp. 135–150.

8. T. M. Bown, M. J. Kraus, S. L. Wing, J. G. Fleagle, B. H. Tiffney, E. L. Simons, C. F. Vondra, "The Fayum Primate Forest Revisited," *Journal of Human Evolution* 11(1982):603–632; R. F. Kay, J. G. Fleagle, and E. L. Simons, "A Revision of the Oligocene Apes of the Fayum Province, Egypt," *American Journal of Physical Anthropology* 55(1981):293–322; and E. Delson and P. Andrews, "Evolution and Interrelationships of the Catarrhine Primates," in *Phylogeny of the Primates,* eds. W. P. Luckett and F. S. Szalay (New York: Plenum Press, 1975), pp. 405–446.

9. J. G. Fleagle, R. F. Kay, and E. L. Simons, "Sexual Dimorphism in Early Anthropoids," *Nature* 287:328–330.

10. J. G. Fleagle, "Locomotor Behavior of the Earliest Anthropoids: A Review of the Current Evidence," *Zeitschrift Für Morphologie und Anthropologie* 71(1980):149–156.

11. P. J. Andrews, *A Revision of the Miocene Hominoidea of East Africa, Bulletin of the British Museum* (Natural History), *Geology Series,* Vol. 10, No. 2 (1978); and R. F. Kay and E. L. Simons, "A Reassessment of the Relationship between Later Miocene and Subsequent Hominoidea," in *New Interpretations of Ape and Human Ancestry,* eds. R. L. Ciochon and R. S. Corruccini (New York: Plenum, 1983), pp. 577–624.

12. D. Pilbeam, "The Descent of Hominoids and Hominids," *Scientific American* 250(1984):84–96.

13. M. E. Morbeck, "*Dryopithecus africanus* Forelimb," *Journal of Human Evolution* 4(1975):39–46.

14. D. Pilbeam, "Recent Finds and Interpretations of Miocene Hominoids," *Annual Review in Anthropology* 8(1979):333–352.

15. R. F. Kay, "The Nut-Crackers—A New Theory of the Adaptations of the Ramapithecinae," *American Journal of Physical Anthropology* 55(1981):141–151.
16. L. Greenfield, "A Late Divergence Hypothesis," *American Journal of Physical Anthropology* 52(1980):351–366.
17. E. L. Simons and J. Fleagle, "The History of Extinct Gibbon-Like Primates," *Gibbon and Siamang* 2(1973):121–148.
18. V. M. Sarich, "A Molecular Approach to the Question of Human Origins," in *Background for Man*, eds. P. Dolhinow and V. M. Sarich (Boston: Little, Brown, 1971), pp. 60–81; and V. M. Sarich, "Appendix: Retrospective on Hominoid Macromolecular Systematics," in *New Interpretations of Ape and Human Ancestry*, eds. R. L. Ciochon and R. S. Corruccini (New York: Plenum, 1983), pp. 137–150.
19. M. Goodman, "Toward a Genealogical Description of the Primates," in *Molecular Anthropology: Genes and Proteins in the Evolutionary Ascent of the Primates*, eds. M. Goodman, R. E. Tashian, and J. H. Tashian (New York: Plenum Press, 1976), pp. 321–353; and M. Goodman and J. E. Cronin, "Molecular Anthropology: Its Development and Current Directions," in *A History of American Physical Anthropology*, ed. F. Spencer (New York: Academic Press, 1982), pp. 105–146.
20. D. Pilbeam, "New Hominoid Skull Material from the Miocene of Pakistan," *Nature* 295(1982):232–234; P. Andrews, "Hominoid Evolution," *Nature* 295(1982):185–186; and S. Lipson and D. Pilbeam, "*Ramapithecus* and Hominoid Evolution," *Journal of Human Evolution* 11(1982):545–548.
21. M. H. Wolpoff, "*Ramapithecus* and Hominid Origins," *Current Anthropology* 23(1982):501–522.
22. J. H. Schwartz, "The Evolutionary Relationships of Man and Orangutan," *Nature* 308(1984):501–505.
23. D. Pilbeam and A. Walker, "Fossil Monkeys from the Miocene of Napak, Northeast Uganda," *Nature* 220(1968):657–660.
24. G. H. R. von Koenigswald, "Miocene Cercopithecoidea and Oreopithecoidea from the Miocene of East Africa," in *Fossil Vertebrates of Africa*, vol. 1, ed. L. S. B. Leakey (New York: Academic Press, 1969), pp. 39–52.
25. E. Delson, "Evolutionary History of the Cercopithecidae," in *Approaches to Primate Paleobiology*, vol. 5, ed. F. S. Szalay (Basel: Karger, 1975), pp. 167–217.
26. R. Hoffstetter, "Relationships, Origins, and History of the Ceboid Monkeys and Caviomorph Rodents: A Modern Reinterpretation," in *Evolutionary Biology*, vol. 6, eds. T. Dobzhansky, M. K. Hecht, and W. C. Steere (New York: Appleton-Century-Crofts, 1972), pp. 323–347; and R. Hoffstetter, "Origin and Deployment of New World Monkeys Emphasizing the Southern Continents Route," in *Evolutionary Biology of the New World Monkeys and Continental Drift*, eds. R. L. Ciochon and A. B. Chiarelli (New York: Plenum Press, 1980), pp. 103–122.
27. P. D. Gingerich, "Eocene Adapidae, Paleobiogeography, and the Origin of South American Platyrrhini," in *Evolutionary Biology of the New World Monkeys and Continental Drift*, eds. R. L. Ciochon and A. B. Chiarelli (New York: Plenum Press, 1980), pp. 123–138; and E. Delson and A. L. Rosenberger, "Phyletic Perspectives on Platyrrhini Origins and Anthropoid Relationships," in *Evolutionary Biology of the New World Monkeys and Continental Drift*, eds. R. L. Chiochon and A. B. Chiarelli (New York: Plenum Press, 1980), pp. 445–458.

Suggested Readings

Chivers, D. J., and Joysey, K. A., eds. 1978. *Recent Advances in Primatology. Vol. 3: Evolution.* New York: Academic Press.

Ciochon, R. L., and Chiarelli, A. B., eds. 1980. *Evolutionary Biology of the New World Monkeys and Continental Drift.* New York: Plenum Press.

Ciochon, R. L., and Corruccini, R. S., eds. 1983. *New Interpretations of Ape and Human Ancestry.* New York: Plenum Press.

Fleagle, J. G., and Jungers, W. L. 1982. "Fifty Years of Higher Primate Phylogeny." In *A*

History of American Physical Anthropology, ed. F. Spencer. New York: Academic Press, pp. 187–230.

Goodman, M., Tashian, R. E., and Tashian, J. H., eds. 1976. *Molecular Anthropology: Genes and Proteins in the Evolutionary Ascent of the Primates.* New York: Plenum Press.

Le Gros Clark, W. E. 1971. *The Antecedents of Man.* 3rd ed. Edinburgh: The University Press.

Morbeck, M. E., Preuschoft, Holger, and Gomberg, Neil, eds. 1979. *Environment, Behavior, and Morphology: Dynamic Interactions in Primates.* New York: Gustav Fischer.

Simons, E. L. 1972. *Primate Evolution.* New York: Macmillan.

Simpson, G. G. 1964. "Organisms and Molecules in Evolution." *Science* 146:1535–1538.

Szalay, F. S., and Delson, E. 1979. *Evolutionary History of the Primates.* New York: Academic Press.

Tuttle, Russell, ed. 1972. *The Functional and Evolutionary Biology of Primates.* Chicago: Aldine.

Chapter 7   Primate Behavior

Notes

1. D. B. Meikle and S. H. Vessey, "Nepotism among Rhesus Monkey Brothers," *Nature* 294(1981):160–161.

2. S. B. Hrdy, "Infanticide among Animals: A Review, Classification, and Examination of the Implications for the Reproductive Strategies of Females," *Ethology and Sociobiology* 1(1979):13–40.

3. P. Dolhinow, "Normal Monkeys?" *American Scientist* 6(1977):266.

4. A. F. Richard and S. P. Schulman, "Sociobiology: Primate Field Studies," *Annual Review of Anthropology* 11(1982):231–255.

5. J. F. Wittenberger, "Group Size and Polygamy in Social Mammals," *American Naturalist* 115(1980):197–222.

6. H. F. Harlow, M. K. Harlow, and S. J. Suomi, "From Thought to Therapy: Lessons from a Primate Laboratory," *American Scientist* 59 (1971):538–549.

7. S. L. Washburn, "On the Importance of the Study of Primate Behavior for Anthropologists," in *Anthropological Perspectives on Education,* eds. M. L. Wax, S. Diamond, and F. O. Gearing (New York: Basic Books, 1971).

8. D. Premack, "Language in the Chimpanzee," *Science* 172(1971):808–822.

9. H. S. Terrace, L. A. Petitto, R. J. Sanders, and T. G. Bever, "Can an Ape Create a Sentence?" *Science* 206(1979):891–902.

10. M. Kawai, "Newly Acquired Precultural Behavior of the Natural Troop of Japanese Monkeys on Koshima Islet," *Primates* 6(1965):1–30.

11. R. S. O. Harding and S. C. Strum, "The Predatory Baboons of Kekopey," *Natural History* 85(1976):45–53.

12. S. A. Altmann and J. Altmann, *Baboon Ecology* (Chicago: The University of Chicago Press, 1970).

13. J. B. Lancaster and R. B. Lee, "The Annual Reproductive Cycle in Monkeys and Apes," in *Primate Behavior: Field Studies of Monkeys and Apes,* ed. I. DeVore (New York: Holt, Rinehart and Winston, 1965), pp. 486–513.

14. G. Hausfater, "Dominance and Reproduction in Baboons *(Papio cynocephalus),*" *Contributions to Primatology,* vol. 7 (Basel: S. Karger, 1975).

15. T. E. Rowell, "Forest Living Baboons in Uganda," *Journal of Zoology,* London 149(1966):344–364; and S. L. Washburn and I. DeVore, "The Social Life of Baboons," *Scientific American* 204(1961):62–71.

16. S. D. Singh, "Urban Monkeys," *Scientific American* 221 (1969):108–115.

17. D. S. Sade, "Determinants of Dominance in a Group of Free-Ranging Rhesus Monkeys," in *Social Communication among Primates,* ed. S. A. Altmann (Chicago: The University of Chicago Press, 1967), pp. 99–114.

18. E. A. Missakian, "Genealogical and Cross-Genealogical Dominance Relationships in a Group of Free-Ranging Rhesus Monkeys *(Macaca mulatta)* on Cayo Santiago," *Primates* 13(1972):169–180.

19. R. I. M. Dunbar and E. P. Dunbar, "Ecological Relations and Niche Separation between Sympatric Terrestrial Primates in Ethiopia," in *Primate Ecology: Problem-Oriented Field Studies,* ed. R. W. Sussman (New York: John Wiley and Sons, 1979), pp. 187–209.

20. J. H. Crook, "Gelada Baboon Herd Structure and Movement," *Symposium Zoological Society of London* 18(1966):237–258.

21. U. Nagel, "A Comparison of Anubis Baboons, Hamadryas Baboons and their Hybrids at a Species Border in Ethiopia," *Folia Primatologica* 19(1973):104–165.

22. H. Kummer, *Primate Societies: Group Techniques of Ecological Adaptations* (Chicago: Aldine, 1971).

23. K. R. L. Hall, "Behavior and Ecology of the Wild Patas Monkey, *Erythrocebus patas,* in Uganda," *Journal of Zoology* 148(1965):15–87.

24. C. R. Carpenter, "A Field Study of the Behavior and Social Relations of Howling Monkeys *(Alouatta palliata),*" *Comparative Psychology Monographs* 10(1934):1–168.

25. C. B. Jones, "The Functions of Status in the Mantled Howler Monkey, *Alouatta palliata* Gray: Intraspecific Competition for Group Membership in a Folivorous Neotropical Primate," *Primates* 21(1980):389–405.

26. L. L. Klein and D. J. Klein, "Social and Ecological Contrasts between Four Taxa of Neotropical Primates," in *Primate Ecology: Problem-Oriented Field Studies,* ed. R. W. Sussman (New York: John Wiley and Sons, 1979), pp. 107–131.

27. J. van Lawick-Goodall, *In the Shadow of Man* (Boston: Houghton Mifflin, 1971); and The Behavior of Free-Living Chimpanzees in the Gombe Stream Area, *Animal Behavior Monograph,* no. 1, eds. J. M. Cullen and C. G. Beer (London: Bailliérs, Tindall, and Cassell, 1968).

28. J. Itani and A. Suzuki, "The Social Unit of Chimpanzees," *Primates* 8(1967):355–381; T. Nishida, "The Social Structure of Chimpanzees of the Mahale Mountains," in *Perspectives on Human Evolution. Vol 5: The Great Apes,* eds. D. A. Hamburg and E. R. McCown (Menlo Park, Calif.: Benjamin/Cummings, 1979), pp. 73–121; V. Reynolds and F. Reynolds, "Chimpanzees of the Budongo Forest," in *Primate Behavior: Field Studies of Monkeys and Apes,* ed. I. DeVore (New York: Holt, Rinehart and Winston, 1965), pp. 368–424; and Y. Sugiyama, "Social Organization of Chimpanzees in the Budongo Forest, Uganda," *Primates* 9(1968):225–258.

29. G. B. Schaller, *The Mountain Gorilla: Ecology and Behavior* (Chicago: The University of Chicago Press, 1963); and D. Fossey, "Observations on the Home Range of One Group of Mountain Gorilla," *Animal Behavior* 22(1974):568–581.

30. G. Teleki, "Primate Subsistence Patterns: Collector-Predators and Gatherer-Hunters," *Journal of Human Evolution* 4(1975):125–184.

31. B. M. F. Galdikas and G. Teleki, "Variations in Subsistence Activities of Female and Male Pongids: New Perspectives on the Origins of Hominid Labor Division," *Current Anthropology* 22(1981):241–256.

32. J. Goodall, "Infant Killing and Cannibalism in Free-Living Chimpanzees," *Folia Primatologica* 28(1977):259–282; J. D. Bygott, "Agonistic Behavior, Dominance, and Social Structure in Wild Chimpanzees of the Gombe National Park," in *Perspectives on Human Evolution. Vol 5: The Great Apes,* eds. D. A. Hamburg and E. R. McCown (Menlo Park, Calif.: Benjamin/Cummings, 1979), pp. 405–427.

Suggested Readings

Altmann, S. A., ed. 1967. *Social Communication among Primates.* Chicago: The University of Chicago Press.

Chalmers, N. 1980. *Social Behaviour of Primates.* Baltimore: University Park Press.

Hamburg, D. A., and McCown, E. R., eds. 1979. *Perspectives on Human Evolution.* Menlo Park, Calif.: Benjamin/Cummings.

Jolly, A. 1972. *The Evolution of Primate Behavior.* New York: Macmillan.

Kummer, H. 1971. *Primate Societies: Group Techniques of Ecological Adaptation.* Chicago: Aldine.

Michael, R. P., and Crook, J. H., eds. 1973. *Comparative Ecology and Behaviour of Primates.* New York: Academic Press.

Sussman, R. W., ed. 1979. *Primate Ecology: Problem-Oriented Field Studies.* New York: John Wiley and Sons.

Chapter 8   The Hominidae

Notes

1. P. Andrews and J. H. Van Couvering, "Paleoenvironments in the East African Miocene," in *Approaches to Primate Paleobiology, Contributions to Primatology,* vol. 5, ed. F. S. Szalay (Basel: Karger, 1975), pp. 62–103; and J. H. Van Couvering and J. A. Van Couvering, "Early Miocene Mammal Fossils from East Africa; Aspects of Geology, Faunistics, and Paleo-ecology," in *Human Origins: Louis Leakey and the East African Evidence,* ed. G. L. Isaac and E. R. McCown (Menlo Park, Calif.: W. A. Benjamin, 1976), pp. 155–207.

2. J. Fink and G. J. Kukla, "Pleistocene Climates in Central Europe: At Least 17 Interglacials after the Olduvai Event," *Quaternary Research* 7(1977):363–371; and N. J. Shackleton and N. Updyke, "Oxygen Isotope and Palaeomagnetic Stratigraphy of Equatorial Pacific Core V28-238: Oxygen Isotope Temperatures and Ice Volumes on a 10^5 Year and 10^6 Year Scale," *Quaternary Research* 3(1973):39–55.

3. G. H. Curtis, "Man's Immediate Forerunners: Establishing a Relevant Time Scale in Anthropological and Archaeological Research," *Philosophical Transactions of the Royal Society of London,* B 292(1981):7–20.

4. R. Hedges, "Radiocarbon Dating with an Accelerator: Review and Preview," *Archaeometry* 23(1981):3–18; W. F. Libby, *Radiocarbon Dating,* 2nd ed. (Chicago: The University of Chicago Press, 1955); and E. Ralph, "Carbon-14 Dating," in *Dating Techniques for the Archaeologist,* eds. H. Michael and E. Ralph (Cambridge, Mass.: MIT Press, 1971).

5. H. Faul, "Potassium-Argon Dating," in *Dating Techniques for the Archaeologist,* eds. H. Michael and E. Ralph (Cambridge, Mass.: MIT Press, 1971), pp. 157–163.

6. "Amino Acid Dating," *Masca Newsletter* 9(1973):6–8; and P. E. Hare, "Organic Geochemistry of Bone and Its Relation to the Survival of Bone in the Natural Environment," in *Fossils in the Making: Vertebrate Taphonomy and Paleoecology,* eds. A. K. Behrensmeyer and A. P. Hill (Chicago: The University of Chicago Press), pp. 208–219.

7. W. H. Goodenough, *Culture, Language, and Society,* McCaleb Module in Anthropology (Reading, Mass.: Addison-Wesley, 1971), pp. 1–48.

8. R. L. Holloway, "Culture: A Human Domain," *Current Anthropology* 10(1969):395–412.

9. A. E. Mann, "Hominid and Cultural Origins," *Man* N. S. 7(1972):379–386.

10. C. J. Jolly, "The Seed-Eaters: A New Model of Hominid Differentiation Based on a Baboon Analogy," *Man* N.S. 5(1970):5–26.

11. J. T. Robinson, *Early Hominid Posture and Locomotion* (Chicago: The University of Chicago Press, 1972); and R. H. Tuttle, "Parallelism, Brachiation, and Hominoid Phylogeny," in *Phylogeny of the Primates,* eds. W. P. Luckett and F. S. Szalay (New York: Plenum Press, 1975), pp. 447–480.

12. C. O. Lovejoy, "The Origin of Man," *Science* 211(1981):341–350.

13. G. L. Isaac, "Chronology and the Tempo of Cultural Change During the Pleistocene," in *Calibration of Hominoid Evolution,* eds. W. W. Bishop and J. A. Miller (Edinburgh: Scottish Academic Press, 1972), pp. 381–430.

Suggested Readings

Bishop, W. W., and Miller, J. A., eds. 1972. *Calibration of Hominoid Evolution.* Edinburgh: Scottish Academic Press.

Campbell, B. G. 1985. *Humankind Emerging.* 4th ed. Boston: Little, Brown.

Cornwall, I. W. 1970. *Ice Ages: Their Nature and Effects.* New York: Humanities Press.

Flint, R. F. 1971. *Glacial and Quaternary Geology.* New York: John Wiley and Sons.

Holloway, R. L. 1983. "Human Paleontological Evidence Relevant to Language Behavior." *Human Neurobiology* 2:105–114.

Washburn, S. L. 1968. *The Study of Human Evolution.* Eugene: Oregon State System of Higher Education. Reprinted in *Background for Man,* ed. P. Dolhinow and V. M. Sarich (Boston: Little, Brown, 1971).

Chapter 9   Human Evolution I: The Early Hominids

Notes

1. V. M. Sarich, "A Molecular Approach to the Question of Human Origins," in *Background for Man,* eds. Phyllis Dolhinow and V. M. Sarich (Boston: Little, Brown, 1971), pp. 60–81.

2. R. A. Dart, "*Australopithecus africanus:* The Man-Ape of South Africa," *Nature* 115(1925):195–199.

3. R. Millar, *The Piltdown Men* (New York: St. Martin's Press, 1972); and S. J. Gould, "Piltdown in Letters," *Natural History* 90(1981):12–30.

4. P. V. Tobias, *Olduvai Gorge,* vol. 2, *The Cranium and Maxillary Dentition of Australopithecus (Zinjanthropus) boisei* (Cambridge: Cambridge University Press, 1967).

5. L. S. B. Leakey, P. V. Tobias, and J. R. Napier, "A New Species of the Genus *Homo* from Olduvai Gorge," *Nature* 202(1964):7–9.

6. F. C. Howell and Y. Coppens, "An Overview of Hominidae from the Omo Succession, Ethiopia," in *Earliest Man and Environments in the Lake Rudolf Basin,* eds. Y. Coppens, F. C. Howell, G. L. Isaac, and R. E. F. Leakey (Chicago: The University of Chicago Press, 1976), pp. 522–532.

7. M. G. Leakey and R. E. F. Leakey, eds., *Koobi Fora Research Project,* vol. 1, *The Fossil Hominids and an Introduction to Their Context, 1968–1974* (Oxford: Oxford University Press, 1978).

8. D. C. Johanson and M. Edey, *Lucy: The Beginnings of Humankind* (New York: Simon and Schuster, 1981).

9. M. H. Day and E. H. Wickens, "Laetoli Pliocene Hominid Footprints and Bipedalism," *Nature* 286(1980):385–387.

10. D. C. Johanson and T. D. White, "A Systematic Assessment of Early African Hominids," *Science* 202(1979):321–330.

11. P. V. Tobias and G. H. R. von Koenigswald, "A Comparison between the Olduvai Hominines and Those of Java and Some Implications for Hominid Phylogeny," *Nature* 204(1964):515–518.

12. J. T. Stern and R. L. Susman, "The Locomotor Anatomy of *Australopithecus afarensis,*" *American Journal of Physical Anthropology* 60(1983):279–318.

13. C. O. Lovejoy, "The Gait of *Australopithecus,*" *Yearbook of Physical Anthropology* 17(1973):147–161.

14. H. M. McHenry, "The Pattern of Human Evolution: Studies in Bipedalism, Mastication and Encephalization," *Annual Review of Anthropology* 11(1982):151–173.

15. P. V. Tobias, " '*Australopithecus afarensis*' and *A. africanus:* Critique and an Alternative Hypothesis," *Palaeontologia Africana* 23(1980):1–17.

16. T. R. Olson, "Basicranial Morphology of the Extant Hominoids and Pliocene Hominids: The New Material from the Hadar Formation, Ethiopia and its Significance in Early

Human Evolution," in *Aspects of Human Evolution,* ed. C. B. Stringer (London: Taylor & Francis, 1981), pp. 99–128.

17. J. T. Robinson, "Variation and the Taxonomy of the Early Hominids," in *Evolutionary Biology,* vol. 1, eds. T. Dobzhansky, M. K. Hecht, and W. C. Steere (New York: Appleton-Century-Crofts, 1967), pp. 69–100.

18. R. L. Hay, *Geology of the Olduvai Gorge* (Berkeley: University of California Press, 1976).

19. C. K. Brain, "New Finds at the Swartkrans Australopithecine Site," *Nature* 225(1970):1112–1119.

20. A. E. Mann, "Paleodemographic Aspects of the South African Australopithecines," *University of Pennsylvania Publications in Anthropology,* no. 1 (1975).

21. G. L. Isaac, "The Food-Sharing Behavior of Protohuman Hominids," *Scientific American* 238(1978):90–108.

22. C. R. Peters and E. M. O'Brien, "The Early Hominid Plant-Food Niche; Insights from an Analysis of Plant Exploitation by *Homo, Pan,* and *Papio* in Eastern and Southern Africa," *Current Anthropology* 22(1981):127–140.

23. A. E. Mann, "Diet and Human Evolution," in *Omnivorous Primates: Gathering and Hunting in Human Evolution,* eds. R. S. O. Harding and G. Teleki (New York: Columbia University Press, 1981), pp. 10–36.

Suggested Readings

Campbell, B. G. 1985. *Humankind Emerging.* 4th ed. Boston: Little, Brown.

Clark, W. E. Le Gros. 1967. *Man-Apes or Ape-Men?* New York: Holt, Rinehart and Winston.

Coppens, Y., Howell, F. C., Isaac, G. L., and Leakey, R. E. F., eds. 1976. *Earliest Man and Environments in the Lake Rudolf Basin.* Chicago: The University of Chicago Press.

Day, M. H. 1977. *Guide to Fossil Man.* 3rd ed. Chicago: The University of Chicago Press.

Howell, F. C. 1978. "Chapter 10: The Hominidae." In *Evolution of African Mammals,* eds. V. J. Maglio and H. B. S. Cooke. Cambridge, Mass.: Harvard University Press, pp. 154–248.

Isaac, G. L., and McCown, E. R., eds. 1976. *Human Origins: Louis Leakey and the East African Evidence.* Menlo Park, Calif.: W. A. Benjamin.

Leakey, M. D. 1971. *Olduvai Gorge,* vol. 3, *Excavations in Beds I and II, 1960–1963.* Cambridge: Cambridge University Press.

Leakey, R. E. F., and Walker, A. 1976. "*Australopithecus, Homo erectus* and the Single Species Hypothesis." *Nature* 261:572–574.

Pfeiffer, J. E. 1978. *The Emergence of Man.* 3rd ed. New York: Harper & Row.

Tuttle, R. H., ed. 1975. *Paleoanthropology, Morphology and Paleoecology.* The Hague: Mouton.

Wolpoff, M. H. 1980. *Paleoanthropology.* New York: Alfred A. Knopf.

Chapter 10   Human Evolution II: The Emergence of Modern Humans

Notes

1. A. Mann, "Behavior and Demography of *Homo erectus,*" in *L'Homo erectus et la Place de L'Homme de Tautavel parmi les Hominides Fossiles,* Congrès International de Paleontologie Humaine, 1er Congrès, (Nice: Union Internationale des Sciences Préhistoriques et Protohistoriques, 1982), pp. 997–1014.

2. H. L. Shapiro, *Peking Man: The Discovery, Disappearance and Mystery of a Priceless Scientific Treasure* (New York: Simon & Schuster, 1974).

3. Xia Ming, "Uranium-Series Dating of Fossil Bones from Peking Man Cave — Mixing Model," *Acta Anthropologica Sinica* 1(1982):196.

4. A. Thoma, "L'Occipital de L'Homme Mindelien de Vértesszöllös," *L'Anthropologie* 70(1966):495–534; and M. H. Wolpoff, "Is Vértesszöllös II an Occipital of European *Homo erectus?"* *Nature* 232(1971):567–568.

5. C. B. Stringer, F. C. Howell, and J. K. Melentis, "The Significance of the Fossil Hominid Skull from Petralona, Greece," *Journal of Archaeological Science* 6(1979):235–253.

6. G. J. Bartstra, "*Homo erectus erectus:* The Search for His Artifacts," *Current Anthropology* 23(1982):318–320.

7. H. de Lumley, "A Paleolithic Camp at Nice," *Scientific American* 220(1969):42–50.

8. R. B. Lee and I. DeVore, eds., *Man the Hunter* (Chicago: Aldine, 1968).

9. L. G. Freeman, "The Fat of the Land: Notes on Paleolithic Diet in Iberia," in *Omnivorous Primates: Gathering and Hunting in Human Evolution,* eds. R. S. O. Harding and G. Teleki (New York: Columbia University Press, 1981), pp. 104–165.

10. *L'Homme erectus et la Place de L'Homme de Tautavel parmi les Hominides Fossiles,* Congrès International de Paleontologie Humaine, 1er Congrès (Nice: Union Internationale des Sciences Préhistoriques et Protohistoriques, 1982).

11. J. W. Dawson, quoted in Loren Eiseley, *Darwin's Century* (New York: Doubleday, 1958), p. 274.

12. F. Bordes, "Mousterian Cultures in France," *Science* 134(1961):803–810.

13. S. R. Binford and L. R. Binford, "Stone Tools and Human Behavior," *Scientific American* 220(1969):70–84.

14. W. W. Howells, "Explaining Modern Man: Evolutionists vs. Migrationists," *Journal of Human Evolution* 5(1976):477–495.

15. A. Hrdlička, "The Neanderthal Phase of Man," *Journal of the Royal Anthropological Institute* 57(1927):249–274.

16. D. S. Brose and M. H. Wolpoff, "Early Upper Paleolithic Man and Late Middle Paleolithic Tools," *American Anthropologist* 73(1971):1156–1194.

17. F. C. Howell, "The Evolutionary Significance of Variation and Varieties of 'Neanderthal' Man," *Quarterly Review of Biology* 32(1957):330–347.

18. J. Jelínek, "Neanderthal Man and *Homo sapiens* in Central and Eastern Europe," *Current Anthropology* 10(1969):475–503; and F. H. Smith, "Upper Pleistocene Hominid Evolution in South-Central Europe: A Review of the Evidence and Analysis of Trends," *Current Anthropology* 23(1982):667–703.

19. A. M. ApSimon, "The Last Neanderthal in France," *Nature* 287(1980):271–272; and M. H. Wolpoff, C. B. Stringer, R. G. Kruszynski, R. M. Macobi, and A. M. ApSimon, "Matters Arising — Allez Neanderthal," *Nature* 289(1981):823–824.

20. C. B. Stringer, "Population Relationships of Later Pleistocene Hominids: A Multivariate Study of Available Crania," *Journal of Archaeological Science* 1(1974):317–342.

21. E. Trinkaus, "The Morphology of European and Southwest Asian Neanderthal Pubic Bones" *American Journal of Physical Anthropology* 44(1976):95–103.

22. E. Trinkaus and W. W. Howells, "The Neanderthals," *Scientific American* 241 (1979):118–133.

23. M. H. Wolpoff, Wu Xin Zhi, and A. G. Thorne, "Modern *Homo sapiens* Origins: A General Theory of Hominid Evolution Involving the Fossil Evidence from East Asia," in *The Origins of Modern Humans,* eds. F. H. Smith and F. Spencer (New York: Alan Liss, 1984).

24. G. P. Rightmire, "Implications of the Border Cave Skeletal Remains for Later Pleistocene Human Evolution," *Current Anthropology* 20(1979):23–35.

25. C. S. Coon, *The Origin of Races* (New York: Alfred A. Knopf, 1962).

26. L. L. Cavalli-Sforza, "The Genetics of Human Populations," *Scientific American* 231(1974):80–89.

27. R. S. Solecki, *Shanidar: The First Flower People* (New York: Alfred A. Knopf, 1971).

28. P. Leiberman, E. S. Crelin, and D. H. Klatt, "Phonetic Ability and Related Anatomy of the Newborn and Adult Human, Neanderthal Man, and the Chimpanzee," *American Anthropologist* 74(1972):287–307.

29. A. B. Harper and W. S. Laughlin, "Inquiries into the Peopling of the New World: Development of Ideas and Recent Advances," in *A History of American Physical Anthropology: 1930–1980,* ed. F. Spencer (New York: Academic Press, 1982), pp. 281–304.

Suggested Readings

Howells, W. W., ed. 1962. *Ideas on Human Evolution: Selected Essays, 1949–1961.* Cambridge, Mass.: Harvard University Press.

———. 1973. *Evolution of the Genus* Homo. Reading, Mass.: Addison-Wesley.

Jelinek, A. J., Farrand, W. R., Haas, G., Horowitz, A., and Goldberg, P. 1973. "New Excavations at the Tabūn Cave, Mount Carmel, Israel, 1967–1972: A Preliminary Report," *Paléorient* 1:153–183.

L'Homo erectus et la Place de L'Homme de Tautavel parmi les Hominides Fossiles, Congrès International de Paleontologie Humaine, 1er Congrès. 1982. Nice: Union Internationale des Sciences Préhistoriques et Protohistoriques.

McCown, T. D., and Keith, Sir Arthur. 1939. *The Stone Age of Mount Carmel.* Vol. 2. *The Fossil Human Remains from the Levalloiso-Mousterian.* Oxford: Clarendon Press.

Oakley, K. P., Campbell, B. G., and Molleson, T. I. 1971. *Catalogue of Fossil Hominids. Part II: Europe.* London: British Museum (Natural History).

———. 1975. *Catalogue of Fossil Hominids. Part III: Americas, Asia and Australia.* London: British Museum (Natural History).

———. 1977. *Catalogue of Fossil Hominids. Part I: Africa.* Rev. ed. London: British Museum (Natural History).

Smith, F. H., and Spencer, F., eds. 1984. *The Origins of Modern Humans.* New York: Alan Liss.

Trinkaus, E. 1982. "A History of *Homo erectus* and *Homo sapiens* Paleontology in America." In *A History of American Physical Anthropology,* ed. F. Spencer. New York: Academic Press, pp. 261–280.

Weidenreich, F. 1949. *Anthropological Papers of Franz Weidenreich, 1939–1948.* Compiled by S. L. Washburn and D. Wolffson. New York: Viking Fund.

Wolpoff, M. H. 1980. *Paleoanthropology.* New York: Alfred A. Knopf.

Chapter 11   Human Polymorphisms

Notes

1. Theodosius Dobzhansky, *Evolution, Genetics, and Man* (New York: John Wiley, 1955), p. 177.

Suggested Readings

Brown, Peter J. 1981. "New Considerations on the Distribution of Malaria, Thalessemia and Glucose-6-Phosphate Dehydrogenase Deficiency in Sardinia," *Human Biology* 53:367–382.

Cohen, Bernice H. 1970. "ABO and Rh Incompatibility I. Fetal and Neonatal Mortality with ABO and Rh Incompatibility: Some New Interpretations," *American Journal of Human Genetics* 22:412–440.

Friedman, Milton J., and Trager, William. 1981. "The Biochemistry of Resistance to Malaria." *Scientific American* 244:154–164.

Kan, Y. W., and Dozy, A. M. 1980. "Evolution of the Hemoglobin S and C Genes in World Populations." *Science* 209:388–391.

Mielke, James H., and Crawford, Michael H., eds. 1980. *Current Developments in Anthropological Genetics.* Vol. 1. New York: Plenum.

Mourant, A. E., Kopec, Ada C., and Domaniewska-Sobczak, Kazimiera. 1978. *Blood Groups and Diseases: A Study of Associations of Diseases with Blood Groups and Other Polymorphisms.* Oxford: Oxford University Press.

Pagnier, Josée, Mears, J. Gregory, Dunda-Belkhodja, Olga, Schaeffer-Rego, Kim E., Beldjord, Cherif, Nagel, Ronald L., and Labie, Dominque. 1984. "Evidence for the Multicentric Origin of the Sickle-Cell Hemoglobin Gene in Africa," *Proceeding of the National Academy of Science, USA* 81:1771–1773.

Williams, R. C. 1982. HLA. *Yearbook of Physical Anthropology* 25:91–112.

Wyman, Arlene R., and White, Ray. 1980. "A Highly Polymorphic Locus in Human DNA." *Proceeding of the National Academy of Science, USA* 77:6754–6758.

Chapter 12 Human Variation Morphological Traits

Notes

1. Stanley M. Garn, "Human Growth," *Annual Review of Anthropology* 9(1980):275–292.
2. Walter F. Bodmer and Luigi Luca Cavalli-Sforza, "Intelligence and Race," *Scientific American* 223 (1970):29.

Suggested Readings

Branda, Richard F., and Eaton, John W. 1978. "Skin Color and Nutrient Photolysis: An Evolutionary Hypothesis." *Science* 201:625–626.

Byard, Pamela J. 1981. "Quantitative Genetics of Human Skin Color." *Yearbook of Physical Anthropology* 24:123–138.

Garn, Stanley M. 1980. Human Growth, *Annual Review of Anthropology* 9:275–292.

Lampl, Michelle, and Emde, Robert. 1983. "Episodic Growth in Infancy: A Preliminary Report on Length, Head Circumference, and Behavior." In *Levels and Transitions in Children's Development, New Definitions for Child Development #21*, ed. K. W. Fischer. San Francisco: Jossey-Bass.

Lynn, Richard. 1982. "IQ in Japan and the United States Shows a Growing Disparity." *Nature* 297:222–223.

Malina, Robert M., Little, Bertis B., Stern, Michael P., Gaskill, Sharon P., and Hazuda, Helen P. 1983. "Ethnic and Social Class Differences in Selected Anthropometric Characteristics of Mexican American and Anglo Adults: The San Antonio Heart Study." *Human Biology* 55:867–883.

Morse, Dan, Duncan, Jack, and Stoutmire, James, eds. 1983. *Handbook of Forensic Archaeology and Anthropology*. Tallahassee, Fla.: Florida State University Foundation, Inc.

Tanner, J. M. 1978. *Foetus into Man: Physical Growth from Conception to Maturity*. Cambridge, Mass.: Harvard University Press.

Taylor, Howard F. 1980. *The IQ Game: A Methodological Inquiry into the Heredity-Environment Controversy*. New Brunswick, N.J.: Rutgers University Press.

Chapter 13 Human Adaptability

Notes

1. Michael A. Little, "Effects of Alcohol and Coca on Foot Temperature Responses of Highland Peruvians During a Localized Cold Exposure," *American Journal of Physical Anthropology* 32(1970):239.
2. Paul T. Baker, "Ecological and Physiological Adaptation in Indigenous South Americans," in *The Biology of Human Adaptability*, ed. Paul T. Baker and J. S. Weiner (Oxford: Clarendon Press, 1966), p. 291.
3. Sidney Cobb, "Physiological Changes in Men Whose Jobs Were Abolished," *Journal of Psychosomatic Research* 18(1974):245–258.
4. Daniel Z. Gross and Barbara A. Underwood, "Technological Change and Caloric Costs: Sisal Agriculture in Northeastern Brazil," *American Anthropologist* 73(1971):725–740.
5. Alice Brues, "The Spearman and the Archer: An Essay on Selection in Body Build," *American Anthropologist* 61(1959):465.
6. P. Baker, "Ecological and Physiological Adaptation," p. 279.

Suggested Readings

Beall, Cynthia M. 1982. "A Comparison of Chest Morphology in High Altitude Asian and Andean Populations." *Human Biology* 54:145–163.

Frisancho, A. Roberto. 1979. *Human Adaptation: A Functional Interpretation*. St. Louis: C. V. Mosby.

Garruto, Ralph M., 1981. "Disease Patterns of Isolated Groups." In *Biocultural Aspects of Disease*, ed. Henry R. Rothschild. New York: Academic Press, pp. 557–597.

Greene, Lawrence S., ed. 1977. *Malnutrition, Behavior and Social Organization*. New York: Academic Press.

Hanna, Joel M., and Brown, Daniel E. 1983. "Human Heat Tolerance: An Anthropological Perspective." *Annual Review Anthropology* 12:259–284.

Harrison, G. A., Palmer, C. D., Jenner, D., and Reynolds, V. 1981. "Associations between Rates of Urinary Catecholamine Excretion and Aspects of Lifestyle among Adult Women in Some Oxfordshire Villages." *Human Biology* 53:617–633.

Jerome, Norge W.; Kandel, Randy F.; and Pelto, Gretal H., eds. 1980. *Nutritional Anthropology: Contemporary Approaches to Diet and Culture*. Pleasantville, N.Y.: Redgrave Publishing.

Moore, Lorna Grindlay, and Regensteiner, Judith G. 1983. "Adaptation to High Altitude." *Annual Review of Anthropology* 12:285–304.

Pearson, Paul B., and Greenwell, Richard J., eds. 1980. *Nutrition, Food, and Man: An Interdisciplinary Perspective*. Tucson: University of Arizona Press.

Schell, Lawrence M. 1981. "Environmental Noise and Human Prenatal Growth." *American Journal of Physical Anthropology* 56:63–70.

Chapter 14 Biological History of Human Populations

Notes

1. Jon Alfred Mjoen, "Harmonic and Disharmonic Racecrossings," in *Eugenics in Race and State*, vol. 2. Scientific Papers of the Second International Congress of Eugenics (Baltimore: Williams and Wilkins, 1923), p. 46.
2. Jean Hiernaux, "The Concept of Race and the Taxonomy of Mankind," in *The Concept of Race*, ed. M. F. Ashley Montagu (New York: Free Press, 1964), pp. 32–33.
3. Frank B. Livingstone, "On the Nonexistence of Human Races," *Current Anthropology* 3:279.
4. M. F. Ashley Montagu, *Man's Most Dangerous Myth: The Fallacy of Race*, 2d ed. (New York: Columbia University Press, 1945), p. 31.

Suggested Readings

Brace, C. Loring, and Hinton, Robert J. 1981. "Oceanic Tooth-size Variation as a Reflection of Biological and Cultural Mixing." *Current Anthropology* 22:549–569.

Crawford, M. H., and Mielke, J. H., eds. 1982. *Current Developments in Anthropological Genetics, Vol. 2: Ecology and Population Structure*. New York: Plenum Press.

Gould, Stephen J. 1978. "Morton's Ranking of Races by Cranial Capacity." *Science* 200:503–509.

Morton, N. E., Kennett, R., Yee, S., and Lew, R. 1982. "Bioassay of Kinship in Populations of Middle Eastern Origin and Controls," *Current Anthropology* 23:157–167.

Neel, James V. 1978. "The Population Structure of an Amerindian Tribe, The Yanomama," *Annual Review of Genetics* 12:365–413.

Chapter 15 Prospects and Perspectives

Notes

1. Raymond A. Dart with Dennis Craig, *Adventures with the Missing Link* (New York: Viking Press, 1959). See also Robert Ardrey, *African Genesis* (New York: Dell, 1961).

2. D. A. Hamburg, "Psychobiological Studies of Aggressive Behavior," *Nature* 230 (1971):19–23.
3. R. M. Rose, T. P. Gordon, and I. S. Bernstein, "Plasma Testosterone Levels in the Male Rhesus: Influences of Sexual and Social Stimuli," *Science* 178(1972):643–645.
4. Donald Symons, *The Evolution of Human Sexuality* (Oxford: Oxford University Press, 1979).
5. Clifford Geertz, "Review of Donald Symons' *The Evolution of Human Sexuality* (Oxford: Oxford University Press, 1979)," *New York Review of Books* 26(1980):3–4.
6. N. G. Blurton Jones, "An Ethological Study of Some Aspects of Social Behavior of Children in Nursery School," in *Primate Ethology,* ed. Desmond Morris (Chicago: Aldine, 1967), p. 365.
7. G. A. Reichard, "Social Life," in *General Anthropology,* ed. Franz Boas (New York: D. C. Heath, 1938), pp. 471–472.
8. M. A. Tefler, "Are Some Criminals Born That Way?" *Think* 34(1968):24.
9. John Money and Anke A. Ehrhardt, *Man & Woman, Boy & Girl* (Baltimore: Johns Hopkins University Press, 1972).
10. Ernestine Friedl, *Women and Men: An Anthropologist's View* (New York: Holt, Rinehart and Winston, 1975).
11. Patricia Draper, "!Kung Women; Contrasts in Sexual Egalitarianism in Foraging and Sedentary Contexts," in *Toward an Anthropology of Women,* ed. R. R. Reiter (New York: Monthly Review Press, 1975).
12. E. T. Hall, *The Hidden Dimension* (New York: Doubleday and Company, 1966), p. 115.
13. George Gaylord Simpson, *This View of Life: The World of an Evolutionist* (New York: Harcourt, Brace & World, 1947), p. 285.

Suggested Readings

Barash, David P. 1982. *Sociobiology and Behavior,* 2d ed. New York: Elsevier.
Dixon, Bernard. 1984. "Engineering Chimeras for Noah's Ark." *The Hastings Center Report* 14:10–12.
Leibowitz, Lila. 1978. *Females, Males, Families: A Biosocial Approach.* Belmont, Calif.: Duxbury Press.
Weinberg, Robert A. 1983. "A Molecular Basis of Cancer." *Scientific American* 126–142.

Glossary

ABO blood group: a blood group system based on red blood cell surface molecules. Its inheritance is controlled by three alleles, A, B, and O. There are six genotypes and four phenotypes. A, B, and O molecules can be found on cells other than red cells.

Absolute dating: use of radioactive isotopes to date geologic deposits and organic remains and, therefore, to estimate the age of fossils found within these deposits in numbers of years before present. Examples include: Carbon-14, Potassium/Argon, Fission Track, Uranium/Thorium, and the still experimental Electron Spin Resonance.

Acclimatization: adaptive physiological alteration.

Acheulian: a stone tool industry of the Lower Paleolithic, characterized by the presence of hand axes.

Adapis: Eocene fossil primate showing many features similar to living prosimians.

Adaptive radiation: the rapid increase in number of related species following entry into new environments that lack competitors.

Adjustment: a shift in functioning to adapt to stress.

Admixture: the mixing of genes of two or more populations. Often, admixture follows the migration of peoples.

Admixture coefficient: an estimate of the relative contributions of two (or more) parental populations to the gene pool of a hybrid population. The gene pool of the hybrid group, and hence the admixture coefficient, can also be affected by natural selection.

Adrenal cortex: glandular tissue which produces many steroid hormones. Located above each kidney.

Aegyptopithecus: Best known of a number of fossil higher primates found in Oligocene deposits in the Fayum area of Egypt. The skull still retains many primitive attributes, although features like the filled-in eye orbits demonstrate its higher primate status. It appears to be related to the *Proconsul* fossil of the East African Early Miocene, whose ancestor it may be.

Aerobic capacity: a physiological measurement of ability to work.

Agenesis: failure of a biological structure to develop.

Agnatha: a class of primitive vertebrates which lack both jaws and teeth; the major living representative is the lamprey.

Allantois: a structure in the eggs of reptiles and birds and a part of the mammalian placenta that provides for the removal of embryological wastes.

Allele: variant forms of a gene that occupy the same relative position on members of a pair of chromosomes and affect the same trait, but in different ways.

Allen's Rule: the observed tendency of mammals living in cold regions to have shorter extremities than members of the same species living in warm regions.

Altruism: selflessness in the broad sense; in sociobiology, normally referring to acts of selfless or self-sacrificing behavior.

Ambrona: Middle Pleistocene archaeological site in Spain nearby to Torralba.

Amino acid racemization: technique used to determine the age of fossil bone by the examination of the chemical structure of the amino acids present in the collagen of the bone.

Amino acids: compounds that are joined together in specific sequences under the direction of DNA to form the many proteins found in an organism. There are twenty common amino acids.

Anagenesis: one form of speciation in which a species evolves through time into a new species. Anagenesis is contrasted with cladogenesis.

Anatomically modern humans: *Homo sapiens* identical in appearance to living humans. Often placed in their own subspecies, *Homo sapiens sapiens* (to distinguish them from fossil forms of *Homo sapiens*, like *H.s. neanderthalensis*), anatomically modern humans are first found in the fossil record about 30,000 years ago.

Anemia: a deficiency of the oxygen-carrying ability of the blood. It may be produced by a variety of causes: genetic, as in thalassemia or sickle-cell anemia; or environmental, as in iron-deficiency anemia, infections, immune reactions.

Angiosperm: A major grouping of advanced plants, including the deciduous trees (those that lose their leaves in the winter), the fruiting and flowering trees, and all the grasses. The last of the major plant groups to evolve, the angiosperms proliferated during the Cretaceous period, profoundly altering the earth's ecology.

Anthropometry: the measurement of living humans.

Antibody: substance produced as a result of exposure to a foreign substance (an antigen). Through various mechanisms antibodies help eliminate antigens from the body.

Antigen: a substance that the body recognizes as foreign and, as a result, causes the production of an antibody.

Arago: a cave site in southern France with hominid fossils whose morphological features place them in the early or archaic *Homo sapiens* category.

Arboreal: adapted to life in the trees.

Articulation: the joint or point of junction between bones of the skeleton.

Assortative mating, negative: mating with someone who differs from you for a trait.

Assortative mating, positive: mating with someone who resembles you for a trait.

Auditory bulla: paired bulbous boney chambers, located on each side of the bottom of the mammal skull, and which houses the inner ear structures.

Australopithecus afarensis: fossil hominid species found at the sites of Hadar in Ethiopia and Laetoli in Tanzania dated from about 2.9 to 3.6 million years B.P. These are the first known undoubted members of the hominid family. They are fully bipedal, have certain distinctive features in their dentition and small brain sizes.

Australopithecus africanus: fossil hominid species found at sites in East and South Africa, dated from perhaps greater than 3 million years B.P. to 1.5 million years B.P.

Australopithecus boisei: an australopithecine found in East Africa from about 2 to 1.5 million years B.P., noted for the massive size of its teeth, jaws, and face.

Australopithecus robustus: fossil hominids found at the South African sites of Swartkrans and Kromdraai and often related to *Australopithecus boisei* because of their similarity of large teeth and jaws.

B.P.: (years) before present.

Bacteria: any of a wide variety of one-celled organisms. Many cause disease, though not all do.

Balanced polymorphism: the maintenance of two or more alleles as a result of selection favoring the heterozygote.

Bases: the building blocks of DNA and RNA. The four bases found in DNA are adenine, guanine, cytosine, and thymine. In RNA, thymine is replaced by uracil. The specificity of the genetic material rests on the fact that adenine always pairs with thymine (or uracil) and guanine always pairs with cytosine.

Bergmann's Rule: the observed tendency for mammals living in cold regions to be heavier and to be rounder in shape than members of the same species living in warm regions.

Bilateral symmetry: the pattern of symmetry found among vertebrates in which the right and left halves of the animal are almost identical.

Bilophodont: molar teeth characteristic of all Old World monkeys, with four cusps, the front two (one "loph") connected by a transverse ridge, but separated from the back loph by a deep groove.

Bilzingsleben: hominid fossil site in East Germany. The fragmentary skull bones have some features similar to those of *Homo erectus* and a number relating them to early *Homo sapiens;* they are usually assigned to the latter category.

Binomial: the two part name given to every living and extinct form. It is made up of the genus and species names.

Biological species: a group of breeding populations that are reproductively isolated from all other such groups.

Bipedalism: a special form of locomotion on two feet characteristic of all known living and extinct members of the family Hominidae.

Blade tools: stone tools characteristic of the Upper Paleolithic, whose long, relatively thin blades are struck off a core and further worked into projectile points, scrapers, etc.

Blood groups: classes of sugar molecules discernible on the membranes of blood cells, detected by the use of appropriate antibodies. Within each blood group system are two or more alternative types; for example, within the ABO system are types A, B, and O, and AB. At times, blood group substances are found on cells and in fluids other than the blood.

Bodo: a fossil hominid skull from the Afar region of Ethiopia. It is similar in many of its features to the early or archaic *Homo sapiens* fossils from Kabwe, Zambia and Saldanha Bay, South Africa.

Border Cave: a cave site on the border between South Africa and the small kingdom of Swaziland, in which several fragmentary *Homo sapiens* skeletons have been found. The tentative date for these bones, around 75,000 years B.P., if confirmed, would make these the earliest modern humans yet found.

Brachiation: the specialized method of movement of gibbons through the trees, with the body hanging suspended from the treelimb underneath the arms and swinging like a pendulum.

Branching evolution: see cladogenesis.

Breccia: rock and bone cemented together by calcium carbonate (lime).

Breeding population (or Mendelian population): a group of animals of the same species living in the same environment, all of which have an equal chance of breeding with any other member of the group of the opposite sex. The breeding population is the level on which evolution operates.

Broken Hill: older, now disused name for the Kabwe fossil skull from Zambia, southern Africa (see Kabwe).

Bruhnes Normal: the current paleomagnetic time. Earth magnetic polarity reversed to the current orientation about 690,000 years B.P., marking the beginning of the Bruhnes Normal Epoch, and the end of the previous period, the Matuyama Reversed Epoch.

Buluk: a locale in western Kenya where fragmentary pieces of the jaws of a *Sivapithecus* have recently been found. Dated to about 17 million years B.P., the fossils are said to be very similar to those of the South Asian *Sivapithecus*.

Calorie: a unit of heat; the amount of heat needed to raise the temperature of one gram of water from 15 degrees C to 16 degrees C. The unit is used to measure the amount of energy in food and the amount of energy required to perform work. When written with a capital C, it refers to a kilocalorie, which is one thousand times as large.

Canalization: developmental phenomenon wherein relatively large environmental variations produce minimal variations in overall growth.

Canine fossa: a depression above the canine tooth on the cheek of modern humans, resulting from the reduction in the size of the face.

Carbon-14: an absolute dating method used on organic remains, and based on the knowledge that all living things maintain a constant ratio of the unstable isotope C-14 to the stable common element C-12, which begins to change after the living form dies and the C-14 breaks down.

Carnivorous animal: an animal that subsists on a diet of meat.

Catastrophism: a theory of earth history developed by Baron Georges Cuvier, which hypothesizes a series of worldwide periodic catastrophes in which all animal life was destroyed, with life created anew after each catastrophe.

Catch-up growth: accelerated growth following a period of sub-normal growth.

Center-edge model: an evolutionary theory concerned with the way changes in physical attributes originate and over time, spread throughout a population. In the context of human evolution, it suggests a model explaining the origins of modern humans and their relationships with the archaic sapiens that preceded them.

Cerebellum: part of the hindbrain, which along with the cerebrum (part of the forebrain), became elaborated and convoluted in the evolution of the mammals due to its role in coordinating muscular activity.

Cerebrum (cerebral cortex): part of the forebrain which becomes elaborated and convoluted in mammals but especially so in humans.

Cerumen: ear wax.

Chancelade: Upper Paleolithic hominid site in France.

Chesowanja: a site in western Kenya where an *Australopithecus boisei* skull was discovered.

Chignon: a French word for a hair style in which the hair is twisted into a coil or "bun" and fixed on the back of the head, but used in this context for the development of the bony occipital protuberance found on some European neandertals.

Chopping tool tradition: a Lower Paleolithic stone tool industry which apparently evolved from the Oldowan and is found at various sites throughout the Old World including Zhoukoudian, China.

Choukoutien: older term, no longer used, for the large cave site, now called Zhoukoudian, outside of Beijing (formerly Peking), in northern China (see Zhoukoudian).

Chromosomes: paired bodies present within the nucleus of the cell. They are composed primarily of DNA.

Chronospecies: a series of ancestor-descendant populations with its own evolutionary trends; characterized primarily on the basis of anatomy.

Cilia: microscopic hair-like processes which beat rhythmically; found in human respiratory tract and elsewhere.

Cladogenesis: one form of speciation in which one species evolves through time into two or more descendant species. Cladogenesis is contrasted with anagenesis.

Clavicle: collarbone, connecting the breastbone (sternum) with the shoulder blade (scapula).

Cline: continuous gradation over space in the form or frequency of a trait.

Clone: a group of genetically identical cells.

Coadapted gene complex: a series of genes, governing different traits, that work well together.

Cobble tool: a stone tool which uses a cobble or pebble as its core. A cobble or pebble is a stone worn smooth by the action of water or sand.

Codominance: condition in which neither of two alleles for a trait masks the presence of the other in a heterozygote.

Codon: a group of three bases that specifies a particular amino acid; part of the genetic code; stated in terms of mRNA sequence.

Collagen: a protein (made up of amino acids) which is the organic component of bone.

Colostrum: first milk from mother's breast.

Concordance rate: the frequency with which pairs of people, often genetic relatives, exhibit the same form of a trait or disorder. Used to estimate the genetic contribution to the trait.

Conspecifics: members of the same species.

Continental drift: the major land masses of the planet are set on a series of plates which, over the course of earth's history, have moved extensively in relation to one another.

Continuous traits: traits for which variation falls along a continuum; e.g., weight.

Convergent evolution: the evolution of similar adaptations in distantly related groups.

Core area: in the study of primates in the wild, the area within home range where a group spends most of its time.

Core tool: a stone tool manufactured from a core, rather than from a flake or blade taken off the core. Acheulian hand axes are core tools.

Corneum: horny stratum of the epidermis or outer skin layer.

Cranial capacity: the volume of the braincase, expressed in milliliters (ml), from which a rough estimate of brain size can be derived.

Crepuscular: referring to activity during the twilight hours.

Cro-Magnon: a cave site in southern France where anatomically modern humans and Upper Paleolithic tools were found.

Crossover: the exchange of genetic material between members of a pair of chromosomes during meiosis.

Cultural adaptation: adjustment to environmental changes through the medium of culture, such as through dietary or technological changes.

Cusps: pointed or rounded bumps on the occlusal or chewing surface of a tooth.

Deciduous teeth: baby teeth, or the first of the two sets characteristic of mammals to erupt in the jaws. They are smaller in size and fewer in number than the adult set.

Dental formula: a formula expressing the number of different kinds of teeth (incisors, canines, premolars, and molars) characteristic of a particular mammalian species. Humans and other hominoids have a formula of 2.1.2.3.

Dentin: a bone-like material that forms the core of vertebrate teeth.

Dentition: the complete set of upper and lower teeth of an animal.

Diastema: a space between teeth, such as the space in monkey and ape jaws between the enlarged lower canine and the premolar, and into which the upper canine fits, thus allowing the jaws to close.

Discontinuous traits: traits for which variation falls into discrete categories; e.g., blood groups.

Diurnal: referring to activity during the daylight hours.

Divergent evolution: the accumulation of genetic differences in reproductively isolated groups.

Dizygotic (DZ) twins: fraternal twins who are no more similar genetically than any other sibling pair.

Djetis Beds: oldest faunal level on the island of Java, Indonesia. Early Pleistocene in age, these beds underlie the Trinil faunal beds.

DNA: the genetic material, deoxyribonucleic acid. Its base sequence directs the production of proteins.

DNA hybridization: a molecular technique using the double helical structure of DNA to determine the relationship of living primates to each other and thus to shed some·light on primate evolution.

Dominance: the ability of one allele for a trait to mask the presence of another allele. The latter allele is said to be recessive to the former.

Dominance hierarchy: a system of organization seen among some groups of primates in which the males, through the use of predictable behavioral interactions, are sorted into a hierarchy from the alpha or top ranking male to the lowest male. Females are also sometimes formed into hierarchies, which tend to be more stable than those of the males.

Down's syndrome: a genetic defect in which a person has three rather than two copies of the twenty-first chromosome.

Dryopithecidae: a Miocene hominoid family that includes *Proconsul* and *Dryopithecus*.

Dryopithecus: a genus of extinct hominoids from the Middle to Late Miocene of Europe. They appear to share features with the Early Miocene fossil hominoid, *Proconsul*, from whom they may have descended.

Dysmenorrhea: painful menstruation.

Early or archaic sapiens: a general term used to identify all *Homo sapiens* fossils from their first appearance at the end of the Middle Pleistocene to the appearance of anatomically modern humans at about 35,000–40,000 years B.P.

East Turkana: early hominid fossil-bearing deposits located along the shores of Lake Turkana in north Kenya. First searched by Richard Leakey in 1968, this area has yielded the remains of over 100 individuals of the genera *Australopithecus* and *Homo* in the time range from about 2 to 1.3 million years B.P.

Ehringsdorf: Upper Pleistocene hominid site in East Germany.

Electrophoresis: a technique used to separate proteins or other molecules based on differences in molecular size and/or electrical charge.

Endogamy: marrying within one's group.

Enzyme: a protein that speeds up a biochemical reaction.

Epicanthic fold: a fold in the skin of the eyelid that produces the "almond-shaped" eyes found primarily in Oriental and Native American populations.

Erythroblastosis foetalis: destruction of fetal/newborn red blood cells by the mother's antibodies to Rh+ blood.

Erythrocytes: red blood cells.

Estrus: the reproductive cycle in female nonhuman primates, accompanied by physiological, anatomical, and behavioral changes.

Ethnocentrism: view that the cultural values and practices of one's own society are superior to all others.

Ethology: the study of animal behavior

Eucaryote: an organism whose cells contain a nucleus.

Eugenics: methods of improving the species by controlled breeding.

Evolution: genetic change in a population.

Evolutionary species: see chronospecies.

Exogamy: choosing a mate from another group.

Exon: the sections of a gene which code for protein (see also intron).

Faceted butt: in stone tool manufacture, the flattened end of a core stone. A stage in the production of a flake using the Levallois technique.

Fauna: animals, especially those of a particular region.

Fayum: a fossil-rich locale near Cairo, Egypt, from which an extensive series of Oligocene primate fossils have been recovered.

Femur: the thighbone.

Fibula: the bone lateral to (outside) the shinbone in the lower leg.

Fission track dating: one of a number of dating techniques that provide results in years before the present, and are therefore termed absolute dating methods.

Fixed action pattern: a stereotyped behavior, usually biologically based (not learned), that is often the response to a very specific stimulus (a sign stimulus).

Flake tool: a stone tool made from a flake chipped off a core; flakes are generally not as long as blades.

Flora: plants.

Florisbad: Upper Pleistocene fossil hominid site in South Africa.

Forebrain: the most forward of the three swellings at the head end of the nerve cord. In the early vertebrates, this area dealt solely with olfaction (smell) but later development of this part of the brain into the cerebrum led to its increasing importance in mediating and initiating behavior.

Founder's effect: one form of genetic drift that results when the founders of a new population do not carry all the alleles present in the original population.

Frugivorous: subsisting on a diet of fruit.

Gauss Normal: a long period of normal earth magnetic polarity that ranged from about 3.3 to about 2.4 million years B.P. Preceding the Gauss Normal Epoch was the Gilbert Reversed Epoch and following it was the Matuyama Reversed Epoch.

Gene: the sequence of DNA that results in the production of a functioning protein or a subunit of a protein.

Gene flow: the movement of genes from one population into another; an evolutionary force.

Gene frequency: the frequency of a gene or an allele in a population.

Gene pool: all the genes possessed by members of a population.

Genetic drift: fluctuations in the frequency of an allele due to chance. An evolutionary force.

Genetic fitness: a measure of the reproductive capability of a genotype.

Genetic polymorphism: the existence of more than one allele for a trait (see also balanced polymorphism and transient polymorphism).

Genotype: the alleles that one possesses for a particular trait (see also phenotype).

Genus: a category of the taxonomic system above species but below family. Scientific convention requires that valid genus names be written in italics.

Geographic isolation: the division of one species into two or more sub-groups by a geographic barrier which prevents breeding. A prerequisite for cladogenesis. Allows for the evolution of behaviorally and/or biologically based reproductive isolation.

Gibraltar: several neandertal fossils, including a child's bones, have been discovered on Gibraltar.

Gigantopithecus: an extinct hominoid characterized by the huge size of its chewing teeth. Known from deposits in India and south China, and extending in time from the late Miocene to the early Pleistocene, *Gigantopithecus* has often been placed with *Sivapithecus* in the family Sivapithecidae because of similarities in their teeth.

Glacial: over the last two million or so years, changes in planetary climate have led to the periodic advance and retreat of glaciers or ice sheets in many parts of the northern hemisphere. Those times when the climate cooled and glaciers advanced are known as glacial times, while the intervening times of warming and retreat are termed interglacials.

Globins: a family of proteins, the manufacture of which is directed by a family of genes related through evolution. Humans produce different globins at different stages of ontogeny.

Goiter: an enlargement of the thyroid, a gland important in regulating metabolism. Goiters can be caused by several different factors, such as too much PTC or too little iodine.

Gondwanaland: the imaginative name used to describe the continents of South America, Africa, Australia, Antarctica, and the South Asian sub-continent during the late Paleozoic and Mesozoic when they were part of one large connected land mass.

Grade: a level of organization based on the presence of common biological features, and used in assessing different evolutionary lines of animals.

Grimaldi: see Chancelade.

Group selection: in sociobiology, a model of evolution in which natural selection operates on a number of animals, as a group, rather than on the features of an individual, which is the traditional Darwinian level that natural selection is thought to operate on.

Growth distance: amount of growth up to a point in time.

Growth velocity: the rate of growth.

Hadar: an area of rich early hominid fossil-bearing deposits in the Afar region of north central Ethiopia and ranging in time from 2.9 to greater than 3.2 million years B.P. Hominids found at this site have been placed, along with those from Laetoli, in the taxonomic category *Australopithecus afarensis*.

Half-life: the time it takes for half of a radioactive isotope to decay to its byproduct; for example, Carbon-14 to nitrogen.

Hard palate: the structure separating the oral and nasal cavities; composed of bone in mammals.

Hardy-Weinberg equilibrium: an idealization of the behavior of alleles in a population. This model predicts the frequency of the various phenotypes and genotypes in the absence of selection, mutation, drift, and admixture.

Harris lines: dense transverse areas or lines appearing in the bones of people who have encountered periods of arrested growth.

Haua Fteah: Upper Pleistocene fossil hominid site in Libya, north Africa.

Heel strike: in human walking, a stride is taken and distance is covered when the foot swings forward and leaves the ground at toe off. The defined end of the swing phase, when the foot regains the ground, is marked by the heel touching first, thus, heel strike.

Helix: a spiral. DNA occurs as a double helix — two spirals twisting around each other.

Hemoglobin: the most abundant protein inside the red blood cell; it serves to transport oxygen. Hemoglobin is composed of globin protein plus iron (heme).

Hemolysis: destruction of red blood cells.

Hemolytic anemia: reduced oxygen-carrying abililty due to destruction of red blood cells.

Herbivorous: subsisting on a diet of vegetable material.

Heritability: the ratio of genetically caused variation in a trait to the total amount of variation observed for that trait in a particular population at a particular time. It is abbreviated h^2.

Heterodont: a dentition composed of specialized kinds of teeth, serving a variety of functions. In most mammals, incisors, canines, premolars, and molars can be distinguished.

Heterozygote: an individual who has two different alleles for a given trait; for example, a person who has one A and one O allele for the ABO blood group trait.

Hexian: a Middle Pleistocene *Homo erectus* site in central China.

Hindbrain: the most posterior (nearest the nerve cord) of the three swellings which mark the beginnings of the vertebrate brain. Originally, the hindbrain dealt with hearing, balance, and muscular coordination.

Histocompatibility antigens: proteins which are markers of immunological individuality; important in tissue transplantation.

HLA: see histocompatibility antigens.

Home range: the geographical area occupied by a group of animals.

Hominidae: a taxonomic family within the order Primates, composed of modern humans and their extinct close ancestors. Members of this family are called hominids.

Hominids: members of the family Hominidae.

Hominoidea: a taxonomic superfamily within the order Primates, composed of the lesser and greater apes and humans. Members of this superfamily are called hominoids.

Homodont: a dentition having teeth of only one type. This type of dentition is characteristic of lower vertebrates.

Homo erectus: fossil hominid group which occupied much of the temperate and tropical Old World, except perhaps Europe, from about 1.5 million to 3–400,000 years B.P.

Homo habilis: the taxonomic name given to a number of hominid fossils found at Olduvai Gorge and dated from about 1.85 to 1.7 million years B.P. They are distinguished from members of the genus *Australopithecus* by a larger brain size; a smaller sized posterior dentition and a dental arcade more similar to later hominids.

Homologous chromosomes: the members of a chromosome pair, i.e., chromosomes having the same gene loci.

Homozygote: an individual who has two identical alleles for a given trait; for example, a person who has two O alleles for the ABO blood group trait.

Humerus: the bone of the upper arm.

Hyoid: a horse-shoe shaped bone suspended from the base of the skull and forming part of the system of ligaments and muscles which control tongue movement.

Hypoplasia, dental: improper tooth development resulting in pitting and discoloration of the enamel.

Hypoxia: oxygen starvation; often encountered when first arriving at high altitudes.

Ileret: a fossil rich series of deposits north of the Koobi Fora peninsula area east of Lake Turkana in northern Kenya, where a number of early hominid fossils have been found.

Ilium: the blade of the pelvis.

Immunoglobins: classes of antibodies.

Immunological memory: ability of the immune system to remember how to produce a specific antibody.

Initiation codon: a three-base sequence found at the start of every gene.

Innate releasing mechanism: a term used by animal behaviorists to describe the way a specific sensory perception (sign stimulus) unvaryingly leads to a stereotyped behavior (fixed action pattern).

Inbreeding: breeding between genetic relatives. Inbreeding results in a decrease in heterozygosity.

Innominate: the pelvis is made up of three bones, the right and left innominate and the sacrum, which fits between the two innominate bones at the back.

Insectivorous: subsisting on a diet of insects.

Intelligence: a term used both in the description of modern humans to indicate differences in reasoning ability and mental processing; and in the comparative sense to describe the characteristic flexibility in the behavior of mammals, based on their ability to construct a perceptual model of reality during the prolonged period of infant dependency.

Intergenic: between the genes. Long sequences of DNA separate the genes in most eucaryotes.

Interglacial: time between glacial periods when the climate warmed and the glaciers retreated.

Interstadial: a relatively brief interval of warming within a major glaciation.

Intron: sequences of bases which interrupt the coding portions of a gene. Also called intervening sequences or IVSs (see also exon).

Ischial callosities: an area on the buttocks of Old World monkeys which is covered by an insensitive layer of connective tissue that allows the animal to sit for long periods of time without discomfort and without limiting blood supply to the lower limb.

Isolate: a genetically isolated group; one evidencing little interbreeding with other groups.

Jebel Irhoud: Upper Pleistocene fossil hominid site in Morocco.

Jebel Qafzeh: cave site in the Galilee in Israel which yielded a number of fossil hominids whose attributes are much like those of modern humans, in association with Mousterian tools.

Kabwe: a fossil hominid skull from Zambia, southern Africa, which may date to 200,000 years B.P. Along with the Bodo and Saldhanha Bay specimens, it can be considered an African representative of early *Homo sapiens*. It was formerly known as the Broken Hill skull.

Kalambo Falls: Middle Pleistocene site in southern Africa.

Kanapoi: a site in western Kenya where a hominid arm bone was found and dated to about 4.5 million years B.P.

Karyotype: an illustration of the chromosomes of a cell.

Kenyapithecus wickeri: fragmentary jaws and teeth of a hominoid primate from the site of Fort Ternan in western Kenya. Dated to the middle of the Miocene, it may represent the hominoid ancestor of the hominids.

Kin selection: a concept suggested by sociobiologists to account for behaviors that might otherwise be unexplainable. It suggests that acts of altruism or other self-sacrificing behaviors can be understood, not from the perspective of the individual who performs the action, but rather by examining the genetic benefits to the relatives of the actor.

KNM-ER 406: fossil hominid skull from east of Lake Turkana dated to about 1.5 to 1.6 million years B.P. It is a member of the species *Australopithecus boisei.*

KNM-ER 1470: fossil hominid skull from east of Lake Turkana, probably dated at about 1.8 million years B.P. It possesses a large brain, but also apparently large teeth.

KNM-ER 1590: fossil hominid skull from east of Lake Turkana, Kenya; enigmatic because of the combination of a large brain with large teeth.

KNM-ER 1813: hominid fossil skull from east of Lake Turkana, Kenya; enigmatic because of the combination of a small brain with small teeth.

KNM-ER 3733: fossil hominid skull from east of Lake Turkana, Kenya, dated at about 1.5 to 1.6 million years B.P. It is probably *Homo erectus.*

Koobi Fora: a peninsula of fossil-rich sediments east of Lake Turkana in northern Kenya in which a large number of important early hominid fossils, like ER 1470, ER 1590, ER 1813, etc. have been uncovered.

Kow Swamp: a late Pleistocene site in Australia.

Krapina: Upper Pleistocene neandertal site in Yugoslavia.

Kromdraai: one of the early hominid sites in the Sterkfontein Valley, South Africa, from which robust australopithecines have been recovered.

Kuru: fatal viral disease transmitted by cannibalism.

Kwashiorkor: protein deficiency disease.

La Chapelle-aux-Saints: neandertal site in France.

Laetoli: early hominid fossil bearing site in Tanzania dated to about 3.6 million years B.P. Hominids from this site are grouped with those from Hadar and placed in the taxonomic category *Australopithecus afarensis.*

La Ferassie: rock shelter in France which yielded a number of neandertal fossils.

Lantian: *Homo erectus* site from central China.

La Quina: a neandertal site in France.

Laurasia: the name given to the continents of North America and Eurasia when, from the late Paleozoic through the early part of the Cenozoic, they were part of one large continental mass connected across northeastern North America and Western Europe.

Law of independent assortment: Mendelian principle that different, segregating (unlinked) gene pairs are independent in their movement into sex cells during meiosis.

Law of segregation: Mendelian principle that members of a pair of homologous chromosomes enter separate cells during meiosis.

Le Moustier: neandertal site in southern France. The site has also given its name to the Middle Paleolithic Mousterian Industry.

Leukocyte: white blood cells, important in immune response.

Levallois technique: a flint-chipping technique usually associated with the Middle Paleolithic Mousterian stone tool industry.

Linkage: close association of two or more genes for different traits on the same chromosome.

Linkage disequilibrium: greater or less than random occurrence of a particular combination of linked genes.

Living floor: represents the remains of a surface where hominids lived at some point in the past, which is excavated by archaeologists.

Lobe-fins: bony fishes of the Order Crossopterygii with modifications of the lateral fins for support during bottom-feeding and locomotion. The ancestral group from which the land vertebrates probably evolved.

Locus (plural: loci): the position on a chromosome occupied by a particular gene.

Loph: a ridge which connects two cusps on the surface of a molar. See bilophodont.

Lothagam Hill: a fossil locale in western Kenya where a small fragment of an australopithecine lower jaw was found in a context dated to 5.5 million years B.P.

Lufeng: a fossil site in south China where some rather complete, though smashed, fossil bones of *Sivapithecus* have been uncovered.

Lumbar curve: an acute curve, characteristic of bipeds, in the lower part of the back where the bones of the spinal column join the pelvis.

Maba: an Upper Pleistocene, early *Homo sapiens* site in China.

Maka: an early hominid site in north central Ethiopia where a fragmentary hominid skull bone and thigh bone have been found and dated to about 4.0 million years B.P.

Makapansgat: an australopithecine site in the northern Transvaal, South Africa.

Maramus: calorie deficiency.

Marsupial: pouched mammals.

Masseter: one of the major chewing muscles, which runs from the arch (zygomatic arch) on the side of the skull to the bottom outside edge of the lower jaw.

Matuyama Reversed: a long epoch of reversed planetary magnetic polarity which began about 2.4 million years ago and ended about 690,000 years ago with the beginning of the current period of normal polarity, the Bruhnes Normal Epoch. The Matuyama/Bruhnes boundary is often used as a marker to separate the Lower and Middle Pleistocene.

Mauer: the Mauer or Heidelberg jaw, representing either a European *Homo erectus* or, more probably, an early *H. sapiens*, was found at Mauer, near Heidelberg, Germany.

Meiosis: the process that results in the formation of sex cells. During meiosis, members of the chromosome pairs separate and enter different sex cells; therefore, each sex cell has one-half the number of chromosomes found in other cells.

Melanin: a dark pigment present in many human cells, including skin, hair, and eyes.

Melanocyte: a cell which produces melanin.

Menarche: onset of menstruation.

Microevolution: small-scale evolutionary changes, often the change in the frequency of a gene resulting from natural selection, genetic drift, mutation, and/or admixture.

Midbrain: second swelling at the head end of the nerve cord. In the midbrain of early vertebrates, motor responses were initiated and sensory information terminated. In mammals the midbrain is largely bypassed.

Mitosis: the process by which chromosomes replicate in the cell before division, thus retaining the number of chromosomes in each new cell.

Molecular clock: if DNA evolves at a constant rate, then the degree of DNA divergence between living species can be used as a clock to date past evolutionary events. Not all agree to the existence of such a clock.

Monophyletic: the evolutionary development of a group of animals from a single ancestral species.

Monotreme: egg-laying mammals.

Monte Circeo: Italian for Circe's Mountain, in which was found a cave with a neandertal skull in the center of a stone ring.

Monozygotic (MZ) twins: genetically identical twins.

Morphological variability: the variation in biological features in all sexually reproducing animals, from the obvious such as height, weight, and hair color; to the not-so-obvious such as expression of molar cusp differences; to the invisible-to-the-eye such as ABO blood groups and nerve cells in the brain. It is on this variation that natural selection operates.

Mount Carmel: a series of important late Pleistocene hominids, associated with Mousterian tools, have come from two neighboring caves, Skhūl and Tabūn, both on Mount Carmel, outside Haifa, in northern Israel.

Mousterian: a Middle Paleolithic flake-tool industry, usually, but not always, associated with neandertal fossils.

Mutagen: anything that can cause mutations.

Mutation: a change in the genetic material. Mutations are usually very small alterations involving the change of only one DNA base. An evolutionary force.

Mutationism: the disproved theory that major evolutionary changes represent the appearance of single, major mutations.

Napak: Early Miocene site in Uganda yielding a fragment of a fossil primate skull and a tooth. The tooth is bilophodont like the molars of Old World monkeys, and may represent the earliest documented appearance of these primates.

Natural selection: differential reproduction of genotypes, the mechanism proposed by Darwin and Wallace to underlie much evolutionary change; often misstated as "survival of" rather than "reproduction of the fittest."

Neandertal: a descriptive term given to archaic *Homo sapiens* who lived during the later part of the last Interglacial and the early part of the last, Würm, Glacial in eastern and western Europe, the Middle East and parts of North Africa. They may or may not have been the direct ancestors of living Europeans.

Neandertal phase of man: a view suggesting an evolutionary trend all over the Old World from *Homo erectus* to modern *Homo sapiens* which includes a neandertal phase.

Neander Valley: The cave site in Germany where a skeleton was discovered in 1856, and which gave its name to the neandertal fossil group.

Neotony: retention of infantile characteristics into adulthood.

Ngandong: village in eastern Java on the Solo River near where a number of fossil hominids were found. It is also the name given to deposits which overlie and are therefore younger than both the Trinil and Djetis faunal beds.

Nocturnal: referring to activity during the night.

Nuclear family: a social unit composed of an adult male, adult female, and dependent young. This unit is characteristic of modern humans and some nonhuman primates, such as the gibbon.

Nucleic acids: DNA and RNA.

Nucleus: the structure inside an eucaryotic cell that contains the chromosomes.

Occlusion: a term describing the precise interdigitation between teeth in the upper jaw and lower jaw.

OH-9: *Homo erectus* skull cap from Upper Bed II, Olduvai Gorge, Tanzania.

Oldowan: cobble-tool industry, known from a number of sites in East Africa, and representative of the earliest stone tools manufactured by hominids.

Olduvai Events: several short lived periods of normal earth magnetic polarity within the long Matuyama Epoch of reversed polarity. Occurring at about 1.8 million years, these events are used as the marker between the Pliocene and succeeding Pleistocene.

Olduvai Gorge: a deep gorge in northern Tanzania, East Africa, where Louis and Mary Leakey have excavated a number of hominid fossils, stone tools, and living floors.

Olorgesailie: large series of Acheulian sites located near Nairobi, Kenya.

Omnivorous: subsisting on a diet of both animal and vegetable materials.

Omo: river basin in southern Ethiopia where a number of australopithecine fossils have been discovered in particularly well-dated deposits. Also found along the Omo River, but in layers of much more recent date, are the remains of three archaic *Homo sapiens.*

Ontogeny: the course of development of an individual from conception to death (see also phylogeny).

Opposability: the ability of most primates to bring the thumb into contact with the tips of the other fingers on the same hand in order to grasp objects.

Paleoanthropology: the study of human evolution.

Paleolithic: the stone age, usually divided into three units, the Lower, Middle, and Upper.

Paleomagnetic epoch: long intervals of time when the polarity of the earth remains mostly in one orientation (see Bruhnes Normal or Matuyama Reversed).

Paleomagnetic event: short-lived periods of polarity change within a longer period of opposite magnetic polarity (see Olduvai Event).

Paleomagnetic reversal: times when the earth's magnetic polarity shifts 180 degrees. During times of normal polarity, a compass needle points to magnetic north, while at times of reversed polarity, the needle would be directed to magnetic south.

Paleontology: the study of extinct life.

Paleopathology: the study of ancient diseases, as found in fossil bones or mummies.

Paleospecies: see chronospecies.

Parallel evolution: the continuing evolution of similar adaptations in two closely related groups.

Paranthropus robustus: the original classification of early hominid fossils by Robert Broom at the site of Kromdraai, South Africa. These fossils, plus others found at Swartkrans, are now placed in the genus *Australopithecus* but with the separate species name *robustus*.

Pebble tool: a stone tool which uses a pebble or cobble as its core. A pebble or cobble is a stone worn smooth by the action of water or sand.

Pedomorphism: in ontogeny, retaining a juvenile feature into adulthood.

Peninj: a fossil site at Lake Natron, northern Tanzania, where a robust australopithecine jaw was discovered.

Perigordian: Upper Paleolithic tool industry, characterized by a high frequency of blade tools, which seems to have evolved from the Mousterian industry about 35,000 to 40,000 years B.P.

Petralona: Middle Pleistocene fossil hominid skull from Greece. Although the skull has a number of features relating it to both late *Homo erectus* and early *Homo sapiens*, it is usually placed in the latter category.

Phenotype: the observable or testable appearance of an organism for a particular trait. If dominance is not present for the alleles controlling the trait and if the trait is genetically controlled, the phenotype is the same as the genotype. If the alleles do exhibit dominance, the homozygous dominant and the heterozygote have the same phenotype but different genotypes. The homozygous recessive exhibits a different phenotype.

Phosphate bonds: the type of chemical bond found in the DNA backbone.

Phyletic gradualism: a term used to describe how Darwin viewed the action of evolution through slow but constant change in biological features generation after generation.

Phylogeny: the evolutionary development of a species.

Physiological fitness: a person's state of health, particularly in reference to a stress such as heat, cold, high altitude, or overcrowding.

Piltdown hoax: a carefully assembled fossil fraud. The fossil, a cranium of a modern human with a lower jaw of an orangutan with typical human-like tooth wear patterns, was not totally dismissed as fraudulent until 1953, about 40 years after its "discovery."

Pithecanthropus erectus: "Erect apeman." Name given to hominid fossils discovered by Eugene Dubois on the island of Java. Later this name was changed to *Homo erectus*.

Pituitary gland: gland located under the brain. Important in regulation of many body processes.

Placenta: the organ providing for the exchange of material between mother and fetus.

Placoderms: extinct class of primitive vertebrates characterized by heavy armour plating at the head end and a movable jaw.

Plasmodium: a genus of parasites that cause various types of malaria.

Pleiotropy: the ability of one gene to influence more than one trait.

Plesiadapis: primitive mammal of the Paleocene with biological structures of the limbs adapting it for life in the trees. It is thought by many to be a very primitive member of the primate order.

Plesiadapiformes: a major suborder of wholly extinct Primates which includes the primitive early members of this order from the Cretaceous and Paleocene periods.

Plesianthropus transvaalensis: taxonomic term originally given by Robert Broom to the fossil hominids from the Sterkfontein site in South Africa. These fossils are now placed in the category *Australopithecus africanus*.

Pliopithecus: small-sized Miocene fossil hominoids which possess some resemblances to the gibbon, but whose skeletal features, like a tail, make it difficult to directly relate as the direct ancestor of the living lesser apes.

Polygenic trait: a characteristic influenced by more than one set of alleles.

Polymorphism: genetic variability for a trait.

Population: ideally, those members of a species that share a common gene pool.

Postorbital bar: a rim of bone around the outside of the eye orbit which provides a measure of protection to the eyes. It is commonly found in the prosimians, while anthropoid primates possess not only bars, but totally enclosed boney orbits.

Potassium-argon (K-Ar dating): absolute dating method which is applied to rocks that contain the radioactive isotope K-40 which decays slowly to its byproduct argon. Since the half-life of K-40 is much greater than C-14, this method can be used to date deposits at much older fossil sites.

Predators: animals, especially carnivores, that prey on other animals.

Předmostí: a fossil hominid site in Czechoslovakia yielding the remains of 46 individuals buried in a common grave. These early anatomically modern humans, found with Upper Paleolithic tools, show a great deal of morphological variability.

Prehensile tail: a tail which is able to grasp objects like a fifth limb. It is a unique characteristic of some New World monkeys.

Procaryote: organisms that lack nuclei.

Proconsul: Early Miocene fossil hominoids from East Africa. Possessing a number of primitive features of the skull and teeth, *Proconsul* may be the descendent of the earlier *Aegyptopithecus* of the North African Oligocene.

Prognathism: having jaws which project out in front of the braincase.

Prosimians: one way to classify primates is to divide the order into prosimians and anthropoids. In this view, the living prosimians are composed of the lemurs, indriids and aye-aye, all on Madagascar; the loris group, including bush babies, found in Africa and Asia; and the tarsiers, with a limited distribution in southeast Asia.

Protein: molecules composed of long chains of amino acids. The function of the genetic material is to direct the production of proteins.

Pseudogene: a gene which contains one or more defects that prevents it from producing a protein.

Punctuation: a view of evolution in contrast with traditional Darwinian concepts of gradual change. It pictures the evolution of animals as long periods of little or no change (stasis) punctuated by very short intervals of rapid change resulting in new species.

Purgatorius: fossil mammal from Cretaceous and Paleocene deposits in Montana; thought to be the earliest evidence of the evolution of the primates.

Qualitative traits: see discontinuous traits.
Quantitative traits: see continuous traits.

Rabat: *Homo erectus* site in Morocco, North Africa.
Racemization: a chemical change in the structure of amino acids. A dating technique for fossil bones is based on the various rates of racemization that characterize different amino acids.
Radius: a bone of the lower arm (on the thumb side).
"Ramapithecus": fossil hominoid from Middle and Late Miocene deposits of the Siwalik Hills of north India and Pakistan. At one time "Ramapithecus" was thought to be an early member of the human family Hominidae, but additional fossil discoveries have now shown that it is a small form of the Miocene genus *Sivapithecus,* and "Ramapithecus" has now been incorporated into this group.
Recessive: the masking of one allele for a trait by the presence of another allele. The latter allele is said to be dominant to the former.
Recombinant DNA: DNA which is constructed in a laboratory so as to be part viral and part from a species under study, e.g., human.
Recombination: formation of new combinations of genes at separate loci on a chromosome as a result of crossing-over.
Red blood cells: those cells that carry oxygen through the bloodstream. The red color comes from the protein hemoglobin inside the cells. Many other proteins are found within the red cell. The molecules determining one's blood type are found on the outside surface of the cell. Red blood cells are also called erythrocytes.
Reflectance spectrophotometer: a machine that measures the amount of light of a specific wavelength reflected by a surface; it is used in the study of skin and hair color.
Regulatory gene: a gene which regulates the functioning of another gene — turning it on or off.
Relative dates: estimation of the age of geologic deposits based on the comparison of that deposit to other deposits, to some event in earth history, or to the evolutionary history of a better known animal group.
RNA: ribonucleic acid, a chemical similar in structure to DNA. The two types of RNA considered are: messenger RNA, which transcribes the genetic information from the DNA and carries it to the site of protein manufacture; and transfer RNA, which incorporates amino acids into their proper position in a protein.
Reproductive isolation: the inability of members of two species to mate and produce viable offspring for biological or behavioral reasons.
Reproductive strategy: strategies for maintaining adult population numbers adopted by different groups of animals. For example, the strategy among many mammals is to limit the number of offspring produced but at the same time to insure survival of these offspring to reproductive maturity by providing postnatal (after birth) nurturing.
Restriction endonuclease: an enzyme, such as Eco R1, which cuts DNA wherever a particular base sequence occurs; also called restriction enzymes.
Restriction enzyme maps: a chart showing the distribution of various restriction enzyme sites within a piece of DNA.
Retrodiction: a form of prediction; making a statement about the outcome of a past event but about which information is currently unavailable.

Saccopastore: Upper Pleistocene archaic *Homo sapiens* site in Italy.
Sacrum: a bone of the pelvis, fitting in the back, between the two innominate bones.
Sagittal crest: a bony crest or ridge on the top of the skull of some apes and the robust australopithecines, to which the large *temporalis* chewing muscles attach.

Saint-Césaire: a site in southern France with a neandertal in association with Upper Paleolithic tools of the Perigordian Industry.

Šala: fossil hominid frontal bone found in Czechoslovakia. It possesses features reminiscent of both neandertals and anatomically modern humans.

Saldanha Bay: a hominid skull cap from the west coast of South Africa. Along with the Kabwe and Bodo fossils, it can be considered an African representative of early *Homo sapiens*.

San: the correct name for the living human groups of gatherer/hunters of the Kalahari Desert of southern Africa. Formerly called "Bushmen."

Sangiran: a fossil locale on the island of Java, Indonesia, from which a large number of *Homo erectus* fossils have been recovered.

Scapula: the shoulder blade.

Sciatic notch: a strongly angulated sciatic notch is a characteristic feature on the pelvis of bipeds; it is the result of the shortening and broadening of the pelvis.

Secretor: a genetically determined trait which determines whether water soluble forms of one's ABO molecules are found in body fluids, as well as on the surface of red blood cells.

Sectorial premolar: the first lower premolar of monkeys and apes, has only one cusp and that one pointed and caninelike, differing from the first lower premolar of modern humans which has two fairly flat cusps.

Secular trend: a trend over time; often applied to growth and development phenomena.

Semi-species: populations which are in the process of becoming separate biological species.

Sex linkage: genes that are carried on the sex chromosomes.

Sexual dimorphism: differences between males and females of the same species.

Shanidar: a cave site in Iraq from which nine neandertals have been recovered.

Shovel-shaped incisors: upper incisor teeth reinforced at their edges, on the tongue side, with extra enamel.

Sickle-cell anemia: an inability of the blood to carry sufficient oxygen because of homozygosity for the sickle-cell allele.

Sickle cell: red blood cells that have "collapsed" and assumed a sicklelike appearance. This phenomenon occurs most markedly in people homozygous for the sickle-cell allele for hemoglobin type.

Side chain: a variable region in the chemical structure of amino acids. Each amino acid has a different side chain.

Sidi Abderrahman: see Rabat.

Sign stimulus: an action, sign, or other sensory stimulus, which when received by an animal, results in a characteristically stereotyped behavior (fixed action pattern).

Sinanthropus pekinensis: category established for the hominid fossils found at the cave site of Zhoukoudian in China. These fossils are now placed in *Homo erectus*.

Sivapithecus: Miocene hominoids known from discoveries in north India and Pakistan, and also from south China, East Africa and perhaps Europe. "Ramapithecus" is now included within this genus. *Sivapithecus* shares certain characteristics of the jaws and teeth with *Gigantopithecus* which might be related to dietary adaptations.

Sivapithecidae: a family of Miocene hominoids which includes the genera *Sivapithecus* and *Gigantopithecus*.

Skhūl: cave site at Mount Carmel in Israel. Hominid fossil remains, associated with the Mousterian industry, of at least ten individuals were excavated which show a great deal of morphological variability, some reminiscent of neandertals and others with characteristics resembling anatomically modern humans.

Socialization: the process of learning the normative behaviors of a group or society.

Sociobiology: a perspective within the study of animal behavior which seeks explanations for various patterns of animal behavior and adaptation within the context of the processes of natural selection.

Solo hominids: eleven skulls and two shinbones found on the banks of the Solo River near the village of Ngandong. The age of these bones is unclear and morphologically, they can either be early sapiens or late *Homo erectus;* they are usually placed in the latter category.

Species: the smallest working unit in taxonomy (see also biological species and chrono-species).

Spy: neandertal site in Belgium.

St. Acheul: French village that lends its name to the Lower Paleolithic stone tool industry, the Acheulian Industry, which is characterized by a high frequency of hand axes.

Stance phase: in human bipedal stride, the leg that remains on the ground, supporting the body, is said to be in stance phase.

Steatopygia: a genetically influenced, increased deposition of fat in the buttocks.

Steinheim: badly crushed hominid skull from the village of Steinheim in Germany. Dating to the latter part of the Middle Pleistocene, it is probably an early representative of *Homo sapiens.*

Stereoscopic vision: depth-perceiving vision that enables the eyes to look forward and focus together on an object.

Sterkfontein: an australopithecine site in the Sterkfontein Valley, Transvaal, South Africa.

Sternum: the breastbone, to which the ribs and the collarbone (clavicle) attach at the front of the rib cage.

Sticky ends: short segments of single-strand DNA often produced after DNA is treated with a restriction endonuclease.

Straight-line evolution: see anagenesis.

Striding gait: the characteristic bipedal mode of movement of known living and extinct hominids, composed of alternating stance and swing phases.

Structural gene: a gene which directs the structure of a protein.

Subcutaneous fat: fat deposits lying just under the skin.

Suspensory hanging: a pattern of arboreal adaptation suggested for the early hominoids, in which major biological changes developed in the upper trunk and arms as a result of hanging by the arms while suspended in the trees.

Swanscombe: a Middle Pleistocene fossil site along the River Thames in southern England where bones of the back of the skull of an early sapiens have been found.

Swartkrans: a robust australopithecine site, but also with some fragments from a later time of *Homo erectus,* located in the Sterkfontein Valley, Transvaal, South Africa.

Swing phase: in hominid bipedal stride, the leg that leaves the ground and swings forward is said to be in swing phase.

Synthetic theory of evolution: the modern view of evolution, based on an amalgamation of genetic and evolutionary thought.

Tabūn: cave site at Mount Carmel in Israel. The hominid fossils associated with the Mousterian industry share many morphological features with neandertals. Estimates of age place these fossils perhaps as early as 70,000 years B.P.

Talus: the ankle bone of the foot.

Taung: the fossil site in the Cape Province, South Africa, from which the first australopithecine fossil was recovered in 1924.

Taxonomy: the classification of plants and animals into categories based on common biological features.

Temporalis: one of the major chewing muscles, it attaches from the side of the braincase (at the temporal line, or in robust australopithecines and some apes, from the sagittal crest) and runs down the skull, inside of the arch (zygomatic arch), ending on the top back of the lower jaw.

Ternifine: Acheulian site in Algeria, several *Homo erectus* jaws and pieces of skull cap have also been found.

Terra Amata: Middle Pleistocene open air site in France. Stone tools of the Acheulian industry and evidence of fire were found, but no hominid remains were unearthed.

Terrestrial: adapted to life on the ground.

Territory: a home range which is defended from other members of the same species outside the group.

Teshik Tash: a Mousterian site in southern U.S.S.R. where a deliberately buried neandertal youngster was uncovered.

Testosterone: hormone found in greater amounts in males. "Male hormone."

Therapsids: the order of mammal-like reptiles of the Mesozoic that represent the transition between reptiles and mammals.

Tibia: the shinbone of the lower leg.

Titer: a measure of the strength of an antibody.

Toe-off: at the time in bipedalism when swing phase begins, the foot is pushed off from the ground with some muscular force, the last element to leave the ground, being the big toe, hence toe-off.

Topography: the description of a surface; in this context, surfaces depicting the genetic fitness of populations as propounded by Sewall Wright.

Torralba: see Ambrona.

Transient polymorphism: a polymorphism that is in the process of disappearing as a result of some evolutionary force; that is, one allele is disappearing.

Trinil: a locale along the Solo River in Java, Indonesia, where Dubois discovered the first *Homo erectus* fossil; also, a faunal level characteristic of the Middle Pleistocene of Java, and above the earlier Djetis level.

Typology: the study of idealized types; sociological assignments as to race are highly typological.

Ulna: a bone of the lower arm (on the little finger side).

Uniformitarianism: a theory elaborated by Charles Lyell that the appearance of the earth today represents the action of natural forces like wind, rain, and temperature changes operating slowly and constantly over very long periods of time.

Vértesszöllös: an archaeological site along the Danube River in Hungary where a hominid occipital bone was discovered. Although it possesses some features reminiscent of *Homo erectus*, it is usually considered an early representative of *Homo sapiens*.

Victoriapithecus: Middle Miocene fossil primate from Kenya. This genus possesses teeth showing the bilophodont character of Old World monkey molars.

Villafranchian: a relative time period in southern Europe marked by the presence in the deposits of the modern genera of horse, cattle and Asian elephants, hence "Villafranchian fauna." Relatively, the Villafranchian lies just below the first evidence for Pleistocene glaciations.

Virus: any of various very small microorganisms which consist of a protein shell and a core of nucleic acid.

Wadi Amud: Upper Pleistocene cave site in northern Israel, with hominid specimens similar to both the Tabūn and Shanidar fossils.

Wadjak: Upper Pleistocene hominid site in Java.

Wallace's line: the imaginary line marking the boundary between the fauna of Europe/Asia and Australia/New Guinea.

White blood cells: see leukocyte.

Willandra Lakes: an Upper Pleistocene site in southern Australia with early evidence of modern human occupation of the Australian continent.

Y-5 Molars: lower molars characteristic of the hominoids, the apes, and humans, that have five cusps so arranged that the grooves separating the inner cusps look like the letter Y when viewed from the tongue side of the tooth.

Zinjanthropus boisei: taxonomic category for a fossil hominid found in Bed I, Olduvai Gorge. The fossil is now considered *Australopithecus* but with the separate species name *boisei*.

Zhoukoudian: a cave site in the village of Zhoukoudian, just outside of Beijing, People's Republic of China, where a large sample of *Homo erectus* fossils was discovered prior to World War II. The village was formerly known as Choukoutien.

Zygomatic arch: arch of bone on the side of the skull which is the origin of the *masseter* muscle, a major muscle of mastication.

Credits

(continued from page iv)

William C. Brown, 1981), p. 149. Reprinted by permission. 3.6 From P. A. Moody, *Introduction to Evolution*, Third Edition, p. 30, Harper & Row. 3.9 Reproduced by permission of D. F. Roberts from *Ciencia y Cultura*. 3.14 From S. Stanley, *Macroevolution: Pattern and Process* (W. H. Freeman, 1979). 3.16 From A. H. Schultz, *The Life of Primates* (N.Y.: Universe Books), p. 157; and *Evolution* (Time-Life Books), p. 185. 3.17 From A. H. Schultz, *The Life of Primates* (N.Y.: Universe Books), p. 165. **Chapter 4:** 4.2 Adapted from Kent C. Condie, *Plate Tectonics and Crustal Evolution*, p. 214. N.Y.: Pergamon Press (1976). 4.3 Redrawn from J. Z. Young, *Life of the Vertebrates*, fig. 48. Used with permission of the Oxford University Press, Oxford. 4.4 Redrawn from Figure 13 by Lois M. Darling in Edwin H. Colbert, *Evolution of the Vertebrates*, Third Edition (1980). Reprinted by permission of Lois M. Darling. 4.5 Courtesy of the American Museum of Natural History. 4.8 Redrawn by permission of Quadrangle/The New York Times Book Company from *The Antecedents of Man* by W. E. LeGros Clark. Copyright © 1959, 1962, 1971 by Quadrangle/The New York Times Book Co. Also used with permission of Edinburgh University Press. 4.11 *top* Redrawn from *Osteology of the Reptiles* by Alfred Sherwood Romer by permission of The University of Chicago Press, © 1956 by The University of Chicago; *bottom* Redrawn after L. B. Arey, *Developmental Anatomy*, 7th (revised) edition, p. 403, W. B. Saunders Company, Philadelphia (1974). 4.14 From *The Study of Instinct* by N. Tinbergen, published by Oxford University Press, 1951. 4.16 Adapted from Dyna-Vue, Ward's Natural Science Establishment, Inc. 4.17 From "Specializations of the Human Brain" by Norman Geschwind. Copyright © 1979 by Scientific American, Inc. All rights reserved. **Chapter 5:** 5.1(a): Courtesy of The American Museum of Natural History. 5.1(b) and (c): From F. S. Szalay, "Phylogeny of primate higher taxa: the basicranial evidence," in Lucket and Szalay, (eds.), *Phylogeny of the Primate: A Multidisciplinary Approach* (1975). Reprinted by permission of Plenum Publishing Corporation. 5.2 Redrawn by permission of Quadrangle/The New York Times Book Company from *The Antecedents of Man* by W. E. Le Gros Clark. Copyright © 1959, 1962, 1971 by Quadrangle/The New York Times Book Co. Also used by permission of Edinburgh University Press. **Chapter 6:** 6.1, 6.2 From Edwin H. Colbert, *Men and Dinosaurs*. Copyright © 1968 by Edwin H. Colbert. Reprinted by permission of E. P. Dutton, Publisher. 6.4 From J. J. Grand, "The functional anatomy of the lower limb of the Howler Monkey *(Alouatta curaya)*." *American Journal of Physical Anthropology* 28: 163. Reprinted by permission. 6.6 *left* Redrawn from E. Genet-Varcin, *a la Recherche du Primate, Ancêtre de L'Homme*. Boubée et Cie. Editions N, France. *right* Redrawn from W. E. Le Gros Clark, *History of the Primates*, fig. 4.24. University of Chicago Press, Fourth Phoenix Books Editions, published 1963. (Eighth edition published by Trustees of the British Museum. 6.14 From Elwyn L. Simons, *The Earliest Apes*. Copyright © December 1967 by Scientific American, Inc. Redrawn by permission of the photographer, Lee Boltin. All rights reserved. 6.16 Redrawn from W. E. Le Gros Clark and L. S. B. Leakey, *The Miocene Hominoidea of East Africa*, figs. 213 and 216 (1951), British Museum (Natural History) Fossil Mammals of Africa. By permission of the Trustees of the British Museum (Natural History). 6.19 From M. Goodman and J. E. Cronin, "Molecular Anthropology: Its Development and Current Directions," in Frank Spencer (Ed.) *A History of American Physical Anthropology*. Reprinted by permission of Academic Press, Inc. 6.21 Redrawn from L. S. B. Leakey, *Fossil Vertebrates of Africa*, Vol. I, Plate I, 1969. Published with the permission of the National Museum, Kenya. 6.22 Redrawn from Theodosius Dobzhansky, et al., *Evolutionary Biology*, Vol. 6, fig. 5; *Relationships, Origins, History of the Ceboid Monkeys and Caviomorph Rodents: a Modern Reinterpretation*, Plenum Publishing Corp. **Chapter 7:** 7.11 From Alison Jolly, *Evolution of Primate Behavior*, © 1972. Reprinted by permission of Macmillan Publishing Company. 7.13 Redrawn from "Chimpanzees of the Budongo Forest" by Vernon Reynolds and Frances Reynolds in *Primate Behavior: Field Studies of Monkeys and Apes,* edited by Irven DeVore. Copyright © 1965 by Holt, Rinehart and Winston, Inc. Originally published in R. M. Yerkes, *Chimpanzees: A Laboratory Colony,* 1943, Yale University Press. 7.14 From R. H. Tuttle, "Knuckle-walking and the Problem of Human Origins," *Science* 166:953–961. Copyright 1969 by the American Association for the Advancement of Science. **Chapter 8:** 8.1 Redrawn from J. Chaline, *Le Quaternaire,* Doin Editeurs, Paris, 1972. **Chapter 9:** 9.2 Redrawn from Ashley Montagu, *Introduction to Physical Anthropology,* figs. 62, 132, 112, and 113, Charles C Thomas, Publisher. Used by permission of the author. 9.5 Redrawn after C. K. Brain from *Nature,* C. K. Brain, "New Finds at the Swartkrans Australopithecine Site." Vol. 225, figs. 1 and 6, March 21, 1970. 9.8 Redrawn from A. K. Behrensmeyer, "Plio-Pleistocene sequences in the northern Lake Turkana basin," in W. W. Bishop (Ed.), *Geological Background to Fossil Man,* Scottish Academic Press, University of Toronto Press. 9.14 *top* Redrawn from "The Antiquity of Human Walking," by J. R. Napier. Copyright © April 1967 by Scientific American, Inc. All rights reserved. Used with permission of the author. *bottom* From A. L. Zihlman and W. S. Hunter, "A biochemical interpretation of *Australopithecus,*" *Folia Primat.* 18:1–19, S. Karger AG, Basel. 9.16 *left* From W. K. Gregory, *The Anatomy of the Gorilla,* New York: Columbia University Press, 1950. Reprinted by permission of the publisher. *right* Redrawn from "The Antiquity of Human Walking," by J. R. Napier. Copyright © April 1967 by Scientific American, Inc. All rights reserved. 9.19 Redrawn from *Early Hominid Posture and Locomotion* by John T. Robinson, by permission of the University of Chicago Press. 9.21 Redrawn from *The Antecedents of Man* by W. E. Le Gros Clark. Copyright © 1959, 1962, 1971 by Quadrangle/The New York Times Book Co. Reprinted by their permission and by Edinburgh University Press. 9.23 Redrawn from R. Broom and J. T. Robinson (1952) "Swartkrans ape-man, *Paranthropus crassidens.*" Transvaal Museum Memoirs, No. 6. Pretoria, South Africa. With permission from Dr. C. K. Brain. 9.31 Redrawn from L. S. B. Leakey and Mary Leakey, 1964, "Recent discoveries of fossil hominids in Tanganyika at Olduvai and near Lake Natron," *Nature* 202:5–7. 9.36 From Mary Leakey, *Olduvai Gorge: Excavations in Beds 1 and 2, 1960–1963* (volume 3 in the Olduvai Gorge series), Cambridge University Press, 1971. 9.37 Reprinted by permission of Faber and Faber Ltd. from *The Archaeology of Early Man* by J. M. Coles and E. S. Higgs. **Chapter 10:** 10.1, 10.17 From *Atlas of Fossil Man* by C. Loring Brace, Harry Nelson, and Noel Korn. Copyright © 1971 by Holt, Rinehart and Winston, Inc. Reprinted by permission of the publisher. 10.8 and 10.19 *left:* Reprinted by permission of Faber & Faber Ltd. from *The Archaeology of Early Man* by J. M. Coles and E. S. Higgs. 10.9 Redrawn from *The Emergence of Man* by John Pfeiffer, p. 143, Harper & Row, Publishers (1972). Used by permission of Henry de Lumley, Université de Provence. 10.13, 10.18 Redrawn from J. Chaline, *Le Quaternaire,* Doin Editeurs, Paris, 1972. 10.19 *right* From François Bordes, *A Tale of Two Caves.* Copyright © 1972 by François Bordes. Reprinted by permission of Harper & Row, Publishers. 10.25 Redrawn from "Neanderthal Man and *Homo sapiens* in Central and Eastern Europe," by Jan Jelineck in *Current Anthropology* 10, December 1969, 475–503 by permission of The University of Chicago Press. **Chapter 11:** 11.8, 11.9, 11.10, 11.11, 11.12, 11.13, 11.14, 11.20 Adapted by permission of Random House, Inc. from *The Human Species: An Introduction to Physical Anthropology,* Second Edition, by Frederick S. Hulse. Copyright © 1971 by Frederick S. Hulse. Copyright © 1963, 1971 by Random House, Inc. 11.17 Redrawn by permission of Alice Brues and Wistar Institute from Alice Brues, "Selection and Polymorphism in the A-B-O Blood Groups," *American Journal of Physical Anthropology* 21:297, 295. 11.21 Adapted from map "Epidemiological Assessment of Status of Malaria, December 1976" from WHO Weekly Epidemiological Record, No. 43, 1977. 11.23 Adapted from Y. W. Kan and A. M. Dozy, "Evolution of the Hemoglobin S & C Genes in World Population," in *Science* 209:388–391. 11.24 Adapted from *Evolution,* Vol. 18, 1964, Time-Life Books. 11.25 Adapted from *Evolution,* Vol. 18, 1964, Time-Life Books, and F. S. Hulse, *Human Species.* Copyright © 1971 by Frederick S. Hulse. Adapted by permission of Random House, Inc. **Chapter 12:** 12.1 Redrawn from N. A. Barnicot, "Human Pigmentation," *Man* (old series): 57-5, Royal Anthropological Institute of

Great Britain and Ireland. 12.2 (a) Redrawn by permission from Fitzpatrick, Miyamoto and Ishikawa, 1966, *The Evolution of Concepts of Melanin Biology in Advances in Biology of Skin*, Vol. 8, *The Pigmentary Skin*, Plenum Publishing Corp. (b) Redrawn from Gerrit Bevelander, *Essentials of Histology*, Sixth Edition, (St. Louis: C.V. Mosby Company, 1970), p. 140. 12.3 From *The Living Races of Man*, by Carleton S. Coon with Edward E. Hung, Jr. Copyright © 1965 by Carleton S. Coon. Reprinted by permission of Alfred A. Knopf, Inc. 12.5 Adapted from "Rickets," W. F. Loomis. Copyright © December 1970 by Scientific American, Inc. All rights reserved. 12.8 Adapted from graph from article by N. A. Barnicot in *Man* (old series) 57:2, Royal Anthropological Institute of Great Britain and Ireland. 12.18 From *Digging Up Bones: The Excavation, Treatment and Study of Human Skeletal Remains* by Don R. Brothwell. Reprinted by permission of the Trustees of The British Museum (Natural History). 12.19 From G. A. Harrison, J. S. Weiner, J. M. Tanner, and N. A. Barnicot, in *Human Biology*, Second Edition, Oxford University Press. Originally in J. M. Tanner, *Growth at Adolescence*, Second Edition. Reprinted by permission of Blackwell Scientific Publications. 12.20 Redrawn from *Digging Up Bones* by Don R. Brothwell, after I. Schour and M. Massler, "The Development of the Human Dentition," in *Journal of the American Dental Association*, 28:1153–1160. **Chapter 13:** 13.2 From Cynthia Beall, "A Comparison of Chest Morphology in High Altitude, Asian and Andean Populations," in *Human Biology* 54:145–163. 13.3, 13.6 From A. R. Frisancho, *Human Adaptation: A Functional Interpretation* (1979), C.V. Mosby Company. 13.8 Reprinted by permission of the American Anthropological Association from *American Anthropologist* 55(3), 1953. 13.11 From Joel M. Hanna and Daniel E. Brown (1983) "Human Heat Tolerance: An Anthropological Perspective," in *Annual Review of Anthropology* 12:259–284. 13.14 Adapted from Sir Macfarlane Burnet and David O. White, *Natural History of Infectious Disease*, 4th Edition, p. 124, Cambridge University Press. 13.15, 13.16, 13.17 Reprinted with permission from *Journal of Psychosomatic Research*, Vol. 18; Sydney Cobb, "Psychological Changes in Men Whose Jobs Were Abolished," 1974, Pergamon Press, Ltd. 13.18, 13.19 From "The Effects of Light on the Human Body." Copyright © 1975 by Scientific American, Inc. All rights reserved. 13.23 After R. A. McCance and W. M. Widdowson (1968), *Calorie Deficiencies and Protein Deficiencies* (London: J. & A. Churchill). 13.25, 13.26 G. B. Spurr, M. Barac-Nieto, and M. G. Maksud, "Childhood Undernutrition: Implications for Adult Work Capacity and Productivity," in *Environmental Stress* (proceedings of a symposium held at University of California, Santa Barbara, Aug. 31–Sept. 3, 1977), Lawrence J. Folinsbee et al., eds. (Academic Press, 1978). **Chapter 14:** 14.10 From N. E. Morton, R. Kennett, S. Yee, and R. Lew (1982) "Bioassay of Kinship in Populations of Middle Eastern Origin and Controls," in *Current Anthropology* 23:157–167. 14.11 From C. Loring Brace and Robert J. Hinton (1981) "Oceanic Tooth-size Variation" in *Current Anthropology*, Vol. 22, No. 5, 549–569.

Photograph Credits

Chapter 1: *Opening photo* Ellis Herwig/Stock, Boston. 1.1 The Granger Collection, New York. 1.2 Alinari/Art Resource, NY. 1.3 Brown Brothers. 1.4, 1.5 Robert Harding Picture Library/Rainbird Ltd. 1.6 Dr. I. Eibl-Eibesfeldt. 1.7 *left* Robert Harding Picture Library/Rainbird Ltd.; *right* BBC Hulton Picture Library. 1.8 Courtesy of the Department of Library Services, American Museum of Natural History. 1.9 Culver Pictures. **Chapter 2:** *Opening photo* Museum of Science, Boston. 2.2(b) Porter, K. R. and Bonneville, M. A.: *Fine Structure of Cells and Tissues,* 4th ed., Lea & Febiger, Philadelphia, 1973. 2.12 Dr. Marion I. Barnhart, Wayne State University. 2.14(b) Courtesy of Harold W. Fisher and Robley C. Williams. 2.16 Brown Brothers. 2.18 Courtesy of Evan Weiss and Matthew Fillmore. 2.19 Leonard Atkins, M.D., Massachusetts General Hospital. 2.20(c) Dr. A. Al Saadi; (d, e) From A. Redding, K. Hirschhorn, "Guide to Human Chromosomes." D. Bergsma (ed). White Plains: The National Foundation—March of Dimes, BD:OAS IV(4), 1968; (f) From J. W. Bianchine, *Noonan Syndrome and Trisomy 21 in Sibs*. In D. Bergsma (ed): Part XV. "The Cardiovascular System." Baltimore: Williams & Wilkins for The National Foundation—March of Dimes, BD:OAS VIII(5):247, 1972; (g) In D. Bergsma (ed) 1973. *Birth Defects: Atlas & Compendium.* Published for The National Foundation—March of Dimes by Williams & Wilkins: Baltimore. Figure 562. 2.25 Wide World Photos. 2.28 The Gernsheim Collection, Harry Ransom Humanities Research Center, University of Texas at Austin. 2.29 *top* Ann L. Koen; *bottom* In D. Bergsma (ed) 1973. *Birth Defects: Atlas & Compendium.* Published for the National Foundation—March of Dimes by Williams & Wilkins: Baltimore. Figure 579. **Chapter 3:** *Opening photo* Courtesy of the Department of Library Services, American Museum of Natural History. 3.1 Gabriel Benzur, LIFE Magazine © 1945 Time Inc. 3.2 Country Life Newspaper, Australia. 3.7 Courtesy of the Department of Library Services, American Museum of Natural History. 3.15(2) Russell French. **Chapter 4:** *Opening photo* George Laycock/Photo Researchers, Inc. **Chapter 5:** *Opening photo* Russ Kinne/Photo Researchers, Inc. 5.6 *right,* 5.11 Sarah Blaffer Hrdy/Anthro-Photo. 5.9 Nina Leen. 5.10 Michael Lyster, Zoological Society of London. 5.12 Courtesy of Norris M. Durham. 5.13 Courtesy of the Department of Library Services, American Museum of Natural History. **Chapter 6:** *Opening photo* Courtesy of the Department of Library Services, American Museum of Natural History. 6.7, 6.10 *right* Courtesy of the Department of Library Services, American Museum of Natural History. 6.10 *left* Ralph Morse, LIFE Magazine © 1965 Time, Inc. 6.11 From O. L. Lewis, 1972. "Evolution of the hominoid wrist" in *The Functional and Evolutionary Biology of Primates,* Russell Tuttle (ed.), Cambridge University Press. 6.12 *left* From D. R. Swindler and C. D. Wood, 1973. *An Atlas of Primate Gross Anatomy: Baboon, Chimpanzee, and Man* (Seattle: University of Washington Press); *right* "Knuckle-Walking and the Problem of Human Origins," Tuttle, R. H., *Science* Vol. 166, pp. 953–961, Figs., 21 November 1969. Copyright 1969 by the AAAS. **Chapter 7:** *Opening photo* Jim Moore/Anthro-Photo. 7.1, 7.15, 7.16, 7.17 Courtesy of Geza Teleki. 7.2, 7.3, 7.5, 7.8 Irven DeVore/Anthro-Photo. 7.6 Courtesy of Dr. Sherwood L. Washburn, University of California, Berkeley. 7.7 Courtesy of the Department of Library Services, American Museum of Natural History. 7.8 Irven DeVore, Anthro-Photo. 7.10 Bruce Coleman, Inc. and Wolfgang Bayer. 7.11 Reprinted with permission of Macmillan Publishing Co., Inc. from *Evolution of Primate Behavior* by Alison Jolly. Copyright © 1972, Alison Jolly. 7.14 R. H. Tuttle, "Knuckle-Walking and the Problem of Human Origins," *Science* 166:953–961. Copyright 1969 by the American Association for the Advancement of Science. **Chapter 8:** *Opening photo* Hillel Burger, Peabody Museum, Harvard University. Copyright © President & Fellows of Harvard College, 1980. All rights reserved. **Chapter 9:** *Opening photo* National Geographic News Service, February 1978. 9.3, 9.4 Courtesy of the Department of Library Services, American Museum of Natural History. 9.9 From D. C. Johanson, "Ethiopia yields first 'family' of early man," *National Geographic* Dec. 1976:802. 9.10 National Geographic News Service, February 1978. 9.32 *left* 9.33 Reprinted with permission of the National Museums of Kenya. Copyright reserved; *right* Dorothy Mann. 9.34 Courtesy of Clarendon Press. **Chapter 10:** *Opening photo* Jay Kelley/Anthro-Photo. 10.4, 10.21 Courtesy of the Department of Library Services, American Museum of Natural History. 10.9 Redrawn from *The Emergence of Man* by John Pfeiffer, p. 143, Harper & Row, Publishers, Inc., 1972. Used with permission of Henry de Lumley, Université de Provence. 10.14 From *Paleoanthropology,* by M. H. Wolpoff. Copyright © 1980 by Alfred A. Knopf, Inc. Reprinted by permission of Alfred A. Knopf, Inc. 10.26 From J. Matiegka, *The Fossil Man of Předmostí in Moravia* (Prague: Nákladem České Akademie Věd A Uměmí, 1934), Table 2. **Chapter 11:** *Opening photo* Dr. Marion I. Barnhart. 11.1 From Komai and Fukuota, *Journal of Heredity,* Vol. 25, p. 425, 1934, American Genetic Association. 11.2 Courtesy of Major M. Ash, Jr., D.D.S., M.S., from Kerr, Donald A., Ash, Major M., Jr., and Millard, H. Dean: *Oral Diagnosis,* 6th ed., 1983, The C.V. Mosby Co., St. Louis. 11.3 Henry McHenry, *American Journal of Physical Anthropology* 29:7 (plate 1), July 1968. Courtesy of H. M. McHenry. 11.19 Reprinted by permission from *The Structure and Action of Proteins* by R. E. Dickerson and I. Geis, W. A. Benjamin, Inc., Publishers, Menlo Park, Calif. Copyright © 1969 by Dickerson and Geis. 11.26 Culver Pictures. **Chapter 12:** *Opening photo* Ellis Herwig/Stock Boston. 12.4 From Michael C. Latham, Robert B. McGandy, Mary B. McCann, and Frederick J. Stare, 1972. *Scope Manual of Nutrition,* Second Edition (Kalamazoo: The Upjohn Company). Courtesy of Dr. Rosa Lee Nemir and

Ward C. Morgan Studios. 12.7 Courtesy of the Department of Library Services, American Museum of Natural History. 12.16(b & c) Reprinted from *Radiographic Atlas of Skeletal Development of the Hand and Wrist,* 2cd. ed., by William Walter Greulich and S. Idell Pyle, with the permission of the publishers, Stanford University Press. Copyright © 1950 and 1959 by the Board of Trustees of the Leland Stanford Junior University. 12.17 Courtesy of Harry Israel, D.D.S., Ph.D., Director of Dental Research, 1 Children's Plaza, Children's Medical Center, Dayton, Ohio, Associate Clinical Professor of Pediatrics, Wright State University School of Medicine, Dayton, Ohio and Harold H. Sandstead, M.D., USDA Human Nutrition Research Center on Aging at Tufts University, Boston, MA. Reprinted from Falkner & Tanner, *Human Growth/2: Postnatal Growth,* Plenum Publishing Corp., New York. 12.24 *left* Jiro Tanaka/Anthro-Photo; *right* Brian M. Fagan. **Chapter 13:** *Opening photo* George Holton/Photo Researchers, Inc. 13.1 Courtesy of Norris M. Durham. 13.5 Stanley Washburn/Anthro-Photo. 13.10 *left* Reproduced by permission of D. F. Roberts from *American Journal of Physical Anthropology; right* Photo: Knutsen. Arktisk Institut, Denmark ©. 13.20 Joel Gordon/Design Photographers International. 13.21 *left* John Dominis, LIFE, © Time Inc.; *right* From *Kabluna,* copyright © 1941 Gontran de Poncins, by permission A. Watkins, Inc. 13.22 Marc Ribaud, Magnum Photos, Inc. 13.24 Courtesy of Dr. Alex F. Roche. Reprinted from Falkner & Tanner, *Human Growth/2: Postnatal Growth,* Plenum Publishing Corp., New York. 13.27 Plate #DCG59DNGII Reprinted from "Disease Patterns of Isolated Groups" in *Biocultural Aspects of Disease,* H. R. Rothschild, ed., Academic Press, 1981. Courtesy of Ralph M. Garruto and D. C. Gajdusek. **Chapter 14:** *Opening photo* Peter Menzel/Stock Boston. 14.1 The Detroit Institute of Arts, Gift of Edsel B. Ford. 14.2 Neal Menschel. 14.3 *left* Paul Conklin, Monkmeyer Press Photo Service; *right* Michal Heron. 14.4 through 14.6 Courtesy of the Department of Library Services, American Museum of Natural History. 14.7 Monkmeyer Press Photo Service. 14.8 Irven DeVore/Anthro-Photo. 14.9 Courtesy of Napoleon A. Chagnon, from *Yanomamö The Fierce People,* Holt, Rinehart and Winston. **Chapter 15:** *Opening photo* Bettye Lane/Photo Researchers, Inc. 15.1 Charles L. Thompson/Black Star. 15.2 Rita Freed/Nancy Palmer. 15.3 Oliver Pierce/Stock Boston.

Index

Page numbers in *italic* indicate illustrations.

characteristics of, 398
Diego group, 408
and evolution, 410–419
MN group, 63, 65–67, 391–392, 397, 398, *398*, 405
MNS group, 405, *407*
Rh group, 397, 401–405, *406*
Sutter group, 408
test for, 398
Xg group, 408
Blurton Jones, N. G., 548–549
Boaz, Noel, 335
Bodo skull, 359–361
Body build, 520–521. *See also* Stature
and climate, 489–493, *492*
Body composition, 454–456
Body measurements, 451–459
Body size, 506
of puma, 489, *490*
Bone growth, *136*, 136–137
Bordes, François, 367, 369
Boundary marking, 264–265
Brace, C. Loring, 539–540
Brachiation, 188, *194*, 196
Brachymesophalangia-5, 514, *514*
Brain. *See also* Skulls
australopithecine, 287, 288, 320–321, 337
of early sapiens, 380
growth of, 454, 512–513
hominid, 274, 278, 280–281
human, *141–143*, 142–143, 287
mammalian, 138–143
neandertal, 366, 380, 381
primate, 186–188, 230
of reptile, 138
size of, 280–281, 528
of Taung child, 287
vertebrate, 138, 141–142
Brain, C. K., 330
Brain damage, and malnutrition, 512
Branda, Richard F., 445
Breast feeding, 494, 509–510
Breeding population, 62, 120
Broken Hill specimens. *See* Kabwe
Broom, Robert, 291, 292, 295
Brown, Peter, 428
Brues, Alice, 417, 520–521
Bruhnes Normal Epoch, 268, 269
Buffon, Georges de, 3–4, 5
Buluk fossils, 204, 211, 212–213
Burial, 379–380
Burt, Cyril, 471
Bushmen. *See* San Bushmen

adjustment to cold stress of, 485–486
status among !Kung San, 556
steatopygia of, 467

Calcium
absorption of, *505*
deficiency, 444
Callithricidae, 158, 218
Calories, 507–509. *See also* Diet
Canalization, 456
Cancer, 499
skin, 444
Canine fossa, 370
Canine teeth
in apes, 289–290
australopithecine, 321–323
in hominoids, 206
in humans, 273
in mammals, 132
sexual dimorphism in, 200, 207, 245, 321
tension display, 230, *230*
Cannibalism, 519
Carbohydrates, 507–509. *See also* Diet
Carbon-14 dating technique, 269–270, 281
Carnivores, 120, 132, 184
Carpenter, C. R., 245
Cartmill, Matt, 157, 184–185, 188
Catastrophism theory, 12
Catecholamines, 500–501
Cebidae, 158, 197, 217–219
Ceboids, 158. *See also* New World monkeys
Cell
meiosis (division), 28, 47–48, 50, 51, 55–56, 69, 394
mitosis (duplication), 48–50
schematic view of, 26
Cenozoic era, 129–130, 144, 179, 184
Center-edge model of evolution, 378–379
Cephalic index, 466
Cercopithecines, 160, 161, 217. *See also* Old World monkeys
Cercopithecoids, 158. *See also* Old World monkeys
Chagnon, Napoleon, *537*
Childhood
of australopithecines, 334
of gatherers/hunters, 355
of hominids, 549
learning in, 549–550

and malnutrition, 512–513
socialization in, 548
Childhood dependency period
of australopithecines, 334, 549
of gatherers/hunters, 355
of hominids, 549
of mammals, 138, 228
of primates, 227, 228
Chimpanzees, 162, 180, 215, 227, 235–236
aggression in, 545–547
behavior of, 250–256
dentition of, 250–251, *314*
diet of, 252–254, *253*, 256
distribution of, 250, *250*
and evolutionary theory, 76
language and, 231
locomotion of, 251, *251*
social organization of, 228, 251–257, *252*
use of tools by, 255, 256, *256*, 275, 276
China, hominid fossils in, 343–345. *See also* Zhoukoudian specimens
Chomsky, Noam, 7
Chondrichthyes, 119, 124
Chordata, 121
Choukoutien specimens, *see* Zhoukoudian specimens
Chromosomes, 43–44
halving of, 47–48
homologous, 47, *55*
human, *44–46*
in Klinefelter's disease, *59*
linkage of, 54–56
in sex determination, 56–60
Chronospecies, 80, *80*, 81
Circe's Mountain. *See* Monte Circeo.
Cladogenesis, 81, 82, 83, 114
Clark, W. E. Le Gros, 151, 185
Climate
in Eocene, 189–190, 191–192, 219
during glacials, 265–267
and hominid evolution, 276
human adaptation to, 485–494
in Miocene, 264, 276
in Oligocene, 192
and primate evolution, 191
and skin color, 444
Cline, 99–100, 533–535
for puma body size, *490*
for skin color, *443*
Clone, defined, 38, 106

Cloning, 560
  and recombinant DNA, 38
Cobb, Sidney, 501
Cocaine, and cold stress, 485
Codons, 32, 33. *See also* Amino
  acids
  initiation, 33
Cohen, Bernice, 411
Cold, adaptation to, 267, 485–488
Cold stress, 485–488
Collectors/predators, 254
Colobines, 160, 216–217
Colonialism, 8
Color blindness, 408, *409*, 521
Columbus, Christopher, *4*
Communication. *See also* Language
  among higher primates, 227,
    230–231
  systems of, 6–7
Comparative anatomy, 12, 76, 182
Comparative sciences, as evidence
  for evolution, 76, 114
Computer simulation, of ABO
  blood group evolution, 416–
  417
Conservatism, 552
Continental drift, 121, *122*, 184,
  191, 263–264, 281
Contraception, 556
Convection, 492
Convergence, 180
Cooperation, among hominids, 353
Coppens, Yves, 297
Corruccini, Robert, 467
Crelin, E. S., 380–381
Cretaceous period, 129, 130, 183,
  184
Cretinism, 519–520
Cri du chat (cat's cry) syndrome,
  46, 48
Cro-Magnon specimen, *370*
Crook, John, 243
Crossing-over, 55, *55*
Culture
  and adaptation to stress, 477–
    479, 484, 485–486, 493–494,
    495–498
  and biology, 6, 8, 9
  hominid, 273–274
  and malnutrition, 517–520
Cusps, 134
Cuvier, Georges, 12, 13
Cystic fibrosis (CF), 53, 479

Dart, Raymond, 276, 286–288,
  291, 292, 335, 342, 545

Darwin, Charles, 3, 13, 14, *14, 19,
  20*, 76, 103, 114, 126, 147
  Beagle voyage of, 14–18, *15*
  Descent of Man, 20, 263, 288
  The Origin of Species, 8, 19, 102
  theory of evolution of, 11, 14,
    18–20, 21, 41, 73, 102
Darwin, Erasmus, 13
Dating
  absolute, 269–272
  of hominid fossils, 267–269
  methods of, 269–272, 281
  relative, 272
Davenport, Charles and Gertrude,
  440
Dawson, Charles, *288, 289*, 291
DDT, insect resistance to, 77, 78
Decker, R. L., 189
Delson, E., 152, 216
deLumley, Henry, 350–351, 359
Dental formula, 134, 197, 218–
  219, 313
Dental hypoplasia, 392, *392*
Dentin, in vertebrates, 124
Dentition. *See also* Teeth
  australopithecine, 286–289,
    313–315, 316, 318–320,
    321–323
  hominoid, 197–199, 205–207
  human, 215–216, 280, 282,
    313–315, *314*
  mammalian, 130–134, *132, 133,*
    197–199
  primate, 197–199, 203–204,
    216
  reptilian, 130, 131, *131*
  of savanna baboons, 238
  vertebrate, 124
Depth perception, of primates, 185,
  189
Descent of Man (Darwin), 20, 263,
  288
Devonian period, 124, 127, 128,
  144
DeVore, Irven, 241
Diastema, 313–315. *See also* Dentition
Diego blood group, 408
Diet. *see also* Nutrition
  adequate, 507–509
  of Australian aborigines, 508
  of chimpanzees, 252–254, 256
  of Eskimos, 507–508
  of gorilla, 252
  of hominids, 276
  and intelligence, 473

  of monkeys, 237, 246–248, 249
  of Quechua Indians, 508
  of savanna baboons, 237
  of seeds, 276
  synthetic foods in, 515–517
  and variability, 506–507
Dinosaurs, 129–130, 181–182, *182*
Disease. *See also* Epidemiology
  effects of, 391, 455, 456
  infectious, 414–416, 494–498,
    511–512
  noninfectious, 413–414, 430,
    498–499
  parasitic, 518
  socioeconomic factors in, 498,
    502
Djetis Bed specimens, 342–343,
  383
DNA (deoxyribonucleic acid), 25,
  27, 28, 29
  cloning and recombinant, 38–40
  functions of, 25, 28–33, 68–69
  hybridization of, *169*, 169–170,
    170
  intergenic, 34
  and mutation, 34–38, 69
  recombinant, 558–560
  replication, 32, 44, 48
  and restriction enzyme poly-
    morphisms, 433–434
  sequencing, 172–174
  structure of, 25–28
Dobzhansky, Theodosius, 86, 392–
  394, 395, 526, 529, 541
Dolhinow, Phyllis, 225
Dominance, genetic, 43, 52–54, 69
Dominance hierarchies
  among baboons, 238–240, 241
  among macaques, 241, 242
Double helix, 25, *27, 28*, 32
Down's syndrome, *46*, 48, 56
Draper, Patricia, 556
Drills, 233, 234
Drosophila, 86
Dryopithecidae, 202, 204, 211,
  220, 272
Dryopithecus, 205–206, 211
Dubois, Eugene, 340–342
Dunbar, R. I. M. and E. P., 243
Dunkers, 61–62
Dutt, James, 484
Dwarfism, nutritional, 513
Dysmenorrhea, 459

Earlobes, variability in, 42–43, *43,*
  67